# Prentice Hall Studies in International Relations
## *Enduring Questions in Changing Times*

CHARLES W. KEGLEY, JR., *SERIES EDITOR*

In the era of globalization in the twenty-first century, people cannot afford to ignore the impact of international relations on their future. From the value of one's investments to the quality of the air one breathes, international relations matter. The instantaneous spread of communications throughout the world is making for the internationalization of all phenomena, while the distinction between the domestic and the foreign, the public and the private, and the national and the international is vanishing. Globalization is an accelerating trend that is transforming how virtually every field of study in the social sciences is being investigated and taught.

Contemporary scholarship has made bold advances in understanding the many facets of international relations. It has also laid a firm foundation for interpreting the major forces and factors that are shaping the global future.

To introduce the latest research findings and theoretical commentary, a new publication series has been launched. *Prentice Hall Studies in International Relations: Enduring Questions in Changing Times* presents books that focus on the issues, controversies, and trends that are defining the central topics dominating discussion about international relations.

*Series Editor*
**Charles W. Kegley, Jr.**
University of South Carolina

## Series Editorial Advisory Board

**Shannon Lindsey Blanton**
University of Memphis

**Linda P. Brady**
Georgia Institute of Technology

**Leann Brown**
University of Florida

**Steve Chan**
University of Colorado, Boulder

**William A. Clark**
Louisiana State University

**Charles F. Hermann**
Texas A & M University

**Margaret G. Hermann**
Syracuse University

**Ole R. Holsti**
Duke University

**Steve W. Hook**
Kent State University

**Loch K. Johnson**
University of Georgia

**Christopher C. Joyner**
Georgetown University

**Jack S. Levy**
Rutgers University

**Craig Murphy**
Wellesley College

**Nicholas G. Onuf**
Florida International University

**Gregory A. Raymond**
Boise State University

**Neil R. Richardson**
University of Wisconsin

**Volker Rittberger**
Eberhard-Karls-Universitat Tubingen

**J. Martin Rochester**
University of Missouri, St. Louis

**Joel Rosenthal**
Carnegie Council on Ethics
and International Affairs

**Alpo Rusi**
Helsinki University

**Peter Schraeder**
Loyola University, Chicago

**Bengt Sundelius**
Uppsala University

**John Vasquez**
Vanderbilt University

**Thomas Volgy**
University of Arizona

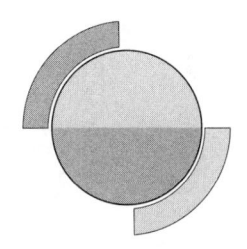

# REALISM AND THE BALANCING OF POWER
## A NEW DEBATE

JOHN A. VASQUEZ
*Vanderbilt University*

COLIN ELMAN
*Arizona State University*

Prentice Hall

UPPER SADDLE RIVER, NEW JERSEY 07458

Library of Congress Cataloging-in-Publication Data

Realism and the balancing of power: a new debate/[edited by] John A. Vasquez, Colin Elman.
p. cm.—(Prentice Hall studies in international relations)
Includes bibliographical references and index.
ISBN 0-13-090866-5
1. Balance of power. 2. International relations—Research. 3. International relations—Political aspects.
I. Vasquez, John A. II. Elman, Colin. III. Series.

JZ1313 .R43 2002
327.1'01—dc21

2002014769

Senior acquisitions editor: Heather Shelstad
Editorial assistant: Jessica Drew
Marketing manager: Claire Bitting
Marketing assistant: Jennifer Bryant
Editorial/production supervision: Kari Callaghan Mazzola
Prepress and manufacturing buyer: Ben Smith
Electronic page makeup: Kari Callaghan Mazzola and John P. Mazzola
Interior design: John P. Mazzola
Cover director: Jayne Conte
Cover design: Kiwi Design

This book was set in 10/12 Electra by Big Sky Composition
and was printed and bound by Courier Companies, Inc.
The cover was printed by Coral Graphics.

**Prentice Hall**  © 2003 by Pearson Education, Inc.
Upper Saddle River, New Jersey 07458

All rights reserved. No part of this book may be
reproduced, in any form or by any means,
without permission in writing from the publisher.

Printed in the United States of America
10 9 8 7 6 5 4 3 2 1

ISBN 0-13-090866-5

Pearson Education LTD., London
Pearson Education Australia PTY, Limited, Sydney
Pearson Education Singapore, Pte. Ltd
Pearson Education North Asia Ltd, Hong Kong
Pearson Education Canada, Ltd., Toronto
Pearson Educación de Mexico, S.A. de C.V.
Pearson Education—Japan, Tokyo
Pearson Education Malaysia, Pte. Ltd
Pearson Education, Upper Saddle River, New Jersey

*For Marie and Miriam*
*with love*

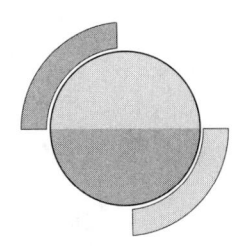

## Contents

Preface    xi

About the Contributors    xix

CHAPTER 1
Introduction: Appraising Balance of Power Theory    1
   *Colin Elman*

### PART I   THE INITIAL DEBATE

CHAPTER 2
The Realist Paradigm and Degenerative versus Progressive Research Programs:
An Appraisal of Neotraditional Research on Waltz's Balancing Proposition    23
   *John A. Vasquez*

CHAPTER 3
Evaluating Theories    49
   *Kenneth N. Waltz*

CHAPTER 4
The Progressive Power of Realism    58
   *Stephen M. Walt*

CHAPTER 5
Progressive Research on Degenerate Alliances    66
   *Thomas J. Christensen and Jack Snyder*

CHAPTER 6
New Realist Research on Alliances: Refining, Not Refuting, Waltz's Balancing Proposition    74
   *Randall L. Schweller*

CHAPTER 7
Lakatos and Neorealism: A Reply to Vasquez    80
   *Colin Elman and Miriam Fendius Elman*

CHAPTER 8
The New Debate on Balancing Power: A Reply to My Critics    87
   *John A. Vasquez*

## PART II   NEW CONTRIBUTIONS

CHAPTER 9
Why Realism Does Not Work Well for International History (Whether or Not It Represents a Degenerate IR Research Strategy)    114
   *Paul W. Schroeder*

CHAPTER 10
Balances and Balancing: Concepts, Propositions, and Research Design    128
   *Jack S. Levy*

CHAPTER 11
Is There a Balance of Power?    154
   *Richard Rosecrance*

CHAPTER 12
Neorealism's Logic and Evidence: When Is a Theory Falsified?    166
   *Bruce Bueno de Mesquita*

CHAPTER 13
Paradoxical Functions of International Alliances: Security and Other Dilemmas    200
   *Zeev Maoz*

CHAPTER 14
Alliances, Balances of Threats, and Neorealism: The Accidental Coup   222
   *Michael Barnett*

CHAPTER 15
Measuring Power—and the Power of Theories   250
   *William C. Wohlforth*

CHAPTER 16
The Necessary and Natural Evolution of Structural Realism   266
   *Charles L. Glaser*

## PART III   CONCLUSION

CHAPTER 17
Closing Dialogue   280
   *Colin Elman and John A. Vasquez*

References   305

Index   326

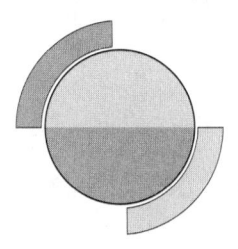

# Preface

*Realism and the Balance of Power: A New Debate* presents a conversation about the merits of the most recent phase of realist research on international relations. For at least sixty years, realists and nonrealists alike have been occupied with defining, defending, and defeating different versions of realist theory. On the one hand, successive groups of realist scholars have presented their own preferred interpretation, always on the bones of preceding accounts. Classical realists, for example, were critiqued by structural realists, who were in turn opposed by neotraditionalists. On the other hand, while nonrealist scholars offered radically different views of how the international system works and of what drives state behavior, they, too, juxtaposed their accounts with the then prevailing version of the realist canon. In short, although differing on what they wanted to replace it with, both realists and their critics have largely taken realist theory as their target of choice. The bull's-eye in that mark has often been the subset of realist theory that might loosely be described as "balance of power theory"—the various arguments that realists have offered about why and how great powers respond to their threatening external environment, especially the accumulation of a threatening concentration of power by another state—and associated observations about the implications of those responses for the international system.[1]

The editors position themselves on different sides of this conversation. John Vasquez is a longstanding and trenchant critic of realism.[2] Colin Elman, by contrast, has been characterized as a "defender of the faith."[3] While acknowledging these differences, however, the editors concur on the importance of IR theorists engaging in a sustained dialogue on the different standards by which research, including realism, can be judged. Scholars need to explicate what frameworks they will use to evaluate and appraise a theory. In philosophy of science such frameworks are referred to as metatheories (i.e., theories about the nature of theory). Thus, scholars should add a prefix to their appraisals of realism: "*According to metatheory x*, how well is realism doing?"[4]

IR scholars describe and judge their theories in terms of the larger theoretical groupings with which they identify or disagree.[5] Members of the subfield often categorize groups of scholars with loyalties to particular theoretical aggregates and seek to make judgments about the trajectory of those aggregates. They rarely make explicit statements of the metatheory on which they are relying, or the grounds on which they calculate the comparative merits of competing theories.

This book is structured around the argument that scholarly judgments about theories should be based on consciously chosen metrics, and that those selections should be made with due consideration of the different standards' strengths and limitations.[6] The book takes as its starting point an essay by John Vasquez (1997) contending that, when judged using a particular metatheory's criteria, recent realist research is problematic. Vasquez applies Imre Lakatos's Methodology of Scientific Research Programs (MSRP) to a succession of recent variants of realist theory and finds them wanting. In a series of articles responding to that claim, seven realists questioned Vasquez's choice and use of MSRP, as well as his conclusions. Several additional essays (commissioned for this book) follow, further expanding the discussion. Thus, the book is intended to be read and used in at least four different ways:

- First, the book is the most recent iteration in the long running dialogue between realists and their critics. While pursuing a usefully different approach from previous accounts, the book builds upon this distinguished academic tradition.
- Second, while taking realism as their substantive focus, more generally the essays investigate how political scientists decide that they know what they think they know. The essays provide a series of different perspectives on how the field should be described and on how theories should be appraised. In particular, several essays discuss the use of Lakatos's MSRP for conducting theory appraisal in international relations. In laying out their disagreements about Lakatos's metatheory, the contributing authors provide an in-depth analysis by political scientists of the possibility for rational and objective choices among different theories. Although framed here in terms of realism and balance of power theory, the conversation on how scholars should group and appraise theories can be applied to any research in political science.
- Third, while each of the essays addresses a series of common questions, they can also be read as stand-alone pieces. In particular, the contributions in Part II of the book represent the latest word on their subject from leading scholars in the field.
- Fourth, by presenting an important debate in its entirety, the book provides an unparalleled pedagogical device. Much of the introduction and the "Editors' Commentary" following each succeeding chapter are written to help students learn how to read scholarly articles. In an age in which undergraduate education has become increasingly pablumized, we believe that it is important that majors leave a course being able to digest material that they may not have been able to read before they took the course. Learning how to read and evaluate scholarly debates is not always easy, but to leave college without gaining those skills is to miss the core of the discipline in which one is majoring.

## Plan of the Book[7]

Part I of the book reprints John Vasquez's (1997) essay from the *American Political Science Review*, and the subsequent multiauthor forum. In Chapter 2, Vasquez suggests that successive versions of realist theory have demonstrated serious problems. Vasquez argues that contemporary research on balancing of power constitutes a degenerative realist research program. Utilizing Imre Lakatos's criterion that research programs should be progressive rather than degenerating in the way they reformulate theories, Vasquez maintains that neotraditional research investigating Kenneth Waltz's proposition on balancing of power fails to satisfy this criterion. He suggests that the research program can be seen as degenerating because of (1) the protean character of its theoretical development, (2) an unwillingness to specify what constitutes the true theory, which if falsified would lead to a rejection of realism, (3) a continual adoption of auxiliary propositions to explain away flaws, and (4) a general dearth of strong research findings.

Vasquez's article provoked vigorous responses, reprinted as Chapters 3 through 7. These responses, published with Vasquez's article as an *APSR Forum*, engaged the larger philosophical and theoretical issues raised by Vasquez's critique and took issue with his substantive findings. In his essay "Evaluating Theories," Kenneth Waltz suggests that Vasquez's argument is flawed by both epistemological and substantive errors. Waltz charges that Vasquez misunderstands the nature of theories (which Waltz defines as pictures, mentally formed, of bounded realms or domains of activity) and how they should be tested. While Vasquez cites MSRP, Waltz claims that he actually distorts Lakatos's criteria by trying to falsify neorealism. Noting that facts and theory are interdependent, Waltz suggests that a theory can be validated only by working back and forth between its implications and an uncertain state of affairs that observers take to be the reality against which theory is tested. Because of that uncertainty, the results of such tests are always problematic. Waltz also suggests that Vasquez (in part because of epistemological errors) mistakenly conflates different theories, in particular by placing structural and classical realists within the same paradigm.

In Chapter 4, arguing for "The Progressive Power of Realism," Stephen Walt contends that Vasquez's assessment of realism is flawed by its reliance on MSRP, its underestimation of realist research, and its limited sampling of relevant literature. Walt suggests that Vasquez's reliance on Imre Lakatos's (1970) model of scientific progress is problematic because the Lakatosian model has been largely rejected by contemporary historians and philosophers of science. Second, Vasquez understates the range and diversity of the realist research program and mistakenly sees disagreements among realists as evidence of theoretical degeneration. Finally, Walt argues that Vasquez overlooks the progressive character of contemporary realist theory, largely because he does not consider all the relevant literature. Disagreements within and across competing research programs are essential to progress and should be welcomed, but criticism will be most helpful when it seeks to do more than merely delegitimate a particular research tradition, which seems to be Vasquez's intent.

Chapter 5 presents Thomas Christensen and Jack Snyder's "Progressive Research on Degenerate Alliances." Christensen and Snyder grant that Vasquez was right to use Lakatosian criteria to judge realist research. They disagree, however, with the conclusions Vasquez reaches. Christensen and Snyder acknowledge that their 1990 article on alliance dynamics in multipolarity differs from some neorealist approaches by incorporating variables from the theory of the security dilemma, including perceptual factors. But they insist that their argument meets Imre Lakatos's criteria for a progressive problemshift insofar as it explains more than the original theory, does so parsimoniously, has been successfully applied to new domains, and does not introduce new assumptions that contradict the core of the original theory.

In Chapter 6, Randall Schweller's "New Realist Research on Alliances: Refining, Not Refuting, Waltz's Balancing Proposition" suggests that realism is both a scientific research program and, more traditionally, a political philosophy. Schweller argues that all realists share a pessimistic world view that posits perpetual struggle among groups for security, prestige, and power, and that denies the capacity of human reason to create a world of peace and harmony. Schweller disputes Vasquez's conclusion that recent realist research disconfirms Waltz's balancing proposition. Instead, these works have tended to add unit-level variables in order to transform Waltz's theory of international politics into one of foreign policy. Schweller argues that history clearly shows that states both balance and bandwagon, and that realism's task is to determine under what conditions states choose one strategy or the other.

In Chapter 7, Colin Elman and Miriam Fendius Elman's "Lakatos and Neorealism" takes issue with Vasquez's characterization of their response to an article by Paul Schroeder in *International Security*. Elman and Elman (1995) argued that Schroeder's reading of European history was not necessarily inconsistent with realism. Schroeder may be right that balancing is not ubiquitous in the historical record of European international relations, but contrary to Schroeder and Vasquez's assertions, neorealist theories do not invariably predict that states will balance, that they will always balance effectively (they are less likely to under multipolarity when structural pathologies are present), or that balances will always form. Vasquez's conclusion is based on a mistaken conflation of the neorealist research program with the proposition that balancing is a common foreign policy. In addition, while welcoming Vasquez's use of MSRP, Elman and Elman suggest that he misstates Lakatos's criteria.

Part I closes with Chapter 8, which presents a new essay by Vasquez. In "The New Debate on Balancing Power," Vasquez responds to the criticisms made in Chapters 3 through 7. While Vasquez addresses each of his critics, indicating where he agrees and disagrees, he focuses on three areas. First, he finds it remarkable that many of his critics do not focus on the question of whether neotraditional reformulations of Waltz are degenerating, but rather seek, in various ways, to deny that there is much wrong with Waltz's balancing proposition in the first place. He therefore specifies a set of tests—historical and quantitative—that would resolve this prior question of whether the proposition is empirically accurate. Second, he points out that the debate illustrates the need to develop more precise rules for distinguishing degenerative from progressive research programs with an emphasis on how to handle discrepant evidence, how to tell when specifying the domain of a proposition is potentially degenerative (and when it is not), and how to determine what are "novel facts." Third, the debate raises the question of what are legitimate criteria for appraising theory. He defends the utility of using Lakatos against Walt's criticisms, and he addresses the points raised by Elman and Elman that his use of Lakatos has been incomplete, indicating where he agrees and disagrees.

In Chapter 9, Paul Schroeder leads off Part II of the book by picking up Vasquez's challenge to see if Waltz's claim—that the major hegemonic threats posed by Charles I of Spain (Charles V, Holy Roman Emperor), Louis XIV, Napoleon Bonaparte, Wilhelm II, and Adolph Hitler were met by a balancing of power—actually conforms to the historical record. He maintains that a close examination of historical research raises serious questions about this claim. With the possible exception of Louis XIV, Schroeder does not see balancing as a response to hegemonic threats. More often than not, states are willing to make a deal, and in the end go to war primarily because they are attacked.

In Chapter 10, Jack Levy addresses the same question as Schroeder: Do great powers balance against hegemonic threats? Levy, however, takes a different approach. Rather than attempting to provide an empirical answer in light of the historical record, Levy delineates some of the terminological and conceptual ambiguities that must be resolved before such a question can be answered. He provides some valuable insights about how we can determine when balancing and nonbalancing occur, a key question that must be answered if the theory is to be tested. After pointing out that there are a variety of balance of power theories, he identifies two key propositions that most of them share and that can provide a test of this family of theories—states will balance in the face of serious hegemonic threats and (because of this) hegemonies will rarely if ever occur. He proposes that the debate can move forward by investigating whether these propositions hold for the European continental system. If the theory does not hold there then it probably will not hold anywhere and it will be seriously damaged.

Richard Rosecrance examines, in Chapter 11, some of the analytical problems associated with defining the balance of power and therefore identifying its presence in history. In particular, he points out that there is a danger of making the concept so broad that it could include a variety of actions, thus ensuring that one could always find some sort of balance of power. As a result, the analytical rigor and theoretical insights that attract us to the concept in the first place would be lost. Given some reasonable definitions, Rosecrance questions the frequency with which balancing can be found. This does not mean that hegemonies are common, however. He points out that there are other mechanisms that prevent hegemonies from forming.

In Chapter 12, Bruce Bueno de Mesquita moves away from a focus on the concept of the balance of power to an appraisal of Waltz's broader theoretical claims, especially those on the stability of bipolarity. Bueno de Mesquita argues that theories can be considered to be falsified if they can be shown to be logically incoherent or if they fail to explain as many relevant facts as an alternative theory. He finds Waltz's theory deficient on both grounds. For Bueno de Mesquita, Waltz's claims about bipolarity do not hold. Empirically, he shows that the post-1945 bipolar era is not any longer than previous multipolar periods. Nor does he find that the Cold War bipolar period is characterized by a significantly longer period of peace than some multipolar periods. He concludes by offering an alternative theory that he believes is more consistent with the empirical evidence.

Zeev Maoz also employs data to test claims on the balance of power in Chapter 13. Unlike Bueno de Mesquita, however, he does not focus on Waltz's theory specifically, but rather on the general family of realist theories and what propositions can be derived from it about alliance formation and the relationship between alliances and militarized conflict. He then asks what kinds of propositions on these questions can be derived from the family of liberal theories. He tests the realist and liberal propositions against each other and finds, on the whole, that the liberal propositions perform better.

In Chapter 14, Michael Barnett focuses on Stephen Walt's balance of threat theory and examines Middle Eastern, specifically Arab, alliances to assess Walt's theory. He does not disagree with Walt that Arab states form alliances with reference to threat rather than power, but he maintains that this behavior cannot be logically derived from neorealist assumptions about the effect of anarchy. For Barnett, alliance formation and perceptions of threat do not derive from material factors, but from ideas and social constructions. States find each other threatening and form alliances against each other not because of differences in power, but because they believe in different things. For Barnett, Walt's reformulation does not save neorealism but points to a tension that is better explained by a constructivist approach.

In "Measuring Power—and the Power of Theories," presented in Chapter 15, William Wohlforth suggests that Vasquez and other critics of Waltzian structural realism simply misunderstand what Waltz thinks theories can do in general, and what balance of power theory predicts in particular. Wohlforth argues that Waltz makes very moderate demands upon his theory, which is only designed to make weak and indeterminate claims. Critics who prefer their theories to make clear and firm predictions should choose another target to attack (indeed, Wohlforth argues that by misstating Waltz's theory, they essentially already have). Second, Wohlforth maintains that the best way of testing Waltz's modest claims is by careful case study research. Neither formal theory nor quantitative research can uncover whether the causal mechanisms claimed to be at play when hegemonic bids failed were really operating or not. Third, Wohlforth launches a scathing broadside at "Lakatos boosters," and the use of a theory-appraisal metric that he argues is self-referential, divorced from reality, and "at best irrelevant and at worst downright damaging to scholarly inquiry." He finds very little in MSRP to recommend itself, and argues that a focus on paradigmatic description and appraisal will encourage unhelpful and destructive scholarly behavior.

Charles Glaser's "The Necessary and Natural Evolution of Structural Realism," in Chapter 16, provides a sympathetic overview of the trajectory of realist research since the publication of Waltz's *Theory of International Politics*. Glaser suggests that it is entirely expected and beneficial that subsequent realist theories have made divergent predictions from Waltz's book and from each other, largely because these successor theories have tightened up and improved the logic of structural arguments. Glaser suggests that Waltzian structural realism subsequently divided into two separate camps: defensive and offensive realism. The two variants were based on theorists deriving different deductions from similar structural models. Glaser then distinguishes defensive and offensive realism from neoclassical realism, which modifies structural realism by adding unit level variables. Glaser notes that neoclassical realists are willing to layer on additional variables because of a sensible modesty about the limitations of their theories. In addition, while the resulting multilevel theories that rely on additional variables may not be as "pure" as the theories they modified, without those original theories the multilevel variants would probably not have been developed.

Part III of the book consists of the concluding chapter. In Chapter 17, Elman and Vasquez review the main arguments in the book as a whole and enter into a dialogue with each other about the outstanding issues of the debate. They review each of the chapters to set forth the case against paradigmatism (looking at IR theory in terms of paradigms, written by Elman), the case for it (written by Vasquez), the case against the balance of power (written by Vasquez), and the case for the balance of power (written by Elman). In the last section, they outline some of the main lessons that can be derived from the debate and briefly look toward how future work might help resolve some of the unsettled questions.

## Acknowledgments

A number of people helped in preparing this book, not the least of which are our contributors, who agreed to participate in print and, in many cases, on panels at the American Political Science Association and the International Studies Association, where several of the chapters in Part II were initially presented. We thank Akan Malici, who spent countless hours reading and checking drafts of the manuscript, and the following Prentice Hall reviewers, who made helpful comments: Gregory A. Raymond, Boise State University; J. Martin Rochester, University of Missouri at St. Louis; Robert A. Denemark, University of Delaware; and Robert J. Lieber, Georgetown University. We also thank Heather Shelstad, our acquisitions editor at Prentice Hall, her assistant, Jessica Drew, and our production editor, Kari Callaghan Mazzola.

Lastly, for John Vasquez: I dedicate this book to Marie Henehan, my wife, intellectual partner, and companion in life's journey. For Colin Elman: This book is dedicated to Miriam Fendius Elman, who taught me to live in Holland.

*Colin Elman*
*John A. Vasquez*

## NOTES

1. For example, as Stephen Walt (1997, 933; Ch. 4 herein, 65*n*7) notes, realist scholars have provided explanations for (inter alia) the failure of modern efforts to gain hegemony over the international system, and for the difficulty of maintaining cooperation among states.
2. See Vasquez 1983, 1998.
3. Brecher 1999, 234. See Elman and Elman 1995 and 1997; Elman 1996a, 1996b, and 2001a.
4. Metatheories have other theories as their subject matter. They describe a second order inquiry, a reflection on our knowledge of things as distinct from our knowledge of things. See Mautner 1996, 267; and Polyani 1962, 344.
5. This tendency toward paradigmatism is nicely illustrated by a series of recent stock-taking symposia and special journal issues. See, for example, Dunne, Cox, and Booth 1998; and Katzenstein, Keohane, and Krasner 1998. These and similar efforts bore out Ada Finifter's (1997) remarks to the effect that "critical evaluations and assessments of research traditions and literatures" are particularly timely.
6. See, for example, Elman and Elman 2002b.
7. The paragraphs describing the essays reprinted from the *APSR* are partly redacted from the article abstracts, which are not reproduced in the chapters.

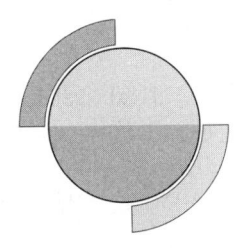

# About the Contributors

MICHAEL BARNETT is professor of political science at the University of Wisconsin at Madison. He has published in the areas of international relations theory, Middle Eastern politics, and the United Nations. Among his books are *Confronting the Costs of War: Military Power, State, and Society in Egypt and Israel* (1992); *Dialogues in Arab Politics: Negotiations in Regional Order* (1998); *Security Communities* (1998); and *Eyewitness to a Genocide: The United Nations and Rwanda* (2002).

BRUCE BUENO DE MESQUITA is a professor in the department of politics at New York University and a Senior Fellow at Stanford's Hoover Institution. He is the author or co-author of twelve books, including *The War Trap*; *War and Reason* (with David Lalman); *Principles of International Politics*; the forthcoming *Logic of Political Survival* (with Alastair Smith, Randolph M. Siverson, and James D. Morrow); and a novel, *The Trial of Ebenezer Scrooge*. He has written over one hundred articles for scholarly journals, as well as numerous pieces for newspapers and magazines. Bueno de Mesquita received an honorary doctorate from the University of Groningen (the Netherlands) in 1999 and was president of the International Studies Association for 2001–2002. He is a member of the American Academy of Arts and Sciences and the Council on Foreign Relations.

THOMAS J. CHRISTENSEN is professor of political science at the Massachusetts Institute of Technology, and the author of *Useful Adversaries: Grand Strategy, Domestic Mobilization, and Sino-American Conflict, 1947–1958* (1996). He is also the author of many articles and book chapters on Chinese foreign policy, international relations theory, and international security affairs.

COLIN ELMAN is assistant professor of political science at Arizona State University. His work has appeared in *American Political Science Review, International Security, Security Studies, International History Review,* and *International Studies Quarterly,* and he is the co-editor (with Miriam Fendius Elman) of *Bridges and Boundaries: Historians, Political Scientists, and the Study of International Relations* (2001) and *Progress in International Relations Theory: An Appraisal of the Field* (forthcoming). Elman is currently executive director of the Consortium for Qualitative Research Methods.

MIRIAM FENDIUS ELMAN is associate professor of political science at Arizona State University. She is the editor of *Paths to Peace: Is Democracy the Answer?* (1997); and co-editor (with Colin Elman) of *Bridges and Boundaries: Historians, Political Scientists, and the Study of International Relations* (2001) and *Progress in International Relations Theory: An Appraisal of the Field* (forthcoming). Elman's work appears in *American Political Science Review, British Journal of Political Science, International Security, International History Review, Security Studies,* and other scholarly journals.

CHARLES L. GLASER is deputy dean and professor at the Irving B. Harris Graduate School of Public Policy Studies, co-director of the Program on International Security Policy (PISP) at the University of Chicago, and the author of *Analyzing Strategic Nuclear Policy* (1990). Glaser researches international relations, focusing on issues of international security and defense policy, and is the author of several articles and book chapters on missile defense, NATO, defensive realism, the security dilemma, and the offense-defense balance.

JACK S. LEVY is Board of Governors' professor of political science at Rutgers University. He is author of *War in the Modern Great Power System, 1495–1975* (1983) and numerous articles and book chapters. His research interests focus on the causes of war and on foreign policy decision making. He is vice-president of the International Studies Association for 2001–2002.

ZEEV MAOZ is professor of political science and head of the Graduate School of Government and Policy at Tel-Aviv University. His most recent books include *Bound by Struggle: The Strategic Evolution of Enduring International Rivalries* (with Ben D. Mor) and *Domestic Sources of Global Change* (1996). He has published in *American Political Science Review, World Politics, International Security, Journal of Conflict Resolution, International Studies Quarterly,* and other journals in political science.

RICHARD ROSECRANCE is professor of political science at the University of California, Los Angeles, and adjunct professor at the John F. Kennedy School of Government, Harvard University. His books include *The Rise of the Virtual State: Wealth and Power in the Coming Century* (1999), which has been translated into

Chinese, Japanese, and German. A French commentary will appear shortly. Most recently, he edited *The New Great Power Coalition* (2001). He has served as director of the UCLA Burkle Center for International Relations and has been president of the International Studies Association. His work has appeared in many professional journals.

PAUL W. SCHROEDER is professor of history and political science emeritus at the University of Illinois (Urbana). He is the author of four books and many articles on the history of European international politics and the relation of history and theory in international relations from the seventeenth to the twentieth century. His most recent book, a volume in the Oxford History of Modern Europe series, is *The Transformation of European Politics, 1763–1848* (1994, 1996).

RANDALL L. SCHWELLER is associate professor in the Department of Political Science at Ohio State University. He is the author of *Deadly Imbalances: Tripolarity and Hitler's Strategy of World Conquest* (1998), and has published articles in numerous journals, including *International Security, Security Studies, World Politics,* and *International Studies Quarterly*.

JACK SNYDER is the Robert and Renée Belfer Professor of International Relations in the Department of Political Science and the Institute of War and Peace Studies at Columbia University. His books include *From Voting to Violence: Democratization and Nationalist Conflict* (2000); *Myths of Empire: Domestic Politics and International Ambition* (1991); and *Civil Wars, Insecurity, and Intervention,* co-edited with Barbara Walter (1999).

JOHN A. VASQUEZ is professor of political science at Vanderbilt University. He has published eleven books, including *The Power of Power Politics: From Classical Realism to Neotraditionalism; The War Puzzle;* and, most recently, *What Do We Know about War?* (editor). His scholarly articles have appeared in *International Studies Quarterly, World Politics, Security Studies, American Political Science Review, Journal of Peace Research, IO, Journal of Politics, International Political Science Review, Millennium,* and *British Journal of Political Science,* among others. He has been president of the Peace Science Society (International) and the International Studies Association.

STEPHEN M. WALT is Robert and Renee Belfer Professor of International Affairs at the John F. Kennedy School of Government, Harvard University. He is the author of *The Origins of Alliances* and *Revolution and War* (1987), as well as numerous scholarly articles on international relations and foreign policy. His recent works include "Rigor or Rigor Mortis? Rational Choice and Security Studies," *International Security* (spring 1999), and "The Enduring Relevance of the Realist Tradition," in *Political Science: State of the Discipline III,* ed. Ira Katznelson and Helen Milner (2002).

KENNETH N. WALTZ is Ford Professor emeritus of the University of California, Berkeley. He is now a senior research associate of the Institute of War and Peace Studies and adjunct professor of political science at Columbia University. He is most recently a co-author of *The Spread of Nuclear Weapons: A Debate* (1995), and is the author of other books and many articles.

WILLIAM C. WOHLFORTH is associate professor in the department of government at Dartmouth College. He is author of *The Elusive Balance: Power and Perceptions During the Cold War* (1993), and editor of *Witnesses to the End of the Cold War* (1996) and the forthcoming *Cold War Endgame*. His articles have appeared in *International Security*, *World Politics*, *Security Studies*, *Review of International Studies*, *Journal of Cold War Studies*, and *Diplomatic History*.

# INTRODUCTION

## APPRAISING BALANCE OF POWER THEORY

### COLIN ELMAN*

Questions about the balance of power have been discussed and disputed since at least the mid-sixteenth century.[1] It would not be unreasonable for International Relations (IR) theorists to suppose that everything that could be said has been said, perhaps several times over. Despite the longevity of the subject material, however, John Vasquez's 1997 essay published in the *American Political Science Review* (reprinted herein as Chapter 2) opens a genuinely new phase in this long conversation. The great virtue of Vasquez's chapter is in its intentional application of tools developed by philosophy of science to determine whether recent developments in balance of power theory have given us any added value. The mechanisms employed by Vasquez are here applied to realism and the balancing of power, but are potentially extendable and germane to any body of social science in the IR subfield and beyond.

Responding to the arguments and claims made in Vasquez's essay, the chapters that follow collectively address two related questions: First, how should IR theorists portray and appraise the knowledge statements they make? These statements often take the form of theories, from which hypotheses are drawn, linking causes and effects. For example, a subset of realist theories commonly observe that states very rarely accumulate preponderant power in the international system. How can we determine whether statements like this are "true" or "valuable"? How can we ascertain whether theories that change over time, and accordingly that make different empirical claims, are improving? Second, having decided how to describe and appraise the work to be judged, scholars then need to determine which scholarship is to be aggregated, and to detail the empirical claims made by the old and new versions of the theories.

---

*The author thanks Stephen Walt, Jack Snyder, and especially John Vasquez and Miriam Fendius Elman for helpful comments on earlier drafts of this chapter.

The next two sections of the chapter provide a menu of possible answers to these questions, offering an overview of different theory choice metrics, positioning the contemporary realist research that Vasquez critiques vis-à-vis the larger realist tradition, and detailing some different empirical claims made by various versions of balance of power theory.

## How Should We Describe and Judge Theories?[2]

Karl Popper (1989) suggests that the best way of determining the value of a theoretical claim is by attempting to contradict it with evidence. For Popper, the way that science improves is by writing propositions in ways that allow them to be confronted and falsified with empirical observations.[3] Science, regardless of chronology, social context, or particular content, is falsifiable; nonscience is not. A theory is to be preferred if it has been subjected to severe tests and has not yet been falsified. According to this view, an IR theory is judged in isolation vis-à-vis empirical evidence, and is doing well if it survives to fight another day. For example, in the case of the prediction that states will rarely be allowed to achieve hegemony, we could search the historical record looking for states that managed to do so. If almost every would-be hegemon failed, perhaps because they were frustrated by a blocking coalition of their threatened neighbors, the claim would be considered "not yet falsified."

For at least two reasons, however, basing our views of a theory's validity on the absence of direct contradictory evidence may be problematic. The first reason provides the means to save theories in the face of discrepant evidence, the second suggests a motive for doing so. First, falsification is too easy a test to pass.[4] It is usually possible to make minor amendments to theories that will accommodate contradictory data. To save the prediction that hegemony is rare, for example, scholars could simply raise the bar for what constitutes preponderant power.[5] Or they could suggest that in a given deviant case, neighboring states misperceived the rising challenger's capabilities.

Second, philosophers of science have noted that groups of scholars tend to share basic world views and assumptions that circumscribe theoretical and empirical work and that are resistant to change. These common and durable beliefs are the basis for relatively stable schools or traditions in the sciences, variously described as paradigms, research programs, research traditions, and so on. Philosophers suggest that loyalty to these aggregates make it likely that they will be amended, rather than abandoned, when challenged by contradictory information.

The best-known account of how scientists cluster into communities, and how their hard-wearing common commitments prevent early rejection of their theories, is provided by Thomas Kuhn. Arguing contra Popper that scientific advance does not consist of the gradual accumulation of ever truer theories that have yet to be falsified when they fail to pass critical tests, Kuhn's *The Structure of Scientific Revolutions* (1962) gives a very different view of science and scientific progress. Kuhn suggests that mature sciences are characterized by dominant paradigms that determine both the trajectory of puzzle solving "normal science," and the paradigm-specific criteria for deciding whether such activity is successful or not. By contrast, much less common "revolutionary science" occurs when scientific communities switch between paradigms, after the dominant approach becomes mired in increasingly damaging anomalies.[6]

Kuhn argues that, because paradigms are based on competing world views and are consequently not directly comparable, the decision to discard one paradigm for another cannot be based on "external" objective criteria. Because paradigms are incommensurable, the choice "between competing paradigms proves to be a choice between incompatible modes of community life." For Kuhn (1970a, 94), "there is no standard higher than the assent of the relevant community."[7] Since Kuhn maintains that that there is no common metric by which work in two different paradigms can be judged—criteria do not (by definition, cannot) span paradigms—extra-scientific sociological factors direct theory choice.[8] For example, a Kuhnian might argue that the unpopularity of political realism in the 1990s was an artifact of the more optimistic social milieu that arose after the Cold War.[9]

Imre Lakatos sought to bridge the gap between Popper and Kuhn's positions.[10] Lakatos recognized that scientists develop shared and lasting commitments to their theories, but he believed that it was nevertheless possible to develop external criteria that transcended those understandings, and that would permit more than purely sociological theory assessment. His solution borrowed elements from both Popper and Kuhn but both in this juxtaposition, and in the layering-on of additional features, provided a different approach to describing and appraising scientific theories.[11]

Lakatos's Methodology of Scientific Research Programs (MSRP) suggests that theories should be judged as a series of research programs (SRPs), each of which has a unique substantive and methodological configuration. SRPs have four elements: a hard core; a negative heuristic; a positive heuristic; and a protective belt of auxiliary hypotheses. The program's hard core consists of unchanging, privileged content. The hard core is protected by a negative heuristic that forbids this knowledge from being directly challenged or tested. In addition, SRPs have a protective belt which "bear[s] the brunt of tests and get[s] adjusted and re-adjusted, or even completely replaced, to defend . . . the core."[12] As Spiro J. Latsis (1976, 23) notes, the "protective belt may consist of various types of propositions from specific auxiliary hypotheses, accounting for predictive failure, to redefinitions of the conceptual apparatus." This protective belt is developed in accordance with the program's positive heuristic, "a partially articulated set of suggestions or hints"[13] that "guides the production of specific theories within the programme."[14] Lakatos also provides metatheoretic criteria that can be applied to determine whether theoretical developments add value. Most notably, Lakatos insists that changes in theories must do more than simply cover known empirical anomalies: They have to lead to new information.[15]

A fourth candidate metatheory is offered by Larry Laudan (1977, 81) who argues that scientific development should be described in terms of durable research traditions, which consist of "a set of general assumptions about the entities and processes in a domain of study, and about the appropriate methods to be used for investigating the theories in that domain." Research traditions determine the problems science seeks to solve; they provide heuristic guidance for future developments; and they help justify and rationalize theories.[16] Laudan's research traditions are more malleable than Lakatos's research programs. Their hard cores at any given time are rigid, but over time the elements that are considered sacrosanct can change.[17] Research traditions are also much less connected to their theories than in MSRP's research programs. For Laudan, research traditions do not entail theories, and theories do not entail research traditions. Contradictory theories can belong to the same research traditions, and different research traditions can "provide the presuppositional base for any given theory."[18] Laudan also moves away from Lakatos's criteria for determining the validity of theoretical trajectories. His metric is to "choose the theory (or research tradition) with the highest problem-solving adequacy,"[19] which leads him to accept as progressive ad hoc changes that are only capable of solving existing anomalies, a position that Lakatos categorically rejects.[20]

It is clear that, at a very general level, use of these candidate metatheories requires undertaking similar tasks. Regardless of which metatheory is being used, appraisers need to offer defensible descriptions of the elements that the aggregate's adherents share, and to apply the metatheory's criteria for determining whether successive theoretical moves provide added value.[21] But despite these very general similarities, metatheoretic choice *necessarily predates* other considerations. Each metatheory advocates different ways to delineate theories, describe their development over time, and to reach conclusions from their changing degree of conformity with empirical evidence. Different metatheoretic units are made of different things and are judged by different standards. Depending on which of Kuhn's two definitions one employs, a paradigm can be as specific as an exemplar, or as general as a world view.[22] Lakatos's research program consists of hard core and auxiliary belt, and of negative and positive heuristic. Laudan's research tradition is "a set of general assumptions about the entities and processes in a domain of study, and about the appropriate methods to be used for investigating the theories in that domain."[23] These are not picayune details to be left to the philosophers. They are the basic dimensions to be described, and as such their choice cannot be postponed until after the depiction is done.

## What Substantive Body of Material Should Be Described and What Theoretical Claims Does That Aggregate Make?

While differing on how they should be portrayed and appraised, all the metatheories described above anticipate that theories will change over time. Whichever metatheory is employed, scholars need to provide *before* and *after* accounts, to determine what the old and new theories claim. While this is a seemingly straightforward exercise, it turns out that what balance of power theory says is almost as contested as the more abstruse philosophical matters discussed above. Accordingly, this section positions the contemporary balance of power research that Vasquez critiques vis-à-vis the larger realist tradition, and provides a typology of different relevant empirical claims.

## REALISM

Conventional descriptions of realist literature trace the tradition as far back as circa 400 BCE and the writings of Thucydides.[24] For instance, Smith (1986) and other surveyors find in Thucydides' history of *The Peloponnesian War* both a concern with power relations among "states" and a rejection of the importance of morality. Thucydides (1972, 49) attributes the war to the interaction among the leaders of two powerful rival alliance systems, famously observing that: "What made war inevitable was the growth of Athenian power and the fear which this caused in Sparta." In addition, in a particularly stark illustration of realism's skepticism for the restraining effects of morality, Thucydides (1972, 402) notes in a speech attributed to the Athenians in the Melian dialogue that: ". . . the standards of justice depend on the equality of power to compel and that in fact the strong do what they have the power to do and the weak accept what they have to accept." Realists also claim among their number Niccolo Machiavelli, from whom they take the lesson that while morality may guide the lives of individuals, "any action that can be regarded as important for the survival of the state carries with it a built-in justification" (Smith 1986, 12). In addition, realists identify with Thomas Hobbes's notion of a "state of nature" where the absence of overriding authority allows human appetites to be unrestrainedly pursued—individuals engage in constant conflict, with their lives being concomitantly "nasty, brutish and short." Contemporary realists apply that image to the international system, where the absence of an overarching authority is seen as either a permissive or proximate cause of conflict.

Twentieth-century realism went through three succeeding phases: classical, neorealist, and neoclassical.[25] Classical realism, the first modern variant of this (perhaps) very old tradition is usually dated from 1939 and the publication of Edward Hallett Carr's seminal *The Twenty Year's Crisis*.[26] The approach's pessimistic and skeptical view of world politics was given a major boost by the Second World War.[27] During the 1950s, Hans Morgenthau's *Politics Among Nations: The Struggle for Power and Peace* became, as John Vasquez (1998, 36) notes, "the single most important vehicle for establishing the dominance of the realist paradigm within the field."[28] The 1960s saw classical realism coming under increasing scrutiny. Scholars who disagreed with Morgenthau and other classical realists on substantive grounds closely parsed their work to find inconsistencies and contradictions.[29] In addition, advocates of new behavioral and quantitative methodologies questioned the value of the traditional approach to inquiry. The 1970s saw the pendulum swing further against realism, with work focusing on interdependence and nonstate actors finding new prominence and popularity.[30]

The realist tradition was revived and revised with the publication of Waltz's neorealist *Theory of International Politics* (1979), which replaced Morgenthau's *Politics Among Nations* as the standard-bearer for realists, and is arguably the most influential book on international politics written in the last part of the twentieth century.[31] Such a prominent target was bound to attract criticism and, as time went by, detractors chipped away at the volume's dominance.[32] Nonrealist work, in particular neoliberal institutionalism and investigations of the democratic peace, became more popular.[33] Realists in their turn developed new understandings that addressed their own concerns with some aspects of Waltz's theory. Perhaps the most important strand of post-Waltzian realism is to be found in what subsequently came to be described as the neoclassical school.[34] The works Vasquez critiques in his 1997 essay can be coded as belonging to this neoclassical grouping.

The main substantive distinction between classical, neorealist, and neoclassical realism is the extent to which unit level causes—independent variables within the state—are thought to play a causal role. According to classical realism, because the desire for more power is rooted in the flawed nature of humanity, states are continuously engaged in a struggle to increase their capabilities. For classical realists international politics can be characterized as evil: Bad things happen because the people making foreign policy are sometimes bad. The absence of the international equivalent of a state's government is a permissive condition that gives human appetites free reign. In short, classical realism explains conflictual behavior by human failings. Wars are explained, for example, by particular aggressive statesmen, or by domestic political systems that give greedy parochial groups the opportunity to pursue self-serving expansionist foreign policies.[35]

By contrast, in *Theory of International Politics*, Waltz uses a sparse and deliberately simplified theoretical picture of a tightly bounded international political domain in which structure is generative. Contra classical realism, the internal makeup of different states is excluded from the theory. Waltz notes that international politics is characterized by a disheartening consistency; the same depressingly familiar things happening over and over. This repetitiveness endures despite considerable differences in internal domestic political arrangements, both through time (contrast, for example, seventeenth- and nineteenth-century England) and space (contrast, for example, the United States and Germany in the 1930s). Waltz's purpose is to explain why state systems all seem to be characterized by similar outcomes, even though their units (i.e., member states) have different domestic political arrangements and particular parochial histories. Waltz concludes that it must be something peculiar to, and pervasive in, international politics that explains these commonalities. He therefore excludes as "reductionist" all but the most minimal of assumptions about the units that make up the system.

By focusing only minor attention on unit level variables, Waltz aims to separate out the persistent effects of the international system. Because systems are generative, the international political system is characterized by complex nonlinear relationships and unintended consequences.[36] Outcomes are produced by something more than simply the aggregation of individual states' behaviors. In short, there is a gap between what states want and what states get. One important consequence is that wars can occur in the absence of revisionist intent. According to Waltz, an anarchical international system populated by states that, at a minimum, want to survive is *by itself* sufficient to generate conflict, even absent the revisionist motives attributed to states by classical realists. Neorealists suggest that wars can result because even benign states take steps to ensure their survival, and these steps threaten the survival of others.[37] Unlike classical realists, neorealists see international politics as tragic, not evil: Bad things can happen because states (some good, some bad) are placed in difficult situations.[38]

An additional consequence of the gap between foreign policies and international political outcomes is that it becomes meaningful (and indeed necessary) to separate them out as discrete categories of dependent variables. System-level dependent variables describe international outcomes, which occur regardless of the idiosyncratic behavior of individual units. These would include, for example, the predictions that multipolar systems will be less stable than bipolar systems; that interdependence will be lower in bipolarity than multipolarity; and that regardless of unit behavior, hegemony by any single state is unlikely or even impossible. Foreign policy predictions, by contrast, describe what individual states do. Whereas classical realism made predictions about foreign policy as well, Waltz suggests that his theory only accounts for international politics.

In part because they are uncomfortable with this modesty in declining to address individual state behavior and foreign policy, neoclassical realists seek to retain neorealism's insights about the generative nature of international structure, while reintroducing unit level causal factors back into their theories. This concern is nicely summarized by Jack Snyder's (1991, 19) observation that

> realism must be recaptured from those who look only at politics between societies, ignoring what goes on within societies. Realists are right in stressing power, interests, and coalition making as the central elements in a theory of politics, but recent exponents of Realism in international relations have been wrong in looking exclusively to states as the irreducible atoms whose power and interests are to be assessed.

The works Vasquez critiques in his 1997 essay can be regarded as fitting in this neoclassical category. All, either implicitly or explicitly, employ unit level variables in their theories, and all are interested in making overt foreign policy predictions.[39]

It is these post-Waltzian realist works at which John Vasquez takes aim. His argument is that they amended Waltz's claims to accommodate known empirical anomalies without satisfying Imre Lakatos's central criterion that new versions of theories must comply with: the prediction of novel facts that are eventually corroborated. In particular, Vasquez argues that post-Waltzian realists have watered down Waltz's "balancing proposition." Accordingly, a central disagreement in the book is what, if any, claims Waltz made about balance of power theory, and how those claims relate to those made by the other authors Vasquez criticizes. The next subsection considers different interpretations of balance of power theory.

## Balance of Power Theory

As with (indeed as part of) realism, scholars disagree about balance of power theory's claims to a long and venerable tradition. David Hume (1882), for example, suggests that "in all the politics of [ancient] Greece, the anxiety, with regard to the balance of power is apparent." According to Seabury (1965, 7) Kautilya's *Arthasastra*, written between 321 and 300 BCE, "clearly instructs . . . in the principles of a balance of power system."[40] In a similar way, Polybius commends Hiero, the king of Syracuse, for aligning with weaker Carthage, notwithstanding a pre-existing treaty with stronger Rome. Polybius suggests this was wise and prudent since the fall of Carthage would have left Rome as the dominant power "able, without contrast or opposition, to execute every purpose and undertaking . . . such a force [ought never] to be thrown into one hand, as to incapacitate the neighboring states from defending their rights against it." [41]

Notwithstanding these examples, the relative antiquity of balance of power thinking is contested. Herbert Butterfield (1966, 132–133) for example, argues that Hume is mistaken in his interpretation of Polybius's account of Hiero, and that "the idea of the balance of power . . . did not exist in the ancient world." There is somewhat more consensus about its emergence (or perhaps reemergence) in Europe, especially in sixteenth-century Italy.[42] Butterfield (1966, 136–139) suggests that Guicciardini's (1537) *History of Italy* gives "the first vivid picture of the balance of power" but still fell short of a fully developed theory. It is not until the mid-seventeenth century that references "begin to come in an amazing flood" and "the doctrine has its remarkable development." From that point on there also developed a proliferation of different understandings, as well as criticisms of them.[43]

Writing at least several hundred years after its inception, Robert Jervis (1997, 131) observes that "Balance of Power is the best known, and perhaps the best, theory in international politics, although there is no agreement as to exactly what the theory holds, let alone whether it is valid." Part of the confusion arises because scholars with quite different perspectives have appropriated the surprisingly malleable term. A. F. Pollard (1923, 58), for example, wrote ". . . the term balance of power may mean almost anything; and it is used not only in different senses by different people, or in different senses by the same people at different times, but in different senses by the same person at the same time."[44]

There have been several attempts to provide comprehensive definitions as well as typologies of the different claims that various balance of power theories have made.[45]

International relations theorists often draw a distinction between "balancing" as state behavior and "balance" as an international political outcome. "Balancing" describes foreign policy: that is, what a state does. A working definition is that balancing is *a countervailing policy designed to improve abilities to prosecute military missions in order to deter and/or defeat another state*. States can balance in a variety of ways, including co-opting the resources of other states by making alliances (external balancing) or by improving their own military abilities (internal balancing). For the latter, enhancements can be achieved in several different ways, including: acquiring more of the material that forms or pays for military units, for example, steel, coal, people, or money; extracting more resources from the endowments the territorial state already controls (Zakaria 1998); directing more of the resources the state has already extracted away from societal consumption toward defense (Powell 1999); and using the resources the state already applies to defense more wisely, with a military doctrine that is better suited to its security needs (Posen 1984).

"Balance" describes a systemic outcome, an equilibrium of military capability in the international system. It is important to note that while often operationalized as a distribution of resources among two or more states, the balance concept itself is centrally concerned with the ability (or lack thereof) to prevail in a military conflict. Counting factor endowments only satisfactorily reflects this concern by virtue of a number of *ceteris paribus* (other things being equal) clauses: that states are equally capable in extracting resources from their societies; that they commit comparable proportions of those resources to defense; and that the resources so committed are employed with similar levels of skill.[46]

Considering endowment, extraction, commitment, and planned use separately allows for a more nuanced treatment of balance. First, since the *ceteris paribus* clauses will often not hold, counting the distribution of capabilities may not be an accurate operationalization of states' abilities to prevail in a military contest. Second, the four elements interact, but not necessarily in an intuitive linear "more is better" fashion. Overextraction, which one might expect in a command economy, can stifle productivity and reduce the availability of resources in the future. In addition, a state could surrender control over resources and, nevertheless, become a greater threat in the future because of resulting improvements on the other three dimensions. A smaller efficient Russia is likely to be more powerful than a larger stagnant Soviet Union. Third, the trigger event that signals that a state has accumulated sufficient resources to become a would-be hegemon or a dyadic threat may not be a straightforward increase in factor endowments following territorial expansion. Arguably, a state could become a threat by improving on any of the other three dimensions, which could be done without interfering with its neighbors (or indeed, as with the demise of the Soviet Union, actually retrenching from the near and not-so-near abroad).

A central argument in this book is about whether balancing and/or balances are predicted by the different theories under investigation. There are also disagreements about the connection between the two phenomena: Is balancing necessary for balances to form? Is the existence of a balance evidence that balancing has taken place? Theorists take different positions on these questions depending on which type of balance of power theory they advocate. For the purposes of this chapter, three versions are particularly important, and are represented in Table 1.1: manual, dyadic, and automatic balance of power theory.

TABLE 1.1   DIFFERENT CATEGORIES OF BALANCE OF POWER THEORY

| OUTCOME IS | DEPENDENT VARIABLE | |
| --- | --- | --- |
|  | EQUILIBRIUM IN THE SYSTEM | COUNTERVAILING STATE BEHAVIOR |
| INTENTIONAL | Manual balance of power theory | Dyadic balance of power theory |
| INEVITABLE | Automatic balance of power theory | [Self-defense—not balance of power theory][47] |

Some theorists argue that balance of power theory predicts that states will deliberately act with a view to balancing the system. *Manual balance of power* theory (Claude 1962, 48–49) sees equilibrium resulting from the intentional acts of statesmen, who prefer a balanced system to possible alternatives. The reasons for that preference can be the belief that a balanced system is most likely to result in state survival, or the view that equilibrium carries with it some additional intrinsic benefits, such as a lower prevalence of war. It is important to note that theories that predict that states will act to countervail a would-be hegemon belong in this manual category: States perceive the likelihood of a systemic outcome they wish to avoid (hegemony by another state) and act to bring about a systemic outcome they prefer (balance). For example, this seems to be the kind of balancing Rosecrance (Ch. 11 herein) has in mind when he suggests that "balancers must aim to create the public good of security against hegemony of the system as a whole, not simply to defend themselves."[48]

Other theorists suggest that states will act to balance against other states' rising power, but without any explicit preference for a particular systemic outcome. *Dyadic balance of power* theory anticipates that state actions will be designed to countervail threats posed by other states. Those threats may be operationalized differently, for example, by relative capabilities alone, or in combination with other indicators such as proximity and intentions. Dyadic balance of power theory does not require that the threatening state is likely to achieve hegemony, just that it is posing a threat that needs to be countervailed.[49]

*Automatic balance of power* theory (Claude 1962, 43–46) suggests that the system will tend toward balance, regardless of the intentions or actions of individual states. This view was famously captured by Jean Jacques Rousseau (1756, Hoffman and Fidler 1991, 62) when he observed that the balance is not

> the work of any man, or that any man has deliberately done anything to maintain it. It is there; and men who do not feel themselves strong enough to break it conceal the selfishness of their designs under the pretext of preserving it. But, whether we are aware of it or not, the balance continues to support itself without the aid of any special intervention; if it were to break for a moment on one side, it would soon restore itself on another....[50]

Thus the acid test for distinguishing automatic and manual variants is to ask whether equilibrium is achieved because statesmen intend to bring or keep the system in balance.[51]

Automatic balance of power theory is designed to explain why balances form in the international system, but is agnostic about why (or even whether) individual states will balance. As described in Table 1.2, a would-be hegemon's challenge, and states that bandwagon (join in) with it, represent what systems theorists describe as positive feedback, moving the system away from equilibrium. Balances can only form in the presence of negative feedback, an impetus back in the direction of equilibrium. Balancing behavior is one obvious source of negative feedback. An important question

TABLE 1.2   FEEDBACK IN THE INTERNATIONAL SYSTEM

**NEGATIVE FEEDBACK**

| | |
|---|---|
| Manual balancing | State(s) prepare to deter or defeat a rising hegemon to maintain system's equilibrium |
| Dyadic balancing | State(s) prepare to deter or defeat a threatening state in order to neutralize that threat |
| Mutual Expansion | Two expansionist states struggle with one another, each providing a drag on the other's expansion |
| Self-encirclement | Expansionist state(s) attack state(s) that have sufficient capabilities to defeat the expansionist(s) |
| Predators' Quarrel | Initially successful expansionist states fall out over division of the spoils, and provide a drag on the other's expansion |

**NEUTRAL FEEDBACK**

| | |
|---|---|
| Buck-passing | Free ride on other state(s)' balancing efforts, either to avoid costs, or because relative position will be advanced by conflict between other parties (Christensen and Snyder 1990, 141) |

**POSITIVE FEEDBACK**

| | |
|---|---|
| Manual Expansion | State attempts to achieve regional or global hegemony (manual, because state is driven by a preferred view of the system) |
| Dyadic Expansion | State attempts to improve its relative capabilities vis-à-vis another state |
| Bandwagoning | State surrenders to overwhelmingly powerful aggressor to avoid adding unnecessary costs to inevitable defeat (Walt 1987) or state joins with aggressor to share in spoils of victory, to avoid punishment by the victor, or because they believe the aggressor represents the "wave of the future" (Schweller 1998a, 77–81). |

for automatic balance of power theorists then is how much (if any) balancing is required in order to bring the system into equilibrium. There are at least three different possibilities: widespread balancing; sufficient balancing; and little or no balancing because of the presence of other types of negative feedback.

If either dyadic or manual balancing were widespread, we would expect balances to form in the international system. A state can balance manually by preparing to deter or defeat a rising hegemon because it values a system in which no state possesses preponderant power. Alternatively, a state can balance dyadically by preparing to deter or defeat a threatening state in order to neutralize that danger. If such balancing behavior is very common, balances are likely to form.

It is, however, possible to sustain the argument that balances materialize without prevalent manual or dyadic balancing. In other words, even if the *only* source of negative feedback were manual or dyadic balancing, the related behavioral prediction is *not* necessarily that states on the aggregate balance, or that a majority of states balance.[52] It simply requires that states with sufficient military capabilities act to check the rising challenger or threat. Just how much is enough is in each instance an empirical question. If the then prevailing technology or geographical circumstances favor the defense, if seized resources do not cumulate easily with those already possessed by the metropole, if dominoes do not fall, and if power is difficult to project at a distance, that may not be too heavy a burden to satisfy.[53] In a world in which conquest is hard it may not take too much manual or dyadic balancing for balances to form.

Finally, as indicated in Table 1.2, there are other kinds of negative feedback than balancing. In a situation of *mutual expansion*, two rising expansionist challengers might stop each other in their tracks without balancing against each other, and without either being balanced by other states.[54] Similarly, as noted earlier, most (although not all) invaded states fight back, even when they have made negligible arrangements to do so in advance. Invaders might engage in *self-encirclement* by attacking an enemy that has made no preparations to deter or vanquish particular aggressors, but which is nevertheless too powerful to defeat. Hence the system returns toward equilibrium, and automatic balance of power is supported, even in the absence of balancing behavior.[55] Finally, initially successful expansionist states may fall out over division of the spoils, resulting in their mutual retrenchment. Rousseau (1756; Hoffman and Fidler 1991, 63–64) captures the dynamic of this kind of *predators' quarrel* when he describes the aftermath of a successful joint offensive action:

> [T]hat very success would sow the seeds of discord among our victorious allies. It is beyond the bounds of possibility that the prizes of victory should be so equally divided, that each will be equally satisfied with his share. The least fortunate will soon set himself to resist the further progress of his rivals, who in their turn, for the same reason, will speedily fall out with one another. I doubt whether, since the beginning of the world, there has been a single case in which three, or even two, powers have joined forces for the conquest of others without quarreling over their contingents [of forces that they supply to fight in the war], or over the division of the spoil, and without, in consequence of this disagreement, promptly giving new strength to their common enemy.[56]

In sum, it is arguable that neither widespread manual nor dyadic balancing are required to produce a balanced international system. In some circumstances, limited countervailing may be enough. It may also be the case that a combination of the different kinds of negative feedback will be sufficient to keep the system in (or tending toward) equilibrium.[57]

Before proceeding we should note that the three categories of manual, automatic, and dyadic balance of power are not exhaustive and that scholars and policymakers sometimes use the term more loosely.[58] My own view is that we should reserve the phrase for one of the three situations described above, but readers should be aware of other popular usages. Inis Claude's (1962) inventory is particularly useful, and as indicated by the contemporary examples cited below, all are very much still in play. Balance of power is used to describe a *situation* when it refers to a snapshot of the current configuration of power, the objective situation as it currently is.[59] Peter Biles (2000, 11), for example, uses the term this way when he asks rhetorically, "How did Ethiopia so rapidly change the balance of power in its two-year dispute with neighboring Eritrea?" Similarly, John Mearsheimer (2001, 403n3) defines balance of power as "the actual distribution of military assets among the great powers in the system." Balance of power is used to describe a *policy* when it delineates the actions a state takes in pursuit of a particular, or in cognizance of the current, configuration of power. James Chace (1998, 105), for example, is sympathetic to the suggestion that "the United States . . . play a central role in seeking a balance of power among nations." Tim Huxley (1998, 90) observes that "in East Asia, the regional security landscape is still molded to a large extent by balance of power thinking, in which relative military power is a central consideration." The third use of the term balance of power is as a *symbol*. Claude (1962, 36–39) suggested that balance of power is used in this way when the phrase is invoked to support the speaker's realistic and prudent approach to foreign affairs, or to suggest that another's neglect of the concept is a serious failing.[60] George W. Bush used the term symbolically in his inaugural presidential address when he said: "The enemies of liberty and our country should make no mistake, America remains engaged in the world, by history and by choice, shaping a balance of power that favors freedom."[61]

Setting these more colloquial usages aside, we must nevertheless determine which (or which combination) of the three different categories of balance of power theory (manual, dyadic, and automatic) Waltz, Walt, Schweller, and Christensen and Snyder use. Waltz's *Theory of International Politics* is first and foremost an automatic balance of power theory. According to Waltz (1979, 118), in an anarchic international system populated by states that at a minimum seek their own preservation, balances will recurrently form, whether states intend them or not.[62] Waltz explicitly eschews predicting that states will balance a dyadic threat, or that states will act to bring the system into balance because they value equilibrium. As Jack Levy (Ch. 10 herein) notes, this raises a tricky question for Waltz. While Waltz may decline to predict any individual state's foreign policy, his expectation of balance as an international political outcome is likely to have some implications for the incidence of balancing behavior by states. But in order to test those implications, we need to know what they are. Unfortunately, it is simply unclear how widespread Waltz believes balancing behavior to be.

Thomas Christensen and Jack Snyder's 1990 article addresses an indeterminacy in Waltz's theory. Waltz distinguishes between two kinds of balancing: *internal balancing*, when a state relies on its own efforts, and *external balancing*, when a state makes alliances with other states. In bipolar systems, the only state that has the wherewithal to balance against a superpower is the other superpower. Accordingly, the two poles will almost always rely on their own efforts, and will not greatly value their alliances with smaller states. In multipolarity, by contrast, two external balancing dynamics can occur. Because more than one state has the opportunity to respond to a competitor, each has an incentive to "pass the buck," hoping that another threatened state will expend the necessary blood and treasure to stop a rising hegemon.[63] A mutual buck-pass could result in neither balancing, with the consequence that the rising state could achieve hegemony. A second possible multipolar balancing dynamic, chain-ganging, results when states "chain themselves unconditionally to reckless allies."[64] Interlocking alliance commitments result in "hyperactive balancing behavior [which] threatens the stability of the system by causing unrestrained warfare that threatens the survival of some of the great powers that form the system's poles."[65]

While anticipating that both dynamics are possible in multipolarity, Waltz is silent on when each is likely to occur. This is not a problem for his theory, since it only claims to account for the reason multipolar systems are less stable than bipolar systems, not to predict behavioral variation within multipolar systems.[66] By contrast, Christensen and Snyder are explicitly concerned with explaining individual states' foreign policies—whether states are likely to balance dyadically. For these purposes, the indeterminacy needs to be squeezed out of Waltz's theory. Christensen and Snyder do so by incorporating into the theory perceptions of whether offensive or defensive military technology and doctrine have the advantage—the offense-defense balance. Christensen and Snyder argue that when states believe the defense has the advantage, they are much more likely to buck-pass. That is, they sit back and wait for another threatened state to act. By contrast, when they believe the offense has the advantage they will briskly respond, leading to chain-ganging and a rapid widening of the war.[67]

TABLE 1.3  THEORIES VASQUEZ CRITIQUES

| Author | Independent Variables | Predicted State Behavior | Predicted Systemic Outcome | Type of Balance of Power Theory |
|---|---|---|---|---|
| Waltz | Distribution of capabilities | Indeterminate | Balance of capabilities | Automatic |
| Christensen and Snyder | Distribution of capabilities plus perception of offense-defense balance | Depends on perceived offense-defense balance Buck-passing and hyper-balancing | Indeterminate | Partly dyadic |
| Walt | Distribution of capabilities plus offense-defense balance plus proximity plus intentions | Balancing (some rare bandwagoning) | Balance of threat | Dyadic |
| Schweller | Distribution of capabilities plus state motives (fear or greed) | Depends on whether states are fearful or greedy Balancing and bandwagoning | Indeterminate | Partly dyadic |

For Christensen and Snyder, the prevalence of balancing behavior under multipolarity will depend on the perceived offense-defense balance. Where offense is regarded as dominant, states will be quick to make external alliances and to live up to their commitments under them. Where defense is seen as dominant, buck-passing will be widespread and balancing rare. The predicted systemic outcome is indeterminate. Chain-ganging is a strong form of positive feedback, and while it may be unnecessarily costly, it is also likely to help restore equilibrium. However, it should be recalled that chain-ganging is associated with a perception of offense dominance. In a truly offense dominant world, would-be hegemons are likely to be able to roll up the system quickly, and balances will not form.[68]

By contrast, buck-passing is a form of neutral feedback that, if widespread, would give a potential hegemon the opportunity to amass preponderant power. But buck-passing is associated with a perception of defense dominance. A correct perception of defense dominance would suggest a reduced requirement for negative feedback. That is, if the defense really were dominant, such that invaded states could cope without much preparation and without outside assistance, balances would form even with widespread buck-passing. In a truly defense dominant world, almost all aggression would be self-encirclement. In sum, while Christensen and Snyder's perception of offense-defense variable may allow for determinate behavioral predictions under multipolarity, there is still substantial room for different systemic outcomes.[69]

Although there is considerable overlap between Waltz's version of balance of power theory and Stephen Walt's balance of threat theory, there are also differences in both their dependent and independent variables. Walt, like Christensen and Snyder, explicitly seeks to explain foreign policy. In order to do so, Walt expands the number of causal variables.[70] For Walt, states do not simply balance against other states' rising capabilities, but also take into account other factors that determine how threatening those capabilities are. Hence Walt (1987, 21–28; 1991, 54) argues that in deciding whether or not to balance, states look not just at aggregate power (more is more threatening), but also at geographical proximity (closer is more threatening), offensive capabilities (more is more threatening), and offensive intentions (states that have them are more threatening).[71] Walt expects balancing against threat to be a prevalent foreign policy behavior, although he does suggest (1987, 28–32; 1991, 53) that some states may have no choice but to bandwagon and join forces with the more menacing state. Walt (1987, 29) argues, however, that potential bandwagoners are aware that increasing the capabilities of a threatening state carries great risks, and will usually opt to balance against them instead.

Walt, unlike Waltz, is willing to argue that his theory can explain particular cases of dyadic balancing, as well as explain widespread balancing behavior in the international system. As for international political outcomes, the negative feedback in Walt's system arising from common dyadic balancing against threatening states clearly means that balances will form. What is not so clear, however, is balances of *what*? Walt (2000, 203) observes that "[e]very modern attempt to achieve hegemony in Europe has been thwarted by a powerful balancing coalition." But every state in modern Europe that attempted hegemony was near to states it threatened, possessed offensive capabilities, and had malign intentions. Given the different elements that make up Walt's main causal variable, it is at least possible that a more distant state that possessed mainly defensive means and benign intentions could be allowed to build up overwhelming relative capabilities without other states reacting. Such a state would be a hegemon for Waltz, and a clear anomaly for his balance of power theory. But it is not clear whether it would be a hegemon for Walt's balance of threat theory. It is possible that, when states are approaching capabilities of hegemonic proportions, those resources alone are so threatening that they "drown out" distance, offense-defense, and intentions as potential negative threat modifiers. If that were so, both Walt and Waltz would agree that a state is unlikely to accumulate preponderant power.

Randall Schweller's "balance of interests" theory travels the most distance from Waltz's approach, and is perhaps the most explicit of all neoclassical works in its insistence that realism is best served by acknowledging and including different state motivations (1993, 76–77, 84; 1994, 92–99). Instead of using Waltz's assumption that states will at a minimum seek survival, Schweller develops a typological theory based on whether states are primarily motivated by, and the extent of, their fear and greed.[72] Using zoological imagery, Schweller suggests that "wolves" with unlimited aims seek to maximize their power at every turn. They are primarily opposed by "lions," satisfied states that seek to maintain the current status quo. Schweller's theory also contemplates a second class of greedy states: "jackals" with limited aims. In a major departure from the preceding realist theories, Schweller suggests that these second-class revisionists (at least initially) bandwagon with the rising challenger. Unlike Walt, who mainly argues that if states are sometimes compelled to bandwagon it will be because they are outclassed, Schweller (1994, 93–95) maintains that greedy states will bandwagon in anticipation of gain, feeding off the wolf's kill. For Schweller, bandwagoning is much more common than in either Waltz's balance of power or Walt's balance of threat theory. While Schweller's theory is a dyadic balance of power theory for lions, it is clearly not so for wolves and jackals.

Schweller (1993, 75; 1994, 100–106) is interested in explaining both unit-level foreign policy and systemic level international political outcomes. At the system level, it is unclear whether sufficient negative feedback occurs to bring the system toward equilibrium. There are at least two different potential sources. Initially, the main impetus in the direction of balance will be from status quo lion states seeking to countervail the revisionists.[73] However, if smaller status quo powers conclude that the revisionist coalition is too powerful to confront, they may "distance" themselves, and refuse to join the defensive alliance.[74] Taking fearful distancing and greedy bandwagoning together, it is quite possible that balances might not form at all. Schweller (1994, 104) notes that "the stability of the system depends on the balance of conservative and revisionist forces. . . . When a revisionist state or coalition is stronger than the defenders of the status quo, the system will eventually undergo change. . . ." The system may be a little more stable than this formulation suggests, however, because of a second type of negative feedback, which takes the form of a predators' quarrel.[75] While they may be initially successful, the wolf and its attending jackals are likely to fall out over future strategies and relative capabilities. Wolves have unlimited aims, and so will continue to push for greater expansion. Jackals have restricted appetites, and so are likely to be satiated by the early success, and are therefore much less likely to agree to further risky attacks. In addition, since wolves claim a greater share of the spoils than jackals, success leaves the wolf relatively more powerful. This raises the question in the jackals' minds of when they are likely to end up on the menu. At some point the combination of satiation, unwillingness to undertake further risks, and fear of the rising hegemon leads to the jackals' defection to the status quo coalition.

## QUESTIONS TO KEEP IN MIND WHILE READING THIS BOOK

As suggested in the preface, philosophy of science is sometimes difficult to digest. Accordingly, it might be helpful to keep some signpost questions in mind while reading the chapters. All of the authors address some of these questions; some take on all of them.

1. What do the different authors suggest is the appropriate way to describe and judge theoretical developments? Answers range from the Vasquez's (Chapters 2 and 8) and Elman and Elman's (Chapter 7) endorsements of Lakatos's MSRP, to Walt's (Chapter 4) suggestion that it is outdated, and Wohlforth's (Chapter 15) unqualified rejection of paradigmatism.
2. If the authors' answer to question 1 requires tracking the development of large theoretical aggregates and noting the commonalities and discontinuities between them, how do they think realism and balance of power theory should be configured? In particular, what do the authors believe is the correct degree of overlap between the works cited and critiqued by Vasquez in Chapter 2? Is there, as Vasquez suggests in that chapter, one large realist paradigm with several constituent research programs, one of which is balance of power?
3. What do the different authors suggest balance of power theory predicts, particularly in respect to the crucial distinction between foreign policies (balancing) and international political outcomes (balances)? Waltz (Chapter 3) and Wohlforth (Chapter 15) argue for an indeterminate theory that is only capable of making predictions about systemic outcomes, not individual state behavior.
4. Given their answers to the preceding questions, do the authors believe that balance of power theory passes the test they set? What are the implications of their findings for realist understandings of international politics?
5. What are the implications of the authors' answers to these questions for how America should be acting abroad, and for the prospects for sustainable peace and security in world politics? Is the best that realism has to offer the world an armed and watchful peace anchored in mutual deterrence, punctuated by inevitable war?[76] Or would a reliance on alternative theories lead to a failure to deter potential adversaries, and an America unprepared to prevail against its enemies if deterrence failed?

6. Are the disagreements among the authors more about the ways in which theories should be described (what work should be grouped under the rubric of a common theory); what kinds of tests will determine a theory's value (for example, surviving Popperian falsification versus providing Lakatos's increased novel content); what substantive claims balance of power theory makes (balancing, balances, or both); or the empirical observations made in support of, or to undermine, the theories (for example, disagreements about whether a particular state's foreign policy amounted to balancing or not)?

## Why This Book Matters

While negotiating the thicket of philosophy of science, we must remember that this volume's subject is, without exaggeration, dealing with issues of life and death on a scale that is hard to imagine. The twentieth century witnessed over one hundred and eleven million deaths caused by war.[77] Given the extraordinary forces of destruction still waiting to be unleashed in the world, it does not require much effort to establish the importance of improving our understanding of how states behave abroad. This volume can be seen, in some respects, as the latest exchange between scholars with commitments to competing realist, liberal, and other nonrealist understandings of that behavior and its outcomes.

Pessimistic and prudential, political realism suggests that state behavior is driven by selfish human appetites for power, or by the need to accumulate the wherewithal to be secure in a self-help world. Liberal competitors, grounded in a more hopeful and optimistic point of view, hold out the promise of progress toward a more peaceful and enlightened world.[78] Taken as prescriptive guides, these approaches provide very different menus of foreign policy choices. The stakes in this disagreement are enormous, and go well beyond the parochial concerns of a subfield of an academic discipline. Accordingly, we should welcome developments that might help us arrive at a better understanding of world politics, and minimize the likelihood that the previous century's ghastly record will be equaled or exceeded.

By spelling out the epistemological rules he intends to follow, and then making a good faith effort to comply with them, Vasquez offers an entrée to better IR theory. Detractors may (and indeed do) quarrel with his choice or use of those rules and with his rendition of the substance of the realist theories he seeks to describe and appraise. But even Vasquez's harshest critics must acknowledge that, were he mistaken in every particular, his application would nevertheless serve a vital purpose. By tracking part of the trajectory of realist scholarship, and by self-consciously using a particular epistemology to describe and appraise it, Vasquez forces IR theorists to deconstruct and reexamine their taken-for-granted paradigmatism.[79]

It is commonplace to acknowledge that IR scholars structure their subfield, and their arguments, around a few large theoretical aggregates.[80] The great majority of disciplinary surveys are written in paradigmatic terms. In addition, when new theoretical developments are offered, or empirical tests are performed, it is most often in the name of bolstering or undermining one of the subfield's "isms," particularly realism or liberalism. IR theorists have maintained this commitment to paradigmatism, even while it has fallen out of fashion with contemporary philosophers of science.

While remaining steadfastly committed to such an approach, however, when it comes to asking *how* to be paradigmatic, most IR theorists have a very wide comfort zone for ambiguity and unspoken assumptions. They seem comfortable applying Potter Stewart's test for pornography: "I know it when I see it."[81] The problem is that there are various kinds of paradigmatism, each bounded by a separate metatheory that offers a different road map for how to proceed. As discussed above, what is to be included in a theoretical aggregate, and how it will be appraised, depends on which metatheory is being employed. For example, Kuhnian paradigms, Lakatosian research programs, Laudanian research traditions, and other metatheoretic units are constituted by different elements and are judged by different criteria. IR theorists often cite one or more of these candidate metatheories while paying little or no attention to its associated complex of concepts and conventions. In addition, since different IR scholars pursue paradigmatism while applying different metatheories, the subfield has become characterized by a muted but nonetheless consequential incommensurability.

Vasquez's (1997) essay provokes IR scholars into consciously reconsidering their own views on philosophy of science, forcing the reacquisition of the epistemological underpinnings of the subfield's attachment to paradigmatism. To be sure, the philosophers of science who are referenced by Vasquez and others in this volume are hardy perennials, and readers might be tempted to ask what can be gained from revisiting such seemingly familiar territory. The answer, as Giovanni Sartori (1994, 14) suggests, is that if "'methodological discussions are often reinventing what has been forgotten,'" rediscovering "the 'forgotten known' is just as important as discover[ing] (anew) an unknown."

## Notes

1. Wright 1975, ix–xii; Sheehan 1996, 29–36; Wight 1966, 149; Butterfield 1966.
2. This section draws partly on Elman and Elman 2002a and 2002b, and Elman 2001b.
3. See also Lakatos 1974, 310–312; Suppe 1977a, 167; Diesing 1991, 31–32; Blaug 1992, 14; Donovan, Laudan, and Laudan 1992, 4–5; and Leplin 1997, 38.
4. This view is captured in the labels "dogmatic" and "naïve" that are sometimes attached to this kind of falsificationism. To be fair to Popper, he did recognize that scientists could trivially restate their propositions in a way that avoided contradiction by known empirical evidence. Accordingly, he bolstered falsification with "methodological rules that forbid what he first called 'ad-hoc auxiliary assumptions,' later 'conventionalist stratagems,' and finally 'immunizing stratagems'" (Blaug 1992, 19; see also Caldwell 1991, 96).
5. For example, possessing 51 percent of the system's resources rather than the capability to defeat simultaneously the next two (i.e., second and third) most powerful states in the system.
6. Suppe 1977a, 143–144; and Backhouse 1998, 352.
7. See also Suppe 1977a, 149–150.
8. It should be noted that this reading is disputed by some Kuhnians, who argue that there are some rules or practices that are so ubiquitous as to amount to multiparadigmatic standards, for example maintaining logical consistency, not deliberately faking data, and so on.
9. The events of September 11, 2001, however, have probably ended this brief hiatus. See Elman 2001b.
10. Popper (1970, 52–53) strongly disputed Kuhn's sociological account of science (see also Mayo 1996, 22; Diesing 1991, 34). Popper's view that a scientific community was the finest example of an open

society was completely antithetical to Kuhn's suggestion that science was nothing more or less than the powers-that-be said it was (Suppe 1977a, 170; Larvor 1998, 45).
11. Larvor 1998, 45–46. Imre Lipsitz was born on November 9, 1922, to a Hungarian Jewish family. Hungary was allied with Nazi Germany in the second world war, and Lipsitz took the name Tibor Molnar to avoid conscription into forced labor and eventual deportation to Poland, where his mother and grandmother perished at Auschwitz. After taking the third name Lakatos, and continuing his training in mathematics, physics, and philosophy, he joined the Hungarian Ministry of Education in 1947. In 1950 he was arrested, charged with "revisionism," and spent four years in prison. Subsequent to returning to academia for two years, Lakatos fled Hungary after the 1956 uprising was put down by the Soviet Union. Between 1957 and 1960 Lakatos attended, and wrote a Ph.D. thesis at, King's College, Cambridge. In 1960 he joined Karl Popper at the London School of Economics, where he remained until his death in February 1974. This biographical summary is redacted from Larvor 1998, 1–7.
12. Lakatos 1970, 133.
13. Lakatos 1970, 135.
14. Worrall 1978, 59.
15. See the chapters by Vasquez and Elman and Elman in this volume for more discussion of Lakatos's metatheory.
16. Laudan 1977, 86–93.
17. Laudan 1977, 99–100.
18. Laudan 1977, 85.
19. Laudan 1977, 109.
20. Laudan 1977, 114–118.
21. For Popper, Lakatos, and Laudan these criteria are separate and separable from the substance of the aggregate in question. For Kuhn, they are not.
22. Kuhn acknowledges that, in the first edition of *The Structure of Scientific Revolutions* he used "paradigm" with multiple different meanings. In the postscript to the second edition, he narrows the list to two. See Kuhn 1970a, 175.
23. Laudan 1977, 81.
24. See, for example, Smith 1986, 4–15, which provides a very useful review and which I draw on heavily for the remainder of this paragraph. For the ways in which Thucydides has been (ab)used by IR theorists, see also Garst 1989; Bedford and Workman 2001, 51; Lebow 2001; Sheehan 1996, 27–28, and Forde 1995.
25. This is a much simplified account. For a more nuanced version, which differentiates post-Waltzian realism into several different schools, see Elman 2002.
26. Vasquez 1998, 35 (though, see Jones 1998 for a dissenting view). In addition to Carr, work by Frederick Schuman (1933), Harold Nicolson (1939), Reinhold Niebuhr (1940), Georg Schwarzenberger (1941), Martin Wight (1946), Hans Morgenthau (1948), George F. Kennan (1951), and Herbert Butterfield (1953) are all credited with having contributed to realism's postwar dominance. While it is commonly agreed that realists were critical of idealism, there is disagreement about how monolithic and dominant that competing school was. Jack Donnelly (1995, 179), for example, suggests that "international relations was . . . completely dominated by liberal internationalists. . . ." By contrast, Miles Kahler (1997, 24) argues that "Realism did not mount its theoretical charge against a field that was monolithic in its allegiances." The disagreement between Donnelly and Kahler rests in part on a judgment of the relative influence of proto-realist research in the 1930s. For example, Kahler (1997, 25) cites Frederick Schuman as the author of an influential anti-idealist text, while Donnelly notes that when he published his *International Politics* in 1933, Schuman was still only a junior faculty member at the University of Chicago.
27. Bueno de Mesquita, Chapter 12, page 166.
28. The volume went through six editions between 1948 and 1985. Morgenthau died in 1982, and the sixth edition was issued posthumously with the assistance of Kenneth W. Thompson. Bueno de Mesquita (Chapter 12, page 166) also notes the importance of works by Morton Kaplan (1957) and Kenneth Organski (1958).
29. Donnelly 1995, 186–189.
30. See especially Keohane and Nye 1977.
31. Jervis 1997, 4. Richard K. Ashley (1986, 257) coined the term *neorealism*. Traditionally in the international relations subfield, attaching the prefix "neo-" to the description of a body of work has been done by critics of the work in question (see also Joseph M. Grieco [1993, 117] on neoliberal institutionalism and Michael Desch [1997] on neoculturalism).

32. See, for example Keohane 1986a. Although much of this criticism predated the end of the Cold War, there is no doubt that the subfield's failure to anticipate (indeed, even to contemplate) such a major event contributed to neorealism's difficulties. See, for example, Gaddis 1992/1993; Hopf and Gaddis 1993; Lebow 1994; Wohlforth 1994/1995; and Lebow, Mueller, and Wohlforth 1995. To be sure, realist and nonrealist theories alike failed in this respect, but it was only to be expected that the then leading theory would be the most damaged.
33. Works arguing in favor of democratic peace theory include Rummel 1983; Doyle 1986; Maoz and Russett 1993; Russett 1993; and Ray 1995. Critical treatments include Mearsheimer 1990, 48–51; Layne 1994; Spiro 1994; and Elman 1997. On institutional theory or neoliberal institutionalism see Keohane 1983/1986; 1984; 1993; Martin 1992; and Martin and Simmons 1998. For criticism see Grieco 1988; Baldwin 1993; and Mearsheimer 1994/1995.
34. Rose 1998.
35. Spirtas 1996, 387–400.
36. Jervis (1997, 7) observes that: "We are dealing with a system when (a) a set of units or elements is interconnected so that changes in some elements or their relations produce changes in other parts of the system; and (b) the entire system exhibits properties and behaviors that are different from those parts." Jervis provides several compelling illustrations of unintended consequences, including demonstrating multiple potential problems with the seemingly straightforward argument "if [oil] tankers had double hulls, there would be fewer oil spills." For example, forced to spend more on hulls, oil companies might cut back on navigational or safety equipment, leading to an *increase* in oil spills. Such interconnectedness is ubiquitous in social life. A recent *New York Times* report, for example, observes that an increase in the use of bicycle safety helmets is correlated with an increase in injuries, possibly because riders feel safer and so ride faster. On systems, see also Luard 1992, x–xv.
37. Note that theorizing about the security dilemma predates neorealism (see particularly Herz 1962, 231, 243; and Wolfers 1962, 158–159). For a critique of Waltz's use of the security dilemma, see Schweller 1996.
38. Spirtas 1996, 387–400.
39. See Glaser's Chapter 16 for a similar, although somewhat more extended, typology.
40. Though see Wight 1966, 149, for a less expansive reading of the *Arthasastra*.
41. Polybius (Book I, Chapter 4). Hume (1882) argues that, by contrast to the widespread concern in ancient Greece, Hiero was unique among the contemporaries of Rome in his understanding of the balance of power.
42. See Luard 1992, 2–4; and Sheehan 1996, 29–36.
43. Luard 1992, 15–18, 21–25. See also Morgenthau 1985, 209–210.
44. Cited by Gulick, 1967. See also Haas, 1953; Wight 1966, 151; Zinnes 1967.
45. See Jack Levy's Chapter 10 herein for an excellent survey of different conceptual issues raised by balance of power theory.
46. See Mearsheimer 2001, 55–82 for an outstanding discussion of these issues.
47. The bottom right quadrant of the two-by-two matrix refers to situations in which states spontaneously countervail threats. The most obvious circumstance in which this is likely to occur is when a state that fails to build up its armed forces internally, or to make alliances with other threatened states externally, is invaded by an aggressor. The invaded state may belatedly respond, but to call its policy balancing would be like describing a little old lady who successfully hangs onto her purse during a mugging as engaging in crime prevention. Accordingly, this fourth possibility is excluded as a category of balance of power theory. Rosecrance (Ch. 11 herein, 157) makes a similar point when he argues that "self-defense is not enough. . . ." See also Levy, Ch. 10.
48. See also Gulick 1967.
49. Note that self-denial or self-abnegation by a rising state would be considered a subset of dyadic balancing if the self-denial was to avoid countervailing action by the threatened state. Since the self-denial was an anticipated reaction to the balancing, it can be considered part of the same category. Also note that it is possible for self-denial to be a subset of manual balancing if a state forgoes the opportunity to upset the balance because "a balanced system is best."
50. See also Wight 1966, 166–167.
51. A hybrid "semi-automatic" system combines elements of the automatic and manual arrangements (see Claude 1962, 47–48). A state acting as the "holder of the balance" manually intervenes when an otherwise automatic system appears to be heading out of equilibrium. This view is typically associated with British balance of power policies from the seventeenth through the twentieth centuries, but can be discerned as early as 1520 in Henry VIII's motto at the Field of the Cloth of Gold: *Cui adhaereo prae est*, rendered by Butterfield (1966, 138) as "the one that I join is the one who will turn the scales"

and by Luard (1992, 4) as "the one that I join will prevail." For the view that the United States should be pursuing a similar "offshore balancing" strategy, see Layne 1998.
52. Miriam Fendius Elman and I overstated this argument in our response to Paul Schroeder.
53. In essence, this possibility "reads into" neorealism several of the elements in Stephen Van Evera's (1999, 10) Type III "fine grained structural" realism. On the offense-defense balance see also Christensen and Snyder 1990; on cumulation of resources see also Liberman 1993; on falling dominoes see Jervis and Snyder 1991; on the stopping power of water see Mearsheimer 2001.
54. The image here is of a head-on collision between two speeding vehicles. While not designed to bring them to a halt, such a collision is as effective as an intentional static roadblock in doing so.
55. By the same token, it is possible for there to be an absence of negative feedback even in the presence of dyadic balancing. France took great pains before the Second World War to prepare for a German invasion, but nevertheless failed to cope when it occurred.
56. Jervis (1997, 133–134) discusses a more general form of this argument in his treatment of the hypothesis that losers in war usually survive, because the winners will be unable to agree on a fair division of the spoils.
57. See Rosecrance, Ch. 11, 162 for additional discussion of negative feedback, including "aggressor ambition, effective self-defense, and diseconomies of territorial scale."
58. The situation and symbol usages are rarely used in contemporary realism. The term *distribution of capabilities* is preferred when describing the current configuration of capabilities, qualified with *preponderant* or *equilibrium* if relevant. Symbolic uses of balance of power should similarly be avoided.
59. This breaks down into three sub-uses: to denote equilibrium; to describe preponderance; or to delineate the current distribution of power without evaluation as to whether it is in equilibrium or not.
60. We might note that in the twenty-first century, the term is also used emblematically to delineate an outmoded or outdated concern with "old-fashioned power politics."
61. Depending on the listener's degree of cynicism, this might also be coded as falling in the second category, the pursuit of a particular configuration of capabilities, in this case American preponderance.
62. Waltz 1979, 118.
63. Christensen and Snyder 1990, 138, 140–141.
64. Christensen and Snyder 1990, 138.
65. Christensen and Snyder 1990, 141.
66. Christensen and Snyder 1990, 138, 142.
67. Christensen and Snyder 1990, 145.
68. Jack Snyder mentions this possibility in an e-mail to the author.
69. Interestingly, Christensen and Snyder's article suggests that *mis*perceptions of the offense-defense balance drove the two different dynamics before World War I and World War II. In the latter case, even though statesmen buck-passed when they should not have, the system eventually returned to equilibrium.
70. Walt (1991, 54) argues that because "capability" in Waltz's theory is also a composite variable, his expansion of the independent variable does not lead to a loss of parsimony.
71. It is these additional factors, for example, that explain why Western Europe sided with the more powerful United States against a nearby and malign Soviet Union.
72. Schweller (1996) disputes the neorealist claim that structural dynamics, absent malign intent by one or more parties, are sufficient to generate conflict. For Schweller, bad things happen because bad states make them happen.
73. Schweller 1994, 101, 104.
74. Schweller 1993, 84.
75. The following description is redacted from an e-mail from Schweller to the author.
76. Elman 2001b, 759.
77. Rourke 2001, 322.
78. Elman 2001b, 758.
79. "Paradigmatism" does not necessarily connote a commitment to a Kuhnian understanding of scientific development. All Kuhnians are paradigmatists; not all paradigmatists are Kuhnians.
80. See Jones (1998, 5) for the view that IR theorists' attachment to these aggregates is misplaced: "However necessary they may be as heuristic devices, these attempts at generalisation are inimical to scholarship to the extent that they suppress significant distinctions. Detailed and empathetic investigation of specific theorists offers a more fruitful path into the study and criticism of political realism than repeated attempts to draft the perfect formulation of a supposed realist creed, whether for worship or sacrifice."
81. Cited in Jervis 2001, 385.

# The Realist Paradigm and Degenerative versus Progressive Research Programs

## An Appraisal of Neotraditional Research on Waltz's Balancing Proposition

*JOHN A. VASQUEZ*

Within international relations inquiry, the debate over the adequacy of the realist paradigm has been fairly extensive since the 1970s. In Europe it is often referred to as the interparadigm debate (see Banks 1985; Smith 1995, 18–21). In North America, the focus has been more singularly on realist approaches and their critics (see Vasquez 1983). Toward the end of the 1970s, it appeared that alternate approaches, such as transnational relations and world society perspectives, would supplant the realist paradigm. This did not happen, partly because of the rise of neorealism, especially as embodied in the work of Waltz (1979). Now the debate over the adequacy of the realist paradigm has emerged anew.

In this analysis, *realism* is defined as a set of theories associated with a group of thinkers who emerged just before World War II and who distinguished themselves from idealists (i.e., Wilsonians) on the basis of their belief in the centrality of power for shaping politics, the prevalence of the practices of power politics, and the danger of basing foreign policy on morality or reason rather than interest and power. The *realist paradigm* refers to the shared fundamental assumptions various realist theorists make about the world. Derived primarily from the exemplar of realist scholarship, Morgenthau's ([1948] 1978) *Politics among Nations*, these include: (1) Nation-states are the most important actors in international relations; (2) there is a sharp distinction between domestic and international politics; and (3) international relations is a struggle for power and peace. Understanding how and why that struggle occurs is the major purpose of the discipline (see Vasquez 1983, 15–19, 26–30 for elaboration and justification).

While much of the debate over realism has focused on a comparison to neoliberalism (see Kegley 1995),[1] the debate has also raised new empirical (Rosecrance and Stein 1993), conceptual (Lebow and Risse-Kappen 1995, Wendt 1992), and historical (Schroeder 1994a) challenges to the paradigm as a whole. Some call for a sharp break with the paradigm (e.g., Vasquez 1992), while others see the need to reformulate on the basis of known empirical regularities (Wayman and Diehl 1994). Many still see it as the major theoretical framework within which the field must continue to work (Hollis and Smith 1990, 66), and even critics like Keohane ([1983] 1989) and Nye (1988) see the need to synthesize their approaches (in this case neoliberalism) with the realist paradigm.

If any progress is to be made, scholars must have a set of criteria for appraising the empirical component of theories and paradigms (see Vasquez 1992, 1995). Appraising a paradigm, however, is difficult because often its assumptions are not testable, since they typically do not explain anything in and of themselves (e.g., nation-states are the most important actors). Essentially, a paradigm promises scholars that if they view the world in a particular way, they will successfully understand the subject they are studying. In Kuhn's ([1962] 1970a, 23–24) language, paradigms do not so much provide answers as the promise of answers. Ultimately, a paradigm must be appraised by its utility and its ability to make good on its promise. Thus, a paradigm can only be appraised indirectly by examining the ability of the theories it generates to satisfy criteria of adequacy.

Within mainstream international relations, the work of Lakatos (1970) has attracted the most consensus as a source of such criteria among both quantitative and traditional scholars (see Keohane [1983] 1989). Although the appraisal of theories and the paradigms from which they are derived involves a number of criteria (see Simowitz and Price 1990), including, in particular, the criterion of empirical accuracy (the ability to pass tests) and the principle of falsifiability, the present analysis will apply only the main criterion on which Lakatos laid great stress for the evaluation of a series of theories: They must produce a progressive as opposed to a degenerating research program. Lakatos's criteria clearly stem from a more positivist perspective, but since realists and neorealists accept them, they are perfectly applicable.[2]

One main difference between Lakatos and early positivists is that Lakatos believes the rules of theory appraisal are community norms and cannot be seen as logically compelling, as Popper (1959) had hoped. The case that any given research program is degenerating (or progressive) cannot be logically proven. Such a stance assumes a foundationalist philosophy of inquiry that has been increasingly under attack in the last two decades (see Hollis and Smith 1990). A more reasonable stance is that exemplified by the trade-off between type 1 and type 2 errors in deciding to accept or reject the null hypothesis. Deciding whether a research program is degenerating involves many individual decisions about where scholars are willing to place their research bets, as well as collective decisions as to which research programs deserve continued funding, publication, and so forth. Some individuals will be willing to take more risks than others. This analysis seeks to present evidence that is relevant to the making of such decisions.

The task of determining whether research programs are progressive or degenerating is of especial importance because a number of analysts (e.g., Hollis and Smith 1990, 66; Wayman and Diehl 1994, 263) argue that, despite anomalies, the realist paradigm is dominant because it is more enlightening and fertile than its rivals. While the ability of the realist paradigm to reformulate its theories in light of conceptual criticism and unexpected events is taken by the above authors as an indicator of its fertility and accounts for its persistence, the proliferation of emendations may not be a healthy sign. Indeed, it can be argued that persistent emendation exposes the degenerating character of the paradigm. This analysis will demonstrate that the "theoretical fertility" apparently exhibited by realism in the last twenty years or so is actually an indicator of the degenerating nature of its research program.

## The Criterion

Imre Lakatos (1970) argued against Popper (1959) and in favor of Kuhn ([1962] 1970a) that no single theory can ever be falsified because auxiliary propositions can be added to account for discrepant evidence. The problem, then, is how to evaluate a *series of theories* that are intellectually related.

A series of theories is exactly what is posing under the general rubrics of realism and neorealism. All these theories share certain fundamental assumptions about how the world works.[3] In Kuhn's ([1962] 1970a) language, they constitute a family of theories because they share a paradigm. A *paradigm* can be stipulatively defined as "the fundamental assumptions scholars make about the world they are studying" (Vasquez 1983, 5).[4] Since a paradigm can easily generate a family of theories, Popper's (1959) falsification strategy was seen by Lakatos (1970) as problematic, since one theory can simply be replaced by another in incremental fashion without ever rejecting the shared fundamental assumptions. It was because of this problem that Kuhn's sociological explanation of theoretical change within science was viewed as undermining the standard view in philosophy of science, and it was against Kuhn that Lakatos developed his criteria for appraising a series of theories. To deal with the problem of appraising a series of theories that may share a common paradigm or set of assumptions, Lakatos stipulated that a research program coming out of this core must develop in such a way that theoretical emendations are progressive rather than degenerating.

The main problem with this criterion is that, unless it is applied rigorously, with specific indicators as to what constitutes "progressive" or "degenerating" research programs, it will not provide a basis for settling the debate on the adequacy of the realist paradigm. In an early application of this criterion to structural realism, Keohane ([1983] 1989, 43–44, 52, 55–56, 59), for example, goes back and forth talking about not only the fruitfulness of neorealism but also its incompleteness and the general inability of any international relations theory to satisfy Lakatos's criteria (see also Nye 1988, 243).

Eventually, it would be highly desirable to construct operational indicators of the progressive or degenerating nature of a paradigm's research program. Since these are not available, this analysis will explicitly identify the characteristics that will be used to indicate that a research program is degenerating. Lakatos (1970, 116–117) sees a research program as degenerating if its auxiliary propositions increasingly take on the characteristic of ad hoc explanations that do not produce any novel (theoretical) facts, as well as new empirical content. For Lakatos (p. 116), "no experimental result can ever kill a theory: any theory can be saved from counterinstances either by some auxiliary hypothesis or by a suitable reinterpretation of its terms." Since Lakatos (p. 117) finds this to be the case, he asks: Why not "impose certain standards on the theoretical adjustments by which one is allowed to save a theory?" Adjustments that are acceptable he labels progressive, and those that are not he labels degenerating.

The key for Lakatos is to evaluate not a single theory but a series of theories linked together. Is each "theoryshift" advancing knowledge, or is it simply a "linguistic device" for saving a theoretical approach?[5] A theoryshift or problemshift is considered (1) theoretically progressive if it theoretically "predicts some novel, hitherto unexpected fact" and (2) empirically progressive if these new predictions are actually corroborated, giving the new theory an excess empirical content over its rival (Lakatos 1970, 118). In order to be considered progressive, a problemshift must be *both* theoretically and empirically progressive—anything short of that is defined (by default) as *degenerating* (p. 118). A degenerating problemshift or research program, then, is characterized by the use of semantic devices that hide the actual content-decreasing nature of the research program through reinterpretation (p. 119). In this way, the new theory or set of theories are really ad hoc explanations intended to save the theory (p. 117).

It should be clear from this inspection of Lakatos's criterion that progressive research programs are evaluated ultimately on the basis of a criterion of accuracy, in that the new explanations must pass empirical testing. If this is the case, then they must in principle be *falsifiable*. The generation of new insights and the ability to produce a number of research tests, consequently, are not indicators of a progressive research program, if *these do not result in new empirical content that has passed empirical tests*.

How can one tell whether a series of theories that come out of a research program is degenerating? First, the movement from $T$ to $T'$ may indicate a degenerating tendency if the revision of $T$ involves primarily the introduction of new concepts or some other reformulation that attempts to explain away discrepant evidence. Second, this will be seen as degenerating if this reformulating never points to any novel unexpected facts, by which Lakatos means that $T'$ should tell scholars something about the world other than what was uncovered by the discrepant evidence. Third, if $T'$ does not have any of its new propositions successfully tested or lacks new propositions (other than those offered to explain away discrepant evidence), then it does not have excess empirical content over $T$, and this can be an indicator of a degenerating tendency in the research program. Fourth, if a research program goes through a number of theoryshifts, all of which have one or more of the above characteristics *and* the end result of these theoryshifts is that collectively the family of theories fields a set of contradictory hypotheses which greatly increase the probability of at least one passing an empirical test, then a research program can be appraised as degenerating.

This fourth indicator is crucial and deserves greater explication. It implies that while some latitude may be permitted for the development of ad hoc explanations, the longer this goes on in the face of discrepant evidence, the greater is the likelihood that scientists are engaged in a research program that is constantly repairing one flawed theory after another without any incremental advancement in the empirical content of these theories. What changes is not what is known about the world, but semantic labels to describe discrepant evidence that the original theory(ies) did not anticipate.

How does one determine whether semantic changes are of this sort or the product of a fruitful theoretical development and new insights? An effect of repeated semantic changes which are not progressive is that they focus almost entirely on trying to deal with experimental outcomes or empirical patterns contrary to the initial predictions of the theory. One consequence is that collectively the paradigm begins to embody contradictory propositions, such as (1) war is likely when power is not balanced and one side is preponderant, and (2) war is likely when power is relatively equal. The development of two or more contradictory propositions increases the probability that at least one of them will pass an empirical test. If a series of theories, all derived from the same paradigm (and claiming a family resemblance, such as by using the same name, e.g., Freudian, Marxist, or realist), predict several competing outcomes as providing support for the paradigm, then this is an example of the fourth indicator. Carried to an extreme, the paradigm could prevent any kind of falsification, because collectively its propositions in effect pose the bet: "Heads, I win; tails, you lose." A research program can be considered blatantly degenerative if one or more of the behaviors predicted is only predicted after the fact.

To be progressive, a theoryshift needs to do more than just explain away the discrepant evidence. It should show how the logic of the original or reformulated theory can account for the discrepant evidence and then delineate how this theoretic can give rise to new propositions and predictions (or observations) that the original theory did not anticipate. The generation of new predictions is necessary because one cannot logically test a theory on the basis of the discrepant evidence that led to the theoryshift in the first place, since the outcome of the statistical test is already known (and therefore cannot be objectively predicted before the fact). The stipulation of new hypotheses that pass empirical testing on some basis other than the discrepant evidence is the minimal logical condition for being progressive. Just *how* fruitful or progressive a theoryshift is, beyond the minimal condition, depends very much on how insightful and/or unexpected the novel facts embodied in the auxiliary hypotheses are deemed to be by scholars within the field. Do they tell scholars things they did not (theoretically) know before?

It should be clear that the criteria of adequacy involve the application of disciplinary norms as to what constitutes progress. The four indicators outlined above provide reasonable and fairly explicit ways to interpret the evidence. Applying them to a body of research should permit a basis for determining whether a research program appears to be on the whole degenerative or progressive.

It will be argued that what some see as theoretical enrichment of the realist paradigm is actually a proliferation of emendations that prevent it from being falsified. It will be shown that the realist paradigm has exhibited (1) a protean character in its theoretical development; which plays into (2) an unwillingness to specify what form(s) of the theory constitutes the true theory, which if falsified would lead to a rejection of the paradigm; as well as (3) a continual and persistent adoption of auxiliary propositions to explain away empirical and theoretical flaws that greatly exceed the ability of researchers to test the propositions; and (4) a general dearth of strong empirical findings. Each of these four characteristics can be seen as "the facts" that need to be established or denied to make a decision about whether a given research program is degenerating.

## The Research Program to Be Analyzed

Any paradigm worth its salt will have more than one ongoing research program, so in assessing research programs it is important to select those that focus on a core area of the paradigm and not on areas that are more peripheral or can be easily accommodated by a competing paradigm. It also is important that the research program be fairly well developed both in terms of the number of scholars and the amount of time spent on the program.

If one uses Kuhn's ([1962] 1970a) analysis to understand the post–World War II development of the field of international relations, there is a general consensus that the realist paradigm has dominated international relations inquiry within the English-speaking world and that Morgenthau's *Politics among Nations* can be seen as the exemplar of this paradigm (see Vasquez 1983 for a test of this claim; see also Banks 1985; Smith 1995; Olson and Groom 1991; and George 1994). Neorealism can be seen as a further articulation of the realist paradigm along at least two lines. The first, by Waltz (1979), brought the insights of structuralism to bear on realism and for this reason is often referred to as structural realism. For Waltz (1979), structure (specifically the anarchic nature of the international system) is presented as the single most important factor affecting all other behavior. The second, by Gilpin (1981), brought to bear some of the insights of political economy with emphasis on the effect of the rise and decline of hegemons on historical change. Both of these efforts have developed research programs. Generally, it is fair to say that Waltz has had more influence on security studies, whereas Gilpin has been primarily influential on questions of international political economy. Since the main concern here is with security, peace, and war, this appraisal will concentrate on the work of scholars who have been influenced by Waltz.

A complete case against the realist paradigm needs to look at other aspects of neorealism and to examine classical realism as well. Elsewhere, the quantitative work guided by classical realism has been evaluated (Vasquez 1983). Gilpin's work on war is best treated in conjunction with the power transition thesis of Organski and Kugler (1980), with which it shares a number of similarities (for an initial appraisal see Vasquez 1993, chapter 3; 1996). So, part of the reason for focusing on Waltz and the research agenda sparked by his analysis is that only so much work can be reviewed in depth in a single article.[6] The more compelling reason is that Waltz's analysis has in fact had a great impact on empirical research. His influence on those who study security questions within international relations in what may be called a neotraditional (i.e., nonquantitative) manner is without equal.

Waltz (1979) centers on two empirical questions: (1) explaining what he considers a fundamental law of international politics, the balancing of power, and (2) delineating the differing effects of bipolarity and multipolarity on system stability. While the latter has recently given rise to some vehement debates about the future of the post–Cold War era (see Mearsheimer 1990, Van Evera 1990/91; see also Kegley and Raymond 1994), it has not yet generated a sustained research program. In contrast, the first area has. The focus of this appraisal will be not so much on Waltz himself as on the neotraditional research program that has taken his proposition on balancing and investigated it empirically. This work is fairly extensive and appears to many to be both cumulative and fruitful. Specifically, the analysis will review the work of Walt (1987) and Schweller (1994) on balancing and bandwagoning, the work of Christensen and Snyder (1990) on "buck-passing" and "chain-ganging," and historical case studies that have uncovered discrepant evidence to see how these works have been treated in the field by proponents of the realist paradigm.

In addition, unlike the work on polarity, that on balancing focuses on a core area for both classical realism and neorealism. It is clearly a central proposition within the paradigm (see Vasquez 1983, 183–194), and concerns with it can be traced back to David Hume and from him to the Ancients in the West, India, and China. Given the prominence of the balance of power concept, a research program devoted to investigating Waltz's analysis of the balancing of power, which has attracted widespread attention and is generally well-treated in the current literature, cannot fail to pass an examination of whether it is degenerating or progressive without reflecting on the paradigm as a whole—either positively or negatively.

Before beginning this appraisal it is important to keep in mind that the criterion on research programs being progressive is only one of several that can be applied to a paradigm. A full appraisal would involve the application of other criteria, such as accuracy, to all areas of the paradigm. Clearly, such an effort is beyond the scope of this analysis. This article provides only one appraisal, albeit a very important one, of a number that need to be conducted. As other appraisals are completed, more evidence will be acquired to make an overall assessment.

Likewise, because only the research program on balancing is examined, it can be argued that logically only conclusions about balancing (and not the other aspects of the realist paradigm) can be made. This is a legitimate position to take in that it would be illogical (as well as unfair) to generalize conclusions about one research program to others of the paradigm. Those obviously need to be evaluated separately and appraised on their own merit. They may pass or fail an appraisal based on the criterion of progressivity or on other criteria such as empirical accuracy or falsifiability. Nevertheless, while this is true, it is just as illogical to assume in the absence of such appraisals that all is well with the other research programs.[7]

In fact, the conclusions of this study are not inconsistent with other recent work which finds fundamental deficiencies in the realist paradigm on other grounds, using different methods and addressing different questions—for example, that by Rosecrance and Stein (1993), who look at the role of domestic politics (cf. Snyder and Jervis 1993); Lebow and Risse-Kappen (1995), who examine realist and nonrealist explanations of the end of the Cold War; and George (1994), who examines the closed nature of realist thinking and its negative effects on the field.

Logically, while this analysis can only draw conclusions about the degeneracy (or progressiveness) of the research program on balancing, the implication of failing or passing this appraisal for the paradigm as a whole is not an irrelevant issue. If Waltz's neorealism is seen as reflecting well on the theoretical robustness and fertility of the realist paradigm (Hollis and Smith 1990, 66), then the failure of a research program meant to test his theory must have some negative effect on the paradigm. The question is, how negative? The concluding section will return to this issue, since such matters are more fruitfully discussed in light of specific evidence rather than in the abstract.

## The Balancing of Power: The Great New Law That Turned Out Not to Be So

One of Waltz's (1979) main purposes was to explain what, in his view, is a fundamental law of international politics: the balancing of power. Waltz (pp. 5, 6, 9) defines theory as statements that explain laws (i.e., regularities of behavior). For Waltz (p. 117), "whenever agents and agencies are coupled by force and competition rather than authority and law," they exhibit "certain repeated and enduring patterns." These he says have been identified by the tradition of *Realpolitik*. Of these the most central pattern is balance of power, of which he says: "If there is any distinctively political theory of international politics, balance-of-power theory is it" (p. 117). He maintains that a self-help system "stimulates states to behave in ways that tend toward the creation of balances of power" (p. 118) and that "these balances tend to form whether some or all states consciously aim to establish [them]" (p. 119). This law or regularity is what the first six of the nine chapters in *Theory of International Politics* are trying to explain (see, in particular, Waltz 1979, 116–128).

The main problem, of course, is that many scholars, including many realists such as Morgenthau ([1948] 1978, chapter 14), do not see balancing as the given law Waltz takes it to be. In many ways, raising it to the status of a law dismisses all the extensive criticism that has been made of the concept (Claude 1962; Haas 1953; Morgenthau [1948] 1978, chapter 14) (see Waltz 1979, 50–59, 117, for a review). Likewise, it also sidesteps a great deal of the theoretical and empirical work suggesting that the balance of power, specifically, is not associated with the preservation of peace (Organski 1958; Singer, Bremer, and Stuckey 1972; see also the more recent Bueno de Mesquita 1981; the earlier work is discussed in Waltz 1979, 14–15, 119).

Waltz (1979) avoided contradicting this research by arguing, like Gulick (1955), that a balance of power does not always preserve the peace because it often requires wars to be fought to maintain the balance. What Waltz does here is separate two possible functions of the balance of power—protection of the state in terms of its survival versus the avoidance of war or maintenance of the peace. Waltz does not see the latter as a legitimate prediction of balance of power theory. All he requires is that states attempt to balance, not that balancing prevents war.

From the perspective of Kuhn ([1962] 1970a, 24, 33–34) one can see Waltz (1979) as articulating a part of the dominant realist paradigm. Waltz is elaborating one of the problems (puzzles as Kuhn [1962] 1970a, 36–37, would call them) that Morgenthau left unresolved in *Politics among Nations*; namely, how and why the balance of power can be expected to work and how major a role this concept should play within the paradigm. Waltz's (1979) book can be seen as a theoryshift that places the balance of power in much more positive light than does Morgenthau (cf. 1978, chapter 14). This theoryshift tries to resolve the question of whether the balance is associated with peace by saying that it is not. Waltz, unlike Morgenthau, sees the balance as automatic; it is not the product of a particular leadership's diplomacy but of system structure. The focus on system structure and the identification of "anarchy" are two of the original contributions of Waltz (1979). These can be seen as the introduction of new concepts that bring novel facts into the paradigm. Such a shift appears progressive, but whether it proves to be so turns on whether the predictions made by the explanation can pass empirical testing.

It should come as no surprise, therefore, that the proposition on balancing is the focus of much of the research of younger political scientists influenced by Waltz. Walt, Schweller, Christensen and Snyder, and the historian Schroeder all cite Waltz and consciously address his theoretical proposition on balancing. They also cite and build upon the work of one another; that is, those who discuss bandwagoning cite Walt (e.g., Levy and Barnett 1991, Schweller 1994); those who talk about buck-passing cite Christensen and Snyder (1990). More fundamentally, they generally are interested (with the exception of Schroeder, who is a critic) in working within the realist paradigm and/or defending it. They differ in terms of how they defend realism. Because they all share certain concepts, are concerned with balancing, and share a view of the world and the general purpose of trying to work within and defend the paradigm, they all can be seen as working on the same general research program. Thus, what they have found and how they have tried to account for their findings provide a good case for appraising the extent to which this particular research program is progressive or degenerating.

## Balancing versus Bandwagoning

A passing comment Waltz (1979, 126) makes about his theory is that in anarchic systems (unlike domestic systems), balancing, not bandwagoning (a term for which he thanks Stephen Van Evera), is the typical behavior.[8] This is one of the few unambiguous empirical predictions in his theory; Waltz (p. 121) states: "Balance-of-power politics prevail wherever two, and only two, requirements are met: that the order be anarchic and that it be populated by units wishing to survive."

The first major test is conducted by Walt (1987), who looks primarily at the Middle East from 1955 to 1979. He maintains that "balancing is more common than bandwagoning" (Walt 1987, 33). Consistent with Waltz, he argues that, in general, states should not be expected to bandwagon except under certain identifiable conditions (p. 28). Contrary to Waltz, however, he finds that they do not balance power!

Instead, he shows that they balance against threat (chapter 5), while recognizing that for many realists, states should balance against power (pp. 18–19, 22–23).[9] He then extends his analysis to East-West relations and shows that if states were really concerned with power, then they would not have allied so extensively with the United States, which had a very overwhelming coalition against the USSR and its allies. Such a coalition was a result not of the power of the USSR but of its perceived threat (pp. 273–281).

Here is a clear falsification of Waltz (in the naive falsification sense of Popper 1959; see Lakatos 1970, 116), but how does Walt deal with this counterevidence or counterinstance, as Lakatos would term it? He takes a very incrementalist position. He explicitly maintains that balance of threat "should be viewed as a refinement of traditional balance of power theory" (Walt 1987, 263). Yet, in what way is this a "refinement" and not an unexpected anomalous finding, given Waltz's prediction? For Morgenthau and Waltz, the greatest source of threat to a state comes from the possible power advantages another state may have over it. In a world that is assumed to be a struggle for power and a self-help system, a state *capable* of making a threat must be guarded against because no one can be assured when it may actualize that potential. Hence, states must balance against power regardless of immediate threat. If, however, power and threat are independent, as they are perceived to be by the states in Walt's sample, then something may be awry in the realist world. The only thing that reduces the anomalous nature of the finding is that it has not been shown to hold for the central system of major states, that is, modern Europe. If it could be demonstrated that the European states balanced threat and not power, then that would be a serious if not devastating blow for neorealism and the paradigm.[10]

As it stands, despite the rhetorical veneer, Walt's findings are consistent with the thrust of other empirical research: The balance of power does not seem to work or produce the patterns that many theorists have expected it to produce. For Walt, it turns out that states balance but not for reasons of power, a rather curious finding for Waltz but one entirely predictable given the results of previous research that found the balance of power was not significantly related to war and peace (Bueno de Mesquita 1981; see also Vasquez 1983, 183–194).

The degenerating tendency of the research program in this area can be seen in how Walt conceptualizes his findings and in how the field "refines" them further. "Balance of threat" is a felicitous phrase. The very phraseology makes states' behavior appear much more consistent with the larger paradigm than it actually is. It rhetorically captures all the connotations and emotive force of balance of power while changing it only incrementally. It appears as a refinement—insightful and supportive of the paradigm. In doing so, it strips away the anomalous nature and devastating potential of the findings for Waltz's explanation.

This problemshift, however, exhibits all four of the characteristics outlined earlier as indicative of degenerative tendencies within a research program. First, the new concept, balance of threat, is introduced to explain why states do not balance in the way Waltz theorizes. The balance of threat concept does not appear in Waltz (1979) or in the literature before Walt introduced it in conjunction with his findings. Second, the concept does not point to any novel facts other than the discrepant evidence. Third, therefore this new variant of realism does not have any excess empirical content compared to the original theory, except that it now takes the discrepant evidence and says it supports a new variant of realism.

These three degenerating characteristics open up the possibility that, when both the original balance of power proposition and the new balance of threat proposition ($T$ and $T'$, respectively) are taken as two versions of realism, either behavior can be seen as evidence supporting realist theory (in some form) and hence the realist paradigm or approach in general. Waltz (1979, 121) allows a clear test, because bandwagoning is taken to be the opposite of balancing. Now, Walt splits the concept of balancing into two components, either one of which will support the realist paradigm (because the second is but "a refinement" of balance of power theory). From outside the realist paradigm, this appears as a move to dismiss discrepant evidence and explain it away by an ad hoc theoryshift. Such a move is also a degenerating shift on the basis of the fourth indicator, because it reduces the probability that the corpus of realist propositions can be falsified. Before Walt wrote, the set of empirical behavior in which states *could* engage that would be seen as evidence falsifying Waltz's balancing proposition, was much broader than it was after Walt wrote.

The danger posed by such theoryshifts can be seen by conducting a mental experiment. Would the following theoretical emendation be regarded as a progressive shift? Let us suppose that the concept of bandwagoning now becomes the focus of empirical research in its own right. Waltz (1979, 126) firmly states: "Balancing not bandwagoning is the behavior induced by the system." (Walt 1987, 32, agrees.) If someone finds bandwagoning to be more frequent, should such a finding be seen as an anomaly for Waltz's $T$, Walt's $T'$, and the realist paradigm, or simply as the foundation to erect yet another version of realism ($T''$)? If the latter were to occur, it would demonstrate yet further degeneration of the paradigm's research program and an unwillingness of these researchers to see anything as anomalous for the paradigm as a whole.

By raising the salience of the bandwagoning concept and giving an explanation of it, Walt leaves the door open to the possibility that situations similar to the experiment may occur within the research program. Through this door walks Schweller (1994), who argues in contradiction to Walt that bandwagoning is more common than balancing. From this he weaves "an alternative theory of alliances" that he labels "balance of interests," another felicitous phrase, made even more picturesque by his habit of referring to states as jackals, wolves, lambs, and lions. Schweller (1994, 86) argues that his theory is even more realist than Waltz's because he bases his analysis on the assumption of the classical realists—states strive for greater power and expansion—and not on security, as Waltz (1979, 126) assumes. Waltz is misled, according to Schweller (1994, 85–88), because of his status quo bias. If he were to look at things from the perspective of a revisionist state, he would see why they bandwagon: to gain rewards (and presumably power).

Schweller (1994, 89–92), in a cursory review of European history, questions the extent to which states have balanced and argues instead that they mostly bandwagon.

To establish this claim, he redefines bandwagoning more broadly than Walt; it is no longer the opposite of balancing (i.e., siding with the actor who poses the greatest threat or has the most power) but simply any attempt to side with the stronger, especially for opportunistic gain. Because the stronger state often does not pose a direct threat to every weak state, this kind of behavior is much more common and distinct from what Walt meant.

Two things about Schweller (1994) are important for the appraisal of this research program. First, despite the vehemence of his attack on the balancing proposition, this is nowhere seen as a deficiency of the realist paradigm; rather, it is Waltz's distortion of classical realism (however, see Morgenthau [1948] 1978, 194). The latter is technically true, in that Waltz raises the idea of balancing to the status of a law, but one would think that the absence of balancing in world politics, especially in European history, would have some negative effect on the realist view of the world. Certainly, Schweller's "finding" that bandwagoning is more prevalent than balancing is something classical realists, such as Morgenthau ([1948] 1978), Dehio (1961), or Kissinger (1994, 20–21, 67–68, 166–167) would find very disturbing. They would not expect this to be the typical behavior of states, and if it did occur they would see it as a failure to follow a rational foreign policy and/or to pursue a prudent realist course (see Morgenthau [1948] 1978, 7–8).

Second, and more important, Schweller's theoryshift (T″) has made bandwagoning a "confirming" piece of evidence for the realist paradigm. So, if he turns out to be correct, his theory, which he says is even more realist than Waltz's, will be confirmed. If he is incorrect, then Waltz's version of realism will be confirmed. Under what circumstances will the realist paradigm be considered as having failed to pass an empirical test? The field is now in a position (in this research program) where any one of the following can be taken as evidence supporting the realist paradigm: balancing of power, balancing of threat, and bandwagoning. At the same time, the paradigm as a whole has failed to specify what evidence will be accepted as falsifying it—a clear violation of Popper's (1959) principle of falsifiability. Findings revealing the absence of balancing of power and the presence of balancing of threat or bandwagoning are taken by these researchers as supporting the realist paradigm; instead, from the perspective of those outside the paradigm, these outcomes should be taken as anomalies. All their new concepts do is try to hide the anomaly through semantic labeling (see Lakatos 1970, 117, 119). Each emendation tries to salvage something but does so by moving farther and farther away from the original concept. Thus, Waltz moves from the idea of a balance of power to simply balancing power, even if it does not prevent war. Walt finds that states do not balance power but oppose threats to themselves. Schweller argues that states do not balance against the stronger but more frequently bandwagon with it to take advantage of opportunities to gain rewards.

Walt and Schweller recognize discrepant evidence and explain it away by using a balance phraseology that hides the fact the observed behavior is fundamentally different from that expected by the original theory. The field hardly needs realism to tell it that states will oppose threats to themselves (if they can) or that revisionist states will seize opportunities to gain rewards (especially if the risks are low). In addition, these new concepts do not point to any novel theoretical facts; they are not used to describe or predict any pattern or behavior other than the discrepant patterns that undercut the original theory.

Ultimately, under the fourth indicator, such theoryshifts are also degenerating because they increase the probability that the realist paradigm will pass some test, since three kinds of behavior now can be seen as confirmatory. While any one version of realism (balance of power, balancing power, balance of threats, balance of interests) may be falsified, the paradigm itself will live on and, indeed, be seen as theoretically robust. In fact, the protean character of realism prevents the paradigm from being falsified because as soon as one theoretical variant is discarded, another variant pops up to replace it as the "true realism" or the "new realism."

The point is not that Walt or others are engaged in "bad" scholarship or have made mistakes; indeed, just the opposite is the case: They are practicing the discipline the way the dominant paradigm leads them to practice it. They are theoretically articulating the paradigm in a normal science fashion, solving puzzles, engaging the historical record, and coming up with new insights—all derived from neorealism's exemplar and the paradigm from which it is derived. In doing so, however, these individual decisions reflect a collective degeneration.

Even as it is, other research on bandwagoning (narrowly defined) has opened up further anomalies for the realist paradigm by suggesting that a main reason for bandwagoning (and indeed for making alliances in general) may not be the structure of the international system but domestic political considerations. Larson (1991, 86–87) argues antithetically to realism that states in a similar position in the international system and with similar relative capabilities behave differently with regard to bandwagoning; therefore, there must be some intervening variable to explain the difference. On the basis of a comparison of cases, she argues that some elites bandwagon to preserve their domestic rule (see also Strauss 1991, 245, who sees domestic considerations and cultural conceptions of world politics as critical intervening variables). Similarly, Levy and Barnett (1991, 1992) present evidence on Egypt and Third World states showing that internal needs and domestic political concerns are often more important in alliance making than are external threats. This research suggests that realist assumptions—the primacy of the international struggle for power and the unitary rational nature of the state will lead elites to formulate foreign policy strictly in accord with the national interest defined in terms of power—are flawed. Theories need to take greater cognizance of the role domestic concerns play in shaping foreign policy objectives. To the extent bandwagoning is a "novel" fact (even if not a predominant pattern), it points us away from the dominant paradigm, not back to its classical formulation.

## BUCK-PASSING AND CHAIN-GANGING

The bandwagoning research program is not the only way in which the protean character of realism has been revealed. Another and perhaps even more powerful example is the way in which Christensen and Snyder (1990) have dealt with the failure of states to balance. They begin by criticizing Waltz for being too parsimonious and making indeterminate predictions about balancing under multipolarity. They then seek to correct this defect within realism by specifying that states will engage in chain-ganging or buck-passing depending on the perceived balance between offense and defense. Chain-ganging occurs when states, especially strong states, commit "themselves unconditionally to reckless allies whose survival is seen to be indispensable to the maintenance of the balance"; buck-passing is a failure to balance and reliance on "third parties to bear the costs of stopping a rising hegemon" (Christensen and Snyder 1990, 138). The alliance pattern that led to World War I is given as an example of chain-ganging, and Europe in the 1930s is given as an example of buck-passing. The propositions are applied only to multipolarity; in bipolarity, balancing is seen as unproblematic.

This article is another example of how the realist paradigm (since Waltz) has been articulated in a normal science fashion. The authors find a gap in Waltz's explanation and try to correct it by bringing in a variable from Jervis (1978; see also Van Evera 1984). This gives the impression of cumulation and progress through further specification, especially since they have come up with a fancy title for labeling what Waltz identified as possible sources of instability in multipolarity.

A closer inspection reveals the degenerating character of their emendation. The argument that states will either engage in buck-passing or chain-ganging under multipolarity is an admission that in important instances, such as the 1930s, states fail to balance the way Waltz (1979) says they must because of the system's structure. Recall Waltz's (1979, 121) clear prediction that "balance-of-power politics will prevail wherever two, and only two, requirements are met: anarchy and units wishing to survive." Surely, these requirements were met in the period before World War II, and therefore failure to balance should be taken as falsifying evidence.

Christensen and Snyder (1990) seem to want to explain away the 1930s, in which they argue there was a great deal of buck-passing. Waltz (1979, 164–165, 167), however, never says that states will not conform overall to the law of balancing in multipolarity, only that there are more "difficulties" in doing so. If Christensen and Snyder see the 1930s as a failure to balance properly, then this is an anomaly that needs to be explained away. The buck-passing/chain-ganging concept does that in a rhetorical flourish that grabs attention and seems persuasive. Yet, it "rescues" the theory not simply from indeterminate predictions, as Christensen and Snyder (1990, 146) put it, but explains away a critical case that the theory should have predicted.

This seems to be especially important because, contrary to what Waltz and Christensen and Snyder postulate, balancing through alliances should be more feasible under multipolarity than bipolarity, because under the latter there simply are not any other major states with whom to align. Thus, Waltz (1979, 168) says that under bipolarity *internal* balancing is more predominant and precise than external balancing. If under bipolarity there is, according to Waltz, a tendency to balance (internally, i.e., through military buildups), and under multipolarity there is, according to Christensen and Snyder, a tendency to pass the buck or chain-gang, then when exactly do we get the kind of alliance balancing that we attribute to the traditional balance of power

Waltz has decreed as a law? Christensen and Snyder's analysis appears as a "proteanshift" in realism that permits the paradigm to be confirmed if states balance (internally or externally), chain-gang, or buck-pass (as well as bandwagon, see Schweller 1994). This is degenerative under the fourth indicator because the probability of falsification decreases to a very low level. It seems to increase greatly the probability that empirical tests will be passed by some form of realism.[11]

Imprecise measurement leaving open the possibility for ad hoc interpretation is also a problem with identifying buck-passing and chain-ganging. Were Britain, France, and the USSR passing the buck in the late 1930s, or were they just slow to balance? Or were Britain and France pursuing an entirely different strategy, appeasement, because of the lessons they derived from World War I? If the latter, which seems more plausible, then buck-passing is not involved at all, and the factor explaining alliance behavior is not multipolarity but an entirely different variable (see Rosecrance and Steiner 1993). What is even more troubling is that while Christensen and Snyder (1990) see pre-1939 as buck-passing and pre-1914 as chain-ganging, it seems that Britain was much more hesitant to enter the war in 1914 than in 1939, contrary to what one would expect given the logic of Christensen and Snyder's historical analysis.[12] After Hitler took Prague in March 1939, domestic public and elite opinion moved toward a commitment to war (Rosecrance and Steiner 1993, 140), but in 1914 that commitment never came before the outbreak of hostilities (see Levy 1990/91). The cabinet was split, and only the violation of Belgium tipped the balance. Thus, the introduction of the new refinement is far from a clear or unproblematic solution to the anomaly on its own terms.

The refinements of Waltz produced by the literature on bandwagoning and buck-passing are degenerating because they hide, rather than deal directly with, the seriousness of the anomalies they are trying to handle. A theory whose main purpose is to explain balancing cannot stand if balancing is not the law it says it is. Such an anomaly also reflects negatively on the paradigm as a whole. Even though Morgenthau ([1948] 1978, chapter 14) did not think the balance of power was very workable, power variables are part of the central core of his work, and he does say that the balance of power is "a natural and inevitable outgrowth of the struggle of power" and "a protective device of an alliance of nations, anxious for their independence, against another nation's designs for world domination" (Morgenthau [1948] 1978, 194, and see 173, 195–196). Waltz's (1979) theory, which has been characterized as a systematization of classical realism (Keohane 1986b, 15) and widely seen as such, cannot fail on one of its few concrete predictions without reflecting badly (in some sense) on the larger paradigm in which it is embedded.

## HISTORICAL CASE STUDIES

Unlike the explicitly sympathetic work cited above, several historical case studies that focus on the balancing hypothesis give rise to more severe criticism of realist theory. Rosecrance and Stein (1993, 7) see the balancing proposition as the key prediction of structural realism. In a series of case studies, they challenge the idea that balancing power actually occurs or explains very much of the grand strategy of the twentieth-century major states they examine; to explain grand strategy for them requires examining domestic politics (Rosecrance and Stein 1993, 10, 17–21). In contradiction to structural realism, they find that balance of power concerns do not take "precedence over domestic factors or restraints" (Rosecrance and Stein 1993, 17). Britain in 1938, the United States in 1940, and even the Soviet Union facing Reagan in 1985 fail to meet powerful external challenges, in part because of domestic political factors (Rosecrance and Stein 1993, 18, and see the related case studies in chapters 5–7). States sometimes under- or overbalance. As Rosecrance (1995, 145) maintains, states rarely get it right—they either commit too much or too little, or they become so concerned with the periphery that they overlook what is happening to the core (see Kupchan 1994, Thompson and Zuk 1986). And, of course, they do this because they are not the unitary rational actors the realist paradigm thinks they are. Contrary to Waltz, and even Morgenthau, states engage in much more variegated behavior than the realist paradigm suggests.

This last point is demonstrated even more forcibly by the historian Paul Schroeder (1994a and b). He shows that the basic generalizations of Waltz—that anarchy leads states to balancing and to act on the basis of their power position—are not principles that tell the "real story" of what happened from 1648 to 1945. He demonstrates that states do not balance in a law-like manner but deal with threat in a variety of ways; among others, they hide, they join the stronger side, they try to "transcend" the problem, or they balance. In a brief but systematic review of the major conflicts in the modern period, he shows that in the Napoleonic wars, Crimean War, World War I, and World War II there was no real balancing of an alleged hegemonic threat—so much for the claim that this kind of balancing is a fundamental law of international politics. When states do resist, as they did with Napoleon, it is because they have been attacked and have no choice: "They resisted because France kept on attacking them" (Schroeder 1994a, 135; see also Schweller 1994, 92). A similar point also could be made about French, British, Soviet, and American resistance to Hitler and Japan.

Basically, Schroeder shows that the historical record in Europe does not conform to neorealists' theoretical expectations about balancing power. Their main generalizations are simply wrong. For instance, Schroeder does not see balancing against Napoleon, the prime instance in European history in which it should have occurred (see also Rosecrance and Lo 1996). Many states left the First Coalition against revolutionary France after 1793, when they should not have, given France's new power potential. Periodically, states bandwagoned with France, especially after victories, as in late 1799, when the Second Coalition collapsed. According to Schroeder (1994a, 120–121), hiding or bandwagoning, not balancing, was the main response to the Napoleonic hegemonic threat, the exact opposite of the assertions not only by Waltz but also by such long-time classical realists as Dehio (1961). For World War I, Schroeder (1994a, 122–123) argues that the balancing versus bidding for hegemony conceptualization simply does not make much sense of what each side was doing in trying to deal with security problems. With World War II, Schroeder (1994a, 123–124) sees a failure of Britain and France to balance and sees many states trying to hide or bandwagon.[13]

For Schroeder (1994a, 115, 116), neorealist theory is a misleading guide to inquiry:

> The more one examines Waltz's historical generalizations about the conduct of international politics throughout history with the aid of the historian's knowledge of the actual course of history, the more doubtful—in fact, strange—these generalizations become. . . . I cannot construct a history of the European states system from 1648 to 1945 based on the generalization that most unit actors within that system responded to crucial threats to their security and independence by resorting to self-help, as defined above. In the majority of instances this just did not happen.

All this suggests that the balancing of power was never the law Waltz thought it was. In effect, he offered an explanation of a behavioral regularity that never existed, except within the logic of the theory. As Schroeder (1994b, 147) concludes:

> [My point has been] to show how a normal, standard understanding of neo-realist theory, applied precisely to the historical era where it should fit best, gets the motives, the process, the patterns, and the broad outcomes of international history wrong . . . it prescribes and predicts a determinate order for history without having adequately checked this against the historical evidence.

## SHIRKING THE EVIDENCE AND PROVING THE POINT

How have scholars sympathetic to realism responded to Schroeder? They have sought to deny everything and done so precisely in the degenerating manner that Lakatos (1970, 116–119) predicted. The reaction by Elman and Elman (1995) to Schroeder in the correspondence section of *International Security* illustrates best the extent to which the last ten years of realist research have cumulated in degenerating problemshifts. Elman and Elman (1995) make three points against Schroeder (1994a). First, although his evidence may challenge Waltz's particular theory, it still leaves the larger neorealist approach unscathed. Second, Waltz recognizes balancing failures so that not every instance of these necessarily disconfirms his theory. Third, even if Schroeder's evidence on balancing poses a problem for Waltz, "only better theories can displace theories. . . . Thus, Waltz's theory should not be discarded until something better comes along to replace it" (Elman and Elman 1995, 192).

The first point somewhat misses the mark, since so much of neorealism is associated with Waltz. There remains mostly Gilpin (1981) and Krasner (1978). It is primarily Gilpin whom Elman and Elman have in mind when they argue that Schroeder's "omission of entire neo-realist literatures" leads him to fail to understand that "balancing is not the only strategy which is logically compatible with neo-realist assumptions of anarchy and self-help" (Elman and Elman 1995, 185, 186; see also Schweller 1992, 267, whom they cite).[14] They argue that for Gilpin (1981) and power transition theory "balancing is not considered a prevalent strategy, nor are balances predicted to occur repeatedly" (Elman and Elman 1995, 186). The problem with using Gilpin and the more quantitatively oriented power transition thesis of Organski and Kugler (1980) is that the two main pillars of neorealism predict contradictory things. Thus, between Waltz and Gilpin, threat can be handled by either balancing or not balancing. It certainly is not a very strong defense of neorealism to say that opposite behaviors are both logically compatible with the assumptions of anarchy.

The Elmans are technically correct that evidence against balancing does not speak against all the larger realist paradigm in that neorealism also embodies Gilpin. But it is this very correctness that proves the larger point being made here and illustrates what so worried Lakatos about degenerating research programs. At the beginning of this article, four indicators of a degenerating research program were presented. Elman and Elman (1995) serves as evidence that all these are very much in play within the field. On the basis of their defense of neorealism and the review of the literature above, it will be shown that the protean nature of realism, promulgated by the proliferation of auxiliary hypotheses to explain away discrepant evidence, has produced an unwillingness to specify what evidence would in principle lead to a rejection of the paradigm. The result has been a continual theoretical articulation but in the context of a persistent dearth of strong empirical findings.

Using Gilpin and power transition in the manner of the Elmans is degenerating because permitting the paradigm to be supported by instances of either "balancing" or "not balancing" reduces greatly the probability of finding any discrepant evidence. As if this were not enough to cover all sides of the bet, Elman and Elman (1995, 187–188) maintain that, within the neorealist assumption of self-help, threat can be handled by bandwagoning, expansion, preventive war, balancing, hiding, and even what Schroeder has labeled "transcending."[15] In other words, there is always some behavior (in dealing with threat) that will prove realism correct, even though most versions will be shown to be incorrect, and even though neorealists "often consider balancing to be the most successful strategy for most states most of the time" (Elman and Elman 1995, 187). But if this caveat is the case, then why do states not regularly engage in this behavior? Elman and Elman rightly capture the theoretical robustness of the realist paradigm—showing that Waltz, Gilpin, and others are part of the paradigm—but they fail to realize the damning protean portrayal they give of its research program and how this very theoretical development makes it difficult for the paradigm to satisfy the criterion of falsifiability.

Instead, they conclude about Schroeder's (1994a) historical evidence that "no evidence could be more compatible with a neo-realist reading of international relations" (Elman and Elman 1995, 184). They conclude this because each of these strategies (bandwagoning, etc.) does not challenge the realist conception of a rational actor behaving in a situation of competition and opportunity. For them, so long as states choose strategies that are "consistent with their position in the global power structure and pursue policies that are likely to provide them with greater benefits than costs" (Elman and Elman 1995, 184), this is seen as evidence supporting the broad realist approach. Only Wendt's (1992) claim that states could be "other-regarding" as opposed to "self-regarding" is seen as discrepant evidence (see also Elman 1996a, Appendix, Diagram 1). Basically, these are "sucker bets" of the "I win, you lose" variety. Let it be noted that these are not bets that Elman and Elman are proposing; they are merely reporting what, in effect, the entire realist research program has been doing—from Walt, to Christensen and Snyder, to Schweller, and so forth. Collectively, the realist mainstream has set up a situation that provides a very narrow empirical base on which to falsify the paradigm.

What kinds of political actors would, for example, consciously pursue policies that are "likely to provide" them with greater costs than benefits? To see only "other-regarding" behavior as falsifying leaves a rather vast and variegated stream of behaviors as supportive of the paradigm. Schroeder (1995, 194) has a legitimate complaint when he says, in reply: "The Elman argument . . . appropriates every possible tenable position in IR theory and history for the neo-realist camp." He concludes: "Their whole case that history fits the neo-realist paradigm falls to the ground because they fail to see that it is their neo-realist assumptions, as they understand and use them, which simply put all state action in the state system into a neo-realist mold and neo-realist boxes, *by definition*" (Schroeder 1995, 194, emphasis in the original).

Instead of defending the paradigm, Elman and Elman (1995) expose the degenerating nature of its research program and the field's collective shirking of the evidence through proteanshifts. Many neotraditionalists, such as Mearsheimer (1990), have eschewed quantitative evidence challenging the adequacy of the realist paradigm; if realists will now refuse to accept historical evidence as well, then what kind of evidence will they accept as falsifying their theories? Only "other-regarding" behavior? That simply will not do.

The cause of this problem is the lack of rigor in the field in appraising theories. The nature of the problem can be seen in Elman and Elman's (1995) second point against Schroeder. Drawing upon Christensen and Snyder (1990), they note that balancing under multipolarity, for Waltz, is more difficult than balancing under bipolarity: "Thus Schroeder's finding that states failed to balance prior to World War I (pp. 122–123) and World War II (pp. 123–124) does not disconfirm Waltz's argument. . . . In short, a failure to balance is not a failure of balance of power theory if systemic conditions are likely to generate this sort of outcome in the first place" (Elman and Elman 1995, 190–191). This sets up a situation in which any failure to balance under multipolarity can be taken as confirmatory evidence because, according to Elman and Elman (1995, 90), "Waltz's theory also predicts balancing *failures*" (emphasis in the original). This again poses an "I win, you lose" bet. If the periods before World War I and World War II are not legitimate tests of Waltz's prediction of balancing, then what would be? The implication is that balancing more easily occurs under bipolarity, but here external balancing is structurally impossible by definition. If this is the case, how is balancing a "law," or the main outcome of anarchy? This is especially problematic because there is a tendency in Waltz to see only the post-1945 period as a true bipolarity (see Nye 1988, 244), which means the rest of history is multipolar and subject to balancing failures.

In the end, Elman and Elman (1995, 192) concede that Waltz does believe that, "on aggregate," states should balance, so "Schroeder's evidence that states rarely balance does indeed pose a problem for Waltz's theory." They conclude, however, by citing Lakatos—only better theories can displace theories—and therefore Waltz's theory should not be discarded until something better comes along. They then outline a general strategy for improving the theory, namely, adding variables, identifying the domain to which it is applicable, and broadening definitions (especially of threat). All these, however, are precisely the tactics that have produced the degenerating situation the field now faces. Thus, they say, by broadening the definition of threat to include internal threats from domestic rivals, decision makers could still be seen as balancing, and bandwagoning "would not necessarily disconfirm the prediction that balancing is more common" (Elman and Elman 1995, 192). This would take the discrepant evidence of Levy and Barnett (1991, 1992) and of Larson (1991) and make it confirmatory. This is precisely the kind of strategy that Lakatos (1970, 117–119) decried.

What is also evident from this appraisal of the realist paradigm is that Lakatos's (1970, 119) comment that "there is no falsification before the emergence of a better theory" can play an important role in muting the implications of a degenerating research program, especially when alternative paradigms or competing mid-range theories are ignored, as has been the case in international relations. There have been too many empirical failures and anomalies, and theoretical emendations have taken on an entirely too ad hoc nonfalsifying character for adherents to say that the paradigm cannot be displaced until there is a clearly better theory available. Such a position makes collective inertia work to the advantage of the dominant paradigm and makes the field less rather than more rigorous.

If one wants to take the very cautious position that Schroeder's historical evidence affects only Waltz, one should not then be incautious and assume that other research programs within the realist paradigm are doing fine. A more consistent position would be to hold this conclusion in abeyance until all aspects of the paradigm are appraised. The lesson from Schroeder's (1994a and b) discrepant evidence should *not* be that his "article leaves the general neo-realist paradigm unscathed" (Elman and Elman 1995, 192), but that a major proposition of the paradigm has failed to pass an important historical test.

## Where Do We Go from Here?

It seems that the internal logic of the Lakatos rules requires that a warning flag on the degenerating direction of the research program on balancing be raised. Theorists should be aware of the pitfalls of setting up realist variants that produce a "heads, I win; tails, you lose" situation, which makes realism nonfalsifiable. In addition, greater efforts need to be made in specifying testable differences between realist and nonrealist explanations before the evidence is assessed, so as to limit the use of ex post facto argumentation that tries to explain away discrepant evidence.

If one accepts the general thrust of the analysis that the neotraditional research program on balancing has been degenerating, then the question that needs to be discussed further is the implications of this for the wider paradigm. Two obvious conclusions are possible. A narrow and more conservative conclusion would try to preserve as much of the dominant paradigm as possible in face of discrepant evidence. A broader and more radical conclusion would take failure in this one research program as consistent with the assessments of other studies and thus as an indicator of a deeper, broader problem. It is not really necessary that one conclusion rather than the other be taken by the entire field, since what is at stake here are the research bets individuals are willing to take with their own time and effort. In this light, it is only necessary to outline the implications of the two different conclusions.

The narrow conclusion is that Waltz's attempt to explain what he regards as the major behavioral regularity of international politics was premature because states simply do not engage in balancing with the kind of regularity that he assumes. It is the failure of neotraditional researchers and historians to establish clearly the empirical accuracy of Waltz's balancing proposition that so hurts his theory. If the logical connection between anarchy (as a systemic structure) and balancing is what Waltz claims it to be, and states do not engage in balancing, then this empirical anomaly must indicate some theoretical deficiency.

The neotraditional approach to date has muted the implications of the evidence by bringing to bear new concepts. The argument presented here is that such changes are primarily semantic and more clearly conform to what Lakatos calls degenerating theoryshifts than to progressive theoryshifts. If this is accepted, then at minimum one would draw the narrow conservative conclusion that the discrepant evidence (until further research demonstrates otherwise) is showing that states do not balance in the way Waltz assumes they do. Realists then can concentrate on other research programs within the paradigm without being susceptible (at least on the basis of this analysis) to the charge of engaging in a degenerating research program. Those who continue to mine realist inquiry, however, should pay more attention to the problem of degeneration in making theoretical reformulations of realism. Specifically, scholars making theoryshifts in realism should take care to ensure that these are not just proteanshifts.

The implication of the broader and more radical conclusion is to ask why a concept so long associated with realism should do so poorly and so misguide so many theorists. Could not its failure to pass neotraditional and historical "testing" (or investigation) be an indicator of the distorted view of world politics that the paradigm imposes on scholars? Such questions are reasonable to ask, especially in light of appraisals that have found other aspects of realism wanting (see Lebow and Risse-Kappen 1995, Rosecrance and Stein 1993, Vasquez 1983), but they are not the same as logically compelling conclusions that can be derived from the analysis herein. It has been shown only that one major research program, which has commanded a great deal of interest, seems to be exhibiting a degenerating tendency.

Such a demonstration is important in its own right, particularly if analysts are unaware of the collective effect of their individual decisions. In addition, it shows that what admirers of the realist paradigm have often taken as theoretical fertility and a continuing ability to provide new insights is not that at all, but a degenerating process of reformulating itself in light of discrepant evidence.

Regardless of whether a narrow or broad conclusion is accepted, this analysis has shown that the field needs much more rigor in the interparadigm debate. Only by being more rigorous, both in testing the dominant paradigm and in building a new one that can explain the growing body of counterevidence as well as produce new nonobvious findings of its own, will progress be made.

## Editors' Commentary

### Major Query

Can neotraditional realist research on Waltz's balancing of power proposition be considered degenerating, and hence inadequate?

### Major Points

In this article, which opened the new debate on the balancing of power, Vasquez makes two basic claims. The first is that Waltz's assertion that balancing of power is a law of international politics is simply not true: There is not much evidence in favor of it, and there appear to be many discrepancies. The second is that attempts by researchers to reformulate or emend the theory have offered little added value when measured according to the criteria outlined by philosopher of science Imre Lakatos. Vasquez's article focuses primarily on the latter claim. His analysis can be regarded as a **theory appraisal** in that it outlines and applies an explicit set of criteria that a theory or set of theories must satisfy.

Vasquez begins by talking about the broad debate in the field of international relations over the adequacy of realist research. He then outlines Lakatos's criterion of **degenerative versus progressive research programs**. Next, he applies the criterion to the neotraditional research program on balancing, looking at the work of specific researchers (who then reply to him herein, Chapters 3–7).

Lakatos is concerned that falsification and rejection of a theory can be avoided by reformulating the theory. Since these emendations can occur continuously, and refutation can be postponed indefinitely, surviving falsification is an insufficient measure of value. Lakatos suggests that we need additional rules for determining when emendations are legitimate. Simply put, we need to ask our theories to do more than accommodate embarrassing evidence. Changes can legitimately solve existing puzzles, but they must also produce new knowledge if they are to be judged progressive. More technically, a new theory, $T'$, must explain all that the original theory, $T$, explains plus make new predictions. These new predictions must then pass tests, i.e., be empirically corroborated. If it does the latter, $T'$ is said to have greater empirical content than $T$.

Lakatos's analysis makes it clear that because theories are reformulated, the acceptance or rejection of a theory is not a matter of logic as some philosophers of science have argued. Rather rejection of a theory is a *decision* about how the research program is doing. (Of course, once criteria are agreed upon, then whether the given facts satisfy the criteria becomes once again a matter of logical reasoning). Because theory rejection now becomes a matter of decision, there can be scholarly disagreement about: (1) what rules should be used to make the decision, in general, and (2) how those rules should be applied to a specific research program. Most of the disagreements in the debate stem from the latter, although some deal with the former, especially when scholars question the use of Lakatos.

Vasquez maintains that the neotraditional research that has been conducted on Waltz's balancing of power proposition has uncovered important evidence inconsistent with the proposition. Instead of recognizing this as evidence against the proposition, however, various realist scholars have tried to save the theory by emending it. Their primary method of doing this has been to take discrepant evidence and call it a form of "balancing," and then say this is a new realist theory. Vasquez argues that the new label does not tell us anything other than that there are counter-instances. It has not explained some phenomenon separate from the body of discrepant evidence. Therefore, it has made no new prediction that was unknown prior to the research being completed. By definition, this means it has produced no new (novel) facts. Since there are no new predictions, they cannot have been corroborated and hence there can be no empirical progress.

According to Vasquez, what neotraditional realists believe is that the discrepant evidence is both a new prediction and corroboration of that new prediction. But as Elman and Elman (herein, Ch. 5) point out, the evidence used to create a new theory cannot also be used as evidence that corroborates the theory because prediction did not precede knowledge of the evidence. Hence, the new theory appears to be, as Lakatos says, merely semantic relabeling that hides the fact that the original theory has been falsified. This shift makes us think we have increased the body of knowledge when all we have done is labeled the evidence that refutes the original theory. The new theory has not done two major things Lakatos says it must do to avoid being degenerative—it has not produced new predictions and these predictions have not passed empirical tests.

Vasquez first examines the work of Walt (1987), who finds that states do not balance against power, as both Waltz and Morgenthau would expect, but balance against threat. Vasquez argues that using the term *balancing* to describe the failure of states to balance against the most powerful states in the system (which they should see automatically as threatening if realism were correct) hides the discrepant nature of the evidence that was uncovered and is a label meant to save the neorealist approach. The concept of *balancing threat* does not point to any novel facts other than the discrepant evidence, i.e., it does not make any new predictions other than that states will not balance against the most powerful and that they will not automatically see the most powerful as inherently threatening. Therefore, it does not satisfy Lakatos's requirements that progressive theoryshifts have excess corroborated empirical content over the original theory.

Vasquez also points out that this sort of emendation over the long run produces contradictory hypotheses that increase the probability that at least one variant of realism will be supported. Thus, before Walt wrote, if states balanced power this would support the theory and if they did not this would be inconsistent with the theory. Now states can fail to balance power, but this can still support a form of realism if they balance against threat. Both Waltz and Walt see bandwagoning (siding with the stronger side) as evidence against balancing.

Schweller's work is used by Vasquez to point out how the research program further narrows the evidentiary base that could falsify realist theories. Schweller argues that states not only fail to balance power, but that they often bandwagon. This, however, is seen by Schweller not as refuting Waltz but as evidence that classical realism is a better theory. He calls his new theory *balance of interests*. From Vasquez's perspective, this narrows the evidentiary base of the realist research program even further, in that now balancing of power, balancing of threat, and bandwagoning in one's interest are all seen as supportive of realism. Vasquez sees this evolution of theory within the research program as an indicator of its degenerative tendency because when any one version of realism produces falsifying evidence, a new theory is constructed labeling that discrepant evidence as consistent with realism. This is what Vasquez means by the **protean** character of realism—it keeps changing the evidence that would lead scholars to reject realist theory.

Vasquez next discusses the work of Christensen and Snyder. They recognize that the 1930s prior to World War II do not appear to conform to Waltz's balancing of power proposition. But instead of seeing the failure to balance in the 1930s as a serious anomaly, Christensen and Snyder explain it away as a product of *buck-passing*. Vasquez argues that Britain and France were not buck-passing in the 1930s, but following a different strategy—appeasement—a strategy they should not be following if Waltz's proposition is correct.

Vasquez ends his review by looking at discrepant evidence on Waltz's balancing proposition uncovered by those who have conducted historical research—Rosecrance and Stein and Paul Schroeder. He maintains that much of this discrepant evidence has been ignored or pushed aside. He argues against Elman and Elman who claim that such evidence can be seen as supportive of a more broadly defined neorealism. Vasquez insists that it is precisely such broadening of the research program that should be taken as an indicator of its degenerative nature.

Vasquez makes two conclusions—one narrow and one broad. The narrow conclusion is that Waltz's attempt to explain a law-like pattern in international politics was premature because states do not engage in balancing of power with the kind of regularity he assumes. Attempts by researchers who have uncovered discrepant evidence to explain it away as balancing of threat, balance of interests, or buck-passing are indicators of strong degenerative tendencies. Those who continue to work within the research program must take greater care to show that their reformulation of the theory conforms more clearly with the characteristics of progressive theoryshifts.

The broader conclusion is that a degenerative research program in the core of the realist paradigm implies a fundamental problem with the paradigm as a whole and not just the research program on balancing of power. That such an old concept should produce so few findings suggests that the need to view the world in new and different ways may be in order for at least some of the field, if not the whole.

## Key Terms

**theory appraisal** Evaluating the adequacy of a theory in terms of some explicit set of criteria, such as how accurate it is, its explanatory power, its policy relevance, whether its research program and problemshifts are degenerative or progressive.

**problemshifts** Shifts from one theory or theoretical problem to another in light of research that produces discrepant evidence. These problemshifts or theoryshifts, as Lakatos also calls them, can be either progressive or degenerative.

**degenerative versus progressive research programs** Criterion developed by Imre Lakatos to determine whether a given theoretical reformulation is legitimate or simply an ad hoc explanation or set of explanations intended to save the theory from falsification. A progressive shift must make a new prediction and must have that new prediction corroborated by empirical research. Emendations that do not do this are degenerative and can be seen as simply semantic relabeling intended to save the theory from counter-instances. Degenerative research programs become involved in a series of efforts to save the theory from an increasing number of counter-instances without ever developing new predictions that are supported by new tests.

**protean** Changing one's form or shape as needed; from the Greek mythical story of Proteus, the sea god who could change his shape at will.

## Notes

1. *Neoliberalism* is a label employed by a number of scholars (see Nye 1988, 1993, 36–40) to refer to a theoretical approach associated with a cluster of three ideas: (1) Democracies do not fight one another (an idea going back at least to Kant); (2) free trade and growing wealth will create a harmony of interests that will reduce the need for war (the position of the early free traders); and (3) reason can be used to reduce global anarchy and produce more orderly relations among states in part through the creation of global institutions (ideas associated with Grotius and, later, Wilson). For a complete review, see the authors in Kegley 1995; see also Doyle 1986.
2. Vasquez (1995) deals with antifoundationalist postpositivist criticisms of such criteria. On the latter, see Lapid (1989).
3. Theory is defined here as a set of interrelated propositions purporting to explain behavior; see Vasquez 1992, 835–836. Given this definition, which is noncontroversial, the realist paradigm can have many different theories; see Vasquez 1983, 4–6.
4. Masterman (1970) has criticized Kuhn for using the concept of paradigm ambiguously. This stipulative definition is meant to overcome this objection, while still capturing the essence of what Kuhn ([1968] 1970, postscript) was trying to do with the concept.
5. Lakatos (1970, 118n3) notes that by "problemshift" he really means "theoryshift" (i.e., a shift from one specific theory to another) but does not use that word because it "sounds dreadful." Actually, it is much clearer. On the claim that the problemshifts which are degenerating are really just linguistic devices to resolve anomalies in a semantic manner, see Lakatos 1970, 117, 119.
6. For reason of space I also do not examine formal models of the balance of power, such as those of Wagner (1986) or Niou, Ordeshook, and Rose (1989).

7. I am currently engaged in a project to appraise various aspects of the realist paradigm on a variety of criteria; see Vasquez 1998.
8. For Waltz (1979, 126), bandwagoning is allying with the strongest power, that is, the one capable of establishing hegemony. He maintains that such an alignment will be dangerous to the survival of states. Walt (1987, 17, 21–22) defines the term similarly but introduces the notion of threat: "*Balancing* is defined as allying with others against the prevailing threat; *bandwagoning* refers to alignment with the source of danger" (italics in original).
9. Walt (1987, 172) concludes: "The main point should be obvious: Balance of threat theory is superior to balance of power theory. Examining the impact of several related but distinct sources of threat can provide a more persuasive account of alliance formation than can focusing solely on the distribution of aggregate capabilities."
10. Schroeder (1994a, b) provides this devastating evidence on Europe (see also Schweller 1994, 89–92).
11. Of course, one may argue that Christensen and Snyder's (1994) proposition on offense-defense is falsifiable in principle, and that is true, but this points out another problem with their analysis; namely, Levy (1984) is unable to distinguish in specific historical periods whether offense or defense has the advantage (see Christensen and Snyder 1990, 139, 6, 7). They, in turn, rely on the perception of offense and defense, but such a "belief" variable takes us away from realism and toward a more psychological-cognitive paradigm.
12. Christensen and Snyder (1990, 156) recognize British buck-passing in 1914, but they say Britain was an outlier and "did not entirely pass the buck."
13. Numerous other deviant cases are listed in Schroeder (1994a, 118–122, 126–129, 133–147).
14. By saying that Schroeder leaves much of the neorealist approach unscathed, Elman and Elman (1995) seem to fall into the trap of assuming that Gilpin (1981) is empirically accurate unless proven otherwise. In fact, as related to security questions, Gilpin (1981) has not been extensively tested, and existing tests are not very encouraging (see Spiezio 1990, as well as Boswell and Sweat (1991) and the discussion in Vasquez 1993, 93–98).
15. Transcending is seen by Schroeder (1994a) as particularly discrepant for realism, but Elman and Elman (1995, 188) view it as part of the realist approach.

# Evaluating Theories

*KENNETH N. WALTZ**

Having previously covered the criticisms John Vasquez makes (see especially Waltz 1979, 1986), I respond to his article reluctantly. One is, however, always tempted to try again.

Following Lakatos (1970), albeit shakily, in moving from paradigms to theories to research programs, Vasquez says he places theories in a single paradigm if they "share certain fundamental assumptions" (1997, 900; Ch. 2 herein, 25). He thereupon lumps old and new realists together in one realist paradigm. This is odd since, as he recognizes, old and new realists work from different basic assumptions. Believing that states strive for ever more power, Hans Morgenthau took power to be an end in itself. In contrast, I built structural theory on the assumption that survival is the goal of states and that power is one of the means to that end. Political scientists generally work from two different paradigms: one behavioral, the other systemic. Old realists see causes as running directly from states to the outcomes their actions produce. New realists see states forming a structure by their interactions and then being strongly affected by the structure their interactions have formed. Old realists account for political outcomes mainly by analyzing differences among states; new realists show why states tend to become like units as they try to coexist in a self-help system, with behaviors and outcomes explained by differences in the positions of states as well as by their internal characteristics (see Waltz 1990). If the term "paradigm" means anything at all, it cannot accommodate such fundamental differences.

Vasquez puts old and new realists in the same pot because he misunderstands realists. He makes odd statements about what paradigms do because he misunderstands paradigms. He believes that paradigms easily generate a family of theories (1997, 900; Ch. 2 herein, 25). Paradigms are apparently like sausage machines: Turn the crank,

---
*The author is grateful to Karen Ruth Adams for her assistance.

and theories come out. Yet no one in any field is able to generate theories easily or even to say how to go about creating them.

Vasquez finds lots of realist theories because he defines theories loosely as "interrelated propositions purporting to explain behavior" (fn. 3). If interrelating propositions were all it took to make theories, then, of course, we would have many of them. I can, however, think of any number of propositions purporting to explain something that would not qualify as theories by any useful definition of the term. I define theory as a picture, mentally formed, of a bounded realm or domain of activity. A theory depicts the organization of a realm and the connections among its parts. The infinite materials of any realm can be organized in endlessly different ways. Reality is complex; theory is simple. By simplification, theories lay bare the essential elements in play and indicate necessary relations of cause and interdependency—or suggest where to look for them (see Waltz 1979, 1–13). Vasquez, following his definition, finds many theories; I find few.

Vasquez's belief that theories are plentiful and easy to produce reflects the positivist tradition that permeates American political science. At the extreme, positivists believe that reality can be apprehended directly, without benefit of theory. Reality is whatever we directly observe. In a more moderate version of positivism, theory is but one step removed from reality, is arrived at largely by induction, is rather easy to construct, and is fairly easy to test. In their book on interdependence, Keohane and Nye provide a clear example when they "argue that complex interdependence sometimes comes closer to reality than does realism" (1989, 23). Yet, if we knew what reality is, theory would serve no purpose. Statements such as "parsimony is a judgment . . . about the nature of the world: it is assumed to be simple," neatly express the idea that theory does little more than mirror reality (King, Keohane, and Verba 1994, 20).

Faced with an infinite number of "facts" one must wonder, however, which ones are to be taken as pertinent when trying to explain something. As the molecular biologist Gunther Stent has put it: "Reality is constructed by the mind . . . the recognition of structures is nothing else than the selective destruction of information" (1973, E17). Scientists and philosophers of science refer to facts as being "theory laden" and to theory and fact as being "interdependent." "Every fact," as Goethe nicely put it, "is already a theory." Theory, rather than being a mirror in which reality is reflected, is an instrument to be used in attempting to explain a circumscribed part of a reality of whose true dimensions we can never be sure. The instrument is of no use if it does little more than ape the complexity of the world. To say that a "theory should be just as complicated as all our evidence suggests" (King, Keohane, and Verba 1994, 20) amounts to a renunciation of science from Galileo onward.

Because of the interdependence of theory and fact, the construction and testing of theories is a more problematic task than most political scientists have thought. Understanding this, Lakatos rejected "dogmatic falsification" in favor of judging theories by the fruitfulness of the research programs they may spawn. Following Lakatos, Vasquez faults the realist paradigm for what he takes to be the regressive quality of its research program. Forsaking Lakatos, he then adduces evidence that in his view falsifies balance of power theory in its structural-realist form. I shall consider both claims.

I disagree with Lakatos on some points, but not on his rejection of the notion that tests can falsify theories. To explain why falsification won't do, I all too briefly mention two problems. First, proving something false requires proving something else true. Yet the facts against which we test theories are themselves problematic. As Lakatos rightly says, in italics, *"theories are not only equally unprovable, . . . they are also equally undisprovable"* (1970, 103; cf. Harris 1970, 353). Among natural scientists, falsification is a little used method (Bochenski 1965, 109; cf. Harris 1970). Social scientists should think about why this is so.

Second, citing Popper (1959), Vasquez insists that "paradigms" should specify the evidence that would disprove them and criticizes realism for not doing so (p. 905). In contrast, Lakatos observes that *"the most admired scientific theories simply fail to forbid any observable state of affairs"* (1970, 100, his italics). This is true for many reasons. Lakatos himself points out that we always evaluate theories with a *ceteris paribus* clause implied, and we can never be sure that it holds. To express the same thought in different words, scientific theories deal in idealizations. If the results of scientific experiments are carried to enough decimal points, hypotheses inferred from theories are always proved wrong. As the Nobel Laureate in physics, Steven Weinberg, puts it: "There is no theory that is not contradicted by some experiment" (1992, 93). Ernst Nagel (1961, 460–466, 505–509) expressed a similar thought when he pointed out that social-science predictions fail because social scientists do not deal in idealizations. It is because falsification is untenable that Lakatos proposes that we evaluate theories by the fruitfulness of their research programs. Ultimately he concludes, as others had earlier, that a theory is overthrown only by a better theory (p. 119; cf. Conant 1947, 48).

Despite claiming to follow Lakatos's advice to evaluate theories through their research programs, Vasquez emphasizes what he takes to be evidence falsifying balance of power theory. According to him, the historian Paul Schroeder (1994) has presented "devastating evidence" against it. One must understand, however, what a theory claims to explain before attempting to test it. Early in his piece, Schroeder (p. 109) draws a picture of neorealism's logic. All of his arrows run in one direction, from the system downward. Realizing that many people have trouble understanding theory, I drew a few pictures myself. Figure 3.1 depicts one of them (Waltz 1979, 40). Structural theory emphasizes that causation runs from structures to states *and* from states to structure. It also explains, among other things, why balances of power recurrently form. Schroeder rejects structural theory because it fails to account for the motives of statesmen. Yet, as William Graham Sumner wrote: "Motives from which men act have nothing at all to do with the consequences of their action" ([1911] 1968, 212). I would say "little" rather than "nothing," but the point is clear, and structural theory explains why it holds. What Vasquez takes to be Schroeder's "devastating evidence" turns out to be a melange of irrelevant diplomatic lore. Like Vasquez, Schroeder ignores the basic injunction that theories be judged by what they claim to explain. Moreover, both fail to notice that Morgenthau's understanding of balances of power differs fundamentally from mine. For Morgenthau, balances are intended and must be sought by the statesmen who produce them. For me, balances

```
┌─────────────────────────┐
│  International Structure │
└─────────────────────────┘
        ↑       ↓
┌─────────────────────────┐
│    Interacting Units    │
└─────────────────────────┘
```

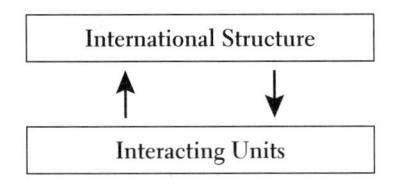

FIGURE 3.1

are produced whether or not intended. Schroeder's "evidence" may apply to Morgenthau's ideas about balances of power; it does not apply to mine. This again shows how misleading it is to place all realists in a single paradigm.

Vasquez and Schroeder note that power is often out of balance. Is structural theory invalidated because the actions of states sometimes fail to bring their system into balance? In answering this question, it is helpful to think of similar problems in economics. Classical economic theory holds that, in the absence of governmental intervention, competitive economies tend toward equilibrium at full employment of the factors of production. Yet one rarely finds an economy in equilibrium. Further, theory leads one to expect that competition will lead to a similarity of products as well as of prices. Illustrating the result, Harold Hotelling (1929) pointed out that autos, furniture, cider, churches, and political parties become much like one another. But a tendency toward the sameness of products may not be apparent at a given moment, for a competitor may successfully outflank its rivals by offering a design that breaks the mold. Do economies in disequilibrium and variations in product design cast doubt on hypotheses inferred from theories of competition? Hardly. Economic theory predicts strong and persistent tendencies rather than particular states or conditions. Similarly, no contradiction exists between saying that international political systems tend strongly *toward* balance but are seldom *in* balance.

Vasquez's attempt to apply Lakatos's ideas about research programs to balance of power theory is as unsuccessful as his attempt to adduce evidence that would falsify it. Lakatos defines a series of theories as progressive "if each new theory has some excess empirical content over its predecessor, that is, if it predicts some novel, hitherto unexpected facts" (1970, 116). Newtonian science is a wonderful example of a progressive series of theories, incorporating the same basic assumptions about the universe in theories covering successively more phenomena. Classical economics, able to explain the working of national and of international economies as well, is another example. In international politics, where can one find such a use of fundamental concepts to develop theories covering ever more phenomena? Vasquez claims to find several, but his claim rests sometimes on placing in a single realist program work that belongs in different ones, and sometimes on taking work done when applying a theory as being the creation of a new one.

One cannot judge the fertility of a research program by evaluating work done outside of it. Vasquez takes Randall Schweller's (1994) essay on bandwagoning as work done within the realist paradigm and argues that it provides an example of its degeneration. Schweller, however, sets out to show that the central theory of neorealism is wrong. He rejects neorealism's assumptions about power as a means and survival as the goal of states in favor of Morgenthau's assumption that states seek ever more power. He claims to show that bandwagoning is more common than balancing, believing that if it is, then neorealist theory fails. Schweller and I work within different research programs. The question therefore shifts from the quality of the program to whether his claims about bandwagoning invalidate structural theory.

Structural theory assumes that the dominant goal of states is security, since to pursue whatever other goals they may have, they first must survive. Bandwagoning and balancing, by the logic of the theory, are opposite responses of security-seeking states to their situations. States concerned for their security value relative gains over absolute ones. At the extremes, however, with very secure or very insecure states, the quest for absolute gains may prevail over the quest for relative ones. Very weak states cannot make themselves secure by their own efforts. Whatever the risks, their main chance may be to jump on a bandwagon pulled by stronger states. Other states may have a choice between joining a stronger state and balancing against it, and they may make the wrong one. States sometimes blunder when trying to respond sensibly to both internal and external pressures. Morgenthau once compared a statesman not believing in the balance of power to a scientist not believing in the law of gravity. Laws can be broken, but breaking them risks punishment. One who violates the law of gravity by stepping from a nineteenth-story window will suffer instant and condign punishment. A state that bandwagons when the situation calls for balancing runs risks, as Mussolini's Italy discovered after it jumped on Hitler's bandwagon, although in international politics punishment may not be swift and sure. By joining the stronger side, Italy became Germany's junior partner and Mussolini lost control of his policy. Bandwagoning by some states strengthened Germany and encouraged Hitler to further conquest. Only balancing in the middle and later 1930s could have stopped him. Various states, including Italy, paid a great price for their failure to balance earlier. Theory does not direct the policies of states; it does describe their expected consequences.

States' actions are not determined by structure. Rather, as I have said before, structures shape and shove; they encourage states to do some things and to refrain from doing others. Because states coexist in a self-help system, they are free to do any fool thing they care to, but they are likely to be rewarded for behavior that is responsive to structural pressures and punished for behavior that is not.

Vasquez requires that theories predict, since prediction seems to make falsification possible. He therefore seizes upon Schweller's claim that bandwagoning is more common than balancing. Whether this looks like falsifying evidence depends on what is predicted. Like classical economic theory, balance of power theory does not say that a system will be in equilibrium most or even much of the time. Instead, it predicts that, willy nilly, balances will form over time. That, Vasquez would no doubt say, is not much of a prediction. Yet Charles Kegley (1993, 139) has sensibly remarked that if a multipolar system emerges from the present unipolar one, realism will be vindicated. Seldom in international politics do signs of vindication appear so quickly. Multipolarity is developing before our eyes: To all but the myopic, it can already be seen on the horizon. Moreover, it is emerging in accordance with the balancing imperative.

In the light of structural theory, unipolarity appears as the least stable of international configurations. Unlikely though it is, a dominant power may behave with moderation, restraint, and forbearance. Even if it does, however, weaker states will worry about its future behavior. America's founding fathers warned against the perils of power in the absence of checks and balances. Is unbalanced power less of a danger in international than in national politics? Some countries will not want to bet that it is. As nature abhors a vacuum, so international politics abhors unbalanced power. Faced by unbalanced power, states try to increase their own strength or they ally with others to bring the international distribution of power into balance. The reactions of other states to the drive for dominance of Charles I of Spain, of Louis XIV and Napoleon Bonaparte of France, of Wilhelm II and Adolph Hitler of Germany, illustrate the point.

Will the preponderant power of the United States elicit similar reactions? Unbalanced power, whoever wields it, is a potential danger to others. The powerful state may, and the United States does, think of itself as acting for the sake of peace, justice, and well-being in the world. These terms, however, will be defined to the liking of the powerful, which may conflict with the preferences and interests of others. The powerful state will at times act in ways that appear arbitrary and high-handed to others, who will smart under the unfair treatment they believe they are receiving. Some of the weaker states in the system will therefore act to restore a balance and thus move the system back to bi- or multipolarity. China and Japan are doing so now.

In international politics, overwhelming power repels and leads others to balance against it. Stephen Walt (1987, viii, 5, 21, 263–265) has offered a reformulation of balance of power theory, believing that states balance not against power but against threat. Vasquez sees Walt's "refinement" as placing a semantic patch on the original theory in an attempt to rescue it from falsifying evidence. I would agree if I took Walt's reformulation to be the correction of a concept that increases the explanatory power of a defective theory and makes it more precise. Changing the concepts of a theory, however, makes an old theory into a new one that has to be evaluated in its own right. I see "balance of threat" not as the name of a new theory but as part of a description of how makers of foreign policy think when making alliance decisions. Theory is an instrument. The empirical material on which it is to be used is not found in the instrument; it has to be adduced by the person using it. Walt makes this clear when he describes "threat" as one of the "factors that statesmen consider when deciding with whom to ally" (p. 21). In moving from international political *theory* to foreign policy *application* one has to consider such matters as statesmen's assessments of threats, but they do not thereby become part of the theory. Forcing more empirical content into a theory would truly amount to a "regressive theory shift." It would turn a general theory into a particular explanation. Vasquez, and Walt, have unfortunately taken the imaginative application of a theory to be the creation of a new one.

Vasquez makes a similar mistake in his appraisal of Christensen's and Snyder's (1990) essay, "Chain Gangs and Passed Bucks." "The authors," according to Vasquez, "find a gap in Waltz's explanation [of European diplomacy preceding World War II] and try to correct it by bringing in a variable from Jervis" (1997, 906; Ch. 2 herein, 36). However good or bad my brief explanation of what happened in Europe prior to World War II may be (Waltz 1979, 164–170), an explanation is not a theory. A theory does not provide an account of what has happened or of what may happen. Just as a hammer becomes a useful tool when nails and wood are available, so a theory becomes useful in devising an explanation of events when combined with information about them.

The question is not what should be included in an account of foreign policies but what can be included in a theory of international politics. A theory is not a mere collection of variables. If a "gap" is found in a theory, it cannot be plugged by adding a "variable" to it. To add to a theory something that one believes has been omitted requires showing how it can take its place as one element of a coherent and effective theory. If that were easy to do, we would be blessed with a wealth of strong and comprehensive theories.

I conclude by emphasizing a few points about the testing of theories. A theory's ability to explain is more important than its ability to predict. At least Steven Weinberg and many others think so. Believing that scientists will one day come up with a final theory, he writes that even then we will not be able "to predict everything or even very much," but, he adds, we will be able to understand why things "work the way they do" (1992, 45; cf. Toulmin 1961, 36–38). Success in explaining, not in predicting, is the ultimate criterion of good theory. Theories of evolution, after all, predict nothing in particular.

Vasquez makes the testing of theories seem easy by adopting a positivist standard: Does the observation made correspond with a theory's prediction? His adoption of such a standard is shown by his crisp assertion that the failure of states to balance "in the period before World War II . . . should be taken as falsifying evidence" (1997, 906; Ch. 2 herein, 36). Yet what is to be taken as evidence for or against a theory is always in question. Some attempts to balance were made in the prewar years, but a balance formed, so to speak, only in the end. Should delay in completing a balance be taken as evidence contradicting balance of power theory? One may not be able to answer the question decisively. Testing theories is an uncertain business. In this case, however, one should certainly remember that the theory being tested explains the process of balancing as well as predicting that balances recurrently form. The theory cannot say how long the process will take.

The title of Errol Harris's (1970) book, *Hypothesis and Perception*, implies a criticism of Popper's claim that a critical test of a hypothesis, if flunked, falsifies a theory once and for all. As Harris suggests, our perceptions count; the results of tests require interpretation. Evaluating a theory requires working back and forth between the implications of the theory and an uncertain state of affairs that we take to be the reality against which the theory is tested. Whether or not events in the 1930s tend to validate or to falsify my version of balance of power theory depends as much on how one interprets the theory as on what happened. However thorough the evaluation of a theory, we can never say for sure that the theory is true. All the more, then, we should test a theory in all of the ways we can think of—by trying to falsify and to confirm it, by seeing whether things work in the way the theory suggests, and by comparing events in arenas of similar structure to see if they follow similar patterns. Weinberg suggests yet another way. "The most important thing for the progress of physics," he writes, "is not the decision that a theory is true, but the decision that it is worth taking seriously" (1992, 103). The structural theory set forth in my *Theory of International Politics* at least passes that test.

## Editors' Commentary

### Major Query

What is **neo- or structural realist theory**, what does it claim to explain, and how well does it perform?

### Major Points

Waltz argues that Vasquez misstates and misjudges Waltz's structural realist **theory**. Their disagreement is both about epistemology (what are theories and how are they to be appraised) and substantive (what does Waltz's theory say).

Waltz agrees with Lakatos that simple falsificationism is problematic. But Waltz suggests that, despite rhetoric to the contrary, Vasquez is engaging in simple falsificationism when he insists that scholars must specify the evidence that would *disprove* their theories. If Vasquez were truly employing MSRP he would apply its criteria to the structural realist research program's trajectory. Instead he looks for Popperian empirical contradictions, and uses evidence from nonstructural realist theories.

Waltz argues that Vasquez (and Paul Schroeder, whom Vasquez cites favorably) misunderstands what structural realism says about balance of power. One of their errors is to mistakenly combine **classical** and **structural realism**. Structural realism argues that the international political system shoves and shapes but does not determine state behavior. The patterns of actions and outcomes that result are attributed to this shoving and shaping, not to the internally generated desires of individual states. One such outcome is that balances will tend to form in the international system, whether or not states intend them. Accordingly, evidence that states often act as if they did *not* intend the system to be in balance leaves structural realism undamaged. Similarly, structural realism says the international political system tends toward, not that it necessarily achieves or maintains, equilibrium. Hence, findings that the system is sometimes not balanced are also irrelevant to the theory's claims.

Waltz suggests that Vasquez mistakenly groups different realist theories into the same research program. In particular, Schweller's work falls outside of structural realism because it attributes behavior to internally generated motives, not to the external constraints engendered by the international political system. In addition, even if empirically correct, Schweller's substantive finding that states bandwagon would not contradict structural realism. The theory only suggests that states will suffer if they ignore structural constraints; it does not predict that they will obey them.

## Key Terms

**theory** Theory is defined differently by different scholars. For Waltz, a theory is a mental picture that depicts the organization of a realm and the connections among its parts. While a simplification of reality, a theory's selection and juxtaposition of explanatory factors may not look like the world it is designed to explain.

**classical realism** Argues that because states are engaged in a constant struggle to increase their power, international politics is conflictual and cooperation rare. This desire for power is rooted in human nature. Hans Morgenthau's (1948) realism is often referred to today as classical realism to distinguish it from Waltz's structural realism. Waltz sees the struggle for power as emanating from the system of anarchy and a desire for security, rather than from a flawed human nature.

**structural realism** Excludes the internal makeup and appetites of states from the theory, and argues instead that conflict and the absence of cooperation can be attributed to the effects of an enduring international political structure. That structure is comprised of three parts: (1) the absence of an overarching authority, the condition of anarchy; (2) the absence of functional differentiation, since states cannot rely on other states to perform needed services or supply necessary materials; and (3) the distribution of capabilities, which can range from bipolar (two great powers) to multipolar (three or more great powers). The juxtaposition of two or more great powers creates an international system that has enduring, but not determining, effects. One of these is that systems will tend toward balance.

# THE PROGRESSIVE POWER OF REALISM

*STEPHEN M. WALT**

John Vasquez's evaluation of the realist research program is a misstep on the road to better international relations theory. By portraying realism as "degenerating," Vasquez hopes to influence both "individual decisions about where scholars are willing to place their research bets, *as well as collective decisions as to which research programs deserve continued funding, publication, and so forth*" (1997, 900; Ch. 2 herein, 24, emphasis added). In other words, his main goal is to discredit realism as a legitimate approach to the study of world politics, discourage scholars from pursuing a realist research agenda, and make it less likely that scholars working in the realist tradition will receive research funds or access to prominent journals.

What evidence does Vasquez present to justify this extreme position? Vasquez's (1997) criticism of realism is based on one philosopher of science (Imre Lakatos) and a handful of contemporary realist writings. Specifically, to support his charge of "degeneration," he has selected two "realist" books (Waltz 1979, Walt 1987), two articles (Schweller 1994, Christensen and Snyder 1990), and an eleven-page letter to the editor (Elman and Elman 1995). Does such a cursory survey justify discarding a respected intellectual tradition? Would we consider abandoning rational choice theory, the cognitive approach to decision making, organization theory, liberal theory, or the quantitative analysis of voting behavior on the basis of a similar sample? Even if every one of Vasquez's criticisms were valid (which is not the case), his evaluation would say little about the value of the realist perspective.[1]

The foundation of Vasquez's critique is Lakatos's (1970) well-known essay on scientific research programs. Lakatos argued that a research program consists of (1) a "hard core" of basic propositions accepted by all members of the research

---

*The author thanks Michael Desch, David Edelstein, Markus Fischer, Keir Lieber, John Mearsheimer, and Rebecca Stone for comments on earlier drafts.

community, (2) a "negative heuristic" that deflects criticism away from this hard core, and (3) a "positive heuristic" that identifies legitimate puzzles and sets the research agenda. According to Lakatos, a research program is "progressive" if new theoretical refinements lead to "excess empirical content" (i.e., to newly confirmed predictions) when compared with the earlier theory. By contrast, a research program is said to be "degenerating" if each new theory is merely an ad hoc or semantic adjustment that explains an anomaly but does not anticipate some "novel fact."

Influenced by the Lakatosian model, Vasquez portrays realism as a narrow, tightly unified research program that is exhibiting clear signs of degeneration. After describing what he takes to be realism's hard core, he argues that recent theoretical refinements are merely ad hoc adjustments designed to rescue the entire paradigm from its purported empirical failings. He does this by showing that a handful of realists have advanced different theories about alliance formation. Vasquez sees these disagreements as a symptom of degeneration because the presence of several competing realist theories increases "the probability that the realist paradigm will pass some test" (1997, 906; Ch. 2 herein, 35).

There are three main problems with Vasquez's criticism. First, his reliance on Lakatos is problematic, both because that model of scientific progress is flawed and because Vasquez's interpretation of it would justify abandoning most (if not all) of social science theory. Second, Vasquez's characterization of the realist tradition is misleading and understates its range and diversity. Third, Vasquez overlooks the progressive character of contemporary realist theorizing, in large part because he did not consider all the relevant literature. In particular, his treatment of my own work is both inconsistent and demonstrably inaccurate. Taken together, these errors explain why his article leaves realism largely unscathed and sheds little light on how it might be improved.

## How Not to Judge Social Science Theories

Vasquez relies on Lakatos's model of scientific progress because he believes that it "has attracted the most consensus" as a source of criteria for judging theoretical merit, at least among mainstream scholars of international relations (1997, 899–900; Ch. 2 herein, 24). Even if this assertion were correct, however, it would not be a persuasive justification. Lakatos's now-dated analysis has been largely rejected by contemporary historians and philosophers of science (Diesing 1991, Laudan 1977, Suppe 1977b, Toulmin 1972). Why should social scientists embrace a model of scientific progress that has been widely discredited by experts in that field?

Lakatos's analysis has been discarded mainly because it does not square with what we now know about scientific discovery. For example, Lakatos argues that scientists in a particular research program share a "hard core" of common assumptions, but the historical record shows that scientists working in such a program often disagree about its central elements.[2] Similarly, Lakatos's model implies that progress takes place only at the research frontier, while the hard core of a research program remains unchallenged. In fact, the hard core is often the object of debate, and it evolves in response to new empirical discoveries and conceptual innovations. Thus, Lakatos's model of scientific progress is doubtful on purely historical grounds.

Second, although Lakatos emphasizes that the key criterion in choosing between rival theories is "excess empirical content," he never explains how to perform this sort of comparison. For Lakatos, theory $T_2$ is progressive if it explains everything that the old theory $T_1$ did, while simultaneously accounting for some unanticipated "new fact." Yet, comparing the empirical content of rival theories turns out to be especially difficult in practice, which helps explain why "neither Lakatos nor his followers have been able to identify *any* historical case to which the Lakatosian definition of progress can be shown strictly to apply" (Laudan 1977, 77; see also Grunbaum 1976a; McCloskey 1994, chapter 7). A measure of progress that is difficult to operationalize is not a useful guide.

Third, Lakatos's rejection of ad hoc adjustments is inconsistent with actual scientific practice. An ad hoc adjustment that resolves an existing anomaly but does not lead to any other new facts is still an advance in our understanding; after all, it does answer a puzzle. Such an adjustment is problematic only if it simultaneously creates additional conceptual or empirical difficulties. Similarly, a refinement that limits the domain of a theory (i.e., by showing that it only operates under circumscribed conditions) is still an improvement over the prior but incorrect claim that the theory possessed a broader explanatory range. Thus, working scientists routinely embrace ad hoc adjustments and correctly regard them as part of normal scientific procedure.[3]

These points suggest that Lakatos's model is not a sound basis for judging realism or any other research program. Indeed, taken to its logical conclusion, Vasquez's application of Lakatos would justify abandoning virtually all social science theory. Vasquez sees a research program as degenerating if (1) new theories offer no new empirical content and (2) if the program "goes through a number of theoryshifts ... the end result [of which] is that collectively the family of theories fields a set of contradictory hypotheses which greatly increase the probability of at least one passing an empirical test" (1997, 901; Ch. 2 herein, 26). As we shall see, his claim that certain realist theories have not produced "new facts" is simply wrong. Moreover, his claim that the emergence of contradictory hypotheses is a sign of degeneration in effect means that when scholars in a particular research program advance different theories or reach different conclusions, then that research program is ipso facto beginning to degenerate. This conclusion ignores the possibility that one scholar is correct and another is incorrect, as well as the possibility that a particular disagreement can be reconciled by empirical testing or by a more precise specification of intervening variables or boundary conditions (Schweller 1997). Adopting this standard would force us to reject virtually every research tradition in the social sciences.

## What Is Realism?

Vasquez appears to regard realism as a single, tightly unified research program, centered around the ideas of Kenneth Waltz. This view leads him to see any major disagreement among realists—and especially any departure from Waltz—as a sign of degeneration, which in turn leads him to portray other realists as trying to salvage the larger paradigm through a series of ad hoc amendments. This perspective also allows him to count the discrediting of any particular realist theory as a blow against the entire paradigm.

Vasquez's view rests on an inaccurate picture of contemporary realist thought. In fact, realism is a broad research program that contains a host of competing theories. Realists begin with some general assumptions (such as states are the key actors, the international system is anarchic, power is central to political life).[4] As with all successful research programs, however, realists also disagree about a host of fundamental ideas. For example, Hans Morgenthau assumes that competition between states arises from the human lust for power (which he termed the *animus dominandi*), while Kenneth Waltz ignores human nature and assumes that states merely aim to survive (Morgenthau 1946, Waltz 1979). "Offensive" realists, such as Mearsheimer (1994-95), argue that great powers seek to maximize security by maximizing their relative power, while "defensive" realists, such as Jack Snyder (1991) or Charles Glaser (1994-95), argue that great powers are generally more secure when they refrain from power maximization and seek to defend the status quo. Realists also disagree about the relative importance of domestic versus systems-level causes, the relative stability of bipolar versus multipolar worlds, and the importance of intentions in shaping the calculations of national leaders (to name but a few possibilities). Thus, far from being a narrow intellectual monolith, realism is a large and diverse body of thought whose proponents share a few important ideas but disagree about many others.[5]

Two implications follow. First, it is hardly evidence of degeneration when realists advance contradictory arguments or reach different conclusions, just as it is not a major issue whenever neo-Keynesian economists, Skinnerian psychologists, Darwinian sociobiologists, or quantum physicists are at loggerheads. There are a host of competing theories within the realist paradigm, and not all of them are going to be equally valid or useful. Second, the failure of a particular realist theory does not discredit the entire paradigm, especially since realism deals with a very wide variety of international phenomena. Vasquez focuses on a handful of authors in his attempt to discredit the entire approach, but this step mischaracterizes the broader research tradition and the many different theories it contains.[6]

The real question to ask is whether realism—with all its limitations—has advanced or impeded our understanding of international relations. On this issue, even well-known critics of realism concede that it has been an influential tradition precisely because it sheds considerable, if only partial, light on a number of important international phenomena (Keohane 1984, 1986b; Ruggie, 1983; Wendt n.d.).[7]

## Power, Threat, and Empirical Content

The problems with Vasquez's analysis are evident in his discussion of my own work. To begin with, he cannot make up his mind about the theoretical status of balance-of-threat theory. He begins by portraying my theory as a direct refutation of Waltz's neorealist balance of *power* theory, based on my assertion that states tend to balance against *threats* rather than against power alone. In his view, this challenge to Waltz has "devastating" consequences for the realist paradigm. As Vasquez puts it, "if . . . power and threat are independent, as they are perceived to be by the states in Walt's sample, then something may be awry in the realist world" (1997, 904; Ch. 2 herein, 32).

Yet, it is hardly clear why refuting Waltz would lead us to abandon the realist paradigm in toto. Vasquez clearly regards my work as part of the realist paradigm, so if I have correctly refuted Waltz, then realism is a progressive program after all. To avoid this obvious challenge to his argument, Vasquez reverses course and argues that balance-of-threat theory is merely a "felicitous phrase" that "makes states' behavior appear much more consistent with the larger paradigm than it actually is." In particular, he claims my theory "does not point to any novel facts other than the discrepant evidence [and] . . . does not have any excess empirical content compared to the original theory, except that it now takes the discrepant evidence and says it supports a new variant of realism" (1997, 904–905; Ch. 2 herein, 33). In short, Vasquez begins by calling balance-of-threat theory a "devastating" challenge to Waltz, based on the claim that power and threat are wholly independent concepts. But he quickly backtracks to argue that balance-of-threat theory is merely a semantic repackaging of Waltz's theory that does not point to any novel facts. He cannot have it both ways.

As it turns out, both assertions are incorrect. With respect to the first, I do not see power and threat as independent. Balance-of-threat theory openly incorporates power, subsuming it (along with geography, offensive capabilities, and intentions) within the more general concept of *threat*.[8] Balance of *power* theory predicts that states will ally against the *strongest* state in the system, but balance-of-threat theory predicts they will tend to ally against the most *threatening*. Thus, the latter can explain not only why a state may align against the strongest power (if its power makes it the most dangerous) but also why one state may balance against another state which is not necessarily the strongest but which is seen as more threatening on account of its proximity, aggressive intentions, or acquisition of especially potent means of conquest. The two theories are not the same, although they share certain elements.

With respect to the second assertion that balance-of-threat theory is merely a semantic repackaging, I point to several of my works that offer novel facts. Balance-of-threat theory was originally laid out in my 1987 book, which examined alliance behavior in the Middle East. The final chapter showed, however, that it can also explain the anomalous distribution of power between the Soviet and American alliance systems during the Cold War. In a subsequent article (not cited by Vasquez), the theory was used to explain the alliance behavior of four different states in Southwest Asia (Walt 1988). Another article (also not mentioned by Vasquez) shows how balance-of-threat theory explains alliance dynamics in Europe during the 1930s, a period that poses an especially demanding test for the theory. In particular, the theory explains why (1) the East European states failed to balance effectively against both Nazi Germany and the Soviet Union, (2) the United States was the last great power to mobilize for World War II, and (3) Great Britain and France balanced more slowly than hindsight might dictate. Parenthetically, this article also shows that Britain and France did not fail to balance the rising threat from Nazi Germany, as Vasquez, Schroeder, and others imply (Walt 1992b). Other scholars have successfully used balance-of-threat theory to explain the formation of the Gulf War coalition in 1990–91 and to analyze the grand strategy of the United States in the post–Cold War period (Garnham 1991, Mastanduno 1997). Finally, Vasquez does not refer to my recent efforts to apply the theory to a new realm—the international consequences of domestic revolutions (Walt 1992a, 1996). Thus, Vasquez's central claim—that balance-of-threat theory does not have "excess empirical content"—is false. And with this error exposed, his argument collapses.

## Conclusion

Viewed as a whole, Vasquez's essay is a classic illustration of the hazards of small sample size. First, he relies on one modern work on the history and philosophy of science. Second, he relies on five contemporary realist works. Finally, he cursorily surveys the writings he examines, thereby missing the novel facts they uncover. This combination of problems is fatal to his argument, and prevents him from offering a useful criticism of realism in general or the specific body of literature under examination.

This failure is unfortunate, because realism is not without flaws and certainly should be exposed to criticism. The realist perspective offers a simple and powerful way to understand relations among political groups (including states) and offers compelling (albeit imperfect) accounts of a diverse array of international phenomena. But it is hardly the only way to study international relations. In the future, as in the past, scholars will continue to revise and extend the diverse body of realist thought. In doing so, they will inevitably disagree in various ways. At the same time, other scholars will pursue a variety of nonrealist research programs, and the resulting competition among different approaches will help us refine our understanding of international politics. The clash of theories both within and across competing research programs is essential to progress in the social sciences and should be welcomed. Progress will be swifter, however, if criticism seeks to do more than merely delegitimate realism, or any other approach a critic happens to dislike.

## Editors' Commentary

### Major Query

How should realism be evaluated, and does it satisfy those criteria?

### Major Points

Walt argues that Vasquez mistakenly relies on Lakatos's MSRP, a metric which has been rejected by contemporary philosophers of science as a flawed way to organize and assess knowledge. Science simply does not work the way that MSRP expects it to. For example, research programs are supposed to have hard cores, a list of elements that the program's adherents agree are indispensable, and which do not change over time. But an investigation of the history of science reveals that both consensus and stability are rare. Walt also suggests that Lakatos's measure of progress, excess empirical content, is hard to measure, and excludes many of the most important advances, which would be dismissed by MSRP as mere puzzle solving.

In addition, Walt suggests that Vasquez overstates the unitary nature of the realist research program, as well as the centrality of Waltz's *Theory of International Politics*. Realism is better viewed as a broad research program that contains a host of competing theories. These theories share some assumptions but disagree about others. It is nonsensical to regard this diversity as a sign of degeneration, or to regard the failure of any single theory as a failure of the whole research program.

Finally, Walt argues that even if one were to apply MSRP, there is strong evidence that realism has experienced a progressive trajectory in terms of the discovery and corroboration of new (or novel) facts. For example, Walt's own balance-of-threat theory represents a progressive problemshift because it predicted new facts. These included alliance behavior in the Cold War, in Southwest Asia, and in interwar Europe. The theory has also been extended to explain the formation of the Gulf War coalition in 1990–91, to analyze the grand strategy of the United States in the post–Cold War world, and to explain the international consequences of domestic revolutions.

## Key Term

**balance-of-threat theory**   Best contrasted with dyadic balance of power theory, which suggests that states will react to increases in other states' capabilities. Balance-of-threat theory suggests that, in deciding whether or not to balance, states look not just at aggregate power (more is more threatening), but also at geographical proximity (closer is more threatening), offensive capabilities (more is more threatening), and offensive intentions (states that have them are more threatening).

## Notes

1. As discussed below, Vasquez's sample is not even a comprehensive survey of the relevant works on the (relatively) narrow subject of balancing behavior.
2. To note one example, both Charles Darwin and Alfred Wallace worked within the Darwinian "research program," insofar as each believed in the core principle of natural selection. Yet they disagreed on several basic issues, such as the inheritability of acquired characteristics (Richards 1987, chapters 2 and 4).
3. As Laudan (1977, 115) puts it: "If some theory $T_2$ has solved more empirical problems than its predecessor—*even just one more*—then $T_2$ is clearly preferable to $T_1$ and, *ceteris paribus*, represents cognitive progress with respect to $T_1$. . . . Ad hoc modifications, *by their very definition*, are empirically progressive." See also Grunbaum 1976b.
4. Some realists might add the assumption that states are more or less rational actors, although several prominent realists (including the present author) also examine how domestic politics can affect the

"rational" assessment of strategic interests. For a sample of recent attempts to identify the core features of the realist paradigm, see Mearsheimer 1994–95; Van Evera, n.d., chapter 1; Walt 1992b, 473.
5. Recent examples and discussions of the broad body of realist thought include Brooks 1997; Brown, Lynn-Jones, and Miller 1995; Desch 1996; Deudney 1993; Elman 1996a; Frankel 1996a, 1996b; Gilpin 1986; Grieco 1990; Van Evera n.d., chapter 1; and Zakaria 1992.
6. The most egregious example is Vasquez's claim that Colin and Miriam Elman's 1995 letter to the editor of *International Security* illustrates the response to Schroeder of scholars "sympathetic to realism" (1997, 908; Ch. 2 herein, 39). Such an assertion would be valid only if realism were in fact a single theory and if all so-called realists agreed with the Elmans' position. Vasquez offers no evidence that this is the case, which it is surely not.
7. For example, realism provides cogent explanations for (1) the failure of all modern efforts to gain hegemony over the state system; (2) the nearly universal tendency for great powers to be extremely sensitive to shifts in the balance of power; (3) the constancy of security competition among great powers; (4) the difficulty of sustaining effective international cooperation; (5) the tendency for great powers to acquire either formal empires or informal spheres of influence; and (6) the tendency for great powers to imitate one another over time. Realism does not provide the *only* explanation for these (and other) phenomena, but it contains a set of explanations that one would not want to dismiss out of hand.
8. As I wrote in *The Origins of Alliances*: "Balancing and bandwagoning are usually framed solely in terms of capabilities.... This conception should be revised, however, to account for the other factors that statesmen consider when deciding with whom to ally. *Although power is an important part of the equation, it is not the only one*" (Walt 1987, 21, emphasis added; see also 263–264).

# PROGRESSIVE RESEARCH ON DEGENERATE ALLIANCES

*THOMAS J. CHRISTENSEN AND JACK SNYDER*

John Vasquez is right to insist that students of international politics should justify their theories in terms of Imre Lakatos's (1970) criteria for distinguishing progressive research programs from degenerative ones. Indeed, in our article on European alliance patterns (Christensen and Snyder 1990) we paid close attention to these criteria. We are grateful for the opportunity to remind readers of our strategies for theory-building and of the empirical and theoretical puzzles that motivated us to write the original article.

Before responding to Vasquez's (1997) specific criticisms of our arguments, we must clarify the general relationship between our article and the enterprise of neorealism. We are not hard-core neorealist disciples whose main motivation is to "explain away" anomalies in the neorealist research program, as Vasquez contends. In common with neorealists, we believe that considerations of power often play a central role in the calculations of state leaders and that the logic of anarchy often shapes their strategic choices. We also believe, however, that domestic politics, perceptions, ideology, and other factors may play a major role in shaping choices and outcomes. Sometimes these factors may override the considerations that neorealists emphasize. More commonly, we believe that such factors interact with or mediate the effect of neorealist factors, such as the international distribution of power and the degree of military vulnerability. We adopt this perspective in our article on alliances and in many of our other works (for example, Christensen 1996, Snyder 1991). Whether this makes us neorealists is a labeling exercise in which we decline to take part.

We resist being cast in the role of apologists for neorealism. Still less are we interested in trying to reconcile the heterogeneous arguments of the various scholars whom Vasquez calls neorealist. Nonetheless, we do take the view that Waltz and other scholars working in a similar mode have generated insights into international politics that can be employed as tools in our broader, more eclectic research programs. Consequently, we felt we had a stake in sharpening those tools in order to use them more productively to solve a specific problem that concerned us: namely, the conditions that lead to unconditional "chain-gang" alliances as a response to threat in multipolarity, as opposed to "passing the buck" to third parties to parry the threat. We think that our borrowings from neorealism for that specific purpose yielded valid insights, when employed in the context of our overall research design. Moreover, our argument constitutes a progressive problem shift, as judged by Lakatos's criteria.

## Strategic Perceptions and Alliance Choices

Before discussing how our article fulfills those criteria, we will briefly restate our central arguments; except for one footnote (11), Vasquez (1997) misses our main point entirely. We began by noting that alliance patterns before the two world wars were very different, in fact opposite, yet the polarity of the international system, as defined by Waltz, was very similar. For the most part, the European powers chain-ganged as a response to the German threat before 1914 and buck-passed in the face of a similar threat in the 1930s, despite the similar multipolar configurations of power. Therefore, Waltz's ultraparsimonious structural analysis, focused exclusively on polarity, cannot explain the variation.

Of course, Waltz (1979, 1996) explicitly and repeatedly states in his work that, in proposing a structural realist theory, he is not interested in explaining foreign policy. "Waltz is interested in showing that a system of two is more stable than a system of many. He therefore evinces no interest in predicting which pathology of multipolarity will appear in particular circumstances" (Christensen and Snyder 1990, 142). Thus, the problem that interested us could be viewed as largely irrelevant to Waltz's concerns. Notwithstanding these differences in objective, we found Waltz's analysis of the dynamics of multipolar and bipolar worlds a useful starting point. This, however, no more makes us slavish neorealists than emphasizing the economic sources of political power makes one an orthodox Marxist. Although multipolarity was a factor in both the quick escalation of the July crisis in 1914 and the lethargic response to Hitler in the late 1930s, identifying which multipolar malady occurs in which circumstances requires looking for additional causal factors.

To unravel this puzzle, we argued that, if leaders in a multipolar setting believe that offensive doctrines are likely to be effective, then they are more likely to form tight alliances; if they believe defenses are hardy, then they are more likely to attempt to pass onto their current or potential future allies the high costs of initial resistance to aggressors. Under multipolar conditions, when leaders believe wars will be decided early, chain-gangs are likely, and when they expect war to be attritional, buck-passing is likely. Strategic realities are filtered through leaders' perceptions, however, and leaders often misperceive the objective strategic environment, as they did before both world wars. So, in our approach, leaders' perceptions of the strategic environment, not objective conditions, constitute the central variable that determines outcomes.

Except for one footnote, Vasquez ignores this perceptual aspect of our argument, misreading it as a purely structural account intended to save Waltzian neorealism's arguments about states' tendency to balance against threats. This misreading is also the source of Vasquez's claim that our argument constitutes a degenerative problem shift for neorealism, on the grounds that it "hides" or "explains away" what he sees as the failure of interwar states to balance. Far from hiding lacunae in the realist account about multipolar instability, we ourselves uncovered and explained them using perceptual variables that orthodox neorealists typically underrate.

Vasquez also fails to recognize that our dependent variable is not "balancing" but alliance maladies that complicate the balancing process. Failures to balance properly occurred before both wars, not just World War II. We wrote: "In multipolarity, two equal and opposite alliance dilemmas impede efficient balancing" (Christensen and Snyder 1990, 140). Before World War I, states were hyperactive; before World War II, they were lethargic. Thus, we are not testing some generic proposition about "the law of balancing." Rather, we are exploring implications of Waltz's more specific arguments about the mechanisms that make multipolar worlds less stable than bipolar ones. This means that, all things being equal, balancing occurs less smoothly in multipolar worlds than in bipolar ones. Vasquez's claim that Waltz should expect multipolar alliances to form smoothly runs counter to one of the major themes, if not the major theme, of Waltz's work. Thus, Vasquez's arguments about alliance dynamics before the world wars are unhelpful as criticisms either of our work or that of Waltz.

## Meeting Lakatos's Standards

Having clarified the objectives of our article, we can now assess whether it satisfies Lakatos's criteria for a progressive problem shift. One criterion is whether the new theoretical formulation can explain phenomena that the original one cannot. We pass that test, since we explain when chain-ganging occurs and when buck-passing occurs, whereas Waltz only explained that both were more common in multipolarity than in bipolarity. A second criterion is whether the new formulation can explain a large number of new observations, or whether each additional observation demands ad hoc adjustments to the theory. As we argue in the historical section below, we pass that test, too, insofar as our formulation adequately explains the alliance choices of all the major European powers before both world wars. A third criterion is whether the new formulation can be generalized successfully to new domains, and whether any theoretical adjustments needed to extend its range can be accomplished parsimoniously. We pass that test, too, given that a simple extension of our original argument allowed Christensen (1997), in a follow-up article, to explain a variety of nineteenth-century alliance choices. Unlike degenerative Ptolemaic astronomy, we explain a lot with a little.

A final criterion is whether modifications to the original theory introduce assumptions that contradict the theory's core logic. Our article took great pains to show that Waltz's basic assumptions overlap extensively with the core axioms of Robert Jervis's (1978) theory of the security dilemma. This theory has always been understood as having dove-tailed structural and perceptual elements. In anarchy, actors may misperceive structural constraints, but insofar as their perceptual antennae remain focused on figuring out what those structural constraints are, we contend that perceptual arguments are neither contradictory to structural ones nor especially degenerative. Moreover, as Waltz argues, alliance dynamics are more complex and uncertain in multipolarity. Therefore, under these structural conditions, miscalculation and misperception should be more likely.

## Vasquez's Historical Analysis

Aside from his theoretical arguments, Vasquez calls into question some of our historical interpretations. He criticizes our account of alliance behavior before the two world wars on two counts. Before World War I, he argues, Britain did not behave in a way consistent with our theory. It did not chain itself tightly to allies and, according to Vasquez, did less than it did in the early phases of World War II. He also suggests that in the 1930s there was really no balancing against the rise of German power. Instead there was appeasement, something he believes is fundamentally at odds with balancing.

Once again, Vasquez misrepresents our article. We stated clearly that Britain did not chain-gang in 1914 to the same degree that France and Russia did, in part because Britain's off-shore strategic position gave it a defensive advantage that the continental states lacked. Thus, British behavior differed for reasons that our hypothesis readily explains (Christensen and Snyder 1990, 155–156).

Consistent with our argument, Britain responded rather slowly to the security challenges on the continent before both world wars. It is inaccurate to state that it was slower to respond in 1914 than in 1939. British faith in defensive advantage on land was much stronger in 1939 than in 1914, and Britain's commitment to Europe was therefore much smaller and slower to arrive than its commitment to France in summer 1914. London managed to assemble no more than ten divisions for the British Expeditionary Force by the time Germany invaded the Low Countries and France in May 1940 (eight months after the Anglo-French declaration of war). That force was only about half the size sent to Europe by the first half of 1915, and it constituted only 10% of joint Anglo-French forces on the continent (Christensen 1997). Finally, regarding Vasquez's comparison between August 1914 and March 1939, our theory readily explains why the Serbian question sparked quick escalation in 1914, whereas the strategically much more important issue of German control of Czechoslovakia did not do the same in 1938–39.

On the issue of "appeasement versus balancing" Vasquez asks (1997, 907; Ch. 2 herein, 37): "Were Britain, France, and the USSR passing the buck in the late 1930s, or were they just slow to balance. Or were Britain and France pursuing an entirely different strategy, appeasement?" In fact, Britain, France, and Russia were slow to balance and also were buck-passing. The reasons for both postures were similar: British and Russian leaders in particular underestimated the threats posed by German offensives against France and the Low Countries. Therefore, in both their internal balancing efforts (arming) and their external balancing efforts (alliances) they responded anemically in the short term in order to preserve fighting power for the longer war that they anticipated would follow Germany's initial attempts to subdue either Britain or France.

British, French, and Russian leaders were still concerned about the growth of German power and aggressiveness, however. It is wrong to suggest that they were "appeasing" instead of "balancing." Once again, they did both. It is strange that Vasquez takes an "either/or" view of realist balancing and diplomatic appeasement. One of the first major realist works (published 40 years before Waltz's *Theory of International Politics*) was E. H. Carr's classic *Twenty Years' Crisis*. The 1939 edition of this book called on England to appease Hitler in the short term and to build up military power to balance against German expansionism in the longer term (Carr 1939). Appeasement is a diplomatic strategy that can either accompany or preclude balancing strategies, in the same way that "talking tough" and leveling coercive threats can accompany or preclude taking concrete measures to improve one's power position in the world.

Moreover, Britain's misguided and dangerous appeasement policy was largely abandoned after March 1939. By then, British strategists were thinking almost solely in terms of balancing against German power. Britain and France both increased their defense spending in 1939–40. Moreover, they formed an alliance in early 1939. Clearly, some balancing was occurring. Yet, Britain continued to adopt rather anemic responses to the threat posed to France and the Low Countries, even after the formation of a formal Anglo-French alliance. The pace and direction of the British rearmament effort as well as the deployment of available forces all demonstrated Britain's false faith in the hardiness of defensive positions in northern and eastern France (Christensen 1997).

As for the Soviet Union, Stalin's appeasement of and collusion with Hitler were accompanied by a serious arms build-up. As we reported in the original article, Stalin was shocked that France fell so quickly in spring 1940 (Christensen and Snyder 1990, 157). He not only underestimated the effectiveness of German offensives but also grossly overestimated the comprehensive power of Britain and France in comparison to Germany. Given his confidence about French defenses and the power of the Anglo-French condominium, Stalin was much less interested in alliance formation in the months leading up to Guderian's blitz than he likely otherwise would have been (Christensen 1997).

Stalin's misjudgements and the ways that they affected Soviet strategy demonstrate particularly well the real shortcomings in straightforward realist foreign policy analysis. Even when state leaders think of their security in terms consistent with realist tenets—weighing the general balance of power and the ways in which military power can be used to threaten national security—leaders still will often analyze their security environment so badly that they will adopt policies that should appear puzzling to realists.

By underreacting to the threat posed by Hitler, the British, French, and Soviet leaders did not maximize the security of the future alliance. But to suggest that they did not balance at all is simply wrong. The most obvious fact in this regard is that Germany was defeated. If no one balanced, then how did this happen? Soviet, French, and British leaders built up their militaries beginning in 1938, and Britain and France formed an alliance several months before the German invasion of Poland. Britain sent ten divisions to its ally before the German invasion of France; British leaders considered sending more immediately thereafter, until they received the shocking news of the total collapse of allied forces; finally, after the fall of Paris, London guaranteed support for the remaining French forces, thus assuring that Britain would be Hitler's next target. Though Britain should have done more to help France and should have done so earlier, it hardly "distanced" itself from the crisis in France (Christensen 1997).

When designing their security policies before the Cold War, European leaders did think in terms of the balance of power (both the number of great powers and the distribution of power among them) and the relative efficacy of offensive versus defensive strategies. Although they worried about their national security in ways familiar to realists, they often misread their strategic environments on both counts, and thus behaved in ways that should confound realists. This is true not only for the early twentieth century but also for the late nineteenth century (Christensen 1997).

This does not mean that all regions in all times have leaders who are obsessed first and foremost with Realpolitik. Rather than offering a theory of all foreign policy, we were offering a perceptual approach to explain why behaviors vary greatly even in structurally similar worlds in which leaders are generally thinking in terms of power and military doctrine. So, in this limited sense, our article may be seen as truly critical of realism. It uncovers the problems of straightforward realism in explaining the cases in which realism should prove most effective, and it explains the anomalies using perceptual variables. But we never meant to suggest that even our "emendation" of realism would prove decisive in analyzing all international settings. Just as it would be very dangerous to try to ignore power-related factors such as multipolarity, leaders' calculations of the balance of power, and beliefs about the offense-defense balance in analyzing security relations in pre–Cold War Europe, it would be equally dangerous to assume that power politics is always primary in the thinking of all leaders in relations with all outsiders. Both dogmatic realism and dogmatic antirealism will prove crippling in understanding many aspects of international relations. Ideology, institutions, domestic politics, and interdependence may indeed combine in various ways that make balance of power considerations irrelevant to various regions or bilateral relationships (Goldgeier and McFaul 1992; Jervis 1991/92). Yet, there have been, there still are, and there likely will be again times and places in which Realpolitik thinking prevails. Our 1990 article and Christensen's 1997 article merely emphasize that, to understand such worlds, we will have to know more about the region in question than the balance of power or the relative efficacy of offensive and defensive doctrines. We will have to know what leaders think about those factors in order to explain and predict the likely patterns of alliance formation and potential causes of conflict escalation.

## Editors' Commentary

### Major Query

What was the purpose of Christensen and Snyder's 1990 article on **chain-ganging** and **buck-passing**, and does it satisfy Lakatos's criteria?

### Major Points

Christensen and Snyder agree that Lakatos's metric is an appropriate way to assess research, and that social science should meet MSRP's requirements. They suggest, however, that Vasquez mischaracterizes their 1990 article both in the tasks it was designed to fulfill and the extent to which it meets Lakatosian criteria.

Christensen and Snyder insist that they do not consider themselves neorealists. In particular, unlike Waltz, they are eager to combine international structure with domestic politics, perceptions, ideology, and other factors in order to explain state foreign policy choices. Contra Vasquez, their 1990 argument was not an attempt to bolster neorealism by explaining away balancing failures before World War II. They were interested in amending Waltz's theory so that it could be extended into a new domain for which it was not originally designed: foreign policy analysis.

All Waltz's structural theory says is that because two different pathological balancing dynamics—chain-ganging and buck-passing—can take place in multipolarity, war and resulting system change is more likely than in bipolarity. Christensen and Snyder were interested in taking Waltz's structural theory and layering on additional nonstructural variables to determine *when* each of the two possible multipolar balancing pathologies is likely to occur. To make that determination, scholars need to be able to predict when individual states are likely to sit tight and do nothing, and when they are likely to have a hair-trigger response. The solution was to combine neorealism with perceptual variables from security dilemma theory.

Christensen and Snyder argue that their theoretical innovation meets Lakatosian criteria because it can explain something Waltz's theory cannot explain when either buck-passing or chain-ganging is likely to occur. In addition, in a 1997 article Christensen subsequently used the theory to explain a variety of nineteenth-century alliance choices.

Finally, Christensen and Snyder take issue with Vasquez's interpretation of the historical record as well as his insistence that appeasement and balancing are mutually exclusive policies. For example, there is no reason why Britain and Russia in the 1930s could not simultaneously acquiesce to German demands in the hope that it would become satiated and lose its revisionist aspirations, at the same time that they balanced as a hedge in case it did not. Indeed, this is the foreign policy mix that those states pursued before World War II.

## Key Terms

**chain-ganging**  A multipolar balancing dynamic that results when interlocking alliance commitments pull states into wars that they might otherwise have avoided. Christensen and Snyder argue that this dynamic is most likely to occur when states perceive that offense has the advantage over defense, since states must then lend quick and decisive support to their allies. The result is that all the members of an alliance become hostage to the behavior of the least restrained state, with hyperactive balancing producing unrestrained war. The archetype of this dynamic is the role respective alliance commitments to Austro-Hungary and Serbia played in causing World War I. Ironically, states' perceptions of offensive advantage were misplaced, and the Western Front experienced four years of static trench warfare.

**buck-passing**  A multipolar balancing dynamic that occurs when a state refuses to balance against a rising state, hoping that another threatened state will expend the necessary blood and treasure. A mutual buck-pass could result in none of the threatened states balancing, with the consequence that the rising state could achieve hegemony. Christensen and Snyder argue that this dynamic is most likely when states perceive that defense has the advantage over offense. The archetype of this dynamic is British and French half-hearted responses to Germany's rise before World War II, each hoping that others would pick up the slack. Largely relying on their World War I experiences, states again misperceived the offense-defense balance and overlooked the possibilities offered by new mobile combined arms operations. Poland and then France both fell within weeks.

# 6

# NEW REALIST RESEARCH ON ALLIANCES
## REFINING, NOT REFUTING, WALTZ'S BALANCING PROPOSITION

### RANDALL L. SCHWELLER

Vasquez's (1997; Ch. 2 herein) essay is a useful contribution to the enduring controversy over the merits of the realist approach to international relations theory. Disclaimers aside, Vasquez suggests that there is (or should be) one "true theory" of realism and that Waltz's (1979) balancing proposition provides a litmus test for deciding whether realism is a degenerating research program. My response begins with an overarching critique of the piece, in which I challenge both of these claims. This is followed by specific points on Vasquez's treatment of my own work. I conclude by suggesting that realism suffers not from proliferating emendations but rather from underspecified scope conditions.

There is no definitive or "single" theory of political realism; there are, instead, many realist theories derived from the same first principles and basic set of assumptions. Taken together, this large and growing body of work forms a theoretical perspective that has achieved the status of dominant research program in the study of world politics. Like all research programs, political realism consists of an irrefutable "hard core" and a surrounding "protective belt" of auxiliary hypotheses that "bear the brunt of tests and get adjusted and readjusted, or even completely replaced, to defend the thus-hardened core" (Lakatos 1970, 133). In my view (see Schweller and Priess 1997, 6–8), the "hard core" of the realist school of thought consists not of Waltz's balancing proposition but of seven propositions (or, rather, assumptions) about international politics. (1) Humans do not face one another primarily as individuals but as members of groups that command their loyalty (Gilpin 1986, 304–305; 1996, 7). (2) International affairs take place in a state of anarchy. (3) Power is the fundamental feature of international politics (Morgenthau 1967); it is the currency of international politics required to secure any national goal, whether world mastery or simply to be left alone. (4) The nature of international interaction is essentially conflictual: "A world without struggle would be a world in which life had ceased to exist"

(Spykman 1942, 12). (5) Humankind cannot transcend conflict through the progressive power of reason to discover a science of peace (see Morgenthau 1946, 90–95, chapter 8). (6) Politics are not a function of ethics; morality is the product of power (Carr [1946] 1964, 63–64; Spykman 1942, 18). (7) Necessity and reason of state trump morality and ethics when these values conflict (Wolfers 1962, 244).

The centrality of realism's hard core in the field of international relations is similar to that of rationality in the field of economics: It serves as *the* baseline expectation for empirical observations; that is, anomaly appears primarily, if not only, against the background of the realist research program. All other competing theoretical perspectives in international relations—for example, neoliberal institutionalism, bureaucratic politics, social constructivism, and so forth—have been defined in opposition to realism. When anomaly does appear, or ambiguity arises as the realist perspective is applied to new areas of interests, or when empirical or experimental work is undertaken to improve the explanatory and predictive precision and power of different auxiliary hypotheses, change takes place in the "protective" belt, but it must not occur in the hard core. Because the formulation of a new research program is a relatively rare event, devising and testing amendments to the program's protective belt of auxiliary hypotheses makes up the bulk of the work that scientists do. (In some ways, the development of a research program's auxiliary hypotheses can be seen as analogous to Thomas Kuhn's description of normal science [see Kuhn 1970a, 33]). Thus, no one should be surprised, much less shocked or alarmed, to find that political realism has been continually revised, reformulated, and amended for the purposes of (1) better explanations and more determinate predictions, (2) refinement and clarification of the research program's theoretical concepts, and (3) extension of the research program to cover new issue areas.

Political realism is more than a "scientific" research program, however; it is also a political philosophy or world view—one that is profoundly pessimistic about the human condition, moral progress, and the capacity of human reason to create a world of peace and harmony. These recurrent pessimistic themes, more than any specific proposition or testable hypothesis, make it possible to speak of a tradition of realist thought that includes Thucydides, Machiavelli, Hobbes, Rousseau, Weber, Kissinger, Waltz, and Mearsheimer. All political realists, whether philosophers or scientists, share this pessimism about human relations, which they depict as a perpetual struggle for security, prestige, and power and influence (control over territory, the behavior of other states, and the world economy).

In more technical terms, realists see a world of constant positional competition among groups under conditions of scarcity. By positional I mean that what counts is not the players' absolute skills or capabilities but how they perform relative to their opponents. In such situations, a change in the absolute capability of any actor (holding constant the remaining actors' capabilities) has important effects not only for that player but also for the other contestants (see Frank 1991; Schelling 1978, chapter 7). By competition I mean that the goal of the players is to win (viz., primacy; see Huntington 1993) or, at a minimum, to avoid relative losses (see Grieco 1990). Neorealism's assumption that states seek to maximize their security (not power or influence) transforms classical realism from a game of pure positional competition to one of collaboration with mixed motives. This is because, among security-seeking states, there is no inherent competition—no one winner (see Schweller 1996). In theory, security is a positive-sum value; it can, under certain conditions, be both commonly desired and commonly shared without diminishing its enjoyment for any individual actor. The same cannot be said for positional goods, such as prestige, status, political influence, leadership, political leverage, a positive trade balance, or market shares (see Hirsch 1976; Jervis 1993, 58–59). All states cannot simultaneously enjoy a positive trade balance; and if everyone has status, then no one does. Indeed, scarcity confers status (see Mishan 1982, chapter 17; Shubik 1971). Positional competition is therefore zero-sum: a gain (loss) for one player becomes a corresponding loss (gain) for the opponent(s). Here one is reminded of Francis I, who, when asked to list the disagreements underlying the perpetual warfare between him and his archrival Charles V, replied: "None whatever. We agree perfectly. We both want control of Italy!" (quoted in Waltz 1959, 187–188).

Turning to my own work, Vasquez maintains that I redefine "bandwagoning more broadly than Walt; it is no longer the opposite of balancing (i.e., siding with the actor who poses the greatest threat or has the most power) but simply any attempt to side with the stronger, especially for opportunistic gain" (1997, 905; Ch. 2 herein, 34). Vasquez acknowledges that I define bandwagoning as "any attempt to side with the stronger" but then claims that this is somehow different or inconsistent with "siding with the actor that . . . has the most power." Perhaps the key words are "any attempt." They are not my words, however. Like Waltz, I simply define bandwagoning as siding with the stronger state or coalition.[1]

It is Walt (1987), not I, who redefines bandwagoning. In order to retain the balancing/bandwagoning dichotomy and to make it fit his balance-of-threat framework, Walt (1987, 17) redefined bandwagoning as "alignment with the source of danger." As I pointed out (Schweller 1994), the problem with Walt's definition is that it (1) confuses bandwagoning with strategic surrender,[2] (2) defies conventional usage and the common meaning of the term, and (3) by viewing bandwagoning solely as a response to threat, ignores the primary motivation for bandwagoning, namely, the expectation of profit and easy gains. The more general point is that alliances are responses not only to threats but also to opportunities. By defining bandwagoning as a response to threat, Walt's theory overlooks the principal reasons states, particularly nonthreatened ones, would engage in this behavior.

Vasquez further claims that my "new concepts do not point to any novel theoretical facts" (1997, 906; Ch. 2 herein, 35). This charge would be true if I had simply confirmed the standard hypothesis that weak states sometimes ally with strong states when it is to their advantage. I did not do this, however. Instead, my bandwagoning argument and my cases focused on *great powers*, not weak ones; that is, I examined the behavior of precisely those states that realists claim are most likely to balance dangerous accumulations of power. Therefore, my conclusion that great powers typically bandwagon with rising dissatisfied challengers is, indeed, theoretically important and novel. I observed that England and the Habsburgs bandwagoned with Louis XIV's France in

1667–79, when France achieved hegemonic status in Europe (Schweller 1994, 89–90). Similarly, during the Napoleonic wars, every great power (Prussia, Austria, Russia, Spain) with the exception of Great Britain bandwagoned with France at one time or another (1994, 90–92). Likewise, Japan, Italy, and the Soviet Union bandwagoned with Hitlerite Germany (1994, 94), and some scholars even suggest that France did so in 1940.

My argument is straightforward: Unthreatened revisionist states (those overlooked by Walt and Waltzian neorealists) often bandwagon with the stronger revisionist state or coalition for opportunistic reasons. My use of the term conforms to the standard definition of bandwagoning as joining the stronger side; and I show that this behavior is quite prevalent throughout history among a certain class of states (Schweller 1994, 1998). This is an important theoretical insight that explains novel facts. I did not claim, however, that I had falsified the "balancing predominates" proposition. Instead, I wrote: "Balancing is an extremely costly activity that most states would rather not engage in, but sometimes must to survive and protect their values. Bandwagoning rarely involves costs and is typically done in the expectation of gain. This is why bandwagoning is more common, I believe, than Walt or Waltz suggest" (Schweller 1994, 93).

But even if I had shown conclusively that more states bandwagon than balance (a claim I did not make), this would not necessarily contradict or disconfirm Waltz's balancing proposition. Balancing forces may still prevail at the systemic level (that is, balances of power may recurrently form after their disruption), as Waltz's theory predicts. This is because satisfied great powers are typically the most powerful ones with the greatest interest in maintaining the status quo. They are therefore likely to balance against revisionist aggressors and to be successful, even when outnumbered.

Finally, Vasquez writes: "Schweller . . . argues that his theory is even more realist than Waltz's, because he bases his analysis on the assumption of the classical realists—states strive for greater power and expansion—and not on security, as Waltz . . . assumes" (1997, 905; Ch. 2 herein, 33). Here again, Vasquez is only partially correct. Contemporary realists, such as Waltz and Walt, treat *all* states as if they were satisfied, status-quo powers that seek primarily to maximize their security rather than their power. I argue that this status-quo bias overlooks the main protagonists or catalysts of balance of power theory: revisionist, dissatisfied powers that seek to expand their power at the expense of others. Without these states, there would be little need for security (or security studies) in world politics (see Schweller 1996). Consistent with traditional realism, therefore, my balance-of-interests theory includes *both* revisionist states (those that seek to increase their power) and status-quo states (those that seek merely to keep what they already possess). By relaxing neorealism's assumption that all states value what they possess more than what they covet, my theory allows for the full range of state interests.

The essential point is that, for neorealists, conflict and competition are framed in terms of self-preservation; that is, states fear being dominated or even destroyed by others. As a result, neorealism is relatively silent about other important state goals, such as "tranquility, profit, and power," which Waltz (1979, 126) views as secondary interests that can only be safely sought "if survival is assured." History, however, shows otherwise (see Zakaria 1998). In the words of fellow realist, Raymond Aron (1966, 598): "All great states have jeopardized their survival to gain ulterior objectives. Hitler preferred, for himself and for Germany, the possibility of empire to the security of survival. Nor did he want empire—or an accumulation of power—as a means to security." Even if we concede Waltz's point that survival is the sine qua non for the pursuit of other goals, the question arises: When survival is assured, what does neorealism explain? Not enough, in my view; that is why I developed balance-of-interests theory.

By highlighting apparent theoretical contradictions and discrepant patterns of evidence within the realist research program, Vasquez's appraisal of neotraditional research serves a useful purpose. Yet, it seems to me that the problem is not one of a degenerating research program but of underspecified scope conditions. Realists, like most other theorists in the discipline, have done a poor job of identifying the conditions required for their theories to operate; as Bobrow (1972, 15) put it, "one reason for conflicting generalizations is the failure to state the necessary conditions for one rather than the other to hold." With regard to the balancing proposition, I agree with Walt's conclusion that states typically respond to threats by balancing against, not aligning with, the source of danger. But because states align for reasons other than security, I disagree with his more general claim that states usually balance and rarely bandwagon. As I wrote: "Walt does not offer a theory of alliances so much as a theory of how states respond to external threats" (Schweller 1994, 83). Both his theory and his "balancing predominates" proposition apply only to threatened states. In contrast, I looked at how unthreatened states respond to opportunities in their environment and found that bandwagoning is a common form of behavior, especially among dissatisfied states. The two findings are not inconsistent. When proper attention is devoted to the scope conditions of our theories, much of what appears to be contradictory and discrepant proves consistent and complementary.

## Editors' Commentary

### Major Query

Is there "one true" theory of realism, and does the accuracy of Kenneth Waltz's views on balance of power provide an authoritative test for its success or failure?

### Major Points

Schweller suggests that realism is dominant in the international relations subfield, both as a political philosophy and a research program. All other approaches define themselves by reference and in opposition to it.

Viewed as a research program, there are many realist theories derived from the same set of unchanging assumptions. Contra Vasquez, these assumptions, not Waltz's theory of international politics, form the irrefutable hard core. While the hard core is stable, realism's refutable auxiliary belt is amended over time and thus new realist theories are created.

Schweller argues that the major difference between realism and neorealism arises from how they view states' motives. Neorealism argues that states want to maximize their security. Under some circumstances, therefore, states can be better off without making others worse off. By contrast, in the older and harsher classical realist view, states are pure positionalists: the things they want they can only get by taking them away from others.

Schweller contends that Vasquez simply misunderstands his views on **bandwagoning**, in particular conflating Schweller's position with that of Walt. Schweller views alliances as tools to make gains, as well as to avoid losses. Walt argues that while *fearful* states usually balance, they are occasionally forced to bandwagon when faced with overwhelming odds. Schweller suggests that Walt is correct that fearful states will usually balance. But because Walt underplays greed as a motive, he undercounts bandwagoning in the international system. Sometimes states bandwagon because they want a cut of the take, not because they fear the rising challenger.

Schweller argues that his theory is not an incremental widening of balance-of-threat theory in order to incorporate empirical anomalies. It offers a different account of states' motives (fear *and* greed) and makes a genuinely novel prediction: Unthreatened revisionist states sometimes bandwagon with stronger revisionist states.

## Key Term

**bandwagoning**  Joining with a rising state, either (a) from fear because when faced with overwhelming odds a threatened state has no choice; or (b) from greed, because a secondary revisionist state (what Schweller describes as a "jackal revisionist") calculates that joining with the major revisionist state will deliver additional resources.

## Notes

1. In fact, the term "bandwagoning" as a description of international alliance behavior first appeared in Quincy Wright's *A Study of War* ([1942] 1964, 136) and only much later in Waltz (1979, 126; also see Wolfers 1962, 124). Both Wright and Waltz employ the concept to serve as the opposite of balancing behavior or what Wright ([1942] 1964, 136) called "the underdog policy." Bandwagoning refers to joining the stronger coalition; balancing means allying with the weaker side. Contrary to neorealist logic, however, Wright correctly points out that bandwagoning can, under certain circumstances, preserve the balance of power. This occurs when "the stronger in a given war is a relatively weak state whose strengthening is necessary to hold a more powerful neighbor in check" (Wright [1942] 1964, 136).
2. Walt's bandwagoning is a preventive form of strategic surrender. The prospective loser agrees not to initiate hostilities and to transfer its residual military capability to the prospective winner in exchange for immunity of life, the avoidance of losses it would incur in a certain military rout, and (if the loser retains some bargaining assets) the possibility of political concessions, e.g., the survival of the loser's authority structure. Sometimes the weaker side capitulates rather than fights in order to conserve its strength for a future battle under more favorable conditions. By giving in without a fight, it gains a breathing spell, during which it expects the balance of power to shift against the more powerful aggressor. See Kecskemeti 1958, Chapters 1 and 2.

# LAKATOS AND NEOREALISM

## A REPLY TO VASQUEZ

COLIN ELMAN AND MIRIAM FENDIUS ELMAN*

John Vasquez (1997) provides an account of Lakatos's (1970) methodology of scientific research programs and then uses the criteria to conclude that the neorealist scientific research program is degenerating. In support of his claim, Vasquez references our commentary (Elman and Elman 1995) on Schroeder's (1994a) thoughtful and important critique of neorealism. In particular, Vasquez insists that two of our arguments are signs of degeneration: (1) Evidence that states do not balance may challenge Waltz's (1979) theory without necessarily undermining the neorealist research program; and (2) a program should be improved before it is discarded and, in any event, should not be rejected until an alternative is devised to take its place. We stand by both arguments and maintain that they do not constitute evidence of neorealism's degeneration. We suggest that Vasquez's conclusion is based on a misstatement of Lakatos's criteria and on a mistaken conflation of the neorealist program with the proposition that states balance.

Vasquez presents four indicators of a degenerating research program and argues that "Elman and Elman (1995) serves as evidence that all these are very much in play within the field" (1997, 909; Ch. 2 herein, 40). His critique, however, is based on a problematic account and application of Lakatos's criteria of appraisal. Vasquez suggests that "it would be highly desirable to construct operational indicators of the progressive or degenerating nature of a ... research program. Since these are not available, [I] will explicitly identify the characteristics that will be used to indicate that a research program is degenerating" (1997, 900; Ch. 2 herein, 25). In fact, there is a voluminous literature on Lakatos's methodology, including extended discussions of the operational criteria for appraising scientific research programs. These criteria address two sorts of

---

*The authors thank Stephen G. Walker and Brian Taylor for helpful comments on an earlier draft of this article.

scientific development: *intra-* or within program problemshifts that consist of modifications to the protective belt of auxiliary hypotheses, and *inter-* or between program problemshifts that occur when, despite the prohibition against modification, elements of the hard core of the research program are rewritten. Problemshifts are degenerative to the extent that they are ad hoc. Lakatosians distinguish among three notions of ad hocness: ad hoc$_1$, the theory predicts no novel consequences; ad hoc$_2$, the theory's novel predictions have not been corroborated; and ad hoc$_3$, the theory is obtained from its predecessor through a modification of the auxiliary hypotheses that does not accord with the positive heuristic of the program (Lakatos 1970, 175n2 and 3, 182; Musgrave 1974, 20; Zahar 1973, 101). While interprogram problemshifts need only satisfy the two novel fact criteria, intraprogram problemshifts must also correspond with the research program's positive heuristic (Lakatos 1970, 175–176). In light of these widely recognized Lakatosian measures, Vasquez's four "operational criteria" of degeneration (1997, 900–902; Ch. 2 herein, 25–28) prove to be either otiose or incomplete.

Vasquez's first sign of degeneration, that problemshifts are driven by a need for repair in the face of existing empirical anomalies (1997, 901; Ch. 2 herein, 26), is superfluous. Anomaly solving is neither a necessary nor sufficient indication of degeneration. It is not necessary because anomaly solving is only one motive that may produce problemshifts that do not satisfy the need for novelty (Carrier 1988, 206). It is not a sufficient sign of degeneration because solving an anomaly can be an entirely legitimate exercise, so long as the problemshift also satisfies the three Lakatosian criteria.

The second operational indicator mentioned by Vasquez roughly corresponds to the ad hoc$_1$ criterion of the prediction of novel facts, but he fails to note the extensive debate among Lakatosian scholars as to what counts as a novel fact (Carrier 1988, 206; Hands 1991a, 70, 1991b, 94). There are at least seven definitions, all following what Musgrave (1974, 3) describes as a "historical approach to confirmation." This is not merely a matter of semantics, because the way factual novelty is defined crucially affects whether a problemshift will be appraised as progressive or degenerating. Since employing different definitions of novel fact will produce contrasting conclusions concerning the progressiveness or degeneracy of the research program under scrutiny, it is quite impossible to apply Lakatos's methodology without first recognizing, and then making a choice from among, the menu of available meanings.[1] This Vasquez fails to do. Indeed, he seems to rely on several different definitions throughout his essay.

Vasquez's third operational indicator is an incomplete version of the ad hoc$_2$ criterion that the new theory's novel predictions are not borne out by empirical evidence (Zahar 1973, 101n1). Vasquez fails to tackle the thorny issue of dating the novel predictions made by the research program (Rosenberg 1986, 135). One can make a case for a variety of different starting dates for the neorealist research program and variants created by problemshifts both within and from it. Vasquez also declines to choose from between the two available versions of ad hoc$_2$: that none of the excess content is corroborated or that all its excess content is refuted (Zahar 1973, 101n1). Nor does Vasquez specify the time we should allow for either of these two conditions to be satisfied before concluding that a problemshift is ad hoc$_2$. We do, however, get the impression that Vasquez ignores Lakatos's (1970, 116, 133–134, 155) injunction that scholars should not require instant gratification or be too impatient.

Vasquez's fourth indicator suggests that if "collectively the family of theories fields a set of contradictory hypotheses which greatly increase the probability of at least one passing an empirical test, then a research program can be appraised as degenerating" (p. 901). This indicator is misleading, since it simply describes the ordinary development of a research program. According to Lakatos, changes in the protective belt of auxiliary hypotheses are *designed* to protect the hard core. These intraprogram problemshifts combine the hard core with different auxiliary hypotheses to produce dissimilar predictions. That is, contrary to Vasquez's claim, Lakatos *anticipates* that a family of theories based on the same inviolable core will make contradictory predictions. Thus, for example, the fact that Gilpin (1981) and Waltz (1979) "predict contradictory things" (1997, 908–909; Ch. 2 herein, 40) is not an indicator of the degenerating nature of the neorealist research program.

Finally, Vasquez does not mention the ad hoc$_3$ criterion, modification of the protective belt of auxiliary hypotheses in ways that do not accord with the positive heuristic of the research program. Lakatos (1970, 175) argues that "in the positive heuristic of a powerful programme there is, right at the start, a general outline of how to build the protective belts." He defines "a research programme as degenerating even if it anticipates novel facts but does so in a patched-up development rather than by a coherent, pre-planned positive heuristic" (Lakatos 1971b, 125). Vasquez does not specify the neorealist positive heuristic, nor does he address this form of ad hocness in his overview of contemporary international relations theory.

Accordingly, although Vasquez argues that our 1995 essay provides evidence of neorealism's Lakatosian degeneration, his critique is based on incomplete and inconsistent operational measures. We suggest, however, that even when judged by the true Lakatosian criteria, our 1995 arguments fail to support his conclusion that the neorealist program is degenerating. Vasquez first cites our point that evidence that states do not balance may challenge Waltz's theory without directly undermining the neorealist research program. Vasquez charges that permitting both balancing and nonbalancing behavior to be consistent with neorealism is evidence of the research program's degenerating character (1997, 909; Ch. 2 herein, 40). This assertion is based on a misspecification of the neorealist program.

Recall that Lakatos argues that research programs have four elements: a hard core consisting of unchanging, privileged knowledge; a negative heuristic which forbids that knowledge from being directly challenged; a protective belt of auxiliary hypotheses, which "bear the brunt of tests and get adjusted and re-adjusted, or even completely replaced, to defend . . . the core" (Lakatos 1970, 133); and a positive heuristic that "guides the production of specific theories within the programme" (Worral 1978, 59; see also Lakatos 1970, 135). An application of the methodology of scientific research programs requires that all these components be specified (de Marchi 1991, 17). Vasquez fails to provide such a description. Instead, he observes that Walt, Schweller, and Christensen and Snyder are working within the same research program because they "all share certain concepts, are concerned with balancing, and share a view of the world and the general purpose of trying to work within and defend the paradigm" (1997, 904). This rendition of the neorealist program is methodologically and substantively unsatisfactory. It makes no attempt to delineate neorealism's hard core and heuristics, and it mistakenly conflates the entire neorealist program with balancing.

While we do not have the space to elaborate, we can provide a preliminary and illustrative description of the neorealist hard core.[2] (1) States interact in an anarchic environment, without the protection offered by an overarching authority. (2) States are self-regarding, and consequently self-help is the system-mandated behavioral rule. (3) Threat to survival is the main problem generated by the system, and consequently state behavior is designed to ensure survival. (4) States are the primary actors in international politics. (5) States have limited resources that they can employ to improve their chances for survival, and accordingly they are concerned to maintain or enhance those capabilities. (6) States select those strategies in which the expected gain is likely to exceed the expected loss. (7) States weigh options and make decisions based on their strategic situation and an assessment of the external environment.

Our main criticism of Schroeder's (1994a) article was that his reading of European history is largely consistent with this neorealist hard core. Schroeder may be right that the historical record of European international relations does not conform to Waltz's (1979) prediction of balancing, but contrary to Schroeder and Vasquez's assertions, neorealist theories do not invariably predict that states will balance; that they will always balance effectively (they are less likely to under multipolarity when structural pathologies are present); or that balances will always form. Specific behavioral predictions depend upon a combination of the hard core with different versions of the protective belt of auxiliary hypotheses. Although we cannot provide a full account of these different versions here, one brief example may be helpful. It is common practice to distinguish between offensive neorealists, who assert that states are power maximizing revisionists, and defensive neorealists, who contend that states defend the status quo and minimize relative power losses (Frankel 1996, xv–xviii; Mearsheimer 1994/95, 11–12n27). These two broad strategic assumptions funnel neorealist theories in particular directions. It is the particular costs and benefits suggested by these and other elements of the protective belt, in combination with the unchanging hard core, that lead neorealists to predict different behaviors. Employing some versions of the protective belt, strategies other than balancing will have lower costs and a better chance of coping with the external threat. Hence, as we argue in our rejoinder to Schroeder, neorealist theories can predict policies other than balancing, including bandwagoning and integrating (Elman and Elman 1995; see also Elman 1996a).

But this is not to argue that virtually any behavior is compatible with the neorealist research program. Vasquez misrepresents our position (1997, 909; Ch. 2 herein, 40–41) when he claims we assert that *only* "other-regarding" behavior is inconsistent with the hard core of neorealism (see, for example, Elman and Elman 1995, n6). Neorealism will never, indeed, by definition *cannot*, predict behavior that is incompatible with any elements of the hard core. Hence, it cannot predict that states will behave irrationally, or will respond primarily to demands internal to the state, or behave as if they had other-help identities, and so on.[3] Thus, contrary to Vasquez (1997, 909–910; Ch. 2 herein, 41) and Schroeder (1995, 194), neorealism does not "appropriate every possible tenable position in IR theory and history." The nonneorealist box is not empty.

Vasquez also notes as a sign of neorealism's degeneration our argument that, consistent with Lakatos (1970, 115), if a research program is found wanting, it should be improved before it is discarded; in any event it should not be thrown away until an alternative is devised to take its place. Again, as with his fourth operational indicator, Vasquez mistakenly presents what Lakatosians see as the typical trajectory of scientific development as evidence of degeneration. The tactics we suggest in our 1995 essay require amending the protective belt of auxiliary hypotheses in accordance with the research program's positive heuristic. While these problemshifts may turn out to be degenerative when judged by the three Lakatosian criteria of ad hoc$_1$, ad hoc$_2$, and ad hoc$_3$, our suggestion that scholars should amend the protective belt rather than discard the program is entirely consistent with standard Lakatosian metatheory.[4] In and of itself, it certainly does not constitute evidence of degeneration. Moreover, acknowledging that only a better theory can replace a theory recognizes that the methodology of scientific research programs is a comparative metric. A complete judgment of neorealism's progress cannot be made without reference to its rivals (e.g., classical realism, liberal institutionalism) and the extent to which these have been progressive or degenerating (Blaug 1976, 155, 177; Carricr 1988, 276–278; Lakatos 1971a, 177, 1971b, 105; Nunan 1984, 271–273, 281–282, 290).

Although we disagree with Vasquez's critique of our 1995 essay, and with his conclusions regarding the neorealist program, we welcome his attempt to apply the methodology of scientific research programs to international relations theory. Scholars in the field often claim to be following Lakatos's philosophy of science, but usually this amounts to little more than a boilerplate footnote reference to Lakatos's (1970) seminal essay. Only rarely do we find substantive discussions and applications of the methodology.[5] We applaud Vasquez's effort, and we hope that this exchange of views will induce other scholars to employ this useful and powerful approach.

## Editors' Commentary

### Major Query

Does Vasquez deploy an accurate version of Lakatos's Methodology of Scientific Research Programs? Does Vasquez apply MSRP in a way that allows for a useful assessment of realism?

### Major Points

Vasquez's essay lays out a contestable version of MSRP that insufficiently reflects Lakatosian metatheory. In particular, it wrongly identifies degeneration with puzzle solving, as opposed to failing to satisfy **novel fact criteria**. Lakatos is unconcerned with why theoretical modifications are introduced (they may or may not be aimed at solving anomalies) but is concerned that the modifications produce "new knowledge." Accordingly, interrogating a few realist works to find solved puzzles is an insufficient basis for concluding that the research program is degenerating. A complete analysis requires a survey to determine whether new theoretical mechanisms have been employed (possibly by scholars other than those who introduced the amendments) to discover new facts.

In addition to metatheoretic problems, Vasquez's essay is blemished by an ambiguous and misleading definition of the realist **research program**. Vasquez makes little or no attempt to delineate the hard core, negative heuristic, protective belt, or positive heuristic of the research program(s) he seeks to investigate and assess.

Operationally, Vasquez's descriptive failing may not be fatal to his enterprise, since novel fact criteria are applicable to both inter and intraprogram problemshifts. In other words, Waltz and the other respondents may be entirely correct that Vasquez mistakenly puts them all in the same research program; but Vasquez may still be entirely correct that the succession of theoretical modifications has to satisfy novel fact criteria. The difference is that the criteria will only be applicable to theories in the new research program, and cannot be applied retrospectively to theories in the old research program. Contrast the following hypothetical scenarios:

- Walt's balance of threat theory is part of the same research program as Waltz's structural realism. On investigation, analysts conclude that balance of threat produced no novel facts. This absence reflects on the whole research program, and so would impact upon both Waltz's and Walt's work.
- Walt's balance of threat theory is not part of the same research program as Waltz's structural realism. Its creation amounted to an interprogram problemshift. On investigation, analysts conclude that balance of threat theory produced no novel facts. This absence reflects only on the new research program, since the old research program cannot be held responsible for the failings of its successors. Only Walt's theory (and other theories in the new research program) will be impacted by this negative finding.

Since there is a strong case for suggesting that Waltz is working in a different research program from Walt, Snyder and Christensen, and Schweller he had no need to defend his theory from Vasquez's charges, even if they turned out to be true.

## Key Terms

**novel fact criteria**   MSRP suggests that where a theory $T$ is contradicted by fact $e$, a slightly modified theory $T'$ can be easily developed that will accommodate the anomaly. If $T$ and $T'$ share the same hard core, they belong to the same research program. If $T$ and $T'$ have different hard cores, they belong to different research programs. Regardless whether the move from $T$ to $T'$ takes place intra (within) or inter (between) program, Lakatos insists that the second theory $T'$ must do more than just accommodate the anomaly *e*: it must also predict "something else." Philosophers disagree about what this "something else" must be. In what sense must it be a "new" or "novel" fact? There are, at least, four kinds of possible novelty: (1) temporal novelty (Lakatos$_1$), where the fact must be something unknown to science at the time a theory was proposed; (2) new interpretation novelty (Lakatos$_2$), where the new theory must explain an "old" fact in a new way, thus converting it into a novel fact; (3) heuristic novelty (Zahar/Lakatos$_3$), where the new fact being offered to buttress a theory played no heuristic role in that theory's construction; and (4) background theory novelty (Musgrave), where the second theory predicts something that is not also predicted by its background theory.

**research program** A metatheoretic unit consisting of four elements: a hard core; a negative heuristic; a positive heuristic; and a protective belt of auxiliary hypotheses. The program's hard core consists of unchanging, privileged content. The hard core is protected by a negative heuristic that forbids this knowledge from being directly challenged or tested. In addition, research programs have a protective belt of auxiliary hypotheses, which can be adjusted or replaced to defend the core. The protective belt is developed in accordance with the program's positive heuristic, which Lakatos suggests will guide the production of specific theories within the research program.

## Notes

1. The different definitions of novelty can be grouped into four categories: (1) Lakatos$_1$, or strict temporal novelty (Hands 1991b, 96; Lakatos 1970, 118; Nunan 1984, 275; Worral 1978, 46 and 66*n*7; Zahar 1973, 101); (2) Lakatos$_2$, or new interpretation novelty (Carrier 1988, 206; Lakatos 1970, 157; Musgrave 1974, 11; Nunan 1984, 275; Zahar 1973, 102); (3) Zahar/Lakatos$_3$, or heuristic novelty (Lakatos and Zahar 1975, 375–376; Worral 1978, 48–49; Zahar 1973, 103); and (4) Musgrave's background theory novelty (Carrier 1988, 213; Musgrave 1974, 15–16). Although lack of space prevents an extensive discussion of this debate, we favor Worral's (1978, 48–49) reformulation of Zahar/Lakatos$_3$, novelty: "One can't use the same fact twice: once in the construction of a theory and then again in its support."
2. This list is derived from, and supporting citations may be found in, Elman and Elman 1995 and Elman 1996.
3. There are, of course, nonneorealist theories suggesting otherwise. Hence, some argue that foreign policy behavior can be explained as the product of nonrational choice mechanisms (Katzenstein 1996); internal demands (Milner 1988); or other-regarding identities and corollary behavioral rules (Wendt 1992).
4. Some Lakatosians would strongly disagree with our suggestion that the methodology of scientific research programs can be used to advise scholars on how to respond to degeneration rather than as a retrospective tool of appraisal (Musgrave 1976, 474). Lakatos (1971a, 174, 178, 1971b, 125) explicitly argues that he offers no advice to the working scientist. He only insists that practitioners should be aware of their alternatives, publicize the decisions they are making, and accept the consequences of their choices (Lakatos 1971b, 104–105). We agree with Blaug (1992, 37) that this position amounts to intellectual schizophrenia, and with Musgrave (1976, 473–482) that Lakatos's attempts to deny the methodology's role in providing advice for working scientists are inconsistent, unwise, and unnecessary.
5. For scarce examples, see Bueno de Mesquita 1984; Bueno de Mesquita, Krasner, and Jervis 1985; Grieco 1995; Keohane 1986b; and Simowitz and Price 1990. By contrast, economics has produced extensive discussions and applications (de Marchi 1991, 29–30).

# 8

# THE NEW DEBATE ON BALANCING POWER

## A REPLY TO MY CRITICS

### JOHN A. VASQUEZ*

### INTRODUCTION

Three lessons are clear from the preceding debate on the neotraditional research program on balancing power (herein, Chs. 2–7): First, the original thesis I laid out (herein, Ch. 2; Vasquez, 1997) was that the theoretical emendations of Waltz's balancing proposition were not an indicator of the fruitfulness of the realist paradigm but a sign that the research program on balancing was engaged in a series of degenerating problemshifts, in Lakatos's (1970) terminology. What is remarkable about some of the replies is that, rather than trying to resolve the debate primarily on Lakatos's criterion of what constitutes a degenerative or progressive problemshift, they seek to deny that Waltz's balancing proposition is empirically inaccurate in the first place — thus shifting the focus of the debate from the criterion of progressivity to the criterion of empirical accuracy and from the theoretical emendations of the neotraditional research program back to the actual proposition itself. This suggests that further empirical research may resolve the debate.

Second, and as would be expected, all of those accused of making theoretical emendations that are not progressive have denied it and insisted that their emendations have been progressive either in terms of specifying the domain of Waltz's original proposition on balancing and/or in uncovering novel facts. This aspect of the debate points out the need in the field to have more precise rules (if not indicators) to distinguish degenerative from progressive problemshifts, as well as the need to apply these in a rigorous and objective manner both before and after theoretical emendations are made.

---

*The author thanks Marie T. Henehan for valuable comments.

Lastly, in order for the debate to move toward some resolution, there must be a consensus on what criteria of adequacy are most appropriate. With one exception (Walt, herein, Ch. 4, but see also Wohlforth, herein, Ch. 15), there seems to be agreement that Lakatos (1970) provides a good starting point for such appraisals, but there remains some disagreement on how his criteria should be applied and, in general, on how the criteria of empirical accuracy, explanatory power, and progressivity should be combined to provide an overall appraisal. Each of these lessons will be analyzed seriatim.

## Is the Balancing Proposition Empirically Accurate?

Three of the replies to my original analysis maintain that the balancing proposition (fundamentally) is accurate (Waltz, herein, Ch. 3; Walt, herein, Ch. 4; and Christensen and Snyder, herein, Ch. 5). Even Schweller (herein, Ch. 6, 77; 1997, 929), who is the most critical of Waltz, denies that his evidence has falsified the balancing proposition. While it is logically consistent for Waltz to take such a tack, this is more difficult for Walt and Christensen and Snyder, since they amend the proposition quite a bit. If the proposition were empirically accurate in the first place, as Waltz avers, then there would be no need for theoretical emendation.

Nevertheless, each of the three replies explicitly maintains that all or the essential part of the balancing proposition is empirically accurate. Thus, Waltz (herein, Ch. 3, 54; 1997, 915) states:

> Faced by unbalanced power, states try to increase their own strength or they ally with others to bring the international distribution of power into balance. The reactions of other states to the drive for dominance of Charles I of Spain, of Louis XIV and Napoleon Bonaparte of France, of Wilhelm II and Adolph Hitler of Germany, illustrate the point.

Likewise, Walt (herein, Ch. 4, 65n7; 1997, 933n7) states:

> ... realism provides cogent explanations for (1) the failure of all modern efforts to gain hegemony over the state system ...

Finally, Christensen and Snyder (herein, Ch. 5, 71; 1997, 921) quip:

> By underreacting to the threat posed by Hitler, the British, French, and Soviet leaders did not maximize the security of the future alliance. But to suggest that they did not balance at all is simply wrong. The most obvious fact in this regard is that Germany was defeated. If no one balanced, then how did this happen?

These three claims are clearly empirical, and they form one basis on which a possible resolution of the debate could rest. For those who have denied the accuracy of the proposition, the above specifications would constitute a set of falsifying evidence (in Popper's [1959] formulation) that would permit all sides to see if the proposition was rejected or passed a crucial test. For defenders, it would permit their claims to be substantiated on an evidential basis that would establish the central importance of balancing behavior in the modern nation-state system. For the community of scholars, as a whole, it would provide a way for determining whether the evidence on balancing of power was discrepant or not, and if so, how discrepant.

For social scientists, trying to make a debate turn on an empirical disagreement has an obvious advantage, since presumably there are clearer rules and procedures for resolving empirical questions than for resolving conceptual and terminological disagreements. The problem is to come up with a mutually acceptable set of tests that would be binding. I challenge my critics to work with me in coming up with such a set of tests. In the remainder of this section, I will outline what I think would be acceptable empirical tests of Waltz's balancing proposition.

First, any set of tests should involve both comparative historical case studies and systematic quantitative tests with both methods producing the same or consistent results. Second, there has to be some agreement on what sets of behavior constitute attempts to balance and what do not; i.e., there has to be agreement on what evidence (retrodictions) will be reasonable grounds for rejecting one's belief. As Waltz (1979, 125) puts it when discussing the testing of his proposition and some of the difficulties raised by the Dual Alliance of 1879 between Germany and Austria-Hungary: ". . . we should examine diplomacy and policy . . . to see whether the theory serves to explain and broadly predict the actions and reactions of states. . . ."

Given Waltz's comments (herein, Ch. 3, 54; 1997, 915) on reactions to Napoleon and Hitler (quoted above), a key test of balancing of power has to be the response of states to hegemonic threat (see also Levy 1989; herein, Ch. 10). Note that Waltz does not say that balancing occurs only when there is a hegemonic threat (in Europe), since that would contradict his general proposition that: "Balance-of-power politics prevail wherever two, and only two, requirements are met: that the order be anarchic and that it be populated by units wishing to survive" (Waltz 1979, 121).[1] Nonetheless, since balance-of-power politics are a response to potential or actualized threat, one would presume that since the clearest and greatest threat a group of states could face would be the drive for dominance over all the other major states, this would most likely give rise to attempts to balance. Thus, it is no surprise that Dehio (1961) focuses on such drives in his analysis of the balance of power. Even Morgenthau (1960, 187), who has a number of qualms about the operation of the balance of power and speaks about its "uncertainty," its "unreality," and its "inadequacy" (Ch. 14), maintains:

> While the balance of power as a natural and inevitable outgrowth of the struggle for power is as old as political history itself, systematic theoretic reflections, starting in the sixteenth century and reaching their culmination in the eighteenth and nineteenth centuries, have conceived the balance of power generally as a protective device of an alliance of nations, anxious for their independence, against another nation's designs for world domination, then called universal monarchy.

Looking at so-called hegemonic threats, therefore, would constitute a legitimate sample to test not only Waltz's version of "balance-of-power politics," but also that of some classical realists, like Morgenthau (1960, 187). Both quantitative analyses of data restricted to these cases and in-depth historical analyses and process tracing could be used to test the proposition. For the purpose of this test, the question of whether each of these actors (e.g., Louis XIV) really constituted a hegemonic threat or really sought world domination (see Kaiser 1990) can be held in abeyance, and the cases that Waltz and other realists have traditionally seen as hegemonic threats can be taken as the sample.

The real problem is how to determine what constitutes "balancing" and "balance-of-power politics," as Waltz puts it, so that it is possible to ascertain before an in-depth examination of the evidence whether this phenomenon occurs. This is a classic problem of clear conceptual definition, operationalization (selection of indicators), and measurement, even if one does a case study and does not collect statistical data. If there cannot be any agreement on what will count as instances of "balancing," then it will be difficult to come up with a mutually acceptable test.

Hopefully, this problem will not be too serious an obstacle, since balancing as an international relations concept has several explicit empirical referents. Historically, it has been used to refer to an attempt by a state(s) to equal (balance) the power (often seen in terms of capability) of the other. Waltz (herein, Ch. 3, 54; 1997, 915) explicitly mentions this criterion in the passage quoted above. He states that "[f]aced by unbalanced power, states try to *increase* their own *strength* or they ally . . . to bring the international *distribution of power* into balance" (emphases added). Morgenthau (1960) uses a similar empirical referent and provides a useful list of the elements of national power (in Ch. 9) that can be used as possible indicators. Gulick (1955, 70–72, Ch. 11), in his discussion of the balance of power, argues that states distributed territory with a keen eye as to what specific pieces of territory would contribute to the power of a state in terms of its demographic and material resources (see also Morgenthau 1960, 179–180).

Some realists (like Kissinger 1994, 20–21, 67–68, 166–167) then go on to argue that, when sides are truly balanced in their capability (see the discussions in Morgenthau 1960, 173–177, 194–197; and Organski 1958, 292–293), this will inhibit an attack or "aggression." Others realize that such an equality will only reduce the chances of victory to 50–50; in fact only when the odds in favor of defense are much higher (say 75–25 or 80–20) could a real inhibiting effect be expected.[2] Thus, Morgenthau (1960, 194–197) speaks of the need for a "holder" of the balance that would swing back and forth, always giving the defending coalition overwhelming power over an "aggressor." Organski (1958, 292–293) is more explicit, arguing that only a "preponderance of power" will secure a state from attack; hence states seek not a balance of power but a preponderance.

Gulick (1955, 35–37) and Waltz (1979, 204) reject the idea that a balance of power will prevent war (although Gulick often insists a balance is necessary to maintain a peace), since wars may be fought to maintain a balance of power. For Waltz, the key law of international politics is not that balances prevent war, but simply that balancing arises out of anarchy as a typical kind of behavior in the system. In many ways his phrase, "balance-of-power politics" more clearly conveys the notion that "balancing" constitutes a key element in the set of power politics behavior (what some would call a game of power politics) that naturally arises out of the condition of anarchy. Balancing in this sense refers not just to attempts to increase one's capability so as to move toward equality, but also refers to attempts to increase capability that have the end result of checking and limiting the power and actions of the other side (i.e., the potential "aggressor") (Waltz 1979, 121).

Balancing-of-power politics involves blocking the ambitions of the other side, taking actions to prevent it from achieving its goal of dominance. From this perspective, certain actions would not be balancing. For example, siding with the potential aggressor (what Waltz calls bandwagoning) would not be balancing because it would aid the goal of the "aggressor," not block it. Nor would what Schroeder (1994a, 117) calls "hiding" check a potential "aggressor." Likewise, explicit declarations of neutrality cannot be seen as checking or blocking and should be seen as one of the ways in which states can "hide." Nor can policies of accommodation, like appeasement, be counted as instances of balancing, unless they are part of an explicit carrot and stick policy.[3]

Traditionally, the balance of power has been associated with alliance making as the key practice by which not only to balance a potential threat by increasing one's capability, but also as a way of building a coalition that will "check" and "block" the designs of an "aggressor," preferably before they get out of hand (see Morgenthau 1960, 181–197). Waltz (1979, 118, 168) refers to this as external balancing. He also introduces a new phrase, "internal balancing," by which he means relying on one's own (military) capabilities "rather than on the capabilities of allies" (see also Morgenthau 1960, 180 on armaments and balancing).

From this conceptual analysis, it is possible to construct a more operational definition of "balancing" in terms of the way Waltz uses it. First, balancing behavior must involve checking, blocking, and taking some action that inhibits the goals and designs of a potential "aggressor." Second, this usually involves states trying (in effect) to be at least equal to the power of other states (whether that is the intended policy or not—Waltz (1979, 119)—or of one coalition trying to be at least equal to another). The making of alliances among states is considered a feasible and traditional practice to achieve this end in the modern nation-state system. States also try to meet this end by maintaining or increasing their internal sources of power—i.e., their demographic growth, economic potential, access to mineral resources, the size of their military forces, the quality of their weaponry, and so forth.

A valid operationalization of balancing must use both sets of indicators. It is not sufficient to look just at the presence of alliance making or the building up of militaries. These actions can be taken by states that might bandwagon. Even neutral states might, as in the Cold War, come together in a coalition, if not an alliance, which might aid rather than block a potential "aggressor." The traditional practices of realism—alliance making and military buildups—must be seen as balancing only if the effect of balancing is present; i.e., these actions must be taken for the purpose of checking and blocking ambitions or have that consequence.[4] They must be used to make power meet power and thereby inhibit "aggression."

One set of tests that would seem to assess whether Waltz's claim on balancing is empirically accurate would be to see if, in the historical record, the evidence supports the claim that states, particularly major states, met the drive for dominance posed by Charles I (of Spain), Louis XIV, Napoleon, Wilhelm II, and Hitler by balancing (as defined above). Did they make alliances and take other actions that clearly checked the designs and power of these potential "aggressors"? Did they block and inhibit the actions of these states (or from a classical perspective did they seek to do so)? Did they confront these states; stand up to them—making power meet power? Or did they try to avoid the situation? Did they hide? Did they declare their neutrality? Did they engage in wishful thinking hoping the problem would go away? Were they paralyzed by inertia or fear? Did they save themselves or exploit the situation by joining up with the stronger side (i.e., bandwagon)? Did they try to transcend (Schroeder 1994a, 1994b) the game of balance-of-power politics, the struggle for power, the zero-sum relative gains perception of realism by going beyond this form of politics through accommodation or revamping a harsh peace (appeasement)?

What is not an acceptable test of Waltz's balancing proposition is to drop the first indicator on checking. To do this would give rise to an overly wide range of behavior that is consistent with the proposition. Christensen and Snyder (herein, Ch. 5, 71; 1997, 921) do this, inadvertently, when they ask if no one balanced Hitler, then how was Germany defeated? The mere fact that Hitler, Wilhelm II, and Napoleon were defeated does not mean they were defeated because their opponents balanced. In fact, Napoleon and Hitler were defeated because they did not know when to stop. As Schroeder (1994a, 120–121, 135) says, Napoleon insisted on attacking his opponents and his allies until all were against him. Likewise, Hitler was defeated not because of any balancing by Britain and France but because Hitler attacked his own ally (USSR) and because he declared war on the United States (being unable or lacking the foresight to restrain his ally from attacking the United States). Without these attacks, the USSR would have continued to bandwagon and the United States would probably have remained neutral, and without their intervention Britain alone could not have defeated Hitler. Balancing did not defeat Hitler or Napoleon; overexpansion did (see Rosecrance and Lo 1996, 491n29). This is not the place to conduct a historical debate; that should await the case studies. My point is, what is and is not an instance of balancing must be delimited before conducting a test. From my operational definition, resisting an open attack or invasion is not a valid indicator of balancing.

One of the differences between Waltz, Walt, Christensen and Snyder, and myself is that they seem to think (in various ways) that balancing in each of the above instances of hegemonic threat is an established fact. Waltz (herein, Ch. 3, 54; 1997, 915), for example, says that these historical instances illustrate his point, as if everyone who knew the historical record would understand this. Likewise, Walt (herein, Ch. 4, 65n7; 1997, 933n7) assumes that the historical record demonstrates "the failure of all modern efforts to gain hegemony. . . ." (see also his analysis of the 1930s in Walt [1992a]). My point is that existing research has not established these patterns, and that the consensus in contemporary historical research, for several of these cases, may in fact be the opposite. Indeed, for me, the kinds of emendations Walt, Schweller, and Christensen and Snyder make would be unnecessary if they themselves had not found some of the evidence on balancing discrepant with Waltz's (1979, 121) general proposition. Nevertheless, these are questions of fact that, in principle, should be answerable, even though we may have to go through a period of debate over particular interpretations of specific facts.

Such a test would be crucial for Waltz, since he suggests it. If his cases failed to pass such a test then that would undermine his claim. However, passing such a test would not in itself lead to the opposite conclusion. The main reason for this is that his cases are those he thinks best illustrate his points; they are not the entire population of hegemonic threats, nor a random sample. They may even be a sample biased in favor of the proposition. A more complete test would be to develop some indicators or criteria for determining when states attempt to achieve dominance and hegemony (or when in fact they succeed) and then examine whether this gives rise to balancing. Schroeder (1994a, 144–147), for example, takes what he sees as the failure to balance British hegemony in the nineteenth century as evidence against Waltz's proposition. Waltz (1993, 74–75, 77) himself suggests that if in the post–Cold War era the United States becomes dominant, then other states, specifically China and/or Japan, will begin to balance the United States (compare Walt, 1987, 273–284).

Of course, an even broader and more difficult test for Waltz's proposition would be to test it in its universal form and not limit it to just drives for dominance or hegemonic threats. In this instance, it would be expected that in anarchy, balancing—in terms of checking and blocking—is going to be part of the normal pulling and hauling of international politics. It would be the typical behavior states engage in, while hiding and bandwagoning would not be.

These last two tests are important and will go a long way in determining whether the balancing proposition is empirically accurate. They differ from the first one, however, in that in the first (Charles I, Napoleon, Hitler, etc.) power and threat are concomitant, so that both Walt and Waltz can be tested simultaneously. As one tries to look at the population of possible "targets against whom other states should balance," the question arises as to whether states should balance against power or against threat. Waltz is clear that states should balance against power. He does not talk about threat. The reason for this is that he, like Morgenthau, assumes that the most powerful state in the system must always be seen as at least a potential threat, because power (regardless of intentions) is what is important to those who are realistic. Walt (herein, Ch. 4, 62; 1997, 933) underestimates the theoretical implications of instances of when threat and power are separate. For Walt (1987), states rarely balance power unless these states also pose a threat, and sometimes the most powerful state in the system, as with the United States in the Cold War, is not seen (at least for capitalist states) as posing a threat (see also Walt 1988, 280).[5] The differences between Waltz and Walt lead them to make different predictions about the United States. Waltz (1993, 50, 66, 74–75, 77), as noted above, predicts that in the post–Cold War era China and/or Japan will balance the United States (a prediction he repeats in Waltz [herein, Ch. 3, 54; 1997, 916]), whereas Walt will presumably assume that, as in the

Cold War, so long as the United States poses no vital threat to states, there will not be an attempt to balance against it.

It was for this reason that I saw Walt's test, as well as the cursory review of European history provided by Schweller, as discrepant evidence that should be taken as falsifying Waltz's (1979, 121) proposition. Likewise, Christensen and Snyder's (1990) notion that states do not always balance but sometimes pass the buck should be taken as discrepant evidence undermining Waltz's theoretical proposition. Walt (herein, Ch. 4), Christensen and Snyder (herein, Ch. 5) and Schweller (herein, Ch. 6), however, all see this evidence as a basis for emending Waltz's proposition, rather than rejecting it. Reformulation is the conventional incremental decision scholars make in normal science, but the problem, as Lakatos (1970, 117) has pointed out, is how to tell when a series of such reformulations constitutes a degenerating research program. To make such a determination, he attempted to lay out a set of rules. Here we move from a purely historical disagreement to a theoretical and interpretive disagreement over what constitutes degenerative or progressive problemshifts in the neotraditional research program.

## Is the Research Program a Series of Degenerative or Progressive Problemshifts?

One of the main disagreements I have with the neotraditionalists under review and the one that gave rise to the analysis in the first place is that they have in their research program insufficiently recognized the extent to which their own evidence has undermined Waltz's proposition; instead they have sought to save some form of the proposition and/or the general realist perspective by introducing new concepts and propositions. These concepts and propositions have often been taken as a sign of theoretical growth and progress. I argued that they really are a series of degenerating shifts in theory (theoryshifts) that serve the function of ad hoc explanations intended to dismiss discrepant evidence.

Such a disagreement is not over what the historical record says per se, but over how to interpret evidence and whether the theoretical reformulations satisfy or fail to satisfy Lakatos's criterion on progressivity (the question of whether this is the appropriate criterion and whether it was properly applied in Vasquez (herein, Ch. 2) will be discussed in the next section). There are two questions here—one, as it was put in the debate, whether evidence is being "shirked" by neotraditionalists and another as to whether the reformulations are progressive or degenerating according to Lakatos's criterion. Each will be discussed in turn. Let me begin by illustrating how each of the theorists mute discrepant evidence.

What is particularly disturbing about the research program on balancing is the extent to which the discrepant evidence is downplayed and, at times, outright rejected as undermining the theory. The replies do not improve upon this, and that of Waltz (herein, Ch. 3; 1997) actually worsens the situation. Instead of taking some of the historical work seriously, including Schroeder's rather extensive historical work, he states: "What Vasquez takes to be Schroeder's 'devastating evidence' turns out to be a melange of irrelevant diplomatic lore." From the scholar who became renowned for dismissing all quantitative evidence as "correlational labors" (Waltz 1979, 12), we now hear that serious discussion of the historical record is simply "diplomatic lore" (Waltz herein, Ch. 3, 51; 1997, 914). This rejection of Schroeder's evidence, as that of quantitative evidence earlier, is so dismissive that one wonders whether any evidence will ever be sufficient to test his proposition.

He then goes on to assert that the behavior of Charles I of Spain, Louis XIV, Napoleon, Wilhelm II, and Hitler all conform to his balancing proposition. Yet Schroeder (1994a, 1994b), and even Schweller (1994), question this one-line history (see also Kaiser 1990). From their research, the major states as a group did not balance against Napoleon and Hitler. As Rosecrance and Lo (1996, 482) point out: "During this period, it appears that other states sought to co-opt, reward, avoid, or bandwagon with France instead of balancing against Napoleon." The major states often reacted only to invasion or attack, as did the USSR and the United States in 1941. Similarly, in the summer of 1914, Britain did not clearly commit against Germany before the invasion of Belgium, and so failed to provide a possible "deterrent effect."

Morgenthau's (1960, 187) original claim that states balance against attempts of "world domination," which Waltz presents here as one representative of his broader balancing generalization, must mean something more theoretically useful than simply the truism that states that are invaded will eventually get into the war. One hopes that Waltz will agree to some sort of test based on his statement as I proposed in the previous section (but see his qualms about testing in the closing section of Waltz, herein, Ch. 3, 55; 1997, 916).[6] In the meantime, there should be some recognition that existing historical evidence (like that of Schroeder 1994a, 1994b; and of Rosecrance and Lo 1996; and Rosecrance and Stein 1993) has raised questions that at least need to be investigated further.

Christensen and Snyder (herein, Ch. 5) are not so dismissive; their very concept of buck-passing recognizes that there is a problem and they rightly state that they are not "apologists for neorealism." They also state that to claim that British, French, and Soviet leaders "did not balance at all is simply wrong." This implies that the balancing that did occur did not quite live up to what one would expect. Here the disagreement is once again empirical and can be tested to reach a more precise judgment on the historical record. From my perspective, appeasing while building up one's military but hoping appeasement will work (U.K. 1938),[7] surrendering in 1940 (France), bandwagoning in 1939 (USSR), and remaining isolated but supportive (the United States)[8] cannot be taken as evidence of a law-like pattern of balancing permeating history just because these countries found themselves, at one time or another, at war with Hitler. If the theoretical import of balance of power is to be reduced to this and Waltz's descriptive truism, then we have wasted centuries of time on the trivial. Waltz's (herein, Ch. 3, 54; 1997, 915) claim on Napoleon and Hitler, Christensen and Snyder's (herein, Ch. 6, 71; 1997, 921) claim on the defeat of Hitler, and Walt's (herein, Ch. 4, 65n7; 1997, 933n7) claim that realism provides a cogent explanation for the failure of any modern state to gain hegemony must mean more than just that states fight wars when physically attacked or that they arm and seek allies when they feel threatened.

It must mean that they follow a balancing strategy in preference to other strategies or have such behavior induced by the system as opposed to other behavior; i.e., that, at minimum, these states *actually* move diplomatically to check the power (or threat) of a challenging state with their own power (usually in the hope that this will limit that power or threat).[9] It must mean what Waltz (herein, Ch. 3; 1997, 915) says it means, that "states try to increase their own strength or they ally with others to bring the international distribution of power into balance." If states fail to do this, then the balancing proposition is not supported. If adherents to the balancing proposition cannot accept such a test (or some reasonable emendation of it), then the entire debate will have moved from the purview of scientific inquiry to the purview of scholasticism. Schroeder's evidence cannot be shirked, unless it can be shown that its details are incorrect.

Schweller (1994) gives the most evidence against balancing, yet he too in his reply denies the discrepant nature of his evidence. He states (Schweller herein, Ch. 6; 1997, 929) that he did not show that bandwagoning predominates over balancing, only that it "is more common . . . than Walt or Waltz suggest." My complaint is that the instances he lists of both the failure to balance and the incidents of bandwagoning that do occur are much more serious failures of predictions for Waltz's proposition than he seems to think. Schweller (1994, 89–92) points out that Louis XIV and Napoleon were able to conquer and win as much as they did at their height because other major states bandwagoned with them—the British and Swedes for example in the Dutch War (1672–1679). Of the Napoleonic wars, Schweller (1994, 92) says:

> But the victory of the Allies over the would-be hegemon was not as inevitable as the "balancing predominates" view would have us believe. The Allied coalition, whose forces doubled those of France by February of 1814, would never have come together in the first place, much less held together, had Napoleon not attacked his own allies and neutrals.

Here again we see that what brought about defeat of a hegemonic threat was not balancing but over-ambition and attacking states that would have preferred to let the hegemon keep its conquests rather than try to check or block it (see also Rosecrance and Lo 1996, 481–483, 487–488, 491–493). Surely, in at least these two instances—Louis XIV and Napoleon—Schweller should have qualms about Waltz's balancing proposition being a "law" of international politics.

Lastly, Walt (1987) clearly finds in the Middle East and in the Cold War period that states tend to balance not against the strongest state in a system but the state that poses the greatest threat to a particular state. Similarly, Priess (1996, 169) finds that the Gulf states reacted to Iranian threat, not its power, which was declining from 1978 to 1980. Yet if realism and neorealism are correct, states should find the most powerful state as potentially the most threatening, and therefore they should balance against it because the world is a jungle in a permanent struggle for power. This is especially the case when we are dealing with the central system of major states. In my original article (Vasquez herein, Ch. 2, 32; 1997, 904) I asked why balancing of threat should be taken as a "refinement" of balance-of-power theory and not as an unexpected anomalous finding, given Waltz's unambiguous prediction. It makes all the difference in the world whether one sees the failure of states to balance power as a falsification of Waltz, or at least the failure to hold in a number of instances.

The above three responses contrast to that of Elman and Elman (1995, 192) who in their initial criticism of Schroeder (1994a) concede:

> While Waltz does not specify how prevalent balancing is likely to be, he clearly believes that, *in the aggregate*, states are constrained by the system and will tend to balance. Consequently, Schroeder's evidence that states rarely balance does indeed pose a problem for Waltz's theory (italics in the original).

With this exception, the replies to my original argument still fail to recognize the discrepant evidence they and others have presented against Waltz's proposition. It would help move the debate forward if they would indicate, as Christensen and Snyder (herein, Ch. 5) do for the Second World War, which of the cases Waltz lists as examples of hegemonic threat (herein, Ch. 3, 54; 1997, 915) resulted in balancing and which did not.

One of the reasons Walt, Schweller, and Christensen and Snyder underestimate the nature of discrepant evidence is that they relabel it in terms that make it appear consistent with some variant of realism. The question is whether, in doing so, they have moved the research program in a progressive direction, as they think, or a degenerating one. They claim, however, that they have not just relabeled discrepant evidence but have come up with new concepts that have, among other things, specified the domain of Waltz's proposition and thereby advanced knowledge.[10] Is this the case?

Specifying the domain of a proposition is a typical procedure by which to advance research while incorporating discrepant evidence. Waltz (1979, 121), of course, did not specify any domain to his proposition other than the anarchic system. The problem is how to distinguish a legitimate specification of the domain of a proposition from a degenerating trend. This can be difficult and complex, but there are some obvious rules.

Let us suppose that research shows that 50 percent of the cases support the proposition and 50 percent do not, clearly a random relationship. A reformulation that was degenerative would simply group the cases that supported the proposition, give them a label (e.g., balancing states or prudent states) and say that this is the domain of proposition; whereas the other group could be given another name (say impaired states) and it could be "hypothesized" that in this domain the proposition did not hold. If the labels lack any ability to predict (before examining the evidence) which states will be prudent and which impaired, then the reformulation is just semantic relabeling. Likewise, if the labels are merely hunches that borrow the paradigm's phraseology, but lack a clear theoretical explication distinguishing what the cases have in common that makes them behave in two different ways, then the reformulation is degenerative. Lastly, if the theoretical explication of why one set of cases behaves one way and the other set the opposite way can only explain the outcome of this experiment, then its explanatory power is *ex post facto* (and it fails to provide any novel facts; i.e., new predictions separate from the discrepant evidence). Likewise, if it can explain other patterns or predict novel facts but these new explanations and predictions do not survive testing, then the reformulation lacks excess corroborated empirical content and is degenerative.

One cannot, therefore, simply assume that a specification of a domain will be progressive, as Elman and Elman (1995, 193) do, without examining how that specification is made (see also Schweller herein, Ch. 6, 78; 1997, 929; Christensen and Snyder, herein, Ch. 5, 67; 1997, 919). Elman and Elman (herein, Ch. 7) argue that what I have seen as degenerating shifts are simply the changes Lakatos (1970, 133–138) would expect to occur in the positive heuristic of the research program (i.e., the logic that guides the construction of auxiliary hypotheses intended to protect its core). The Elmans imply that none of these theoretical emendations challenge the hard core (or negative heuristic); hence they are what is to be expected (see also Walt herein, Ch. 4, 61; 1997, 933 on disagreements among realists).

Yes, they are to be expected, but do they successfully protect the core or do they fail to deal with discrepant evidence? How well are they protecting is the question the criterion of progressivity is intended to address. If the emendations cannot explain the discrepant evidence and predict and corroborate novel facts, then they are degenerating, especially if the attempts to explain away are themselves problematic (see Laudan 1977, 117). Repeated failures at protecting the core are indicators that the hard core may be a problematic way of looking at the world. If the theory and its research program are successful, then research corroborates the main proposition(s) of the original theory and the anomalies are minor. Changes and reformulations fill in the details; they are not focused on anomalies.[11] Findings and "discoveries" proliferate. Domains are clearly established. Changes that are progressive produce these kinds of effects.

This has not been the case with neotraditional research on Waltz's balancing proposition. No basic pattern has been established. Nor has this research been very successful in establishing a domain where the proposition holds. Walt (1987) does not find that under certain circumstances states balance power and in others they balance threat. He maintains that they generally balance threat and do not balance power unless threat is present.

In my original argument, I maintained that this evidence was potentially devastating for Waltz's theory and that Walt's balance of threat theory hid this by semantic relabeling (Vasquez, herein, Ch. 2, 32, 27; 1997, 904, 901 respectively); i.e., by calling the discrepant behavior balancing of threat instead of seeing it as a failure to balance power. In his reply, Walt (herein, Ch. 4, 62; 1997, 933) argues that I cannot say that balance of threat theory is both a "'devastating' challenge to Waltz" and "merely a semantic repackaging of Waltz's theory." I do not say the first. What is "devastating" for Waltz is the *evidence* that states do not balance power, not balance-of-threat *theory*, which by its very phrasing mutes the negative impact of the finding.

Walt (herein, Ch. 4, 62–63; 1997, 933–934) argues that his theory is a progressive shift because, contrary to what I state, his theory presents "novel facts." He states that several of his analyses, including some of his articles not discussed (Walt, 1988, 1992a, 1992b), do offer novel facts—for example, that states did not balance against the United States in the Cold War and that East European states failed to balance against both Germany and the USSR in the 1930s. This is "new information" in the sense that it is evidence brought to bear by Walt that shows that states do not balance power, but meet threats posed against them. With respect to Waltz's balancing proposition, however, this new information is "discrepant evidence" that is then explained (away) by "balance of threat" theory. Any particular fact relating to the failure to balance cannot be a "novel fact" because it is part of the discrepant evidence, by definition. To be progressive, Walt's theory needs to predict and explain something other than the failure of states to balance power because they balance threat or (as with the East European states) did not balance because the threat was not clear enough (see Lakatos 1970, 124).

Perhaps what is causing the problem here is the phrase "novel facts." It is true that after Walt (1987) we know that states in his sample tend to balance threat rather than power, but this finding was unexpected beforehand by balance-of-power theory (theory *T* as Lakatos would call it). Thus in order to be progressive, theory *T'* must now make a new or novel prediction; i.e., it must predict something other than the fact that states balance threat. If it does not, then it cannot be tested and thus, logically, it cannot be falsified. Hence for Lakatos (1970, 124) it would be a degenerating theoryshift.

Even under Laudan's (1977, 115–120) terms of progress, which Walt (herein, Ch. 4, 60; 1997, 932) cites approvingly in contradistinction to Lakatos, Walt's theory is not progressive because it does not resolve the puzzle of why states fail to balance power in terms of the logic of Waltz's or Morgenthau's theory—it merely describes the fact that states generally balance threat and not power.[12] Walt fails to derive a plausible explanation from the logic of realism of why states balance against threat rather than power. As Elman and Elman (herein, Ch. 7, 82; 1997, 924) correctly point out, a problemshift that would be progressive must flow from the logic of the theory (see below). For Laudan (1977, 116), an ad hoc change must increase the problem-solving capacity of a theory. On this basis, Walt must show how a theory of power would lead states to balance threat instead of power. This is also important because competing paradigms or explanations—like psychological explanations of the security dilemma or hostility—can predict and better explain attempts to check threat. They need not see threats or responses to them as solely the product of rationalistic calculations of power. A psychological theory would be superior to Walt's reformulation because on Laudan's criterion it would have more problem-solving capacity—it would predict the failure to balance in the first place and accurately predict threat as more likely to generate a response when power and threat are separate (as with the United States during the Cold War).[13]

These criticisms raise a more basic question. If states balance threats and not power, as Walt avers, then where do threats come from? Barnett (1996, herein Ch. 14) maintains that in Middle Eastern alliances, which are the focus of Walt's book (1987), threat comes not from power (or the logic of its strategic extensions) but from conceptions of identity. Pan Arabism is seen as a threat to some individual states and so they ally against external and internal proponents of this ideology. Barnett (1996, 413) aims to show that strategic behavior, and alliance formation specifically, is better seen as deriving from shared conceptions of identity than from the anarchy problematique of neorealism or material forces From his constructivist perspective, identity shapes preferences and thereby informs states of who should be seen as an attractive ally and who should be seen as a possible threat. Ideas and not power are what determines threat.

Such a constructivist critique undercuts Walt's reformulation because it uses a nonmaterialist logic, derived from a potentially competing paradigm (constructivism), to explain how states choose alliances, how they perceive threat, and how preferences are formed. Barnett's analysis thus shows how one can take Walt's finding to enhance a competing explanation. In addition, it can be argued that constructivism can make a better case, that it does provide "novel" facts in that it not only explains why states might balance against threat rather than power, but also provides a new theory of preference formation separate from a realist or material theory and separate from prevailing psychological theories.

Schweller (herein, Ch. 6, 77; 1997, 928–929) clearly specifies a domain for his hypothesis about bandwagoning (namely, revisionist major states), but remains neutral as to whether states balance outside this domain. However, he is not entirely successful in explaining away why balancing should not generally occur by establishing the domain of when bandwagoning can be expected. For Schweller (herein, Ch. 6, 77; 1997, 928), bandwagoning rather than balancing will occur among "[u]nthreatened revisionist states" that are great powers. He then goes on to cite examples that fit his claim, like Italy and Japan in the Second World War, but other important cases he cites do not fit—namely Prussia, Austria, Russia, and Spain in the Napoleonic wars, and the Soviet Union (and perhaps Vichy France) in the Second World War. These states do not fit the domain because they were not unthreatened states. Their bandwagoning must count against Waltz and cannot be explained away by Schweller's analysis. In addition, as with Walt, Schweller (1994, herein, Ch. 6) must show theoretically, in his classical realist approach, why major states (especially) do not perceive themselves to be threatened by the strongest states in the system—why they do not fear that the most powerful revisionist state will be able to dominate them by picking them off one by one if some bandwagon and thereby make a later balance ineffective (compare Rosecrance and Lo 1996, 493, 496).

Christensen and Snyder (1990; herein, Ch. 5) come closest to successfully specifying a domain—namely, states are most likely to balance in multipolar systems when the offensive has the advantage. In this domain, they predict that chain-ganging tends to occur; however, this term has a negative connotation, suggesting something aberrant though not quite pathological. In part, this is because they are concerned with instabilities within multipolarity; yet nowhere do they specify where *normal* (what Morgenthau would call *prudent*) balancing occurs.

In their reply, Christensen and Snyder (herein, Ch. 5, 68; 1997, 920) merely restate that "balancing occurs less smoothly in multipolar worlds than bipolar ones," but I do not see how using alliances to balance can proceed more smoothly in bipolar periods, when there are no countries who, by Waltz's definition of bipolarity, can shift the balance of power in a bipolar system—if there were, then the system would be multipolar. All that Waltz can mean by this is that internal balancing (a terrible expression for military buildups) is more smoothly implemented, but why is it necessarily any more smoothly implemented in bipolar than multipolar systems? What he is also implying is that arming is easier than alliance making, but as Morrow (1993) shows, this really depends on the interaction of the domestic and international political environment and not on the external structure per se.

If this is the case, this means that the key concept in their specification of the domain is "perceived offensive advantage" and not "multipolar systems." However, once perceived offense/defense becomes the domain, it becomes difficult to precisely measure the perceptions that count, leaving open the possibility for ad hoc interpretations. For example, some domestic political actors may perceive the offensive as having the advantage, while others may not. In the 1930s, Christensen and Snyder (1990) argue that states saw the defensive as having the advantage and therefore passed the buck. Yet as Morrow (1993, 228) reports, the French general staff feared in 1938 that its air force "would be wiped out in a few days," as General Vuillemin put it. Neville Chamberlain also felt that German air power was very threatening and an offensive weapon for which there was not much defense. Even Christensen (1997, 85) has recognized, in his recent article, British fear of a "knockout blow from Germany against the home islands," which means that a defensive advantage on the Continent would be irrelevant to Britain. The Germans, of course, believed in *Blitzkrieg*. So, it is not clear whether perceptions of the defensive having the advantage was uniform in the 1930s or even dominant. More importantly, the fact that one can differentiate offensive and defensive advantages depending on the theatre of operation and for different weapon systems shows how slippery this concept can be and how fruitful it is for an endless series of ad hoc explanations.[14]

It must also be pointed out that Christensen and Snyder's (1990) analysis is only illustrated by two cases and not systematically tested. Morrow (1993, 211–213) argues that offense was perceived as having the advantage in the 1860s, yet in 1866 and again in 1870 threatened states did not chain-gang as Christensen and Snyder's explanation predicts. Systematic testing of more cases will be needed before their proposition is accepted as empirically accurate. The point here is not to prejudge that research (see Christensen's [1997, 70–81] discussion of Morrow), but to emphasize that in order for their theoryshift to be progressive, it cannot just *"explain when chain-gaining occurs and when buck-passing occurs"* (Christensen and Snyder, herein, Ch. 5, 68; 1997, 920)(emphasis added); their explanation must pass *empirical* testing as well (Lakatos, 1970, 116).

That research may not get off the ground, however, because Christensen (1997, 66) has reformulated his and Snyder's "original thesis," which placed great weight on perceptions of the offense/defense, into a very refined calculation of perceived power and offensive/defensive advantage of the various actors. In terms of the critique being made here, two important points must be kept in mind about Christensen (1997). First, he admits "de facto" that not only Waltz's proposition on balancing, but even the more refined Christensen and Snyder (1990) proposition, must be further refined to account for cases. It is far from clear after reading Christensen (1997) that this "new formulation" is one that "can explain a large number of new observations" and is not one where "additional observations demand ad hoc adjustments to the theory," as Christensen and Snyder (herein, Ch. 5, 68; 1997, 920) put it. Second, the need to examine calculations of perceptions shows why anarchy provides no invisible hand that automatically institutes Waltz's balancing, and it makes it clear why Morgenthau's prescription that balancing be brought about by prudent leaders is difficult to implement in any given circumstance.[15] Christensen's (1997) analysis demonstrates further the weakness of focusing on realist power variables, while his introduction of perceptions to save these variables drives analysts away from both the core of the paradigm and from nomothetic explanation.

The end result of Christensen's (1997, 69) analysis is that the domain of the balancing proposition is further delimited to frontline states whose perceived power is not superior to their immediate rivals, and the situation is one where the offensive has the advantage. Such an emendation is required because there are many states (like Britain in 1914) that do not balance even under conditions where the offensive is perceived to have the advantage in a multipolar system.[16] Yet it is far from clear why this further specification of domain is not just a reaction to the discovery of additional discrepant cases; i.e., why it, too, is not a degenerative shift.

My objection to Christensen and to Snyder is not with their criticisms of neorealism, but their apparent unwillingness to admit the extent to which the evidence they present poses such a damning portrayal of Waltz's balancing proposition. I can agree that balancing often does not occur because of misperception (generally), because of uncertainty (i.e., low information), or because of the role of domestic politics, but for those outside the realist paradigm, all this is another way of saying that balancing never occurs in the systematic fashion that Waltz believes, and "power" is not the core of what shapes world politics.[17]

With the various emendations of Walt, Schweller, and Christensen and Snyder, we have come a long way from Waltz's (1979, 121) claim that balancing prevails "wherever two, and only two, requirements are met." It would help the field to progress if those who emend a general proposition like Waltz's would recognize that, in certain arenas (and in Waltz's case very large arenas), the proposition does not hold. "De facto recognition" of realism's failings needs to be replaced by "de jure recognition." Then analysts should go on to provide some discussion of why a proposition does not hold and what the theoretical implications of that "fact" are for the field. It would also help if scholars in addressing the last two questions followed

Jervis's (1976) example of not only providing one explanation of the discrepant evidence, but alternative explanations (from the perspective of competing paradigms).

What is more central to the debate, however, is that these attempts to specify the domain of the proposition do not constitute progressive theoryshifts (in the technical sense of Lakatos (1970). They do not do so for three reasons. First, they do not predict anything new other than the discrepant evidence; hence they do not provide novel facts. The new concepts introduced simply label the anomalous evidence. This is particularly true of Walt and of Christensen and Snyder, but to a lesser extent of Schweller. Second, some of the ad hoc propositions are either not fully tested or themselves are problematic on conceptual grounds or on the basis of existing research. This is true of Schweller and of Christensen and Snyder (including Christensen [1997]). Third, with the exception of Schweller, the emendations do not ground their proposition in the logic of a power theory (as Walt fails to do), or they move beyond the positive heuristic of power politics to introduce nonrealist variables, like perceptions (as Christensen and Snyder [1990, herein, Ch. 5, 67; 1997, 920] do) that are consistent with competing paradigms.

## WHAT CRITERIA SHOULD BE USED TO APPRAISE THEORIES?

The last set of concerns raised by the debate deals with the question of what are legitimate criteria by which to evaluate theories. This is a major focus of Elman and Elman (herein, Ch. 7; 1997), but it also plays an important role in Walt (herein, Ch. 4) and Waltz (herein, Ch. 3).

The most fundamental criticism comes from Walt (herein, Ch. 4, 59; 1997, 932), who rejects the very use of Lakatos's (1970) criterion of progressive vs. degenerative problemshifts. He refers to Lakatos (1970) as a "now-dated analysis [that] has been largely rejected by contemporary historians and philosophers of science (Diesing 1991; Laudan 1977; Suppe 1977b; Toulmin 1972)." He goes on to ask "[w]hy should social scientists embrace a model of scientific progress that has been widely discredited by experts in that field?" *Discredited* is a very strong term, especially since what is at issue here is not Lakatos's historical description of progress, but his recommendation of how auxiliary propositions should be treated.

Contrary to Walt, I would maintain that Lakatos is very much at the epistemological core of political science. Lakatos (1970) has been widely cited by both quantitative and nonquantitative scholars, most of whom seem to accept his criteria as legitimate (see Keohane 1983; Bueno de Mesquita 1989, 151; Organski and Kugler 1989, 171; King, Keohane, and Verba 1994; and Lustick 1997), and he is generally seen as an advancement over the more "naive falsificationist" approach of Popper (1959). The debate over balancing of power has also resulted in several international relations scholars applying Lakatos to a number of other research programs (Elman and Elman, 2002b). Lustick (1997, 88n1 and 2) sees Lakatos's criteria as the most legitimate to use in his appraisal of a key research program in comparative politics. He also points out that the recent debate over rational choice, sparked by the Green and

Shapiro (1994) volume, uses Lakatos's criterion and that "[b]etween 1980 and 1995 the *Social Science Citation Index* lists an annual average of 10.5 inches of citations to works by Lakatos."

In this regard, it comes as a bit of a surprise that Walt (herein, Ch. 4, 59; 1997, 932) objects to the use of Lakatos. Such an appraisal, of course, is only worth conducting if scholars accept Lakatos's criterion as useful. Nevertheless, since Hollis and Smith (1990, 66) have employed Lakatos to speak of realism as being progressive and more enlightening and fertile than its rivals, it is perfectly appropriate to employ this criterion even though an individual scholar might object to it—although one cannot help noting that Walt (herein, Ch. 4) entitled his response "The *Progressive* Power of Realism" (emphasis added), presumably a reference to Laudan (1977) rather than Lakatos (1970).

Walt (herein, Ch. 4, 60; 1997, 932) goes on to say that adopting Lakatos's standard on progressivity would "force us to reject virtually every research tradition in the social sciences." This is a very alarmist reaction. To claim that a research program is degenerating, there must be at least several theoretical reformulations, and these must fail to have corroborated excess empirical content. This effort, as Elman and Elman (herein, Ch. 7, 82; 1997, 924) recognize, must take some time (see also Lakatos 1970, 134, 179). The debate over multipolarity initiated by Mearsheimer (1990), for example, could not be a candidate for appraisal on the progressivity criterion and be rejected as degenerating, because it does not involve a series of reformulations based on research. Rather it is a fairly straightforward disagreement about the effects of multipolarity and the nature of the future.

Conversely, the research program on balancing is a legitimate candidate because it has embodied both theoretical reformulation and empirical investigation. The *mere* necessity of theoretical reformulation, however, does not of itself indicate degeneracy, as Walt (herein, Ch. 4, 60; 1997, 932) states. Such a conclusion can only be reached if there is persistent emendation because of repeated discrepant evidence and the reformulation provides no new basis (other than the discrepant evidence itself) to test the theory.

Walt (herein, Ch. 4, 60; 1997, 932) also objects that: "Lakatos's rejection of ad hoc adjustments is inconsistent with actual scientific practice. An ad hoc adjustment that resolves an existing anomaly but does not lead to any other new facts is still an advance in our understanding; after all, it does answer a puzzle" (Walt, herein, Ch. 4, 60; 1997, 932). First, it must be remembered that a philosophy of science, which is what Lakatos is offering here, is not the same as a history of science. Lakatos is clearly (see his p. 117) trying to come up with a set of rules to end a practice that he says leads to the nonfalsification of a series of theories, so it is not surprising that what Lakatos suggests is inconsistent with practice. Walt, and Laudan (1977, 115) for that matter, underappreciate the logical problems that led Lakatos (1970) to establish these rules. It is worth quoting (Lakatos 1970, 116–117) at length:

> First, we have to remember . . . that no experimental result can ever kill a theory: any theory can be saved from counterinstances either by some auxiliary hypothesis or by a suitable reinterpretation of its terms. Naive falsificationists solved this

problem by relegating . . . the auxiliary hypotheses to the realm of unproblematic background knowledge, eliminating them from the deductive model of the test-situation and thereby *forcing* the chosen theory into logical isolation, in which it becomes a sitting target for the attack of test-experiments. . . . Why aim at falsification at any price? Why not rather impose certain standards on the theoretical adjustments by which one is allowed to save a theory?

It was from this logical and practical problem that the criterion of progressivity was born. Adjustments that meet Lakatos's standards are defined as progressive and those that do not are defined as degenerative. This is not to say that it will be easy to determine when theoretical emendations meet these standards, as this debate has shown (see also Walt herein, Ch. 4, 60; 1997, 932). But it is to say that these standards cannot just be ignored because they are difficult to operationalize. They appear to be essential to the conducting of theory appraisals.[18]

Even if they are essential, however, that does not mean that there are not other criteria that might be more fundamental, if they can be applied. As already noted, several critics insist on having the debate focus more on the criterion of empirical accuracy. There is nothing wrong with that if an agreement can be made as to what would constitute a fair set of tests to settle the matter. The criterion of empirical accuracy is fundamental. So too, however, is the criterion of falsifiability, for if adherents are not willing to specify, at some point, what evidence would lead them to say the theory was inaccurate, then the theory can never be tested. What is crucial is that theories be able to pass tests, both in principle and in fact. The criterion of progressivity is applied only when the outcomes of tests are not accepted as findings, but are the basis for theoretical emendations intended to save the theory.

Other criteria that are often presented, such as parsimony or explanatory power, must be seen as of lesser importance (see Vasquez 1998, Ch. 10). The reason for this is simple: Having great explanatory power is of little use if the explanation is untrue. It is for this reason that one must reject Waltz's (herein, Ch. 3, 55; 1997, 916) position that "success in explaining, not predicting, is the ultimate criterion of good theory." This cannot be the ultimate criterion for evaluating theories. Waltz (herein, Ch. 3) tries to make this point by defining "predicting" somewhat narrowly, so as to focus only on the future and not to include "retrodiction," but this is not how "positivists" usually define the term when speaking of testing. It makes no sense to explain patterns that do not exist when the conditions that are supposed to give rise to them have long been in existence.[19]

Elman and Elman (herein, Ch. 7) support the use of Lakatos (1970), but they have a number of concerns about how I have conceptualized and applied his criterion. They would prefer that I be much more detailed and precise in my use of Lakatos—that I discuss the different types of ad hoc propositions he delineates, that I discuss differences between the positive and negative heuristics, that I distinguish the hard core of a research program from its "protective belt of auxiliary hypotheses," that I recognize that there are different types of novel facts. They then go on to say that if I had done these things, I would have reached a different conclusion about the neotraditional research program and about their specific criticisms (Elman and

Elman 1995) of Schroeder (1994a). Let me say that while I agree, in principle, with their first set of points, I do not agree with the second.

Let me begin by indicating why I did not use all of Lakatos's framework and specifying briefly which parts of the framework are more useful than others for international relations theory. Their suggestion (Elman and Elman herein, Ch. 7, 81; 1997, 923) that I should have used Lakatos's three types of ad hoc explanations is useful and would have made clearer some of the different types of problems theoretical emendations can encounter. For Lakatos (1970, 175n2 and 3) there are three kinds of (what he calls) *adhocness* that are degenerating. Ad hoc$_1$ are "theories which [have] no excess content over their predecessor (or competitors), that is which [do] not predict any novel *facts*" (Lakatos 1970, 175n2). Ad hoc$_2$ make new predictions but these do not get corroborated (Lakatos 1970, 175n2). Ad hoc$_3$ are theoretical emendations that are not derived from the logic of the theory's positive heuristic or hard core (Lakatos 1970, 175).

These three distinctions are useful and most of my analysis has relied on the first two types of ad hoc explanations, although I have not labeled them as such. I do not see the need, however, given the current state of neotraditional research, to further specify ad hoc$_2$ by choosing between two different meanings of research success—(1) whether none of the new content is corroborated or (2) all of it is refuted (Elman and Elman, herein, Ch. 7, 81; 1997, 924, citing Zahar 1973, 101n1). No doubt, partial satisfaction of either would be persuasive, if central propositions were involved. Lakatos (1970, 116) insists only that *some* of the new content be verified.

I was hesitant to apply Lakatos's third type of ad hoc explanation because it might have been seen as too stringent. Ad hoc$_3$ is an emendation that does not flow from the logic of the original theory. Such emendations appear to be attempts to "patch up" in an "arbitrary" even "trial-and-error" fashion (Lakatos 1970, 175), rather than showing how the emendation can be logically derived from the assumptions of the core. Since so few theories in international relations, let alone emendations, are logically or even tightly derived from a set of assumptions, use of this rule might be overly dismissive. Nevertheless, while I have pointed out above when reformulations move away from the core, Elman and Elman (herein, Ch. 7) are correct in pointing out that a more formal labeling of these deviations from the core's logic as ad hoc$_3$ would make the analysis clearer and more trenchant. I have taken this suggestion in this reply, especially in my discussion of Christensen and Snyder.

Likewise, it would be useful if someone went through the neotraditional research program and classified the various emendations in terms of the four categories of possible novel facts that Elman and Elman (herein, Ch. 7, 86n1; 1997, 923n1) delineate. Suffice it to say I agree with them that the most important factor that should be used in denying an emendation the status of a novel fact is if it is used—"once in the construction of a theory and then again in its support." As I noted above in the discussion of Walt, the word *fact* may be misleading, and we should consider using the term *novel prediction*.

I have not used Lakatos's (1970) language of heuristics and of hard core and protective belt because I have, on the whole, preferred Kuhn's (1970a) language of paradigms, normal science, anomalies, and so forth (see Vasquez 1983, 1998, 2002). This is because I have found Kuhn more useful for discussing the history of a science, and Lakatos more useful for theory and paradigm appraisal. This has led me to see the wider field of international relations theory in a slightly different way from the Elmans and as such probably to reach different conclusions about the evolution of theory within our field and of realism and neorealism.

I agree that Lakatos would see the theoretical emendations of a hard core (or a paradigm, to use Kuhn) as something that is to be anticipated, and that "the belt of auxiliary hypotheses are *designed* to protect the hard core" (emphasis in the original) (Elman and Elman herein, Ch. 7, 82; 1997, 924). While such developments are to be expected, not all of them are *approved* by Lakatos. He is concerned that certain auxiliary hypotheses can lead to nonfalsification, especially, I would think, if they produce contradictory predictions. Thus, in a sense, he wants to declare certain ways of protecting the hard core an *illegal defense*. This is why he wants to "impose certain standards on the theoretical adjustments" (Lakatos 1970, 117).

Amending the protective belt, as opposed to discarding the research program entirely, is a legitimate activity (Elman and Elman herein, Ch. 7, 84; 1997, 925) *if it is done according to the rules*. The problem is that it is not always obvious when the rules are being violated, especially since a research program must be given a decent amount of time to gestate (Elman and Elman herein, Ch. 7, 82; 1997, 924); there may be disagreement as to what constitute novel facts, and corroboration of novel predictions takes time. But many emendations, decades of discourse (if not centuries), and lack of clear corroboration of the original proposition are not indicators of good health.

Elman and Elman (herein, Ch. 7, 84; 1997, 925) are on very solid ground when they lay claim to Lakatos's (1970, 119) statement that "[t]here is no falsification before the emergence of a better theory." My concern is that realists cannot just sit back on a pile of anomalies and say there is no better theory. I do not disagree with Elman and Elman (herein, Ch. 7, 84; 1997, 925) that judgments about progress should be made with reference to neorealism's rivals, but these rivals must not be just sibling rivals (like classical realism, defensive realism, etc.). This is because a fundamentally flawed paradigm, like alchemy, will not ever produce an adequate theory. Once things appear to be going badly for the dominant theory or paradigm, then critics should only have to come up with a truly different view of the world that is plausible, and not, in the short run, show that that view is better. The question of which is better should be held in abeyance until there is some research done on the new paradigm.

Perhaps the most serious disagreement I have with Elman and Elman (herein, Ch. 7, 83; 1997, 924–925) that stems from my not using Lakatos's framework of hard core and protective belt is with their specification of the neorealist hard core. I would not try to specify the neorealist hard core, but would look at how the neorealist analyses of Waltz (1979) and Gilpin (1981) are attempts to articulate the realist paradigm (see Vasquez 1998, Ch. 9). Instead of looking at the "hard core" I would look at the fundamental assumptions that constitute the realist paradigm and then see how these along with the exemplar of the paradigm—in this case Morgenthau's *Politics among Nations*—guided theory construction in the field. To me the realist paradigm makes three fundamental assumptions that all realist variants, including Waltz's, should not violate if they are to remain within the paradigm:

1. Nation-states or their decision makers are the most important actors for understanding international relations.
2. There is a sharp distinction between domestic politics and international politics.
3. International relations is the struggle for power and peace. Understanding how and why that struggle occurs and suggesting ways for regulating it is the purpose of the discipline. All research that is not at least indirectly related to this purpose is trivial (Vasquez 1983, 18; see also Vasquez 1998, 37).[20]

This specification is quite different from that of Elman and Elman (herein, Ch. 7, 83; 1997, 924). My objection to their list is that it contains too many assumptions or propositions that could be shared by other (competing) paradigms, especially any paradigm that incorporated a cost-benefit framework as does Marxism, for example, or the issue politics paradigm (Mansbach and Vasquez 1981, 192–197). There are a number of nonrealist explanations that would not object to assumptions 2, 6, and 7 on their list.[21] For me, any specification of the "hard core" of neorealism would have to include power politics as a central element. Once this is done, though, a number of things they would see as within the purview of neorealism, I would see as either outside or better explained by a nonrealist paradigm. This would certainly be the case with what Schroeder calls "hiding" or "transcending." It would also be the case with West European integration and the creation of transcending peace systems, like the Concert of Europe.[22] It is important when appraising theories and evaluating paradigms to establish testable differences. By not focusing more on power politics and having instead several broad assumptions, the Elmans garner in support of neorealism a variety of behaviors while they leave to nonrealist approaches only a narrow base from which to gain support. When a research program or paradigm becomes so broad and has so many contradictory predictions then it becomes virtually, if not logically, impossible to falsify it. This is a danger both with the neotraditional program on balancing and the broader realist paradigm from which it is derived.

I shall not dwell on the latter here, since I discuss the broader question of the realist paradigm at length elsewhere (Vasquez 1998). Let me just repeat that a critique of balancing cannot logically imply that other parts of the realist and neorealist research agenda are degenerating or inadequate. These other research programs must be appraised separately and by the criteria most appropriate to them. I have done that elsewhere through a series of case studies applying different criteria of adequacy. Those case studies, as the one on balancing, raise serious questions about specific realist explanations. Only a systematic appraisal and comparative evaluation of realist and nonrealist theories will be definitive, but as each study of a specific explanation is completed and debated, it cannot help but enhance or diminish the power of a paradigm to keep adherents.

For the purpose of this debate, I have chosen to focus on the research program on balancing so that details could be explored. Only if we are committed as a community of scholars to exploring those details and debating them within the context of a rigorous set of criteria will we be able to advance our understanding of world politics. Regardless of the outcome of these appraisals, we can all agree that *Theory of International Politics* has not only been worth taking seriously but has enhanced the role of theory within the field, both by making scholars think more theoretically and by providing an informative guide to research that might otherwise have been overly inductive, if not idiosyncratic.

## Editors' Commentary

### Major Query

How can we tell if Waltz's balancing of power proposition is true and if empirical research related to it is degenerating?

### Major Points

Vasquez makes three major points. First, he argues contra Waltz, Walt, and Christensen and Snyder, who in varying degrees think that Waltz's balancing proposition is fairly accurate, that it is not an empirical law and can be considered generally false. Since this disagreement is primarily empirical, it should be easily resolved by historical and quantitative research. He then tries to develop a test that all sides might agree would resolve the matter, and he calls upon those who support the proposition to specify what historical and/or quantitative evidence they would accept as showing that the proposition has been falsified. He outlines several different tests, the most important being one suggested by Waltz (herein, Ch. 3) in his reply—that states balanced against Charles I of Spain (Charles V Holy Roman Emperor), Louis XIV, Napoleon, Wilhelm II, and Hitler. He maintains that if the record shows that this did not occur as a general pattern, then the proposition should be rejected.

To conduct such a test, however, there must be agreement on what constitutes balancing. This is a question that will occupy several of the chapters that follow (e.g., Schroeder, Levy, and Rosecrance). Vasquez addresses the question by building upon what Waltz states in his reply; namely, that states faced by unbalanced power will automatically behave in a way that results in strengthening their power to bring the international distribution of power into balance. In other words, actions will be taken to make states that were (becoming) unequal, more equal. In addition, Vasquez draws upon Waltz's (1979) original statement on the subject to maintain that balancing does not merely result in a more equal distribution of capability, but must also attempt (whether consciously or not) to check and block the ambitions of the "aggressor" state.

From these two basic **defining criteria**, Vasquez stipulates that certain things cannot be seen as balancing: siding with the stronger or not blocking the stronger (i.e., being neutral or hiding or appeasing). Likewise, he maintains defense against a direct attack should not be seen as balancing. This leads Vasquez into discussing specific historical cases where he deals with disagreements he has with Christensen and Snyder (herein, Ch. 5). He closes this section by indicating that whereas realists think that balancing is an established fact, he maintains that it is a generalization that has not been established either by historians or political scientists, and therefore should not be accepted (but he is willing to pursue the matter if a set of tests can be agreed upon).

Second, in response to his critics, who maintain that their reformulations are progressive, he argues why they are not. Early on, he asks rhetorically of Christensen and Snyder, Walt, and Schweller, why they needed to reformulate Waltz's basic proposition if it is accurate. He has two objections to the way they emend Waltz's theory. First, they fail to recognize that there is serious discrepant evidence that falsifies Waltz, and second they develop new theories that fail to satisfy Lakatos's criteria as to what constitutes a progressive shift. Beginning with Waltz, he points out how each of his critics, with the major exception of Elman and Elman, play down, or in some cases outright reject, discrepant evidence they have uncovered in their case analyses. Vasquez asks: Where is the evidence in support of balancing and how extensive is it? He maintains that too many of his critics are prepared to say that maybe they have uncovered some discrepancies, but these are exceptions to a general pattern well-documented elsewhere. He maintains that too many assume that the pattern has been established, but when you look at the whole body of research you see that it has not.

He goes on to argue that the two main strategies with which neotraditionalists have defended the way they have dealt with discrepant evidence — to establish the **domain** of the proposition and to show that their reformulation has produced novel facts — are deficient. He uses a hypothetical example to show that simply establishing a domain does not mean the emendation is progressive. One could take evidence that shows a random relationship and try to turn it into support for a proposition by saying that the proposition's domain encompasses only the cases that are consistent with it. Establishing the domain must do more than that. The new theory must explain the reasons the discrepant cases need not have followed the pattern, and what it is about the cases that follow the pattern that make them do that. It should, according to Lakatos (see Elman and Elman, herein, Ch. 7) do this using the logic of the original theory and not by bringing in some "alien" logic from outside the research program. In the end, progressive emendations, although they may not all be made at once, need to explain all that the original theory ($T$) explains and more (new areas not heretofore covered by the original theory). In addition, Lakatos maintains that these new propositions must have been tested and corroborated before they can be accepted.

Many scholars refer to explaining new areas as establishing "novel facts." The question of what is a novel fact has been a subject of discussion in the debate on balancing of power. Walt (herein, Ch. 4) maintains that his theory of balancing of threats embodies novel facts. Vasquez argues that only balancing threat from power can be supportive evidence for a realist theory. What is novel about Walt's (1987) finding is not that states balance (block) against threat, but that they do not find the strongest state threatening, as Waltz and Morgenthau would expect. From a Lakatosian perspective, this is not a novel fact but unexpected evidence against the proposition. To be a novel fact a theory must predict something other than the discrepant evidence it has uncovered. Vasquez goes on to use Barnett's analysis (1996; herein, Ch. 14) of Walt (1987) to maintain that balancing of threat is better explained by constructivist theory, which is a nonmaterialist (and nonrealist) explanation of the source of threat that explains when the strongest actor is seen as threatening and when someone else is. Replies are also made to specific points raised by Schweller and by Christensen and Snyder.

Third, he defends the use of Lakatos's MSRP (methodology of scientific research programs) and the conclusions he derived from his application of it. Here, he replies in detail to Walt (herein, Ch. 4) who argues that Lakatos is irrelevant. He concludes by discussing why he has not used certain aspects of Lakatos's MSRP, as Elman and Elman (herein, Ch. 7) say he should. He agrees that using Lakatos's idea of ad hoc$_3$ explanations would have been useful, but points out that this would have actually strengthened his critique against the neotraditional realist research program rather than weakened it.

## Key Terms

**defining criteria**   Criteria that identify what should and should not be included in a definition; delimiting what empirical referents are part of the definition and which are not.

**domain**   The phenomena, situation, locale, or historical era to which a theory is meant to apply.

## Notes

1. See also Morgenthau (1960, 167), who says from a foreign policy perspective, "The aspiration for power on the part of several nations, each trying either to maintain or overthrow the status quo, leads of necessity to a configuration that is called the balance of power and to policies that aim at preserving it."
2. I have not used deterrence language here because I feel, given its logic of war as unwinnable, that it should only be used for nuclear situations or situations that would be perceived as resulting in an Armageddon.
3. Christensen and Snyder (herein, Ch. 5, 70; 1997, 921) argue that Chamberlain's appeasement is a "strategy that can either accompany or preclude balancing." I do not disagree with this as a logical possibility, but Chamberlain's policy was based on trying to cope with German revisionism by revamping what they now considered an unreasonable Versailles settlement. Balancing, if it came into the picture at all, came in only after the takeover in Prague made it clear that the Munich settlement and the strategy of accommodation was a failure (see Bell 1986, 252–253). See also the discussion in endnotes 7 and 9.

4. I have emphasized "effect" and "consequence" in this sentence because Waltz (1979), as a systems theorist, eschews intentions or motives and relegates them to the purview of foreign policy, which his theory does not cover; see also Morgenthau (1960, 6–7 on motives). Waltz (1979, 122) states: "Balance-of-power theory is a theory about the results produced by the uncoordinated actions of states." From a more classical realist perspective, actions could be seen as balancing if that were the actors' intention, purpose, or goal, even if they did not actually have that effect. From my perspective such "confirmation" would be acceptable, even though it does not support the "market mechanism" embodied in Waltz's logic.
5. From a Waltzian perspective, it is clear that the most powerful state in the system from 1945–1991 was the United States, and it was balanced by the Soviet Union.
6. Waltz (herein, Ch. 3, 55; 1997, 916) worries that I find testing to be an easy and definitive process. Testing is never easy, nor is measurement, but the alternative is never knowing whether one's beliefs about the world are true.
7. From a realist perspective, adopting appeasement in the face of such an increase in power and in threat should not occur because it will only "whet the appetite of the aggressor" as realists claim. The use of appeasement, therefore, must be considered as something that realists see as both unexpected and imprudent (compare Christensen and Snyder herein, Ch. 5, 70; 1997, 921). On the use of appeasement as a traditional British strategy, see Rosecrance and Lo 1996, 480.
8. FDR should not be seen as buck-passing, since U.S. policy was due to constraints of isolationist sentiment rather than trying to avoid costs (FDR's policy suggests a noncollective goods reason for the failure of balance). Nor should it be assumed that the external threat posed by Hitler would have made any U.S. leader adopt FDR's pro-British stance. The latter was also probably a function of his anglophile tendencies. Certainly a Charles Beard or a Charles Lindbergh, if one of them were president, would have interpreted the external threat and national interest in different terms.
9. It is for this reason that I do not accept Walt's (1992b, 452–463) position that the 1930s is an example of balancing. Britain and France did build up their militaries, but this was not their main strategy for dealing with Hitler—appeasement was. The buildup of their militaries is better interpreted as a fall-back strategy that would provide insurance if the main strategy failed. It can also be seen as an effort to reduce potential criticism of the main strategy by domestic hard-liners. Because arming was a secondary strategy, it lacked the concomitant diplomatic moves necessary to make it a credible balancing strategy and thereby did not have a real chance of producing an inhibiting effect (i.e., what some would call a "deterrent" effect). From a hard-line realist perspective, the adding of "the stick" of rearmament had no benefit—it did not intimidate Hitler because appeasement undercut that possibility, while further whetting his appetite.

In addition, it must be pointed out that the making of alliances and building up of militaries is a major prediction of a nonrealist explanation of the steps to war (Vasquez 1993, Ch. 5), which maintains that such practices among equals (even when they include genuine balancing) increase hostility, hard-liners, and the probability of war, and do not produce an inhibiting effect (posited by realists)(see the application to the 1930s in Vasquez 1996c).
10. Similarly, Elman and Elman (1995, 193) hope to advance the field by specifying the domain under which the proposition holds.
11. Lakatos (1970, 137) says the problems scientists choose to work on in powerful research programs are "determined by the positive heuristic of the programme rather than by psychologically worrying ... anomalies. The anomalies are listed but shoved aside. ... Only those scientists have to rivet their attention on anomalies who are either engaged in trial-and-error exercises or who work in a degenerating phase of a research programme when the positive heuristic ran out of steam."
12. Contrast his reformulation of the problem with that of Rosecrance and Lo (1996), who use "nested games" to show not only why balancing does not occur in a specific era, but why it is generally rare when the "aggressor" offers side payments.
13. This is not the place to compare a psychology-based paradigm with the power-rational choice paradigm of realism. However, such a comparison based on Laudan's criteria would be worth undertaking. In summary, Laudan (1977, 119) states: "The *adequacy* or *effectiveness* of individual theories is a function of how many significant empirical problems they solve, and how many important anomalies and conceptual problems they generate" (emphasis in original) (cf. Lakatos 1970, 137 quoted in endnote 11 above). Psychological theories, especially if grounded in the biology of emotions and of territoriality (see Damasio 1994; Devlin 1997) would do well in explaining several of realism's anomalies, such as why deterrence does not always work (see Jervis, Lebow, and Stein 1985) and why weak states attack stronger ones (cf. Paul 1994, and Roy 1997).

14. One way to ease this measurement impasse is to look at whether leaders expect the next war to be short or a war of attrition, as Christensen and Snyder (herein, Ch. 5, 67; 1997, 920) suggest, rather than looking at perceptions of the offensive/defensive advantage. A study of perceptions of the length of the coming war, however, may take research even further away from the hard-core realist variable of power, since perceptions of a war's length might be subject to psychological overconfidence (White 1966) or to lessons derived from the previous war (Jervis 1976, 266–269), rather than cold "objective" calculations of capability.
15. See Rosecrance and Lo (1996) for some insights and game theoretics on why balancing may not be "rational" for individual states.
16. One of the minor disagreements between Christensen and Snyder (herein, Ch. 5) and me has to do with whether Britain was slower to balance (in terms of making a commitment to go to war) in 1939 than in 1914. If the offense had the advantage in 1914 as Christensen and Snyder (1990) maintain, then Britain should have been quicker to balance than in 1939. Christensen and Snyder (herein, Ch. 5, 69; 1997, 920) support their claim by saying that Britain was slower to respond with troops in 1939 than in 1914 because it saw the defensive as having the advantage. I am not concerned here with troop deployment. My point is that the *political* commitment and *decision to go to war* in the event of a German attack on the continent was much slower in 1914 than in 1939. The lack of a clear British commitment in 1914 to fight affected German calculations and, in the view of some analysts, was an important factor in failing to "deter" Germany (Levy 1990/91; see also Rosecrance and Lo 1996, 497). If this is the case, then 1914 is an instance when a major state failed to balance power (and even threaten when it was supposed to), resulting in revisionist states' taking risks they otherwise might have avoided.
17. In Lakatos's (1970, 175) terms, Christensen and Snyder come close to an ad hoc$_3$ explanation here (see below and Elman and Elman herein, Ch. 7, 82; 1997, 924), because it so undercuts the rationality of the power politics of Morgenthau's realism and Waltz's anarchic system (i.e., their respective positive heuristics).
18. It should be noted that there are two distinct definitions of progress employed in the debate. One is the technical meaning stipulated by Lakatos (1970), which refers to progressive as opposed to degenerative problemshifts. The other is the normal dictionary definition of any sort of advancement or improvement in knowledge. The two need to be kept distinct. (For a general review of problems of progress in the social sciences based on the dictionary definition, see Rule 1997). I do not claim that neotraditionalist research is without merit nor that it has not improved our understanding of international relations; only that one of its most important contributions — the uncovering of discrepant evidence — has not been properly labeled as such.
19. Likewise, I find Walt's (herein, Ch. 4, 65n7; 1997, 933n7) emphasis on "cogent explanations" and Christensen and Snyder's (herein, Ch. 5, 68; 1997, 920) references to what the buck-passing/chain-ganging frame can *explain* of less importance than whether these explanations will pass rigorous empirical investigation.
20. I have included Waltz (1979) as part of the larger realist paradigm because he does not violate any of these three fundamental assumptions. Waltz (herein, Ch. 3, 49; 1997, 913) objects to this because he says he has a structural theory and Morgenthau does not. I have not said there are no differences between the two "theories," but they clearly share a family resemblance just as Lenin's and Marx's theories do, even though they are quite different. In addition, Waltz (1979) builds upon propositions on balancing found in Morgenthau (1960, 167, 187–189; see endnote 1 above and the text following it) and can be seen as articulating the larger paradigm. Where he differs is on how he explains why states balance and in his assumption that the goal of states is security (or survival) and not a striving for ever more power (Waltz, herein, Ch. 3, 49; 1997, 913; cf. Mearsheimer 2001). These differences are not so fundamental that they must be seen as constituting two paradigms, rather than two different theories within the same paradigm. If this were not the case, then no one would think of calling Waltz's theory structural *realism* (emphasis added) (for additional discussion on the connections between Morgenthau and Waltz, see Vasquez 1998, Ch. 9).
21. These assumptions refer respectively to self-help, expected gains, and strategic decision making. While power politics is consistent with these assumptions, so are a number of other behaviors — e.g., capitalist behavior.
22. This is not to say that realists cannot explain such institutions (see the recent effort by Schweller and Priess 1997), but that in doing so they must give attention to how competing paradigms differ in their understanding and in their retrodictions.

# WHY REALISM DOES NOT WORK WELL FOR INTERNATIONAL HISTORY
## (WHETHER OR NOT IT REPRESENTS A DEGENERATE IR RESEARCH STRATEGY)

*PAUL W. SCHROEDER*

As an international historian, I am an outsider in this debate over Lakatosian theory and international relations theory in general and in particular over the proposition that realism, especially structural realism, represents a degenerate IR research program. The vantage point and concerns that originally brought me into the ongoing controversy over realism in IR theory were strictly historical—how to use international relations theory in doing international history—and remain so. Therefore if, as is the case, I tend to agree with the "degenerate strategy" proposition, it is as an interested observer rather than a judge or an expert witness.

To be sure, as a historian I could make some contribution to the debate by discussing the historical generalizations about balance of power, balancing, bandwagoning, and other tactics and strategies in international politics offered by various parties in the debate, and for the most part will do this here. But such bare-boned comments, allusions, and assertions about history as can be made in a brief essay can only be suggestive rather than decisive. There is another important reason, moreover, for not confining myself to a historical critique of these generalizations: the conviction that, important though it is to test the generalizations made by political scientists and other social scientists about international politics by historical data, this kind of critique, here at least, finally does not reach the main problem. The generalizations in question seem to me unhelpful and misleading not, in many cases, because they are demonstrably wrong, falsified by the weight of historical evidence (though in fact some are), but because they mislead scholars, or at least historians, by failing to reach a deeper reality about international politics. Hence this will primarily be an attempt to state briefly and broadly why my advice to historians (I do not presume to advise other scholars) is that realism is not the best theoretical approach to international history, and why they should not discard or totally reject it but get beyond it. At the same time, in hopes of a more or less graceful exit from the debate, I offer an irenic proposal at the end—or at least as irenic a one as I can manage.

Let me start with Kenneth Waltz's contribution. He makes two charges: first, that I do not understand what theory is and what it is supposed to do in scientific explanation; and second, that as a result of this misunderstanding of the purpose and role of theory I expect Waltz's theory to explain foreign policy behavior and to account for the motives and purposes of statesmen, when it never claims to do this and no theory can. Therefore the historical evidence and argument I offer in criticism of realist theory is "a melange of irrelevant diplomatic lore." The first charge, that I misunderstand the nature and purpose of theory is, I think, incorrect, but not important for our purposes here even if true. I could have a defective understanding of the nature and purpose of theory without being guilty of the other error he attributes to me. The second charge, I feel sure, is wrong. I have never said or thought that structure and system determine the actual conduct of foreign policy, or that Waltz's structural theory claims that they do. I could show by quotations that instead I have long independently believed what Waltz says here, that structures do not determine individual foreign policy decisions, but that "structures shape and shove; they encourage states to do some things and to refrain from doing others." We further agree that "success in explaining, not predicting, is the ultimate criterion of good theory" and that any theory should be expected to explain not the details of foreign policy but the broad patterns and outcomes of international history. This is once again what Waltz claims for his theory here—that structural realism explains the broad course of history, that history, past and current, broadly vindicates its explanation. Unipolarity, he asserts, is "the least stable of international configurations"; "willy nilly, balances will form over time":

> As nature abhors a vacuum, so international politics abhors unbalanced power. Faced by unbalanced power, states try to increase their own strength or they ally with others to bring the international distribution of power into balance. The reactions of other states to the drive for dominance of Charles I of Spain, of Louis XIV and Napoleon Bonaparte of France, of Wilhelm II and Adolph [sic] Hitler of Germany, illustrate the point (1997, 915; Ch. 3 herein, 54).

In fact, this precisely illustrates mine. These are the same generalizations about history that I argued were historically untenable. The case is made fairly briefly but clearly and explicitly in the article in *International Security* alluded to (Schroeder 1994a), and at greater length with much more evidence in other works (especially Schroeder 1994b). Yet they are asserted here once again as if they were as obvious and unchallengeable as the multiplication table. Waltz's procedure would seem to indicate a belief that if he shows to his own satisfaction that I misunderstand theory in general or his theory in particular, he may then ignore any historical evidence I or others may present disputing the broad historical patterns that he asserts both illustrate his theory and demonstrate its explanatory power. This is not new. In rereading his books (Waltz 1959, 1967, 1979), I am struck with how little international history is in them—much theory, much discussion of political philosophy and science, and frequent allusions to history, but no serious effort to see whether the generalizations he makes and the patterns he sees square with historical research. He repeatedly says, "Look at history," but gives us the results of not really looking at it.

It is impossible here to develop a serious historical critique of his assertions about the natural, inevitable, and recurrent incidence of balancing as a reaction to imbalances of power, but I can at least indicate superficially why as a historian I reject it. In a long book on European politics in 1763–1848 (Schroeder 1994b), I tried to show in detail how the normal reaction of other European states, small and large alike, to the massive imbalance of power represented by Napoleonic France and its satellites and allies was not to try to balance against it, but to accept the fact of Napoleonic domination and try to join his empire for the sake of sharing the profits, or to work out an accommodation with it, or simply to try to escape any involvement with it at all. In other words, they pursued various strategies of hiding or bandwagoning (and also, as will be discussed below, transcending and grouping) in preference to balancing. Not only did every smaller power on the Continent accept Napoleonic hegemony more or less willingly and try to live under it, but so, at times, did every other continental great power—Prussia, Austria, and Russia. It is not an exaggeration to say that a major occupation of many leading statesmen in large and smaller European countries alike in the Napoleonic era was trying to work out ways by which they could survive and prosper in and under Napoleonic hegemony rather than challenge it. Even Great Britain, never defeated by France and essentially invulnerable to conquest, showed itself more than once (in 1802–1803 and 1807–1808) ready to come to terms with Napoleonic hegemony on the Continent, if France would accept a corresponding British hegemony at sea and in the colonies. The central reason that these states finally ended up resisting Napoleonic domination and, in the end, overthrowing it lay not in some imperative compelling them to balance against excessive power, but in Napoleon—in the repeated, constant proofs he gave that he would never be content with any kind of stable and tolerable hegemony, but understood no relationship save exploitative empire. They resisted ("balanced," if you insist), in other words, because he would not allow them not to—denied them any stable, reasonably autonomous status in an international system under his hegemony.

Nor is it the case that after Napoleon's overthrow the international system worked on the basis of a balance of power in any other but the crude and anodyne sense that no single state was so powerful as to be able to conquer or dominate all the rest—virtually a self-understood part of the definition of an international system. The Vienna system was, instead, a solidarity system, resting on a general consensus in favor of a settlement based on legitimacy and operating through various forms of hegemony—the hegemony of all the great powers in the European Concert over all the smaller ones—of Great Britain generally in Western Europe and overseas, Russia generally in Central and Eastern Europe, Austria particularly in Italy, and Austria and Prussia jointly in Germany. France, the one major power that seriously resented and opposed this scheme of divided and shared hegemonies did so because it had no acknowledged sphere of influence of its own. It tried to change this scheme not by balancing against other powers and trying to create a new balance of power, but by trying to join the scheme—to become Britain's ally and junior partner in Western Europe and in overseas ventures, sharing its hegemony—and to force Austria to grant France a sphere of its own in Italy.

In most of the other cases of supposed balancing behavior cited by Waltz, similar explanations apply. For example, the dominant initial response to Nazi Germany's rise in power was certainly not balancing but appeasement, hiding, and bandwagoning, until Nazi aggression made continuance of these strategies impossible. As for Wilhelmine Germany, even assuming that it actually posed a hegemonic threat to the balance, one can make a powerful case that what Great Britain, France, Russia, and even in a limited sense the United States were actually doing in the decades before 1914 was not mainly balancing against this supposed German threat, but making profitable deals over shares in imperialist domination of the non-European world—a strategy that required limiting or excluding German competition. As for Charles I of Spain (simultaneously Emperor Charles V of the Holy Roman Empire), he claimed a sort of universal monarchy on both old medieval and newer Age of Discovery grounds. The challenge to his claims and exercise of power however came not just from power-political struggles with rival aspirants for hegemony, France and the Ottoman Empire, but even more from typical sixteenth- and seventeenth-century obstacles to royal or imperial power in general: resistance by provinces, nobles, and estates in Spain, the Low Countries, and elsewhere to Charles's centralized rule, taxes, and infringement of their privileges, and in Germany especially to his attempts to enforce religious uniformity. Only with Louis XIV does the notion of hegemonic threat evoking balancing behavior work, and even here only with major qualifications, the most important being that here too the states that resisted Louis did so only after trying appeasement and coexistence and failing because he regularly pushed his pretensions too far.

The realist answer might be that this is merely the usual historian's insistence on a picture more detailed and nuanced than structural realism or any theory can supply or needs or is interested in. The fact remains that all these bids for unipolar hegemony ultimately ran into resistance and failed, and this pattern is what structural realism explains. My response is that this is not a call for more detail and nuance, but a claim that the so-called pattern is an optical illusion produced by too flat and superficial a view of the historical evidence. The pattern (insofar as there is any) is not one of smaller powers being driven by their security imperative more or less automatically and regularly to balance against excessive power and fight bids for hegemony; it is one of some hegemonic powers (not all) compelling or inducing resistance by their failure or refusal to make their hegemony tolerable or profitable to other powers who in principle are willing to accommodate it.

This pattern, moreover, is confirmed by the other side of the coin: Hegemonies that are considered tolerable (either because they are in fact relatively benign or because they seem so strong as to be unchallengeable, or both) prove durable in history. Unipolarity in the form of particular hegemonies appears to me in the international history of the last five centuries not the least stable of international configurations, but the most stable. British maritime, colonial, and imperial hegemony lasted over two hundred years, and finally gave way not to a rival coalition or new balance of power but to a partner, ally, and new stable naval and imperial hegemon, the United States. Russian hegemony in Eastern Europe proved stable for over a hundred years. Even Soviet hegemony, though anything but benign, lasted forty-five years and disappeared, not because of the internal or external resistance of its enemies, but by the voluntary surrender of hegemony by the hegemon. American hegemony in North America, the Western Hemisphere, the Pacific, and now much of the world has lasted for more than one hundred fifty years. While one doubtless can look at the end of the Cold War in many ways, one obvious view is that it represents the end of another failed or abandoned attempt to balance against the United States, like the attempts of Great Britain and France to balance against the United States in the Western Hemisphere in the nineteenth century, or Hitler's dreams of doing so. Why Professor Waltz thinks China and Japan are bound to make a similar effort today, or even contemplate doing so, escapes me. In contrast, I know of no so-called balance of power in history (most of which were in any case concealed hegemonies or attempts at hegemony) that ever proved stable.

This leads to a general point. The international history that Waltz and some other neorealists (not by any means all or most) know and use is the history everyone knows. This is not good enough. The problem is partly that the usual neorealist historical paradigm ignores too much historical evidence and has too flat and undifferentiated a picture of historical development. Beyond this, it rests on the fundamentally unsound basis of what has been called the sameness principle: the assumption that since the structural elements of international politics are supposedly always the same, the broad outcomes and patterns of international history must remain the same as well. One cannot do good international history using this principle. This is not to say that all history done by neorealists is bad—the contrary is true—but rather that, to the extent it is good, it is so in spite of this principle rather than because of it, in the way that some Marxist political history is good because it mainly ignores Marxist doctrines, or gets round them, or consigns them to the edges.

This criticism does not hold for all realism or all realists, of course. Much realist writing, both theoretical and historical, actually seems to me an attempt to deal with the difficulties faced by structural realism in dealing with history. My disagreements with the others in this current debate are therefore less profound, and include again the stipulation that many political scientists in all camps take history seriously, understand its nature and requirements, use it responsibly, and do good history themselves. Hence these are only comments on certain points rather than any extended argument.

First, Stephen Walt's argument that states balance against threats more than against power (Walt 1987), while it has some advantages in explaining particular historical cases of balancing conduct, still does not satisfactorily answer the question of whether balancing behavior has historically been dominant in international politics. There are difficulties with how both terms, *balance* and *threat*, are to be defined. If balancing means overt power-political actions of some sort taken to counter some power-political danger, then I agree that such balancing actions, when they occur, are more commonly directed against perceived threats than against power per se—but not that such balancing is historically the dominant response to perceived threats any more than it is to excessive power. Here too balancing has historically been more often a fall-back position than a first choice; states that perceive real threats usually try to handle them, if they can, not by balancing but by other means. The range of alternative responses and strategies, moreover, is not limited to the usual IR categories—bandwagoning, hiding, and buck-passing. One further strategy is what I have called *transcending*, i.e., trying to deal with the dangers both of concentrations of power and of concrete threats by taking the problem to a higher level, establishing norms of a legal, religious, moral, or procedural nature to govern international practice, with these norms to be somehow maintained and enforced by the international community or by a particular segment of it. The fact that this strategy fails more often than not does not diminish its significance in this context. It has often been tried in the early modern era as well as our own (Duchhardt 1979, 1991), and has arguably grown in frequency and effectiveness over time. A much more common and frequently successful strategy for managing threats, especially since the early nineteenth century, is called *grouping* (the actual term used by Austria's Prince Metternich and others). Grouping means attempting to draw a state that poses a threat to one's vital interests into a larger group so that group suasion and group norms, pressure, and incentives will control its actions and possibly turn the threat into cooperation. The Concert of Europe worked on the grouping principle; so did restraining alliances, perhaps the most important and effective means of threat and crisis management in the nineteenth century (Schroeder 1976).

Two examples illustrate how grouping could be effective even in situations of serious competition and crisis. A persistent recurrent threat to the vital interests of several major powers throughout the nineteenth century (Austria, Britain, France, and ultimately Germany) arose from the Russian menace to the Ottoman Empire, a threat derived both from Russia's formidable power and invulnerable position vis-à-vis Turkey, and from particular Russian ambitions and moves. Throughout the history of the perennial Eastern Question in the nineteenth century, two different strategies were promoted to check Russia—balancing and grouping. Britain, sometimes joined by other powers, especially France, usually wanted to stop the Russian threat by various forms of balancing—using its own navy or a combination of fleets to threaten Russia at the Straits or in the Black Sea, trying to strengthen the Turks or ally with them against Russia, and above all trying to get the Continental powers, especially Austria and Prussia/Germany, to oppose Russia on its western frontier or its flank in the Balkans. The strategy regularly promoted by other states, especially Austria, Prussia, and later Bismarck's Germany, as a conscious alternative to the British balancing policy was to group Russia, using pressure and inducements, to persuade it to act toward Turkey only as part of a group, either the whole European Concert or its particular conservative partners. I think one can show convincingly that grouping was more effective than balancing, both in restraining Russia and in avoiding war. In any case, regardless of its effectiveness, it was clearly the preferred, dominant strategy most of the time for most Continental powers.

A second prominent example of grouping: In the late nineteenth century Britain faced major, multiform threats to the naval, colonial, commercial-industrial, and imperial hegemony it had enjoyed almost unchallenged since the Napoleonic Wars. These threats developed in general out of Britain's decline industrially and commercially in relation to new rivals, especially the United States and Germany, and more specifically from challenges posed to its far-flung empire at various places by both old imperial competitors (Russia and France) and new ones (Germany, the United States, Japan). There is no denying that the British government sometimes responded to particular threats by balancing—outbuilding Germany and others in the naval race, facing France down at Fashoda, standing up to Russia at times in Central Asia, defying world opinion in the Second Anglo-Boer war, etc. But a more common, pervasive, and successful British strategy was to meet these threats by grouping, that is, making deals with competitors both in order to protect the main British interests and to manage the threat these other powers posed by drawing them into cooperation. All Britain's major moves in this era—the Entente Cordiale with France, the Anglo-Japanese alliance, rapprochement with the United States, the Anglo-Russian Convention of 1907, various colonial deals in Africa, even ultimately its agreement with Germany over the Bagdad railway project—were part of this strategy of grouping. As some historians have long contended (Monger 1963; Klein 1968; Bridge 1972; Schroeder 1972a) and more are now arguing (Wilson 1985, 1987; Neilson 1996; French 1986; and Bridge 1990), the main aim of British policy before 1914 was not to balance against Germany so as to preserve a balance of power on the Continent. That purpose, though subjectively genuinely believed and proclaimed, actually represented a subordinate aspect and necessary consequence of the central British concern, which was to meet the pressing threats to its empire by preserving the alliances, ententes, and partnerships it had achieved with Russia, France, the United States, and Japan. The most important of these, the so-called Triple Entente with Russia and France, required Britain to side generally (i.e., "balance") with them in Europe against Germany—a policy which, though dictated more by British imperial needs and motives, was rendered more plausible and saleable by the fact that Germany was also a naval, commercial, and colonial rival to Britain. In other words, sustaining Britain's worldwide position by forming a cooperative hegemonic partnership with Russia, France, and other states (principally Japan and the United States) represented the real purpose behind the British "balancing" policy against Germany.

It might be said that grouping is still a form of balancing against threats in that it involves an element of coercion, namely, the implicit or explicit threat of exclusion from the group, thereby incurring the loss of group benefits and the dangers of the open enmity of its members. But surely this stretches the definition of balancing beyond recognition or usefulness. It would be like arguing that a wife who guards against the threat that her husband will leave her by trying to meet his needs and make him happy in the marriage is really balancing against the threat of his unfaithfulness or desertion by implicitly threatening him with the prospect of losing the benefits of marriage and facing a costly divorce. Grouping, like transcending, must be seen as an alternative to balancing, bandwagoning, buck-passing, hiding, or any other realist power-political strategy; its aim and modus operandi are not essentially power-political, but managerial and societal.

A similar problem arises with the definition of *threat*. If this means, as it ought to, a genuine, objectively verifiable power-political danger and menace, then states undoubtedly tend to balance against these if they feel they must, and if they have any chance of success in doing so. (There are, of course, many instances in which states perceive a threat but do not even try to balance against it because they see resistance as futile and counterproductive. Denmark's and Norway's responses to the German threat in 1939–1940 are examples.) However, states actually perceive or name as threats to their vital interests so many actions or conditions, real, imagined, or deliberately concocted, and what is supposedly threatened includes so many divergent things, tangible interests like territory or military security and intangible and imponderable ones such as honor, prestige, credibility, status, national feeling, etc., that any action taken by a government against some alleged wrong or danger can be called balancing against a threat. (For examples of the many different things nineteenth century European statesmen cited as threats to their vital interests and thereby to the European balance, see Schroeder 1989; for a discussion of threat perception in general, see Jervis 1976). The fact that both the perceptions of threats and the concepts of the interests supposedly threatened are inherently subjective and often gravely distorted does not of course make them any less real as factors in international politics. Intangible and imponderable interests can be as real and vital as tangible ones, and highly distorted and exaggerated perceptions can be convincing and powerful motives for policy. Though this is almost a truism, a concrete illustration of it may help. From 1909 on, Russia's European policy especially in the Balkans was dominated by a conviction dominant in the Russian government and public opinion that Austria-Hungary and Germany had deliberately humiliated Russia in the Bosnian Crisis. In my view, Russian perceptions were at least badly distorted and grossly exaggerated in regard to the Bosnian Crisis itself, and demonstrably wrong about Austria's and Germany's aims thereafter, which though ill-coordinated, consistently represented an attempt to conciliate Russia and restore good relations. Yet the political offensive Russia thereafter waged in its attempt to gain complete control over Balkan affairs, excluding Austria-Hungary from influence in the region, was genuinely viewed by Russians as a defensive measure, balancing against a perceived (largely nonexistent) threat of further Austro-German humiliation. In situations like this, which are by no means uncommon, the terms *threat* and *balancing* become so inflated as to be almost useless for analysis and explanation. The proposition, "States balance against threats" reduces to little more than "States do various things to counter things they do not like."

My comment on the Elmans' depiction of realism as a broad camp or tendency that embraces many stances and views is that, besides detecting in it a general tendency to make the realist theorist into Gilbert and Sullivan's John Wellington Wells, the dealer in magic and spells who can provide a different version of the theory to meet every objection (a tendency Vasquez points out), I sense a difficulty with their version of the shared hard core of realism. This consists of seven propositions (1997, 924; Ch. 7 herein, 83), all of which, they claim, both fit the historical account of developments given in my essay and explain it. Now even if I were to concede (as I do not) that all the examples of state actions discussed in that essay, along with many others not there, could be explained by these seven propositions and thus reconciled with hard core realism, a vital question remains. The crucial distinction between a realist and a nonrealist approach to international politics, according to the Elmans, is the distinction between self-regarding and other-regarding behavior. This distinction, and the insistence that state action is and must be self-regarding, keeps the realist core coherent and keeps the opposing nonrealist category from being empty. What happens, however, if a state, in the course of acting upon realist imperatives, concludes that to succeed at self-help it must adopt a deliberate policy of other-help; that it can only survive and prosper by promoting the strength and security of a rival, even though it thereby increases the potential danger of that rival's becoming a still more dangerous threat and enemy?

This, I contend, is not at all an abstract possibility. It has happened numerous times in the past, and is becoming increasingly common as an insight and basis for action today. Again, a few examples. Prince Metternich, no sentimental idealist, concluded in 1813 that the only way Austria could achieve real security was as part of an independent European center that it needed to lead but not dominate or control, because any attempt to do this would exceed Austria's capabilities and ruin the tranquility it needed in order to survive and recover. To build this independent center, Austria had to promote the independence of Prussia as a great power and recognize the independence of Bavaria and other smaller states in order to secure them as willing partners in the endeavor, even though (as Metternich knew) Prussia was sure to remain a rival and potential threat to Austrian leadership, and the other German states, especially Bavaria, would be suspicious of Austria and hard to manage. (Kraehe 1963, 1983; Schroeder 1994b). The leading historian of Weimar Germany's foreign policy (Krüger 1985) has shown that in the 1920s, while the foreign minister Gustav Stresemann was seeking German security through traditional Realpolitik, trying to restore Germany's great power status and freedom of maneuver in secret opposition to France by hollowing out the Treaty of Versailles, Carl Schubert, political director at the German Foreign Office, and a number of his coworkers had already concluded that Germany could never attain real security except by becoming economically and politically integrated with Western Europe, in particular with its main rival France. This insight, though impossible to act upon in the 1920s, became the basis of policy for both France and Germany under the leadership of Jean Monnet, Robert Schuman, Konrad Adenauer, and others, laying the basis for Franco-German reconciliation and West European integration after 1950.

It will not do to reply that these are instances where a so-called "other-help" stance is merely part of a larger self-help strategy—a policy of recruiting and supporting allies in order to meet a larger threat. In these instances and others the distinction between self-help and other-help, supposedly vital to the coherence of realist doctrine, breaks down. An essential, central security problem is met not by balancing or by any other power-political strategy, but by transcending it—by interweaving self-help and other-help to make them inseparable.

Nor is it the case that states that do this thereby surrender their sovereignty and independence and cease to be rational unitary actors playing the normal international game. As Alan Milward (1992) and others argue, the major members of the European Union have deliberately used the EU to rescue and preserve their status as nation-states, investing certain aspects of their sovereignty in common in order to exercise sovereignty more effectively in other ways. This is not new. The German states that joined the Prussian-led German Customs Union (*Zollverein*) from 1834 on did the same thing for the same reasons (Hahn 1984). To the reply that such policies are still clearly motivated by enlightened self-interest, the answer is, "Of course." The point is that enlightened state self-interest is not always bounded and governed by self-regarding realist propositions. Enlightened self-interest can under certain circumstances lead or even compel states to get beyond these supposedly insuperable limits, and at certain points in history, becoming more frequent and compelling all the time, the distinction between self-regarding and other-regarding policy breaks down and becomes meaningless and unworkable.

Finally a comment on Randall Schweller's argument that realism is "more than a 'scientific' research program," but rather that it rests on and derives from a sober appraisal of the incurably self-centered, competitive, and conflictual nature of international society and the world economy (1997, 927–928; Ch. 6 herein, 75). My reaction is that one could share both his pessimistic view of the world and humankind and his skepticism about ever achieving a world of peace and harmony without conceding that this general world view determines what the nature of international politics must be—"a perpetual struggle for security, prestige, and power and influence"—any more than the ineluctable fact that we will all die and during our lives be subject to sickness, suffering, and want determines how much change and progress can be made over time in prolonging human life and alleviating sickness and suffering. Both these concepts, that of human mortality and its inescapable concomitants and that of the intractability of human self-centeredness and evil even in the face of rationality, represent what Germans call a *Grenzbegriff*, a boundary or limiting concept. Boundary concepts set certain limits within which we conceive and understand the problem and the task, but that is all they do; in practical terms they neither dictate nor govern the amount or character of possible action and change within those boundaries. To understand what has already been done or tried within these limits, one looks to history. To predict what can still be done, one looks to current science, technology, politics, economics, and other areas—in other words, to what is happening and being learned and tried now, not to fixed notions of the nature of the world, society, or humankind.

This distinction applies not just to that world view which, according to Schweller, informs realist thought, but to all its hard core of assumptions and principles. These are, at bottom, boundary concepts. They do not dictate what has always been done and can be done in international politics, but indicate certain broad and elastic limits marking its outer boundaries. Within those limits, the answers on what is possible in international politics are found not in its supposedly unchanging structure, but in the record of how it began, what it has become, how it has changed, and what it seems to be becoming—in other words, in human history and current human action.

This brings me to my last point. No response to an opposing position is more patronizing than to say, "I used to believe that;" nothing more self-indulgent than to discuss one's own intellectual development as if this made any difference or anyone cared. Yet doing this seems the best way to indicate why realism now seems to me an inadequate approach to international history. For a fairly long time I was a realist historian in the unreflecting, untheoretical manner of most historians. My working assumptions, though unarticulated, were exactly those Stephen Walt identifies as generic realism; I would have accepted the Elmans' seven propositions. Out of ordinary historical research, done without much theoretical knowledge or reflection, I gradually became convinced that my generic-realist assumptions were inadequate. This was not because they were flatly untrue, worthless for purposes of explanation, or grossly incompatible with the facts, but because they left too much out, could not handle important parts of the evidence, explained too many things away. Much later, I reached the conclusion that this was because the central assumptions and propositions of realism, though not simply false, were flawed in two ways. First, as already stated, they represented boundary concepts being understood and used as if they were central, constitutive structures. Second and closely related, they were penultimate or antepenultimate realities or truths being seen and used as if they were the ultimate ones. When boundary concepts are taken as constitutive structures, and penultimate truths taken as final ones, then what emerges, it seems to me, is a theory and history of international politics that is quite coherent and persuasive, hangs together and works for a long time, but eventually breaks down like the wonderful one-horse shay. Moreover, this theory and history serves to conceal and obscure a deeper history of international politics (and possibly a deeper theory of it), one which is finally more true to the facts and serves better to integrate international history into general history and into our wider understanding of the human condition.

Obviously I cannot prove any of this but only try to indicate some central differences in understanding that getting beyond realism can make. Realism (meaning, as I have defined it, taking realist propositions as constitutive structures rather than boundary concepts and as final rather than penultimate truths) results in an emphasis on sameness, continuity, the common insistence that international politics has not changed in its essence since Thucydides. Getting beyond realism enables one to see the centrality of change—that the only permanent, unchanging historical reality in international politics is change. Seventeenth-century European politics changed markedly in the early eighteenth century; that of the eighteenth in the early nineteenth; nineteenth again in the early and mid-twentieth, and mid-twentieth most decisively in the late twentieth. Realism further leads to a concept of international politics as an ongoing contest for power and security, essentially marked by competition, conflict, and war. Getting beyond realism enables one to conceive international politics as an ongoing quest for order and peace, and to recognize the considerable historic advances made in this quest. The main problem for international history is not to explain and account for war and conflict—that is the easy part—but to explain and account for the growth of order and peace, the surprising extent to which many vital international activities once entirely or mainly in the zone of war are now firmly in the zone of order, peace, and law. Explaining order and peace takes one beyond realism. Realism, finally, leads one to emphasize the structural differences between international politics and domestic governance so that the two never can become the same, and to see international history as fundamentally unlike other aspects of human history. They go somewhere, become radically different over time; international history remains in its nature and structure always the same, recounts the same story with different actors and scenery. Getting beyond realism means seeing international politics, though in some respects unique, as in other important respects not really different from domestic politics and governance, but part and parcel of the activity of politics as found everywhere in human society: the exercise of leadership and governance in groups organized for collective endeavor. Thus the history of international politics becomes basically like the history of other human institutions, such as capitalism or representative government—a history that goes somewhere.

To sum up my reasons for not being a realist: Realism treats boundary concepts as constitutive structures and penultimate truths as ultimate ones; it ignores the central reality of change; it does fairly well at explaining conflict and war, but much worse at explaining order and peace; and it underestimates the capacity of the human spirit and misses the real direction of international history. Despite this, however, realism is not to be despised or discarded. It remains an important doctrine responsible for much valuable scholarship, and it contains vital penultimate truths that cannot be forgotten because, in a practical sense, they once fit certain dominant traits of international politics, characteristics that still prevail in some quarters and could become dominant again.

It seems to me that this conclusion is not very far removed from the moderate and conciliatory conclusions of Stephen Walt and the Elmans. This encourages me to make my irenic proposal—not that we continue this debate hoping for greater light, reconciliation, or closure, but that we declare a religious peace, like the Lutheran-Catholic agreements in the mid-sixteenth century that kept Germany at peace for fifty years while much of the rest of Europe was plagued with religious war. Though we do not agree, the differences are not all that crucial, and each of us might reflect that we have worse opponents and threats to worry about. Political scientists are opposed by hard-line model-builders who believe that the discipline international relations scholars should emulate is theoretical economics, and who believe that the elegant sophistication of the political science model is more important than its connection with empirical reality or practice. Opposed to historians are post-modernists and metahistorians, for whom the notion that international history embodies a coherent narrative covering centuries of time and resting on solid evidence is an illusion, and the narratives that international historians construct are arbitrary inventions no more true or meaningful than fictional ones. Against such foes, we could at least be united in sympathy, if not action.

## Editors' Commentary

### Major Query

Is structural realism and its version of balance of power theory the best theoretical approach for understanding international history?

### Major Points

Schroeder's answer to the above question is "no." He shows systematically that, in almost all of the cases Waltz mentions, European states did not really react to hegemonic threats the way balance of power theory expects them to.

Schroeder begins by chastising Waltz for asserting historical patterns as if they were obvious and incontrovertible without a "serious effort" to see if these claims are consistent with historical research. In fact, he says he is struck with how little international history is in Waltz's (1959, 1967, 1979) books. Schroeder's most recent historical work (1994b) is on the transformation of European international politics from 1763–1848. He is well-equipped to look at whether reactions to Napoleon fit the realist generalization on the balancing of power. He states that in this work (Schroeder 1994b) he has shown "in detail how the normal reaction" of European states to Napoleonic France "was not to try to balance against it, but to accept the fact of Napoleonic domination." Balancing was never the preferred strategy of small states or the Continental great powers, as would be expected according to Waltz's proposition. Instead, states followed a number of strategies, including trying to share in the profits, working out some accommodation, "grouping" Napoleon into an alliance that would control him, or escaping as best one could. Even Britain, Schroeder argues, was willing to make a deal.

The reason there was any opposition to Napoleon and the reason he was defeated is not because states sought to balance his "excessive power," but because he would not leave them alone and let them accommodate themselves in a reasonable fashion to the hegemony he created.

Schroeder also points out that the coalition that ultimately overthrew the Napoleonic system did not go on and create a balance of power system but attempted to create a new system in 1815 (the Vienna System and Concert of Europe) that would transcend power politics, be based on a consensus among the great powers, and use conference diplomacy. Schroeder argues that, far from a balance of power, this arrangement amounted to shared hegemonies (a kind of spheres-of-influence strategy). This system worked to preserve the peace by basing it on a concert of the European powers.

Nor does Schroeder see most of Waltz's other cases of balancing holding. For example, the initial response to Hitler was not balancing but appeasement and bandwagoning. Schroeder questions whether Wilhemine Germany posed a hegemonic threat. More pertinent, however, is that regardless of this, diplomacy before 1914 centered not on balancing Germany but on making deals to divide up colonies. Similarly, the main challenges to Charles V were not efforts to balance by his main rivals—France and the Ottoman Empire—but local nobles and others who resisted taxes, etc. Of the various cases Waltz lists, Schroeder sees only Louis XIV as evoking balancing, and even here balancing follows only after other strategies, like appeasement, fail.

In each of these cases, it is the revisionist states' own continuing attacks that induce resistance and result in war. Accordingly, for Schroeder there is no pattern of states regularly balancing against power and hegemonic bids. In fact, hegemonies that are tolerable—British maritime hegemony, Russian hegemony over Eastern Europe, and U.S. hegemony in the Western Hemisphere—are quite stable and long-lasting.

Although a critic of structural realism, Schroeder does not conclude that realism should be "despised or discarded." He notes that realism continues to provide "penultimate truths" that cannot be forgotten, and captures characteristics that still prevail in some regions of the world. Nevertheless, one of Schroeder's main points is that realist theory puts history in a straitjacket that obscures what really happens by leaving too much out. It does not see important strategies, like "grouping" and attempts to transcend power politics to create order and peace.[1] Realists see international politics as essentially the same since Thucydides. For Schroeder, international history is characterized by change; it is open-ended—to see that, one must understand that international history is a real "history that goes somewhere" and not just the repetition of a law.

## KEY TERMS

**hegemonic bid**   The attempt to gain control or dominance of a region or the world.

**grouping**   A strategy whereby major states attempt to control another state by making an alliance with it for the purpose of limiting what that state will and can do (such alliances are called *pacta de contrahendo* [pacts of restraint]).

## NOTE

1. For the view that *binding*, a strategy similar to *grouping*, is consistent with realism, see Grieco 1995. For the view that it is not, see Keohane and Martin 2002.

# 10

# BALANCES AND BALANCING

## CONCEPTS, PROPOSITIONS, AND RESEARCH DESIGN

### JACK S. LEVY*

Over a decade ago, in the context of a review essay on the causes of war, I began a discussion of balance of power theory by writing that

> the balance of power is one of the oldest concepts in the literature on international relations, but also one of the most ambiguous and least tractable. . . . The central concepts . . . [of] balance, power, equilibrium, stability, are rarely defined in any rigorous manner. . . . Ambiguity is increased further by the tendency by some to equate balance of power theory with realist theory or with any theory utilizing power as a central organizing concept. . . . There is no single balance of power theory, but instead a multiplicity of theories. . . . The confusion is all the greater because balance of power theorists cannot even agree on what it is they are trying to explain. (Levy 1989, 228–229)

Nearly all of these ambiguities in conceptualization and causal specification continue to plague the literature on the balance of power. There are still many variations of balance of power theory, many variations of realist international theory, and considerable confusion about how best to conceptualize the relationship between them. Although most balance of power theories are realist theories,[1] not all realist theories are balance of power theories.[2]

In this paper I focus on balance of power theories and in particular on their hypotheses about balances and balancing, not on realist theory as a whole. I attempt to

---

*Earlier versions of this paper were presented at the Annual Meeting of the International Studies Association in February 2001, the International Studies International Convention in Hong Kong in July 2001, and at seminars at Harvard University, Dartmouth College, and McGill University. I thank Robert Art, Stephen Brooks, Michael Glosny, Ronald Krebs, Kevin Narizny, Henry Nau, Jon Pevehouse, William Thompson, William Wohlforth, and the editors of this volume for their helpful comments.

identify a common set of propositions shared by nearly all balance of power theorists, with the aim of developing some generally acceptable empirical tests that would help shift the debate from the level of abstract argument to the level of empirical evidence, a shift that is necessary if we are to resolve some long-standing debates about the empirical validity of balance of power theories.[3] In the process I highlight a number of conceptual issues that must be resolved before hypotheses about balancing can be tested empirically, and I try to identify the scope conditions under which key balance of power propositions are most likely to hold.

On one level, finding some common ground should be an easy task. Balance of power theorists have long argued that states demonstrate a strong tendency toward balancing behavior, and that as a result it is extraordinarily rare for any one state to achieve a position of hegemony or dominance over the system. Rarely, however, do these theorists define what constitutes balancing, power, or hegemony, or specify who balances against whom, in response to what kinds of threats, in what systems.

More recent theorizing associated with the balance of power tradition has helped to refine some aspects of the argument and generate additional hypotheses. Walt (1987) questioned whether Waltz (1979) was right that states balance against the strongest power in the system, and argued instead that states balance against the greatest threats to their interests, defining threats as a product of perceived intentions, ideology, and distance, as well as capabilities. Others posed more fundamental questions about balancing and asked whether states balance against power/threats or bandwagon with them (Waltz 1979; Labs 1992; Kaufman 1992; Walt 1992b), and Arquilla (1992) and Schroeder (1994a) argued that bandwagoning with the strong or hiding from them was more common than balancing. Schweller (1994) argued that status quo states may balance to preserve their security while revisionist states often bandwagon with the strong in order to secure economic gains and otherwise expand their influence; Barnett (1996) meanwhile, suggests that states sometimes balance against threats to national identity rather than against more narrowly defined security threats.[4]

Shifting the debate to a different level, Vasquez (Ch. 2, herein; 1997) examined the evolution of the neorealist research program on balancing behavior. He concluded that this aspect of neorealism was degenerating rather than progressive (Lakatos 1970) because it involved a series of ad hoc attempts to resolve theoretical and empirical anomalies in the balancing hypothesis without generating "novel facts" that could be tested over new empirical domains. Proponents of the balancing hypothesis responded to Vasquez's criticisms, with the debate focusing on the utility of Lakatosian metatheory as a normative standard for scientific progress, on the question of what counts as balancing, and on the historical record (Waltz 1997; Christensen and Snyder 1997; Elman and Elman 1997; Schweller 1997; Walt 1997; Chs. 3–7, herein). Still, there is no agreement on what might constitute a reasonable test of the balancing proposition, and certainly nothing that resembles a systematic (quantitative or comparative historical) empirical test.

The balancing/bandwagoning debate has potentially important implications for contemporary American foreign policy as well as for theory. If states tend to balance, arguments about the need for the United States to intervene around the world to stop regional aggressors and falling dominoes are less compelling, because states in the region will form new coalitions to restore an equilibrium of power and thus increase the anticipated costs of conquest.[5] If states tend to bandwagon, however, aggression can pay for itself by generating new resources and new allies, and external intervention becomes more imperative. Applied to the United States itself, some have argued that if balancing works, a new coalition will soon form in response to American hegemony in the world. If states tend to bandwagon, however, the United States can continue to extend its influence without much worry about generating a counterbalancing coalition; at the same time, however, it must anticipate that blocking coalitions will be slow to form against any rising military power in the future (Arquilla 1992). One of my primary arguments in this essay is that historically the leading states in the system have balanced against dominant continental states but not against dominant economic and maritime powers, and consequently we should not necessarily expect great power balancing against the United States in the early twenty-first century.

The question of whether or not states engage in balancing is very complex. There remains considerable confusion about what balancing is and what the theory predicts, and further conceptual clarification is necessary before ongoing theoretical debates can be fruitfully engaged at the empirical level. I am neither a committed proponent nor a committed critic of balance of power theory and its balancing hypotheses, but I think that it is imperative that debates about balancing be informed by the evidence. In this study I tackle some of the conceptual issues that plague the study of balancing, identify and refine some key hypotheses on balancing that are shared by most balance of power theorists, and identify the scope conditions for these hypotheses, with the aim of facilitating a shift in debates about balancing from the theoretical to the empirical level. Thus my focus is more on the level of theory specification and research design than on metatheory, and I leave aside the question of the progressive or degenerative nature of the realist research program as a whole or of its theory of balancing in particular.[6]

## WHAT DOES BALANCE OF POWER THEORY PREDICT?

This is not the place for a thorough review of balance of power theory (see Gulick 1955; Claude 1962; Morgenthau 1967; Aron 1973), but some background is necessary in order to identify the key propositions of the theory.[7] There is no single balance of power theory but, instead, a variety of balance of power theories.[8] Each begins with the hard core assumptions of realist theory—the key actors are states, who act rationally to maximize power or security under constraints in an anarchic international system—and then adds empirical content through the operationalization of power and other key concepts and through the specification of additional assumptions. As a result, different balance of power theories generate conflicting propositions about the actions and interactions of states. One example is the well-known debate about whether bipolar systems are more stable than multipolar systems (Waltz 1979; Deutsch and Singer 1969). Tests of the polarity hypotheses might constitute a test of a central proposition of Waltzian neorealism, but they do not necessarily bear on the validity of many classical balance of power theories.

Some balance of power theorists have argued that the purpose or function of a balance of power system is to maintain the peace (Wolfers 1962, Ch. 8; Claude 1962, 55).[9] Let us leave aside the analytical problems involved in postulating the purposes or goals of a system, which not only attributes to systems the properties of individuals but also confounds state preferences with international outcomes that are the joint product of the behavior of two or more actors.[10] The basic problem is that in most formulations of balance of power theory, states generally rank other goals higher than peace and conceive of war as an acceptable instrument to advance those ends, if only as a last resort. Such goals include the maintenance of the independence of states (Gulick 1955; Organski 1968; Waltz 1979; Wagner 1986; Jervis 1997,131), the avoidance of hegemony (Morgenthau 1967; Blainey 1973, 112; Sheehan 1996), or perhaps the general maintenance of the status quo (Kissinger 1964).

While balance of power theorists disagree over the relative importance of these goals, these objectives are in fact interrelated and can be conceived as a nested hierarchy of instrumental goals. The primary aim of all states is their own survival, defined in terms of some combination of autonomy and territorial integrity. There is a hierarchy of instrumental goals for achieving that end. The first is the avoidance of hegemony, a situation in which one state amasses so much power that it is able to dominate over the rest and thus put an end to the multistate system. There are several other goals that are seen as instrumental to the avoidance of hegemony. One instrumental goal is maintaining the independence of other states in the system, or at least the independence of the other great powers, which facilitates the formation of balancing coalitions against potential hegemons.[11] Another is maintaining an approximately equal distribution of power in the system, defined in terms of some combination of individual state capabilities and the aggregation of state capabilities in coalitions.

None of this is meant to suggest that individual states aim to limit their own power or objectives for the sake of the system. They often seek to maximize their own power and/or security, but maintain an equal distribution of power among others; pursue whatever aims they choose, but induce others to pursue more limited aims; promote the status quo, but only if it serves their own interests. They engage in balancing strategies, not for the primary purpose of maintaining a balance, but because limiting the power of others is necessary to maintain their own security and independence. That is, the maintenance of the "system" is the unintended consequence of the actions of many states, each of whom attempts to maximize its own interests under existing constraints.[12]

There are two causal paths leading to the absence of hegemony in balance of power theory, two reasons why the balancing mechanism almost always works successfully to avoid hegemony: (1) potential hegemons anticipate that expansionist behavior will lead to the formation of a military coalition against them, and refrain from aggression for that reason; or (2) potential hegemons pursue expansionist policies and are defeated in war by a blocking coalition. The first results in peace but the second does not, so that the outbreak of war, even major war, cannot necessarily be taken as evidence against balance of power theory or the balancing hypothesis. Balancing hypotheses predict either state strategies of balancing or an outcome of balance (or nonhegemony), not peace (Levy 1994).

It is true that the *power parity hypothesis* predicts that an equality of power between two states is likely to lead to peace, or at least that parity is more likely than preponderance to lead to peace.[13] But the power parity hypothesis is a dyadic-level hypothesis that assumes that alliances play no role,[14] while balance of power theory is a systemic-level theory in which alliances are central and in which the outcome of any particular dyadic-level balance of power between two states is theoretically indeterminate. For this reason, Walt's (1987) conception of bandwagoning to include the appeasement of threats in a dyadic relationship is an excessively broad conception of balancing, and Schweller (1994, 83) rightly criticizes Walt for providing a theory of how states respond to threats rather than a theory of alliances, which is an integral part of balancing.

Another point of disagreement among balance of power theorists, noted above, is whether states balance against the strongest power in the system (Waltz 1979) or against the greatest threats to their interests (Walt 1987).[15] Without trying to resolve that debate here, let me emphasize that one thing both sides of this debate would agree on is that states, and particularly great powers, will balance against a state that threatens to achieve a position of hegemony over the system, because any state strong enough to threaten hegemony will in most cases be the greatest single threat to the interests of any other great power.

In emphasizing that balance of power theory generates predictions of both strategies of balancing and outcomes of balance, I acknowledge that some scholars, most notably Waltz (1979) and some other structuralists, argue that his neorealist theory predicts only outcomes, not state strategies or foreign policies. He predicts that balances of power naturally occur but leaves open the question of *how* they occur. For Waltz, outcomes of balanced power do not necessarily require deliberate balancing behavior by states.[16]

It is important to note that Waltz is not always consistent in his argument that neorealism predicts balanced outcomes but not balancing behavior. At times he makes unambiguous statements about balancing behavior. He argues, for example, that "faced by unbalanced power, states try to increase their own strength or they ally with others to bring the international distribution of power into balance" (Waltz 1997, 915). He goes on to talk about "the reactions of other states to the drive for dominance of Charles I of Spain, of Louis XIV and Napoleon Bonaparte of France, of Wilhelm II and Adolph Hitler of Germany. . . ." (Charles I became Charles V when he became emperor.) In his allusions to balancing behavior, however, one thing that Waltz does not emphasize is the specific motivations for that behavior or the degree of rationality underlying it. His arguments best fit Claude's (1962) "automatic" conception of the operation of the balance of power.

It is clear that balanced outcomes and balancing strategies are analytically distinct, and that it is possible in principle to have one without the other. Certainly it is possible in principle to have balancing strategies that fail and end up in hegemonic outcomes. It is also possible in principle to have nonhegemonic outcomes without deliberate balancing strategies by states. This would be the result if no state had hegemonic ambitions. But if this outcome were the result of the fear of balancing, then balancing strategies play an important causal role even if states do not actually resort to them.[17] Another possible explanation for the absence of hegemony might be that even in the absence of constraints no state prefers hegemony. While this is possible, it seems to run against the basic thrust of most realist theories. Even Kant argued that "It is the desire of every state, or of its ruler, to arrive at a condition of perpetual peace by conquering the whole world, if that were possible" (in Wight 1986, 144). Waltz is free to argue that balancing is not a necessary condition for balanced outcomes, but it is incumbent on him to specify the alternative causal mechanisms through which nonhegemonic outcomes repeatedly (or always) arise, and to do so in a way that is consistent with the basic assumptions of neorealist theory.

Specifying the causal mechanisms leading to balanced outcomes is important for another reason. A theory that predicts only that balances will form, or that multistate systems will not be transformed into universal empires, has far less empirical content, and can explain far less variation in the empirical world, than a theory that predicts state strategies as well as international outcomes.[18] The loss of empirical content is particularly serious for neorealism, which generates relatively few testable propositions as it is (Keohane 1986c). In Lakatosian terms, a theory that predicts not only outcomes but the causal processes through which they occur is a scientific advance over one that predicts outcomes alone.

Because most balance of power theorists predict strategies of balancing as well as the absence of hegemony; because that is the stronger form of the theory (in terms of amount of empirical content, degree of falsifiability, and hence analytic power, but not necessarily empirical accuracy); and because the burden falls on those who do not hypothesize about balancing to specify the alternative mechanisms through which balances occur, I focus on versions of balance of power theory that predict strategies as well as outcomes.

## Conceptual Problems in the Analysis of Balancing

I have suggested that the two propositions that nearly all balance of power theorists would accept is that (1) hegemonies do not form in multistate systems because (2) perceived threats of hegemony over the system generate balancing behavior by the other leading states in the system. States with expansionist ambitions are either deterred by the anticipation of blocking coalitions or beaten back by the formation of such coalitions.[19] Most of the literature on balancing behavior focuses on the second proposition. Before hypotheses on balancing can be investigated empirically, however, we must be able to recognize balancing behavior when we see it. This raises a host of analytical problems that have either not been acknowledged or not been resolved in the literature. These are related to the degree and timing of balancing, preventive war and other forms of strategic interaction between the balancer and the target of balancing, and endogeneity and case selection. Let us consider each in turn.

## The Degree and Timing of Balancing

Waltz (1979) raised the question of whether states balance against stronger power or bandwagon with it. Most scholars have accepted this basic formulation of a dichotomy between balancing and nonbalancing, though some have specified numerous forms of nonbalancing behavior. These include the overlapping concepts of "shirking," "bystanding," or "noninvolvement/distancing" (Arquilla 1992) or "hiding" (Schroeder 1994a), perhaps because of "buck-passing" (Christensen and Snyder 1990). Schroeder (1994a) also suggests that states sometimes attempt to "transcend" threats by creating new international institutions and norms that will absorb or deflect those threats (see also Schroeder, Ch. 9, herein).

Critics have questioned Waltz's (1979) balancing hypothesis and argued that bandwagoning and other forms of nonbalancing are historically more common than balancing (Arquilla 1992; Schroeder 1994a).[20] This literature has been extremely useful in drawing attention to apparent historical violations of balancing hypotheses and in stimulating further research. Before we can make statements about the relative frequencies of balancing and nonbalancing behavior, however, we need rigorous operational criteria for distinguishing between the two, because balancing comes in different degrees and forms. The literature, which has to date been primarily qualitative in orientation, has yet to address this question of how to draw the line between balancing and nonbalancing behavior for the purposes of classifying behavior.

Two important issues concern the kind of behavior that constitutes balancing and the timing of balancing. Both proponents and critics of balancing agree that Britain balanced against Germany in World War I because Britain entered the war fairly quickly against Germany. But in the years leading up to the war, and even during the July crisis, Britain failed to make an unequivocal commitment to intervene in defense of France in the event of a German attack. This failure may have contributed in significant ways to the German and Austrian decisions for war (Fischer 1967).[21] Similarly, Britain engaged in appeasement in the late 1930s but eventually entered the war. As Vasquez asks (1997, 907; Ch. 2 herein, 37), "Were Britain, France, and the USSR passing the buck in the late 1930s, or were they just slow to balance?" Similar questions can be raised about the behavior of the United States, which intervened in each of the world wars but which made no effort to balance early in an attempt to deter the aggressor.

Intervention against the stronger state after the outbreak of war should not be excluded as a form of balancing. We know in retrospect that the course of certain wars led to overwhelming military victories by one side and subsequent intervention by third parties to limit or roll back the extent of those victories. Military outcomes are not always anticipated in advance, however, and intrawar balancing to maintain or restore equilibrium is an important form of balancing. Indeed, intrawar balancing may be more common than prewar balancing.

Still, the phenomenon of intrawar balancing leads to the question of how late a state might be in entering the war and still be classified as engaging in balancing behavior? Would we still classify Britain as a balancer if it had not entered the war in early August 1914 but instead waited until German armies had occupied Paris? Would we classify the United States as a balancer if it had not intervened until Hitler's armies had conquered nearly all of Europe? It seems to me that late balancing is still balancing, but it suggests the need to distinguish the fact of balancing from the timing of balancing, and to include the latter as a separate variable.

There are two qualifications. First, to qualify as balancing, military intervention must be directed against the strongest power or the greatest threat.[22] It would not be balancing if a third party enters the war against the expansionist state only after it has become clear that the aggressor would be defeated in war (the Soviet Union's late entry into the Pacific War against Japan in August 1945, for example).

Second, it would not be balancing if war is forced on the potential balancer by a direct military attack by the aggressor. As Schweller (1994, 83) argues, balancing involves a situation in which "a state is not directly menaced by a predatory state but decides to balance against it anyway to protect its long-term security interests." During the Napoleonic Wars, for example, the great powers of Europe generally did not balance against France, and when they did resist it was only because they were attacked by France (Schroeder 1994a, 135; Rosecrance and Lo 1996) Similarly, Stalin was forced into the war with Hitler when German armies invaded the Soviet Union, and Vasquez (Ch. 2, herein) is correct to argue that this should not be classified as balancing.

Questions also arise as to whether military alliances in peacetime (against stronger states) constitute balancing. Presumably formal, written defense pacts calling on all signatories to intervene in the event of a third party attack on any of them would be balancing, but nonaggression, neutrality, and entente pacts (as defined by the Correlates of War Project [Singer and Small 1968]) would not. The fact that Britain and France closely coordinated naval planning in the decade prior to the war and structured their respective war plans around those agreements (Williamson 1969) is a reminder, however, that balancing comes in degrees and that we need a separate dimension for the degree of balancing.

There are also questions relating to the intentions and motivations of the balancer and the perceptions of targets. States do not always live up to their commitments, and states sometimes intervene despite the absence of a formal alliance. Would it be balancing if a state signs a defense pact directed against an expansionist state but has no intention of honoring its commitment in the event of war? What if that alliance successfully deterred an external attack? Would it be balancing if a state does not form a formal alliance but has every intention of intervening in a war that would put an expansionist state in an unacceptably strong position (Britain and Germany in World War I, for example)? There is a wide range of ways in which states signal their intentions with respect to intervention (Morrow 2000), and we need to incorporate this fact into our conception of balancing.

Another question is how to classify behavior involving a combination of strategies, some of which may be consistent with balancing but others inconsistent. How do we aggregate these into an overall judgment on balancing? Churchill (1948) writes that the strategy of appeasing Germany was not necessarily a mistake as long as it was combined with one of using the time purchased by appeasement to undertake a major military buildup in preparation for the inevitable war. In fact, Carr (1939) called on England to pursue such a strategy, and Christensen and Snyder (1997, 921; Ch. 5 herein, 69–70) use this to argue that appeasement and balancing are not necessarily alternative strategies but in fact may be complementary ones. This might be true in principle, but whether it was true for Britain prior to World War II is open to question, as Britain made little effort to prepare for war while it attempted to appease Hitler (Watt 1989). Britain pursued a strategy of appeasement and, only after it failed, shifted to a strategy of balancing.

The Soviet Union adopted nearly the reverse strategy. It first tried to balance against Germany, and in fact went to great efforts to form an anti-German alliance with France and Britain. When Stalin could not come to terms with the Western powers, however, he reversed course and bandwagoned with Hitler by agreeing to the Nazi-Soviet Pact (Read and Fisher 1988). We talk about state strategies of balancing, and that makes sense in the context of intervention in an ongoing war, but prewar balancing through the formation of defensive alliances involves the actions of two or more states, not a single state. Intentions of balancing do not always materialize.

As this discussion and various historical examples and counterfactual possibilities make clear, balancing is a multidimensional concept that cannot easily be captured by a simple dichotomy of balancing and nonbalancing. While this dichotomy may be useful for some theoretical purposes, for many other purposes it is too limiting, and we need to think in terms of a range of balancing behavior that is characterized by different dimensions and degrees. We should distinguish the scale or magnitude of balancing (absent, weak, moderate, strong), the timing of balancing (early, late), and perhaps also the extent of balancing, defined in terms of the number or proportion of states (or of great powers) that engage in balancing behavior. There was great-power balancing against Revolutionary and Napoleonic France and against Nazi Germany, but in these wars states balanced at different times and with different intensities; some states switched from balancing to bandwagoning; and some states did not balance at all. We need, for many theoretical purposes, a more nuanced set of categories to help capture this variation in behavior.

## Preventive War

In the last section I noted that Vasquez and others argue that military resistance against an expansionist state does not count as balancing if it is a response to a direct attack. I accept this argument, but it raises an interesting analytical question and more difficult historical issue that we need to deal with in classifying balancing in particular cases. The interactive nature of decisions for war requires that we look not only at the behavior of the aggressor as well as that of the hypothesized balancer, but also that we ask why the aggressor attacks in the first place. It may be that the stronger state attacks the weaker one not because of blatantly expansionist motives, but because it anticipates balancing behavior by the defender and decides to take preemptive or preventive action (Levy 1987).

Frederick the Great initiated an attack on Austria in 1756, for example, but this is widely interpreted as a preventive war in anticipation of the formation of an offensive alliance and war against Prussia, which Frederick knew was planned for the following spring (Anderson 1966, 34; Dorn 1940, 312–314). If this interpretation is correct, then I would conclude that Austria and its allies intended to balance and Frederick acted in anticipation of balancing, so that balancing played a major role although Frederick initiated the war by attacking Austria.[23]

The possibility of preventive or preemptive attack in response to the anticipation of balancing raises a very difficult problem for the analyst who wants to differentiate between balancing and a response to military attack. It forces the analyst to make a judgment about the motivations of the attacker, and consequently to engage the historical literature on this question. This is rarely conclusive, given the conflicting interpretations of historians, but some judgments are more defendable than others.

Consider Vasquez's (1997) argument that the Soviet Union did not balance but was attacked by Germany in 1941. An alternative explanation is that Hitler assumed that Stalin would eventually enter the war against Germany, recognized that German power relative to the Soviet Union was peaking in 1941, feared that within two years Stalin would be a much more potent adversary, particularly in the context of a two-front war, and took advantage of a closing window of opportunity to invade the Soviet Union (Copeland 2000). Balancing plays a role in the second interpretation but not in the first. While one can find some evidence in support of the preventive war interpretation, there is enough written on the role of *Lebensraum* in Hitler's foreign policy and on planning for eastward expansion to suggest to me that Hitler planned this all along (Weinberg 1994).[24] On this basis I would tentatively conclude that the preventive motivation affected only the timing of Hitler's move against Russia, that this was an attack by an expansionist state, and consequently that the Soviet Union did not engage in balancing in summer 1941.[25]

## Endogeneity and the Problem of Case Selection

The possibility of preemptive or preventive action by an expansionist state against a prospective balancer raises an interesting problem of interpretation. If A attacks B in the anticipation of balancing by B, then balancing has a causal impact even though we do not actually observe B's balancing behavior. We encountered this problem of unobserved balancing before in our discussion of the two causal paths that lead to the absence of hegemony in realist theory: (1) restraint by potential hegemons because they anticipate that aggression would lead to a blocking coalition and a costly and possibly fatal war; and (2) the lack of restraint, aggressive expansion, the formation of a blocking coalition, and (usually) the defeat of the expansionist state. Balancing is central to each of these causal paths, but is observed only in the second. Behavior that is off the equilibrium path has no less a causal impact than behavior that we observe.

The possibility of unobserved balancing raises some important questions of empirical case selection, questions that have been mostly ignored in the literature (but see Jervis 1997, 137–139) and that seriously complicate the assessment of the relative frequency and causal importance of balancing. The problem with nearly all of the recent literature that tries to bring historical evidence to bear on the balancing proposition is that it focuses on the wars that have occurred and asks whether states balance or not. It does not look at the wars that have not occurred and ask whether the absence of war might be due to the anticipation of balancing by the potential aggressor. By ignoring strategic behavior by the potential aggressor and its impact on what we observe, existing studies of balancing systematically underestimate the causal importance of balancing in international politics.

It is conceivable that scholars' observations of a substantial number of cases in which states fail to balance against strong and/or threatening states reflects the possibility that balancing behavior is not particularly common. But the possibility of strategic selection leads to an alternative explanation. If states frequently balance in international politics, but if there is some uncertainty as to which states balance and under what conditions and in response to what kinds of threats, and if potential aggressors recognize this, aspiring hegemons will engage in expansionist behavior only in those situations in which they have some reason to believe that their potential enemies either will not balance or will balance ineffectively. These are the only cases that we observe, and consequently it is not surprising that we find a fair number of cases of nonbalancing. This is a biased sample, however, and it results in a systematic underestimation of the causal importance of balancing in international politics.

Analytic problems like these are now familiar in the literature, as researchers have become increasingly sensitized to problems of endogeneity and strategic selection (which makes it all the more surprising that this problem has not been given much attention in the literature on balancing). Consider the question of the relative success or failure of economic sanctions. Most of the empirical literature finds that economic sanctions frequently fail to accomplish their objective (Hufbauer, Schott, and Elliot 1990). The problem is that, until recently, the literature generally looked at sanctions and asked whether they succeeded or failed, but ignored the problem of strategic selection. If targets can anticipate that threatened sanctions would be successful, they will alter their behavior before sanctions are actually applied. Consequently, successful sanctions will seldom be observed. If, on the other hand, targets anticipate that sanctions will not be effective or that the cost of compliance would be too great, targets will not alter their behavior, sanctions will then be applied, and they will frequently fail (Morgan and Miers 1999).

There is thus a close parallel between the study of the relative success and failure of economic sanctions and the relative frequency of balancing and nonbalancing in international politics. Analyses of economic sanctions based on cases in which sanctions are actually applied will systematically underestimate the causal impact of sanctions by ignoring cases in which sanctions succeed by inducing "anticipatory compliance" with expected sanctions. Analyses of balancing that are based on cases in which balancing actually occurs will systematically underestimate the causal impact of balancing by ignoring cases in which balancing works because potential aggressors' anticipation of balancing leads them to strategically alter their behavior.

While there is no doubt that an empirical study of balancing that focuses on observable wars or grand coalitions underestimates the causal importance of balancing by ignoring unobserved balancing, what is not clear is the magnitude of this bias or how to estimate it. The basic problem is that the relevant cases are nonevents resulting from the potential aggressor's calculated restraint. It is hard to identify what this population of nonevents looks like or what criteria we should use for the selection of cases, because the potential population of such nonevents is extraordinarily large.[26] One thing that is clear, however, is that the common approach of selecting cases in which wars occur and then examining the presence or absence of balancing behavior in those wars is a form of "selection on the dependent variable" that has the potential to generate very biased results (King, Keohane, and Verba 1994).

It is far preferable to focus on the independent variable, the conditions or actions that are hypothesized to lead to balancing. Proponents of Waltz's theory, which hypothesizes that states balance against power, should examine cases of high concentrations of military power and analyze how frequently states balance in response to that power.[27] Those who hypothesize that states balance against threats rather than against power should devise a way of measuring the intensity of threats, generate a database, and then see if balance of threat hypotheses are consistent with the evidence.[28] Because balance of power theory and balance of threat theory lead to similar predictions if one state begins to approach a position of military dominance in the system, selecting all such cases (or a sample from them) would provide the basis for a test of both sets of hypotheses.

## THE SCOPE CONDITIONS OF BALANCE OF POWER THEORY

Our earlier review of the literature on balance of power theory suggests that despite the many different versions of balance of power theories, there are two core propositions that most balance of power theorists would accept: (1) if a state becomes strong enough to threaten to gain a position of hegemony over the system, other leading states in the system will balance against it, and consequently (2) hegemonies will rarely if ever occur.[29] I think that most critics of balance of power theory would accept these propositions as correct inferences from most versions of balance of power theory. This brings us closer to an empirical test that both proponents and critics of balance of power theory would accept as a "fair" test of the theory. There are some additional ambiguities in the meaning of the central concepts of states, system, hegemony, and power, however, and further clarification and operationalization of these concepts are necessary before we can think seriously about testing balancing propositions empirically.

First consider the domain of the proposition that states balance against hegemonic threats. Balance of power theorists speak very loosely about "states" balancing, but implicit in most versions of balance of power theory is a strong sense that it is the great powers that are expected (descriptively and perhaps normatively as well) to do the balancing. While both great powers and lesser states prefer that the power of an aspiring hegemon be limited, only the former are strong enough to make a difference. The weak know that they can have only a marginal impact on outcomes, and given their vulnerability and short-term time horizons, they will sometimes balance and sometimes bandwagon, depending on the context.

The great power bias in the balancing proposition is reflected in the long tradition of balance of power theory. As Claude (1989, 78) argues, "balance of power theory is concerned mainly with the rivalries and clashes of great powers and—above all ... *world wars.*" This bias is shared by most (but not all) traditional realist theories and most diplomatic histories (Levy 1989).[30] Waltz (1979, 72–73) is explicit in saying that any theory of international politics must necessarily be based on the great powers, for they define the context for others as well as for themselves. Formal theorists create stylized balance of power models consisting of just a handful of actors (Wagner 1986; Niou, Ordeshook, and Rose 1989; Powell 1996a). Theories of hegemonic decline, power transition, and hegemonic war clearly focus on the causes and consequences of the behavior of the leading powers in the system (Organski 1968; Gilpin 1981; Kennedy 1987; Thompson 1988; Rasler and Thompson 1994).

The very concepts of balance of power or equilibrium in the literature generally refer to a balance or equilibrium among the great powers, not among states in general. Many balance of power theorists, including those involved in debates over the relative stability of bipolar and multipolar systems, use stability to mean the absence of war, and by this they mean the absence of war between the great powers, not the absence of war in general.[31] Balance of power theorists do not regard wars between the weak, or between the strong and the weak, as constituting instability in the system. On the contrary, some balance of power theorists argue that imperial wars on the "periphery" of the system serve as a "safety valve" and play a stabilizing role.[32]

This conception of stability in terms of the absence of major war rather than the persistence of key structural features of the system is reflected in the fact that most balance of power theorists regard the periods of 1618–1659, 1672–1714, 1914–1918 as extremely unstable precisely because of the severity of general wars in those periods, even though the multipolar distribution of power in the system or other key structural properties of the system did not change. The collapse of the Soviet Union, the end of bipolarity, and the emergence of a single "hyperpower" was a fundamental structural change around 1989, but this process is not viewed as constituting instability because it was not accompanied by a major war.

Some recent formulations and applications of balance of power/threat theory, and the balancing hypothesis in particular, have focused on smaller states in regional systems (Walt 1987; Labs 1992). We need to be careful, however, in applying balance of power hypotheses drawn from the experience of the great powers to regional systems in which the assumptions underlying balance of power theory might not fully hold. In particular, the assumption of anarchy—the absence of any mechanism for enforcing agreements—is not fully satisfied in regional systems, where smaller states can sometimes appeal to actors outside of the system. Great powers in the larger system do not have this option. As a result, behavior in systems that are nested within larger systems may differ from behavior within the larger system.

Under some conditions, a state might choose to forego balancing against the strongest regional power (or greatest regional threat) if its survival and security are guaranteed by an external great power. How often this occurs, and under what conditions, remains to be theorized. In terms of outcomes, while hegemonies rarely form in larger great power systems, they occasionally form in local systems, often because such local hegemonies are not contrary to the interests of more powerful states outside the region.[33] This does not mean that Walt (1997) and others are wrong to apply balance of power/threat theory to regional systems, only that scholars must be very careful in doing so and must acknowledge the different structural contexts and their possible consequences.

Thus when most balance of power theorists talk about states balancing power, there is generally an unstated assumption that it is the most powerful states in the system (which might include the strongest regional states in regional systems) who do the balancing, not states in general. In addition, while balance of power theorists disagree about exactly what it is that great powers balance against, they agree that at a minimum great powers balance against states that threaten to achieve a position of hegemony in the system.

This hypothesis is not yet fully specified because the concepts of hegemony and system remain ambiguous. As I have argued elsewhere (Levy 1985, 1994), a key limitation of most hypotheses about polarity and the balance of power more generally is that scholars have failed to identify (1) the system under consideration and (2) the basis of power in that system. Until this is done, we cannot identify hegemons or hegemonic threats and consequently we cannot specify testable propositions about balancing behavior.

A reading of balance of power theorists who have had the greatest impact on the international relations literature over the past several decades (for example, Morgenthau 1967; Gulick 1955; Claude 1962) suggests that there is a strong Eurocentric orientation in balance of power scholarship. Most of the literature is written by Europeans (especially the British) and Americans (whose security outlook was primarily Eurocentric until the late twentieth century). This literature focuses on the modern European great power system going back to 1648 or perhaps to 1494/5 or the Italian city-state system (Mattingly 1955), and until the twentieth century the leading powers in that system have all been European. Even if we were to focus on the "modern world system" over the last five centuries, the "system leaders" have all been European (Wallerstein 1974; Thompson 1988).

There are numerous manifestations of the Eurocentric bias in balance of power theory. The concept of a "balancer" or "holder of the balance," while it can be generalized in principle, is nearly always equated with Britain's role in maintaining an equilibrium of power on the European continent by shifting its weight to the side of the weaker coalition (Dehio 1962; Morgenthau 1967). The hypothesis that the system tends to be most stable if there is a colonial frontier into which the dominant actors in the system can expand their power and influence without directly threatening the vital interests of other dominant actors also reflects a Eurocentric orientation (Morgenthau 1967, Ch. 14; Gulick 1955, Ch. 1; Hoffmann 1968; Wright 1965, Ch. 20).

Even the central claim that the balance of power mechanism works effectively to prevent hegemonies from forming (or the weaker claim that for whatever reason hegemonies have not formed) reflects the European experience, which has been characterized by the continuation of a multistate system and the absence of a sustained period of dominance of a single great power over the European continent over the last millennium.

While Waltz (1979) and many other balance of power theorists imply that the same patterns of balancing and balance hold in any system of two or more states, this was not true for the Chinese multistate system at the end of the Spring and Autumn period and Warring States period.[34] At this time a succession of military conquests transformed the multistate system in China into universal empire (within China) under the hegemony of the Qin Dynasty by 221 B.C.[35]

This raises the interesting questions of why a universal empire was established in China but not in modern Europe (Hui 2001), whether the European or the Chinese experience is the more common one (and thus whether the European experience is relatively unique), and the extent to which balance of power theories arising from the European tradition are applicable to (or are valid in) other historical systems. The answers to these questions have important implications for the extent to which key balance of power propositions can claim to be universal in their applicability, or whether even the most powerful of those propositions (hegemonies do not form) are themselves temporally and spatially bounded.

It is also clear that most international relations theorists and historians writing about the balance of power have implicitly conceived of hegemony in terms of dominance over the European system. For most of the literature on the balance of power, the foundation of potential hegemonic power is land-based military power based on large armies, supported in recent times by armor. Thus balance of power theorists talk about balancing coalitions against the Habsburgs under Charles V in the early sixteenth century, Philip II at the end of the sixteenth century, and the combined strength of Spain and the Holy Roman Empire in the Thirty Years War; against France under Louis XIV and then Napoleon; and against Germany under Wilhelm and then Hitler (Gulick 1955; Dehio 1962; Claude 1962; Morgenthau 1967; Aron 1973; Kennedy 1987). It is revealing that even Waltz (1997, 914; Ch. 3 herein, 54), who speaks in broader theoretical terms about balancing and balances in the international system as a whole, illustrates his arguments with examples of balancing against Charles I, Louis XIV, Napoleon, Wilhelm II, and Hitler.

Although it is common to refer to the Pax Britannica of the nineteenth century and to treat Britain as a hegemon or leader during much of that period,[36] that is a view associated with hegemonic stability theory (Keohane 1984), which generally conceives of power in terms of financial and commercial strength; power transition theory (Organski 1968), which operationally defines power in terms of gross national product; or leadership long cycle theory (Thompson 1988), which defines power in terms of naval capability and dominance in leading economic sectors. This is not to say that global economic power is unimportant, only that it is not a central concern of balance of power theories. One of the most important trends in the international system over the last five hundred years is globalization, but as Sheehan (1996, 115) notes, "the voluminous balance of power literature is almost completely silent on this issue."

Balance of power theorists, on the contrary, conceive of power in terms of military power and potential, and their identification of the leading threats to hegemony over the last five centuries (Charles V, Philip II, Napoleon, Wilhelm II, and Hitler) make it clear that military power is land-based military power. For balance of power theorists, it was Germany, not Britain, that was the leading power in the "system" by the end of the nineteenth century.[37] If Britain was a hegemon, it was a hegemon in finance, trade, and naval power on a global scale, not a military hegemon over Europe. Similarly, to the extent that the United States was a hegemon after World War II, it was because of American dominance in the world economy; in terms of military power, the situation was one of parity between the United States and the Soviet Union.[38]

From a balance of power perspective, it is not surprising that a blocking coalition did not form against Britain at the peak of its global economic and naval strength in the 1870s, but that one did form against Germany, the leading power on the continent, in the period leading up to World War I. Nor is it surprising that a great power balancing coalition formed in the late 1940s against the Soviet Union, the primary military threat to the major states of Europe, and not against the United States, by far the leading power in the world in terms of economic strength and naval and air power.[39] Similar logic explains why a balancing coalition did not form against the Netherlands in the seventeenth century despite its dominance in world trade, finance, and (until midcentury) naval strength (Israel 1989), but instead against Louis XIV and his massive armies (Levy 1985, 368).[40]

Maritime powers, as compared to continental powers, have fewer capabilities for imposing their will on major continental states, fewer incentives for doing so, and a greater range of strategies for increasing their influence by other means. One explanation for the lower levels of threats posed by maritime powers, at least to other great powers, the majority of which have been European over the last five centuries, derives from the fact that effective military power significantly diminishes over distance, especially over water (Mearsheimer 2001).[41] Large armies massing on borders, threatening to mass on borders, or simply having the potential to mass on borders threatens the territorial integrity of other states in a way that strong naval power or financial strength does not. Whereas European hegemons threaten their neighbors by virtue of their very existence, maritime hegemons do not.

Another explanation for the lower threat posed by maritime powers derives from the recent literature on territory and international conflict, which suggests that a disproportionately high number of wars involve territorially contiguous states; that unsettled territorial disputes are an important predictor of war; and that rivalries are significantly more likely to escalate to war if they involve territorial disputes (Vasquez 1993, 1996b; Huth 1996; Hensel 2000; Vasquez and Henehan 2001). The absence of territorial contiguity removes both a direct path for conquest and a source of many of the disputes that escalate to war, and hence removes an important source of threat.

Maritime powers differ from continental states in their interests as well as their capabilities, and those interests lead to different strategies. The goals of increasing commercial, financial, and naval power on a global scale do not require military or political control on the continent, and this leaves them less threatening to the major European states. Maritime powers may impose their will on smaller states and other actors, but that is not directly relevant for testing balancing hypotheses or balance of power theories more generally. Even with respect to small states, however, maritime powers often exert their influence through means other than overt military force. The "imperialism of free trade" (Robinson and Gallagher 1953) was as potent as military force in establishing British dominance in far corners of the globe.

Thus global maritime powers define their interests on a global scale and have fewer incentives to expand their influence in Europe, appear less threatening to European great powers, and are consequently less likely to trigger balancing coalitions. This does not imply that they have no stake in what happens on the European continent. They often perceive that their overall interests require that no single state achieve a hegemonic position in Europe, for fear that such a position might provide the resources for mounting a challenge to the dominance of the leading global maritime power on a worldwide scale. Thus the leading maritime power often plays a central role in balancing coalitions against potential European hegemons. It is not an accident that the global leader in economic and naval power plays the role of the "balancer" in balance of power theory.

There is another reason why most balance of power theorists have implicitly conceived of the absence of hegemony as the absence of European hegemony and of the balance of power as the balance of military power on the continent rather than the balance of naval and economic power on a global scale. That is because much of the literature that we read on the balance of power is British or American in national origin. Britain has long defined its interests in term of pursuing a balance of power on the continent but a preponderance of naval and colonial power, and the restriction of the balance of power concept to the continent provided a useful rationalization for those interests. The same can be said for American interests in American global dominance and a balance of power in Europe.

The Vienna settlement is often interpreted in terms of the balance of power (Gulick 1955; Kissinger 1964), but the system emerging from Vienna constrained France and possibly Russia while doing nothing to limit British naval or colonial power. As Bullen (1980, 15) notes, "the concept of the balance of power was hardly ever used except by British governments. The continental powers certainly did not consciously seek to uphold it." To the contrary, continental statesmen and scholars were often quite skeptical of the concept and the uses to which it was put. As the Duc de Choiseul pointed out, "the English, while pretending to protect the balance on land which no one threatens, are entirely destroying the balance at sea which no one defends" (quoted in Sheehan 1996, 115).[42]

The European orientation inherent in balance of power theories, as well as their potentially self-serving basis, is recognized by Sheehan (1996, 115):

> The balance of power concept for some 200 years after its confirmation as the basis of the European state system remained a purely European phenomenon. Its logic was not applied beyond the boundaries of the European continent. This may have been because the strongest proponent of the theory, Britain, had the most to lose from such a development. It may also have been related to the fact that the European balance of power idea was, in terms of its origins, part of a peculiarly European solution to the problems afflicting the European imagination.[43]

Although there is no necessary link between state policy interests and the scholarship conducted within its borders, it is no coincidence that scholars from the global maritime powers have generally emphasized a balance of power on the European continent while remaining silent on balance of naval, colonial, or economic power, while many on the continent advocate a balance of power on the seas and in the colonies as well as on land. This need not adversely affect the scientific evaluation of balance of power hypotheses, however, if we accept the view that the logic of confirmation is distinct from the logic of discovery (Popper 1959). Nevertheless, a sensitivity to the origins of an intellectual tradition can alert the researcher to the normative biases and scope conditions underlying those propositions and facilitate efforts to minimize the effects of those biases in empirical tests.

The great power, Eurocentric bias of most balance of power theories has important implications for American global hegemony and reactions to it in the early twenty-first century. Zakaria (2001) notes the puzzle of "why is no one ganging up against the United States? Throughout modern history countries have regularly resisted a rising global power. The world mobilized against Napoleon's France, imperial and Nazi Germany, the Soviet Union." There is an inconsistency between Zakaria's theoretical statement about responses to global power and his historical examples, which all deal with responses to land-based military powers. In terms of the implicit analytic and perhaps normative biases of balance of power theory, the absence of balancing against the United States is not a puzzle at all.

Nor is the absence of balancing against the United States a puzzle from the perspective of hegemonic stability theory, power transition theory, leadership long cycle theory, and other hegemonic perspectives, which emphasize the tendency for coalitions to form around the leading state to create a stable global political economy and security system—assuming the leading state is committed to a liberal international economy. Far from being a source of threat, liberal leaders can be the source of reassurance and stability. Thus Charles Maier (1987) speaks of "consensual hegemony," and Geir Lundestad (1986) speaks of an American "empire by invitation." From this perspective it is possible to have a "benign hegemon" (Friedman 1999, cited in Waltz 1999, 694). A balance of power theorist would never say this (but see Schweller and Wohlforth 2000, 74). For them, hegemonic powers are threatening not because of what they do but for what they are capable of doing. From a balance of power perspective, therefore, the failure of a grand coalition to form against the United States, if it continues, should not be taken as disconfirming evidence for balance of power theory's central proposition that great powers balance against hegemonic threats, just as the absence of balancing against Britain in the nineteenth century or the Dutch in the seventeenth century should not be taken as evidence against the balancing hypothesis.[44]

It is true that Waltz (1997, 915–916; Ch. 3 herein, 54; 1999) argues that the world will begin to balance against American hegemony, and implies that the absence of such balancing would constitute evidence against his neorealist balance of power theory.[45] Waltz is to be commended for specifying with such precision the kinds of evidence that he would take as falsifying his theory (though he does not make a similar argument about Britain in the nineteenth century), because the more precise we are in specifying what observable behavior and outcomes would lead us to abandon our theories, the greater the analytic power of those theories. Regardless of how Waltz wants to treat neorealism, however, any failure to balance against the United States should not be taken as evidence contrary to other formulations of balance of power theory, most of which have a strong Eurocentric orientation.

I have spoken of the implicit biases in balance of power theories, but let me frame this in a slightly different way. Waltz (1979) argues that his neorealist theory and its key propositions about the stability of multistate systems and the strong tendencies for hegemonies not to form are derived from a very limited number of assumptions: the existence of an anarchic system of two or more states who wish to survive. My argument is that Waltz's formulation of neorealist theory's balancing proposition as a universal law is probably incorrect. Waltz's theory—and indeed all theories of balancing behavior and balanced outcomes—is much more plausible if we add a scope condition that limits the domain of the theory to continental systems. Whether hypotheses of balancing and balances are valid for all continental systems, and not just for the European system over the last five centuries, is an important question that requires much more attention in the literature.

## Conclusions

The question of whether states balance or bandwagon is extraordinarily and deceptively complex. There is considerable confusion about what balancing is and what it is not, who balances against whom and how, how to identify balancing when it occurs, and the conditions under which propositions about balancing and balances are expected to hold. The critics of balance of power theory and its balancing proposition have made an important contribution by demonstrating that historically states do not always balance against the strongest states in the system or the greatest threats to their interests, but sometimes adopt other strategies. They have convinced me that if the question is whether states nearly always balance, the answer, based on the historical record, is almost certainly no. But if the question is whether states balance more frequently than they do not, or the conditions under which states balance, then we need a much more refined conceptualization of balancing and a method for measuring different dimensions of balancing before we can come up with an empirically-based answer to that question. One of my primary objectives in this study has been to add some conceptual clarity to debates about balancing.

My other objective, not unrelated to the first, has been to identify some key propositions that are shared by nearly all balance of power theorists, in order to help structure an empirical test that would be accepted by most balance of power theorists and their critics as a good test of the theory. I have argued that the core propositions shared by most balance of power theorists is that the emergence of any single state with the potential to dominate the international system will generate a blocking coalition of other great powers, and that consequently hegemonies over the system will not form. I have also argued that it is necessary to qualify these propositions by specifying their scope conditions: Balancing propositions apply to continental systems, and particularly to the European state system over the last five centuries, but not necessarily to global systems. We know that the European multistate system has not been transformed into a single empire, which leaves the question of whether European great powers have systematically adopted balancing strategies whenever a single state amasses a disproportionately large share of power in the system.

In terms of the logic of comparative inquiry, this is the "most likely" case for the balancing proposition (Przeworski and Teune 1970; Meckstroth 1975). If the balancing proposition does not hold here, our confidence in its more general validity would be significantly diminished, and in this sense this constitutes a good test of the balancing hypothesis.[46] Evidence that such balancing occurs would provide some support for the theory, but supporting evidence would increase our confidence in the theory less than discrepant evidence would diminish it, given the asymmetry in most-likely research designs. Because the United States is a global maritime power rather than a continental power, it falls beyond the scope conditions of the theory, and the failure of a general coalition to form against the United States in the twenty-first century would not necessarily contradict the assumptions underlying most formulations of balance of power theory.

## Editors' Commentary

### Major Query

Which hypothesis or hypotheses would best assess balance of power theory, and how should it or they be tested?

### Major Points

Levy attempts to identify the key problems that arise when trying to test propositions associated with balance of power theory, to provide solutions to these problems, and ultimately to come up with an empirical test.

He begins by pointing out that there is no one balance of power theory, but several. Accordingly, a prerequisite for testing is to determine what each theory predicts and what common propositions they share. Once this is done, it is still necessary to set out explicit criteria for determining when balancing and nonbalancing occur, so that it can be observed. Each of these tasks, which seem simple enough, turns out to be more complicated than meets the eye.

In terms of what balance of power theories predict, Levy documents that early theorists, going back at least to the Italian Renaissance, originally saw a balance of power system as a way of maintaining peace (see also Bueno de Mesquita, Ch. 12, herein). The problem, however, is that other balance of power theorists posit that states will go to war to balance power and/or prevent hegemony, and so they deny the connection between balance of power and peace. Still another disagreement is whether states balance against power (i.e., the strongest state in the system) or against threat. Then there are dyadic versions of the theory, which Levy sets aside because some see alliances as playing no role at this level. However, Levy argues that despite these differences "most balance of power theorists predict strategies of balancing as well as the absence of hegemony." The absence of hegemonic outcomes and the tendency for threats of hegemony to generate balancing behavior are the two key tests that most balance of power theorists should accept.

However, there is still the problem of determining when balancing behavior exists. Levy discusses several major problems. One of the more important is the timing of balancing. How late can balancing occur in order for it still to be seen as balancing? Recall in the previous chapter, Schroeder sees the failure of states to choose an initial strategy of balancing as evidence against Waltz. Levy agrees with Vasquez and Schroeder, as well as Schweller, that responses to a direct attack are not balancing. Nevertheless, he is prepared to admit some cases of late balancing as evidence in favor of the theory: for example, balancing that occurs during a war would count if it involves balancing against the stronger state or if it limits or rolls back the victories of that state.

Levy also analyses several more subtle questions, such as whether only certain kinds of alliances can be considered balancing (defense pacts for sure, but not nonaggression pacts or ententes); whether the intentions of states are relevant to the analysis of observed or unobserved balancing; and the role of backup strategies, or pursuing a combination of strategies such as using appeasement to buy time in order to balance more effectively later.

In addressing these questions, all of which are nicely illustrated by historical examples, Levy makes the point that balancing is a multidimensional concept that cannot be treated as a dichotomy (balancing or nonbalancing). This implies that a proper test will need to measure different aspects of balancing. These include: the *scale* or *magnitude* of balancing (whether it is absent, weak, moderate, or strong); the *timing* of balancing (when it occurs—early or late); and the *extent* of balancing (the number or proportion of great powers that balance).

Such measurement will go a long way in helping scholars marshal evidence for and against the balancing proposition. However, there are two instances where such measurement alone does not get at important evidence—preventive war and unobserved balancing. Levy points out that it is analytically possible that an expansionist state might anticipate balancing and therefore initiate a preventive attack before this balancing behavior can be actualized. Here, there would be no observable evidence of balancing on the part of other states, but the anticipation of balancing nonetheless affected the initiator's behavior. According to Levy, these cases of "dogs that do not bark" should count in favor of balance of power theory.

Preventive war is a special case of this more general problem of unobserved balancing. Levy maintains that the most effective form of balancing may be when a potential aggressor abandons expansionist goals in anticipation of balancing. Such unobserved cases never make it into the test sample, yet they constitute relevant evidence. A sample of cases that leaves out these **nonevents** can underestimate the evidence consistent with the proposition. Problems due to unobserved balancing are difficult to handle statistically, since they involve intentions and counterfactuals. Often they have to be discussed on a case-by-case basis, and Levy's analysis illustrates the kind of specific detailed discussion of historical cases that will need to take place to resolve these sorts of problems.

Levy concludes his chapter with a discussion of the scope of balance of power theory; i.e., to what domain it is applicable and to what it is not applicable. Based on the literature, he maintains that it applies to great powers and that it is especially relevant to Europe. In a more original vein, he goes on to argue that the balance of power propositions apply to military rather than economic power, and specifically to concentrations of land rather than naval forces. This leads him to conclude that it is primarily the attempt to prevent a hegemonic threat to a continental system containing major states that is the most natural domain for balance of power theory (which means for the modern state system—the European continental system). He points out that states did not balance against British maritime and economic hegemony in the nineteenth century or against Dutch maritime and economic hegemony in the seventeenth century, and he argues that this is not inconsistent with the logic of balance of power theory. He also engages current debates about responses to American hegemony, and using the implicit assumptions of traditional balance of power theory, he argues that the absence of great power balancing against the United States today is not surprising.

For Levy, a global naval power does not pose a threat to European land powers and therefore is less likely to evoke a balancing response. He states that Waltz's formulation of the balancing-of-power proposition as a universal law requiring only anarchy and a desire to survive "is probably incorrect," but a balance of power theory with a narrower scope might not be.

Levy suggests that most proponents and critics of balance of power agree that the theory predicts balancing against hegemonic threats in Europe (Waltz would predict balanced outcomes but does not insist that it is necessarily balancing foreign policy behavior that leads to those outcomes). If the main propositions of balance of power theory do not apply to the European continent, then it is unclear where they would apply. The European continent is the "most likely" case where it should hold. If it did not pass such a test, the credibility of balance of power theory would be severely undermined. Conversely, if it passed it would provide only limited evidence in favor of the theory, because it would be regarded as an easy test. In sum, Levy succeeds in stipulating a test that balance of power theory must pass, if it is to be taken seriously.

## Key Terms

**"most likely" case**  A case in which a theory is expected to hold; therefore, an easy test for the theory to pass. Failure to pass an easy test would lead many scholars to conclude that the theory is false and should be rejected.

**non-events**  Events that do not result in observable behaviors when measured using the theory's concepts and operationalized variables. For example, a would-be hegemon may anticipate a countervailing balancing coalition, and so moderate its actions. The case will appear to contain neither expansion nor balancing, when in fact it provides strong support for balance of power theory.

## Notes

1. Exceptions might include Grotian conceptions of a balance within international society (Bull 1977; Sheehan 1996, 199–200).
2. Realist international theory includes both hegemonic realism and balance of power realism, which generate diametrically opposed predictions about the consequences of extreme concentrations or deconcentrations of power in the system (Levy 1994, 2002a). Balance of power realism includes both classical theories as reformulated by Morgenthau (1948), Gulick (1955), and Claude (1962), and the more systematic structural realism of Waltz (1979). Hegemonic realism includes power transition theories, hegemonic stability theory (Gilpin 1981; Keohane 1984), and leadership long cycle theories (Thompson 1988; Rasler and Thompson 1994). This distinction is obscured by standard classifications of realist theory that focus on the differences between various forms of classical realism and contemporary structural realism (Frankel 1996c; Doyle 1997; Schweller and Priess 1997; Rose 1998; Brooks 1997). Waltz's (1979) neorealist propositions about the balance of power, for example, have far more in common with classical realist balance of power theories than with Gilpin's (1981) structural realism.
3. This is an important theme in Vasquez's introductory essay in this volume. Distinguishing between balance of power theory and realist "theory" is a necessary step toward the construction and testing of falsifiable theories, because the conflicting predictions of different versions of realism mean that nearly any behavior or outcome is consistent with some version of that paradigm, leaving realism as a whole nearly immune to empirical falsification.
4. Alliance formation in pursuit of economic gain is not limited to revisionist states, as Barnett and Levy (1991) demonstrate in their study of the domestic political economy of alliance formation in the Third World.
5. This raises the question of whether there are strategies by which the United States might diffuse any potential opposition and prevent blocking coalitions from materializing. For a theoretical discussion of how leading states construct an institutional order that helps to co-opt their potential adversaries, see Ikenberry 2001.
6. For my own views of the utility of Lakatosian metatheory for the analysis of international relations, and for an application to the research program on power transitions, see DiCicco and Levy 2002.
7. On the varied uses of the balance of power concept, see Haas 1953, Claude 1962, and Sheehan 1996. I treat the balance of power as a theory of state behavior and international outcomes in anarchic systems

consisting of two or more states. The use of balance of power in a descriptive sense to refer to a particular distribution of power in the system (an equal balance, a favorable balance, or any distribution) is confusing, and it is better to use the term distribution of power. The concept of a "balance of power system" generates additional conceptual baggage and provides no value-added over a view of the balance of power as a theory of behavior that includes variations in system structure as key independent variables. Systems are not real; they are analytical constructions that theorists use to describe and explain reality.

8. It might be more accurate to say that most balance of power theories are sets of discrete hypotheses rather than logically interconnected theories. More formal attempts to model balance of power theory include Wagner 1986, Niou, Ordeshook, and Rose 1989, and Powell 1996a. For a formalized argument that key predictions of Waltzian neorealism cannot be derived from the theory's assumptions, see Bueno de Mesquita's essay in this volume.
9. This goes back at least to Giovanni Botero, who wrote in 1589 that balances produce peace and that by balancing power Lorenzo de Medici had kept Italy at peace for many years (Sheehan 1996, 33).
10. States might prefer peace over war, yet find themselves locked in a structural dilemma (such as a prisoners' dilemma) that leads to war.
11. The term *independence of states* is ambiguous in balance of power theory. It is necessary to distinguish between one's own state, other great powers, and other states. Maintaining the independence of one's own state is an irreducible national value. Maintaining the independence of other great powers is a means to that end, not an end in itself. Maintaining the independence of weaker states in the international system as a whole is not generally regarded by most balance of power theorists as being among the highest priority goals of states, particularly of great powers. In traditional formulations of balance of power theory, for example, the partitioning of weak states is often mentioned as a possible strategy for maintaining equilibrium in the system (Gulick 1955).
12. This is Claude's (1962) "automatic" conception of the balance of power, formalized by Waltz (1979); see also Jervis 1997,132. An alternative view of the balance of power argues that a stable balance of power system requires some degree of restraint by individual actors (Gulick 1955, 33; Kaplan 1957) or a "moral consensus" (Morgenthau 1967, 208–215) as to the legitimacy of the system. For a more systematic argument regarding the role of norms of restraint and conceptions of self-interest in terms of the security of the broader community, see Schroeder 1993.
13. Waltz's (1979) neorealist theory also predicts that bipolar systems are more stable than multipolar systems, but Waltz defines stability in terms of the persistence of key structural characteristics of the system (anarchy, number of major actors), not the relative frequency of war or peace.
14. Most quantitative empirical research demonstrates that at the dyadic level peace is associated with a preponderance of power (Kugler and Lemke 1996), not a parity of power.
15. Waltz (1979), Mearsheimer (2001), and most "offensive realists" argue that because under conditions of anarchy security is scarce and the intentions of others are always uncertain and subject to change, power is inherently threatening, there are no benign hegemons, and consequently states balance against power. Walt (1987) and most "defensive realists" argue that anarchy does not necessarily imply insecurity, that states judge security threats in terms of others' intentions as well as capabilities, and that consequently they balance against the greatest perceived threat rather than against the greatest power. On the distinction between offensive and defensive realism, see Frankel 1996a and Levy 2002a.
16. Arguments over whether or not states consciously and deliberately balance power is reminiscent of Claude's (1962) distinction between automatic, semiautomatic, or manual conceptions of balance of power systems. Balances form without the conscious calculations of states in the first conception, only with conscious and calculating balancing strategies by all states in the third conception, and with deliberate balancing by one state (the "balancer") in the second conception.
17. This is what game theorists refer to as behavior "off the equilibrium path."
18. On the debate over whether neorealism incorporates a theory of foreign policy, see Elman 1996a and Waltz 1996.
19. I use deterrence in the broad sense of an actor being dissuaded from taking an action for fear that the expected costs and risks of that action exceed the expected benefits, either because of successful defense on the battlefield or, particularly in the nuclear age, threats of punishment away from the battlefield. While the deterrence concept was not commonly used before the nuclear era, political leaders and scholars would have clearly understood its meaning.
20. Similarly, Schweller (1994a, 99) argues that contemporary realist theory has underestimated the frequency of bandwagoning.

21. Thus Britain's failure to balance against Germany before August 1914 contributed to the outbreak of the war while its balancing after the outbreak of war helped avoid a German hegemony over Europe.
22. It must also be a substantial, not token, intervention. The context is different, but would we say that Western states "balanced" against the Bolshevik threat in the Russian Civil War, given the limited nature of their intervention?
23. Similarly, Louis XIV declared war against the Holy Roman Emperor in 1688, beginning the War of the League of Augsburg. This war involved balancing, however, because a defensive coalition had already formed and Louis may have acted preventively out of a defensive strategy to maintain the status quo in Europe rather than an offensive strategy to expand his influence (Lynn 1999).
24. An argument that Stalin had planned an aggressive war against Nazi Germany but was preempted by the German invasion is made by Suvorov (1990) and persuasively rebutted by Gorodetsky (1999).
25. But remember that the Soviet Union tried to balance earlier but could not reach an agreement with the West on the terms of an alliance.
26. This is similar to the problem of general deterrence. Did American military might and the NATO alliance successfully deter the Soviet Union from invading Europe, or did the Soviets have no intentions of invading in the first place?
27. A secondary hypothesis might be that higher concentrations of power lead to stronger balancing, though this is more difficult to analyze because many instances of strong concentration of power will be unobserved because balancing will take place at lower levels of concentration.
28. The difficulty of identifying and measuring threat perception independently of the behavior that is hypothesized to follow from those threats is one reason why it is far easier to test Waltz's (1979) hypothesis of balancing against power than Walt's (1987) hypothesis of balancing against threats. Schroeder (1994a) goes further and argues that balance of threat hypotheses have little meaning because they cannot be empirically falsified.
29. Recall that individual states seek the absence of hegemony not as an end in itself but rather as a means to self-preservation.
30. The majority of Western diplomatic historians have followed Leopold Von Ranke (1833/1973) in conceiving European history as the history of great power relations. A. J. P. Taylor (1954, xix), for example, argues that "the relations of the great powers have determined the history of Europe."
31. Waltz (1979) is in the minority in defining stability in terms of the persistence of key structural characteristics of the system.
32. This is one basis for the common argument that in any given period wars are either frequent but limited, or infrequent but serious, but not both frequent and serious (Morgan and Levy 1990).
33. Similarly, Jervis (1997, 133) notes that "although the overall balance of power system has never failed, local ones have."
34. The fact that the multistate system was transformed, for a time, into a hegemonic system does not necessarily imply that states did not adopt balancing strategies. The absence of balance does not necessarily imply the absence of balancing.
35. Though this lasted less than two decades, a universal empire was reestablished under the Han Dynasty.
36. For different assessments of the influence of British leadership in the nineteenth century, see Ingram 2001 and Thompson 2001.
37. As I have argued elsewhere, balance of power theories and "hegemonic realist" theories generate diametrically opposed predictions regarding the consequences of various distributions of power, which is right at the heart of realism (Levy 1994, 2002a).Whereas balance of power theories see hegemony as rare, hegemonic theories see it as quite common. Whereas balance of power theories suggest that the probability of a major war is quite high when concentrations of power are high, hegemonic theories predict that the probability of major war is quite low under conditions of high concentrations of power. Whereas balance of power theories imply that the probability of a major war is relatively low when there is a fairly equal distribution of power among the individual great powers and among great power coalitions in the system, hegemonic realists see that as the point of the highest probability of a major war, when the declining leader is being overtaken by the rising challenger. For an argument that balance of power theory and power transition theory are complementary, see Schweller and Wohlforth 2000, 73).
38. My arguments about the differences between the European and global systems emerged from my critique of Thompson's (1988) leadership long cycle theory and its primary focus on the global system. In part because of the influence of Thompson's work, however, I now emphasize the interactions between the European and global systems.

39. There is another sense in which the NATO alliance is consistent with my argument regarding the fear of concentrations of continental power and the absence of fear of concentrations of global power. In the often-quoted words of Lord Ismay, the purpose of NATO was to "keep the Russians out, the Germans down, and the Americans in."
40. There are enough cases of balancing against naval power to suggest the desirability of more research on the theoretical conditions under which this is most likely to occur and how these differ, if at all, from balancing against land-based power on the continent. France, Spain, and the Netherlands entered the War of the American Revolution against Britain, for example.
41. This "loss of strength gradient" (Boulding 1963) is to a certain extent a function of technology, but for much of the past five centuries of the modern system even fairly narrow bodies of water significantly diminished the ability to project military power. Palmerston's midcentury observation that before the steam engine, the English channel was "impassible by a military force" (quoted in Brodie 1941, 49) is quite revealing, and most observers argue that Palmerston overstated the impact of steam on British vulnerability to a cross-channel invasion. Even today analysts debate whether China has the military capability of mounting a successful military conquest of a much weaker Taiwan.
42. The argument that the territorial balance of power in Europe should be combined with a balance of colonial and maritime power was made by the Germans as well as the French. In fact, Sheehan (1996, 137) argues that German writers made a distinctive contribution to balance of power thinking through their willingness to discuss the concept in global terms, which, he argues, the British rarely did. Of course, the German argument was also a convenient rationalization for their repeated charges that their own efforts to acquire territories and influence beyond Europe were being blocked by Britain and other global powers.
43. While one can find occasional reference to balance and the balance of power going back to ancient Greece, Sheehan (1996, Ch. 2) argues that the systematic use of the concept originated in the intellectual uncertainty and crisis of authority that followed the Renaissance and Reformation and that led to a search for intellectual order and harmony.
44. For another perspective on the absence of balancing against the United States, see Brooks and Wohlforth (2002, 24–27).
45. Kegley (1993) argues that the emergence of a multipolar system from the present unipolar system would constitute vindication of realist theory. Waltz (1999, 915) agrees, and goes on to say that "to all but the myopic . . . [multipolarity] can already be seen on the horizon." This is consistent with Layne's (1993b) argument that new great powers always rise in response to unipolarity.
46. Whereas least-likely research designs are based on what I call the "Sinatra inference" (if I can make it there I can make it anywhere), most-likely research designs are based on the inverse Sinatra inference—if I cannot make it there I cannot make it anywhere (Levy 2002b).

# 11

# IS THERE A BALANCE OF POWER?

*RICHARD ROSECRANCE*

This collection of essays considers whether decreasingly credible claims concerning the continuing operation of a balance of power constitute degenerative features of the realist paradigm. In this dispute, much depends on definitions or uses of the key term *balance of power*.

I seek to make four points in this essay. First, if *balance of power* is defined broadly, it may accommodate apparent exceptions to its operation but at the expense of empirical content. Second, if *balance of power* is defined narrowly (and is not subject to definitional extension to cover the deviant case), the essential constituents of balance of power are frequently absent in the international system. Many if not most actions heretofore described as "balancing" do not meet such criteria. Third, individual responses to threat (whether technically balancing or not) typically take a different form than usually assumed in the balance of power literature. Fourth, even if balancing is not a ubiquitous feature, its absence does not constitute an anomaly in our understanding of the interstate system because the absence of *hegemony* in international politics has never depended solely on the presumed existence of balance of power mechanisms.

## BROAD DEFINITIONS OF BALANCE OF POWER

According to some definitions of the term, *balancing* is akin to *competition* in economics. In Glenn Snyder's (1997, 17) words, "competitive security seeking produces equilibrium much as, in classical economic theory, competitive profit seeking gives rise to an equilibrium of supply and demand at the lowest possible price." In like manner, Kenneth Waltz's (1979, 128) "expectation is not that a balance, once achieved, will be maintained, but that a balance once disrupted, will be restored in one way or another. Balances of power recurrently form." He also believes "balance of power theory applies in all situations where two or more units coexist in a self-help system" (Waltz 1979, 57). The validity of these claims depends on a broad definition of the key concepts, *power*, *balance*, and *equilibrium*. Countries often do not "balance" in the narrow meaning of the term. The public goods problem which balancing confronts may lead some states to become shirkers or *free riders*.[1] Others may *bandwagon* on the side of the strongest power for material gain.[2] The particular *equilibrium* that emerges in economics or international relations may leave one or more firms or states in a situation of preponderance. Oligopoly and monopoly may emerge from competition in economics if there are economies of scale. Some states may be strengthened by the competition process, while others are weakened. While no international hegemonic power has been strong enough to transform the state system itself, Charles V's Hapsburg Empire, early-Victorian Britain, and post–World War II America possessed power beyond that of their colleagues and competitors. In addition, all three were remarkably free from *balancing* operations directed at reducing their preponderance. In the seventeenth century, France's Louis XIV encountered opposition but it was largely of his own making, stemming from his attack on other states. As Paul Schroeder points out, British and Austrian reactions to Louis XIV's invasions during the period 1660 to 1713 cannot be explained by simple notions of the balance of power.[3] The British opposition after 1688 was caused by William of Orange's ascension to the throne of England. Prior to his accession, restoration England had been a virtual tributary of France. As we will see in more detail later, there are many exceptions to typical balancing processes both currently and in the historic past.

Imagine a theoretical concept like *balance of power* that correctly arrogates a realm of empirical events. It might be depicted as in Figure 11.1.

Then let us suppose that a series of new events are discovered that do not fall neatly or at all under the old definition of the concept. If the linguistic breadth of the concept is simply extended to cover the deviant cases, we have learned nothing. We have manipulated definitions, but discovered nothing about reality.

| CONCEPT (definition) | Balance of Power | |
|---|---|---|
| REALITY (number of events) | x x x x x x x x x x<br>x x x x x x x x x x<br>x x x x x x x x x x<br>x x x x x x x x x x | x<br>x<br>x (new events)<br>x |

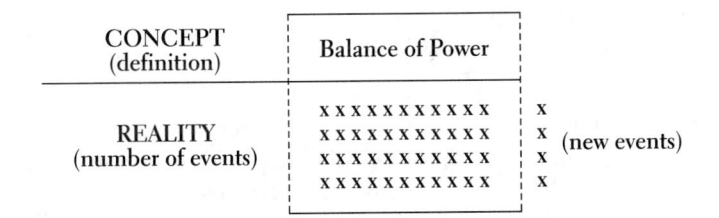

FIGURE 11.1

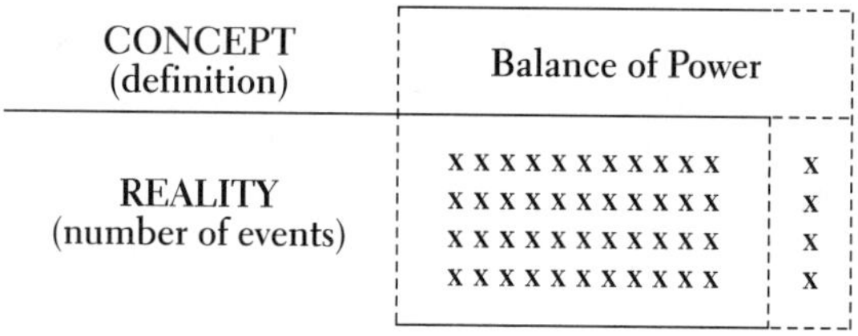

|  | Balance of Power |
|---|---|
| CONCEPT (definition) |  |
| REALITY (number of events) | x x x x x x x x x x x   x<br>x x x x x x x x x x x   x<br>x x x x x x x x x x x   x<br>x x x x x x x x x x x   x |

FIGURE 11.2

In Figure 11.2 (unlike in Figure 11.1), the definition of the term *balance of power* has been extended to cover the anomalies. While this linguistic operation may have protected the key concept against refutation, it does not advance the field of study in any empirical manner. If a series of such amendments occur in which the central definition is progressively extended to cover each deviant case, one may enter a realm in which the paradigm becomes useless in any empirical sense. If, ultimately, one cannot even think hypothetically of a single case that could not be explained by this (indefinitely extensible) theoretical term, the theory loses all value.[4] This will be true even though there may be no alternative paradigm to replace it.[5] The truth of key propositions then comes to depend upon the meaning of words rather than the nature of reality. It was basically the failure to meet such tests that led to the progressive disutility of Hans Morgenthau's initial power theory.[6] Kenneth Waltz's rejoinder to this point is unconvincing.[7] In scientific theories, the structure of a theory may be "undisprovable," but propositions or empirical applications derived from the theory can be tested. This is true in physics, and it is also true in Darwinian evolution. If the theory fails such tests, its validity and empirical application are cast into doubt. In similar fashion, citing and then criticizing Colin and Miriam Elman's version of realism, Vasquez contends:

> Thus Schroeder's finding that states failed to balance prior to World War I . . . and World War II . . . does not disconfirm Waltz's argument. . . . In short, a failure to balance is not a failure of balance of power theory if systemic conditions are unlikely to generate this sort of outcome in the first place" [Elman and Elman]. . . . This sets up a situation in which any failure to balance under multipolarity can be taken as confirmatory evidence because, according to Elman and Elman . . . "Waltz's theory also predicts balancing failures." This poses an: "I win, you lose" bet.[8]

If concepts in international relations undergo progressive (one might even say degenerative) linguistic extension in this manner, then the power paradigm may merely become equivalent with "states pursue their own interests" or "cost benefit criteria apply to state behavior."[9] These formulations may be correct but unless they are further elaborated and developed, they give us little information about international reality.

## Narrow Definitions of "Balance of Power"

As we have seen, when key theoretical terms are broadly defined they can apply to a very wide realm of international behavior, but what we learn empirically from such theories is minimal. The situation is very different when definitions of key terms are precise and narrow in scope. If narrowly defined key terms can still be shown to apply to a wide range of international events and discourse, we have learned a great deal about international reality. Typically, such outcomes result from the normal procedures of natural science. How might they be applied to such a protean concept as the balance of power?

One way to render them applicable is to compile a checklist of the features of balance of power intentions and policies that need to be present for us to claim that a *balance of power* is in effect. The following list seeks to accomplish this objective:

### Essential Characteristics of Balance of Power

1. The existence of opposition between states does not necessarily indicate the presence of a balance of power. In a bipolar opposition, the fact that the weaker side resists the stronger side is not necessarily reflective of a "balancing" motivation on the latter's part. If the stronger pole seeks to annex or aggrandize the weaker pole, the latter's resistance does not indicate "balancing," but simply self-preservation. The victims of Napoleon's aggression resisted individually, but there was no overall balance forged against the French Emperor.[10] Balancing intentions, thus, are critical to the existence of a balance. Self-defense is not enough; it must be accompanied by motivations and policies favoring generic, even systemic, defense.

2. For the balance of power to exist, a state must balance against the stronger side and in favor of the weaker. Any other response is bandwagoning, shirking, or free-riding.[11] Presumably a nation must balance proportionately more strongly as the threat/power of the competitor grows. After 1812, Austria and Prussia turned against France. But their action was bandwagoning in favor of the Russian victor, not balancing against France. They were favoring the stronger, not the weaker side.

3. The existence of war does not necessarily indicate the operation of a balance of power. Wars may be aggressive in their origins and causes. Wars launched by a series of defenders against an individually stronger aggressor, however, would classify as balance of power wars. In this sense, it still remains unclear whether World War I was an aggressive or a balance of power war. The answer to this question depends upon the respective role of Germany and Austria on the one side as against Russia and France on the other in causing the war.

4. Power balancers must aim to create the public good of security against hegemony of the system as a whole, not simply to defend themselves. Glenn Snyder explicitly recognizes this point, but contends that if individual states did not ultimately balance they would be risking their own national security. He believes that resistance is warranted as the aggressor's power mounts.[12] But then, of course, the cost of prevailing is also much greater and continued resistance may amount to national suicide. Sometimes analysts erroneously assume that defeat or surrender is equivalent to national extinction. As Paul Kecskemeti shows, this is

not true.[13] Czechoslovakia was not the only state that rolled over in face of Hitler's pressure. Sweden and Switzerland did so.[14] The former provided steel and other raw materials to Hitler. The latter opened its financial markets to him. In both cases, their pro-German "neutrality" saved them from invasion. Danish and Dutch resistance was minimal. Even France did not initially organize armed resistance against the German dictator, and some Frenchmen remember the early days of the German occupation with nostalgia.

5. The balance of power is not a simple analogue of the competition of market economics. Firms do not seek to maintain each other's existence or to safeguard the stability and integrity of a market system as a whole. They seek to improve their own position and to make a profit. Sometimes they also seek to increase market share.

If we apply these criteria to particular episodes and periods, we observe that the balance of power functions much more rarely than the conventional wisdom presumes. It does not apply to Napoleon. Hitler was not resisted until the end, and the resistance was usually the result of his own aggressive attacks. Neither the Soviet Union nor the United States, it can be argued, would have come into the war had Hitler not attacked or declared war on them. Christensen and Snyder admit that Britain, France, and Russia underreacted to Hitler's threat, but then conclude that since Germany was defeated, someone must have balanced against him. Germany's defeat, however, was the result of Hitler's own vaulting ambition, which allowed him to declare war on and attack countries whose involvement in war against Germany would in fact forge a balance of power against him—not of the patient creation of a balance of power by defending states.[15] As we have seen, the balancing origins of World War I remain an open question, the answer to which depends on which state one believes started the war. German Chancellor Otto von Bismarck was not balanced against, except perhaps in the "War in Sight" crisis of 1875, and yet Germany remained the center of all European alliances and alignments and the dominant land power for a generation.[16] From 1840–1860 Great Britain was the preponderant industrial and naval power and yet did not encounter a continental coalition directed against it, despite Lord Palmerston's occasional bellicosity. Its immunity to balancing provides additional evidence in support of Stephen Walt's argument that if states balance at all, they balance against threat not against power. The same argument provides an answer to those who believe that the United States will today become the target of a counter-coalition of balancers.[17]

The Cold War provides what many believe is the classic case of balancing against an aggressive power, but again the question is not so simple. While the USSR had aggressive as well as defensive motives, some in the Kremlin may have thought they were balancing against the United States, and the American revisionists largely agreed with them. Melvin Leffler sketches an America ready for an expansion of its power in economic and diplomatic, if not territorial terms.[18] Those who joined the United States against the Soviet Union were, from this point of view, bandwagoning in favor of America, not balancing against the Soviet Union. They were also getting economic benefits from the stronger side. In any event, the mere opposition of two power blocs does not by itself indicate the operation of a balance of power. Motives need to be understood for us to know whether one or the other party seeks a balance. While Stalin probably wished to expand Soviet territorial boundaries, America favored ideological and economic expansion. Mutual expansion, however, is not mutual balance.

In short, for "power balancing" operations to exist, a state must (1) entertain defensive, not offensive motives; (2) join the weaker coalition; (3) seek to defend not only itself, but others similarly menaced and (as far as its resources permit) the system as a whole. It must, in other words, seek to solve the public goods problem. Simple inspection of the record shows that these three criteria are infrequently met.

Thus, it is not certain that a rigorous and narrow definition of balancing will turn up as many cases as the conventional wisdom presumes. States may do what is in their own interest, but a much stronger case needs to be made that they would and do place safeguarding the stability of the system over and against their short-term interests in avoiding conflict or war. Nor is it at all clear, despite Snyder's argument, that they will be forced to resist an aggressive power in the longer term (unless that power attacks them). Even then, they may temporize or even resign their struggle.

## THE PATTERN OF INDIVIDUAL RESPONSES TO THREAT

If the system often fails to provide a balance against a putative aggressor, individual nations also respond differently to threat. If the balancing hypothesis is correct, it should involve a direct and increasing response to equally increasing threat. In Figure 11.3, we assume monotonically increasing threat and focus upon the balancing responses of the defending state.

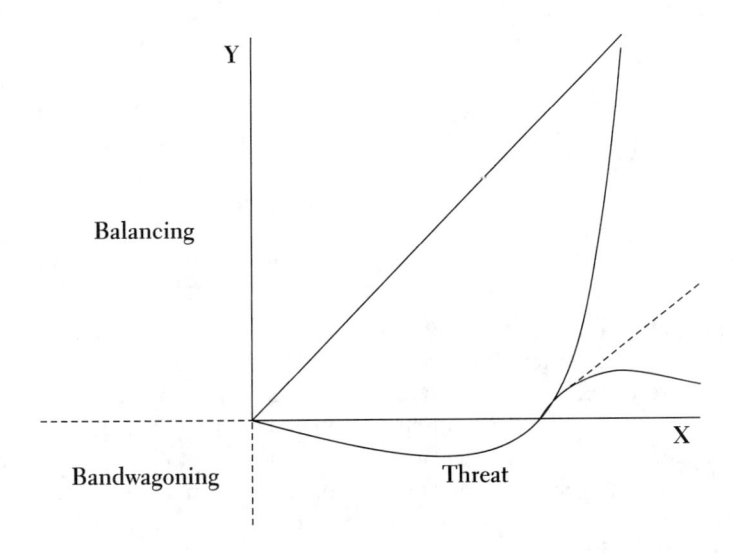

FIGURE 11.3

In Figure 11.3, the typically assumed balancing response is the 45-degree line. Yet rarely if ever does this hold. Much more typical is the response detailed by international historian Paul Schroeder.[19] When a power appears to be advancing aggressive goals, the first tactic is blandishments or reassurance, policies that would fall into the bandwagoning category and represent a movement below the X-axis. A country may seek to deflect an aggressor's thrust away from itself and toward other states. It may temporize. It may seek to convince the aggressor to reconsider its position and goals and lessen its dissatisfaction. Austrian Chancellor Clemens von Metternich successfully used this tactic with Tsar Alexander I of Russia to delay his support of the Greek revolutionists after 1820. As Robert Powell shows, it may simply wait to decide what to do.[20] If the threat persists and increases, however, the defending state may eventually respond in unpredictable ways—suddenly adopting an aggressive stance and mounting to the 45-degree line, or renouncing its defense altogether. If the British Parliament forced Chamberlain to adopt the first course of action on September 2–3, 1939, Czech responses have typically been of the latter kind, in 1938, 1948, and 1968. In 1939–1940 Denmark, Holland, and other powers followed suit and gave up their opposition to Hitler.[21] The British response was later viewed by B. H. Liddell-Hart, the eminent military historian, as a "bulldog," or even an "irrational" action,[22] given the limits of British power.[23]

This raises an even more important question. If the 45-degree line charts the usual response to threat, typical military deterrence can come into play. Potential aggressors may hold back if defense always administers what the Soviets called "a resolute rebuff" to aggression. But expansive powers may be misled by a curvilinear rejoinder. Because the defender has apparently initially accepted threats with little counter-response, an aggressor may expect the path of reaction to follow the mildly rising path of the dotted line. He will not anticipate a sudden shift upward to the 45-degree line. Thus this type of balancing response will not deter challenge or war; it will be more likely to bring them on. This raises the question whether a more determined pattern of resolute balancing actually rests on a degree of irrationality.[24] Whatever one says, the actual pattern of national response to threat is likely to be different from the assumed balancing rejoinder. It is not clear at all that there will be a response to "power" per se.[25]

## Does Absence of Hegemony Equal Presence of a Balance?

Many writers appear to think that the system of a multiplicity of states could not have survived without the existence of a continuing balance of power. Only the balance, so it is said, prevented the extinction of individual states and the creation of world-empire. Of course there is no linear trend in national political scale. In fact, the number of independent political units greatly declined from 1500 to 1900 and then rapidly increased once again. Since the balance of power has been supposed to be in constant operation over the same period, it cannot be quantitatively correlated with the result in question. But even if it were, there are other factors that contributed to the outcome. The first and most potent is probably the tendency for aggressors to attack the very states whose opposition will dictate their defeat. Imperial Germany sunk the Lusitania and then launched unrestricted submarine warfare against the United States in early 1917, bringing the United States into the war. Hitler declared war on the United States on December 11, 1941, four days after the Japanese attack on Pearl Harbor. In 1917, U.S. entry into World War I decisively tipped the military balance in favor of the allied side and determined the outcome.[26] But Hitler's greatest blunder was to place himself at war with the Soviet Union and the United States at the same time. In similar ways, Napoleon sealed his own fate by attacking Russia in 1812. Overreaching ambition was the cause of his and Hitler's demise. Louis XIV also made key mistakes in putting himself at war with England and Holland as well as the German states. Typically, writers think that the balance of power determined these results, but they were actually brought on by the aggressor himself. While the Soviet Union did not go to war with the United States, it would have been better advised to mute its opposition than to express continuing and full-scale hostility to Western ideals and interests. This reaction kept the United States in Europe and guaranteed Western rearmament, the two results Russia sought to avoid. Perhaps there is a congenital fault in aggressors that leads them to overreach.

A second factor is diseconomies of scale in territorial organization. The invention of gunpowder and its introduction to Europe in 1450 did not create much larger states or a single empire. Despite the strength of the Hapsburgs and France, defensive bastions were created in the Low Countries and Italy that were largely impervious to assault. Small manors and duchies were eliminated, but the great powers and the trading cities continued their sway. This feature changed in the nineteenth century and empires bestrode the world, initially facing few governance problems. It was not until after the Second World War that colonial peoples threw off their yoke, and the attempt to acquire and assimilate new territory was rendered increasingly difficult.[27] As Thomas Christensen, Robert Jervis, and Jack Snyder show, the ability to accumulate gains and the degree of validity of the "domino theory" also remain important factors in the equation that determines the scale of territorial organization.[28] So do the relative power of *offense* and *defense*.[29] If defensive (or retaliatory) strength is dominant, countries can maintain their position without untoward reliance upon allies. If governability also is questionable, expansion hits a barrier. Kenneth Boulding's principle of "the further, the weaker" and the presence of a loss of strength gradient in national and territorial power also operated to diminish the size of the state.[30] Finally, self-defense has been a primary means of maintaining a multiplicity of states or at least the territorial integrity of the major great powers. A great power, *ex hypothesi*, was a state that could not certainly be defeated even by a combination of others. It could frequently or even normally maintain its own independence without the assistance of power balancing. There was little if any power-balancing in the Napoleonic period, but no great power was eliminated from the European scene. Individual great powers could stand up to major assaults. Russia proved its durability in both 1812 and 1941. Prussia was not extinguished, despite the Kaunitz Coalition of 1756 and the Seven Years' War against Berlin.

## Conclusion

In answer to the question posed at the outset of this chapter, one may conclude that there is a balance of power. But unless defined in an essentially tautological manner, it operates much less frequently than the conventional wisdom has claimed. This is because cost-benefit calculations would typically decide against power balancing in the short term. States are not disinterested servants of a community or international bond. They do not sacrifice themselves on the altar of international stability. They fight when attacked, and they resist when pressed by others, but they do not generally or necessarily seek to forge an overall balance. The absence of a generalized balance of power, however, does not mean that the state system is in jeopardy. There are other mechanisms including aggressor ambition, effective self-defense, and diseconomies of territorial scale that militate in favor of the existing system. In addition, though not treated here, there is a growing specialization in the world economy that provides for many state needs, obviating traditional territorial expansion.[31] For all these reasons, the realist paradigm is unable fully to comprehend the trend of events, and its grasp on the discipline is withering.

## Editors' Commentary

### Major Query

Has the balance of power ever existed, and, if so, how commonly does it occur?

### Major Points

In order to answer these questions, Rosecrance begins by defining what he considers to be the essential characteristics of the balance of power. These include (1) an *intention* to balance, (2) siding with the weaker side against the stronger, and (3) supporting the public good against hegemony. On the basis of these characteristics, Rosecrance questions the extent to which balances of power are as common as they are supposed.

Rosecrance's version of the theory uses a strongly manual understanding of balance of power. In Rosecrance's view, for balancing to occur statesmen must act to achieve a balanced system because they view a balanced system as best. This definition partially collapses the distinction between balancing behavior and balance as systemic outcome, because the result is defined as the deliberate product of the action. For Rosecrance, neither dyadic balancing (states acting to countervail a particular threatening state) nor automatic balances (a system that is balanced because of an aggregation of different states' actions, none of which were necessarily aimed at a balance) count in balance of power theory's favor.

His analysis of the balance of power in terms of a **public goods** problem is an interesting restatement of the systemic conditions that make buck-passing a possible hindrance to timely balancing, especially in the context of the manual version of the theory.[32] A balance of power protects all states against a hegemonic bid, even if all states do not balance. From this perspective, the balance of power can be seen as a way of providing a "defense" of the entire system of independent states. This poses a public goods problem (and a collective action problem) in that each state that can balance is tempted to let someone else bear all or most of the burden (and thereby get a "free ride"). The danger is that no one or an insufficient number will balance.

By analyzing the balance of power through the lens of public goods, Rosecrance provides two insights. First, he is able to use the public goods aspect of balance of power as a defining criterion for helping to determine what is or is not an instance of balancing. For him, if states are simply defending themselves from an attack, they are not engaged in providing a public good, and hence have not met one of the three essential defining criteria of balancing he presents. Likewise, mutual expansion, which Rosecrance argues occurred during the early Cold War, is not mutual balancing because it involves the ambitions of two states clashing and not the attempt to provide a true public good.

Since mere opposition (as in self-defense) is not balancing per se if there is not an intention to balance, then balancing is rarer than supposed. Rosecrance questions whether Hitler, Napoleon, or Louis XIV, among others, can be seen as having had to confront balancing. For instance, he maintains that it would have been unlikely that either the Soviet Union or the United States would have entered World War II against the axis powers if they had not been directly attacked. Germany's defeat was not due to balancing but to unlimited ambition.

Second, by bringing in public goods theory Rosecrance provides a powerful explanation of why it is difficult to create an authentic (i.e., narrowly defined) balance of power and a prediction that it will not be that common. He then graphs what he thinks is the more typical response to hegemonic threat (see Figure 11.3 on page 159). In the balancing hypothesis, as threat increases (along the x axis), then balancing (along the y axis) should increase on a one to one basis (indicated by the 45 degree straight line). In fact, Rosecrance posits that states typically tend, first, either to do nothing or to bandwagon (the curve below the x axis) in the face of threat. If threat persists, then they move away from bandwagoning and either do nothing or follow one of the other lines coming out of bandwagoning. Under some conditions they may, if threat persists, move dramatically toward balancing (along the 45 degree line).

Of course, the balance of power concept can be broadened to include other phenomena, such as self-defense or just the presence of war, but if this is done then the theory may add little insight into behavior and may be reduced to obvious statements, like "states pursue their own interests," or "may apply cost-benefit criteria." As with other critics, Rosecrance maintains that if the concept is broadened to cover behavior that deviates from the theory, then this does not advance the field empirically but merely constitutes a linguistic operation that saves the theory from refutation.

According to Rosecrance, the failure to see the balance of power operating as commonly as some suppose does not mean, however, that there are no other mechanisms that prevent hegemony. There are several, including: the limits of aggressor ambition, self-defense, and diseconomies of scale for large territorial units. Rosecrance concludes by suggesting that the balance of power (as well as balancing), although it can be found, is comparatively rare in modern European history and does not play a central role in the conduct of international politics.

## Key Terms

**public good**  A good, when purchased, that is automatically available to everyone in a given locale, whether they have paid for it or not. Defense is a classic example of a public good.

**free-riders**  Those who benefit from a public good without having had to pay for it; for example, states that benefit from others' balancing against hegemonic bids while they stand on the sidelines.

## Notes

1. See Powell 1999, Ch. 5, and Snyder 1997, 50–51.
2. See particularly Schweller 1998a.
3. See Schroeder 1994b and Donnelly 2000, 119–120.
4. John Vasquez (herein, Ch. 8, 21) writes: "The criterion of empirical accuracy is fundamental. So, too, however, is the criterion of falsifiability, for if adherents are not willing to specify, at some point, what evidence would lead them to say the theory was inaccurate, then the theory can never be tested."
5. This does not mean in Thomas Kuhn's sense that a "paradigm shift" has occurred. Newtonian mechanics and thermodynamics were in disarray until Max Planck emerged to give them a new regularity, but even this did not represent a paradigm shift.
6. For this debate see inter alia Rosecrance 1961 and Hoffmann 1960.
7. Waltz 1997.
8. Vasquez herein Ch. 2, 41; 1997, 909.
9. For an example of "cost benefit analysis" which reaches conclusions very different from those of typical neorealism, see Powell 1999, particularly Ch. 5.
10. See Rosecrance and Lo 1996.
11. See Kaplan 1957, Ch. 2, especially rule 4 of the balance of power system. Nicholson (1989, 26) observes that principles such as the balance of power "require actors to deviate from narrow self-interest to having goals for the system as such." Stephen Walt (1991, 53) points out that balancing power means aligning with the weaker side.
12. He believes that "at some point the cost of resistance will be assessed as lower than the cost of allowing the aggression to succeed." But this may not be true; see Snyder 1997, 51. See also the analysis in Powell 1999, Ch. 5.
13. See Kecskemeti 1958.
14. See Reiter's (1996) argument on this point.
15. See Christensen and Snyder 1990.
16. See Langer 1950.
17. See Waltz 2000.
18. See Leffler 1992.
19. See particularly Schroeder 1994a.
20. See Powell 1999, Ch. 5.
21. Some later took up passive resistance or organized covert opposition to Nazi rule.
22. See Liddell-Hart's 1970 history of the Second World War.
23. See also Barnett [c. 1972], 1984.

24. In nuclear terms Herman Kahn always referred to this as "the rationality of irrationality." But the phenomenon has relevance for conventional deterrence as well. See Kahn 1960.
25. Weaker states frequently are the threateners as Prussia was in the mid-eighteenth century and North Vietnam or North Korea in the 1950s and 1960s. As we have seen, stronger states do not always evoke opposition or balance of power coalitions.
26. See Paul Kennedy's (1984) calculations on the balance of military and economic power in World War I.
27. See particularly Kaysen 1990.
28. See Jervis and Snyder 1991 and Christensen and Snyder 1990.
29. In addition to Jervis and Snyder 1991, see Quester 1977.
30. See Boulding 1963, c1962.
31. See Rosecrance 1999.
32. See Waltz 1979 and Christensen and Snyder 1990 for discussions of similar issues when employing dyadic and automatic understandings of balance of power.

# Neorealism's Logic and Evidence
## WHEN IS A THEORY FALSIFIED?

*BRUCE BUENO DE MESQUITA*

Knowledge progresses through a dynamic process. Arguments are made for the plausibility of hypotheses. The logic of such arguments is scrutinized and the evidence for and against the inferences drawn from the arguments is evaluated. Progress is made by reducing the set of logically and empirically plausible explanations of the phenomena of interest. Such reduction takes place on at least two levels. Some seemingly plausible explanations are eliminated for want of logical coherence. Others, passing the test of logical coherence, are superceded by alternatives that account for a broader array of empirical phenomena and/or a broader set of facts. In this essay I suggest that on both grounds, the neorealist research program grounded in the core assumptions of Waltz's *Theory of International Politics* (1979) is not a plausible explanation of the central phenomena with which it is concerned.

## Origins of Realist and Neorealist Thought

The Second World War shattered confidence in idealistic, utopian views of international politics. To be sure, after the war there were still the World Federalists and other organizations that believed orderly international affairs could be achieved by bringing people together and educating them to their common interest. In counterpoint to the idealism that dominated prewar scholarship on international security, the postwar years witnessed a renaissance of efforts at positive, rather than normative, analysis. Principal among the early efforts to direct research in a more "realist" way were studies by Hans Morgenthau (1948), Kenneth Waltz (1959), Morton Kaplan (1957), and Kenneth Organski (1958). Each sought to identify the central factors that govern how nations interact with each other. In doing so, each subscribed to certain common principles that continue to dominate thinking about international relations.

The new realists saw the state, rather than individual leaders, as the central actor on the world stage. Because decision makers were relegated to a fairly minor role, sharp distinctions were drawn between domestic politics and international politics. The former was seen to refer to maneuvering within the state and often included foreign policy, while the latter was said to deal with the "international system" and the role states play within that system. The focus of attention was on the system, its central characteristics, and the factors thought to give it stability.

By the 1980s, the leading contender among competing realist theories clearly was Waltz's theory of neorealism. Waltz set out a seemingly elegant theory with both explicit assumptions and criteria for evaluating the theory's performance. His theory, by focusing on security maximization rather than power maximization, appeared to fix the fundamental problem of Morgenthau's realism, namely the existence of the security dilemma. Neorealism appeared to offer a rich argument and certainly stimulated a wealth of new ideas and new research. Neorealism offered the prospect of a progressive research program that could lead to cumulative knowledge. Though the remainder of this essay suggests that neorealism is falsified and superceded, based on its own criteria for judgment as well as more stringent criteria, we should not lose sight of the fact that the inquiries it has stimulated have advanced the field.[1] Plausible hypotheses have been stated and, as is a natural part of scientific progress, these hypotheses are shown to be wanting theoretically and empirically. Therefore, we can infer that they are no longer contenders as explanations of international affairs.[2]

## NEOREALISM: A SUMMARY OF WALTZ'S THEORY

Neorealists, like their realist precursors, examine structural aspects of international politics. The distribution of power among the states in the international system is identified as a major factor determining whether international affairs are stable or unstable. Stability refers to circumstances in which the sovereignty of key states is preserved (Gulick 1955). Instability refers to changes in the composition of the international system, especially changes involving the disappearance or emergence of consequential states, like major powers, following large wars. Consequential or key states are those whose assistance might be needed to counteract a threat from a rival grouping of states. Sometimes I will refer to these states as *essential actors* to highlight their ability to turn a potentially losing situation into a winning one or at least into one that blocks adversaries from victory (Niou, Ordeshook, and Rose 1989). That this is what Waltz has in mind seems evident from his definition of stability:

> To say that an international-political system is stable means two things: first, that it remains anarchic; second, that no consequential variation takes place in the number of principal parties that constitute the system. "Consequential" variations in number are changes of number that lead to different expectations about the effect of structure on units; the stability of the system, so long as it remains anarchic, is

then closely linked with the fate of its principal members. The close link is established by the relation of changes in number of great powers to transformation of the system. (1979, 161–162)

In addressing threats to international stability, neorealism posits the following central assumptions:

1. International politics is characterized by anarchy.
2. States, as rational unitary entities, are the central actors in international politics.
3. States seek to maximize their security above all else, considering other factors only when security is assured.
4. States try to increase their power if doing so does not put their security at risk.

Anarchy means that there is no central authority that can enforce agreements between states. Consequently, international politics involves self-help above all else. No state can count on any other for help except to the extent that others expect to benefit themselves by helping. The assumption of anarchy is equivalent to saying that international politics is played out as a noncooperative game. Noncooperative games are games in which promises are not binding and contracts are enforced by self-interest rather than by some external authority.

The second assumption claims that domestic politics within states are largely irrelevant to international politics. It is because of this assumption that neorealists argue that foreign policy needs to be considered separately from international politics. By assuming that the state is the central actor and that it is unitary and rational, neorealism puts aside internal factors, like those highlighted by bureaucratic or interest group perspectives, when dealing with issues that might jeopardize the state's survival.

The third assumption establishes the primacy of security above all other possible goals. It also establishes that states are not willing to trade away any of their currently assured security for other benefits. Other things of value are only pursued once security is assured. This assumption lends considerable predictability to behavior: Because all states are assumed to have the same goal, there is no need to worry about idiosyncratic factors like the personalities of individual leaders or the domestic political institutions that govern state behavior. Every state is a role player with the role dictated by its security needs and its position in the distribution of power among states.[3]

The final assumption tells us that states are always interested in increasing their influence over other states. No state is content to be weak, but states accept being weaker than they might otherwise be if pursuit of greater power could place their security at risk. This assumption places restrictions on the pursuit of power. The idea is that if a state becomes sufficiently powerful that other states foresee the prospect that their security will be threatened by it in the future, they then join together to deprive the growing state of the power to threaten them. That is, states more often balance than bandwagon, in the jargon of neorealism. So, an increase in a state's power can actually make the state weaker in the long run if, for instance, the increase in power stimulates rivals to form an opposition alliance. A coalition or alliance of states is expected to come together to beat back a growing state if that state's power threatens to become large enough that others face a possible loss of sovereignty as a result of the growing power of the first state. This well-known element of the security dilemma that bedeviled earlier realist theories is solved in the neorealist formulation by the presence of the third and fourth assumption. These two assumptions place a brake on the pursuit of power. Morgenthau (1978, 215, emphasis added) argued that, "Since the desire to attain a maximum of power is universal, all nations must always be afraid that their own miscalculations and the power increases of other nations might add up to an inferiority for themselves which *they must at all costs try to avoid.*"

With his third and fourth assumptions, Waltz set out an important innovation over earlier realist thought. States are not assumed to seek power or to avoid a decrease in power at all costs. Specifically, the quest for power is assumed not to be worthwhile if it costs the state its current security. Power becomes an instrument for security in neorealism, while it was the goal of states in realism.

Together Waltz's four core assumptions provide a parsimonious and powerful view of international politics. Several important hypotheses are said to follow from these assumptions. I focus here only on those that directly concern the risk of instability, especially instability manifested as either changes in the composition of the international system's membership or in large-scale war. The most important neorealist hypotheses about the threat of instability are as follows:

- Bipolar systems are more stable than multipolar systems.
- States engage in balancing behavior so that power becomes more or less equally divided among states over time.
- States mimic or echo each other's successful behavior.

## CRITERIA FOR EVALUATING THE THEORY

Before examining the logical coherence and empirical accuracy of neorealist claims about instability, I pause to review the criteria Waltz (1979) suggests for assessing his and all other theories. I will steadfastly apply these criteria as well as, from time to time, additional criteria. The additional criteria will always be *in addition* to the others, so as to be faithful to the epistemological requirements stipulated by the most important neorealist theorist.[4]

Waltz (1979, 13) proposes seven conditions that should be applied to all theory. These are as follows:

1. State the theory being tested.
2. Infer hypotheses from it.
3. Subject the hypotheses to experimental or observational tests.

4. In taking steps two and three, use the definitions of terms found in the theory being tested.
5. Eliminate or control perturbing variables not included in the theory under test.
6. Devise a number of distinct and demanding tests.
7. If a test is not passed, ask whether the theory flunks completely, needs repair and restatement, or requires a narrowing of scope of its explanatory claims.

The first is a call for making the theoretical argument explicit. To do so, one must state all assumptions; that is, all restrictions on action that are needed to infer the logical implications of the argument. The second requires that hypotheses, that is, proposed relationships among variables, follow from the logic of the theory. The first two conditions, then, are a call for logical consistency within the framework of the restrictions assumed by the theory. Subsequent additional or auxiliary assumptions are not ruled out by these two conditions, but the nature of such additional assumptions is circumscribed. They may be additions to, but not replacements for, the existing assumptions. The existing assumptions are what define a theory and so are the constituent elements of Waltz's first condition. New assumptions can be added, thereby further restricting the domain of applicability of a theory, but the new assumptions cannot contradict the old ones. If they do, either they or some old assumption(s) must be abandoned to avoid incoherence. If even one old, core assumption is abandoned, that is equivalent to the statement of an entirely new theory and not an evolutionary change in the old theory.

The fourth condition requires that terms have explicit meaning and that the meaning is not altered from application to application or test to test or from one discussion of the theory to the next. With conditions one, two, and four, Waltz has stipulated that theories must be clearly and explicitly defined. In the spirit of adhering to these conditions, I frequently quote Waltz's definitions in this essay to be clear about the meaning of his central concepts.

The remaining four conditions concern the empirical evaluation of the hypotheses that follow from a theory. Waltz is careful to note that a single test should be regarded as insufficient to falsify or to confirm a theory, thus the call for a number of distinct and demanding tests. Demanding tests presumably refer to tests that allow the researcher to distinguish between competing explanations of a phenomenon. When two theories make the same predictions about something, tests of those predictions provide no basis for choosing between the theories and so place relatively low demands on either theory. When two theories make different predictions about the same phenomenon, then a test of the explanation offered by each is demanding because, at most, only one of the contending theories can pass the test. If a pattern emerges across several distinct tests that systematically favors one explanation over another when all of the tests are demanding, then a choice can be made between the competing explanations. As I noted earlier, Waltz (1979, 124) stipulates how to make this choice: "In the end, one sticks with the theory that reveals most, even if its validity is suspect." I will try to perform just such distinct and demanding tests here.

Finally, the seventh condition recognizes the possibility that a theory can not be repaired and can be falsified. If a theory fails the many distinct and demanding tests and cannot be made to pass by the addition of auxiliary assumptions that are logically consistent with the core assumptions, then the theory is falsified. I will show that, at least in my judgment and given Waltz's criteria, this is the case for neorealism with regard to the three central hypotheses stated earlier.[5]

The existence of some selected cases that are consistent with a theory's hypotheses is not, by itself, evidence that the theory is supported, just as isolated cases that seem inconsistent with a theory are not a refutation. Such individual cases are not demanding tests. If some variable, such as the presence or absence of a balance of power between states, is hypothesized to increase or decrease stability, the observation of cases of a balance of power and of stability does not demonstrate that the hypothesis is correct. After all, if one observes fifty cases in which balance is accompanied by stability and fifty cases in which balance is accompanied by instability, then the correlation between balance and stability is zero. Correlation does not imply causation, but causation does imply correlation. Of course, the structure of the correlation may be simple or complex and contingent, depending on the specific hypothesis, but that is another matter. The point is, the call for distinct and demanding tests is a call for more than the observation that a case or nonrandom set of cases fits the hypothesis.

A single case is only convincing evidence when a theory stipulates necessary or sufficient conditions (or both) and a case is found that contradicts the claim without itself being controversial. Controversy might swirl around a case because of disagreement about its interpretation (i.e., measurement error) or because of disagreement about the appropriateness of the case as a test of the claim. Absent a case that incontrovertibly falsifies a claim, no case (or large N) can serve to confirm a hypothesis. Rather, the accumulation of supportive evidence over many cases (distinct and demanding tests) bolsters confidence in the claim. It is imperative to remember that if a hypothesized relationship is false in the sense of a zero correlation between the variables, then about half of all cases will, more or less, be consistent with the hypothesis and about half, again more or less, will be inconsistent with the hypothesis. Therefore, as I test neorealist empirical claims (i.e., hypotheses), I rely on large numbers of historical cases, rather than individual events. Neither the theory nor its hypotheses nor its empirical claims are about individual events. They are about patterns of relationships between key independent variables, like polarity, balancing, and mimicking, and key dependent variables, like the survival of major powers or the survival of states in general.

## How Well Does Neorealism Do in Explaining Instability?

The examination of neorealist theory proceeds in stages. First I investigate whether the core hypotheses stipulated earlier are logically implied by the four assumptions of the theory. Then I examine how well those hypotheses describe historical circumstances.

If the neorealist hypotheses are not accurate descriptions of international affairs, then their logical status is not so important because they are wrong about the world in any event. If the hypotheses are logically implied by the assumptions of neorealism but they are not consistent with actual state behavior then they are of little interest and the theory's predictions are falsified. If the hypotheses are consistent with behavior but do not follow from the assumptions, then we will want to think about how the assumptions must be altered to account for the observed facts. In that case, other implications will probably follow from the new assumptions. We will want to know whether or not those new implications are also consistent with the facts. Finally, if the hypotheses follow logically from the assumptions and if the hypotheses accurately account for behavior, then neorealist theory is a powerful tool for understanding international politics.

## Bipolarity and Stability

A bipolar international system is defined in neorealism as a set of states dominated by two especially powerful states, with other nations concentrated around each of the two power blocs. A multipolar system consists of more than two especially powerful states. The great powers in a multipolar environment may also attract the support of other, lesser states. There must be more than two such concentrations of power in a multipolar system.

The argument that bipolar structures are more stable than multipolar ones is inferred largely from the claim that there is more uncertainty in a multipolar system than in a bipolar one. Waltz writes, "In the great-power politics of multipolar worlds, who is a danger to whom, and who can be expected to deal with threats and problems, are matters of uncertainty. In the great-power politics of bipolar worlds, who is a danger to whom is never in doubt" (1979, 170). Neorealists conclude that because there is less uncertainty in a bipolar world, fewer errors are made by the leaders of states in bipolar international politics. They know who their prospective supporters are and who their foes are. This is less true in multipolar environments. Therefore, according to neorealists, bipolar systems are more stable than multipolar systems.

Let us accept the argument that multipolar systems are more likely than are bipolar systems to require that decisions be made under uncertainty. Still, there is a considerable logical leap from the association of uncertainty with multipolarity to the association of multipolarity with instability and bipolarity with stability. Indeed, some have argued that multipolar systems are more stable than bipolar systems exactly because multipolarity produces uncertainty (Deutsch and Singer 1964). It has also been argued that there is no particular reason to expect that bipolarity is more or less conducive to stability than is multipolarity (Bueno de Mesquita 1978).

There are several problems with the argument that, because a bipolar system has less uncertainty than a multipolar one, bipolarity therefore yields greater stability. To start with, this argument is not implied logically by the four key assumptions of neorealism. In fact, those assumptions say nothing at all about uncertainty or how uncertainty effects stability. So, to conclude that there is a relationship between uncertainty and the stability of the international system, we need additional assumptions.

In particular, within the framework Waltz proposes, we need an assumption about how states (or decision makers) respond to uncertainty. For instance, uncertainty might prompt states (or their leaders) to behave cautiously. Relatively greater certainty, by contrast, may inspire the more powerful nations to seize the opportunity to eliminate or diminish weaker rivals just because diminished uncertainty makes the opportunity more evident. If uncertainty provokes caution and certainty encourages someone to seize an opportunity, then bipolarity encourages instability. This is essentially the argument that led Deutsch and Singer (1964) to conclude that multipolar systems are more stable than bipolar systems.

In order to create the argument that bipolarity fosters stability, we can assume that certainty makes states cautious while multipolarity and uncertainty makes states reckless or risk seeking. That is, we logically exclude the possibility that uncertainty breeds caution. So, all states, mimicking each other's behavior, could be assumed to be risk averse in the absence of uncertainty. While this is a strong assumption, it does solve the logical dilemma we face, and it is tautologically consistent with the third neorealist hypothesis that says states echo one another's (successful) actions. Furthermore, it is a view subscribed to in neorealist theorizing.[6] Whether it solves the logical problem we are confronting at the price of departing too much from reality or from neorealist precepts is an empirical question to be resolved by examining evidence rather than making a judgment of whether we think the assumption is realistic or not.[7]

The assumption that states are risk averse when faced with certainty but not when faced with uncertainty specifically precludes the possibility that different leaders or different states respond in different ways to certainty and uncertainty. Indeed, if leaders in different states react to uncertainty each in his or her own way, then we have three immediate problems. First, the unitary rational actor assumption of neorealist theory contends that important choices in international politics are driven by structural factors and not by considerations internal to the state. All structural or system-level arguments preclude just the sort of variation in leader proclivities regarding uncertainty that I am considering at the moment. So, this cannot be a fix for the neorealist argument. It violates a core assumption. Second, if different decision makers respond to uncertainty in different ways, then there is no reason to expect any empirical relationship between bipolarity and stability at all. Some leaders might be cautious when facing an uncertain situation while others might be reckless. If there is a roughly equal mix of states (or leaders) with reckless and with cautious reactions, then, on average, uncertainty would not have any systematic effect on the system's stability. Half the time uncertainty would prompt cautious, stability-enhancing actions, and half the time it would make states more reckless. Naturally, this point of view requires that we weaken the assumption that states act as unitary rational actors and instead focus on differences in the characteristics of individual leaders. From time to time, new leaders may come to power in a given state and the new leader might differ from the predecessor in terms of how to deal with uncertainty. Third, if leaders differ in how they respond to uncertainty, then the third hypothesis, that leaders mimic one another, contradicts an assumption of the theory and so cannot logically follow from it. Therefore, the theory cannot tolerate the possibility that individual decision makers vary in their response to uncertainty. So, a repair that allows us to infer the first hypothesis is to assume that all states respond to uncertainty with greater recklessness than they manifest when there is no uncertainty, and to assume that bipolar structures inherently produce less uncertainty (or no uncertainty) than do multipolar structures.

The bipolarity argument is problematic, however, even if we ignore its silence with regards to the willingness of states to take risks when facing an uncertain situation. The deeper problem is that the hypothesis that stability is fostered by bipolarity is inconsistent with the four assumptions of neorealism. To see that this is so, I must demonstrate that, taking neorealist assumptions into account, it is logically true that more distributions of power are stable in a multipolar world than in a bipolar world. Keep in mind that I am not now making an empirical claim. I am making a claim about the implications of the neorealist assumptions.

To prove this claim, and building on the efforts of Niou, Ordeshook, and Rose (1989), suppose that there are 300 units of power in the international system. Two distributions of power are of interest when it comes to a bipolar world. If the distribution of power for bloc A and bloc B is exactly 150–150, then neither state can destabilize the system by trying to take power away from the other bloc. Each is exactly powerful enough to prevent a defeat by its rival. Such a system would be very stable indeed, as hypothesized by neorealist thinkers. If, however, the distribution of power differs at all from 150–150, then the system *must* be unstable according to neorealist assumptions, if not neorealist conclusions (Niou, Ordeshook, and Rose 1989).

Suppose, for example, that the bloc led by nation A has 151 units of power, while B's bloc has 149. The system is practically balanced, but not quite. A wants more power according to assumption 4. It will not seek more power if doing so can put its security at risk (as indicated by assumptions 3 and 4). But, since power is the ability to make a rival do something it otherwise would not want to do, A has the absolute ability to force B to give up all of its resources (i.e., the 149 units of power). A is stronger than B. If B does not willingly give up its resources, A can just take them; in a bipolar world B cannot turn to anyone else for help because there is no one else. By taking B's resources, A increases its own power and does not place its sovereignty or its security at risk because it knows that it can beat B. That is what it means to say that A is more powerful than B.[8] Therefore, except in the unlikely event that power is *precisely* equally distributed or *believed* to be evenly distributed between rivals, bipolar systems are unstable according to neorealist logic.[9]

One might object that my conclusion really depends on certainty about power being equally distributed. Recall that the introduction of uncertainty in the bipolar setting turns the argument for the stability of bipolar systems on its head. Bipolar systems, according to neorealist theory, are supposed to be devoid of uncertainty. ("In the great-power politics of bipolar worlds, who is a danger to whom is never in doubt" [Waltz 1979, 170].) An argument that appeals to uncertainty to explain bipolar stability, then, contradicts the argument offered by neorealists to support the hypothesized link between bipolarity and stability.

Consider two different multipolar systems, each consisting of five nations (or blocs of nations). Call the nations A, B, C, D, and E. Imagine the following possible power distributions: (A = 75, B = 74, C = 75, D = 74, E = 2) or (A = 78, B = 74, C = 73, D = 73, E = 2). According to the assumptions of neorealism, what can we say about the stability of these systems? They appear to be quite similar, and yet neorealist logic implies that one of them is stable with respect to the survival of the states in the system and could, but need not, lead to a stable distribution of power. In the other, the survival of all the states cannot be assured if we follow the implications of neorealist assumptions.

The first system (75, 74, 75, 74, 2) is sufficiently stable that no country can be eliminated from the international system, not even state E, given the current distribution of power, although E holds only 2/300ths of the total power. Nation E is important in this system because it can help some states to build a coalition strong enough to protect themselves from defeat by any remaining combination of rivals. Nation E can help itself and other states enhance security. E turns out to be essential to the preservation of the structure of this system.[10]

Any combination of states with power totaling more than half the available capabilities can defeat any combination of opponents. For hypothetical systems with 300 units of power, any combination of states that is greater than 150 can defeat the remaining states. Each state has an incentive to prevent the formation of such a coalition if the alliance excludes the state. By forging a *blocking coalition* of 150 power units (that is, if R = resources, the blocking coalition must equal R/2) all the states can assure their security in the sense that their survival is assured. The reason that the earlier bipolar system with 150 power units per bloc was stable was exactly that each pole formed a blocking coalition with R/2 units of power.

In the first illustrative multipolar system, nation E might align with nations B and D (74 + 74 + 2 = 150 = R/2) against A and C. That arrangement is stable in that neither side is strong enough to eliminate any state. Each state is essential because each state can turn a losing coalition into a winning coalition or a blocking coalition. Notice that if A, for instance, attacked E, other states would join to defend E and defeat A. They would do so because if they did not, their own security would be diminished by the lost opportunity to form a blocking coalition with E or a subsequent winning coalition against A. By ignoring E's plight, C and D place their own future security at risk, something they would not do according to the assumptions of neorealist theory. Less obviously, B also places its future security at risk in such a situation. Under the assumptions of neorealism, there is no sustainable additional benefit in terms of security for B (or anyone else) once the power configuration is such that a coalition with R/2 resources can form. When such a distribution forms, the power distribution may or may not remain stable, but all of the states will survive because they all play a crucial role in helping to preserve someone's security. There is no need to redistribute power to assure security, though security could be assured even if the power were to be redistributed. For instance, a redistribution to (75, 75, 70, 70, 10) would also be stable in terms of protecting the survival of each state as would a redistribution that gave any one state 150 units of power.

In the second illustrative multipolar system (A = 78, B = 74, C = 73, D = 73, E = 2) there is no combination of states that cares to insure the survival of nation E because no state requires E's assistance to form a blocking or winning coalition. Nation A can form a winning coalition by just joining with B, or if B is not willing, by aligning with C or D. Adding E to any of these coalitions is superfluous. B likewise can forge winning coalitions by aligning with A or with C and D. C and D of course are included in an option for A and an option for B. No winning or blocking coalition that would otherwise be a losing coalition can form by adding nation E to it. Consequently, E is expendable. A, B, C, and D have assured security—they are each essential in at least one blocking or winning coalition—but E is inessential. Not even E's survival can be assured.

We can see how this second illustrative system might evolve by applying the rules of neorealism to it. A and D might threaten to gobble up B, C, and E. D will only agree to do so if at the end of the ensuing war both A and D control half of the remaining resources or units of power. They would each require an equal number of units of power at the end of the fighting.[11] If either took less it would be destroyed by its erstwhile ally as soon as the war was over. B, C, and E obviously are unhappy with this state of affairs. B and C might approach the leader of A and offer a deal at least as good for A as a proposal by D to form an alliance and destroy B, C, and E. B and C (or either one of them), might suggest that A destroy E, giving A 80 units instead of 78 and, in addition, B and C might each give A an additional 35 units of their own power, say by transferring territory or some other tangible source of power.[12] Then A would possess 150 units without having to fight a big war against B, C, and E, and without having to take the risk that D might come out ahead of A in the war. Under this arrangement, while B and C sacrifice power, they assure their survival because once A has 150 units of power (R/2 = 150), the surviving states are all essential. The new distribution of power might be (A = 150, B = 39, C = 38, D = 73) or, perhaps (A = 150, B = 74, C = 3, D = 73) or any of a number of other possibilities.

In summary, state E is an essential actor in the first hypothetical multipolar system. No one can afford to see state E eliminated. That would needlessly place someone's future security at risk in direct violation of assumption 3. In the first system, for any winning alliance that could form, there is a counter proposal that some other state can make to offer a better deal (that is, more security) to some member of the winning combination in exchange for their supporting some other, blocking coalition. And, in accordance with neorealist assumptions 3 and 4, such an offer will be made. Because of the possibility of switching alliances to get a better deal (i.e., anarchy), no state is expendable in this system and so the system's composition is stable, although the distribution of power may be subject to change.

The second system, although seemingly very similar to the first, is not stable according to neorealism because there is no circumstance in which E can survive that is consistent with neorealist assumptions. Other states can increase their power by destroying E without placing their security at risk. The key to stability, at least in terms of the survival of the states, is that each state is essential to the formation of at least one winning or blocking coalition. Sometimes such states may survive while having to transfer some of their power to rival states, but at least all can survive. States that are inessential cannot survive and so the system's composition cannot be stable (Niou, Ordeshook, and Rose 1989).

It should be evident that many different distributions of power in a multipolar system can be stable, while others would not be. Among the potentially stable multipolar systems, at least in the sense that every state can survive, we must include a system in which power is perfectly evenly distributed among the member states, just as was true for the bipolar world. Such a multipolar system, however, is subject to power being redistributed away from perfect equality if there is an odd number of members. This is so for any odd numbered system with more than one bloc and with an equal distribution of power because a blocking coalition with R/2 resources that ensures the survival of all states cannot be formed without redistributing resources in that case.

Stability in a multipolar world is not limited to the situation of exact power equality. It should also be evident that only a perfectly balanced bipolar system can be stable; any other must be unstable according to neorealist assumptions. Thus the neorealist hypothesis that bipolarity promotes stability while multipolarity promotes instability is logically false given the assumptions of the theory. Further, a true balance of power is essential for stability in a bipolar world, but not in a multipolar one, contradicting the second hypothesis. A vast array of power distributions produce stability so that, in a multipolar environment, an exact or even approximate balance of power is irrelevant. There is no particular reason for the distribution of power in a multipolar environment to gravitate toward balance. Either the balance of power does not matter in multipolarity or the term is defined to mean any system in which each actor is essential. In the latter case, the concept is close to vacuous as so many systems would then qualify as a balance of power.[13]

One might object that the portrayal of the relationship between polarity and stability is too simple, since war or other means of taking a nation's power and threatening its sovereignty are all risky and costly business. The outcome is not a certainty, so probably the more powerful state or alliance of states cannot be sure of its advantage unless that advantage is large (Morgenthau 1978). Otherwise, it might lose or might suffer such high costs in winning that any victory would be pyrrhic. In such a case, the bipolar system may still be stable even though power is not balanced between the rival camps. This argument seems appealing at first blush, but it contradicts fundamental aspects of the neorealist argument. I return to the bipolar example of instability to see why this is so.

Before providing a more elaborate assessment, recall that the basis for the claim that bipolar systems are more stable than multipolar systems hinged on the contention that multipolarity meant greater uncertainty than bipolarity. Now I am going to turn this contention on its head by asserting that uncertainty is especially a problem in bipolar systems. I do so in an effort to try to save the logical foundation for the hypothesis that bipolar systems are more stable than multipolar systems.

Suppose nation A thinks there is some chance (say P, where $0 < P < 1$) that it can defeat B at an acceptable cost. Then there is also a chance $(1 - P)$ that A will be defeated by B in a contest to control their respective power or that the cost for victory will be too high. For convenience, I define P so that it equals the ratio of A's power to the sum of A's and B's power so that I treat the probability as the odds that A can beat B. Also for convenience, I ignore costs in most of the remainder of the discussion, though it should be evident that costs only shift individual thresholds for choosing to fight or not fight and do not alter my fundamental point. A will not try to take advantage of B if the following is true:

> P(Utility for A of Capturing B's Power – Costs) + $(1 - P)$(Utility for A of Losing its Sovereignty to B – Costs) < Utility for A of the Status Quo in terms of maintaining A's level of security.

Suppose (without loss of generality) that A attaches a utility of 1 to capturing all of B's power and a utility of 0 to losing its sovereignty. Of course, A prefers capturing B's power to losing its own sovereignty. In accordance with neorealist assumptions, A also prefers capturing B's power to maintaining the status quo, but naturally A prefers the status quo to losing its sovereignty. With these conditions in mind, I can rewrite A's rule for deciding whether to go after B's power or not as follows:

> Rule 1: Attack B if P > Value of the Status Quo plus costs.
> Rule 2: Do not attack B if P ≤ A's utility for the Status Quo plus costs.

The decision A makes depends on how much it likes or dislikes its status quo level of security. Some states, those who are weak and insecure, could under rules 1 and 2 attack the rival pole in a bipolar system even though the rival pole is stronger than they are, because P could be small and still be bigger than the value they attach to the status quo and anticipated war costs. Imagine, for instance, that the value of the status quo is 0.1 and costs are zero, for convenience. This is more than the value of losing sovereignty (0) and less than the value of gaining B's power (1). Then if P is 0.2 the rule for attacking B and destabilizing the system is satisfied. This is equivalent to saying that it is possible in a bipolar world for A to attack and try to eliminate B when A's power is 60 and B's power is 240. That is what is implied by the measurement of P and the stipulation that P = 0.2 and that the utility for the status quo equals 0.1. Remember, P = A's Power/(A's Power + B's Power) = 60/(60 + 240) in this example. So we have an example in which A attacks B even though A's chance of success in gaining power and possibly eliminating B is very small.

Other states, those that are especially happy with the status quo, might not try to eliminate B in a bipolar system even if B is much weaker than they are. That is,

P might be very large and still be smaller than the value for the status quo, again assuming costs are zero for convenience. Suppose that the value of the status quo is 0.9, for instance. This too is greater than the utility of losing sovereignty for A and less than A's utility for gaining control over B's power. P might be equal to 0.8 and A still would not satisfy the rule for attacking B. So, A's power might equal 240 and B's resources might only total 60 and still A would not feel confident enough to seize B's capabilities, given that the status quo is rather good and the downside for A following its own defeat is disastrous. So whether the system remains stable and whether balancing takes place depends on factors other than the system's structure; it depends, in this example, also on the value individual states place on the status quo. Though the substantive content of the international status quo may be a system characteristic, the value placed on it is not.

Such conclusions make intuitive sense. The problem is that they contradict neorealist assumptions, since the fourth neorealist assumption limits the pursuit of increased power to just those situations in which national security is not at risk. Waltz (1979, 126, emphasis added) has aptly noted the following in explaining neorealism:

> In anarchy, security is the highest end. Only if survival is *assured* can states safely seek such other goals as tranquility, profit, and power. Because power is a means and not an end, states prefer to join the weaker of two coalitions. They cannot let power, a possibly useful means, become the end they pursue. The goal the system encourages them to seek is security. Increased power may or may not serve that end. . . . The first concern of states is not to maximize power but to maintain their positions in the system.

Since the anarchic world almost never assures survival, it is rarely possible in the neorealist view for states to trade between security and other desirable goals. Yet, by assuming that the outcome of a contest for power is probabilistic rather than certain, we necessarily introduce tradeoffs between security (that is, the preservation of sovereignty) and the quest for power. With probabilistic outcomes we can imagine a probability of success large enough to warrant putting security at risk (and I gave an example where that probability of success might be quite low). Doing so violates assumptions 3 and 4. We then are not examining the logic of neorealist theory but rather the logic of some other theory in which security is not of the utmost importance.

The first hypothesis of neorealism, that bipolarity leads to stability, does not follow from the stated assumptions of the theory. Still, we can save the hypothesis logically by introducing an assumption that says states always behave with caution when faced with clarity of information and generally behave recklessly when faced with uncertainty. Whether such an assumption is consistent with observed behavior is, of course, another matter. We cannot save the argument by allowing the outcome of competition for power to be probabilistic because that requires that we contradict some of the core assumptions of the theory. Doing so also contradicts the hypothesis that states mimic one another's actions and deprives a balance of power of any privileged position in the calculations of decision makers. So, it is perfectly fine to add additional assumptions to rescue a theory, but the theory cannot be rescued by contradicting the basic assumptions or by contradicting other important parts of its argument. Therefore, we cannot maintain the neorealist argument and add the possibility that leaders choose differently about gaining power at the possible expense of security, depending on how much they value the status quo, or based on how risky the outcome of pursuing more power might be. Still, with the assumption of risk aversion under certainty and risk seeking behavior under uncertainty we can tautologically conclude that destabilizing risks will be more likely in multipolar systems than in bipolar systems.

To elaborate on the previous point, let us turn our attention to some of the more interesting debates among scholars who describe themselves as neorealists. Charles Glaser (1994/1995) draws an optimistic view of international politics from Waltz's theory. He contends that cooperation certainly is a plausible outcome of international politics in a bipolar world. John Mearsheimer (1994/1995), by contrast, extracts a pessimistic view, inferring that conflict, not cooperation, is the state of international affairs in an anarchic, neorealist environment. How is it possible for two scholars to arrive at diametrically opposed, contradictory conclusions when they both claim to draw their inferences from the same theory? The answer may lie in the selective application of logically contradictory auxiliary hypotheses. Waltz (1979, 109) states that "states face a 'prisoners' dilemma'", but he also states (1979, 70) that "Politics among the European great powers tended toward the model of a zero-sum game. Each power viewed another's loss as its own gain." The prisoners' dilemma is not a zero-sum game, but, like two-player zero-sum games, if played a known amount of times, the prisoners' dilemma leads to conflict. However, if played an indefinite number of times, the prisoners' dilemma can lead to cooperation in equilibrium. A bipolar—two-player—zero-sum game, however, can never lead to a cooperative equilibrium, no matter how many times it is repeated.

## History and Neorealist Empirical Claims

Does it pay to try to save the bipolarity argument of neorealism? Is the record of history sufficiently consistent with the hypothesis that we should care to find some logical explanation for the stability produced by bipolarity? There are a number of ways to go about figuring out whether there is a strong historical relationship between the international system's level of polarity and its stability. I address several of those ways now, mindful of Waltz's (1979, 13) admonition that all theory, including neorealism, should be subjected to distinct and demanding tests.

One perspective that makes sense in light of neorealist arguments is to evaluate how long the structure of the international system remained unchanged under different configurations. There were several multipolar systems between 1648, when the modern state system is said by neorealists to have begun, and about 1945 when the bipolar system that ended around 1990 began. During the multipolar years, there were important changes in the system's structure arising as a consequence of alterations in the makeup of the set of nations who were major powers. Spain, for example, was one of the great powers during the sixteenth and seventeenth centuries, but it certainly was not among this elite group of states in the nineteenth or twentieth centuries. The United States is the most powerful state in the world today; it did not even exist in 1648 and it remained a relatively uninvolved state at least until the Spanish-American War in 1898.

If stability requires that the set of great powers remains unaltered, then each time the list of major powers changes we can say that there is a new multipolar system. That appears to be what Waltz had in mind when he wrote (1979, 162), "The stability of the system, so long as it remains anarchic, is then closely linked with the fate of its principal members." Using Jack Levy's (1983) classification of great powers since 1492 (or especially since the modern state system is said to have begun in 1648) we can determine whether the longevity of the bipolar system was comparatively long or short.

Figure 12.1 shows the longevity of each system defined as the period during which the makeup or number of the major powers remained unaltered.[14] It is evident that the approximately forty-five or so years of the bipolar international system was neither unusually long nor unusually short. Many multipolar great power systems lasted longer and many lasted a shorter time. We cannot conclude on the basis of longevity of the major power systems that multipolarity produces less stability than the one instance of bipolarity.

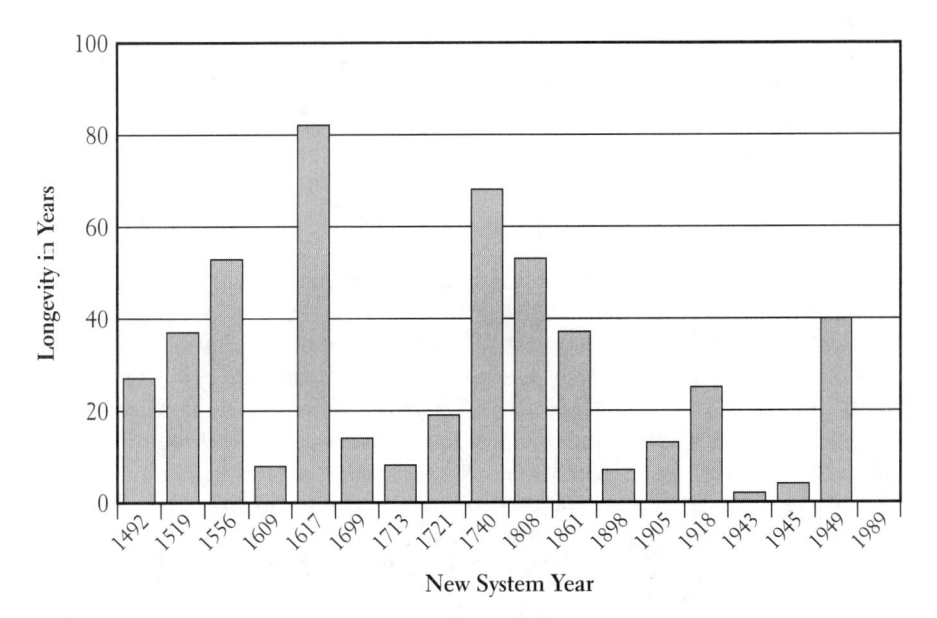

FIGURE 12.1  STABILITY OF INTERNATIONAL SYSTEMS

Of course, the longevity of a given international structure is not the only way to think about system stability. Another way to evaluate the stability of the international system is to examine the frequency of wars among the major powers, the most influential states in the world. Neorealists might object that the theory neither views war as a stabilizing element nor as a destabilizing element. Yet, the most frequently offered evidence for the stability of the bipolar period is the absence of a war between great powers during that period. If that is relevant evidence, then the span between such wars is an appropriate indicator of system stability. If neorealists are prepared to concede that bipolarity and the "long peace" (Gaddis 1980) are unrelated, then we can end the empirical discussion of bipolarity with the evidence already adduced to show that multipolar systems were not, on average, less stable than the one instance of bipolarity.

During the years that neorealists consider bipolar, there were two dominant powers: the United States and the Soviet Union. It is noteworthy that there was no war between these two dominant states during the bipolar years. Still, the United States and the Soviet Union each fought in several wars, just not against one another, and there was at least one war between major powers during the bipolar years. The Korean War from 1950–1953 saw combat between the United States and China. China and Russia also fought repeatedly along their extensive border, with many casualties and deaths, though this is rarely elevated to the stature of a war. The United States, China, and the Soviet Union, of course, were major powers, though only two were superpowers. The peace between the two superpowers has been described by the historian John Gaddis (1980) as "the long peace." Just how long a peace there was and whether it was due to bipolarity are both tricky questions.

With regard to causality, numerous changes in international affairs can be singled out to explain the so-called long peace. Bipolarity is one, but there is no reason to think it more or less plausible a factor than several others. Consider, for instance, the advent of nuclear deterrence. Nuclear deterrence tends to push the international system toward multipolarity, especially when several nuclear powers are each well-enough endowed to make the costs of an attack against them exceed the prospective benefits following a nuclear exchange. Nuclear weapons may well have raised the anticipated costs of instability well beyond any foreseeable benefit. The nuclear era, and its multipolar implications, coincides with the period of bipolarity and, unlike bipolarity, continues today. Waltz himself has argued that nuclear proliferation has a stabilizing impact (Sagan and Waltz 1995).

Some might point to the creation of the United Nations in 1945 as a significant improvement over the pre-war League of Nations in helping to limit superpower warfare. Certainly the United Nations has been involved in numerous peacekeeping missions that have helped contain and resolve disputes that might otherwise have entangled the great powers. The United Nations' most powerful arm is the Security Council. Five great powers are permanent members of the Security Council. Each can veto any resolution brought before the Council and pretty much all major security issues do come before it. The Security Council, then, institutionalizes a multipolar decision-making structure within the United Nations, providing a counterweight to bipolarity as an explanation for the long peace.

Numerous other accounts for the peace between the great powers have been vetted (Mueller 1989). The advent of commercial television and common intercontinental air travel, for instance, have both been claimed as pacifying developments that coincide with the origins of the bipolar system. Each brings people closer together and may foster greater cultural understanding. Of course, it could also be said that familiarity breeds contempt so we should not leap too quickly to endorse these or many other explanations, as each has counterarguments. Still, bipolarity also has counterarguments at least as persuasive as the arguments in its favor.

This leaves the question of just how long the long peace really was. The easy answer is that during all forty-four years between the end of World War II and the end of bipolarity there was no superpower war; there was peace in that limited but important sense. There were, however, only thirty-six years without a war between two major powers if we ignore the Sino-Russian border fighting, and there was barely a moment without some smaller war going on, often involving a major power. Recall that the Korean War involved major powers on each side. Additionally, the French fought in Indochina in the early 1950s, the French and the British fought against Egypt in the Suez War in 1956, the United States fought in the Dominican Republic, Vietnam, Grenada, Panama, and elsewhere; the Chinese fought India, Vietnam, and others, and the Soviet Union engaged in combat in Hungary, Czechoslovakia, Afghanistan, perhaps in the Ogaden, and repeatedly along the Sino-Soviet border against Chinese forces. None of these, however, may count as destabilizing as none led to the elimination of a major power actor. It is reasonable, then, to ask whether forty-four years really is an unusually long time without a major power war. Again I turn to Jack Levy's (1983) compilation, this time on major power wars since 1492. I use the information he assembled to assess whether forty-four years is "the long peace."

Levy's data remind us that thirty-eight years passed without major power war from the end of the Napoleonic Wars (1815) to the beginning of the Crimean War (1853). Forty-three years passed between the end of the Franco-Prussian War (1871) and the beginning of the First World War (1914) without an intervening major power war.[15] Other lengthy intervals without major power war can be found scattered throughout the past several centuries. Perhaps, however, some of these wars are not significant enough to have destabilized the system (though modern Germany and Austria-Hungary were born out of the relatively small Seven Weeks War [1866] and the Franco-Prussian War [1871]).

To evaluate this I look at the record of general wars. Levy identifies seven general wars since the Treaty of Westphalia: the Dutch War of Louis XIV (1672–1678), the War of the League of Augsburg (1688–1697), the War of the Spanish Succession (1701–1713), the Seven Years' War (1755–1763), the French Revolution and Napoleonic Wars (1792–1815), World War I (1914–1918), and World War II (1939–1945). In terms of general war, which seems to be what neorealists have in mind, the average interval between them has been thirty-four years, and the longest interval was ninety-nine years, well above the current period of peace since the last general war. It appears, then, that "the long peace" is not all that unusual after all.

## Other Neorealist Hypotheses and the Historical Record

Still another way to assess the predictive accuracy of the neorealist structural perspective is to examine carefully what does follow logically from the assumptions of this point of view. Then we can determine whether the hypotheses that do follow logically from the theory are historically accurate or not. Several careful studies of the logic of neorealism have been conducted and have derived anew some hypotheses that more casual treatments have identified and also yielded some new hypotheses that they had missed. Emerson Niou, Peter Ordeshook, and Gregory Rose (1989), for instance, have carefully traced out the logic of neorealism. They reach four central conclusions from that logic. Their four conclusions, proven as theorems, given their representation of neorealism, are as follows:

1. Essential states never become inessential.
2. Essential states are never eliminated from the international system.
3. Inessential states never become essential states.
4. Inessential states are always eliminated from the international system.

By essential states, recall, they mean any state that can join a losing coalition and, by dint of its membership, turn that coalition into a blocking coalition or a winner. That is exactly the way the term was used earlier in constructing examples about the stability of multipolar and bipolar systems. Inessential states are states that cannot turn even one losing alliance into a winning or blocking combination.

Although Niou, Ordeshook, and Rose show that these hypotheses follow logically from neorealist assumptions, each is historically false. Austria-Hungary was an essential state at the outset of World War I. By war's end it not only became inessential, it ceased to exist. Likewise, the Soviet Union was an essential state throughout the Cold War. Indeed, it was a superpower. Today it does not exist. In fact, it willingly and peacefully gave up its sphere of influence and its status as a great power. It is not yet clear whether any of its successor states, especially Russia, have reduced their power to ensure survival or are themselves inessential and possibly doomed to extinction. The United States in the late eighteenth and nineteenth centuries was an inessential state. Obviously, today it is an essential player on the world stage; it is the lone superpower in the world. Many other examples can be given to show that the four theorems Niou, Ordeshook, and Rose deduced from a careful, logically coherent representation of neorealism simply are not consistent with history.

Bueno de Mesquita and David Lalman (1992) also constructed a formalized version of neorealist theory. They focused attention on the demands between states that form the core of international disputes. According to neorealist logic these demands between states must be chosen to protect security and enhance national power. Therefore, what is demanded (and what is not) depends on the structure of the situation in which the state finds itself. That is, demands in the international arena are the result of strategic choices; they are endogenous.[16] Because demands are chosen taking the logic of the situation into account, nations would never knowingly choose actions that lead to a war that places their survival at risk, as Bueno de Mesquita and Lalman prove within the context of what they call the *Realpolitik* version of their international interaction game (hereafter IIG). What is more, numerous other game theoretic examinations of war (Powell 1990, 1999; Fearon 1995; Morrow 1997) within a structural perspective also prove that war does not arise without uncertainty, seemingly in support of neorealism's claim about bipolarity (remembering that bipolarity really is a surrogate for the absence of uncertainty and multipolarity is a surrogate for the presence of uncertainty). In fact, states would only knowingly choose actions that protect the status quo or that lead to the negotiated resolution of differences if they did not face uncertainty and lived within a neorealist world.[17] From this perspective, Bueno de Mesquita and Lalman identify another three hypotheses that follow directly from their representation of the logic of neorealism. The three central neorealist hypotheses that they deduce are as follows:

1. Uncertainty promotes war and certainty promotes negotiations or the status quo.
2. Regardless of information circumstances (uncertainty or certainty), no nation will ever acquiesce peacefully to the demands of another state.
3. A necessary, but not sufficient, condition for war is that both parties to the war believe their chances of winning are better than fifty percent.

The record of history does not support any of these hypotheses either.

Using Bueno de Mesquita and Lalman's data, I show that there is not a straightforward historical relationship between uncertainty and the risk of war, as is evident from Figure 12.2.[18] As uncertainty increases, first there is a statistically significant increase in the likelihood of war, followed by a significant decrease in the risk of war

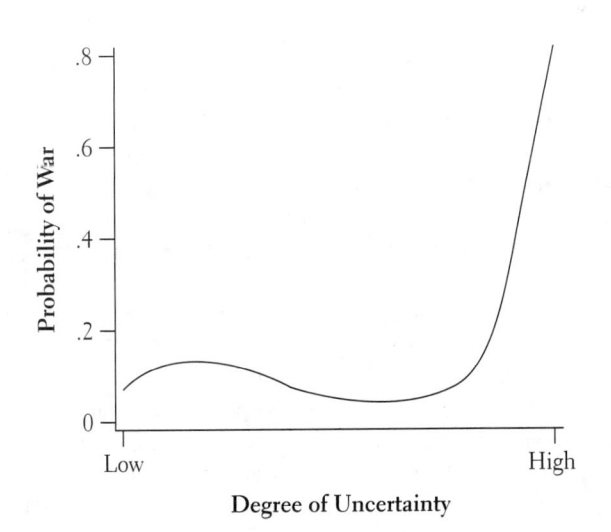

FIGURE 12.2  WAR AND UNCERTAINTY

at moderate to high levels of uncertainty. At extremely high levels of uncertainty, the probability that disputes turn into war turns sharply upwards. For most of the range of degrees of uncertainty, the probability of war stays well below 20 percent, rising above that level only under truly extreme conditions.

The two periods during which uncertainty was so high that it predicted war with near certainty are 1866—when Prussia, Austria, and several smaller German states fought the Seven Weeks War—and 1966–1968, when Cold War tensions were very high in the buildup to the Soviet invasion of Czechoslovakia. In the mid-1860s as in the mid-1960s, long-established ties among nations were under great strain, making leaders more uncertain than usual about who they could or could not count on. In both general instances of extremely high uncertainty it is interesting to realize that the associated conflicts were among states allied to one another. In the 1866 cases, the states involved in the Seven Weeks War were all members of a mutual defense pact with one another. That was also true of many of the cases of tension under high uncertainty in the 1966–1968 period. Conflict among allies precipitates uncertainty because it is difficult to evaluate how states will choose sides between the belligerents, given the great similarities in their discernible foreign policy commitments (Bueno de Mesquita 1981b).

The risk of war and other destabilizing international interactions is not straightforwardly linked to changes in uncertainty. Bueno de Mesquita and Lalman, for instance, show that a particular type of state that they call a pacific dove is especially likely to initiate the use of force when it is very weak relative to its adversaries, provided it is uncertain whether its opponents are also pacifically inclined. In most other instances, however, it is the strong rather than the weak who are likely to initiate violence, according to the results reported by Bueno de Mesquita and Lalman (1992). The prospect that the status quo will continue or that disputes will be resolved through negotiations is also not closely linked to the level of uncertainty. Bueno de Mesquita and Lalman show this using data from 1816 to 1974. Their *Realpolitik* deduction that reductions in uncertainty should increase the odds of peaceful solutions to disputes is a more general form of Waltz's contention that bipolarity reduces the threat of instability. Therefore, the failure of Bueno de Mesquita and Lalman's neorealist proposition to find support in the historical record is quite troubling for neorealist claims, especially in light of all the other evidence against the hypothesis that bipolarity promotes stability.

The second hypothesis derived from the *Realpolitik* variant of the IIG, which concerns the impossibility of a state ever choosing to give in to another state's demand without either negotiating a compromise or fighting to protect its interests, is also historically false. That nations do acquiesce to the demands of others is evident. During the Fashoda Crisis between Britain and France in 1898, for instance, Britain sought to control as much of the Upper Nile as possible. The French, however, controlled the town of Fashoda in the Sudan, exactly in the path of British ambitions. The British were unyielding in their demands. They wanted nothing less than a full acquiescence by the French and were prepared to go to war to pursue their ends. The French were in a militarily weak position and, given domestic dissatisfaction with the French cabinet, the government was in a vulnerable political position indeed. Rather than risk a prolonged crisis and eventual defeat that would almost certainly have led to the downfall of their government, the French gave in. They recognized that their only real alternative was to resist, provoking a British attack that they did not have the strength to repel. In such a situation, they were better off acquiescing, thereby trying to save their domestic political position, than facing a humiliating military defeat.[19] Contrary to the logic of neorealism, but consistent with the domestic variant of the international interaction game, acquiescence was not impossible; in fact it happens quite often in international affairs.

A common claim among some realist theorists is that war only occurs when both sides believe that their chance of winning is greater than 50 percent (Blainey 1973). They appear to hypothesize that a balance of power promotes peace and an imbalance, war. This is a partial statement of what has come to be known as the balance of power theory. Some neorealists, including Waltz, sometimes contend that this is not a prediction made by realism or neorealism.[20] They occasionally maintain that this claim is a foil invented by power transition theorists (Organski 1958; Organski and Kugler 1980; Gilpin 1981). Yet, many eminent realist and neorealist scholars and statesmen suggest that when power is pretty evenly distributed then peace is likely, while an uneven distribution of power tends to increase the risk of war (Wright 1942, see, e.g., Vol. 1, 254; Blainey 1973, especially 109–114; Morgenthau 1973, especially 189 ff; George and Smoke 1974, especially 14 ff; Hartmann 1978, e.g., 316; Kissinger 1979, e.g., 195; Waltz 1979, especially 201–206). To be sure, these scholars and statesmen sometimes disagree with one another about exactly what they mean by a balanced distribution of power. Some emphasize the distribution of power among the most influential states, while others emphasize an equal distribution between coalitions or blocs of states. These can be quite different. Still, many argue that balanced power decreases the risk of war and unbalanced power increases that risk. Waltz himself, theorizing about war, writes (1979, 206, emphasis added) "How can we hope that the wielders of great power will not savage a region in the name of making and maintaining world order? At the level of the international system, *one may hope that power, which has recently come into closer balance, remains there. A military competition, if it is a close one, calls for caution on the part of the competitors.*" I have difficulty seeing how this and the discussion surrounding it can be interpreted other than that the temptation to use force is muted by balanced power.

To see how different alternative views of balanced power can be, consider the estimates of national power in Table 12.1. Table 12.1 shows estimates of the national capabilities, or power, of the seven states that made up the major powers in 1896. The table also shows the capabilities of three blocs of nations that represent the major power blocs in 1896, based on calculations of the similarity in military alliance commitments among these most influential of states. The data are all drawn from the Correlates of War Project. Looking at the capabilities of each of the major powers paints a quite different picture than does looking at the capabilities of the three major power blocs. The individual states were quite unequal in their relative power. Britain alone controlled over 28 percent of the capabilities of the major powers. Japan had less than 5 percent and Italy just barely more than 5 percent of the major power capabilities. Yet the bloc that Italy belonged to (including Germany and Austria-Hungary) possessed almost 35 percent of the capabilities of the major powers. The second bloc, which included Russia, Japan, and France, controlled just under 37 percent of capabilities, with Britain, as already mentioned, in possession of the remaining 28 percent. One easy way to measure how unequally divided power was is to add up the absolute difference between the power of the average nation (or coalition of nations) and the power of each individual nation (or coalition of nations).[21] If every unit had exactly the same amount of power, this method would add up to zero. If one state (or coalition) had all the power and the others had none (the most unbalanced system possible) this method would add up to 100. Focusing on the individual major powers gives a total absolute deviation of 49.5 percent, reflecting great inequality in the distribution of power among the major states in 1896. Focusing on the major power alliance blocs of 1896 suggests that the system was much more balanced. In fact, the sum of the absolute deviations from the mean for each bloc is only 10.3 percent. So, the exact meaning of balance itself can profoundly influence whether we interpret a system as being balanced or unbalanced. Unfortunately, contrary to the epistemological strictures set out by Waltz, neorealism does not provide a precise and explicit definition of the concept "balance of power."

It turns out, by whichever means we measure the balance of power, there is no systematic relationship between the likelihood of war and the balance of power. This fact has been demonstrated by Singer, Bremer, and Stuckey (1972), Organski and Kugler (1980), and Bueno de Mesquita and Lalman (1988) among many others. Nor is there a significant association between estimates of the probability of victory for either side in a war and the likelihood that there would be a war. As Table 12.2 shows, the evidence fails to support the neorealist hypothesis that it is necessary (but not sufficient) for war that each side thinks its chance of victory is greater than 50 percent.

TABLE 12.1   THE BALANCE OF POWER IN 1896

| Country | Power | Bloc | Power |
|---|---|---|---|
| Germany | 21.4% | Germany & Austria-Hungary & Italy | 34.9% |
| Austria-Hungary | 8.4 | | |
| Italy | 5.1 | | |
| Russia | 17.3 | Russia & Japan & France | 36.9 |
| Japan | 4.6 | | |
| France | 15.0 | | |
| Britain | 28.2 | Britain | 28.2% |
| Total | 100.0% | | 100.0% |

TABLE 12.2  IS A GREATER THAN FIFTY/FIFTY CHANCE
OF VICTORY A NECESSARY CONDITION FOR WAR?

| Did War Occur in Europe Dyads, 1815–1992? | Initiator's Probability of Victory > 50 Percent | Initiator's Probability of Victory < 50 Percent |
|---|---|---|
| War Occurred | 52 (13.1%) | 37 (11.9%) |
| No War | 345 (86.9%) | 273 (88.1%) |

Source: Bueno de Mesquita and Lalman (1992, 70).

If the neorealist hypothesis derived from the IIG were correct, then the entry in the cell of Table 12.2 that corresponds with the row labeled "War Occurred" and the column labeled "Initiator's Probability of Victory < 50 Percent" would be zero because that cell violates the hypothesized necessary condition for war. Not only is it not zero, but it is not meaningfully closer to zero than the cell that corresponds to "War Occurred" when the "Initiator's Probability of Victory > 50 Percent." Table 12.2 takes into account all cases of disputes within Europe between 1816 and 1974 and so is a rather broad-based test of this neorealist claim. The evidence forces us to conclude that hypotheses about war and stability that follow from formal statements of neorealism and that also are shown to be stated by Waltz, are not supported by the record of history. One can object that the measurement is too error-prone, though the same data have also been used by Paul Kennedy (1987) and many others. If measurement is an issue, then advocates of neorealist views should identify acceptable indicators of the distribution of power so that appropriate distinct and demanding tests can be performed.

Applying Waltz's standards for evaluating theories, I conclude that the theory's central empirical claims are false. I have reviewed and presented numerous distinct and demanding tests. I have used the definitions provided by Waltz whenever possible. I showed that the central hypotheses do not follow from the stated assumptions. Taking that into account, I have examined ways to modify the theory and then tested the refined propositions. These modifications proved wanting in that either they contradict core assumptions or they prove wanting empirically. In light of the criteria stipulated by Waltz, it is difficult to see how we can avoid the conclusion that the neorealist view is falsified. Still, we should not abandon neorealist theory unless we can demonstrate at least one alternative that does better. This is consistent both with a Lakatosian view of philosophy of science and with Waltz's view that, "in the end one sticks with the theory that reveals most." In the section that follows, I briefly discuss an alternative theory that, on empirical grounds, can be said to supercede neorealism.

## THE INTERNATIONAL INTERACTION GAME AND WAR

Earlier I introduced the neorealist version of the international interaction game (IIG). Bueno de Mesquita and Lalman (1992) also proposed an alternative theory in which policy demands and threats are motivated by domestic political considerations, but choices of action are shaped by the international context. Now I examine a few of the predictions from that theory—the domestic IIG—more carefully. This game identifies eight generic possible outcomes from international interactions: the status quo, negotiations, acquiescence by one side or the other, capitulation by one side or the other, and war started by one side or the other. Bueno de Mesquita and Lalman (1992) propose seven assumptions that define restrictions over the possible ordering of preferences for each decision maker across the eight outcomes.

The domestic version of the international interaction game assumes that leaders select their policy demands based on the domestic political pressures they need to satisfy to retain their jobs. This produces one fundamental difference between the IIG's neorealist variant and its domestic variant. In the neorealist version it is not possible for a decision maker to prefer to compel a rival to capitulate rather than negotiate with the rival. This is so because demands are assumed to be shaped by the structure of the international situation without regard to domestic politics. States choose demands to minimize the risk that they will lose security. Being forced to capitulate following an attack reduces a state's security by compelling it to give in to whatever the adversary has demanded and also to bear a cost in lost lives and resources in the process. To avoid these losses, each state is assumed to structure its response to the adversary's demand so that the state offers just enough concessions to make the would-be aggressor decide to negotiate a compromise settlement rather than use force. That is, each state chooses its own demands to make the adversary indifferent between seeking greater gains, but at a cost, rather than negotiate. By negotiating, the potentially aggressive foe gains less in terms of policy than it might have by using force, but it conserves resources by avoiding the costs it must endure as a consequence of its attack, thereby protecting its current security. As long as the expected utility from negotiating is at least as large as the net expected utility from attacking, the rival is steered toward negotiation and away from aggression.[22] This leaves the rival no worse off and it leaves the state that chose its policy proposals to avoid being forced to capitulate better off.

In the domestic version of the IIG, by contrast, while it is possible to make demands that convince the other side to negotiate rather than attack, the assumptions of the theory do not preclude the possibility that one state's leader will prefer to force a capitulation rather than negotiate. Therefore, the domestic IIG allows some preference orderings that the neorealist version precludes, namely any orderings in which forcing a capitulation is preferred to negotiating. Be careful not to get confused here. In either version of the IIG, any state prefers to negotiate rather than to capitulate. The difference is not in choosing to capitulate or to negotiate; the difference is that, in the domestic version, a state can want to make another state capitulate while, in the Realpolitik variant, it cannot end up preferring to force a capitulation over negotiating because the other state will offer a good enough negotiated settlement to avoid the costs of an attack. The domestic IIG labels actors as doves if they prefer to negotiate with a rival rather than force the rival to capitulate. Hawks are defined as actors who prefer to force a rival to capitulate rather than negotiate with them.

The existence of hawks as well as doves in the domestic version of the international interaction game produces fundamental differences in predictions about war. Bueno de Mesquita and Lalman prove what they call the IIG's *Basic War Theorem*. This logical implication of their game states that war can be a subgame perfect Nash equilibrium of the IIG. This means that the game contains conditions that are both necessary and sufficient for war under complete and perfect information. War is the complete and perfect information equilibrium outcome of the domestic IIG, provided four conditions are fulfilled that are logically permitted, but not required, by the assumptions of the game. These conditions define a subset of the 2,704 logically admissible pairs of preference orderings over the game's outcomes. These conditions are as follows:

1. That player A prefers to initiate a war rather than acquiesce to the demands of the opponent
2. That A prefers to capitulate if attacked rather than retaliate and fight a war in which the adversary gains the advantages of a first strike
3. That player B prefers to fight a war started by A rather than capitulate to an attack by A
4. That B prefers to force A to capitulate rather than negotiate with A

Condition (4) is not possible under the neorealist version of the IIG because when demands are chosen strategically within the international framework, this is the preference by a foe that each actor worries about and so takes action to offset. That action, again, is to make a demand or offer concessions that persuade the would-be aggressive rival that negotiating is at least as good for her state as is trying to force a capitulation. Negotiation is always better for the state that otherwise would have had to capitulate. Negotiation allows the state to avoid the physical costs of being attacked and negotiation provides the state with some chance ($0 < P < 1$) of getting part of what it wants. There is no such chance if the state is compelled to capitulate.

The logical possibility of war under complete and perfect information is controversial. A simple way to think of how such a situation could arise when all players know that all players prefer to negotiate rather than fight a war is to think of a situation similar to a prisoners' dilemma arising in the part of the game known as the crisis subgame. What happens, in essence, is that the threat of being forced to capitulate can lead a state to initiate war if it has a large enough first-strike advantage. Knowing that the rival will take advantage and force a capitulation if the state offers to negotiate, and knowing that it has a valuable first-strike advantage of its own, the state may decide to initiate fighting rather than cede the first-strike advantage to a belligerent foe. In essence, the conditions stipulate that the first-strike advantage makes it difficult for a leader to credibly commit to give up that advantage and negotiate. The derivation of conditions under which war is logically possible with complete and perfect information also implies important differences between the domestic IIG and neorealism.

We have already seen that neorealist theorists suggest that uncertainty in the form of multipolarity increases the risk of instability (and war is often a source of and symptom of instability). In contrast, Bueno de Mesquita and Lalman report conditions under which uncertainty promotes peace and stability, while certainty (or improved information) makes war more likely, and they note other conditions under which uncertainty promotes instability. So, the IIG leads to the inference that the impact of uncertainty on instability is contingent on other factors contained within the IIG. To see how uncertainty can promote peace and stability let us look more carefully at the basic war theorem of the IIG.

If the IIG's logically necessary and sufficient conditions for war are met, then war is expected to take place. Suppose that the four conditions of the basic war theorem are met in the sense that, if preferences were common knowledge, then the conditions for war would be satisfied. Suppose, however, that because of uncertainty, rivals do not know the preferences over outcomes held by their adversaries so that there is incomplete information. This uncertainty reduces the likelihood that the choices made will end in war. If at least one leader mistakenly perceives that the rival's preferences are anything other than what is stated in the basic war theorem, then the risk of war must be reduced by uncertainty. This must be true if the theorem is correct because the probability that an action will be taken when its necessary and sufficient conditions are met is 1.0 (by definition). The theorem, of course, stipulates complete and perfect information. If complete information is absent, but the rest of the theorem's conditions hold, the necessary and sufficient conditions for war as stated above are no longer satisfied because one or both players have mistaken beliefs about the other's expected payoffs. In that case, the probability of the relevant event or action can only decrease as a result of the decision maker's uncertainty.

Similarly, it is possible for decision makers to mistakenly perceive that the conditions for war are met so that their interaction is ripe for war. If the conditions for war under complete and perfect information are not met but, because of uncertainty, leaders believe those conditions are met as a result of a mistaken belief about the preferences of the rival, then uncertainty increases the risk of war because without uncertainty there would be no chance of war at all. Thus, uncertainty should not always have the same effect on the risk of war-created instability in the international system if the IIG hypothesis is supported. Rather, uncertainty can increase the risks of a destabilizing conflict and uncertainty can also decrease that risk, each under specific, identifiable circumstances.[23]

## War and Uncertainty: The IIG and Structural Theories

Bueno de Mesquita and Lalman's results from their domestic IIG can be compared directly to the hypotheses of neorealism. In neorealism, uncertainty makes war (and other sources of instability) more likely and certainty makes war less likely. Put more broadly, the greater the degree of uncertainty, according to neorealism, the higher the probability of destabilizing events like war. By contrast, the domestic IIG identifies conditions under which increases in uncertainty make war more likely and conditions under which increases in uncertainty make war less likely. If the IIG's necessary and sufficient conditions for war under complete and perfect information are not met and there is complete and perfect information, the probability of war (or instability) should be zero, making the same prediction under these conditions as is made by the bipolarity hypothesis of neorealism. When the necessary and sufficient conditions for war under complete and perfect information are not met but there is not complete information so that there is uncertainty, then the international interaction game predicts that the probability of war increases. This is also the prediction made by neorealism. So, under two conditions neorealism and the IIG make the same predictions about the likelihood of war (or other forms of instability), and under two other conditions neorealism makes predictions opposite to those of the IIG. This provides an opportunity to conduct a critical test. The accuracy of the alternative explanations of instability and conflict can be compared by examining the cases in which they make *different* predictions. Of course, we cannot choose among the theories on the basis of the cases where they make the same predictions. In those cases, if one is right so is the other and if one is wrong so is the other. Examining the cases where the theories differ in their predictions is a critical way to choose among theories. It is a demanding test. Both theories can be wrong, one or the other can be consistent with the evidence, but both cannot be supported by the evidence.

Evidence from European disputes since 1816 supports Bueno de Mesquita and Lalman's hypotheses, but refutes the alternative hypothesis about war and uncertainty. Figures 12.3 and 12.4 (on page 194) show the relationship between the probability of war and the level of uncertainty in the European system, using Bueno de Mesquita and Lalman's (1992) indicators, for all disputes in that part of the world since 1816 and through 1974. In Figure 12.3, the IIG's necessary and sufficient conditions for war under complete and perfect information are met and in Figure 12.4 those same conditions are not met. In both figures, uncertainty varies from very low levels to very high levels. If neorealist predictions are supported, then both graphs will slope upwards because these theories predict that uncertainty is destabilizing and less uncertainty enhances greater stability. If the IIG is supported, then the first graph will slope downward and the second upward.[24] Clearly, the two figures support the expectations deduced from the domestic version of the IIG in contradiction to neorealism's expectations. Reevaluations of the claims of the IIG, using more advanced statistical methods or controlling for more potentially confounding factors, have been carried out by Signorino (1998), Smith (1998), Bennett and Stam (1998), Gelpi and Grieco (1998) and others. All of these studies reinforce the IIG findings reported here, with Signorino's results being most equivocal. Smith's show that the IIG is the only theory of the many he tested that does better than the null hypothesis of no relationship when using a stringent, Bayesian inference test. Additionally, the IIG makes numerous predictions not made by neorealist theory so that, in a Lakatosian sense, it contains excess empirical content beyond that possessed by neorealism.

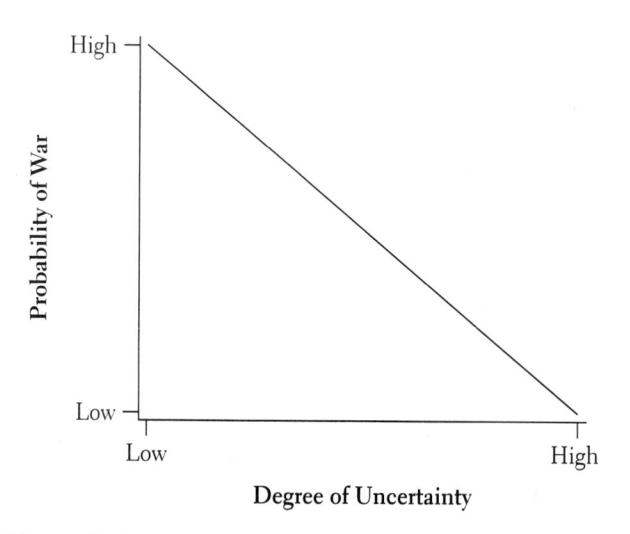

FIGURE 12.3  WAR, IIG CONDITIONS MET, AND UNCERTAINTY

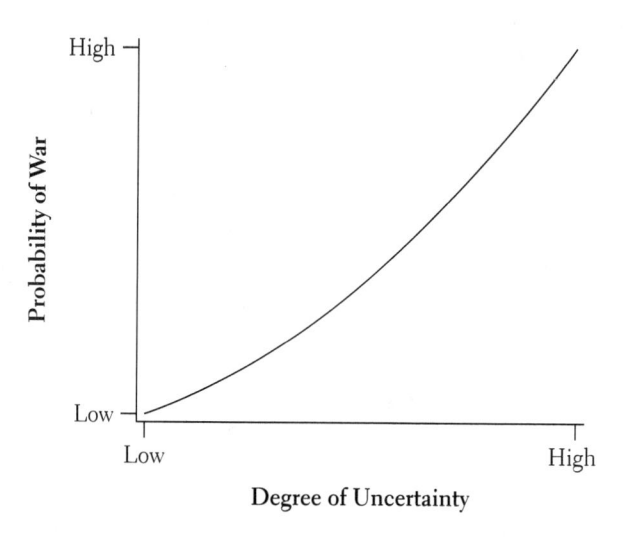

FIGURE 12.4  WAR, IIG CONDITIONS NOT MET, AND UNCERTAINTY

## SUMMARY

I have examined the central hypotheses of neorealism. I showed that the claims that bipolarity promotes stability, uncertainty provokes instability, states routinely mimic each other, and a balance of power helps foster stability are logically flawed and are refuted by the historical record. These contentions must not be taken lightly or accepted casually. Yet at least one alternative theory, the domestic variant of the international interaction game, was shown to be consistent with the historical facts that align with balance of power or neorealist arguments, while also being consistent with central facts that do not align with those other theories. The IIG accounts for the facts accounted for by neorealism, and also accounts for numerous other facts. It also produces novel, tested hypotheses that do not follow from neorealism.

So little evidence exists with which to sustain confidence in neorealist predictions that the burden seems to fall on those who wish to argue that neorealism is not falsified or superceded. Scientific progress is made by building progressively on the ideas we inherit, discarding the parts that clearly fail us when we find superior alternatives. Much valuable debate has been stimulated by neorealism and many useful insights have been gleaned from it. However, mindful of Waltz's rules for judging theories, I now urge us to abandon neorealist balance of power and polarity arguments. The logic behind several game theory treatments of international politics provides an alternative that meets the criteria to be viewed as improvements over the neorealist notions. They account for the facts explained by neorealism, but they also account for many facts not explained by that theory. I have performed here and elsewhere, and have summarized and reported here many distinct and demanding tests. We should not sustain theories out of affection or nostalgia for them, but only if the logic and evidence warrants doing so. If the tests conducted here are not convincing refutation, then those who believe in these structural theories should state clearly what, for them, would constitute a falsifying test or tests.

## Editors' Commentary

### Major Query

Can Waltz's theory on bipolarity be considered falsified?

### Major Points

Bueno de Mesquita follows up on Rosecrance's analysis by asking, when is a theory falsified? He states that, in principle, a theory is falsified either when it is shown to be logically contradictory or incomplete (as when hypotheses do not follow from the logic of the theory) or when it fails to account for as broad an array of facts as competing alternatives. In terms of its logical coherence, Bueno de Mesquita maintains that Waltz's hypothesis that bipolarity is more stable than multipolarity cannot be logically derived from Waltz's four theoretical assumptions. He maintains that the claim is inferred primarily from the assumption that uncertainty is more prevalent in multipolarity than bipolarity. However, Bueno de Mesquita argues that Waltz fails to show that uncertainty per se must be associated with instability, and, more importantly, this conclusion cannot be logically implied by the four assumptions of Waltz's neorealist theory. In fact, he argues that the hypothesis is inconsistent with the assumptions, and that the assumptions would imply the opposite—i.e., that multipolarity is more stable than bipolarity. To save the logical coherence of the theory one must introduce a new assumption; namely, that uncertainty is associated with risk-seeking behavior and certainty with risk aversion.

After examining the logical coherence of the theory, Bueno de Mesquita provides two important tests of the hypothesis. Now that the Cold War and bipolar era are over, it is possible to test some of Waltz's hypotheses. Bueno de Mesquita tests Waltz's claims about stability by seeing: (1) whether the bipolar post–1945 era was longer than previous, especially multipolar, eras, and (2) whether the frequency of wars among the major states was lower. To test the first claim on "stability as longevity," he uses Waltz's (1979, 161–162) criterion that a system changes when there is a major variation in the number of major states. On the basis of this definition, he maintains that the post–1945 era ended in 1990. He collects data going back to 1648 on the length of various systems, and he finds that the post–1945 bipolar era lasted forty-five or so years, which is not unusually long or short compared to other systems (see Figure 12.1). This evidence contradicts the hypothesis that bipolar systems are more stable (i.e., last longer).

He tests the second claim (that bipolar periods have fewer wars) by looking at how long a peace there was between the United States and the USSR compared to other "long peaces" that occurred in the past. He finds that in the Cold War system, the United States and the USSR went without fighting for forty-four years, which is a long time. However, in previous multipolar systems, similar lengthy periods of peace can be found (e.g., 1815–1853 [38 years], 1871–1914 [43 years]). Indeed the average interval between great-power general wars (i.e., world wars) from 1648 on was thirty-four years, and the longest ninety-nine years. From this perspective, he infers that "the long peace" of the bipolar era was not that unusual.

Bueno de Mesquita concludes his analysis by reviewing other discrepant findings on the balance of power and comparing neorealist balance of power theory with his own alternative theory, which incorporates domestic political considerations into an international interaction game (see Bueno de Mesquita and Lalman 1992). He presents evidence that shows that the latter is supported while the neorealist explanation is not. He concludes that the analysis he has presented not only falsifies Waltz's neorealism but also presents a better alternate theory that can explain all the facts the neorealist theory would like to explain, plus more.

## The Argument on Logical Coherence

For Bueno de Mesquita the propositions of a theory must be derived logically from the assumptions of the theory. Bueno de Mesquita lays out a complicated argument to demonstrate that this has not been done. He begins by stating that Waltz assumes that multipolar systems are more prone to uncertainty, and that uncertainty produces instability. However, according to Bueno de Mesquita, Waltz does not show that the uncertainty level of a type of system can be logically derived from the theory's assumptions (nor does Waltz empirically show that uncertainty produces instability).

For Bueno de Mesquita there is this logical gap in the theory that makes it logically incoherent. To "save" the theory, it is necessary to reformulate it, which he does at the end of that section, but this is now a new theory.

## The Empirical Tests

Bueno de Mesquita presents two straightforward tests, as well as reviewing tests he has conducted elsewhere. In testing a proposition, a scholar basically places a "bet" on what the evidence (in a graph or table) should look like, if the theory is correct. The evidence for the first test appears in Figure 12.1. The first test (or bet) is that bipolar periods are more stable and hence longer. Figure 12.1 depicts how long various systems have lasted since 1492. It can be seen from the graph that the post–1945 bipolar period Waltz discusses is hardly longer than other periods.

A second test is to see if the post–1945 bipolar period was more peaceful than other periods. Many scholars refer to this period as "the long peace" (Gaddis 1980). While it is true that the United States and USSR never directly fought each other, examining only the one case does not permit us to infer whether such a long peace is unusual or unique to bipolar periods. Bueno de Mesquita shows that long periods of peace without a general war among major states are not uncommon, with the longest lasting ninety-nine years—considerably longer than the recently passed bipolar era. Therefore, one cannot associate the long peace, necessarily, with bipolarity.

A third test Bueno de Mesquita discusses is represented in Table 12.2 (on page 189). Here he makes the point that if neorealism posits that a necessary condition of war is that the initiator expects its probability of winning the war to be greater than (>) 50 percent, then there should be no cases of a state initiating a war when it expects the probability of winning to be less than (<) 50 percent (top cell on the right). (A *necessary condition* of war is one that must be fulfilled for war to occur.) The table shows that when war occurs there is not much difference between the two expectations—13.1 percent go to war when they believe the probability of winning is greater than 50 percent and 11.9 percent go to war when they believe the probability of winning is less than 50 percent. (If the proposition is correct, there should be no or very few cases in this cell).

On the basis of these tests and other reviewed evidence, Bueno de Mesquita shows that the theory has not *passed* empirical testing, and he concludes that its central empirical claims are false.

## Key Terms

**falsification** Rejection of a theory as a result of its failing to pass an empirical test.

**uncertainty** Doubt in the minds of decisions makers about factors important to a decision, such as what states can be counted on to support them, who their foes will be, and so forth—more generally, lack of information or confidence in the information available.

## NOTES

1. By more stringent criteria I have in mind Lakatos 1978 and Laudan 1977.
2. A careful and thorough debate regarding the logical and empirical standing of the realist paradigm can be found in the exchanges between Vasquez (1997), Waltz (1997), Christensen and Snyder (1997), Elman and Elman (1997), Schweller (1997), and Walt (1997) (reprinted herein as chapters two through seven).
3. Space limitations preclude me from discussing the ways in which the burgeoning research on domestic institutions and international politics challenges central conclusions of neorealism. In this essay I examine other, more direct refutations of neorealist theory. For a summary of other studies that challenge the unitary actor implications of neorealism, see Bueno de Mesquita 1999b.
4. It should be noted that Waltz's seven criteria do not include an evaluation of the relative performance of competing theories. Yet, he later argues (Waltz 1979, 123–124, emphasis added) that "Testing theories is a difficult and subtle task, made so by the interdependence of fact and theory, by the elusive relation between reality and theory as an instrument for its apprehension. Questions of truth and falsity are somehow involved, but so are questions of usefulness and uselessness. *In the end, one sticks with the theory that reveals most, even if its validity is suspect.*" Here Waltz appears supportive of Lakatosian (1978) standards for evaluating theory, though he focuses more on hypothesis testing than does Lakatos.
5. Others may disagree, of course. In that case, I urge them to state explicitly and clearly what standard of rejection they are applying so that additional distinct and demanding tests can be conducted to address their concerns. Neorealists tend to defend their theory with case history examples that purportedly support their perspective. Such studies, however, are not demanding tests in that a single case study cannot show which competing theory, in Waltz's terms, reveals most. Others offer a still weaker defense, arguing that Waltz acknowledges that his theory is not falsifiable (Schweller 1998a, 184; Waltz 1979, 124). Since Waltz explicitly requires that a theory must be falsifiable, to acknowledge that his argument is not falsifiable is to conclude that it is not a theory. I reject this view. Waltz (1979, 124) actually claims that his theory is *difficult* to falsify, not that it cannot be falsified.
6. Waltz (1979, 174) notes, "The simplicity of relations in a bipolar world and the strong pressures that are generated make the two great powers conservative."
7. Notice how quickly the uncertainty condition assumed in Waltz's theory encourages us to consider variations in decision maker responses to uncertainty across states. This leads us to seek a theory of foreign policy, whereas Waltz contends his theory is exclusively systemic. If we cannot derive a common response to uncertainty based on systemic factors alone, then his theory cannot exclude considerations of what he views as foreign policy. But if we introduce foreign policy into the theory, then it is no longer a systemic theory and its fundamental premise is contradicted. One might object that uncertainty is not the key factor for Waltz, the quotation offered above notwithstanding. An alternative candidate might be power balancing on which Waltz also places great emphasis. The difficulty is that risk takers will react to balanced power differently from risk avoiders, so we are back to the same problem. We need either to assume away variation on risk-taking proclivities of leaders or we need to assume, remarkably, that they are all alike in their risk-taking inclinations.
8. Waltz (1979, 112) indicates that victory in war settles questions of relative power at least for the moment: "Wars among states cannot settle questions of authority and right; they can only determine the allocation of gains and losses among contenders and settle for a time the question of who is the stronger."
9. Note that this argument is not circumvented by arguing that victory requires a larger margin of advantage in power as that simply shifts the location, but not the existence, of a knife-edge condition under which bipolar systems are stable. If A has X units of power and B has $1 - X$, and an advantage larger than Y is required to destabilize the situation, then any distribution of power in which $2X - Y > 1$ is unstable and any distribution in which $2X - Y < 1$ is stable. Of course, if for one party $2X - Y < 1$ then, defining X now in terms of the other party's resources, that party calculates that for the newly designated X, $2X - Y > 1$. So, stability only arises when $2X - Y = 1$, a knife-edge condition.
10. If nation E did not exist and the system contained 298 units of power without it, then the configuration would be stable. Any combination of 149 units, including a combination of 75 units and 74 units produces a stable blocking coalition.
11. This raises the issue of credible commitment. How can states credibly commit before a war or other destabilizing event to the distribution of power among them after the event? Because the neorealist world involves self-help, we can infer that some incentive compatible solution to the commitment

problem is worked out, though neorealist theory is largely silent on this issue. As Fearon (1995) has shown, the assumption of anarchy does not preclude cooperation among states when the costs of fighting are expected to be great. Of course, if, as Waltz suggests (1979, 70), bipolar politics are zero-sum, then there can be no cooperation as two-player zero-sum games cannot have cooperative equilibria.

12. To keep the example simple, I treat war costs as zero. The argument does not require this simplification.
13. Waltz (1979, 124–125) himself seems to recognize that the hypothesis that systems move toward balance is vacuous in that he acknowledges that almost any distribution of power satisfies his conception of balance.
14. Using Jack Levy's (1983) data, the periods during which the number of great powers remained fixed and the years during which the list of great powers remained fixed happens to be the same so that the figure shows the duration of systems both in terms of changes in the number and changes in the names of great powers. The multipolar systems varied in terms of the number of members from a low of four (1519–1556) to a high of eight (1905–1918).
15. One might object that there was an intervening major power war, the Russo-Japanese War. In that case, the interval between the Franco-Prussian War and the Russo-Japanese War was thirty-three years.
16. Waltz (1979, 117) maintains, "The elements of Realpolitik, exhaustively listed, are these: The ruler's, and later the state's, interest provides the spring of action; the necessities of policy arise from the unregulated competition of states; calculation based on these necessities can discover the policies that will best serve a state's interests; success is the ultimate test of policy, and success is defined as preserving and strengthening the state."
17. Because demands are chosen strategically in this representation of neorealism, commitment problems are avoided. States make demands designed to be attractive enough to a rival that the foe prefers to negotiate over the demands rather than fight. Therefore, the commitment to negotiate is credible because demands are designed to make negotiation preferable to fighting. This protects the security and survival of states, in keeping with neorealism's core.
18. The measure of uncertainty used here is the annual variance in estimated risk-taking propensities for the states of Europe, as described in Bueno de Mesquita and Lalman 1992. This is a systemic measure of uncertainty in keeping with Waltz's view of uncertainty.
19. Alas for the French politicians, their government fell from power anyway because of domestic considerations.
20. This is an interesting claim, given that this proposition follows logically from the representation of neorealism in the international interaction game, a representation that also produces the hypothesis that bipolarity (i.e., the absence of uncertainty) produces stability through negotiations.
21. Blocs are defined in the manner described in Bueno de Mesquita 1975, based solely on the major power subsystem and using Correlates of War composite capability scores to evaluate capabilities.

$$\text{Balance of Power} = 100 \sum_{i=1}^{n} \mid \text{Capabilities of } i - \tfrac{1}{n} \mid$$

22. The procedure for identifying endogenously chosen demands is explained in Bueno de Mesquita and Lalman 1992, Ch. 3.
23. The general result just explained does not depend on what theory is used to identify the necessary and sufficient conditions for war. That is, the result depends only on the existence of necessary and sufficient conditions under which an action or event is certain to happen and the existence of uncertainty.
24. The figures are based on a Logit analysis that estimates the likelihood of a binary dependent variable (War or No War in this case) as a function of a set of independent variables. The actual statistical test can be found in Bueno de Mesquita and Lalman (1992, 77, and a more demanding test version on ibid., 216). All relevant variables are statistically significant and in the direction predicted by the domestic version of the IIG.

# Paradoxical Functions of International Alliances
## SECURITY AND OTHER DILEMMAS

### ZEEV MAOZ

### Introduction

Most of the literature in international politics views international alliances as security-enhancing devices. Alliances are taken to be, for the most part, a means for extending a state's capabilities, and—as such—they serve as one of the key instruments of security policy (Snyder 1997; Walt 1987). Given the role of alliances in the security policies of states, their origins, structure, process, and consequences have been a major topic of inquiry in the security literature (Ward 1981). The principal incentives for alliance formation, and the various functions of alliances once in existence, are grounded in strategic calculations of states. The key concepts that drive the politics of international alliance concern deterrence, offense, defense, or—to use Walt's (1987) terminology—balancing or bandwagoning. These concepts describe both the principal incentives for alliance formation, and the logic by which alliances function once they are formed.

There appear to be some differences among neorealists as to the motivations for alliance formation and the relationships between alliances and balance of power. For example, Walt (1987; 1997, 932–933) talks about seemingly contradictory alliance behavior patterns, stemming from a single source: balancing against threats. However, he also identifies different varieties of neorealist approaches to alliances that might lead to diametrically contradictory empirical patterns. For example, the distinction between offensive and defensive realism (Elman and Elman 1997, 925), or between chain-ganging and buck-passing (Christensen and Snyder 1990, 1997) may allow explanation of patterns of alliance behavior that seemingly contradict the core assumptions of the neorealist paradigm. According to critics of this paradigm (e.g., Vasquez 1997, 1998), this constitutes evidence that this paradigm is undergoing a degenerative process. According to neorealist scholars (e.g., Waltz 1997; Walt 1997;

Elman and Elman 1997), this merely suggests a normal progression of a scientific research program.

Underlying this debate, however, is the question concerning the motivation for alliance formation, and the resulting behavioral consequences of alliance patterns. The basic neorealist conception of alliances is that they are formed by security concerns. The questions of whether, when, why, and with whom to align should be dealt with in a framework in which states are assumed to respond to security-related events in their external environment. Recent research, however, suggests that alliance formation considerations may well be based on other factors, some of which do not necessarily correspond to the strategic logic derived from strictly realist perspectives. Likewise, some of the consequences of alliance politics—in particular the effects of alliance on conflict and war behavior—exhibit significant cross-state differences. Again, some of these differences may be inconsistent with realist notions of alliance politics (Maoz 1996b, 2000).

One of the problems with many of the theoretical and empirical works on alliance formation and alliance behavior is that they are concerned with only the direct links between nations. Specifically, the questions they address concern the choice of alliance partners in terms of the direct relations between the would-be partners. For example, the notions of balancing/bandwagoning represent two (possibly different, e.g., Walt 1997) patterns of response to threats or distributions of power. However, in examining the alliance choices of states or their behavioral consequences, we often neglect the more complex spatial relationship both between the focal state and other members of the international system, or the relationship between the would-be or actual alliance partner and third parties.

There are many ways in which the debate between realist and other schools of thought in international politics could be framed and perhaps resolved. This study seeks to explore the origins and implications of alliance politics in light of realist and liberal propositions. Rather than focusing on traditional approaches to alliance formation based on direct balancing/bandwagoning or chain-ganging/buck-passing notions, I examine the motivation for alliance formation and the implications of alliances in more general realist versus liberal claims. Specifically, I address the following questions.

1. What is the relative impact of security-related factors compared to political and economic factors on alliance choices of states? More generally, what is the relative impact of security, political, and economic factors on the strategic affinity of states?
2. What is the relationship between alliance ties and conflict? What is the relationship between strategic affinity of states and their propensity for conflict?
3. Is the relationship between alliance ties and conflict affected by regime type?

The chapter is organized as follows. First, I discuss some of the recent theoretical debates and empirical findings about alliance politics and derive some propositions from this literature. These propositions emphasize two perspectives of international politics: realist and liberal. Second, I develop a research design to test these propositions. Third, I examine the empirical results. Fourth, I discuss the implications of these findings.

## Strategic, Political, and Economic Determinants of Alliance Politics

The notion that alliances are an extension of states' power suggests that alliances may be used for defensive or deterrent purposes, or as a prelude for an offensive plan. The question of who allies with whom is typically treated in this context: States choose allies that maximize their ability to advance their national goals. If these goals are defined in terms of the maximization of power, then states ally with those who maximize their power. If states balance not against raw power but against threat (Walt 1987), then the answer to this question is that the choice of allies is based on the most efficient way to defuse the threats directed at them. If we generalize this argument, then alliance portfolios of states reflect the similarity or difference between their strategic interests (Farber and Gowa 1995).

Regardless of which version of realist or neorealist approaches we adopt, there are some basic underlying logical premises that are common to all. The basic premise of realist notions of alliances is that states decide to form alliances when they confront security problems that they feel they cannot resolve on their own. This is the case when the threats emanating from a state's external environment exceed the state's capacity to confront them through the use of its own resources. This is also the case when the state feels it lacks the capability to achieve certain goals on its own and it needs the help of others to accomplish proactive goals (Maoz 1990, Ch. 7). Thus, when examining the origins of alliances from a realist perspective, we explore how strategic factors affect the security calculus of states.

When discussing realist conceptions of alliances, it is important to identify not only what alliances are and what they are supposed to do, but also what they are not designed to accomplish, and what roles they are not supposed to fulfill. First, realist perspectives do not suggest that the alliance formation calculus of states is based on the type of their internal political systems. In other words, the considerations that drive democratic states to form or dissolve alliances are no different from the considerations of nondemocratic states. Likewise, the actual alliance choices of states are not seen to reflect political affinities in terms of the similarity or difference of their political systems—as political affinities may contrast with the strategic calculations of states. If states choose alliance on the basis of political affinities, they may violate the logic of balancing, or—alternatively—they may choose alliances that are inferior in terms of power considerations to other options. Thus, Great Britain was seen as an important player in the balance of power system in Europe in the nineteenth century, despite the fact that, through the late part of this century, it was the only democracy in a region made up of absolutist monarchies.

Second, since realist perspectives of world politics assign an independent reasoning to security policies, alliances are supposed to emerge out of security-related calculations of states, rather than out of political or economic affinities, or as a natural extension of other institutional ties. The reason for that is obvious. Alliances constrain the autonomy of states and require them to relinquish considerable freedom of choice in crucial situations—such as international crises and war—in favor of collective, alliance-based considerations. When an ally gets into trouble, the focal state must decide whether to join the crisis or war. Awareness of the alliance paradox (Maoz 1990, Ch. 7), namely, that a state may be dragged into unwanted war by virtue of its alliance ties, imposes considerable restriction on the choice of alliance partners. States tend to choose those partners that offer them more benefits than costs. Choosing alliance partners on the basis of political or economic affinities may mean trouble in the long run.

The implications of alliances—in particular the effect of alliances on war and conflict—have always been in the center of a major debate in the theoretical and empirical literature of international politics. Some argued that alliance participation increases the likelihood of conflict and war involvement due to the ally's paradox. Others argued that, because alliances serve to balance against threats, they fulfill their function and serve as a substitute for conflict and war. Here too, realist conceptions do not distinguish between the implications of international alliances for democracies and those for nondemocracies; alliances either increase or decrease the propensity of states to engage in conflict, regardless of regime type and economic structure.

Liberal conceptions, in general, do not challenge these ideas. Rather, they argue that, in addition to the role of strategic factors in forming and managing alliances, states make alliance choices on the basis of general affinities based on nonsecurity-related considerations such as regime similarity, economic, or institutional ties. Likewise, these regime, economic, or institutional factors—in addition to alliance participation—constrain states' conflict behavior (Maoz 1996b, 2000).

In previous studies, I attempted to examine the origins, duration, and consequences of alliances using a variety of factors derived from realist and liberal perspectives of international politics (Maoz 1996b, 2000). One of the key findings of these two studies concerned the fact that alliance behavior differs across political systems. Specifically, the factors that drive the formation, maintenance, and use of alliances between democratic states is substantially different from the factors that drive the alliance behavior of nondemocratic states or the alliances between nondemocracies. This finding casts some doubt on straightforward realist notions of alliance politics. This is so despite the fact that power-related, and strategic threat–related considerations do play an important role in alliance politics. Specifically, it suggests that the calculations of states as to when, why, and with whom to ally depend on the domestic structure of the states as well as on the external threats or opportunity they seem to face.

Yet making alliances in a setting where everybody is free to align with everyone else (as realists would have us believe) is just like having sex in a permissive environment: By having sex with a friend, one is having sex with the friend's friends and the friends of the friend's friends, and so forth. By forming an alliance a state also indirectly becomes committed to the other allies of its immediate allies. To the extent that the other allies of the ally drag it to war, the focal state might find itself as a passive war participant. Thus, the study of alliance must focus on both direct and indirect strategic ties between and among states.

The current conception of alliances as direct political ties between states has dominated the IR literature (Singer and Small 1968; Ward 1981; Snyder 1997). I think of alignment in broader terms. The concept I suggest is that of strategic affinity. Strategic affinity refers to the similarity or difference between the alliance portfolios of two states.[1] This concept converges with notions of similarity of interests (Farber and Gowa 1995, 1997). Farber and Gowa may be right in claiming that direct alliance ties between states are not the best indicators to show their similarity of interests (Gartzke 1998).[2] Thus, when discussing the sources and consequences of strategic affinities of states, it is useful to think in terms of general alliance portfolios, which capture the manner in which two states are tied with other states in the system. General alliance portfolios better capture the notion of "the enemy of my enemy is my friend" than do bilateral alliance ties or UN voting patterns.

Thus, in this chapter I examine both the conventional conception of alignments and the more general conception of strategic affinity. My aim is twofold. First, I examine the extent to which strategic threat factors or political factors affect the alignment patterns of states. Second, I explore the implications of strategic affinity of states on their propensity to make conflict. The following general hypotheses refer first to factors that shape individual alignment patterns; second, to strategic affinities in dyads; and third, to the individual and dyadic implications of alliances.

Before going into a discussion of the propositions about alliance behavior, a comment about the unit of analysis used in this study is in order. There are many ways in which we can conceptualize alliance formation processes. We can examine the pattern of alliances that a state chooses to have. In this case, we look at monadic behavior patterns (Maoz 1996b). We can examine patterns of alliances as they appear in the international system. This perspective characterized many studies of system polarization (e.g., Bueno de Mesquita 1975, 1978; Wayman and Morgan 1990; Geller and Singer 1998, 113–119). The third approach that received increased attention recently focuses on alliance choices at the dyadic level (e.g., Morrow 1991; Siverson and Starr 1994; Simon and Gartzke 1996; Gartzke and Simon 1998). In my previous study on this subject, I focused on all three conceptions. Here I restrict myself to the dyadic conception.

This dyadic conception appears to be the most relevant conception to the neorealist-liberal debate for a number of reasons. First, as I have noted elsewhere (Maoz 2000, 118–119), alliance formation processes are at least two-way streets; it requires at least two national choices in order to form an alliance. Very often, the choice of alliance partners involves not only an assessment of the pros and cons of having an alliance with a given state, but also an assessment of the pros and cons of having a set of indirect alliances with this state's other allies. In addition, the notions of bandwagoning and balancing cannot be properly understood in a monadic context; they require at least a dyadic perspective.[3]

Second, a dyadic perspective allows the most meaningful and direct representation of alliance formation as a problem of choice (Smith 1995). If we use actual choices as revealed preferences (that is, we assume that what states do represents their rational choices), then the choice of alliance partners may give us some hint of the kind of goals and interests these alliances were supposed to serve. This kind of logic is represented in realist notions of alignment across political and ideological affinities. For example, if two states that are politically and ideologically different form an alliance against another state that appears to be politically and ideologically similar to one of them, it is fair to conclude that strategic interests override political affinities. Even critics of the democratic peace proposition argued that the fact that democracies appeared not to fight each other in the post–WWII era reflects the fact that they all faced a common enemy rather than a shared set of values (e.g., Mearsheimer 1990; Farber and Gowa 1994; Gowa 1999).

Finally, it is important to examine the relationship between realist factors that affect alliance formation and the consequences of alliances in a dyadic setting because both realist and liberal claims appear to be most directly discernible (see, e.g., Maoz 1998; Gowa 1999). Readers who are interested in analyses of alliance processes at the monadic, regional, and systemic level are referred to my other work on the subject (Maoz 2000, 2001).

Accordingly, I formulate the key propositions about the factors that affect alliance choices and the consequences of alliance formation at the dyadic level.

## STRATEGIC THREAT EFFECTS ON ALLIANCE FORMATION AND THE STRATEGIC AFFINITY OF STATES (REALIST PERSPECTIVE)

The propensity of states to form alliances is a function of the level of strategic threat emanating from their politically relevant international environment (PRIE).[4] This threat varies with the following:

1. *The number of states making up their PRIE.* The more states in one's PRIE the higher the propensity for alliance formation. As discussed elsewhere (Maoz 1996a, 1996b, 2001), the more states exist in the strategic environments of the states making up the dyad, the more potential for conflict, thus the greater the need for security, and consequently, the more likely are such states to align with each other.
2. *The number of alliances in the states' PRIEs that exclude the focal states.* The more potentially threatening alliances in one's PRIE, the higher the propensity to balance these through alliance formation of its own. Increased numbers of alliances that exclude the members of the dyad are likely to push both states into security cooperation, due to the "enemy of my enemy is my friend" logic.
3. *The conflict experience of the states with other members of their PRIE.* The higher the number of past conflicts of both states with other states, the more likely are the states to align. Past conflict of the states with other members of their politically relevant environment is a key indicator of the potential threat that they experience. Thus, it should serve as a key drive to align.

4. *The level of strategic affinity of the focal states with other states in the PRIE.* The higher the past level of strategic affinity of the state with other states in one's PRIE, the lower the propensity to form additional alliances. Strategic affinity is an indication of the convergence or divergence of a state's strategic interests with other states making up its PRIE. This is perhaps the best indication of the degree of threat experienced by a given state. Thus, the greater the convergence of strategic interests of states with members of their respective PRIEs, the less they need each other.
5. *The relative capability of the focal state to states in its PRIE.* The higher this capability, the lower the propensity to seek alliances. This is the balancing conception of alliances. Specifically, the better the balance of capabilities between states making up a dyad and their respective PRIEs, the less they need to balance against capabilities.
6. *The number of alliances the states have with other states.* The higher the number of alliances each state in the dyad has with third parties, the more/less likely it is to form an alliance with the other state making up the dyad. This captures the balancing/bandwagoning debate in the realist literature. Specifically, according to the bandwagoning conception, states are likely to join other states that have already accumulated a number of allies, because this increases the probability of winning a coming confrontation and the right to a share of the spoils of war. On the other hand, the balancing conception argues that the more allies a state has accumulated, the more likely it is to disrupt an existing balance, and hence the less attractive it is as an alliance partner to the other state making up the dyad.

## Effect of Political and Economic Factors on Alliance Formation and the Strategic Affinity of States (Liberal Perspective)

In contrast to the neorealist perspective that sees the relations between states and their strategic reference group as the key drive for alliance formation, the liberal perspective emphasizes the effect of domestic political and external political factors on alliance formation. States respond not only to security concerns but also to domestic pressures as well as to cues stemming from the political structure of, and the processes taking place in, their politically relevant international environment (PRIE). Specifically, the propensity of two states making up a dyad to seek security through an alliance is a function of the following:

1. *The regimes of states making up the dyad and their level of political stability.* Jointly democratic, politically stable states are more likely to form alliances than dyads made up of other types of political regimes or than non–politically stable dyads. My argument is based on Maoz (1996b, 2000). Democratic states are inherently more prone to seek security through alignment because of the domestic cost of seeking security through internal military allocations, which comes at the expense of social spending. Democracies are also more likely to succeed in forming alliances because they are considered more reliable alliance partners. The same applies to the distinction between politically stable and politically unstable states.

2. *The political structure of the states' PRIEs.* The more democratic the respective PRIEs of dyad members, the less likely are its members to seek security through alliances. However, for democratic dyads, democratization in the PRIE pushes them to foster their security through alliances. Thus, for democratic dyads, this relationship between the democratization of the PRIE and the tendency of dyad members to align is reversed.
3. *The degree of violent political change in the states' PRIEs.* The higher the number of political changes in the states' PRIEs, the more likely are they to align. Political instability in dyad members' PRIE generates threat perception. This threat perception is independent from capability ratios or security relations between dyad members and their respective international environments. This instability is due to the uncertainty and the fear of the spread of instability (Maoz 1996a, Ch. 5). This tends to push dyad members toward each other in an effort to stand together against the winds of political change.

Figure 13.1 provides a graphic specification of these relationships. The basic argument is that the propensity of individual states to seek security through alliance is shaped by both strategic threat and by political and economic factors.[5] Moreover, in some cases the impact of political and military security factors on the alliance propensity of states is different for democracies than for nondemocratic states.

**Strategic Threat Factors**

- Number of conflicts between dyad members (−)
- Number of states in members' **PRIE** (+)
- Alliances in **PRIE** not including dyad members (+)
- Past conflict of dyad members (+)
- Strategic affinity of dyad members with their **PRIEs** (−)
- Capability ratio of dyad members to their **PRIE** (−)

→ **Probability of alliance formation** ←

**Political Factors**

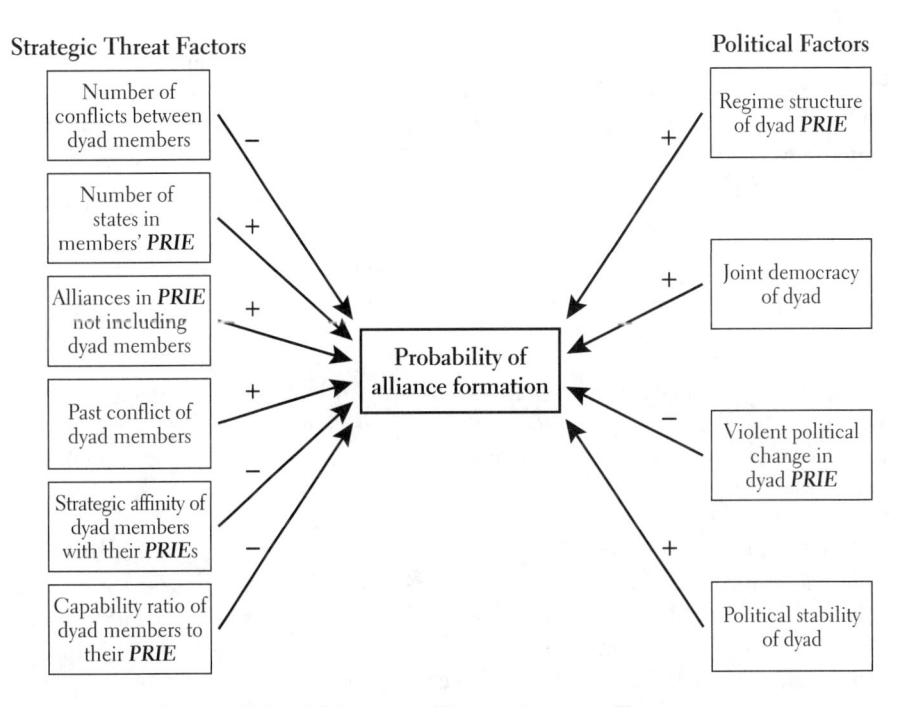

- Regime structure of dyad **PRIE** (+)
- Joint democracy of dyad (+)
- Violent political change in dyad **PRIE** (−)
- Political stability of dyad (+)

FIGURE 13.1  A MODEL OF DYADIC ALLIANCE FORMATION

## The Effects of Alliance and Strategic Affinity on Conflict Behavior

The debates on the origins of alliances both between different versions of neorealism and between realist and liberal approaches also characterize theorizing on the conflict-related implications of alliances and strategic affinity of states. First, if alliances are formed due to states' efforts to balance (against capability or threat), then the implication is that alliances should reduce the probability of conflict in the international system. Alliances, in this context, are seen primarily as a diplomatic and strategic substitute for fixing imbalances through conflict. If, on the other hand, states tend to see alliances as a mechanism that increases the probability of winning a war, they tend to bandwagon, and the implication is that alliances increase the probability of conflict.

This division among realists makes it difficult to find evidence in the relationships between alliances and conflict that could be taken to disconfirm realist predictions. Whatever relationship there exists between alliances and war, it would be consistent with one version or another of neorealist propositions. In this context Vasquez's (1997) contention that the neorealist literature on alliances suggests a degenerative process becomes extremely pertinent, the responses of neorealists notwithstanding.

Second, the debate about the consequences of international alliances also divides realist and liberal approaches. In the realist conception (e.g., Farber and Gowa 1994; Gowa 1999), it is commonality of interests—as reflected in states' alliance portfolios—rather than their internal political structure that prevents dyadic conflict. In the liberal literature, alliances are indeed seen as important mechanisms that regulate interstate relations. However, it is democracy, trade interdependence, and the sharing of norms—as reflected in IGO membership—that are the crucial mechanisms that prevent conflict (Russett and Oneal 2000). Thus, when the predictions of these approaches disagree, it is possible to conduct a critical test of these propositions (Maoz 1997, Maoz 1998).

## Data Analysis

### Alliance Initiation

I start with the analysis of factors affecting alliance formation in dyadic settings. Here I examine what affects the general strategic affinities of states, using the dyadic tau-b score of alliance portfolios (based on a global configuration) as the dependent variable. The results of this analysis are given in Table 13.1.

The results of Table 13.1 show an interesting paradox with respect to the "realist" determinants of dyadic alliance initiation: Both balancing and bandwagoning can find some support in these results. One can support or reject different arguments emerging from realist explanations depending on which particular threat indicators one uses. Specifically, states seem to initiate alliances in response to strategic threats. However, different indicators of threat have diametrically opposite effects on the probability of dyadic alliance initiation.

TABLE 13.1  FACTORS AFFECTING THE PROBABILITY OF DYADIC ALLIANCE INITIATION: COX PROPORTIONAL-HAZARD ANALYSIS OF ALLIANCE INITIATION, 1816–1992

| INDEPENDENT VARIABLE | STRATUM ALL STATES | NON-DEMOCRACIES | DEMOCRACIES |
|---|---|---|---|
| **STRATEGIC THREAT FACTORS** | | | |
| No. of states in PRIE | 0.010 (0.008) | 0.010 (0.009) | –0.008 (0.019) |
| Capability ratio state/PRIE | 5.944** (1.893) | 5.151* (2.802) | 13.962* (6.213) |
| No. of alliances in PRIE excluding the focal state | 0.008** (0.002) | 0.006** (0.002) | 0.010** (0.002) |
| Disputes in PRIE not involving focal state | –0.008 (0.009) | –0.008 (0.009) | 0.030+ (0.018) |
| Minimum strategic affinity of states with PRIE | 0.395** (0.119) | 0.359** (0.129) | 0.623+ (0.376) |
| Minimum no. of allies of dyad members with third parties | –0.329** (0.051) | –0.340** (0.060) | 0.026 (0.111) |
| **POLITICAL FACTORS** | | | |
| Minimum regime score in dyad | –0.001 (0.002) | –0.004* (0.002) | 0.029* (0.014) |
| Average regime of states in PRIE | –0.001 (0.003) | –0.006** (0.002) | 0.062** (0.009) |
| Revolutionary change in PRIE | 0.092 (0.089) | 0.113 (0.099) | 0.647** (0.213) |
| Model Statistics | N = 46,207 Alliance initiations = 304 $\chi^2$ = 117.57** | N = 41,334 Alliance initiations = 255 $\chi^2$ = 97.88** | N = 4,873 Alliance initiations = 49 $\chi^2$ = 131.16** |

*$p \le .05$
**$p \le .01$
+$p \le .10$

First, the probability of dyadic alliance initiation increases with the increase in the number of alliances that are formed in dyad members' respective PRIEs and that exclude the focal states. As each member of the dyad faces a growing number of alliances in its strategic environment, it feels increasingly threatened. If this is the case for both members of the dyad, then the probability of an alliance increases considerably.

Second, the probability of dyadic alliance initiation declines with the number of existing alliances of dyad members. This confirms the notion that states are not eager to take on more commitments than they need. The last result is not robust with respect to the democratic/nondemocratic stratum, a point to which I return below.

Nevertheless, the effect of alliances in dyad members' PRIEs and the effect of dyad members' other alliances on the probability of dyadic alliance initiation seems to be consistent with the balancing notion of alliance formation. However, these results stand in stark contrast to other results in this analysis that strongly suggest bandwagoning effects. Specifically, the capability ratio between dyad members and their respective PRIEs significantly increases the probability of dyadic initiation. This implies that the probability that two states would form an alliance increases with the relative capability of these states compared to their strategic environment. Likewise, the probability that two states would form an alliance significantly increases with the strategic affinity that each of these states has with its environment. Both these results strongly suggest bandwagoning considerations in alliance initiation decisions. It appears that states tend to align when they are stronger rather than weaker with respect to their strategic environment. It also appears that states tend to align when they and their would-be partners are more positively connected with the members of their strategic environment than when their strategic affinity with their PRIEs is weak or negative.

More disturbing is the fact that some key indicators of strategic threat that should have predicted dyadic alliance initiation do not appear related to such processes. Specifically, neither the number of states in dyad members' respective PRIEs nor the extent of dyad members' involvement in militarized disputes with third parties has a significant effect on the probability of alliance initiation.

These findings suggest that realist accounts of the conditions affecting dyadic alliance initiation are both vague and not strongly consistent with empirical data. This brings us back to the effect of political factors on alliance initiation. Here we observe two interesting facts.

First, in the general analysis, neither the regime structure of dyad members, nor the regime structure of dyad members' PRIEs, nor the political stability of their respective PRIEs has a significant effect on dyadic alliance initiation. However, when the entire population is broken down into democratic and nondemocratic dyads, we observe that all three variables are consistently related to alliance formation. Specifically, in nondemocratic dyads, as states become less autocratic, the probability of dyadic alliance formation goes down. For democratic dyads, the more democratic the states, the more likely they are to form an alliance. The same applies to the effect of the degree of democratization in dyad members' PRIEs: For nondemocratic dyads, democratization of their PRIEs decreases the probability of alliance formation. On the other hand, democratization in the respective PRIEs of democratic dyads tends to increase the probability of alliance formation. Finally, revolutionary change in dyad members' PRIEs increases the probability of alliance formation between democratic states.

Taken together, the findings suggest that realist accounts of the factors affecting alliance formation offer contradictory stories. States seem to act on the basis of both balancing and bandwagoning considerations, and more importantly, some of the key predictors of alliance formation derived from realist writings appear to fail the empirical tests. On the other hand, liberal factors appear not only to have a significant effect on the probability of alliance initiation, but they suggest—as in my previous study—that the same factors have opposite effects on democratic and nondemocratic dyads. It turns out that democratic states are likely to form alliances with each other. It also turns out that such states are more likely to align as their PRIE becomes increasingly democratic. The flocking together of democracies in democratic PRIEs is a strong indicator that liberal factors are at work in alliance formation processes.[6]

## THE EFFECTS OF ALLIANCES ON INTERNATIONAL CONFLICT

This brings us to an analysis of the relationship between alliances and conflict. Table 13.2 on page 212 provides the results of a cross-sectional time-series probit analysis of the factors affecting MID and war outbreak between states. Here the key question is how alliance related factors affect that probability. However, instead of using the more traditional measure of alliance (whether or not two states were aligned with each other), which features highly in dyadic analyses of conflict (Bremer 1992, 1993; Maoz and Russett 1992, 1993; Russett, Oneal, and Davis 1998; Russett and Oneal 2000), I employ the measure of dyadic strategic affinity (Signorino and Ritter 1998) to examine the extent to which the convergence of interests between the states affects the probability of conflict between them.

The most important finding in Table 13.2 is probably the fact that the strategic affinity of states does not constitute a potent predictor of their conflict/war behavior. It does not significantly affect the probability of dispute outbreak between states. The strategic affinity of states does negatively affect the propensity of war outbreak, but since the robustness of this effect for jointly democratic dyads cannot be confirmed, we cannot assess how stable this relationship is across strata.[7]

Other alliance indices show again a mixed association with the dependent variables. The extent to which the environment of the state is made up of potentially hostile alliances is again not related to dispute outbreak, but it negatively relates to war outbreak and to dispute escalation. Here too, the robustness of the seemingly dampening effect of environmental alliances on war outbreak cannot be ascertained.

The number of alliances that each of the members of the dyad has with third parties seems to have a dampening effect on the probability of dispute and war outbreak in the general population, as well as for non–jointly democratic dyads. However it does not significantly affect the propensity of conflict between democracies.

If we take these three variables together, we can say again that the expectations of different realist versions about the effect of alliances on conflict are far from being confirmed. There is some evidence that environmental alliances deter states from going into conflict with each other lest these allies enter into the bilateral conflict. This is a crude indication that some balancing behavior may be going on. However, this effect is not general and—to the extent that it exists—it tends to prevent ongoing militarized disputes from escalating into all-out wars.

There is also some evidence that the commonality of interests between states, measured by their strategic affinity score, has a dampening effect on their propensity to escalate disputes into all-out wars. However, strategic affinity does not prevent

TABLE 13.2  CROSS-SECTIONAL TIME-SERIES PROBIT ANALYSIS OF DETERMINANTS OF MID AND WAR OUTBREAK IN DYADS, 1816–1992

|  | MID OUTBREAK ||| | WAR OUTBREAK |||
|---|---|---|---|---|---|---|---|
| INDEPENDENT VARIABLE | ALL STATES | NON-DEMOCRACIES | DEMOCRACIES | | ALL STATES | NON-DEMOCRACIES | DEMOCRACIES |
| *STRATEGIC THREAT FACTORS* | | | | | | | |
| Capability Ratio | −0.001** (0.000) | −0.001 (0.001) | −1.77e-06 (8.5e-05) | | −0.002** (0.001) | −0.002* (0.001) | NA[++] |
| No. of alliances in PRIE excluding the focal state | 0.001 (0.001) | −0.086 (0.067) | −0.001 (0.001) | | −0.004** (0.001) | −0.003** (0.001) | NA |
| Cumulative no. of past disputes between dyad members | 0.043** (0.004) | 0.043** (0.004) | 0.040** (0.047) | | 0.028** (0.004) | 0.027** (0.004) | NA |
| Strategic affinity of dyad members | 0.058 (0.063) | −0.086 (0.067) | 0.320 (0.285) | | −0.555** (0.083) | −0.576** (0.088) | NA |
| Minimum no. of allies of dyad members with third parties | −0.060** (0.015) | −0.064** (0.016) | −0.027 (0.031) | | −0.090** (0.030) | −0.100** (0.030) | NA |
| *POLITICAL FACTORS* | | | | | | | |
| Minimum regime score in dyad | −0.004** (0.001) | −0.002** (0.001) | −0.014[+] (0.08) | | −0.005** (0.001) | −0.002* (0.001) | NA |
| Average regime of states in PRIE | −0.000 (0.000) | 2.01e-06 (0.001) | −0.007** (0.002) | | −0.001 (0.001) | 9.75e-06 (0.001) | NA |
| Revolutionary change in PRIE | 0.054** (0.015) | 0.067** (0.017) | −0.010 (0.045) | | 0.060** (0.025) | 0.072** (0.025) | NA |
| Model Statistics | N = 50,489 Dyads = 1,134 $\chi^2$ = 288.13* | N = 44,320 Dyads = 1,047 $\chi^2$ = 214.89** | N = 6,118 Dyads = 197 $\chi^2$ = 63.31** | | N = 50,489 Dyads = 1,134 $\chi^2$ = 239.13** | N = 44,320 Dyads = 1,074 $\chi^2$ = 205.21** | NA |

**$p \leq .01$  *$p \leq .05$  [+]$p \leq .10$  [++]Only one war case for joint-democracy dyads precludes convergence of probit analysis.

them from entering into militarized disputes in the first place. The only factor that consistently affects the probability of dispute and war outbreak is the capability ratio of the states in the dyad. This factor, contrary to the capability-balancing hypothesis, consistently predicts that parity is related to conflict.

As in the case of the analysis of the determinants of alliance formation, liberal factors, especially the regime type of the dyad, have a robust effect on the probability of conflict and war, and in the direction expected by theory.

## Conclusion

This chapter attempted to examine the empirical implications of various versions of realist theory and some liberal ideas on both the sources and consequences of international alignment processes.

The difficulty of this task was due in large measure to the debates within realist theories about the factors that drive states to align and to the implications of alliances on conflict. As pointed out in the various writings about alignment in realist theory (e.g., Walt 1997; Waltz 1997; Christensen and Snyder 1997), there is not a single version of realist theory with respect to alliances. States may seek alliances to balance against capabilities or against other threats; they may choose in some cases to use alliances as a buck-passing strategy, or as chain-ganging. Likewise, the effects of alliance behavior on conflict are again a matter of interpretation of why certain alliances were formed in the first place. Therefore, the separation of the study of alliance formation from the study of the implications of alliances is a dubious practice (Maoz 2000).

The clearest message of the present essay is that the duality and multiple versions of realist theory with respect to alliance formation and with respect to the implications of international alliances is not at all incidental. It corresponds to a basic ambiguity in the empirical world. Some indices of alliance formation show clear balancing behavior; others show clear signs of bandwagoning. Some indices of alliances suggest that alliances tend to be a deterrent to war; others suggest that they tend to increase the probability of conflict or to be completely irrelevant to the outbreak and escalation of conflict.

Whether or not these results suggest that the neorealist research program that concerns alliance formation and alliance behavior is progressive or degenerative (Vasquez 1997) is not essential for our concern. A more important point that emerges from this study is that the seemingly parsimonious nature of neorealism as a theory of international politics may be highly misleading. In fact, it leaves much to be desired both in terms of conceptual clarity and in terms of empirical rigor. Most importantly, it does not provide a consistent and robust empirical account of the processes of alliance formation and of the relationship between alliances and conflict. This stands in stark contrast to the seemingly consistent and robust effects of political factors—typically associated with liberal perspectives of world politics—on processes of alliance formation and the conflict behavior of states.

Several implications follow. First, we need a more coherent realist account of what kind of functions are served by international alliances; why, with whom, and under what conditions states seek alliances, and in what ways alliances are related to conflict. Deductive theories spelled out in formal mathematical terms (e.g., Smith 1995) would be of great help here, because they require an explicit logical connection between the fundamental assumptions of neorealism and empirically-testable deductions.

Second, as pointed out above, it is not terribly instructive to separate the processes of alliance formation from the processes of alliance management, and from the implications of international alliances. This contributes to the lack of theoretical clarity and to confusing empirical tests; and it certainly contributes to the mixed empirical record of realist hypotheses as suggested by this study.

Third, and most importantly, it is important to integrate realist and liberal accounts in the study of alliances, both at the level of theory formulation, and at the empirical testing level.

## Methodological Appendix

### Spatial-Temporal Domain

This study focuses on the dyadic level of analysis. Specifically, I focus on politically relevant dyads, that is, dyads that are either directly or indirectly contiguous or dyads that contain at least one major power or one regional power. True, a considerable number of alliances exist between non–politically relevant states. Also, it is possible to measure the strategic affinity of any dyad, be it politically relevant or non–politically relevant. However, the focus on politically relevant dyads is due to the fact that conflict-related implications of alliances are particularly pronounced for this group of dyads.

The temporal domain consists of the 1816–1992 period. Hence the analyses in this chapter include all politically relevant dyads over this period.

### Data Sources

The data used for this study were collected from various sources. Data and sources are listed below:

1. *Alliance data.* The alliance data are the COW formal alliance data that have been updated from the list provided by Oren (1990).[8]
2. *Strategic affinity data.* Data were obtained from Richard Tucker's website: http://www.vanderbilt.edu/~rtucker
3. *International conflict data.* The basic data are the COW MID data (Jones, Bremer, and Singer, 1996). Specific data used for this study were obtained from the dyadic MID dataset (Maoz 1999) at http://spirit.tau.ac.il/zeevmaoz/dyadmid.html.

4. *Regime characteristics.* The various measures related to regime structure and regime change are derived from the POLITY III dataset (Jaggers and Gurr 1995).
5. *Capabilities.* Data are derived from the COW military capability dataset (Singer 1990).

## Empirical Measures of Variables

***Dependent Variables*** This study examines the initiation and conflict-related implications of international alliances between states, but it also focuses on a new conception of strategic affinity. They are defined as follows:

1. *Alliance initiation.* The first year of a dyadic alliance is given a score of one for initiation of an alliance, and all years previous to that year are given scores of zero. Alliance years are censored.
2. *Strategic affinity.* Following Bueno de Mesquita (1981b), the strategic affinity of states is defined in terms of the concordance or discordance in their alliance portfolios, not only with each other but also with a group of $n$ third states. Specifically, for each dyad, a 4x4 contingency table is created in which rows represent alliance commitments of state $i$ and columns represent the alliance commitments of state $j$. These commitments range from "defense pact" to "no alliance." Each state is assumed to be in a defense pact with itself, meaning that it would defend itself if attacked. Each cell in this table represents a configuration of alliance commitments of states $i$ and $j$ with another state. Thus, for example, if state $i$ has a defense pact with state $k$ and state $j$ has no alliance with state $k$, then this entry will appear in the first row and fourth column of this table. Since states $i$ and $j$ also appear in this table, then the alliance status of these states will also be expressed. If the two focal states have a nonaggression treaty, then both of them would be listed in the second row-second column of the table. If they have no alliance, then state $i$ will be listed in the first row-fourth column of the table and state $j$ will be listed in the fourth row-first column of the table. Once all states that form the baseline are listed in the table, the table is converted into a joint frequency table and the tau-b score for this table represents the extent to which the alliance portfolios of the two focal states are concordant. If most cases fall around the main diagonal, it implies that the focal states' alliance portfolios are highly concordant. This implies a high degree of strategic affinity, because it implies that those states with which $i$ has some alliance ties are also states with which $j$ has alliance ties. Likewise, third parties with whom state $i$ is nonaligned are also likely to have no alliance with state $j$. However, this tau-b measure of affinity was criticized by Signorino and Ritter (1999), who offered a different measure $S$ to substitute for it. I relied on that measure of strategic affinity.
3. *Conflict involvement.* This variable is defined as one if the dyad experienced at least one day of militarized interstate dispute during the year and zero otherwise.[9] In addition, I assign a score of one to the outbreak of a war and a zero otherwise. Finally, I use a measure of conflict escalation, which looks only at the escalation of existing disputes into wars, with a score of zero for a dispute year that did not escalate into war, a one for a dispute year in which war broke out, and a missing value otherwise.

***Independent Variables*** As a general rule, when a given measure is computed for each state individually, the dyadic measure is the minimum of the two numbers. For example, if the number of states in the PRIE of state A is six and the number of states in the PRIE of state B is four, the latter number is used.

1. *Number of states in PRIE.* Number of states that either (a) are contiguous to the focal state, (b) are regional powers in the region of the focal state, or (c) are major powers with global reach capacity.[10]
2. *Capability ratio state/PRIE.* The ratio of the state's military capabilities (based on the COW capability index) to the capabilities of the states making up its PRIE. (See definition in Maoz 1996b)
3. *Average no. of alliances in PRIE excluding the focal state.* Number of alliances involving members of the focal state's PRIE, which exclude the focal state, averaged over the past three years.
4. *Disputes in PRIE not involving focal state.* The number of MIDs in the state's PRIE, excluding those in which the focal state was involved, averaged over the past three years.
5. *Strategic affinity of focal state with PRIE.* Average S score of state with members making up its PRIE. This measure is averaged over the past three years.
6. *Regime score of focal state.* Regime score is based on the standard definition developed by Maoz and Russett (1993):[11] REGIME = (Democracy Score − Autocracy Score) x Power Concentration.
7. *Average regime of states in PRIE.* Using the REGIME variable, I average the regime score over all states in the PRIE of the focal state.
8. *Revolutionary change in PRIE.* Number of states in the PRIE that have undergone revolutionary political change in the previous five years, using the Maoz (1996b) index of revolutionary political change.

## Dyadic Characteristics

1. *Capability ratio.* Ratio of military capabilities of strongest member of dyad to weakest. Varies between 1.0 and infinity.
2. *Cumulative number of disputes between dyad members.* Number of past dispute years between members of the dyad, lagged one year.
3. *Minimum number of alliances in PRIE of dyad members excluding the members of the dyad.* Defined as above. This denotes the extent to which outside alliances threaten members of the dyad.
4. *Strategic affinity of dyad members.* S score of alliance portfolios of dyad members is averaged over the past three years.

## RESEARCH METHODS

To study alliance initiation, I use the Cox proportional-hazard event-history model that examines the effects of a set of independent variables on the time-related probability of alliance formation of a set of states. Because certain dyads re-form alliances,

I allow for repeated occurrences of hazard event. Also, this allows for right censoring of data at 1992, the last year of our data.

For the test of the conflict implications of alliances, a Cross-Sectional Time-Series (CSTS) analysis was used with dispute, war, and escalation dependent variables. Thus the family-link is a binomial-probit combination, with correction with autocorrelation and robust standard errors (*Stata 6.0 Manual*, 1999).

Several strata are used in most analyses. First, I use a set of analyses for the entire 1816–1992 period. Second, I break down the entire population to non–jointly democratic dyads and to democratic dyads in order to examine the extent to which these results hold for different types of dyads.

## Editors' Commentary

### Major Query

Are realism's hypotheses on alliance behavior more accurate than liberalism's hypotheses on alliance behavior?

### Major Points

Maoz asks broader questions than the others so far. He looks not just at Waltz or the balance of power, but at what various realist theories, in general, have to say about what makes alliances form and what impact they have on conflict and war. He argues that realists, generally, expect states to form alliances because of strategic considerations having to do with highly salient security issues. In other words, regardless of the variations in realist theory, all of them see external relations among states driving alliance formation.

Maoz then contrasts liberal theories to the realist approach. He argues from a liberal perspective that while external relations and strategic considerations are important, of equal and sometimes of more importance are domestic political factors. Different types of countries or regimes, especially democracies, will have different patterns of behavior with regard to alliance formation and dispute and war involvement. After deriving a number of competing hypotheses from the two different perspectives, Maoz produces several interesting results that speak to the ability of realist perspectives, broadly defined, to tell us something about alliance behavior.

He finds, looking at dyadic (i.e., two-party) disputes from 1816–1992 that alliance initiation increases as the number of alliances in a dyad's environment grows. This is consistent with the realist idea that as a state faces more alliances in its neighborhood, it too will feel the pressure to ally. He points out that such a finding is consistent with balancing behavior, but he also presents results consistent with bandwagoning behavior. Specifically, he finds that states are more apt to align when they are stronger than other states in their environment, rather than weaker. Although these two sets of findings support contradictory theoretical expectations,

Maoz is more disturbed that in other tests a number of realist strategic factors do not appear to be associated with alliance formation.

Conversely, the liberal factors, namely, the type of regime, have an important impact on alliance formation in that democratic and nondemocratic states have different patterns of alliance behavior (see Table 13.1 on page 209). Thus, he finds the more democratic states are, the more likely they are to form alliances. Democracies, unlike nondemocratic states, tend to flock together. In addition, revolutionary change in a dyad's neighborhood will increase alliance formation among democratic states, but this has no effect on nondemocratic dyads. All these findings fundamentally undercut the realist assumption, especially pronounced among Waltzian neorealists, that the strategic environment will make all states behave more or less the same with regard to how they form alliances. The fact that alliance formation differs by the regime type of states strongly suggests that domestic political factors play an important role, a point also made by Bueno de Mesquita and Lalman (1992; see also Ch. 12).

The findings on the effect of alliances on dyads becoming involved in militarized disputes and war (see Table 13.2 on page 212) are more complicated. Here, rather than using alliances as an indicator, Maoz employs a measure of commonality of interest (which he calls strategic affinity) that compares the extent to which two states have similar alliances (sometimes referred to as similar alliance portfolios). The assumption is that, for realism, states with similar interests should not get involved in militarized disputes or wars against each other. Maoz finds that while this holds for nondemocracies in terms of war involvement, it does not hold for either type of state for involvement in militarized disputes. The latter shows a random relationship, i.e., sometimes they get involved in disputes when they have similar interests or strategic affinity and sometimes they do not. An analogous finding is reported for the number of hostile alliances in a state's neighborhood: It is unrelated to dispute outbreaks, but does dampen escalation to war.

A more consistent finding using realist factors is that the greater the number of alliances a state has with third parties, the less likely states will become involved in disputes or wars, but this does not hold for democratic involvement in disputes. Another realist factor that is seen as important is the relative capabilities of states, but here the more equal (or balanced) the capabilities, the more likely is war.

Overall, Maoz concludes that there is some evidence in favor of realism in that a commonality of alliance portfolios seems to dampen involvement in war but not militarized disputes, but there are also findings that undercut realism. Chief among these is that democratic dyads have a different pattern of behavior from nondemocracies, especially in that they tend not to fight each other. Of equal significance is that, in terms of dispute involvement, sometimes the factors that are found to be generally important, like capability ratio or alliances with third parties, are found to have different or no effects when examined in terms of democracies and nondemocracies. This suggests again to Maoz that the liberal theory is more accurate, because such deviations from strategic behavior should not occur if external relations were as important as neorealists maintain.

## Using the Scientific Method

Maoz's chapter provides an illustration of how the scientific method is used by political scientists. Typically, scholarly articles that test hypotheses have the following format:

1. Describe the theory or proposition and review the relevant scholarly literature. Maoz does this in the early part of the chapter when he discusses realism and liberalism.
2. Indicate how the hypotheses will be tested and how the concepts will be measured or operationalized so they can be "seen" in the "real world." Maoz does most of this in the Appendix. Note that he wants to test his hypotheses by looking at a state's PRIE (Politically Relevant International Environment—which includes the immediate neighbors of a state and those that can easily reach it, which would include regional and global powers). Measurement is a key element in making science advance. Studying climate is much more precise and easier once the thermometer is invented; then one does not have to rely on individual impressions about what is hot or cold. Measurement tells scholars whether or "how much" of something is present, e.g., *conflict, common interests*. Note that Maoz measures alliances in two different ways—actual membership in a formal alliance and "strategic affinity," which is an index of the extent to which two states share similar alliance configurations. It is assumed that the greater two states' strategic affinity, the greater their common interests.
3. Use statistics to count the number of cases that support the hypothesis and the number that do not, then present the findings. Maoz's tables appear complicated, especially to the untrained eye, but just by being able to understand a few numbers one can learn quite a bit (see "Reading the Tables," below).
4. Interpret the findings in terms of whether the hypotheses are accepted, rejected, or need to be reformulated. In this section, Maoz concludes that the liberal hypotheses often perform better on tests than the realist, primarily because democratic states behave differently than nondemocracies. If realism were correct, all states should behave the same, so every time they do not, Maoz holds this against realism in his assessment (see, for example, in Table 13.1 on page 209, under political factors, sometimes the relationship is negative (−) for nondemocracies and positive (+) for democracies).

## Reading the Tables

If you are a novice, the single number you want to be able to read and understand in the kind of tests Maoz uses is the significance level ($p < .05$, $p < .01$). Maoz asterisks findings that are significant in his tables, so this makes it easy to locate which findings are significant and which are not. Researchers conduct significance tests to tell them if having $x$ (independent variable—such as the number of alliances in PRIE [see Table 13.1, row 3]) affects $y$ (the dependent variable—the probability that a state will form or initiate an alliance). Maoz counts every time the independent variable (a great number of alliances in the PRIE) results in states forming an alliance (in response to this large number of alliances) and every time it does not. The more times a certain value of $x$ occurs and is followed by the same value of $y$ occurring, the more confidence we have that the two variables are related. Significance tests help us determine how many exceptions to a pattern will be tolerated before it is concluded that there is no general rule and things appear to be random. Thus, if half the time when there was a large number of alliances in the PRIE a state formed an alliance and half the time it did not, this would mean that knowing the number of alliances in the PRIE would not help much in predicting whether the state would form an alliance. In fact, Maoz shows in Table 13.1 (on page 209), row 3, that this relationship is not random, and he has accordingly marked it with one or more asterisks (*).

The p value tells the reader how likely it is the given distribution under question is due to chance. In political science, if there are only five chances in a hundred that something is random, we accept that as *not* random and, hence, statistically significant; i.e., we decide that it is safe to conclude that the two variables are statistically related to each other. The same would hold if there were fewer than five chances in a hundred, e.g., less than one chance in a hundred ($p < .01$). Maoz marks these with two asterisks (**). (Note, sometimes Maoz is prepared to stretch this rule and will mark a finding that has only ten chances out of a hundred of being random with a (+) — see Table 13.1, row 5 "strategy affinity," column 3 "democracies"). When medical researchers say that smoking is significantly related to lung cancer, they make this statement on the basis of statistical significance tests, like those Maoz uses. Medical researchers find more smokers get lung cancer than would be expected if the pattern were random.

It should also be noted that numbers that are marked in the two tables also have signs — negative or positive (indicated by the absence of a sign). If the finding is a positive number, this means that as the independent variable increases so does the dependent variable. A negative sign means the opposite. Thus, in Table 13.2 (on page 212), row 5, columns 1 and 4 (the two "All States" columns), the greater number of alliances that a pair of states (a dyad) has with third parties the less likely those two states will have a dispute or go to war ($-0.060^{**}$, $-0.090^{**}$)

## Key Terms

**liberalism (in international relations)** A theory associated with the finding that democratic states do not fight each other — a theory that can be traced back at least to Kant. Liberalism as a family of theories differs from realism primarily in that it expects that the type of government (or regime as it is called) has an important impact on a state's behavior; whereas realists tend to see external factors, like anarchy or the distribution of capabilities, as having the major impact on state behavior.

**dyad** A pair of states; two states, as opposed to one. Dyadic analysis examines what two given states, like France and Germany, do to each other.

## Notes

1. The original idea is probably due to Bueno de Mesquita (1981b) who used this concept to measure the utility of states toward each other.
2. Gartzke offers to use measures of UN voting similarity (tau-b of voting patterns at the dyadic level) as a better indicator of dyadic affinity. This is a very good approach, except for two liabilities. First, data is available only for the post–1947 period. Second, and more importantly, this is a good dyadic indicator, but it does not capture third, fourth, and fifth level affinity as indicated above. For this purpose, I use other measures of affinity more directly related to alliance behavior.
3. A systemic or alliance-based perspective may be even more appropriate, but an indirect representation of this issue can also be developed in a dyadic context, as I show below.
4. The Politically Relevant International Environment (PRIE) of a state consists of all states that are (a) contiguous to the focal state through a land, maritime, or colonial border, (b) all regional powers in the region of the focal states, and (c) all major powers with global reach capacity. The PRIE of regional powers consists of all states in the region and all major powers. The PRIE of minor powers consists of all states in the system. (For a list of major and regional powers see Maoz 1996a, 141).
5. From a liberal perspective it is reasonable to expect that the higher the trade dependency of states making up a dyad, the more likely they are to align. Although this is an interesting proposition, it is not tested in the present study due to the lack of trade data for the period of 1816–1992.
6. It is noteworthy that the probability of an alliance between jointly democratic states is more than twice the probability of an alliance between nondemocratic states or between a democratic and nondemocratic state.
7. A similar analysis was run with a dispute escalation variable, coded as zero if and only if a dispute between states was underway, and as one if a war between these states broke out. When no dispute was underway this variable was coded as missing. Thus this analysis examined the effect of the independent variables given in Table 13.2 (on page 212) on the probability that a dispute would escalate to war. The discussion below is based on the escalation analysis as well.
8. For a discussion of the dataset, see Singer and Small 1968.
9. In both cases I assign a nonzero value to an observation, whether or not the state or dyad was engaged in a new conflict or in an ongoing one that had started in a previous year. The justification for using ongoing dispute measures is given in Maoz 1998, 78.
10. For a discussion of the concept and its implications, see Maoz 1996a.
11. This measure ranges from +100 to –100. In reality, values observed range from -70 to +90 in the POLITY III dataset. For certain breakdowns a regime type variable is used in accordance with the levels given by Maoz (1996a; 1998).

# 14

## ALLIANCES, BALANCES OF THREATS, AND NEOREALISM
### *THE ACCIDENTAL COUP*

*MICHAEL BARNETT*

> The surest symptom of impending change in a theoretical system is increasingly general interest in . . . residual categories.
> —Talcott Parsons (1937, 18)

> When unresolved tensions develop in general theories, theorists will resort to ad hoc ways to resolve them. To cope with these tensions they will introduce, in what is usually an ad hoc and unthought-out way, theoretical categories which are residual to, or outside of, the logically developed systemic strands of their argument. . . . While residual categories are the result of theoretical tensions, for the sake of interpretation it is often more useful to move backwards, from one's discovery of the residual categories back to the basic tensions which they have been developed to obscure.
> —Jeffry Alexander (1987, 124–125)

Like many graduate students of the 1980s, I have a very clear recollection that all conversations about international relations theory had to run through neorealism and all papers had to refer to Kenneth Waltz's *Theory of International Politics*. It is scarcely possible to exaggerate neorealism's intellectual hegemony during this decade. It stamped the discipline's research agenda (keenly evident in the questions asked on graduate comprehensive examinations), the constitution of courses, and the articles accepted in the top journals. It could seem that the scope of the discipline was no wider than those subjects identified by neorealism as important and pressing. For those who did not follow the "Waltzian school," the character and dynamics of the profession seemed better captured by Mannheim's (1991) classic discussion of the sociology of knowledge than by a depoliticized version of Lakatos's (1999, Ch. 5) rendering of scientific progress.

It is now part of the discipline's collective memory that the peaceful end of the Cold War was as transformative for world politics as for those who study it.

Most fascinating, especially from the perspective of those like myself who never sailed under the neorealist flag, were the reactions by neorealists. Three reactions were most curious, each duly suggested by John Vasquez (1997) and his critics. One was the rapid-fire abandonment of neorealism. Although never quite characterized in these terms, the proliferation of realisms could certainly convey the impression that neorealism was not as durable as once assumed. To be sure, there were still those committed to the neorealist enterprise, but it was now widely advertised that realism was bigger than neorealism and neorealism was bigger than Kenneth Waltz. At the very least the willingness to use various modifiers to supplant the "neo" suggested that neorealism was not nearly as muscular as assumed.

These new modifiers signaled a second reaction: There were critical variables contained in earlier versions of realism that had been omitted from neorealism, variables that needed to be recovered in order to address important past and present developments. What was particularly curious was that some of these variables, including state-society relations and national identity, had been previously and categorically excluded by neorealism. Far from signaling the limitations of realism, some of neorealism's advocates claimed that this development demonstrated its ability to uncover and explain novel facts. Perhaps.

At the very least these many emendations complicated the search for neorealism's hard core. What is its core? Walt (1997, 932; Ch. 4 herein, 60–61) notes that neorealism and realism are better understood as a "family of theories." However true this might be, the existence of this very extended family means that blood lines are diluted and it is difficult to identify the core propositions on any founding tablets (Legro and Moravcsik 1999). This problem is particularly evident when auxiliary hypotheses are offered as part of a protective belt for the theory but the hypotheses are disconnected from one another and not easily deducible from core propositions. As Vasquez (1997) suggests, this certainly complicates the desire to develop the research program. The vast menu of choice, moreover, also makes life difficult for those who want to test their theories against the realist alternative (Risse-Kappen 1995, Ch. 1).

A third reaction by many who were sympathetic to neorealism and its variants, and suspicious of constructivism and other theoretical approaches that argued the causal force of "social" variables, was to claim that the former had proven superior to the latter in competitive tests. Michael Desch (1998) argued that the hullabaloo surrounding "culture" was unwarranted on a variety of grounds, including the simple fact that culture did not provide a superior explanation for important outcomes. As Richard Price (1999) argued, however, because Desch did not provide an accurate representation of the epistemological implications of a social ontology, he failed to judge fairly or adequately the difference that culture makes. Stephen Walt's book is, of course, an attempt to demonstrate the causal salience of military threats in a part of the world that supposedly takes its ideology seriously. I will have much more to say about this later. But one particularly instructive moment in his assault against ideational variables comes when he (Walt 1987, 200) dismisses the potential causal force of identity in U.S.-Israeli relations by arguing that "ideological solidarity" between the United States and Israel was not possible because "U.S. is [not] a welfare-state theocracy such as Israel."

This represents, at the least, an interesting characterization of Israel's identity, not easily found in either Israel's presentation of self or the United States's representational practices of Israel. A less charitable observation is that Walt's characterization represents the rather extreme lengths that some scholars will go to maintain materialist barricades. In sum, the combination of testing their theories against contrived alternatives, incorporation of ideational factors that they once claimed were outside the hard core of neorealism, and proliferation of realisms could easily project the impression of a research program in turmoil (Legro and Moravcsik 1999).

This essay represents a modest contribution to this debate over the status of the neorealist research program. Specifically, my observation is that various extensions and reformulations of neorealism have occasionally reached outside core propositions and introduced ad hoc emendations. This development has arguably increased the explanatory accuracy of their models but at a significant cost to neorealism's heart. Said otherwise, the very incorporation of residual categories is best interpreted not as evidence of neorealism's ability to develop auxiliary hypotheses that uncover novel facts but rather as illuminating core theoretical tensions. In this regard I am quite supportive of Vasquez's claim that at least some of the extensions of neorealism reach outside the hard core and into foreign terrain to make sense of the world. While this might not be slam-dunk evidence of a degenerative research program, it is hardly evidence of a vibrant one.

To support these observations I interrogate Stephen Walt's *The Origins of Alliances* and his balance of threat theory. I recognize that there is considerable debate regarding whether Walt's "balance of threat" approach is more properly viewed as part of the neorealist research agenda or as part of a reformulated balance of power school. My position is that it can be fairly treated as part of neorealism. The combination of Waltz's claim that he was placing balance of power on a more scientific and rigorous foundation, and the fact that Walt's theoretical apparatus accepted most of Waltz's claims provide considerable weight behind the argument that Walt was working within and extending neorealist theory (Keohane 1988). Certainly many neorealists favorably cited *Origins of Alliances* as an important extension of neorealism. Therefore, while some might claim that any criticism of Walt's model has little to do with neorealism, my position is that, at the time, Walt's statement was widely received by the discipline as an important and favorable reformulation of some basic neorealist propositions as defined by Waltz.

My interrogation of Walt's argument and its application to inter-Arab politics suggests that Walt's refinement represents an ad hoc emendation because his hypotheses cannot be derived from core neorealist propositions (or even classic balance of power propositions, for that matter). To capture the core dynamics of the region Walt must resort to critical variables that undermine neorealism and are more closely linked to nonmaterial factors than they are to the materialist formulations that inform Waltzian neorealism and most balance of power theories. The result is that, while Walt's empirical generalizations and brief historical narrative are highly informative, they are insights that he arrives at with the critical aid of residual categories and that are far afield from core neorealist propositions. While he is generally read as offering a friendly amendment to neorealism, he accidentally subverts it.

My essay is organized as follows. Section I briefly outlines Walt's understanding of the origin of alliances, and argues that his insistence that power and threat are independent leaves unanswered the critical question regarding what informs the definition of threat. To understand the origins of threat, I observe, requires that he reach far outside the neorealist hard core and consider the role of normative structures such as identity and norms. I then put forward the skeleton of an alternative model that is founded on a constructed Arabism and not a mechanical anarchy.[1] Briefly, Arab leaders were fearful of being viewed as outside the Arab consensus, that is, as violating the norms of Arabism, and worked feverishly to construct interpretations of these norms that were consistent with their various interests. They struggled not over the balance of power but rather over the meaning of Arabism. As such, they defined *threats* as interpretations of those norms that ran counter to their interpretations and those moments when they might be viewed as violating the norms of Arabism and as residing outside the Arab consensus. During their debates over these norms they formed coalitions around specific positions, but once that norm was fixed they exhibited a form of normative bandwagoning, using that norm as a focal point to coordinate their policies and to construct their military alliances.

Sections II through IV briefly examine three salient alliances in inter-Arab politics—the Arab Collective Security Pact (ACSP) of 1950, the Baghdad Pact of 1955, and the alliances created immediately preceding the 1967 War. Arabism—and not anarchy—provided the context for the definition of the threat in all three cases and thereby provides greater leverage over the origins of these alliances. Walt does not discuss the ACSP, but the Pact's stated claim that it was a collective security arrangement designed to protect the Arab world against Israel should be an easy mark for neorealism. Yet its dynamics hardly conform to neorealist predictions and instead represented Egypt's ingenious answer to the growing popularity of unification and the threat of a Syrian-Iraqi unification. That is, the "threat" was a vision of Arabism that spelled political unification—an immediate challenge to the sovereignty and autonomy of Arab states.

The Baghdad Pact implicated Iraq in the Western-led containment strategy against the Soviet Union. While on the surface it was a straightforward attempt by Iraq to increase its security against a feared Soviet Union, the debate it unleashed was a testimony to the fact that it brought into bold relief a tension in the Arab states system as it pertained to the security practices of the Arab states. On the one hand, as *sovereign* states they had an interest in maintaining their security against perceived external threats and demanded their sovereign right to make alliances with whomever they saw fit. On the other hand, as *Arab* states they were, first, quite sensitive to alliances with former colonial powers because of the fear that such relations might simply reproduce colonialism by any other name, and, second, believed that their security interests were interdependent. Sovereignty encouraged them to go their own way while Arabism emphasized their enmeshment. This tension came to a head when Iraq signed an alliance with the West and Arab states debated the conditions under which they were permitted to form strategic alliances with the West. Iraq claimed that it was well within its sovereign rights to form such an alliance. Nasser disagreed and publicly opposed the pact on the grounds that it represented a threat to the Arab state's autonomy and independence. Although other Arab states were sympathetic to Iraq's desire to deepen its relations with the West—after all, many retained ties to their former colonial overseer—at the end of the day they reluctantly sided with an increasingly powerful Nasser who successfully promoted the concept of positive neutrality and the norm against alliances with the West.

The 1967 war illuminates how the desire by Arab leaders to be identified with Arabism—and not the desire to confront an immediate military threat from Israel—led them to stumble into an unwanted war with Israel. Arab leaders were less concerned with the Israeli military threat than they were with maintaining their image as Arab nationalists and as ready to fight for Palestine. Because they feared the threat from their own societies if their Arab credentials were found wanting as greater than the possible military threat from Israel, they knowingly signed alliances and undertook aggressive actions that they knew increased the chances of an unwanted war with Israel. The result, as all said privately at the time and publicly afterwards, was that they allowed "one-upmanship" to trip them into a war that they feared would lead to their collective military defeats. But they knowingly did so to keep up appearances and to maintain regime stability.

These three episodes, in short, suggest the incompleteness of a neorealist theory of alliances, how an examination of the "threat" immediately leads to an incorporation of the ideational realm, and that the origins of alliances in the Arab world derive not from anarchy but rather from a desire to be associated with the norms of Arabism for reasons of social approval and regime survival. While I recognize neorealism's forte is explaining patterns of international politics and not offering pinpoint predictions of foreign policy behavior, it remains that Walt (and others) use these very episodes to bolster their positive case for (neo-)realism in general and balance of threat in particular. This makes a reexamination of these instances fair game, to say the least. The overall explication of the pattern of alliance formation in the Middle East, moreover, does not support neorealism or balance of threat theory. Indeed, Walt's own observations of the region support an alternative, constructivist reading. Specifically, Walt's generalizations about alliance formation in the region is dependent on making analytic claims that undermine neorealism (and realist-inspired balance of power theories) and bolster the case for the sociality of world politics.

## Power, Threat, and the Origin of Alliances

Realist scholarship is unanimous that alliances are driven by expediency rather than principle, that their primary motivation is to enhance state security in the face of some immediate or future external threat, and that ideational and domestic interests are of secondary importance. In this view, states seek alliances primarily to enhance their capabilities through combination with others, which helps to deter a potential aggressor and avoid an unwanted war; to prepare for a successful war in the event that deterrence fails; or more generally to increase one's influence in a high-threat environment or maintain a balance of power in the system. Resting on a foundation of systemic theorizing, realist approaches insist that alliances are a result of expedience and military threats from other states.[2]

Of central importance here is Stephen Walt's (1987) justly influential *The Origins of Alliances*. Walt modifies Waltz's account of alliance formation by claiming that states do not balance against power but rather against threats. Walt's balance of threat theory argues that anarchy and the distribution of power alone are unable to signal which states will be identified as threats. It posits that threats derive from a combination of geostrategic and military factors, and "aggressive intentions" (22–26). Threat assessment requires marrying capabilities and intentions.[3]

Walt's "balance of threat" approach represents an important contribution to neorealist thought. Yet to what extent does Walt's theory and narrative of Middle Eastern politics represent a friendly amendment to the research program? Walt's theoretical framework and observations identify not the logic of anarchy but rather the logic of Arabism. Specifically, Walt assembles strong support for normative rather than materialist forces as driving inter-Arab politics in general and alliance formation in particular.

To begin, consider the variable of "aggressive intentions." Walt elevates this critical variable because of his recognition that the distribution of power alone cannot predict which states will be identified as a threat. But how is intent determined? In his theoretical discussion Walt offers various examples of how intent represents an important component of the construction of the threat, yet the concept of intent is left underspecified and undertheorized. By rejecting the proposition that intent is conceptually linked to anarchy or the balance of power and by failing to offer a conceptual tie in its place, the issue remains: How is intent determined? What constitutes a threat?

Although Walt's theoretical discussion does not offer any guidance concerning how intent is determined, looming large in his historical narrative is the "ideology" of Arab nationalism. Because the ideology of Arab nationalism was the source of the threat, interstate interactions had a different dynamic than predicted by realist formulations. Simply put, rivalry had a strong normative element that was independent of material power. In fact, Walt recognizes as much. After surveying a series of alliances and balancing episodes in Arab politics, he concludes (Walt 1987, 149):

> A different form of balancing has occurred in inter-Arab relations. In the Arab world, the most important source of power has been the ability to manipulate one's own image and the image of one's rivals in the minds of other Arab elites. Regimes have gained power and legitimacy if they have been seen as loyal to accepted Arab goals, and they have lost these assets if they have appeared to stray outside the Arab consensus. As a result, an effective means of countering one's rivals has been to attract as many allies as possible in order to portray oneself as leading (or at least conforming to) the norms of Arab solidarity. In effect, the Arab states have balanced one another not by adding up armies but by adding up votes. Thus militarily insignificant alliances between various Arab states often have had profound political effects.

This is a curious conclusion for someone who is widely perceived as offering friendly amendments to neorealism (and reformulating classic realist balance of power theory). Consider the many ways this paragraph subverts neorealism's core claims. Power comes not from the barrel of a gun but rather from a preened image. Arab leaders spend an exorbitant amount of energy attempting to demonstrate that they are the most ardent supporter of the norms of Arabism; being associated with these norms is a source of power. As a consequence, the definition of threat derives not from material power but rather from a hostile intent that originates in the attempt by one Arab leader to portray a rival as outside the Arab consensus. What Arab leaders fear, in other words, is being portrayed as violating the norms of Arabism. This might be the definition of the threat. Alliance dynamics, therefore, have a very different structure and look in Arab politics. Indeed, if the Arab states' behavior is driven by their desire to be perceived as acting in ways that are consistent with the norms of Arabism, then presumably they will be interested in bandwagoning with those norms (and those Arab leaders most closely associated with them), not balancing against them, for fear of being portrayed as outside the Arab consensus. This single paragraph advances several observations that can hardly be treated as logical deductions from neorealism's or balance of threat's core propositions.

If Walt concludes that Arabism and ideology drove inter-Arab dynamics, why does he not revise his balance of threat model to incorporate more fully normative factors? If Walt is suggesting that images, not anarchy, drive inter-Arab politics, then why not direct attention to normative—not material—forces as primary, independent, and causal? As it stands, Walt's various historical observations are inconsistent with his materialist presuppositions, suggesting the limitations of neorealism for understanding inter-Arab politics. It is always good to know one's limits, a point nicely made by Schweller (1997; Ch. 6 herein, 78) who admonishes neorealists for the failure to impose scope conditions on their theories. But Walt arguably wants to bust out of the scope conditions delineated by a material structure and into a social realm. Doing so, in my view, is absolutely essential for getting a handle on inter-Arab alliance patterns—but at a cost of protecting neorealism's flank.

My suspicion is that there are two reasons why Walt fails to give normative forces their proper due. The first is a commitment to a materialism that compels him to reduce normative factors to the level of ideology and to see them as parasitic on the material. Interests derive objectively from a material structure, that is, the international distribution of power; and while states will argue that their policies are in the interests of the broader community, the real function of these policies is to advance particular interests and the real function of this ideology is to provide the veneer of legitimacy. This formulation is consistent with realism (and many influential studies of Arab politics). The problem is that "threat" is hardly tied to military power and "ideology" seems to come prior to anarchy in terms of the definition of interests. Indeed, although Walt's analytical discussion recognizes that "aggressive intentions" drive the construction of the threat and are autonomous from the distribution of power, he fails to consider what other theoretical field might generate the identification of hostile intent. A fuller consideration of Arab "identity" and Arab norms might provide an answer.

A second possible reason why Walt retreats to anarchy is because of the observation that Arab states, who supposedly shared an identity, showed quite a flair for conflict and not for cooperation. In other words, because a shared identity is more closely associated with conflict than it is with cooperation, there is no conceivable way that normative forces are at work. Yet the observation that the existence of a shared identity is associated with conflict is worth greater reflection. To begin, why assume that a shared identity necessarily generates a pacific structure and cooperation? After all, a community of Saddam Husseins is unlikely to foster a secure environment, while a community of Mahatma Gandhis will encourage all to leave their homes unlocked.[4] Perhaps a more reasonable stance is to consider the possibility that conflict can take place among those actors that have a shared identity.[5] Conflict, after all, is part of any social relationship and has many sources. Realists might want to claim that conflict is a core proposition. But they must recognize that lots of other theories do so as well.

Because interstate interactions and alliance formation are better connected conceptually to identity than to anarchy, reducing identity to ideology and assuming that the ideational is parasitic on the material relegates to a residual category what is, in fact, central. Simply put, Arabism and not anarchy provides greater leverage over the dynamics and alliance patterns of the region. Arabism charged that because the West segmented and divided the Arab nation into separate Arab states, Arab states derived their identity, interests, and legitimacy from the entire Arab nation that enveloped their separate borders. A central feature of this drama was that while the Arab states system was nominally organized around sovereignty, Arabism held that Arab states had an obligation to protect Arabs wherever they resided. This showed up in three celebrated areas. One was pan-Arabism and the expectation that Arab states were expected to work to bring into correspondence the national identity and political authority. Far from honoring the correspondence between statehood and sovereignty, a central debate in Arab politics involved whether its fundamental organization should rest on Westphalia, a gift from the West, or an alternative arrangement of the Arabs' own devising.

Another concerned whether and under what conditions Arab states could enter into strategic arrangements with the West. Colonialism and imperialism gave Arab nationalism a kickstart, and, consequently, a defining concern was how to increase the Arab states' power and security vis a vis the West. Beginning in the mandate period with anticolonialism, picking up steam in the mid-1950s, thanks to Nasser and his concept of positive neutrality, it became an article of faith and fear among Arab leaders that they should shun strategic alliances with the West and practice the art of Arab self-reliance. Consequently, although realism assumes that states can enter into any alliance as they see fit, an emerging property of Arabism cautioned against alliances with the West not simply because it might reduce the state's autonomy but because it might jeopardize the security of the entire Arab nation.

And last but not least was the Arab-Israeli conflict. The very understanding that Israel represents a threat to the Arab nation is derived from the Arab identity, and over the years the Arab states have established a series of norms that not only helped to overcome collective action problems but also served to define the very meaning of Arabism. Regardless of how Arab states calculated their strategic or material interests, what Mohammad Heikal (1996) describes as the "taboo" in Arab politics left unquestioned (until recently) the assumption that there would be no relations or a separate peace with Israel.

Unity, the West, and Zionism have been salient, defining, and identity-expressive issues in Arab politics. These were not simply foreign policy issues, they also were domestic issues. And they were not simply about domestic politics, they also concerned identity politics. Because Arab leaders were dependent on Arabism to authenticate and support their rule among a citizenry who saw themselves as Arab nationals, their very domestic legitimacy was dependent on how they conducted, presented, and carried themselves on these matters. Moreover, because these were Arab issues they properly belonged to—and should be decided collectively by—all Arab states. An Arab leader could hardly insist on his right to act unilaterally because of state sovereignty; because these were Arab issues their position should be collectively considered, debated, and decided. Not only was it bad form to act unilaterally on these issues, other Arab states were quick to remind the possible renegade that it also was bad politics. Finally, Arab leaders were forced to take a stand on these matters and judged accordingly, and it was through their collective positions and interactions on these issues that the debates over the desired regional order were waged, defined, and transformed.

All this suggests that there is a normative structure whose defining element is Arabism. Beginning with Arabism and not anarchy raises several important counterpoints to neorealism and generates an alternative understanding of the dynamics of alliance politics in the Arab world. First, Arab leaders were in a structural condition of mutual dependence: Because of their shared Arab identity they collectively determined the norms of Arabism and could hardly declare a sovereign prerogative over such matters, were expected to honor those norms, and generally did so because of their desire for social approval and recognition that they were Arab leaders in good standing. Arab governments recognized that their ability to execute their interests was dependent on the norms that were established and the actions of other Arab leaders, and they manipulated images in order to increase the likelihood that their desired norm was stabilized. The more "thick" is the normative environment, that is, the more embedded are actors in a network of relations that are invested with symbolic content and that provide a source of identity, the more dependent they will be on each other for social approval. This dependence on social approval, in turn, increases their susceptibility to normative suasion. Because their legitimacy, popularity, and sometimes even survival was dependent on whether they were viewed as adhering to the norms of Arabism, Arab leaders expended considerable energy managing their images because of self-preservation. Arab leaders were deeply committed to their own survival. Recognize that at issue here is not the survival of the state that dwells in anarchy but the survival of the Arab leader who dwells in Arabism.[6]

Second, Arab states fought over the norms that should govern their relations. Those states that share a basic identity and organize themselves into a self-constituted group are likely to construct norms that instruct them on how they are to enact their identity. This suggests two possible sources of conflict. While all proclaimed that they were *Arab* leaders, they held different understandings of what it meant to be an Arab nationalist. That actors who have a shared identity will disagree over what constitutes acceptable behavior for the members of the group represents a potential source of conflict. This disagreement stems not only from principled commitments but also from the recognition that their fundamental interest in regime survival was potentially at stake. In general, Arab politics is rightly renowned for its conflict. But this conflict derived not from anarchy and the desire to preserve the balance of power but rather from Arabism and the desire to define the norms of Arabism.

To define the norms of Arabism, therefore, was an exercise of power and a mechanism of social control. Arab leaders competed not to increase their "relative gains" measured in terms of military or economic power but rather to determine the norms of Arabism. International relations theory tends to focus on economic and military means of influence, reflective of its inclination to treat the international system comprising states who are embedded in a nearly normless environment and whose interests are defined by wealth and security. But if the international environment is recognized as having a social character, if states are conceptualized as involved in patterns of relations that can confer social standing or moral censure, and if scholars are willing to concede that state officials desire social approval, then these leaders can be persuaded and embarrassed into submission through normative weapons.

This suggests that norms can be technologies of power and control. This is certainly true in Arab politics. Arab officials often portrayed their rivals as straying from the Arab consensus—and doing so in the most colorful language—to mobilize a target state's population and to ridicule its leadership. This was Nasser's forte, the real source of his power, and the reason Arab leaders viewed him as a threat. In other words, Nasser's power derived not from Egypt's military capabilities but rather from his ability to impose a meaning on the events of his time, to establish the norms of Arabism, and to weave a compelling image of the future.

Third, the "threat" came not from a barrel of a gun but rather from the establishment of a norm or vision of political life that was contrary to a regime's interests. Arab leaders were more obsessed by the possibility that a rival Arab leader would offer an alternative vision of the future, or an interpretation of a norm, than they were with the possibility that that same leader might go on a weapons-buying spree. Arabism represented a potential threat to the Arab state's domestic and international basis of existence, and an Arab leader who wielded the Arab card could be dangerous indeed.

Fourth, once the norm of Arabism was perceived as sufficiently fixed then Arab leaders who were on the losing side of the argument had a tremendous incentive to demonstrate their loyalty to the interpretation of the norm. In the game of inter-Arab politics, sticks and stones had comparatively little effect but words could really hurt; portraying another Arab leader as acting in ways that were inconsistent with Arabism could potentially unleash domestic challenges and subject him to regional sanctions.[7] Arab leaders could lose tremendous legitimacy, and hence suffer a drop in their domestic and regional standing, if they were viewed as not safeguarding the interests, as failing to live up to the goals and aspirations, of the Arab nation. Furthermore, actors who appropriate society's norms for ulterior motives might be compelled to make good on their talk in order to save face. Arab leaders, therefore, had to practice what they preached. Indeed, at various moments they followed a course of action in order to salvage their reputation even though they privately feared that doing so might jeopardize state power. Solidarity and compliance, therefore, was accomplished because of Arab leaders' sense of self and desire for social approval. This was about identity and interests. Actors will be both self-interested and abide by certain standards and codes of conduct because of the desire to be viewed as a moral agent and to maintain the presentation of self, if only for strategic purposes.

The presence of Arabism and these social dynamics imprinted the nature of inter-Arab alliances. Initial coalitions were formed not over the attempt to maintain a balance of power but rather to preserve or promote a particular interpretation of the norms of Arabism. Once a particular interpretation of a norm was fixed or momentarily advanced, however, then Arab states that were on the other side of the battle either had to fall into line or face ostracism. That is, Arab states tended to demonstrate a kind of "normative" bandwagoning. In this respect, many Arab alliances were bound up with impression management and presentational politics. Arab states routinely joined alliances, but they frequently did so to maintain their image as an Arab state in good standing, a point noted by Walt (1987, 149). As a consequence, there should be no surprise when these security institutions failed to develop any substantive military relations because that was not their purpose. Normative and not military politics provide the best starting point for understanding inter-Arab politics and alliances.

## THE ARAB COLLECTIVE SECURITY PACT

Most Arab states demonstrated a keen interest in fixing a meaning of Arabism that was consistent with sovereignty, an interest born not merely from an exegetical reading of the original texts but also from a desire to preserve the territorial and sovereign basis of their power. Yet there remained an undercurrent of sentiment, particularly so in the Fertile Crescent, that continued to champion the idea of unification and to view these states as artificial entities. Accordingly, Iraqi and Jordanian leaders were at the forefront of expressing such sentiments if only to score easy political points, to raise havoc, or to embarrass their rivals. Iraq's interest in unification had various sources—including personal aggrandizement of the palace, domestic politics, and a desire to cast a longer shadow over Arab politics. Always ready to forward a "Greater Syria" plan with himself crowned as king in Damascus, Abdullah's unification impulse derived from: a desire to break out of his desert kingdom; a belief that the Hashemite thrones in Iraq and Transjordan should be united, and that, by all rights, Syria also should have been Hashemite; the goal of elevating his stature in Arab politics and bolstering his domestic fortunes; the wish to fulfill his Hashemite family's longstanding goals; the concern that his heir apparent, Talal, was unfit to rule; and perhaps the dream of reconquering the Hijaz and settling an old debt with the Saudis (Satloff 1994, 19–20; Maddy-Weitzman 1993, 41; and Wilson 1988). Abdullah had more reasons than not to trumpet unification. In both the Iraqi and the Jordanian cases the unity theme derived from a mixture of regime-survival and nationalism, but their very ability to employ unification as a means to extend their influence or to absorb new territories can be attributed only to the enabling conditions of Arabism.

There were various unification proposals between 1945 and 1955 but none more credible than a proposed Syrian-Iraqi unification in Fall, 1949. The backdrop was the following. Unification became a more frequently mentioned goal after the Palestine War. In the debate over the causes of the loss and how to increase the power and security of the Arab world, one candidate was unification, which offered the promise of both answering the challenge posed by Israel and fulfilling a longstanding goal of Arab nationalism. Then came the first post-1945 coup in the Arab world: On March 30, 1949, Husni Za'im overthrew President Qwattli, motivated by a combination of personal grandeur, nationalist goals, defense of the army against charges of corruption, maintaining the army's material privileges, and assorted other reasons (Maddy-Weitzman 1993, 105). Until Za'im's coup, Syria had been ruled by politicians and parties who originated in the National Bloc, the corpus of the nationalist movement in Syria during the interwar period. Increasingly discredited, it began to rely on the military for support; the military, meanwhile, was becoming increasingly disenchanted with the ruling politicians, caused in part by the government's lackluster performance in Palestine. The result was an awkward standoff and constant friction between the military and the government. Za'im's coup shattered the uneasy truce (Rabinovich 1991, 19; Torrey 1964, 137).

One of Za'im's first actions was to propose that Iraq and Syria conclude a defense treaty, motivated largely by his desire to strengthen his hand vis-a-vis Israel at the armistice talks in Rhodes and against any domestic criticism that he was deficient on Arab nationalism (Torrey 1964, 134–135; Seale 1986, 48). Although Syria and Iraq never concluded a defense agreement, its prospect stimulated a round of discussions concerning future regional arrangements and competition among Arab states for Syria's favor (Mufti 1996, 51–52). Unification talk re-emerged after the overthrow of Za'im by Sami al-Hinnawi on August 14, 1949, and soon thereafter Hinnawi recommended that Syria and Iraq unify, a proposal born from Arabist sentiments and fear of Israel (Seale 1986, 77–83). Their negotiations proceeded cautiously through the Fall but a principal Syrian objection was the Anglo-Iraqi Treaty; it represented a perceived affront to Arab independence and Syria would not consider any formal ties as long as it was standing (Seale 1986, 15, 79–81).

Still, unification talk filled the airwaves and soon settled on the Arab League meeting of October, 1949, where Iraq presented the proposed union to the Council, emphasizing its consistency with Article 9 of the League Charter.[8] Jordan, a longtime proponent of unification, defended unification and cited the Palestine war as an additional reason for its urgency. Egypt, Lebanon, and Saudi Arabia opposed the plan. But no Arab official could outright oppose unification for fear of inviting ostracism. The antiunionist forces would have to find a stealth barricade.

Egypt ingeniously proposed a collective security pact. Building on nationalism, the desire for unity, the reluctance to rely on Britain for defense assistance, and the fear of Israel, Egypt proposed that the Arab states construct a regional security arrangement. By injecting this motion into the debate, the meeting became a contest between Iraq's unification plan—an Iraq that was closely tied to Britain and a plan that was restricted to Syria—and Egypt's defense plan—which would be inclusive and perhaps a better solution to Syria's defense concerns because it included Egypt, the Arab world's largest state and one that also bordered Israel.

Egypt's strategy worked. The all-Arab military agreement became the focal point of the meetings. The Arab League subsequently adopted the proposed military plan forwarded by Egypt, which it compared to the Atlantic Pact, and decided not to "touch the question of Iraqi-Syrian rapprochement since it is an internal affair which should not be interfered with."[9] Egypt used the idea of collective security to defeat a unification plan and to institutionalize sovereignty, and the decision by the Arab League not to formally consider the unification proposal under the guise of the principle of noninterference worked to the same end. Egypt used the idea of a multilateral forum to, first, frustrate Iraq and its goal of unification, and, second, re-enforce the principle of state sovereignty and territoriality. The head of the Saudi delegation, visibly pleased with the result, endorsed the collective security plan, implicitly rejected the proposed union, and added that Saudi foreign policy is "established on an unshakable basis: the necessity of preservation of the independence of every Arab state."[10]

Visibly bitter about the League's deliberations and conclusions, Iraq's Nuri al-Said characterized the military pact as a substitute for action and an attempt to block the proposed Iraqi-Syrian unification, and lamented the fact that "nations with no ties of language or religion or history [are] joining together through pacts and treaties [that are] stronger than those between the Arab League states." He then issued a challenge. Either we cooperate in a manner compatible "with our Governments' responsibilities . . . or we lay down another charter for our League under which every Arab government will openly give up some of its rights and authority as an independent sovereign state. A combination of these two alternatives is nothing but a kind of chaos which will lead us into stumbling upon one failure after another and going from bad to worse."[11] Nuri dared Egypt and other Arab states to stop using institutional devices and the cloak of collectivism to preserve their independence and to frustrate inter-Arab cooperation.

Those Syrians who had opposed unification and/or saw the Iraqi unification proposal as a mechanism to increase Syria's security against Israel now grabbed onto the proposed collective security pact as a viable alternative to unity with Iraq. And then on December 17 and 18, one day after the proponents of closer ties with Iraq had used a major political occasion—the debate over the oath of the constitution—to pledge movement toward unity, Hinnawi was overthrown by Colonel Shishakli, a Syrian nationalist and critic of unification (Seale 1986, 84–85, 124).

Beginning with an Egyptian proposal, the Arab League formed the basis of the Treaty of Joint Defence and Economic Cooperation among the States of the Arab League, better known as the Arab Collective Security Pact (ACSP). Signed April 13, 1950, the Arab states pledged to settle their conflicts through nonviolent means (Article 1), to engage in collective defense (Article 2), and to integrate their military and foreign policies (Article 5). The Arab states never implemented the conditions of the treaty, which was not too shocking because Egypt had proposed the treaty as a way to block unification and not because it was a strong supporter of closer and more encumbered ties between Arab states. Balance of threat theory should have an easy time explaining the origins of the ACSP. This was, after all, an alliance of Arab states proclaiming their intent to coordinate their security policies to confront Israel. But surface impressions can be deeply misleading. Egypt invented the ACSP not to confront the Israeli threat but rather the unification threat. For over a decade Egypt had been steadfastly opposed to all unification proposals; it was joined by other Arab states who believed that unification represented an immediate threat to state sovereignty and regime stability. While many regimes opposed unification for self-interested reasons, a vocal strand in many Arab societies continued to argue for unification because of the view that these Western-created Arab states were illegitimate and that there should be a single Arab state for a single Arab nation. To frustrate the cause of unification and satisfy the desire for a bolder security arrangement, Egypt and other Arab states proposed a collective security pact. While Israel might have been the threat formally mentioned in the treaty, the real threat the pact was designed to quell was unification. No wonder, then, that Arab states demonstrated little interest in coordinating their military policies. The ACSP was established to counter the threat of unification and its very existence served that very function.

## The Baghdad Pact

Ever since independence, Arab states had debated what should be their proper relationship to their former colonial masters. Although there was general sympathy to the claim that some sort of relationship was permissible, a largely pragmatic decision that originated from the desire for military and financial aid, there remained the fear that any relationship might compromise the Arab state's autonomy, introduce a new form of colonialism, and potentially undermine the security of the Arab world. The Cold War and the desire by the Western states to enlist the Arab world into their containment strategy only increased the pressure from the West on the Arab states, not completely unwelcome if the price was right. But because any alliance with the West resurrected the specter of colonialism and represented an affront to Arab nationalism, Arab states generally believed that they required regional approval for any possible alliance. This was the backdrop to the fight over the Baghdad Pact, waged between Iraq's venerable Nuri al-Said, who sought an alliance with the West and believed that it was permissible under Arabism, and Egypt's upstart Gamal Nasser, who believed that such alliances defied the meaning of Arabism and potentially threatened his leadership.

A central issue concerned the conditions under which Arab states might be permitted to join a Western-led alliance. This was the topic of the December 1954 Arab Foreign Ministers meeting in Cairo (Seale 1986, 164). As Nasser welcomed the delegates he urged them to follow Egypt's example by constructing resolutions that reflected the needs of the Arab nation, pledging against joining any outside alliance, and emphasizing their reliance on the Collective Security Pact. This they did. The foreign ministers crafted two resolutions: (1) "that no alliance should be concluded outside the fold of the Collective Arab Security Pact"; and (2) "that cooperation with the West was possible, provided that a just solution was found for Arab problems and provided the Arabs were allowed to build up their strength with gifts of arms."[12] Egypt, which used the Arab League Charter to deter the drive for unification and preserve sovereignty and then designed the ACSP to halt the possible Syrian-Iraqi unification in 1949, now used the ACSP to slow down Iraq's planned alliance with the West. Echoing the neutrality that became a hallmark of Nasser's foreign policy, the foreign ministers proclaimed that the "burden of the defense of the Arab East should fall on the states of the area alone, and that the question of putting the Collective Security Pact into effect has become timely and inevitable if the Arab States are to form a united front in political affairs and defense against any foreign danger that may threaten any or all of them."[13] The foreign ministers publicly proclaimed that they must coordinate their policies because they were Arab states.

But immediately after the meeting was adjourned, rumors began to circulate of an Iraqi alliance with the West. There are more speculations than precise explanations concerning Nuri's rapid defiance, but it appears that he believed that his fellow Arab leaders, many of whom already had ties of various kinds with the West, would give him the green light (Kerr 1970, 4; Heikal 1987, 54). On January 13, 1955, Iraq and Turkey announced that they would sign a defense agreement in the near future. In presenting his case to the Iraqi people and the Arab world, Nuri claimed that the Pact was consistent with the Charter of the League of Arab States and Article 51 of the UN, and furthered the goals of the Arab world, and he asserted that Iraq's "special geographic position" (a reference to the Soviet Union) was acknowledged at the recent foreign ministers meeting.

Iraq's announcement triggered outrage across the Arab world. Nasser manned the lead position. There is no doubt that Nasser viewed the alliance as a threat to his personal prestige and to Egypt's regional political position (Dessouki 1989, 36). Nasser, observed King Hussein (1962, 84), "had to attack the Pact if only to prevent other Arab states from joining and so diminishing his prestige." Nasser's central objections concerned the claim that any alliance would only safeguard the interests of the West and harm those of the Arab nation and that Arab states should seek neutrality and security in their unity (Podeh 1995, 66).

Cairo's persistent and emphatic message was that the Baghdad Pact undermined and represented a grave challenge to Arab nationalism and Arab security. The headline of one Egyptian daily proclaimed: "Iraqi Government Demolishes All Efforts to Strengthen the Arab League and Bolster the Arab Collective Security Pact.[14] Nasser deftly tied the meaning of the Pact to both the security of the Arab states and the future of Arab nationalism. Egyptian Interior Minister Salim Salim, who was one of Egypt's point men in the campaign against Iraq, responded to whether sovereign Iraq has the right to enter into any treaty it wants in the following way: "Although Iraq is an independent sovereign state, she nevertheless has obligations and responsibilities toward the League of Arab States and the Arab Collective Security Pact. Is there any state, in the Atlantic Pact, for example, free to make any decisions it chooses even if it be contrary to that pact?"[15] In a later statement Salim dramatically drew the current challenge: "The Arab World is now standing at a crossroads: it will either be an independent and cohesive unit with its own structures and national character or else each country will pursue its own course. The latter would mean the beginning of the downfall of Arab nationhood."[16] Egypt framed the Pact as a challenge to Arab nationalism.

To try and forge a common front against Iraq and to stop the treaty from being signed, Nasser hosted the other Arab leaders from January 22 though February 6. The Arab representatives filed into Cairo publicly proclaiming their outrage at Iraq's actions, but privately were less exercised and some even contemplated following Baghdad rather than Cairo. Saudi Arabia's position was closest to Egypt's, for it feared that its traditional Hashemite rivals in Jordan and Iraq would use their new-found resources and prestige to launch another bid for Fertile Crescent unification; that is, to initiate a threat to Saudi Arabia's external and internal stability.[17] Yemen, too, came out against the Pact.

Syria, Lebanon, and Jordan were less appalled and somewhat approving. Syrian officials were divided over whether or not to join the Pact. Although espousing neutralism in the early 1950s, Prime Minister Faris al-Khuri and Foreign Minister Faydi al-Atasi were both relatively pro-West and therefore somewhat attenuated in their position: While they might not join the Pact they were unwilling to condemn Baghdad (Gerges 1994, 28; and Torrey 1964, 194–196, 273–274). Syrian leader Faris al-Khoury said his personal view was that Syria should not join the pact, but official government policy might be different (Heikal 1987, 56–58). Lebanon was neutral to the point of being slightly encouraging (Podeh 1995, 105–106).

King Hussein was publicly cool to the idea but privately in favor, a stance informed by strategic, dynastic, and symbolic concerns. As a fellow Hashemite monarchy with close political and military ties to the British, Jordan was something of a natural partner and generally disposed toward joining the pact. Yet he was not oblivious to the rising tide of Arabism in Jordan and the region, believed that any joint Arab-Western defense network might be best realized by first working through the Arab League, worried that siding with Cairo's campaign against Iraq meant exacerbating the already inflamed inter-Arab tensions, and feared alienating Egypt and Syria on whom it would rely in the event of an Israeli attack (Dann 1989, 25).

Nasser attempted to convince Syria, Jordan, and Lebanon to condemn and censure Baghdad. In an early address to the conference, he framed the Pact as representing a stark alternative between an Arab nationalism based on unity and one premised on disunity:

> Egypt proposes to the Arab states a foreign policy based on developing Arab unity and independent stature and offers to put all its economic, military, and moral resources at the disposal of Arab nationalism. Nuri al-Said, on the other hand, proposes a policy under which each Arab state would act alone and decide its own future, which would make it easy for the West to swallow them.[18]

Later he challenged his fellow Arab leaders to answer Baghdad with strong action, including the "establishment of a unified Arab army under one command along the same lines as the proposed European army."[19] But the other Arab states remained unconvinced.

Irritated that the other Arab leaders were not following his dictates, Nasser threatened to go to the press and suspend Egypt's relations with them (Heikal 1987, 56–58). Nasser's ultimatum worked. While Jordan, Syria, and Lebanon refused to follow Nasser's admonitions and directives, the conference passed several resolutions condemning Iraq's actions, pledged themselves not to join the Treaty, and decided to send a delegation to Iraq to try and convince Nuri al-Said of the errors of his ways. Significantly, however, the conference adjourned without issuing a final statement. If in public the Arab governments filed out of Cairo declaring their abhorrence of the Pact and their unwillingness to follow Iraq's deviation from the Arab fold, in private they felt less strongly about Iraq's actions and were seriously considering joining it.

Iraq and Turkey formally signed the Pact on February 24. As Nuri unveiled the Pact to a waiting and watching Arab world, he took great pains to detail what was and was not contained in the Pact, to defend himself against Nasser's accusations, and to portray his actions as consistent with the UN, the Arab League, and Arab nationalism. Nuri's speech was highly defensive, reflecting a sensitivity to the charges raised by Nasser and to the public's concern that his actions had isolated Iraq from the Arab fold. To defend himself against the former and to reassure the latter he spent considerable time detailing various tenets of the Pact and emphasizing its link to the Arab past, present, and future.[20]

Now Nuri and Nasser would mobilize all their energies and tools, symbolic and otherwise, to fight for the hearts, minds, and votes in the Arab world. Syria represented the first stop in the debate over the Pact, which became a sign and cause of its increasingly nationalist and neutralist leanings (Seale 1986, Ch. 17). Initially many Syrian nationalists had welcomed the Pact because it might generate aid, increase security against Israel, and perhaps even professionalize the military and keep it in the barracks and out of politics (Torrey 1964, 270). To bolster the anti-Pact forces, Egyptian Minister Salim Salim arrived in Damascus on February 26 to propose a "federal union" with a joint military command and unified foreign policies in lieu of the now defunct collective security pact. The Syrians, however, viewed the proposal with suspicion (Seale 1986, 223).

Nasser received some timely and unintended help from Israel. On February 28, just four days after the Treaty's signing, Israel attacked a military installation in Gaza. Nasser quickly capitalized on the assault by claiming that it was coordinated with and enabled by the Baghdad Pact, and found himself riding a tide of popular support as protests erupted against the Pact throughout the Arab world. In Syria, Israel's attack increased the domestic pressures against the Pact and in favor of an alliance with Egypt as a deterrent to Israel. The army was now so determined to create a defensive alliance against Israel that several Syrian military officers threatened a coup d'etat unless Syria joined an alliance with Egypt (Podeh 1995, 129, 144).

On March 6, Egypt, Syria, and Saudi Arabia pledged to create their own alliance, which they called the *Tripartite Alliance*; included among its provisions was a rejection of the Baghdad Pact and the strengthening of the collective Arab defense (Torrey 1964, 279–280). Syrian Foreign Minister Khalid al-Azm noted that Jordan could not join the alliance because its army was controlled by Britain and therefore ineligible to serve in the United Arab Command,[21] but nevertheless he insisted that the pact not "exclude Iraq or preclude the possibility of member states joining the Iraq-Turkey Pact" (quoted from Podeh 1995, 144). From the Egyptian and Saudi perspective, the value of the Egyptian-Syrian-Saudi alliance was not its deterrent effect but rather its ability to halt Syria from following Iraq's footsteps (Seale 1986, 224–245). There remained, however, some debate in Syrian circles regarding its foreign policy orientation.

Nasser's arms deal with Czechoslovakia on September 27 radically transformed the climate and shifted the ground toward Nasser in the fight over the Pact (Seale 1986, 233–234). The Pact boldly demonstrated to the Arab world that it did not have to be subservient to the West, rendering anachronistic strategic arrangements such as the Baghdad Pact. And Nasser's move, though not intended for this purpose, rescued the nearly moribund Tripartite Pact; it was signed on October 20 (an Egyptian-Saudi mutual defense pact was signed a week later). The arms deal convinced many Syrian officials that by joining Egypt it could vastly increase its security through an alliance and a parallel arms deal with the Soviet Union that would also allow Syrian officials to be identified with Arab neutrality, independence, and power. Syria was now solidly in the Egyptian camp.

The final battle over the Pact would be waged in and over Jordan. Hussein's initial opinion of the Pact was generally positive, but through the Fall no amount of outside pressure from Britain, Turkey, or Iraq could convince him that he should antagonize Egypt and Arab popular opinion by joining the Pact. Hussein abandoned his position of neutrality in November due to three principal events. The first was the Egyptian-Czech arms deal, which according to Hussein (1962, 106), "changed everything." The arms deal reignited the debate over Jordan's participation in the Pact and increased both neutralist sentiments in the region and pressure from the West for Jordan to join the Pact as a countermeasure to the perceived growth of Soviet influence (Heikal 1987, 88). Second, in early November President Bayar of Turkey visited Amman and told Hussein that Britain might provide the strategic assistance he needed to expand the Arab Legion if he joined the Pact. A similar message was conveyed by Lebanese leader Camille Chamoun. Hussein now decided to join the Pact. In mid-November Hussein informed Britain that he would join the Pact at the right price, replaced one prime minister (Huda) who was unwilling to steer Jordan into the arms of the West with another (Said al-Mufti) who would, and asked Nasser not to destabilize his regime once he made his pro-Pact intentions known.

Hussein must have known that he was asking the impossible from Nasser. Emboldened by the military pact with Syria and angered that Britain had seemingly reneged on its spring agreement to cease recruiting other Arab states, Nasser unleashed a torrid media campaign against Jordan and framed the Pact as undermining Arab nationalism and linking any Arab state who supported it to imperialism. In the midst of an increasingly furious debate, in early December Britain sent a top military official, John Templer, to persuade Hussein to join the Pact. This highly publicized and controversial visit by a British official in the midst of Nasser's campaign against the Pact played right into Nasser's hands. Hussein, who braced himself for some political opposition, now confronted fierce rioting. "Hundreds of thousands of Jordanians," Hussein (1962, 88) reflected, "listening avidly to the propaganda on Cairo Radio, saw in Nasser a sort of mystical savior." During this public outcry against the Pact the Jordanian cabinet continued to debate whether or not to join. Then the cabinet fell. The next government was no more successful, and now faced some of the worst rioting in Jordanian history. Demonstrators were calling for the resignation of this recently formed government and a public pledge to cease any further discussions of joining the Pact. As Hussein (1962, 92–93) later wrote:

> We were virtually helpless.... [A]ll hell broke loose. Riots such as we had never seen before... disrupted the whole country. This time bands of fire-raisers started burning the Government buildings, private houses, foreign properties. I had no alternative but to call out the Legion.... That was the end of Jordan and the Baghdad Pact.

The riots left a deep impression on the king. The streets of Amman were solidly behind Nasser, Hussein was nearly an outcast in his own kingdom, and he reluctantly pledged "no new pacts." Reeling from the challenges to his rule, Hussein attempted to repair his stained image through various actions over the next several months, including the dismissal of Sir John Glubb from his military advisory role and the acceptance of an offer from Egypt, Syria, and Saudi Arabia to replace his British subsidy (Podeh 1995, 187–188).

Arabism rather than balance of threat provides a better understanding of the dynamics surrounding the Baghdad Pact. Walt correctly argues that among Said's motives for creating the Pact was his desire to bolster his security against the Soviets. But he also recognizes that the debate that occurred, Iraq's eventual ostracism, and the regional disposition in favor of Nasser's concept of positive neutrality can hardly be attributed to traditional geopolitical threats. His brief historical account, in fact, acknowledges the role of dual visions of the future of Arab nationalism, a personal rivalry between Nasser and Said for prestige in the Arab world, and what I would call normative bandwagoning with Nasser after the formation of the norm prohibiting alliances with the West.

The Pact, in short, represented a challenge not to the balance of power per se but rather to Arab nationalism and its contested norms by unleashing a debate among Arab states concerning what behavior was and was not proper for *Arab* states. That Nuri and Nasser favored rival schools cannot be disconnected from their interests in regime and state security, but neither were they wholly derivative of them. And which version would stand at the end of the debate could not have been predicted by material power alone. Nasser was largely able to defeat the Pact because of his ability to link it to an imperialist past and an equally divided and dependent future. Once he had demonstrated, through his deft use of the media to destabilize other Arab regimes, that public sentiment was on his side, other Arab leaders (sometimes reluctantly) joined Nasser and pledged not to create any alliances with the West. They did so because they sought the social approval gained by being associated with the norms of Arabism and being viewed as an Arab leader in good standing. That this meant having to further the prestige of an increasingly powerful Nasser who demonstrated a willingness and ability to destabilize them from within was the price to be paid for being viewed as an Arab leader in good standing. Nearly damned if they did and damned if they did not, Arab leaders reluctantly aligned themselves with Nasser. This result is a testimony to the threat posed not by military capabilities but rather by normative sanctions.

## The 1967 War

In the early 1960s the Arab states began demonstrating and defining their commitment to Arabism around the Israeli threat. The implication was that the Arab leaders were increasingly vulnerable to the charge that they were not doing enough for the cause of Palestine. This was especially true of those Arab leaders who claimed or aspired to be in a leadership position. Because of previous setbacks, including the dissolution of the United Arab Republic (Egypt's federation with Syria) and the Yemen civil war, Nasser attempted to rally the Arab world behind his leadership to confront the Israelis. The device he struck upon was a "summit system," essentially a series of conferences between Arab leaders beginning in 1964.

The stated purpose of this quasi-alliance was to get the radical and conservative Arab states to cease slinging arrows at each other and redirect them toward Israel. Nasser's ulterior motive was to control the rebellious Syrians. The summit system, therefore, was designed by Nasser to encourage conservatism rather than radicalism. But his ability to maintain the system was dependent on the willingness of the other Arab states to play along.

The contradiction that proved to be the summit system's undoing was Nasser's attempt to use the summit meetings as a multilateral device to control Syria's Israeli policy and Syria's desire to use the Israeli stick to bolster its own credentials and to embarrass Nasser. Two events brought this tension to a breaking point. The first was an Israeli attack on May 13, 1965, on one of Syria's diverting stations. Israel had inaugurated a national water carrier project that would use water from the Jordan River for irrigation purposes. With Syria in the lead, the Arab states agreed to establish a series of diverting stations that would cripple Israel's project. Israel warned that this could represent an act of aggression and that it would respond with force, and the Arab states countered by saying that an attack on a diverting station located in one Arab country represented an attack against all Arab states. Now Syria was putting that claim to the test. What it illuminated was the contradiction between Syria's need to get the Arab states' backing to respond to Israel and the decision of an earlier Arab summit that each state was responsible for responding to "minor" incidents. Syria presented its case in late May at a conference of the Arab premiers, but its plea for support was rejected. A bitter Syria subsequently launched a full-scale propaganda attack on Nasser, proclaiming that it was ready, willing, and able to confront Israel over the Jordan River or any other issue, but that Nasser was hiding behind the summit resolutions to avoid a war with Israel.[22]

This is exactly what Nasser was doing, but he could not very well admit it. At a meeting of the Palestinian National Congress in June, Nasser attempted to refute the Syrian charges by insisting that Arab states must coordinate their policies before confronting Israel. A United Arab Army, he said, was dependent on unified Arab action, which was difficult at the moment because of significant inter-Arab differences. As troubling as was this reality, Nasser confided, it was an improvement over the early 1960s when there was no Arab summit, no Arab resolutions, and no statements of concrete action. How should the Arabs proceed? Through revolutionary action. But, he emphasized and qualified without a hint of irony, this must be cautious and careful revolutionary action. Defending his go-slow policy against Syria's charges of weakness, Nasser raised a theme that would define his position toward the Arab-Israeli conflict for the next two years:

> We must first of all have a plan. If, for example, an aggression is committed against Syria, do I attack Israel? If the case is so, then Israel can set for me the time at which to attack. Why? Just because it commits an aggression and hits one or two tractors, I am to attack Israel the second day. Is this logical and sound talk? It is we who will choose the time of the battle. It is we who will assess our position. It is we who will fight our battle.

Nasser feared that their pattern of one-upmanship and desire to maintain credibility would force the Arab states into an unwanted war with Israel.[23] The Arab summits became the perfect device for sitting on Syria, but there also was the chance that Syria might eventually engage in unilateral action that not only challenged the summit system but also threatened to call Nasser's bluff.

This is exactly what happened. A coup in Syria in February 1966 brought to power, according to Patrick Seale (1986, 104), the most radical regime in Syrian history. All this spelled bad news for Nasser. The new regime explicitly framed past Arab summits as selling out the Arab nation and the cause of Palestine, and offering little more than feeble excuses for inaction.[24] Less beholden to the notion of an all-Arab consensus if this meant conservatism and more interested in establishing its independence and flushing Nasser out from behind the screen of multilateralism, the Syrian government turned up the heat by encouraging fedayeen raids into Israel. Although Nasser feared that Syria's provocative actions might be the Arab states' undoing, he was more alarmed by this challenge to his Arab credentials. As a result, he played into Syria's strategy: He publicly sided with Syria and began attacking the conservative Arab states. This "public declaration of war" led to the end of the era of summitry.

With the summit period over, Syria and Egypt now began playing a dangerous game of symbolic competition. Syria's earlier challenges had coaxed Nasser out of the very multilateral mechanism that he had designed to control it, and now that it had drawn him out into the open it continued to turn up the heat. Israel's actions played right into Syria's hands, for it faithfully retaliated for every fedayeen action, demonstrating that Syria was in no position to defend itself and increasing the pressure on Egypt to come to Syria's defense. While Nasser watched in horror, fearing that Syria's actions might precipitate a war with Israel, he was equally fearful of confirming Syria's charge that he was indistinguishable from the conservative Arab states and was weak on Palestine.

Nasser, still seeking to control Syrian policy but no longer having the summit format to do so, finally established diplomatic relations with the new regime and signed a joint defense agreement in November, 1966. The agreement, according to Egyptian General el-Gamasy (1993, 19), was formed absent trust and never developed any military coordination. But given the apparent motivations of the Syrians and the Egyptians, the lack of military coordination reflects the nonstrategic basis of the agreement. Syria's motives, according to Samir Mutawi (1996, 175), were not to "revenge the injustices done to the Palestinians but in order to gain supremacy over Nasser as leader of the Arabs." Motivated by a desire to control Syria's actions, Nasser accepted the risky wager that the alliance would leave him in control over Syria rather than Syria in control of Nasser.[25] Nasser lost the bet. Syria continued its provocative ways, increasing the prospect of war and forcing Nasser to keep pace with Syria's taunts or stand accused of being weak on Palestine.

Jordan anxiously watched this "dangerous game of brinkmanship," knowing that it, too, would be forced to keep pace or suffer a loss of prestige (Mutawi 1987, 73). Syria and Egypt accused Hussein of being weak on Arabism, made worse by Israel's retaliation against Jordan for fedayeen raids. Israel launched a particularly deadly reprisal on the West Bank village of Samu on November 13, 1966. The raid also dealt a blow to Hussein's credibility regarding his ability to defend its territory and to protect the Palestinians. Always ready to embarrass Hussein, Cairo and Damascus accused him of following in his grandfather's footsteps (Abdullah had annexed the West Bank and sold out the Palestinians) and failing to protect the Palestinians (Mutawi 1987, 79). The combination of the Israeli attack and the inflammatory broadcasts contributed to rioting among the Palestinians for several weeks; some Palestinian figures even declared the West Bank an independent Palestinian state, and the government imposed martial law to take back the streets. The raid persuaded King Hussein that his credentials and Jordan's security were on the line (Mutawi 1987, 77–78, 81).

The first few months of 1967 were relatively quiet, but beginning in April there commenced a series of incidents and maneuvers between Israel and Syria that signaled that the region was spinning toward war. On April 7, a dogfight between Israel and Syria over the Golan led to the downing of several Syrian MIGs. The remainder of the month remained relatively quiet, but events escalated considerably by early May. Perhaps because of an internal crisis, Syria began publishing reports of a "Zionist-reactionary plot" against itself (Dawn 1996, 155). Attending such reports were highly dramatic and public pleas for Egypt to assist Syria and to live up to its Arab obligations. Jordan also unleashed its own media campaign against Nasser, accusing him of doing little to help his brethren and allies (Mutawi 1987, 28, 85; Dawn 1996, 158–159).

Suspiciously silent on these Israeli-Syrian developments, Nasser found himself increasingly pressured to take dramatic action to support his alliance partner and to maintain his credentials. Nasser was caught between the symbolic and the strategic, and he sacrificed the latter on the altar of the former. "Nasser's concern began not with Israel but with Syria, and pointed eventually not to Sharm al-Shaikh, still less to Tel-Aviv, but to the chanceries and streets of the Arab world" (Kerr 1970, 126–127). Jordan and Syria kept daring him to show his mettle and to stop hiding behind the UN flag, and Nasser accepted each and every dare. On May 14 he sent his army into the Sinai and then on May 22 he closed the Straits of Tiran. Nasser's military advisers cautioned him against taking such actions for fear of provoking Israel and tempting an unwanted war. But Nasser accepted such risks "as a means to end Arab opposition to him, and to maintain his popularity and high esteem in the Arab world" (el-Gamasy 1993, 26–27). That he took this risk can be justly attributed to his unsupported belief that Israel would ultimately not launch a preemptive strike, that the combined Arab forces represented a sufficient retaliatory force, and ultimately, that his Arab credentials were at stake.

King Hussein's decision to cast his lot with Egypt and Syria and war with Israel also can be understood as a desire to remain within the Arab consensus and to gain social approval. The Jordanian cabinet held a fierce debate over how it should position itself in the war climate. Jordanian official Wasfi Tal was nearly alone in arguing against trusting Nasser, claiming that war would bring disaster to Jordan and potentially cost the king Jerusalem and the West Bank (Mutawi 1987, 87). While few shared with Tal his pessimistic appraisal of the Arab states' military capabilities, Arabism was the factor that led Hussein to declare war on Israel. The Syrian and Egyptian campaign against Hussein had been highly effective, stirring up the Jordanian population in general and the Palestinians in particular. The result was that if Jordan stayed out of the war Hussein would have a difficult time containing the inevitable public outcry (Mutawi 1987, 90; Dawn 1996, 159). Simply put, Hussein decided that he would rather take his chances with the Israelis than with his own population. If he went to war with Israel the most he would lose would be the West Bank and Jerusalem, but if he stayed on the sidelines he would probably lose his crown and his country (Mutawi 1987, 100–103, 162, 183).

These calculations help to explain King Hussein's somewhat curious decision to cast his lot with Egypt and Syria when he flew to Cairo and signed a joint defense pact with Egypt on May 30 (Mutawi 1987, 108–109). Hussein was now in league with the same states who had repeatedly attempted to undermine his regime over the years and in the recent past. But Hussein flew to Cairo because of symbolic rather than strategic considerations. A Palace adviser explained: "To meet with Nasser may seem strange when one considers the insults and abuse which Radio Cairo had been hurling at the Hashemite throne for the past year; nonetheless, it would have been impossible for us to justify our remaining aloof from so momentous a matter which engaged the entire Arab world" (quoted from Salibi 1993, 220). "If we were isolated from the mainstream of Arab politics," reflected former Prime Minister Zaid Rifai, "we would be an easy target" (Mutawi 1987, 100–101).

The Arab leaders committed themselves to policies that they thought were unwise strategically but necessary politically. This was a war that few Arab military officials had prepared for or that Arab leaders wanted, but it was a war that they stumbled into and got. Their private thoughts became public soon after the end of the war. Frequently linking the very dynamics that led them into this military debacle to prior episodes that had driven them down the road of unwanted outcomes, Arab intellectuals and officials began tying the 1967 war to a more far-reaching diagnosis of the ills that defined Arab politics. In such commentaries, Arab political elites left little doubt that they found few strategic imperatives in their recent war with Israel, but they did find much evidence of symbolic and political calculations that had left them all worse off.

## Conclusion

Neorealists debate various facets of alliance dynamics, but there is no budging from the singular position that alliances are driven by a specific military threat or by the desire to increase war-making capacity. These totem-like observations derive from the understanding that in an anarchic international structure states will balance against power. Walt's important contribution to neorealism (and realism) is the recognition that states do not balance against power but rather against specific threats, and that anarchy is a poor predictor of threat. To get from anarchy to threat, Walt introduced the concept of "aggressive intentions." This represented an important advance for neorealism; without greater specificity it would be difficult to predict the differentiation of friend from foe—that is, who was perceived to be a threat. "Aggressive intentions" does much work for Walt. But how is the term "aggressive intentions" defined? To fill in this missing link requires not reference to the material world but rather to the social world and the social construction of the threat. This is something that Walt subtly recognizes at important points along the way, particularly when he summarizes his findings on inter-Arab alliance politics.

The problem for Walt and neorealism is that the resort to ideational variables to determine which state has aggressive intentions can be interpreted as an ad hoc emendation that is loosely connected, at best if at all, to neorealism's (or realism's) core propositions. This is nowhere more evident than in the very definition of a threat, which came not from the barrel of a gun and a military threat but rather from the attempt by a rival Arab state to promote an interpretation of an Arab norm that potentially threatened another Arab state's domestic and regional standing. It was this dynamic that generated such heat among Arab leaders. It was the contestation over and construction of the norms of Arabism that helps to account for seminal moments in alliance politics in the Arab world. No wonder that Arab leaders generated alliances around alternative versions of the norms of Arabism. This represented a form of normative balancing. No wonder, however, that once that norm obtained some degree of consensus nearly all Arab leaders worked hard to be associated with it, demonstrating a form of normative bandwagoning. No wonder, finally, that no alliance in Arab politics ever generated much military coordination. They were not constructed for that purpose. It is Arabism and not anarchy that provides greater leverage over alliance politics.

Even if there was space, this is not the place to make a concerted case that Arabism has generalizable properties that have broader theoretical import and contain insights for other regions and place. Nevertheless, two quick points are in order. First, I argued that my model worked under fairly specified conditions that concerned a structural condition of mutual dependence: Because of their shared identity, Arab states collectively determined the norms of Arabism, were expected to honor those norms, and generally did so because of their desire for social approval and recognition that they were Arab leaders in good standing. These conditions—mutual dependence on the creation and honoring of social norms and the desire for social approval as a drive for norm compliance—are not unique to Arab politics but rather are present in varying degrees in all social relations, including international relations. To be sure, because of specific historical, cultural, and political features these properties might be more pronounced in the Arab world than in other regions or places, but that does not mean that they are peculiar to the Arab world or absent in other regional moments. In fact, because of increasing integration European politics might discover that recent Arab history holds a glimpse of its future. Second, this essay, alongside my other contributions on Arab politics, joins with many other constructivist analyses that point to the centrality of culture for understanding the sources of strategic interests, strategic interaction between states, and the mixture of normative and instrumental forces behind compliance with social norms.[26] The point here is that the normative model sketched here, that was originally designed to capture broad patterns and developments in inter-Arab politics, was useful for rethinking alliance dynamics in the region and relevant for thinking about patterns of conflict and cooperation exhibited elsewhere.

I will leave it to others to decide whether neorealism represents an instance of a degenerative research program. It is, however, difficult to escape the paradoxical conclusion that Walt's balance of threat theory represented a devastating blow to neorealism. After all, if Walt is correct that balance of threat is superior to balance of power because the former introduces the critical variable of aggressive intentions, and if the threats underlying aggressive intentions can come from normative forces and ideational properties, then we are far removed from core realist and neorealist propositions. Walt, to his credit, recognized quite clearly that it is difficult to construct a theory of international politics that is devoid of social content. His attempt to inject some feature of sociality into the starkly material neorealist world was a natural impulse, and the only one that could provide a fuller understanding of the origins of alliances, whether those alliances are in the Arab world or elsewhere. But doing so also inadvertently subverted neorealist orthodoxy. It was not Walt's intention to be heretical vis-a-vis the neorealist research program. But sometimes that is the cost for making real progress in social science.

## Editors' Commentary

### Major Query

Is alliance formation in the Middle East (and by extension, elsewhere) better explained by Walt's balance of threat theory or by a **constructivist** approach?

### Major Points

Barnett's main point is that while Walt is correct to widen the class of stimuli to which states respond to include more than just material power, his theory does not go far enough in defining threats or their source. If this is done properly, it will be seen that ideology and ideas about identity and **norms** can be important sources of threat. Ideas, rather than material power, can also serve as the basis of alliance formation. Barnett argues that this ideational explanation falls outside neorealism's core. He shows how this alternate explanation fits inter-Arab politics and alliance making by examining three cases: the Arab Collective Security Pact, the Baghdad Pact, and the alliances created between several Arab states just before the 1967 Six Day War with Israel.

Barnett argues that if Walt's theory of alliances were truly neorealist it would employ the logic of anarchy to explain the origins of threat: Threat should come out of anarchy. Instead, however, Walt argues that threat arises from (among other things) "aggressive intentions." Barnett maintains that for inter-Arab politics, "aggressive intentions" boils down to what it means to be an Arab state and the norms the Arab community of states set down for regulating their relations. For Barnett, it is not the "logic of anarchy" but the "logic of Arabism" that gives rise to perceptions of threat and guides inter-Arab alliance making. Thus, if an Arab leader, like Nasser, can accuse a state of violating an Arab norm—by, for example, making an alliance with a Western state—this can be very threatening. It is so for two reasons, first because it is seen as violating a group norm and second because it can have potentially severe domestic consequences for a leader. What is at issue, says Barnett, is not the survival of a "state that dwells in anarchy, but the survival of the Arab leader who dwells in Arabism."

Much of Arab politics then involves fighting over what it means to be an Arab state and what the norms should be. States, according to Barnett, make alliances not on the basis of power or military threat, but on what norms they prefer. States enter alliances to promote certain interpretations of Arabism, and so they often oppose each other. However, as Barnett points out, once a norm becomes established, then states quickly try to get on that bandwagon so as not to be seen as going against the norm. This can have a big impact on behavior, as in 1967 when some Arab states became involved in a war with Israel that they might have preferred to avoid because they did not want to be charged with not doing enough for the Palestinian cause.

Barnett likes much of Walt's empirical work because he sees him uncovering this pattern. He presents a long quotation from Walt that Barnett says acknowledges that balancing is different in inter-Arab relations and is driven by norms. Walt (1987,

149) says that Arab states balance "not by adding up armies but by adding up votes." For Barnett, this is an admission that materialist factors, like power, cannot explain inter-Arab politics.

Barnett then goes on to argue that Walt's ideas about balance of threat do not fit with the core of neorealism. As such, he sees Walt's analysis as ad hoc and inconsistent with the logic of the theory he is trying to save. To Barnett, international relations has a social character and is not based just on materialist factors or forces. A strong leader, like Nasser, is strong not because of his armies, but because of his ability to command allegiance to a vision of Arab identity and the future of the collective Arab nation. International relations for Barnett reflects a culture of norms and identity that sets up a structure that shapes behavior as powerfully as Waltz thought the culture of anarchy shaped behavior.

Barnett takes an approach to studying international relations that is **constructivist**. This suggests that many of the factors that influence behavior and outcomes are socially constructed by the ideas that people and powerful actors have. It is not just a given, nor is it changeless. In international relations, constructivists look at how the existing structure came about and how it might change. For some constructivists, like Wendt (1992), anarchy is not just a given but is the product of what states choose, in a particular period, to make of it. For Barnett, the Arab world is constructed by the norms of Arabism and conflicts over those norms. Norms are malleable, and actors struggle to have influence over their meaning. Threat originates from that struggle and alliance formation is guided by those threats, not from a struggle over the material factors of military power. Barnett believes that constructivist theory, broadly defined, is an alternative to realist theory that explains inter-Arab politics better than does Walt's realism.

## Key Terms

**norms**   Shared expectations that actors hold about how to behave in a certain social context or situation. Norms can regulate behavior when they tell actors what to do. Norms can inform the identity of actors when they tell them what they must believe and how they must act to be an Arab, a Jew, and so forth. Norms involve collective evaluations of what is approved and disapproved.

**constructivism**   A theoretical approach to the study of international relations that emphasizes the importance of ideas, norms, and knowledge in the creation of a social world (or culture) that in turn shapes identity and interests. It provides a theory of preference formation (i.e., a theory of why actors prefer one thing over another). It argues that ideational factors are a key to understanding politics; they are not simply a product of material factors. The actions of states only have meaning within a shared normative context. Scholars cannot fully understand and appreciate the actions of states without understanding that shared normative context. The norms of any context can be quite varied, and some have argued that realism itself should be seen as a set of norms or a particular culture among a variety of possible cultures.

## Notes

1. I develop this model in Barnett 1998.
2. For various realist and neorealist statements, see Thucydides 1954; Liska 1962; Langer 1964; Walt 1987; Gulick 1955, 58–62; Waltz 1979, Chs. 6, 8; Schweller 1994; Snyder 1997; Morrow 2000.
3. In his response to Vasquez 1997, Walt (1997, 933) insists that power and threat are not independent; he nevertheless provides an opening for that very possibility in his earlier and fuller formulation.
4. See Wendt (1992) for a similar view.
5. Walt (1987, 36, 267) observes that certain ideologies are likely to generate suspicions and fears while others are not. Specifically, he argues that a pan-Arabism that is associated with unification and can only have one "leader" is likely to generate fear, suspicion, and rivalry, while democracies and monarchies are not likely to generate the same dynamics. What is instructive here is that Walt appears to be suggesting that identity, and not anarchy, drives interstate dynamics in important ways.
6. On the importance of distinguishing between state and regime survival, see Ayoob 1994; and Barnett and Levy 1991.
7. This relates to domestic sources of alliance formation. See Barnett and Levy, 1991; David, 1991.
8. "Iraq Press Comments on Council, Union," Baghdad, October 19, 1949; cited in *Foreign Broadcast Information Service (FBIS)*, No. 203 (October 20, 1949), p. 2.
9. "Committee Adopts Military Plan," Sharq al-Adna, October 23, 1949; cited in *FBIS*, No. 205 (October 24, 1949), pp. 1–2. Also see Seale 1986, 90–91.
10. "Yusuf Yassin Favors Egyptian Proposal," Cairo, Egyptian Home Service, October 25, 1949; cited in *FBIS*, No. 207 (October 26, 1949), p. 4.
11. "Nuri: League Chaos Causes Problems," Beirut, October 24, 1949; cited in *FBIS*, No. 206 (October 25, 1949), pp. 1–3.
12. "Egypt to Depend on Arab Defense Pact," Cairo, Egyptian Home Service, December 10, 1954; cited in *FBIS*, No. 239 (December 10, 1954), A1.
13. "Middle East Defense Talks Discussed," Cairo, Egyptian Home Service, December 7, 1954; cited in *FBIS*, No. 237 (December 8, 1954), A2.
14. *FBIS-MES* (January 14, 1955), A1–2.
15. "Salim Answers Questions," January 16, 1955; cited in *FBIS-MES*, No. 11 (January 17, 1955), A7.
16. Quoted from Khalil 1962, 236–237.
17. "Amir Faysal's Statement," Cairo, Egyptian Home Service, January 22, 1955; cited in *FBIS*, No. 16 (January 24, 1955), A5.
18. "Press Comment," Cairo, Egyptian Home Service, February 7, 1955; cited in *FBIS*, No. 26 (February 7, 1955), A2.
19. "Nasser Presents Joint Defense Plan," Limassol, Sharq al-Adna, January 26, 1955; cited in *FBIS-MES*, No. 18 (January 26, 1955), A1.
20. "Premier Reports on Pact with Turkey," Baghdad, Iraqi Home Service, February 26, 1955; cited in *FBIS*, No. 40 (February 28, 1955), A3–5.
21. "Azm Comments on New Arab Alliance," Damascus, March 10, 1955; cited in *FBIS*, No. 49 (March 11, 1955), A7.
22. "Nasir Reveals Weak Attitude Toward Syria," Damascus Domestic Service, June 1, 1965; cited in *FBIS* (June 2, 1965), G3; and Rabinovich 1972, 167–168.
23. "Nasir Opens Palestine National Congress," Cairo Domestic Service, May 31, 1965; cited in *FBIS* (June 3, 1965), B1–17.
24. "Al-Bath: Arabs Denounced Summit Long Ago," Damascus Domestic Service, August 2, 1966; cited in *FBIS* (August 2, 1966), G1.
25. According to Mutawi (1996, 175), the Jordanians feared that this alliance spelled the end of Nasser's conservativism and constituted a trap from which he would not be able to extricate himself. Syria, in the Jordanian view, believed that it would come out victorious over Nasser whether there was a war or not and whether the Arabs won or lost the war.
26. On culture and strategy and security politics, see Barnett 1998; Price 1997; Fierke 1998; and Milliken 2001. On the mixture of forces, see Finnemore and Sikkink 1998.

# 15

# MEASURING POWER — AND THE POWER OF THEORIES

*WILLIAM C. WOHLFORTH*

The search for a moderate standard for evaluating scholarship, grounded in real research practice, is surely a worthy goal. But when philosophical arguments about theory appraisal become self-referential and divorced from reality they are at best irrelevant and at worst downright damaging to scholarly inquiry. Vasquez's initial (1997) portrayal of research on the balance of power risked falling in this latter category for four reasons: (1) Neither he nor other critics have adequately addressed some of the most fundamental challenges involved in testing Waltz's balance of power theory; (2) recent neoclassical realist research suggests (and Vasquez, herein, Ch. 8, agrees) that there are ways to test the theory that have yet to be applied systematically; (3) neither Vasquez nor any of the other Lakatos-boosters in our field have provided convincing reasons to prefer Lakatos's Methodology of Scientific Research Programs over competing rationalist approaches to theory appraisal; and (4) just as realism and international relations scholarship more generally have begun to move in the direction of a pragmatic problem-driven research agenda in which paradigm wars recede in salience, efforts to make authoritative use of Lakatosian ideas threaten to reverse course.

Nevertheless, the exchange prompted by Vasquez may prove helpful in building consensus around the probative value of specific empirical tests. To the extent that efforts such as Vasquez's reduce disincentives to doing the kind of straightforward research that is necessary to conduct such tests, they will have a salutary effect on the development of our discipline.

## THE CHALLENGE: TESTING WALTZ'S BALANCE OF POWER THEORY

Evaluating a theory requires reading it carefully and understanding its purposes, terms, and explanatory claims. Kenneth N. Waltz (1979) offers an elegant theory whose stark and simple portrait of international politics proved powerfully attractive — though mainly as an intellectual foil—to scholars of nearly all inclinations. However, Waltz is extremely pessimistic about what any such theory can do. Waltz has been ambiguous about some things, but not about the fundamental weakness and indeterminacy of his theory. His claims are simply that "structure matters" in explanation, and that his theory has captured, at least in part, how it matters. Because his claims are weak, they are hard to test. Indeed, Waltz takes elements from both economic and sociological theoretical traditions that render his theory immune to many empirical tests. He adopts an instrumentalist view of theoretical assumptions, so they are insulated from empirical evaluation. But his conception of structural causation is so subtle as to be empirically elusive. Structures induce, shape, push, and constrain, without agents necessarily being conscious of it.

The empirical implications of this theory are indeterminate, as Waltz (1979, 124) made quite clear. Balances of power tend to form, whether or not they are intended. That statement sounds robust until one notes that Waltz failed to specify a definition of "balance" or "equilibrium" other than the absence of hegemony (with hegemony presumably meaning one state too powerful to counterbalance). So, rather than saying that the theory predicts a "tendency towards balance" it might be more accurate to say that it predicts a tendency against hegemony. In other words, hegemonies tend not to form, whether or not they are intended. It follows that the theory's behavioral referents (e.g., balancing and bandwagoning) as well as its pre- and postdictions become clearest when one state comes close to achieving hegemony (Wagner 1993). The theory's predictions are less clear concerning those configurations of power in which no state has any possibility of achieving hegemony. If the theory is right, at least some states will respond to the structural incentive to maximize security. "Security maximization" is hard to operationalize, but a good rendition would appear to be: maximizing a state's long-term odds on survival. If this is a faithful rendition, then the theory might yield the expectation that even when a hegemonic challenge is judged to be realistically impossible, some observable state actions (e.g., external and internal balancing) will be hedges against the future emergence of such a power configuration.

Already, we have a fairly flabby prediction whose testing confronts all the standard problems of theory appraisal in international relations: a large part played by unobservables (expectations of power trends); limited degrees of freedom (only a handful of great powers whose capabilities change slowly over only two or three centuries); and implied counterfactuals (e.g., if the theory was wrong, there would have been more or longer-lived hegemonies). But that is only the beginning of the challenge, for power—as Waltz construes it—is much more complex and much harder to measure than is generally recognized.

To begin with, two decades of rhetoric about the "third image" notwithstanding, the distribution of capabilities is not a systemic variable; it is a product of both unit- and system-level factors. Waltz never says that domestic politics are not important in explanation. He only makes the much weaker claim that domestic politics alone are insufficient to explain recurring phenomena such as the tendency against hegemony. International relations scholars consider power a "systemic" variable because it only has political meaning when viewed as a relationship between actors. Though it is systemic in this sense, the distribution of power is nonetheless partly the result of processes internal to states that lie completely outside the purview of Waltz's theory (cf. Zakaria 1998). Though Waltz's theory purports to explain patterns that emerge *given* certain distributions of power among certain numbers of core actors, it says nothing about how many such actors there will be or exactly how powerful they will be. It specifies conditions in which states may face strong incentives to enhance their capabilities, but it does not claim to be able to predict their success at doing so. Therefore, explanations derived from this theory are only "systemic" (meaning "excluding all unit-level attributes") if one takes the number and power of states as unproblematic givens (cf. Fearon 1998). The moment one asks why there are five great powers rather than fifteen, or why one great power is four times stronger than any other, "domestic" factors that are exogenous to Waltz's theory must be brought to bear.

Because Waltz's theory does not account for changes in the distribution of capabilities that occur as a consequence of domestic processes, it might be irrelevant for significant stretches of international history and seems to be flat wrong about others—but still be accurate as a very general portrayal of weak structural incentives. "Nature," may select balances of power that either render the theory indeterminate or seem to contradict its predictions. For exogenous, "domestic" reasons, capabilities may be distributed such that hegemony is so remote as to act as only the weakest of constraints. Or, exogenous changes may cause hegemony, despite system incentives. Some states may become powerful because of things that happen inside them. Others will face incentives to respond, but may fail because of internal processes.

Suppose, for example, a giant asteroid impacted the military-industrial heartland of one of two great powers in a bipolar system. If the two polar powers had shared most of the world's capabilities, the removal of one would instantly create a unipolar system. The other powers would have no choice but to bandwagon with the sole pole until they could develop the capabilities necessary to balance it. Unipolarity—the very state of affairs whose absence Waltz's theory is supposed to explain—would come into being for reasons having nothing to do with the theory. The advent of unipolarity in this hypothetical case would be no grounds for reducing confidence in the theory; and the theory would still have utility in predicting the incentives for other states eventually to create a counterpoise to the sole pole. This appears to be Waltz's take on post–Cold War unipolarity (Waltz 1993, 1997; see also Layne 1993a; and Kapstein and Mastanduno 1999). For reasons entirely outside of the purview of *Theory of International Politics*, the Soviet Union's institutions suddenly collapsed under the burden of its polar status, leaving an unambiguous U.S. hegemony in its wake. Other states face incentives to balance, but unit-level processes (rates of growth and innovation, quality of institutions, etc.) will powerfully condition the pace of the response.

In addition—notwithstanding two decades of rhetoric about neorealism as a "materialist" theory—Waltz's concept of the distribution of capabilities is not material. Just as the definition of power as systemic has caused scholars to downplay the obvious link between domestic processes and the distribution of power, so too has the equation of realism with materialism caused scholars to downplay the crucial role nonmaterial factors play in the distribution of capabilities. The equation of realism with materialism is convenient for many scholarly debates (see Wendt 1999; Legro and Moravscik 1999), but it is not true. For Waltz (1979, 131) the distribution of capabilities is made up of many material factors (size of population, territory, resource endowment, economic capability) *and* nonmaterial factors (political stability and competence).[1]

Waltz's definition of capabilities is entirely traditional and uncontroversial. Yet capabilities, as Waltz defines them, are extraordinarily hard to measure. Without reference to the specific period and context, the relative weighting of the various material components cannot be specified with any precision; nor can the relative importance of material and nonmaterial factors. Measuring the nonmaterial factors is also a demanding task that requires extensive contextual knowledge. One key component of capability—military strength—clearly combines material and nonmaterial elements. The military strength of France under Napoleon, Prussia under Bismarck, and Germany under Hitler was clearly a function of both their material endowments and economic capabilities *and* their organizational and strategic acumen, esprit de corps, quality of institutions, and so forth. The location of power is also obviously crucial in any theory driven by the possibility of hegemony. The fact that Berlin's fraction of world capabilities was in Europe in 1914 while Washington's was in North America was critical in determining which power might threaten hegemony. But technology changes the implications of location—as well as the relative importance of population and resource endowments. Indeed, changes in technology are likely to affect the relative weight of various material components of power, as well as the mix between material and nonmaterial elements.

These considerations render the construction of stand-in measures for the distribution of capabilities an exceedingly uncertain enterprise. When do we observe distributions that contradict Waltz's already admittedly indeterminate expectations? There are perfectly sound reasons to reject many seemingly disconfirming observations. Schroeder (1994) cites the absence of a counter-balance to nineteenth century Britain as evidence against Waltz. Layne (1993a) explains this in faithful Waltzian fashion by reference to unit-level lags in responding to structural incentives. It is doubtful, however, that the British Empire had the capability to credibly threaten hegemony over Europe or Eurasia. At the century's dawn, France was Europe's premier military power, from 1815–1853 Russia assumed that role, and for ten years after the Congress of Paris France again took first place, until she was pushed aside by Prussia. While a great naval and financial power, London lacked the military capabilities to subdue such continental powerhouses, as the war in Crimea showed (Anderson 1967). Or take Walt's (1985, 1987) oft-cited example of the "imbalance" of power arrayed against the Soviet Union in the Cold War. How does he know? His measures of power fail to incorporate its nonmaterial elements and location. The fact that Moscow's share of world capabilities was already in Eurasia is surely crucial to any theory driven by the possibility of hegemony. Indeed, at least until the advent of secure nuclear deterrence, the Soviet Union arguably presented a more credible threat of hegemony over Eurasia than Germany or France had before it (see Trachtenberg 1999). If "power" means "estimated probability of being able to achieve hegemony over Eurasia," there may have been no "imbalance" in the Cold War.[2]

All of these complications in measuring power are obvious to anyone with any knowledge of international history, a category that obviously includes Kenneth Waltz. Indeed, Waltz discusses most of these issues in *Theory of International Politics*. In that book, whenever he discusses testing, he notes that it is hard, given the indeterminacy of his theory, and that it requires disciplined and detailed historical research. He never mentions any ways of testing his theory other than careful historical research. His focus on historical research makes sense, given the difficulty of operationalizing the theory in any other way without transforming it in the process. Thus, these points about testability and the need for historical studies are not emendations to Waltz; they are not devices to explain away disconfirming results in order to save the research program. They were stated clearly in Waltz's 1979 work.

## Existing and Future Tests

What is striking is *how little* extant research tries to meet these basic criteria. In the 1980s, case study researchers translated Waltz's writings into a deterministic structural theory of foreign policy and reported the finding that it could not actually account for state behavior in very specific contexts as disconfirming results. In the 1990s, formal theorists translated the theory into abstract axioms whose patent falsity could be ascertained by the most cursory glance at international history; and quantitative researchers translated those axioms into large-N tests that again disconfirmed them (Niou, Ordeshook, and Rose 1989; Bueno de Mesquita and Lalman 1992; Russett 1995; Bueno de Mesquita 1999a). These are useful evaluations of theories other than Waltz's. They bear on Waltz only insofar as they clarify the indeterminacy of this theory. Scholars who translate Waltz into a precise, robust, deterministic, and predictive theory are actually rejecting his pessimistic epistemology and writing down completely different theories.

Also noteworthy is the fact that the bulk of the empirical work (and the studies that appear most faithful to Waltz's own rendering of his theory) concerns implications other than balancing: the problem of cooperation and relative gains; the differences between bipolar and multipolar systems; and the causes of war.

Vasquez is certainly right that some of the work that has been done—including that by Schweller, Walt, and Schroeder—has clarified the weakness of Waltz's balancing *law*. My own research on the Cold War (1993) also showed Waltz's balancing tendency to be present but weak. While they reduce some of the ambiguity created by Waltz's use of the phrase "law" to describe the propensity against hegemony, these findings are not surprising, given Waltz's construal of his own theory.

The plain fact of the matter is that twenty years after the publication of *Theory of International Politics* we still face a shortage of careful historical case-study evaluations of Waltz's most basic proposition that accurately operationalize the theory's key terms. Vasquez (herein, Ch. 8) appears to agree. While he shares Bruce Bueno de Mesquita's (1999a) view that existing quantitative tests are sufficient to disconfirm the existence of the balancing law (as well as Waltz's explanation of it), unlike Bueno de Mesquita he accepts that other scholars might still reasonably be uncertain of the veracity of these tests. He argues, and I agree, that a good first step toward reducing this uncertainty would be a more focused research agenda on failed bids for hegemony. Waltz has pulled out of classical realism the standard balance of power explanation for failed hegemony (e.g., Gulick 1955; Dehio 1962) and clarified it dramatically by transforming it into a rigorously stated general theory. As Walt (1997, n. 7) notes, this is not the only explanation, it is simply a "cogent . . . explanation that one would not want to dismiss out of hand." Although far less grandiose than many of the explanatory claims others have made on behalf of Waltz's theory, this is a bold and sweeping explanation of recurring phenomena over hundreds of years. Moreover, if the theory helps to explain the outcomes of past hegemonic challenges, our confidence in its other implications may be enhanced.

Careful case studies of these episodes conducted by scholars familiar with Waltz's writings — and willing and able to mine quantitative data where available — would certainly have probative value. I agree with Vasquez that given the small number of cases, the brute outcome — repeated failure to establish hegemony over the system — is insufficient to evaluate the explanation. To have confidence in Waltz's theory, the brute outcome must be the result of the causes central to the theory. Only historical research can reveal whether these causal mechanisms — that is, balancing to prevent hegemony under anarchy — were really linked to the general tendency against hegemony. The result of such research would be a keener sense of the theory's limitations. If the causal mechanisms of the theory were irrelevant to these outcomes, the theory would have suffered a serious reversal on its home turf. If, as is most likely based on past research, it turned out that the theory's causal mechanisms were present but weak, we would confirm the current consensus regarding the theory. If the theory turned out to provide a powerful explanation for these outcomes, its veracity would be enhanced in the eyes of many scholars (mine included). Whatever the outcome, such research would have the wonderful byproduct of teaching us a lot about important episodes in international relations.

Vasquez is also right that tests should not be limited to these bids, which are only known to be "bids for hegemony" in hindsight. Waltz's treatise does imply that at least some security-maximizing states will be wary of hegemony even when its occurrence is a very low-probability event. So, to the degree that the theory is true, there ought to be evidence of preclusive balancing. On the surface, there seems to be a lot of such evidence, since statesmen have explained their policies in terms of the balance of power — precluding possible hegemony — for centuries. For example, U.S. statesmen in the Cold War appeared to be doing exactly this (Leffler 1992; Trachtenberg 1999). So, if some accounts are right, were Soviet statesmen (Zubok and Pleshakov 1996;

Mastny 1996). But Vasquez rightly argues that tests must be very carefully conducted. For example, in 1853 Britain waged an aggressive war against Russia, ostensibly in the name of such preclusive balancing (Wentker 1993). As Schroeder (1972b) has shown, this portrayal cannot be accepted at face value. As Schroeder and other historians know well, statesmen's public self-reports are often (but not always) notoriously poor data.

While I agree with Vasquez that such tests will improve the empirical basis for our relative confidence in Waltz's theory, I doubt that the knife-like conclusions he seeks are likely. The problem is that Waltz's theory does not predict efficient behavior, as Vasquez seems to assume. While the theory does expect preclusive balancing, and it does predict that balance-of-power politics will eventually come to the fore in the face of hegemonic challenges, it says nothing about the efficiency with which these things will occur. The notion that the environment enforces efficiency—which infuses Vaquez's discussion of testing—is another rewriting of Waltz into a more deterministic structuralist. Indeed, given Waltz's discussion of his theory, we should expect a lot of inefficiency: checking of states that in hindsight appear to have had no chance of hegemony, as well as failure to check more plausible hegemonic candidates until they demonstrate their power in war.

Given the difficulty of measuring power, it is entirely consistent with Waltz to find that balancing coalitions frequently only form in wartime, as states learn about each other's actual military strength (see, e.g., Schweller 1998a). It is also not surprising to find preclusive balancing against states that in hindsight do not appear capable of threatening hegemony, as is now commonly thought of U.S. efforts to balance the Soviet Union. I disagree with the common tendency to label all assessments of power that turn out to be wrong "misperceptions." Whether these assessments were misperceptions or the best possible guesses based on available information is an empirical question. Determining whether states are responding to systemic incentives as specified by Waltz requires research on how they estimate the distribution of capabilities and what they do in response to those estimates.

Waltz's theory simply fails to rule out the easily observable patterns in international history. This is not surprising, since Waltz was aware of these patterns when he wrote the theory. To gain a better estimate of the theory's power, research must probe beneath these patterns and confront the problem of measuring power. Those who favor the use of quantitative indicators sometimes argue that it is incumbent on critics to develop better ones (Bueno de Mesquita and Lalman 1992; Bueno de Mesquita 1999). That is not necessarily so—revealing measurement error *is* scientific advance, for it reveals that a theory has not been tested. The theory may not be testable; it may have immeasurable terms. Learning that this is so would represent an advance in knowledge. But quantitative researchers are right that criticism of their measures does warrant further work on new ways of operationalizing and testing Waltz's and all other power-centric theories. This is in part what neoclassical realist research on power is doing—by constructing careful case studies of the influence of power on policies in various contexts (Rose 1998). Moreover, this new research is being undertaken just as the field as a whole is becoming more rigorous about the methodological underpinnings of case-study research (King, Keohane and Verba 1994; Van Evera 1997; Bennett and George, forthcoming). If the field follows Vasquez's interpretation of Lakatos, however, this line of inquiry may be discouraged as a degenerating theory-saving exercise.

## Saving Programs or Solving Problems?

Vasquez (1997, herein, Ch. 8) has made a welcome effort to clarify what empirical research might have probative value for Waltz's balance of power theory. While complete prior agreement on the meaning of tests may be elusive, some narrowing of the usual range of ambiguity on this issue can only be welcomed. Thus, the discussion Vasquez launched may prove to be valuable.

The problem is that the potential value of the exercise has nothing whatever to do with Vasquez's use of Lakatosian ideas. Vasquez agrees that Waltz's balancing prediction has yet to be tested adequately. Yet he views the work of Walt, Schweller and Christensen, and Snyder as degenerate problemshifts undertaken in order to rescue a theory from empirical disconfirmation. This does not make sense in terms of Vasquez's use of Lakatos. If these scholars were rational Waltzians seeking to defend his theory, surely it would have occurred to them to attempt new tests of the theory before engaging in such inventive problemshifts. Indeed, if a neorealist research program existed, surely some of its members would have hit upon the sorts of tests Vasquez outlines in order to try to demonstrate the theory's power. After all, these are exactly the sorts of tests Waltz himself suggested in his foundational text twenty years ago.

As Schweller (1998b) argues, the fact of the matter is that the scholars Vasquez evaluates simply refuse to play the roles assigned to them by his construal of Lakatos. Waltz (1986, 1996, 1997) insists that his theory is a take-it-or-leave-it proposition; he has rejected every effort to amend, modify, or adapt it. For Waltz, there is only his theory; there is no research program. In international relations, the expressed views of a theory's author seem to carry little weight. True, according to Waltz, there have been some applications that have been more or less faithful to the theory (e.g., Mearsheimer, 1990; Mastanduno 1993; Grieco 1988; Layne 1993a). But the scholars whose work Vasquez assesses are not faithful Waltzians seeking to advance and defend their great mentor's theory at all costs. As they make clear in their responses to Vasquez, they are independent scholars advancing their own theories that both complement and compete with Waltz (Christensen and Snyder 1997; Walt 1997; Schweller 1997, 1998b).

In rejecting the role of dutiful Waltzian footsoldiers, these scholars are responding to the incentives in our field. To get tenure in a major department (as they all have done) you must make a "major" theoretical contribution. You do not get promoted by conducting evaluations or minor emendations of other people's theories. More importantly, as I read their works, they were interested in different kinds of problems at different levels of analysis than Waltz. They seem to have read Waltz and taken seriously his statements about the limited utility of so general a theory in accounting for the specific phenomena that preoccupied them. The empirical work that has been produced suggests that Waltz's theory is, like many others in social science, sometimes somewhat true. Given the state of our knowledge and the likely prospects for a robust general theory, the research choices of Walt, Schweller, and Christensen and Snyder reflected sound pragmatic judgment. They accept that power balancing under anarchy may be a part of the puzzles they seek to unravel, but the degree of its importance is an empirical question. Like a great many scholars of all stripes, they appear to have found Waltz's general insights useful in addressing their different research problems. They were willing to tackle the problems before them with Waltz's arguments as one among many potentially useful tools. The effort to characterize those choices as driven by the desire to save a degenerating research program is wrong and misleading.

It was an important step forward when scholars recognized that realism, liberalism, Marxism (and perhaps now constructivism) are nonfalsifiable ideologies or intellectual schools and not theories (Gilpin 1987). To translate these "isms" into "hard cores" and "protective belts" a la Lakatos, as Vasquez tries to do, may simply push us back into unproductive "paradigm wars." The actual research practice of scholars, the complex intellectual connections among them, and the real incentives they face in professional life all seem at first brush to contradict a Lakatosian construal. This is not to say that we should deny the existence and even the positive utility of competing ideologies of international relations. International politics is political, so ideologies matter. Far better to trumpet them than to suppress them and pretend they do not exist. And the competing intellectual schools are useful teaching tools. However, it is open to question whether dressing up these intellectual traditions as Lakatosian research programs aids or hinders the evaluation of scholarship.

Indeed, the notion that there was a "neorealist research program" that somehow achieved "dominance" in the 1980s was always a caricature. The effort to frame research in these misleading terms shoe-horned dramatically different kinds of scholarship (e.g., that of Waltz and Gilpin) into one ambiguous grouping; it set up scores of unconvincing "tests" of this amorphous and imaginary "neorealism" against competing "approaches" that were often no more than congeries of domestic, transnational, ideational, and personal factors specific to individual cases; and it sidelined many important classical realist conjectures about world politics. Ambiguity is fatal to scholarly research. There is no doubt that Waltz's writings contain more than their share of ambiguity. But it was the idea that his theory marked the beginning of the social science equivalent of a Lakatosian research program into which all subsequent realist research somehow had to fit that was the most fatal source of ambiguity in the 1980s.

By the end of the decade, it was apparent to many in the field that there was something deeply wrong with this way of organizing scholarly inquiry. In their view, clarifying important differences within realism is in itself an advance to which Waltz made an important contribution (Brooks 1997; Rose 1998). Waltz pulled the structural-equilibrium element out of realist thought and made it into a very general theory. This represented advance—as long as its limits were recognized. Much earlier, Organski (1958) had pulled the "power transition" hypothesis out of classical realism and began a fruitful line of research investigating it (DiCicco and Levy 1998). A year after Waltz's *Theory of International Politics*, Robert Gilpin published *War and Change in World Politics*, which sought systematically to bring together realist ideas about hegemonic war and change in international politics. Recognizing that neorealism is not an all-engulfing research program but is in fact one theory that has been applied faithfully by perhaps four or five other scholars, neoclassical realists have recently proposed and evaluated other discrete hypotheses that are clearly distinct from neorealism (Rose 1998; Schweller 1998b). Their motivation is not to save Waltz. Indeed, few scholars have been clearer than they about Waltz's limitations. Their motivation was to identify and address important empirical puzzles that were falling between the cracks in the crazy way IR inquiry was organized in the 1980s. Yet now Vasquez takes this much more problem-focused research, which subjects discrete realist hypotheses to different empirical tests, as evidence of degeneration. I don't buy it.

## Why Lakatos?

The thrust of Vasquez's analysis is that theories should be checked against our best approximation of reality. The overwhelming majority of scholars in our field share this conviction. I certainly do, and I judge Lakatos accordingly. Lakatos argues for a rational approach to the selection of research programs. In the same spirit, we should adopt a rational approach to the selection of methodologies for evaluating research on world politics. Lakatos has been criticized extensively on philosophical grounds. For me the question is, can Lakatos's ideas be used, given what we know about the real world of scholarly research in international relations? To date, Lakatosians in our field have failed to make the case that they can (Keohane 1986; Bueno de Mesquita 1984; Elman and Elman 1995, 1997, 1998).

The standard critiques of Lakatos's applicability to international relations center on three practical problems: how to achieve consensus on defining a research program's "hard core" as opposed to its "protective belt"; how to reach consensus on what is to be considered a "novel fact" and thus what counts as a progressive problemshift; and how long a research program should be allowed to suffer empirical reversals before it is officially declared to be degenerating (Elman and Elman 1998). But there is a prior problem: In order to evaluate research programs, there must *be* research programs. The exchange generated by Vasquez demonstrates that the very existence of Lakatosian research programs in international relations is questionable. The assumption that there are such research programs might not only be empirically false but actually damaging to scholarly inquiry.

What *is* the "neorealist research program?" Who belongs? No one can agree on this question. No two lists of neorealists in our field match up. If Waltz insists that his is a take-it-or-leave-it theory that cannot be amended and can only be applied in explanation, and if those whom Vasquez criticizes agree that this is so, I do not see how Lakatos's methodology of research programs can be applied. If none of the principles behaves in ways that are compatible with the method, the method should be questioned. Since the research program does not appear to exist, any effort to define its hard core is likely to founder. Recent efforts to specify realism's (or neorealism's) hard core illustrate this problem (cf. Elman and Elman 1997, 1998; Vasquez herein, Ch. 8; Legro and Moravscik 1999).

Of course, one could still try to use Lakatosian metatheory to assess international relations scholarship even though its basic empirical referents—research programs—do not exist in the real world of international relations research. The question, however, is why? The question is important, given that efforts to make authoritative use of Lakatos are not without costs. The downside of deploying Lakatos is not just that trying to use his rules might lead to valuable research being tarred as degenerate. Rather, the risk is that by distorting the real nature of international relations research it will reinforce some of the field's notoriously bad habits: excessive preoccupation with zero-sum paradigm wars; false competition between theories that are actually complementary; misleading and arbitrary divisions among scholars; false perceptions of incommensurability among research traditions; false empirical tests of mis-specified theories; and fruitless quests for universal theories.

I do not see how Lakatosian ideas can be deployed in the assessment of ongoing scholarly work without eliciting defensive reactions and fostering zero-sum exchanges between scholars. No one wants to be associated with a "degenerating" research program, or to be accused of making "ad hoc" emendations to a theory. Lakatos's most famous dictum is that "there is no falsification before the emergence of a better theory" (1970, 119). In practice, this dictum translates into the assumption that progress for one research program is strictly dependent on degeneration for another. Viewed in this light, social science consists entirely of showing how one's own favored theoretical tradition can account for phenomena while another cannot. While competitive testing does lie at the core of the social scientific enterprise, whenever researchers anticipate Lakatosian assessments of their work, they will be less inclined to explore whether models derived from different research traditions work together to explain phenomena.

However, there is much less competition among international relations scholars than meets the eye. Indeed, it is rare that competing theories actually meet on the same empirical ground. For example, most of the explanatory claims concerning the end of the Cold War that have been advanced by scholars representing different intellectual traditions are not actually competing with each other (Wohlforth 1998). The reason there is so much more apparent than real competition is the excessively zero-sum nature of exchanges between scholars who think they represent research programs whose advance depends on the failure of others. The more important Lakatosian notions are in our field, the fewer the incentives to expose complementarity, and the worse this problem will become.

The fundamental risk associated with the use of Lakatosian criteria is that it reinforces the already strong bias in the field in favor of theory development as opposed to empirical research. As David Dessler (1999a) notes, "the bias in Lakatos's work is that his concerns are drawn exclusively from the theoretical side of science. Indeed, he defines a scientific research program as a *series of theories.*" But most research in international relations concerns the explanation of historical phenomena, such as balancing. To quote Dessler (1999a) again, "nowhere in his writings does Lakatos detail his understanding of scientific explanation. He does not even explicitly acknowledge explanation as a central goal of science." Given Vasquez's own scholarship—a testament to his commitment to empirical research—his selection of Lakatos to assess empirical work on the balance of power is curious. In any event, Lakatos's ideas provide scant guidance for assessing empirical progress: new explanations of old empirical puzzles, the mining of new data, new measures for crucial variables, and so on. The more popular Lakatosian ideas are in our field, the greater the premium placed on claims for theoretical as opposed to empirical contributions.

Given these risks, on what basis do scholars promote Lakatos as the method for assessing research in international relations? After all, there are other rationalistic approaches to evaluating scientific advance that accord with our general antirelativist stance: Bayseanism, for example (see Dessler 1999b), or good old pragmatism (see Diesing 1991). Perhaps these philosophical ideas would better capture research practice in our field and thus command wider acceptance. Maybe they are better suited to evaluate our tentative and weak conjectures about international politics; our heavy emphasis on claiming theoretical innovation; our lack of controlled experiments; our degree-of-freedom constraints; our continued need to be relevant to a changing political world; and the powerful influence of complex political events on the demand for and evaluation of various theories. Perhaps they would produce an assessment of the best research bets radically different from what Vasquez proposes.

I do not have answers to these questions, but neither do the Lakatosians in our field. I see no reason to accept Lakatos's scheme without some effort to demonstrate its applicability to international relations in comparison with other rationalist approaches to theory appraisal. Rational selection of such a methodology would entail careful research on the history of our discipline, a profound and sensitive appreciation of common research practices, and a serious study of post-Lakatosian philosophy of science. Before offering Lakatos-based assessments of the value of major research enterprises, Vasquez should supply his reasons for regarding these steps as unnecessary.

Lakatos and his followers acknowledged that—like most social theory—the "methodology of scientific research programs" can only be applied confidently in hindsight. Most applications of Lakatos to international relations, including Vasquez's, are to the here and now. The use of the method to assess ongoing research would be more convincing if scholars could demonstrate its utility in understanding the history of progress and degeneration in our own field. Colin Elman and Miriam Fendius Elman (1998, 2002b) describe a project that may yield some findings on this score. Perhaps my reservations about deploying Lakatos in international relations will turn out to be unfounded. However, scientific skepticism toward still-unverified conjectures would suggest that Vasquez's 1997 assessment is premature.

Responding to Walt (1997), Vasquez (1998) forwards three objections to this pragmatic line of argument. First, "a philosophy of science . . . is not the same as a history of science." The implication seems to be that while theories of international relations should be held to some empirical account, philosophies of science by which we assess those theories are exempt from such scrutiny. Vasquez proposes to use Lakatos's methodology to help individuals, funding organizations, journals, and universities decide where to place their research bets. Yet he maintains that the methodology that informs these momentous judgments need not be tested or compared carefully to alternatives. I do not understand this position; I do not see how it can be defended. Indeed, in his major book assessing realism, Vasquez (1998) relies more on Kuhn than Lakatos. I do not see how a Kuhnian interpretation of the history of our subfield can be squared logically with the use of Lakatosian notions to assess scholarship. If Kuhn is right, then Lakatos's ideas distort history and bias assessments of ongoing research.

In their writings, Lakatos and other philosophers of science constantly refer to episodes in the history of the natural sciences. In the debate in which Lakatos was engaged, progress in natural science was an accepted fact. It was standard practice in this debate to reject a proposed rule that would have forbidden a recognized scientific advance—thus, for example, a definition of "novelty" under which Galileo predicted no new facts could be rejected out of hand. Because they do not ground their theory appraisals in such an understanding of our own field, IR's "Lakatos boosters" never use this sort of argumentation. Judging by the examples they cite, they seem to know more about the history of the natural sciences than that of the social sciences. If they are unable to make arguments that refer to compelling examples of progress from our own field, it is difficult to see how Lakatosians will win wide acceptance of their favored rules of theory appraisal.

Second, Vasquez argues that "these standards cannot just be ignored because they are difficult to operationalize." Of course they can be. If they can't be operationalized, they can't be applied, and they should be ignored. Vasquez objects that Lakatosian standards "appear to be essential to the conducting of theory appraisals." That is an empirical statement—one that Vasquez apparently does not believe is necessary to test. All scientific progress prior to Lakatos occurred without the benefit of his writings. All social-scientific progress up to now has occurred without the widespread use of Lakatosian ideas to appraise research. If one accepts that there has been progress in the natural and social sciences (as I do), then it follows that explicit application of Lakatos's rules are not necessary for progress. Absent some empirical support for the applicability and veracity of Lakatos, there is no reason to believe that having a herd of self-appointed Lakatosian referees would improve matters. Indeed, if the rules cannot be operationalized objectively, then there is reason to suspect that their application would hinder progress.

Finally, Vasquez argues that international relations scholars cite Lakatos frequently, and therefore accept his guidelines for theory appraisal. As Elman and Elman (1998) show, there is a difference between citing Lakatos and actually applying his ideas. The reasons for his popularity in footnotes are many. He does offer an appealing, rationalistic alternative to Kuhn's more sociological account that still seems compatible with our competing "isms." Using Lakatos, one can cast doubt on entire research traditions, as Vasquez does, without being accused of naïve falsificationism. One can also use him to defend entire research traditions, even in the face of repeated empirical failures. With Lakatos, the competing ideologies of international relations become scientifically acceptable "hard cores." Hence, frequent citations of Lakatos also support the reservations I stated above: that Lakatosian language melds nicely with our field's longstanding tradition of debating ideologies as if they were theories. Resuscitating Lakatos may reinforce the field's tendency to become absorbed in such debates just as we were moving toward what might be a rewarding "problem-oriented" agenda.

## Conclusion

The exchange sparked by John A. Vasquez's assessment of recent scholarship on the balance of power has underscored some old truths and generated some new lessons. Waltz's theory is weak and therefore hard to test, which is not surprising given its extreme level of generality. While empirical studies have confirmed its weakness in general, twenty years after the publication of *Theory of International Politics* the field still faces a shortage of straightforward empirical tests of Waltz's balancing proposition that recognize the difficulties inherent in the enterprise. The scholars whose work Vasquez evaluated are not playing the roles Vasquez's rendering of Lakatos assigns to them. "Neo traditionalist" scholarship shows the promise of setting aside the search for a grand theory of international politics and tackling more discrete explanatory problems. In particular, this new and still small body of scholarship shows that there are ways to evaluate conjectures about power in world politics that have yet to be applied systematically. If successful, Vasquez's effort to discourage further research on balance of power theory would close off potentially promising lines of inquiry. Taken together, these observations suggest that Lakatosian ideas are inappropriate for appraising empirical work in international relations.

Other lessons emerge as well. First, Vasquez's assessment is a case study of the field's bias against empirical research, especially historical research. The incentives in our field do not encourage mundane and workmanlike tests of others' theories that do not make appreciable "theoretical advances." Unless they are able to employ highly technical methods, untenured scholars would be ill-advised to make such testing the focus of their research activity. An untenured scholar who shouldered some of the historical work that Vasquez suggests is necessary to evaluate Waltz's theory would be a tough tenure case in a major department. Second, too many scholars do too poor a job of explaining the intellectual origins of their work. This generates ambiguity concerning the real intellectual connections among scholars and makes it hard to apply Lakatos or any other method of theory appraisal. Again, the culprit seems to be the premium placed on theoretical innovation as opposed to empirical evaluation. No one wants to be seen as making niggling amendments to others' great works; few wish to devote years to conducting tests that may be inconclusive. The result is that each book or article must proudly burst through a (usually open) conceptual door.

Third, fruitful debates on theory appraisal require reliable empirical accounts of the history of scholarly inquiry in a field. Diesing (1991), Kahler (1997), Vasquez (1998), Knutson (1997), and Ross (1991) are beginnings, but only beginnings. We still lack the kinds of empirical referents about our own social science that Kuhn, Lakatos, Musgrave, and their colleagues had about the natural sciences. Absent such references, the discussion is airy and antiempirical. Without concrete cases of social-scientific advance in which to ground the discussion, it is difficult to see how we can reduce the range of disagreement about the proper standards of theory appraisal. At the risk of sounding repetitious, the incentives in our field do not encourage this kind of work either. Does anyone want to take tenure bets on a junior scholar who produces a fine history of international relations research? And finally, scholars of international relations need to stop ending their exploration of philosophy of science with Lakatos. Rational selection of methods of theory appraisal demands comparison. Here, the work of David Dessler should command attention.

## Editors' Commentary

### Major Query

What are the testable empirical claims made by Waltz's *Theory of International Politics*? Is Lakatos's Methodology of Scientific Research Programs a useful way to evaluate scholarship in general?

### Major Points

Wohlforth suggests that Vasquez's essay mischaracterizes the claims made by Waltz's theory, and underestimates the difficulties posed by testing its true empirical claims. These are much more indeterminate, and much harder to falsify, than Vasquez and other critics have suggested. Almost all the important concepts in Waltz's theory are difficult to measure, especially the related concepts of *power* and *distribution of capabilities*. In addition there are types of behavior and outcomes (for example foreign policy behavior and exogenous changes in the distribution of capabilities) that Waltz explicitly excludes from the theory.

Most "tests" of Waltz's theory have proceeded to act as if he had made determinate claims, and then argue that the theory fails when the predictions are not borne out by evidence. But making and testing predictions about things a theory is not designed to predict does not amount to making a theory "clearer": It constitutes writing a different theory. What Waltz's theory needs (and what it has yet to receive) is testing via careful historical case studies of episodes of failed hegemonic bids and self-abnegation by would-be hegemons. Do states, armed with the best information available to them about changes in the distribution of capabilities, attempt to balance rising hegemons?

Wohlforth offers one of the strongest criticisms of Lakatos's MSRP in the volume. He suggests that it makes no sense to characterize Waltz's theory as part of a larger research program. The scholars critiqued by Vasquez as trying to save Waltz's research program are doing no such thing. They are advancing their own theories, in competition with Waltz's, and Wohlforth suggests that it is highly misleading to characterize them as trying to save a theory that they were trying to bury. Finally, Wohlforth suggests that Lakatos's MSRP is simply not a useful way to describe and appraise political science research. It does not reflect the subfield's practices, and it is fatally flawed by a failure among its adherents to reach consensus on a variety of its most important questions: how to describe a hard core; which of several novel fact criteria to apply; and how long to allow a research program before abandoning it as degenerative. In addition, MSRP does the subfield a great disservice by orienting research away from the empirically grounded puzzle solving work that is needed toward more abstract theory generation that is not.

## Notes

1. Indeed, the other crucial component of the system's structure in neorealism—anarchy—is not material either. It is social. See Dessler 1999 for a discussion.
2. Walt's measures of "threat" do include location and some nonmaterial factors, but he provides no compelling logical reasons to exclude analogous factors from "power" as Waltz defines it. The difference between "power" and "threat" surely is important, but it is harder to capture empirically than Walt assumes.

# 16

# THE NECESSARY AND NATURAL EVOLUTION OF STRUCTURAL REALISM

*CHARLES L. GLASER*

A variety of strands of the realist family of international relations theory have evolved and matured over the last couple of decades. Because the strands offer divergent explanations and predictions, critics have recently argued that realism is a failing research program.[1] Critics have also argued that the willingness of prominent scholars to combine realist theories with other levels of analysis reflects an often implicit admission that realism suffers severe weakness.

I argue that the first criticism mistakes divergent predictions for what is in fact theoretical progress.[2] This progress has resulted largely from tightening the logic of structural arguments and does not suffer from ad hoc adaptations of the core theory. What is now important is to appreciate the sources of divergent predictions so that further research can contribute to resolving them. The second criticism overlooks the explanatory power that realism retains when built into a multilevel theory and exaggerates the importance of isolating realism from other levels of analysis.

The following three sections compare key strands of the realist debate—the divide within structural realism between Waltz and the defensive realists, the divide within structural realism between defensive and offensive realists, and the divide between structural realists and neoclassical realists—explaining where progress has been made. I divide the realist family along these lines because doing so enables us to focus on the basic sources of divergence. These strands of the realist debate can be distinguished either in terms of basic assumptions (structural versus neoclassical) or in terms of early steps in the logic chain that leads to predictions of specific types of state behaviors (Waltz versus defensive, and offensive versus defensive). Furthermore, using categories defined in terms of predicted behavior, for example in terms of divergent predictions of alliance behavior, risks losing track of which theories actually underlie predictions, since analysts often combine different types of theories in attempting to explain a specific type of behavior.

The fourth section discusses some of the research that needs to be done to further advance the realist arguments that are currently most promising. One indication of progress is that the recent work on realism is generating and/or focusing on a wide array of research questions both within and beyond the boundaries of the structural-realist paradigm. The final section explores the value of realism when combined with other levels of analysis.

## Structural Realism: The Basics

Waltz's realism, defensive realism, and offensive realism are each forms of structural realism, which start from the same basic assumptions: (1) states live in an international environment characterized by anarchy—the lack of an international entity that can provide security and, more generally, enforce agreements; (2) states are motivated only by the desire for security—or, more precisely, the behavior of states can be predicted by assuming they desire only security, even if they actually have other motives and goals;[3] (3) states are essentially rational unitary decision makers; and (4) states "black box" their adversaries; that is, because they are structural/third-image theories, they assume that states do not base their assessments of others' motives on information about the domestic structure or workings of these states or on the specific characteristics of their leaders.[4]

It is also common to identify the special importance that states place on power as a further assumption of realism. However, it is better to derive from these basic assumptions, as much as possible, the means that states will choose to achieve their security goals and which factors or variables they will consider in making these choices. Thus, I do not identify an assumption about the importance of power relative to other factors that should influence a state's choice of means. What we can say is that, in broad terms, the world view that follows from structural realism's assumptions suggests that states should make the possession of adequate military capabilities—that is, the ability to perform the military missions required to defend and/or deter—a top priority. Maybe less obvious, but also flowing from structural realism assumptions, because insecurity is the key source of conflict, states should be concerned about their adversary's security, and therefore interested in communicating their benign motives and avoiding military capabilities that threaten the capabilities that their adversaries require for defense.

## Defensive Realism versus Waltz: Systematic Progress

Defensive realism is the logical extension of the structural realism developed by Kenneth Waltz.[5] This observation may seem surprising, because defensive realism diverges quite dramatically from the predictions that Waltz's theory provides.

Defensive realism makes three key modifications that generate the divergence from Waltz's theory.[6] In the context of the debate over whether realism is making progress, the essential thing to appreciate is that there is nothing ad hoc about these modifications. Quite the contrary, each of these modifications follows naturally and logically from the theory's structural/third-image perspective and its basic assumptions. It is in this sense that the evolution from Waltz's theory to defensive realism is "necessary and natural." Two of these modifications (the first and third described below) involve correcting deductive errors in the standard Waltzian structural-realist argument. The third modification involves introducing structural variables that capture important variation in the constraints and opportunities facing states that cannot be captured by the standard formulation's focus on power. Each of these modifications stands on its own and would, on its own, lead to conclusions that diverge from Waltz's theory; in addition, when combined, these modifications interact to produce larger possible divergences.

Briefly describing these three modifications demonstrates how they follow from structural realism's core logic and assumptions. First, defensive realism challenges the standard claim that international structure generates a general tendency for security-seeking states to compete. The standard argument holds that a state's desire to gain military advantages combined with its determination to avoid the risks of cooperation—which leave a state vulnerable to cheating—force even states that are interested only in security to choose competitive policies. Defensive realism faults this argument for being incomplete: Although cooperation can be risky, competition can also be risky since the outcome of competition is often uncertain and losing a competition can damage a state's security. Thus, by its own internal logic, structural realism requires that states weigh the risks of cooperation and of competition, and does not predict that one approach generally dominates the other.

Second, defensive realism reorients structural realism by emphasizing both the central role of the security dilemma in the logic of the theory and by explaining that offense-defense variables, in addition to power, should influence states' decisions about how best to achieve security.[7] Although the security dilemma is barely mentioned by Waltz, the basic logic of structural realism necessitates that it play a central role. Structural realism assumes that states are concerned only with security. In fact, its claim to great explanatory power comes largely from being able to explain competitive behavior from such minimal and benign assumptions about states' motives. If states could acquire the means necessary to protect their security without reducing others' security, then competition and conflict would never occur between rational states interested only in security. The possibility that competition should at least sometimes occur therefore requires that states face a security dilemma.

At least in principal, the security dilemma can vary over time and between places; that is, how much a state's efforts to increase its security reduce the security of others is a variable, not a constant. The possibility that the security dilemma varies has dramatic implications for structural realism. Based purely on deductive arguments, we have first moved from a theory that purports to predict a general tendency toward competition, to one that appears often indeterminate once its incomplete treatment of risks is addressed, and now to a theory that predicts variation in competitive and cooperative behavior depending on the severity of the security dilemma.

Once we acknowledge this central role for the security dilemma, the introduction of offense-defense variables follows immediately. If the predictions of structural realism vary with the severity of the security dilemma, the question immediately arises: What influences its magnitude? Jervis explains why two offense-defense variables—the offense-defense balance and offense-defense differentiability—are the key to understanding whether the security dilemma is severe or mild.

We can also establish the necessity of including the offense-defense balance in structural realism from a related, complementary perspective. A state interested in achieving security should assess its prospects in terms of its ability to acquire the military mission capabilities required for defense and deterrence. Considering power (the state's resources compared to its adversaries' resources) is insufficient because power does not translate directly into military mission capability. The relative ease of acquiring offensive and defense capabilities also matters. More precisely, the relative costs of performing offensive missions compared to defensive ones—which reflects the offense-defense balance—influences a state's ability to acquire necessary military capabilities. If defense is relatively easy, that is, the offense-defense balance favors defense, then a state that is less powerful than its adversaries may nevertheless be able to be highly secure; alternatively, if offense has the advantage, the most powerful state in the system may be unable to escape severe insecurity. In other words, while power can tell us a great deal about a state's ability to acquire security, we have strong deductive reasons for adding the offense-defense balance to structural realism's small set of explanatory variables.

Third, defensive realism challenges the commonly stated claim that realism requires states to assume the worst about adversaries' motives and intentions and therefore to focus solely on military capabilities and potential. The basis for this flawed claim appears to be twofold: As a third image theory, structural realism assumes that states do not examine adversaries' domestic characteristics, which leaves them without adequate information to judge motives and intentions; and, given uncertainty about other states' intentions, states cannot afford to risk that others will forego opportunities created by their military capabilities.[8] In contrast, defensive realism argues that relying on worst-case policies can be self-defeating and that under a range of conditions states have preferable alternatives.

The divergence results because the standard claim misconstrues the implications of structural realism's core assumptions. Assuming that states do not rely on unit-level information does not mean that they cannot acquire new information about others' motives. Under a range of conditions, the military policies that a state adopts can communicate information about its motives via costly signals—there are arming policies that a pure security seeker would not adopt, but a greedy state would.[9] Thus, without violating structural realism's third image assumption, states can under certain conditions improve their assessments of others' motives simply by observing and assessing their military policies.

Consequently, states need to consider not only the military capabilities that their policies will provide, but also the information that they will communicate. The possibility that policy choices can communicate information is important because, according to structural realism, a security-seeking state should be interested in convincing its adversary that its motives are benign, since this will make the adversary more secure, which in turn makes the security-seeking state more secure. However, the competitive policies fueled by worst-case planning can have the opposite effect, convincing a rational adversary that the state is more dangerous (i.e., greedy) than it previously believed.[10] Thus, states may often face a difficult trade-off that is entirely overlooked by the standard structural realist argument: Protecting against the worst case risks making the actual adversary more insecure and therefore harder to deter. As a result, states may often want to make this trade-off in the opposite direction—pursuing cooperative or restrained policies that signal benign intentions, even if this somewhat increases the state's own military vulnerability.

Once again, the key point for our discussion here is that defensive realism is not creating a new realist theory, but rather is correcting deductive flaws in what has come to be accepted as the standard structural realist argument. Down the road, the result should not be a proliferation of realist arguments that enjoy equal standing. Instead, either deductively flawed theories should simply be replaced, or they should be amended/narrowed by adding assumptions and/or empirical boundaries that are sufficient to support their conclusions.[11]

## Offensive versus Defensive Realism: Deductive Disputes, Not Empirical Ones

Offensive realists, like defensive realists, start from the same basic assumptions as does Waltz. Offensive realism predicts that states can best achieve security through competitive policies. In this way, it resembles Waltz's neorealism. However, offensive realism expects that states will be even more competitive than does Waltz. This is because, contrary to Waltz, offensive realists believe that to achieve security states should maximize their power.[12] As a result, offensive realists expect states to be more inclined toward a variety of more competitive policies, including, for example, having a greater interest in bandwagoning and a greater willingness to buck-pass than predicted by Waltz, who sees a stronger tendency toward efficient balancing.

Obviously, offensive realists diverge quite substantially from defensive realists, who do not see a general tendency toward competitive policies. Here too the fundamental point of divergence is whether states should maximize power to achieve their security goals.

This is a deductive question, not an empirical one. Defensive realists believe that states should generally not try to maximize their power because they face a security dilemma. Policies required to maximize power will often reduce others' security and therefore could be self-defeating—the state will be stronger, but its adversary will be harder to deter.[13] Moreover, these policies can entail additional risks: As already discussed, launching a buildup to maximize power can result in an arms race that the adversary wins; and bandwagoning can be a means of maximizing power, but it can leave a state more vulnerable than balancing. According to defensive realists, although states should sometimes attempt to maximize their power, under other conditions they should not.

Offensive realists have not yet adequately laid out the logic that underlies their claim that, as a general rule, a state seeking security should maximize its power. John Mearsheimer, who has presented the fullest statement of offensive realism, says, "The reason is simple: the greater the military advantage one state has over others, the more secure it is."[14] However, this statement could be true only if states never face a security dilemma and if the policies required to maximize power are somehow not fraught by the downside risks that can accompany competitive policies. Offensive realists have not explained why this is the case, and consequently offensive realism does not yet appear to be progressive relative to Waltz's theory.

Because this is a dispute over the internal integrity of deductive arguments, it cannot be resolved empirically. Examples of states pursuing competitive, power-maximizing policies cannot provide support to flawed deductions. Instead, at least until the deductive logic of offensive realism is more fully explained, if states are in fact consistently pursuing the power-maximizing competitive policies that offensive realism purports to explain, then, broadly speaking, this behavior must be explained in one of two ways. The first would stay within the boundaries of structural realism and argue that offensive realists find a consistent pattern of competitive behavior because the conditions that defensive realism requires for cooperation simply have been rare in the history of the international system, while the conditions under which power maximization is a state's best option have predominated. In other words, state behavior is well-explained by defensive realism, but only a limited range of structural conditions have occurred, and these conditions have favored competition.[15] Although possible, analysts who work with defensive realism have tended not to make this case, arguing instead that the offense-defense balance has often favored defense.[16] The second approach reaches outside of defensive realism, turning to theories that go beyond the boundaries of structural realism. One possibility is that competitive policies were not a state's best option, and that its decisions must be explained by a unit-level theory of suboptimal behavior. A second possibility is that states competed because they were motivated by greed and not only by security and that this explains the divergence from defensive-realist predictions. It is to that class of explanations I now turn.

## Neoclassical Realism versus Structural Realism: Defensive Realism Rescues Classical Realism

Neoclassical realists argue that the key to understanding competitive and conflictual international behavior lies in the nature of individual states—specifically their motives and goals—not in international structure.[17] From one perspective, therefore, neoclassical and structural realism can be viewed as major theoretical competitors. However, from another perspective, these theories appear to be more complementary than they are competitive. Neoclassical realism would be much less important and interesting if it were not for defensive realism. As I explain below, the progress in moving from Waltz's structural realism to defensive realism was necessary to clarify the importance of neoclassical realism, which has in turn clarified the importance of new avenues of research.

If Waltz (and offensive realists) were correct about the state behavior that flowed from the international system, then variation in states' motives would matter very little. Across the full range of international conditions, pure security seekers and very greedy states would adopt competitive policies and forego opportunities for cooperation and unilateral restraint.[18] From a theoretical perspective, therefore, there would be little reason to develop explanations that focused on differences in states' motives and goals. The more purely structural theory would be clearly preferable, offering much greater parsimony at little if any cost in explanatory power.

Consequently, defensive realism saves the day for neoclassical realism. By explaining that security seekers should sometimes pursue cooperative policies, defensive realism gives neoclassical realism something to explain—namely, competitive behavior that runs counter to the predictions of defensive realism. More specifically, by identifying the conditions under which security seekers should cooperate, defensive realism focuses attention on the structural situations in which neoclassical explanations can best distinguish themselves from structural explanations. When states pursue competitive policies under these conditions, rational explanations that emphasize the role of greedy states are a natural place to turn.[19]

Although neoclassical realism has a solid claim to explaining competition over part of the domain covered by defensive realism, Randall Schweller has greatly exaggerated the extent of this domain. He argues incorrectly that in effect the security dilemma does not exist, therefore competition between rational states cannot be explained by defensive realism, thereby claiming that all rational competition is explained by greed and neoclassical realism.[20] He holds that competition should not occur among states that only want security unless they suffer misperceptions, but these are precluded by structural realism. Schweller's argument is flawed because it overlooks the central role of uncertainty in structural realist arguments.[21] Once the role of uncertainty about the adversary's motives is recognized, the security dilemma can in fact, under a range of conditions, explain competition between security seekers. Although Schweller oversteps, the basic point of neoclassical realism remains: Under a range of conditions, the rational explanation for competitive policies lies in greedy motives and not in the incentives generated by the international system that are emphasized by defensive realism.

This relationship between neoclassical and defensive realism suggests the ways in which they are in fact largely complementary theories, not primarily competitors.[22] First, the theories cover different parts of the possible empirical domain: Defensive realism claims those situations in which the states can actually be reasonably approximated as pure security seekers, while neoclassical realism claims those situations in which at least one state has significant motives that extend beyond security. In this sense, the theories are complementary, with each purporting to explain cases that the other is not designed to explain. Taken together, the theories can offer explanations across the entire distribution of states' motives. Second, these theories are also complementary, or at least not competitors, because neither attempts to provide an explanation for the nature of states or their frequency. Because these realist theories take motives as given, in contrast to theories that try to explain motives, neither type of realism can make an empirical claim about the relative frequency with which states fall within their respective domains. Thus, which theory explains more depends on the distribution of types of states over time—which is a question for which these theories do not offer explanations—and not on disagreements over how states interact and the means they will choose, given the constraints and opportunities they face—which is the focus of theories' efforts.[23] Third, a theory of greedy-state behavior should draw on defensive realism, since virtually all states, including greedy ones, are interested in security. Whereas defensive realism explores the options available to security seekers that are uncertain about the motives of their adversaries, neoclassical realism needs to explore how greedy states pursue their dual goals when facing uncertainty about adversaries, and also how states that know that their adversaries are greedy can best deal with them.[24] Schweller's work on the alliance choices of greedy states is a component of this overall effort.

Of course, from the perspective of theory building, the key issue concerning complementarity is not whether theories' assumptions are accurate across the empirical domain, but instead whether they make different predictions for at least some points in this domain. More specifically, if structure were sufficiently influential to determine outcomes independent of the type of state, then it would be relatively unimportant that states' motives varied significantly, and that the theory's assumptions were only accurate for a fraction of states. However, this is not the case for defensive and neoclassical realism—their predictions do vary for certain states under certain structural conditions. Waltz disagrees, arguing that structure is so influential that the distribution of types of states is not important for explaining behavior, but defensive realism corrects this overstatement.[25]

## A Coherent, Evolving Research Agenda as a Further Indication of Progress

Recent work in both defensive and neoclassical realism suggests research that will contribute to a better understanding of their foundations and explanatory power. The continuing evolution and definition of research that needs to be done is in itself an indication that progress is being made in the realist research agenda.

Defensive realism focuses attention on a number of important empirical and theoretical questions. Because offense-defense variables play a central role in the theory, understanding these variables becomes especially important. We need to have clear and agreed-upon definitions of these variables and of how they can be measured.[26] We also need to know whether measurement is feasible. If the offense-defense balance is too difficult to measure, or the uncertainties in any measurement are very large, then states may have little choice other than to put offense-defense variables aside and focus primarily on power.[27] In this case, defensive realism would collapse into a power-based theory, and its predictions would more closely resemble those of standard power-based realism. And it would be useful to have a better understanding of the value of the offense-defense across time and countries.[28] If the balance has usually favored offense (which seems unlikely given the current state of knowledge), then we would expect most major power behavior to be predicted reasonably well by the standard realist analysis and by offensive realism. However, the explanation offered by defensive realism would remain quite different and its implications for policy under different conditions would remain compelling.

Defensive realism suggests another set of research questions by correcting the standard realist disregard for states' intentions. By identifying the possibility that states can gather important information about motivations from their adversaries' military policy choices, defensive realism suggests that we study whether states do in fact look for, and correctly interpret, costly signals. Related to this, when a state identifies actions that provide information about its adversary's motives and intentions, how well does it incorporate this into its military and foreign policy? On the flip side, defensive realism suggests that we study whether, and how well, states incorporate the possibility of sending costly signals into their own military policy; for example, are they sensitive to the possibility that competitive policies are sometimes likely to damage relations with adversaries and, in these cases, how well do states do at weighing the risks of competitive and cooperative policies?

Another implication of defensive realism is more far-reaching. By explaining that a state's policy should be influenced by its understanding of others' motives and intentions, defensive realism raises doubts about its own defining assumptions. If variation in units matters, then why do states not look inside the "black box," as well as looking for costly signals embedded in foreign policy and military policy?[29] Thus, although outside the boundaries of their theory, defensive realists should be interested in whether states can in fact learn about others' intentions by studying their unit-level features. Among other things, this should help them understand the analytic costs of restricting investigation to the third-image/structural level, and to better judge trade-offs between parsimony and explanatory power. Moreover, as I discuss in the final section of this paper, there is no reason that an analyst who works with structural theory should not combine it with other levels of analysis and/or with other structural or rational theories. There will be a trade-off with parsimony, but sometimes the real world will make trading complexity for parsimony a good deal. While there are strong reasons to be very clear about moves between levels of analysis and assumptions about types of states, there is no good reason for theorists to lock themselves into too narrow a box.

Neoclassical realism, by clarifying the importance of variation in states' motives, highlights the importance of research on the sources of state greed. This research lies outside the boundaries of neoclassical realism, which takes motives as given. However, the two lines of research are obviously complementary, with a theory of greedy states explaining an independent variable in neoclassical realism. For example, research that explains when and why states are greedy would help to identify the conditions under which neoclassical realism would apply; and research that explains the extent of states' greed would contribute to the testing of neoclassical hypotheses, many of which depend on a state's willingness to risk security for non–security goals. Work on when expansion will increase a state's prosperity, on states' construction of identities, on the impact of domestic institutions in aggregating preferences, and on the implications of flawed evaluative capabilities can all contribute to understanding these issues and are therefore highly complementary to the overall realist research program.

## Progress That Combines Realism with Other Levels of Analysis

In addition to the strands of realism discussed above, important work that combines realist theory with other levels of analysis deserves mention as evidence of progress. Obviously this progress cannot be credited entirely to realism, since the work does not rely purely on realist theories. However, realism contributes significantly to this progress, even if at the same time this research suggests limitations to the explanatory power of realist theories. Moreover, these multilevel works are progressive for the field of international relations in general, and this is what really matters.

To ground the discussion, I note a few key examples of this type of work, which develops a defensive realist foundation, and then adds the possibility of misperceptions. Van Evera's work on the causes of war develops some of the key arguments that flow from the combination of security-dilemma and power variables. Van Evera, however, does not insist on a purely structural explanation for the causes of war. Instead, he accepts that structural variables must be analyzed by states, and argues that states often misevaluate the conditions they face because, for example, militaries are often biased in their assessment of the international environment. Snyder and Christensen make a similar move in their effort to analyze the conditions under which states pursue different types of balancing behavior—buck-passing and chain-ganging. They argue that to move beyond Waltz requires adding the offense-defense balance as a key variable. This addition is insufficient, however, because states often misperceive the balance, so they include perceptions of the balance as well. Snyder's study of overexpansion develops a defensive realist explanation of when states should expand and uses this as a baseline against which states' behavior can be gauged. Finding that states often expand beyond what is predicted by this rational baseline, Snyder builds a domestic politics model to explain this suboptimal behavior.[30]

Three observations suggest the important and productive role of realism in this multilevel research. First, in the most effective cases the combination of levels of analysis is not ad hoc but, rather, guided by realist theory. For example, defensive realism identifies the variables and possibilities that should influence states' decisions. Once identified, scholars need to measure these variables to learn if states acted as predicted. If states did not, then one possibility is that they misperceived key variables—for example, the offense-defense balance—in which case a theory of misperceptions can be productively combined with realist theory. Without a theory that identified the importance of offense-defense variables, scholars would not have worked to develop a theory of misperceptions of these variables. Thus, while defensive realism is not sufficient on its own, it is nevertheless providing essential guidance.

Second, realism provides a valuable baseline against which the impact of misperceptions and other distortions can be judged. Although a realist theory of state behavior is not required to measure misperceptions, it is required for assessing the implications of misperceptions, since this requires the ability to compare how states would have acted with and without misperceptions. Consequently, the existence of misperceptions and other flawed evaluations does not eliminate the analytic value of realist theories, even though one of the theory's key assumptions—rational state behavior—is violated.

Third, assessments of realism are often confused by the inclination to categorize all theorists who have employed realist theories as realists, even if they have also employed other types of theories to create multilevel theories. Although sometimes a useful simplification, it risks creating confusion about realism's assumptions. For example, if a scholar starts with a realist argument and then layers on a theory of misperception, and if we categorize this scholar as a realist, then in effect we have converted realism into a theory that no longer assumes that states are essentially clear-sighted and rational. For the sake of clarity, we are much better off categorizing scholars in terms of the theories they use—whether single-level or multilevel—than categorizing theories by scholars who use them. Although nothing really fundamental is at stake, the labeling exercise can contribute to, or detract from, clarity in the debate.

The confusion over categories, in which researchers who are doing multilevel work are categorized as realist, provides critics of realism with a straw man to attack. To start with, it leaves realism open incorrectly to the criticism that its basic assumptions are constantly being changed in an attempt to match the theory to the data, or that realism has degenerated into a generic rational theory.[31] Closely related to this, analysts who develop multilevel theories appear vulnerable to the criticism that realism is failing because they have been forced to turn to other levels of analysis to build adequate theories. However, as described above, this criticism fails to appreciate that realist theories are of substantial value in the development and assessment of these multilevel theories. Moreover, even if categorized as realists, theorists who build multilevel theories do not want to defend realism as capable of explaining everything. The goal of research should be to develop useful theories that explain a great deal about international relations, not to defend realism. Structural realism is often a natural place to start, because it is a rational, parsimonious theory. If, however, the real world does not match with structural realism's predictions, then drawing in other assumptions about types of states and/or other levels of analysis is often a wise move. A strength of realism is that it can provide valuable guidance on how best to do this.

## Editors' Commentary

### Major Query

Can recent changes in realist research programs, which involve generating multiple divergent predictions and incorporating causal variables from different **levels of analysis**, be characterized as progressive?

## Major Points

Structural realist theories have been improved following a tightening of their logic. This exactitude uncovered previous ambiguity in realist research, and more clearly identified distinct subsets of realist theories. Rather than a single structural realist theory producing a cacophony of difference, there are now three families of structural realist theories providing a symphony of divergence. Each set of predictions is clearly deduced from and associated with a distinct theory, and accordingly each subset is now much more vulnerable to empirical assessment and falsification.

As noted in Table 16.1, Glaser argues that there are three structural realist theories, each making distinct predictions:

- Waltz's realism, as presented in his *Theory of International Politics*;
- Defensive realism, which modifies Waltz's theory by suggesting that competition and conflict are not inevitable corollaries to international anarchy; by arguing for a prominent role for the security dilemma and for its mitigation by particular values of related offense-defense variables; and by questioning the unwarranted prominence of worst-case analysis in structural realism, where capabilities are always assumed to trump intentions.
- Offensive realism, which modifies Waltz's theory by suggesting that the best way for states to achieve security is by maximizing relative power.

Glaser also identifies a second, nonstructural strand of theory, neoclassical realism. Unlike the three brands of structural realism, neoclassical realism makes explicit use of variations in state motivations. State behavior is not only the product of incentives offered by an anarchic international system, but also the product of what different states want. In short, neoclassical realism adds variables from nonsystemic levels of analysis.

Glaser concludes that both of these "moves," the development of different structural realisms, and of multilevel neoclassical realism, are progressive. He makes the case that among the variants of structural realism, defensive realism is showing particular promise as a research program, in particular by focusing attention on a number of important empirical and theoretical questions. These include the measurement of offense-defense variables; the conceptualization and measurement of state intentions; and discovering the virtues and limits of third image (or system level) theorizing.

Table 16.1

| Structural Realism | Nonstructural Realism |
|---|---|
| Waltz's realism | Neoclassical realism |
| Defensive realism | |
| Offensive realism | |

Glaser is also hopeful that nonstructural neoclassical realism will continue to prove progressive. Because they use "nonrealist" variables, strictly speaking, these multilevel theories redound neither to structural realism's credit nor to its culpability. But structural realism can provide a baseline against which they can be judged, as well as give guidance on which gaps need to be filled by domestic level variables.

## Key Term

**levels of analysis**  A schema for coding theories by the level at which their independent or causal variable falls. The number of levels varies according to the particular version, ranging from two ("inside the state" and "outside the state") to five or more. The most popular version among neotraditionalists is probably the three-level coding offered by Kenneth Waltz in his *Man, the State, and War* (1959): the individual, the state, and the state system, which are sometimes also described as the first, second, and third images. Theories are placed at their independent variable's level of analysis. For example, first image psychobiographical research gives causal weight to the formative experiences of individuals; second image democratic peace theory suggests that democratic domestic institutions and norms have a benign impact upon state foreign security policy; and third image balance of power theory argues that states respond to changes in the distribution of capabilities. Among quantitative scholars, problems of levels of analysis have been informed by Singer's classic (1961) essay.

## Notes

1. Vasquez 1997.
2. In this paper, although I use a number of terms—including *progress*, *ad hoc*, and *research program*—that have a technical Lakatosian meaning, I use them instead with their everyday meaning.
3. This assumption fits well with the purpose of a structural theory, which attempts to explain variations in behavior primarily in terms of variations in international structure, and not in terms of variations in motives and goals. Assuming further that states not only have the same motives but that they are interested only in security provides structural realism with the most basic and parsimonious assumptions: The reason states desire security is sufficiently obvious as to not demand extensive explanation; and by assuming motives along a single dimension, the theory does not need to focus on trade offs with other motives. The assumption that states are pure security seekers is essentially consistent with Waltz's theory; he says that states may have motives beyond security, but suggests that their behavior can be predicted without focusing on these nonsecurity motives.
4. Although somewhat different from my description, a good brief summary of realism's assumptions is Frankel (1996c, xiv–xviii).
5. Waltz 1979.
6. This discussion draws heavily on Glaser 1994/95, 50–90. Other formulations of defensive realism differ somewhat, but are compatible with the thrust of this discussion; see Snyder 1991, esp. 11–12, and 21–26); and Van Evera 1999. Other theoretical work that integrates offense-defense variables with power, and therefore shares important elements of defensive realism includes Walt 1987 and Christensen and Snyder 1990. Note, however, that most of the above works are multilevel theories,

combining a defensive-realist foundation with other levels of analysis. In a following section, I explain that categorizing these theorists as defensive realists has created confusion and suggest a way around this problem.
7. On the security dilemma, see Jervis 1976, esp. 63–76; Jervis 1978, 167–214; Glaser 1997, 171–210.
8. Two other considerations may also contribute to the need for worst-case planning: First, others' motives can always change, so assuming less than the worst leaves the state vulnerable to these changes; and second, even if a state does examine others' unit-level characteristics it will be unable to resolve uncertainties about its motives. Adding in these considerations does not lead defensive realism to call for worst-case policies.
9. On costly signaling, see Kydd 1997a, 371–400; Glaser 1994/95, 67–70; Fearon 1992; Jervis 1970.
10. For a discussion of the rational foundations of the security dilemma, see Glaser 1997, 174–181; see also Kydd 1997a. Worst-case policies can also increase the adversary's insecurity by reducing its ability to perform military missions.
11. For a similar perspective, see Walt 1997, 932.
12. Mearsheimer 1994/95, 5–49; see also Labs 1997, 1–49, and Mearsheimer 2001.
13. For a more detailed discussion see Glaser 1997, 195–196.
14. Mearsheimer 1994/95, 11–12.
15. Although he does not make this argument, Mearsheimer (1994/95, 23–24) uses a similar one to explain why analyses that challenge the constraining effect of concern over relative gains have little real-world applicability. However, developing this line of argument for power maximization would not save offensive realism. As stressed in the text, doing this would simply clarify that the general competition predicted by offensive realism is actually the competition that defensive realism expects over part of its structural domain.
16. Van Evera 1998, 5–43; and Van Evera 1999.
17. Most prominently, see Schweller 1994, 72–107; and Schweller 1996, 90–121.
18. This level of generality does, however, underplay some differences in the competitive behavior that these theories predict. For example, under a range of conditions, these theories make different predictions about states' propensities to balance versus to bandwagon. My discussion therefore underplays the explanatory power of neoclassical realism relative to Waltz's theory, but the thrust of the argument I present in the text remains sound.
19. Neoclassical/greed-based theories may not provide the best explanations even in these cases. Theories that rely on suboptimal decision making are their key competitors and, as I noted in my discussion of offensive realism, defensive realists have tended to turn to these explanations to explain overly competitive behavior. For examples, see Snyder 1991; and Van Evera 1997.
20. Schweller 1996.
21. Glaser 1997, 195; and Kydd 1997b, 116–117.
22. Schweller (1997, 929) makes essentially this point, arguing that their different scope conditions are the key to understanding the relationship between neoclassical and neorealist approaches.
23. It is in this same spirit that Jervis (1976, Ch. 3, esp. 102) observes that analysts who employ the spiral model or deterrence model do not disagree over general models of international relations, but disagree instead about Soviet intentions.
24. Such a theory would not be purely structural, since it would allow for actual variation in states' motives, but it could nevertheless draw on structural/third-image arguments by preserving uncertainty about other states' motives and continuing to "black box" state interactions.
25. Another set of empirical judgments could however eliminate this complementarity: A defensive realist who believed that the structural conditions that actually occurred always made competition a security seeker's best option might find that neoclassical realism did not provide additional explanatory power and might conclude that the theories were not complementary. However, as noted above, analysts who have worked on defensive realism have tended to find the opposite; that is, that structural conditions have often allowed for cooperation and peace.
26. For recent work and debate on this question, see Glaser and Kaufmann 1988, 44–82; Davis, Finel, Goddard, Van Evera, Glaser, and Kaufmann 1998/99, 179–206; Lynn-Jones 1995, 660–691; and Biddle 1998.
27. Keir Lieber (2000) explores this possibility.
28. The most extensive effort to date is Van Evera 1999.
29. David Edelstein (2000) addresses the question of how states assess others' motives and intentions.
30. Van Evera 1999; Christensen and Snyder 1990; Snyder 1991.
31. Emphasizing the latter criticism are Legro and Moravcsik (1999).

# Closing Dialogue

*COLIN ELMAN AND JOHN A. VASQUEZ*

In this concluding exchange of views the editors offer some reflections on the themes discussed in this volume, with an emphasis on where we differ. We do not disagree on everything. We share the belief that Waltz's *Theory of International Politics*, and the research program(s) that grew out of it, make important claims that need to be rigorously investigated. We agree that such appraisals should be grounded in carefully specified and justified epistemologies that are then rigorously applied. We found the initial forum and subsequent responses very informative. We concur that the interchange with each other and the other authors while working on this book helped deepen our own understandings, while at the same time opening our thinking to new questions and problems that need to be solved.

This chapter is presented in a dialogue format, beginning with theory appraisal criteria, and then discussing realism and the balancing of power. A central reason for choosing a dialogue format for this chapter is that much of the recent discussion on balancing of power and many of the chapters in this book, particularly the first eight chapters, joined a discussion between opposing viewpoints. This continuing conversation is not a debate in the sense that there is a single idea that serves as the point of disagreement: There are several different positions being articulated and more than just one question being addressed by the authors, including the editors, of this book. In addition, as editors we have tried to avoid the temptation of scoring points through rhetorical flourishes. Nevertheless, a dialogue format suits us in that it underlines that we are trying to communicate with each other and understand each other's positions, while at the same time raising questions about positions that we feel have not been adequately answered.

First Elman raises some concerns with paradigmatic approaches in general and Lakatos's Methodology of Scientific Research Programs (MSRP) in particular, as well as noting some unease about the particular applications of Lakatos's metric in this volume. Vasquez then responds. In the second section, Vasquez revisits the critiques of realism and balancing of power that are made in the book, and argues that the conclusion he reached in the original *APSR* essay—that the research program is degenerating—has been strengthened. Elman then responds. In the closing section, we jointly outline some common ground on both the importance of the topic and the need to engage in rigorous theory appraisal. These two commitments initially brought us to the debate and later to collaborate in editing this book.

## SECTION I    THEORY APPRAISAL

### A. PARADIGMATISM IN THIS BOOK, AND IN THE INTERNATIONAL RELATIONS SUBFIELD[1]

#### BY COLIN ELMAN

Although both Vasquez and I are sympathetic to the self-conscious application of metatheory, there are several concerns about this approach that need to be considered. These can be divided into critiques of paradigmatism and Lakatos's MSRP, and of its application in this volume. In this section I mention three concerns: That paradigmatism, as rationalized and justified by the various candidate metatheories, may be unhelpful; that the authors may be using the "wrong" metatheory (e.g., Lakatos's rather than Laudan's); and that the authors may be using the "right" metatheory, but nevertheless misspecifying it.

*Is Paradigmatism, in Any of the Forms Commonly Cited in the IR Subfield, the Wrong Way to Think about Social Science?*    Stephen M. Walt argues (Ch. 4 herein) that Lakatos's MSRP has been overtaken by subsequent philosophizing. The same argument can easily be leveled at works by Popper, Kuhn, and Laudan. Given that a quarter-century has passed since the publication of the most recent of the seminal metatheoretic works offered by the four scholars (Laudan's *Progress and Its Problems*), this is hardly surprising. It would be hard to find any academic traditions that have survived the last twenty-five years unscathed, and philosophy of science is no exception. In short, paradigmatism is out of favor with contemporary philosophers of science, and to some extent the IR subfield's continuing attachment is an epistemological anachronism.

There are alternatives, which include individual hypothesis testing with no commitment to an overarching theoretical structure; adherence to a particular methodological prescription such as rational choice; or perhaps a more fundamental rejection of scientific models altogether. However, Vasquez's *APSR* article (Ch. 2 herein), and the rejoinders it provoked, nicely illustrate the extent to which paradigmatism remains deeply embedded in the subfield. Of the scholars taking part in this debate, only William Wohlforth (Ch. 15 herein) explicitly argues that paradigmatic thinking is misleading and unhelpful. The remaining scholars at the very least implicitly accept Vasquez's basic premise that it is appropriate to group theories into larger constructs, and several explicitly endorse the application of metatheoretic descriptions and/or criteria. Thomas Christensen and Jack Snyder (Ch. 5 herein, 66), for example, suggest that "Vasquez is right to insist that students of international politics should justify their theories in terms of Imre Lakatos's (1970) criteria. . . ." Randall Schweller (Ch. 6 herein, 74) refers to realism as a "dominant research program in the study of world politics." Stephen Walt (Ch. 4 herein, 61) suggests that "realism is a broad research program that contains a host of competing theories."

*Do the Authors Choose the "Wrong" Metatheory?* Preferring one metatheory to another requires a working knowledge of the candidates, and an understanding of their different strengths and weaknesses. Each of the approaches has been subjected to extensive critiques, and there is certainly no shortage of problems. Elman and Elman (2002a), for example, discuss a variety of grounds on which Lakatos's MSRP could be challenged, including that: it is outdated; it may not be applicable to the social sciences; its research programs' descriptions are certain to be contested; its criteria for appraisal are ill-defined, in particular with multiple competing understandings of 'novelty'; it places a disproportionate emphasis on novelty; it biases theory development away from empirical testing; it will encourage "paradigm wars;" and it does not describe scientific practice.

Of the different respondents, only one provided an argument that would fit into this category. Walt (Ch. 4 herein, 64n3) argues against Lakatos's rejection of ad hoc modifications, and favorably cites Laudan's position that such changes "by their very definition, are empirically progressive." In addition, one might note that Laudan's research traditions are more malleable than Lakatos's research program. Their hard cores at any given time are rigid but, over time, the elements that are considered sacrosanct can change. Research traditions are also much less connected to their theories than in MSRP's research programs. For Laudan, research traditions do not entail theories, and theories do not entail research traditions. Contradictory theories can belong to the same research traditions, and different research traditions can "provide the presuppositional base for any given theory."[2]

I take no position on the comparative merits of the different metatheories here, except to note that even the process of considering their virtues and vices, and of determining the grounds for choosing Laudan over Lakatos or vice versa, would go a long way toward curing IR scholars of their epistemological blind spot. It could be argued that if IR theorists are going to be paradigmatists, any well-specified metatheory is to be preferred to none.

*If the Authors Do Choose the Right Metatheory, Do They Misspecify It?* To say that IR theorists need a working knowledge of relevant metatheories is not to suggest that they should become philosophers of science, or that scholars *should* be paradigmatists, or that to do so they should employ one particular epistemology in preference to another. I argue, however, that while IR theorists persist in their paradigmatism, they need to use relevant tools to support that position, and to refrain from heroic reinventions. Paul Feyerabend (1975) notwithstanding, it is not the case that "anything goes." Political scientists do not have the freedom to make up their epistemology as they go along.

To his credit, Vasquez provides a lengthy and learned account of the criteria he intends to apply. Nevertheless, his version of Lakatosian metatheory is blemished by its combination with contradictory (indeed, I would argue competing) approaches, and by its incomplete description of Lakatosian theory appraisal criteria. As Miriam Elman and I argue, Vasquez's melding of Kuhnian and Lakatosian units of analysis and criteria commits the "cuisinart" error, putting epistemology in the great blender.[3] It is, for example, contradictory to say that "[a]ny paradigm worth its salt will have more than one ongoing research program."[4]

There are at least two possible responses to our critique: One potential rejoinder is to argue that Kuhn and Lakatos are really making identical arguments, but with different brand names. If that is the case, Vasquez does no harm combining elements from the "same" metatheory. Indeed, Kuhn (1970b, 256; 1971, 137–146) later claimed that Lakatos had merely relabeled his approach, and that the substance of their metatheories was very similar.[5] The better view, however, is that in this instance Kuhn was engaging in special pleading. As Mark Blaug (1992, 32) suggests, arguing that there is little difference between Kuhn and Lakatos "miss[es] the entire object of Lakatos' argument."[6] Vasquez agrees with this position, since in his *APSR* article (Ch. 2 herein), and in this chapter, he differentiates MSRP from Kuhn's metatheory.

An alternative response to this criticism is that, even if Kuhn and Lakatos are saying different things, the two approaches can be used simultaneously and consistently. This is the tack taken by Vasquez. He maintains that, since there is no logically compelling reason to prefer one set of criteria to another, his epistemological choices are largely instrumental.[7] Because we are a borrowing subfield with limited time to develop our own philosophical tools, we would be wise to use multiple frames simultaneously, thus minimizing the damage if one should later be proven faulty.[8] While I applaud Vasquez's commitment to epistemological pluralism, and his concerns with limiting our exposure from being a borrowing subfield, there seems a natural limit on this otherwise welcome tolerance: the epistemologies being combined cannot be contradictory. An author should have difficulty simultaneously arguing that paradigms are incommensurable and research programs are not; that mature sciences are characterized by a single dominant paradigm and a multitude of competing research programs; that no external objective criteria exist for the comparative judgment of paradigms, but that they do exist for research programs; and so on.

A second problem with Vasquez's specification of MSRP is in his picking and choosing from among MSRP's constituent elements, and deliberately providing an incomplete version of the metatheory. In particular, Vasquez provides an ambiguous definition of novelty for determining whether a problemshift is ad hoc$_1$, and excludes the positive heuristic and the related ad hoc$_3$ criterion altogether. In a later version of the *APSR* essay published as a book chapter in his *The Power of Power Politics*, Vasquez acknowledges this latter criticism, and suggests that he eliminates the ad hoc$_3$ criterion on the grounds that it would be "too stringent."[9] For reasons I note in the section below, the exclusion of ad hoc$_3$ may do little harm in this case, but the absence of a clear and consistent definition of novelty is problematic.

While Vasquez's delineation of metatheory may be imperfect, his respondents' near silence on the topic is even more troubling. The subfield's commitment to paradigmatism, as well as its metatheoretic lacunae, are both clearly demonstrated in the published responses to Vasquez's article, as well as in the new essays in Part II. They starkly illustrate the extent to which the subfield is structured around large theoretical constructs, and the degree to which relevant epistemology is slighted. Most of the rejoinders accepted as given the structuring of the subfield into larger theoretic constructs. By far the most common responses to Vasquez's essay were complaints that he had misdescribed the realist aggregate, or mischaracterized the work of a particular realist scholar. Very few of his critics noticed the metatheoretic commitments embedded in his appraisal, or commented on the description or absence of particular criteria. As described at greater length below, neither did Vasquez's supporters make much effort to advance his central thesis that balance of power theory is degenerating when judged by Lakatosian criteria.

In short, the essays illustrate the tendency of IR scholars to be naïve paradigmatists. They are comfortable describing their work as belonging to, and as having implications for, larger theoretical constructs. They also undertake explicit disciplinary appraisals, and depict and appraise the aggregates' content and trajectory. But, for the most part, IR theorists do these things without engaging much of the epistemology that explains and empowers their understandings of the sub-field.

## B. Metatheory, Paradigms, and Appraising IR Theory

### By John A. Vasquez

Colin Elman raises some important points about how the field of international relations thinks about theory appraisal and the various philosophy of science frameworks that are available for our collective use. We agree on several things, but the two most important are that theories and research within the field should be appraised and that existing work in philosophy of science should be used to make these appraisals in the most rigorous manner possible. This agreement covers very broad areas, so much so that some of the remaining areas might seem more matters of detail—and to a certain extent this is true—but the details have important implications and ultimately affect the conclusions we make about the merits of balancing of power theory, and of realism in general.

One of Colin Elman's concerns, and it is a legitimate concern, is that I do not follow Lakatos's (1970) framework completely, and periodically insert Kuhn's (1970a) ideas about paradigms even when they are inconsistent with Lakatos. Except for the latter conclusion, I agree that I do use both Lakatos and Kuhn but I do this for important reasons, and the combination of the two I believe provides a better and more rigorous appraisal than using one alone. Although there are significant disagreements between Kuhn and Lakatos, parts of their frameworks can complement each other, especially in areas where each has important gaps. I have justified the case for using multiple frames in more detail elsewhere (Vasquez 2002), so here I will focus more on Elman's immediate criticisms, as well as outlining some of the reasons I made the decisions I did as I was conducting the appraisals, in the hopes that this might aid others who seek to conduct theory appraisals.

The philosophical point from which I start is that, while I have an interest in philosophy of science, I am not a philosopher of science, as tempting as that might be, and that we are better off borrowing frameworks and adapting them for our own theory appraisals rather than coming up with new ones out of whole cloth. Once one makes this decision, however, then there is the problem of which metatheory and framework to choose. There are two obvious answers to this—one wants to choose that which is seen as the most legitimate by those within the field being appraised (in this case international relations) and as most valid or useful by philosophers of science themselves. Despite some of Walt's (herein Ch. 4) complaints, there is little doubt that among both mainstream neotraditional and quantitative scholars, Lakatos commands the most legitimacy. There are those who object strenuously to Lakatos and these are postmodernists who prefer Foucault and an entirely different approach to the more positivist position exemplified by the philosophers of science discussed by contributors to this book. If one were really concerned with what was "out of date," as Walt is, then one should, in fact, use Foucault (1972). I was tempted to do that in Vasquez (1998), but I did not because, while Foucault and others in this school of thought are more *au courant*, their criteria are not widely accepted by those who have played a major role in writing about the balancing of power.

Ultimately, however, I do not think the choice of a philosophy of science is as crucial as it appears, so long as the framework's criteria are explicitly delineated and applied in a rigorous manner. There are scholars who believe that there is only one true theory, only one optimal philosophy of science or inquiry, and only one correct way of conducting theory appraisals. There is much to be said for this position, but if there is anything that is out of favor in this postmodern era it is probably this stance (see Smith 1996; Hollis and Smith 1990). My position is more pragmatic and goes back to the idea that Plato captures when he speaks of humans dwelling in a cave and only able to see the shadows of the Forms that dwell in the Light. It is not likely that we have found a path out of the cave and into the light. In these circumstances it behooves us to use multiple reasonable frames to appraise our theories and their underlying paradigms. I believe that the realist paradigm and its theories are so flawed that they are unlikely to do well regardless of the frameworks that are applied, so long as these are applied rigorously. In this sense, either Lakatos (1970), Kuhn (1970a), Popper (1959), or Laudan (1977) all could be applied without much changing the general appraisal, although the details would be changed. Each of these frames are different and each is apt to tell us different things about the weaknesses and strength of any given theory. I applied a combination of Lakatos and Kuhn because I believed that together they were more useful than each applied separately; in Vasquez (1997) (herein Ch. 2), the emphasis is on Lakatos, whereas in Vasquez (1998) more emphasis is placed on Kuhn (1970a).

Kuhn (1970a) raises the problem that working scientists do not engage in the kind of testing and falsification that Popper (1959) talks about, but he does not solve the problem. He points out, as have others, that the presence of a paradigm permits innumerable interrelated theories to emerge, even if the original theory might be rejected, which means that while a specific theory might be falsified, no family of theories can be logically falsified because it is always possible to reformulate a given theory. Rejection of a theory can occur, but the paradigm lives on. In the epilogue to the revised edition, Kuhn (1970a, 199) states that he never says that the normal criteria for choosing theories should not be applied, but that these criteria act like values and are reasons for preferring one theory over another; they do not logically compel a scientist to choose one over another.

Lakatos (1970) never moves beyond the idea that selecting one theory over another is a matter of decision and not logic, but he does provide some new criteria for dealing with the problem of multiple theories. His main criterion is of degenerative as opposed to progressive problemshifts, which sets out rules for determining what is and is not a legitimate way to emend a theory. It is this criterion that is the heart of his MSRP and the major reason most political scientists have been attracted to his work. This is an advance over Kuhn because Kuhn provides no new rules for overcoming the problem he identifies with Popper's falsificationism. In large part, this is because Kuhn is primarily a historian of science and not a philosopher of science. He is more expert at what scientists do than on what they *should* do if we are to have confidence that they are producing knowledge. As a result, Kuhn describes mostly sociological reasons for why (and how) one paradigm displaces another, and in some circles this seemed to raise the spectre of relativism. Lakatos's scheme seems to provide a reasonable path out of this situation.

Lakatos, however, has a much less accurate understanding of the history of any science. Many of his descriptions of how science is practiced and of the nature of theory and research do not resonate well, at least in terms of what we know about international relations and political science. Lakatos never talks about paradigms and seems to think that each theory has its own research program. The idea of a research program with its hard core and positive heuristic is about as close to the idea of a paradigm as Lakatos comes, but these ideas are not as lucid as Kuhn's ideas of paradigm, normal science, and extraordinary science. For one thing, Lakatos seems to imply that science consists of a set of research programs that are not held together by some overarching framework; whereas the merit and contribution of Kuhn's work is to show that a variety of theories on very different subjects (dependent variables) can come out of a single paradigm or fundamental view of the world. In this sense, it is fairly easy to write a Kuhnian history of international relations in terms of the realist paradigm displacing the earlier idealist paradigm and the failure of the Marxist paradigm to ever dominate the Anglo-American IR discipline (see Vasquez 1983; Smith 1987; Smith 1995).

What Kuhn captures that Lakatos obscures is that a single paradigm can have very different theories (each with their own program of research) (Vasquez 1983, Ch. 4; 1998, Ch. 4). The key is not just to compare minor variations to theories within the same program, but to compare the underlying theoretical perspective of competing paradigms (the idea that paradigms are inherently incommensurable is refuted by Scheffler [1967]). Lakatos then is relevant for looking at a specific research program, as I do (Vasquez 1997; herein Ch. 2) with the research program generated by Waltz (1979), but there is also the larger question of the adequacy of the underlying paradigm itself (Vasquez 1998). So my appraisal of the neotraditional research program must be seen as one component of my larger appraisal of the realist paradigm as a whole. Since I think that Kuhn's description of disciplines is more accurate and useful, I do not attempt to identify the hard core or positive heuristic of a research program, as Elman and Elman rightly point out, and in this sense my use of Lakatos is incomplete. The reason for this, however, is that I have used ideas derived from Kuhn that are functional equivalents, like identifying the fundamental assumptions of the realist paradigm (rather than the hard core of a research program) and the idea that theory construction is "paradigm articulation" (see Vasquez 1998, 60–61).

Of course it would have been more elegant to use just Lakatos or Kuhn and not to "mix and match" (or throw them into a cuisinart food processor as Elman colorfully puts it above; see also Elman and Elman 2002a, 244), but this would have two negative consequences, as any future theory appraiser needs to be aware. First, to use Kuhn exclusively is to lose Lakatos's criterion of degenerative research programs. Second, to use Lakatos exclusively is to be confronted with difficult problems like identifying the hard core, the positive and negative heuristics of a research program, and specifying where one research program ends and another begins—none of which are easy tasks, as a recent volume by Elman and Elman (2002b) shows (see also Elman's quote of Blaug 1976, 167).

In addition, Lakatos just is not very useful in making sense of what ties the various theories and research programs of a discipline together, or of what keeps a division of labor from becoming separate disciplines. What keeps a discipline together is an underlying paradigm. Certainly our own history as a discipline makes more sense from this perspective, and certainly the current debate between realism and liberalism resonates with the idea that these are paradigms with their own ongoing normal science research. Our field is not just a set of twenty to thirty or more research programs, from war, to IPE, to foreign policy, IL & IO, environmental politics, etc.; our field is dominated by a few central questions that, since 1918, have tended to be guided by three competing paradigms: idealism (now liberalism), realism, and Marxism, with only the first two ever being dominant. These paradigms set out the fundamental assumptions of the field, tell us how to view the world if we want to understand and explain it, and specify what research is worth doing and what is trivial. In short, paradigms make individual scholars into a collective discipline. Lakatos's conception of fields misses all this, and for that reason is not as useful as a heuristic device.

Of equal importance is that Lakatos has one main criterion for appraising theories, but that does not mean that there are not others or that it is the most relevant for appraising a particular research program, as Elman recognizes when he quotes from Hands (1991a, 77–78). As I have argued elsewhere, there are a number of criteria that can be used to appraise theories. For empirical theories, I have suggested that empirical accuracy, falsifiability, explanatory power, progressive vs. degenerative problemshifts, consistency with what is known in other areas, and parsimony are all important criteria and I have applied some of these to various realist theories (see

Vasquez 1998, Part 2). My point here is that theory appraisal is best done by applying more than one criterion and taking more than one approach, and for that to be done most usefully, at least within IR, it needs to be done with an eye toward the underlying paradigms within the field and their relative success in producing adequate theories and fruitful research. What we mean by "success," "adequate," and "fruitful" will be a matter of discussion that needs to be informed by philosophy of science, but in the end it will be important to have some consensus, because theory appraisal and paradigm evaluation are matters of decision and not of something being logically compelling. Those who construct theories and research should be willing to live by a discipline's rules or "warrants" about what constitutes knowledge or acceptable theory and research—even the contributors to this volume who reject Lakatos are willing to accept this, and in the end that is all that is necessary to conduct theory appraisals.

Let me now turn to two specific points Colin Elman makes about my use of Lakatos, because each addresses important concerns that need to be considered for future appraisals. The first deals with novel facts. Elman is correct that novel facts are difficult to discern. His point that novel facts need not necessarily be predicted by the same author is also correct. However, the claim that the predictions need not be made immediately needs to be qualified. If an author presents a theoretical emendation without novel facts, then it is perfectly legitimate to say the author has failed to show that the new emendation is necessarily superior. Of course, one can suspend one's belief on the adequacy of the emendation, but most of those who reformulated neorealism seem to be saying that their theory was better than the original because it accounted for discrepant evidence, when in fact it may have only labeled it. In this regard, I take it that Elman's claim that Walt's (1996) later work on revolution shows that balancing of interest is a "novel fact," implies that Walt (1987) in the original formulation of the theory did not produce any novel facts, which is what I said in the original article (herein Ch. 2). The more recent work by Barnett (1996; herein Ch. 16) suggests that the discrepant evidence Walt uncovers can be explained better by a nonrealist theory that embodies novel facts than the conception of balancing interests that Walt delineates. In the end, Colin Elman, in this chapter and with Miriam Elman in the original debate, is correct in that specifying more explicitly what is and is not a novel fact will help make theory appraisals more rigorous and less controversial. A similar but broader point has been made for several years by Roslyn Simowitz (1998, 2002; see also Simowitz and Price 1990) when she maintains that each of the criteria used in a theory appraisal needs to be operationalized.

The second point that is important to keep in mind has to do with using Lakatos's three categories of ad hoc explanations. Elman and Elman (herein Ch. 7) correctly point out that I do not place much emphasis on Lakatos's three types of ad hoc explanation. Since then I have tried to correct that, and both in my reply and in this chapter, I employ Lakatos's idea that a theoretical emendation that does not stem from the logic of the theory (or, I would add, the paradigm) is ad hoc and an indicator that the research program may be degenerating. I think that ad hoc$_3$ emendations are particularly damaging if they come from a competing theory or paradigm. Thus, when

Christensen and Snyder (1990) employ cognitive psychological variables, this points to the utility and possible superiority of a nonrealist paradigm or theory, since non-power and often nonmaterialist variables are being used to save a realist theory. Likewise, the inclusion of domestic politics variables (as in "neoclassical" realism) raises questions about a realist paradigm that has historically suggested that external strategic power factors are primary. Bringing them in now suggests that other paradigms, like liberalism, transnational relations, and even Marxism may provide better insights. I think I was correct in saying that criticizing emendations by employing ad hoc$_3$ considerations would only have made my case stronger, but these should have been made in detail. I have suggested in my replies how criticism of neotraditional emendations in terms of ad hoc$_3$ explanations might have been made, but a treatment of ad hoc$_3$ explanations still needs to be done more systematically. In the end, while Colin Elman and I still have several disagreements, we do agree on the need for theory appraisal and on a set of questions that still need to be resolved. We now turn to a dialogue on realism and the balancing of power.

## SECTION II   REALISM AND THE BALANCING OF POWER

### A. PROBLEMS WITH THE BALANCING OF POWER

#### BY JOHN A. VASQUEZ

As the chapters in this book have shown, discourse on the balancing of power is quite varied both in terms of the multiplicity of positions of those sympathetic to realism and those critical of it. The case against Waltz's claim that balancing of power is a law rests on two main pillars. The first is that his assumption that this is a law is simply not true—it is empirically inaccurate to claim that states under anarchy regularly engage in balancing behavior. The second is that those who have researched Waltz's proposition utilizing a neotraditional approach have uncovered evidence that undermines Waltz's claim that balancing of power is a law, but instead of recognizing this as evidence that would lead to a consideration of rejecting or falsifying Waltz's theory, they have sought to reformulate and thereby improve the theory. These reformulations, however, have been conducted in a manner that Lakatos would find illegitimate and as a series of degenerating rather than progressive shifts in theory.

As I argued in my initial reply to my critics (Ch. 8 herein), Waltz and most of the neotraditional researchers who have been criticized have spent a great deal of their time arguing that the balancing of power proposition is either accurate or that the evidence uncovered that leads to a reformulation of the theory is not that discrepant and undermining of the original theory. Elman is correct in arguing that the first pillar of criticism is basically the application of a Popperian criterion of falsification rather than a truly Lakatosian one, in that the former looks at the accuracy of the proposition per se, rather than the *trajectory* of the research program as a whole (see editors' commentary on Ch. 3). Nevertheless, it is Waltz who begins this shift back to an assessment of the evidence on the proposition rather than an evaluation of the quality of the reformulations, and almost all the respondents with the exception of Elman and Elman spend a great deal of time on the former. While this shifts the debate slightly, it is not entirely illegitimate since part of what it means for a research program to degenerate is the pushing aside of discrepant evidence. Thus, it is not surprising that different authors would disagree over the extent (or whether) particular pieces of evidence were discrepant.

A good part of the case against Waltz's proposition and the subsequent research on it is that there is not much empirical evidence in favor of the proposition and that evidence uncovered by some of those who have reformulated the proposition is in fact discrepant evidence. From this perspective, Stephen Walt's evidence that states balance states that threaten them and not necessarily the most powerful state(s) in a system is seen as evidence against Waltz's proposition, since the most powerful state must always be considered as posing a potential general threat, whether or not it is actualized in a particular moment. Waltz (1993) recognizes this when he predicts that after the collapse of the Soviet Union, other states will eventually balance against the United States.

Likewise, the claims of Christensen and Snyder that states sometimes buck-pass, especially during periods of multipolarity, is seen as a failure to balance. So too must Schweller's evidence on bandwagoning be seen by realism's critics as a failure to balance power, since states are joining in predation against the weaker. Though it may not be, as Schweller claims, in the interest of an individual state to balance, it is in the collective interest of the system to balance, and the thrust of Waltz's proposition is that states under anarchy will behave in a manner that results in balancing behavior (with the implication that this will benefit most states and help preserve each state's independence).

Waltz, in his reply (Ch. 3 herein), maintains that the historical record shows that states balanced against Charles I, Louis XIV, Napoleon, Hitler, and others and that this evidence is well-known and illustrative of the law-like pattern he is trying to explain. Critics question that pattern, but are willing to take such a claim about balancing against these states in particular as a key test (see Vasquez, Ch.8, herein). Although such a test is close to Popper's idea of falsification, part of the reason for calling for a test that all sides can agree on (Ch. 8, see also Levy, Ch. 10, herein) is that this would form a basis for determining what discrepant evidence would look like and thereby be a step (but only one step) toward seeing if a research program is degenerating.

In Chapter 9, Schroeder makes it clear that not all serious historians accept Waltz's characterization of modern European history as one in which states have balanced against hegemonic bids. Schroeder argues that the problem with Waltz is that he assumes an historical pattern without any "serious effort" to investigate whether this pattern (let alone a law) exists. Schroeder and other critics like him argue that, at the most fundamental level, the case against Waltz's balancing of power proposition is that there is no substantial body of historical evidence supporting it. It is a myth, believed through consistent repetition rather than clear evidence. Schroeder then goes on to briefly review the evidence on Napoleon, Wilhelm II, Charles V, and Hitler, and finds it wanting.

If states do not balance, what do they do? For Schroeder, balancing is rarely the strategy of first choice for states. They often try to accommodate themselves to the state seeking hegemony as most states, including Britain, did with Napoleon or, as I would add, Vichy France did with Hitler, and Halifax wanted to do (unsuccessfully, because of Churchill) in May 1940 (see Lukacs 1999). If states do engage in the kind of checking and blocking Waltz implies, it is frequently because the "aggressor" state, as we note in our commentary on Schroeder's Chapter 9 (p. 126), "would not leave them alone and let them accommodate themselves in a reasonable fashion to the hegemony . . . created." For Schroeder, being attacked and thereby being forced to defend oneself can hardly count as evidence of balancing.

The question Schroeder raises makes it evident that the long discourse on balance of power has not sufficiently specified what counts as balancing and what the theory actually predicts. This ambiguity (i.e., the presence of several different empirical referents) was recognized as a major problem with the concept long before Waltz wrote (see Haas 1953). Because balancing can mean very different things, scholars can easily disagree as to whether it exists. A research program that cannot agree on the central meaning of its concept is going to have difficulty guiding research in a successful direction. The presence of so many different definitions explains why scholars can so easily disagree with each other. At the same time, the persistence of such ambiguity serves as a negative comment on the trajectory of the research program. Part of the reason for the protean nature of realist explanations of balancing undoubtedly has to do with the ease with which the ambiguity and multiple referents of balancing of power lends itself to shifting the evidentiary base of the theory in light of discrepant evidence. Thus, if balancing does not occur before a war, the war itself (and/or its subsequent expansion) can be seen as a form of balancing, even if the implementation of a hegemonic bid provoked little opposition from the state until the "aggressor's" troops crossed its border.

Levy's (herein Ch. 10) analysis is pertinent because he outlines and dissects these ambiguities in systematic detail. While his purpose is to test Waltz's proposition by delineating what can and cannot count as balancing, his review shows just how slippery the concept has been. For Levy, an adequate concept must delimit the *magnitude* of balancing (how strong it is), the *timing* of balancing (when it occurs) and its *extent* (how many states participate). Without such measures, it is difficult to determine whether the evidence supports the balancing proposition. Critics will be quick to use Levy's analysis to argue that the absence of such measures in the research program has made it easy for theorists to discount discrepant evidence by simply shifting the concept to a magnitude, time, or extent that was not refuted by the test at hand. The presence of multiple referents is one indicator of the protean nature of the theory and the ease with which research in the program can slip into degenerating tendencies. For example, critics of balancing who refuse to count Stalin or the United States as respectively balancing Hitler and Japan in World War II after they have been attacked are essentially saying that the time criterion has been broadened to save the proposition. Critics of the theory, like myself, argue (in Levy's terms) that, in general, balancing of power has not been strong in terms of magnitude (as in buck-passing), has come too late to count as balancing (as in self-defense against overt attack), and has not always drawn in all the states it should (as in bandwagoning or in balancing threat).

Levy, however, raises these points not so much to criticize the concept and the research program, but to try to specify a minimally acceptable test that critics and supporters of the balancing of power proposition would accept. In principle, he is successful in specifying such a test, but it remains to be seen whether the participants will accept it. From the critics' perspective, it is a good place to begin and not that different from the test suggested in my Chapter 8 (herein), but with the added benefit of defining explicitly what counts as balancing.

If Levy delineates how to measure what counts as balancing, Rosecrance (herein Ch. 11) provides a definition that shows us what kind of balancing does not occur in history with any frequency. For Rosecrance, balancing of power has traditionally meant the attempt to check a hegemonic bid, which in turn is in the collective interest of all states. For Rosecrance, balancing is always a public good and hence involves a collective action problem. Rosecrance's framing of balancing of power in these theoretical terms at one and the same time explains the fundamental problem that must be overcome for system members to balance successfully while showing why this behavior would be fairly rare and usually not the first strategy tried. Rosecrance goes a step further, however, and says that unless a state is seeking to provide a public good, it is not really balancing but merely engaging in self-defense (as Stalin did in 1941). He also maintains that attempts at mutual expansion that clash (as the United States and USSR did during the Cold War) are also not balancing because they are not seeking to provide a true public good. By defining balancing in this narrow way, Rosecrance has identified a behavior, which it would be useful and theoretically interesting to document, while at the same time showing why it is fairly infrequent and thus not a law. Nor is it clear that such behavior would be a product of anarchy, although the presence of anarchy would explain the difficulty of implementing such a policy. Collective action theory, thereby, both predicts that Waltz's balancing proposition would not be true and explains why such behavior would be fairly rare. If one takes collective action theory seriously, one is not surprised by Schroeder's assessment of the historical evidence.

Rosecrance's analysis shows that there are many different ways to test the adequacy of balance of power theory. In this regard, it must be pointed out that the test Levy suggests is offered as one that sets the minimal acceptable evidence for the theory. In other words, seeing if states on the European continent balance power against each other is something most supporters and critics expect the theory to predict and, therefore, if states do not do that, then that should be regarded by all as evidence against the theory. Levy recognizes that this is a "most likely" case, or a test that should be easily passed. There are other cases that would be more difficult and that would generate more disagreement as to whether Waltz's original proposition, the research program, or the logic of the theory would predict them. On the face of it, Waltz's (1979, 121) statement that "Balance-of-power politics prevail wherever two, and only two, requirements are met: that the order be anarchic and that it be populated by units wishing to survive," would appear to apply to all states whether they were continental or not, major states or not, or whether they sought to make a hegemonic bid.

To the extent that Levy sees the absence of balancing against naval powers, like Britain and the United States, as an established fact, then this must be taken as evidence against Waltz's original proposition, particularly since Waltz (1993) is still on record predicting that balancing will occur against the United States in the current post–Cold War period. To reformulate the theory in such a way as to confine it to continental states as part of an effort to establish the domain of the proposition in light of an examination of the historical record, without recognizing this failure to balance as discrepant evidence that goes against the theory, would be a degenerating shift of the evidentiary base. This would particularly be the case if one insisted (which Levy does not) that the logic of the theory makes this, rather than Waltz's original (and current) formulation, the true prediction of the theory. Instead of coming from neorealism's logic, Levy's prediction seems to be informed by the importance of naval power stipulated in Modelski and Thompson's (1989) long cycle theory. Thus, evidence of the absence of balancing against naval powers and their hegemonies could be taken as evidence in favor of Modelski and Thompson's emphasis and Levy's reformulation, while simultaneously being evidence against Waltz.

The discussion of whether states do not balance against naval powers but do balance against major continental states raises again the question of whether any given reformulation of a theory, including those that try to specify a domain, is a progressive or degenerating theoryshift. One indicator, but only one, is whether the new theory, T', has produced novel facts. A second indicator is whether these novel facts are derived and best explained by the logic of the theory (or the hard core of the research program). In the debate on balancing of power, the question of novel facts has centered mostly on Stephen Walt's (herein Ch. 4) claim that balancing of threat theory is a progressive problemshift because it embodies a novel fact—a position that Elman and Elman (herein Ch. 7) endorse.

Barnett's analysis (herein Ch. 14), however, raises questions about whether Walt's explanation is a progressive problemshift by arguing that Walt has failed to show how—in the cases he analyzes—threat emerges from anarchy or some other materialist (realist) variable. In Lakatosian terms, this makes Walt's reformulation appear to be an ad hoc$_3$ explanation (see Elman and Elman, herein, Ch. 7) in that it does not use the logic of anarchy (or power) to identify and explain the source of threat. Because the evidence that states balance threat instead of power is not predicted *ex ante* by the theory, but uncovered while seeing if states balance power the way Waltz predicts, this evidence can not be a novel fact. It is, by definition, discrepant evidence. All Walt has accomplished is to label the evidence in a way that hides its discrepant nature by calling it "balancing," when it could just as well be referred to as "states oppose those with whom they disagree." A truly novel fact would have to tell us something that was theoretically new and point to some set of behavior other than the unexpected outcome of a test of Waltz's proposition.

Barnett's reliance on constructivism to specify the source of threat shows how Walt's evidence on the failure to balance could be turned into a truly novel fact. If this behavior were expected by a different theory, and that theory could explain why power did not lead to threat and to balancing, then that would be a novel fact. Barnett's constructivist approach is able to do this because it has a theory of preference formation that is based on nonmaterialist variables. He sees threat as emerging from a clash of norms and identity formation, so for him threat does not stem solely (or in this case primarily) from the distribution of capability. In his approach, balancing against ideational threat that emerges from conflicting conceptions of order reflects behavior that is unexpected from realist theory, but consistent with constructivism. The novel fact that constructivism points to is that much of international relations involves a social construction of reality and these social constructions can be used to explain preference formation and interstate alliance formation. Barnett's analysis shows not only that Walt's balance of threat theory has identified an important anomaly and body of discrepant evidence, but that Walt's reformulation is not adequately derived from the logic of neorealism and thus must be ad hoc. He then goes on to use an alternate theory that can account for this discrepant evidence and explain it on the basis of a nonrealist and nonmaterialist theory of global politics. Each of these moves by Barnett suggests that a different theory of alliance formation would produce a research program that could do better than neorealism has done so far by using its own logic to explain why Walt found the discrepant evidence he did, and then using that same logic to point to new problems (dependent variables) that can be analyzed with new independent (nonmaterialist) variables.

Up to this point, the discussion has focused on Waltz's proposition and less on general patterns of alliance formation or other patterns expected by neorealism. The contributions of Bueno de Mesquita and of Zeev Maoz take a broader look. In different ways, each suggests problems with Waltz's neorealism based on evidence, about predictions, other than balancing. Bueno de Mesquita tests the second most important proposition in Waltz's *Theory of International Politics,* namely, that bipolarity is more stable (and less conflict prone) than multipolarity. Taking the period from 1945 to the end of the Cold War in 1990 as an indicator of bipolarity, Bueno de Mesquita shows that the bipolar era was not statistically different from other eras since 1648, either in its length (an indicator of stability) or the frequency with which it experienced wars. He finds that the so-called *long peace* of the bipolar era was not necessarily longer than other periods of peace that occurred in previous multipolar eras (e.g., 1815–1853; 1871–1914). Bueno de Mesquita's analysis is important because it shows that the absence of evidentiary support for Waltz's neorealism is not confined to just the proposition on balancing, but to both of his major propositions. This suggests that the problems are endemic to the theory as a whole, since it has failed to produce consistent evidence in favor of its theoretical expectations.

Zeev Maoz takes an even broader view. He does not look at specific Waltzian propositions, but rather the general realist expectations on alliance behavior. He argues that there must be something wrong with realist theory because the thrust of the empirical evidence shows that democratic states have different patterns of alliance behavior than other states. Since realism posits that alliance behavior is a function of external and strategic factors and not domestic factors, all states should behave in the same way. The fact that they do not implies that theories like liberalism, that do look at domestic factors, might be superior to realism or at least more consistent with the evidence.

Each of the above chapters has raised serious questions about: the utility of the concept of the balancing of power, Waltz's proposition on it, and the attempts of the neotraditional research program to save it by reformulating it into various "balancing theories." Many of the chapters (Schroeder, Rosecrance, Vasquez, and even parts of Levy) have questioned the extent to which balancing of power occurs in any regular pattern, and thus the extent to which it can be regarded as a law. This is a serious problem for Waltz, since he assumes that anarchy (which he sees as constant) gives rise to balancing-of-power politics; if it does not, then there must be something fundamentally wrong with his theory and its logic.

In addition, several of the chapters have shown that the very concept of balance of power has long had problems of ambiguity—of meaning different things and having more than one empirical referent (Schroeder, Rosecrance, Levy, Vasquez; see also Bueno de Mesquita). These have made it all too easy to shift what the theory and proposition really predict about balancing, as one or another prediction is found to be inconsistent with examinations of the historical record. Unlike the respondents in Part I and Elman (herein Ch. 1), I do not see these various realisms (neorealism, defensive realism, neoclassical realism) as separate and independent theories, even though they make different claims, but as a *family* of theories sharing certain fundamental assumptions about the world that can for certain purposes be treated in aggregate. The presence of different claims and predictions has made it difficult, as Levy has shown in detail, to test the theory in a definitive fashion; yet a research program that is always arguing that none of the tests of its main proposition are definitive is one that is naturally going to raise questions about its scientific viability. In this sense, tests of Waltz's other propositions (Bueno de Mesquita) or realism's other propositions on alliances (Maoz) that also fail to find support, add to these concerns about realism's ability to provide an adequate guide to research and understanding. Lastly, the analyses of Barnett, Maoz, Bueno de Mesquita, and Schroeder all suggest that fundamentally different (i.e., nonrealist) theoretical perspectives would be more consistent with the quantitative evidence and the historical record (although it must be pointed out that none of these authors agree on what the best alternate theory would be).

## B. Parsing Realism and Balance of Power Theory

### BY COLIN ELMAN

Vasquez's 1997 article (reprinted herein as Chapter 2), which incited this collection of essays, claims to apply MSRP to balance of power theory and to its near siblings. It finds that contemporary realism, or some subset thereof, is degenerating. In this section I argue that that conclusion is not supported by the case made in the original essay, nor by the essays contributed by realism's other critics in this book. Vasquez's main problems are an underspecification of the scientific research program (SRP) being critiqued, and a failure to take relevant evidence of corroborated, novel predictions into account. The five other critics of balance of power theory in the book (Schroeder, Levy, Maoz, Bueno de Mesquita, and Barnett) simply declined to employ Lakatos's metatheory. One could argue that they provided cogent discussions of various logical flaws and empirical weaknesses of different balance of power theories, but they do not support Vasquez's central thesis.

Theory appraisal involves the consecutive application of a series of decreasingly abstruse steps. Scholars begin by making epistemological choices—deciding which metatheory to employ and which of its variants to use (for example, with MSRP, which definition of novel fact to employ). They then need to apply that metric to describe and appraise the theoretical aggregate being judged. Employing MSRP requires a specification of theory T in the form of a description of the research program's hard core, negative heuristic, positive heuristic, and auxiliary belt. The appraiser then needs to provide a description of the next theoretical formulation, T', and to determine whether the problemshift from T to T' disobeyed the program's negative heuristic. If not, the problemshift was intra or within program, and all three Lakatosian criteria apply. If the shift disobeys the negative heuristic it represents a move between programs, and only the ad hoc$_1$ (no novel facts predicted) and ad hoc$_2$ (novel facts predicted not corroborated) criteria need to be applied.

It is, I think, a fair criticism that Vasquez underspecifies the hard core of the "balancing of power" research program. To be sure, any delineation of an SRP is likely to be contested (Cross 1982, 331–332). As Blaug (1991, 500–501; see also Blaug 1976, 167) suggests, "there is no way of writing down once and for all the precise content of the hard core of any SRP . . . that would command the universal assent of all the protagonists of that program . . . the notion that this is a simple and unambiguous exercise is, surely, naïve." That being said, such a description has to resonate with at least some of the scholars whose work the hard core is said to describe, and encompass some of the elements traditionally associated with that research. Vasquez's description of the hard core does neither. His account of the hard core of the balance of power research program was limited to the general statement that Walt, Christensen and Snyder, and Schweller

> all share certain concepts, are all concerned with balancing, share a view of the world, and share the general purpose of trying to work within and defend the [realist] paradigm.[10]

Not surprisingly, this description provoked trenchant complaints from the other participants in the initial debate.[11]

As described in greater detail in Chapter 1, Vasquez's rather broad description lumps together at least three different categories of balance of power theory. In manual balance of power theory, equilibrium results from the intentional acts of statesmen, who prefer a balanced system to alternatives. This can be because they believe that a balanced system is more likely to result in state survival, or because equilibrium carries with it some additional intrinsic benefits, such as a lower incidence of war. Dyadic balance of power theories suggest that states' actions are rational responses to threats posed by other states. Those threats can be operationalized by relative capabilities alone, or in combination with other indicators such as proximity and intentions. Automatic balance of power theory suggests that international political systems will tend toward balance regardless of the intentions or actions of individual states.

These different categories of balance of power theory make dissimilar substantive claims about both state behavior and international outcomes. These are summarized in Table 17.1. Both manual and dyadic balance of power theory predict balancing behavior, i.e., a countervailing policy designed to improve abilities to prosecute military missions in order to deter and/or defeat another state. The difference is that manual balancing is necessarily aimed at bringing about a balanced system, whereas dyadic balancing is intended to deal with a threat from a particular state.[12]

Both manual and dyadic theories also predict self-abnegation by states capable of expansionist behavior, although for different reasons. Under manual balance of power, a would-be hegemon declines to expand because it values a balanced system. Under dyadic balance of power, a revisionist state defers expansion in order to avoid provoking countervailing policies from states that would be threatened. The latter is based on an anticipated reaction, the former is not.

Strong versions of both these theories predict not only that states will behave in the manner described above, but that the associated systemic or dyadic outcomes will result. For manual balance of power theory, systemic balance is maintained by the intentional acts of states that believe a balanced system is best. For dyadic balance of power theory, dyadic (and in the case of hegemonic bids, systemic) balance is the result of countervailing action taken by threatened states, or self-denial by potential expanders who wish to avoid provoking such action.

TABLE 17.1  CATEGORIES OF BALANCE OF POWER THEORY AND THEIR ASSOCIATED PREDICTIONS

| Type of Balance of Power Theory | Behavioral Predictions | Systemic Outcome Predictions |
| --- | --- | --- |
| Manual | Balancing because of the virtues of a balanced system. Self-abnegation because of the virtues of a balanced system. | Balanced system as a result of balancing or self-abnegation aimed at bringing about a balanced system. |
| Dyadic | Balancing intended to countervail threatening state(s). Self-abnegation to avoid provoking countervailing reaction from threatened state(s). | Balanced dyad as a result of balancing aimed at a threatening state or self-abnegation to avoid provoking countervailing reaction. |
| Automatic | Indeterminate | Balanced system as a result of multiple sufficient negative feedback mechanisms. |

Automatic balance of power theory predicts that the international system will balance as a result of multiple sufficient negative feedback mechanisms. The system is characterized by equifinality: There are several pathways to balance, each adequate to bring about equilibrium. Since the system might follow any one of these pathways, automatic balance of power theory makes indeterminate behavioral predictions.

Not all categories of balance of power theory are equally represented in contemporary realism. As I noted in the introduction (Ch. 1 herein, 5–6), IR theorists distinguish between classical, neo- and neoclassical realism. The groupings are differentiated by the degree to which unit level causes are thought to influence foreign policy choices, and by the extent to which the theories are considered capable of making foreign policy predictions. Accordingly, while Wohlforth (Ch. 15 herein) trenchantly resists casting the subfield in paradigmatic terms, he is correct to argue that Waltz's critics mischaracterize the *Theory of International Politics* as a dyadic balance of power theory that makes specific foreign policy predictions. Similarly, while the details of Glaser's (Ch. 16 herein) description of the different realist camps differ somewhat from mine, he too notes that there are differences that should divide the scholarship that Vasquez and other critics of realism would aggregate. This might be less troubling if the different realist theories made similar claims about balancing behavior and the resulting distribution of capabilities, but they do not. While the earliest balance of power theories were manual, most modern realists' balance of power theories are either dyadic or automatic. Neorealists, and Waltz in particular, tend to be associated with automatic balance of power theory. Neoclassical realists are most likely to argue in favor of dyadic balance of power theory, where states balance against particular threats, not to bring the system into balance. Accordingly, it is ironic that realism's critics often seem interested in debunking manual balance of power theory by demonstrating the absence of a systemic equilibrium brought about by a state that values balance for its own sake.

While Vasquez's respondents are right to protest that he mistakenly conflates Waltz's *Theory of International Politics* with other theories, however, they are quite wrong to suggest that this excuses them from satisfying some of Lakatos's criteria. Waltz is simply mistaken when he observes that "One cannot judge the fertility of a research program by evaluating work done outside of it. . . . Schweller and I work within different research programs."[13] To be sure, Waltz's particular iteration of balance of power theory may be absolved, but Lakatos's MSRP judges trajectories, not freeze frames. Even interprogram problemshifts have to satisfy two of the three Lakatosian criteria—making novel theoretical predictions that are eventually corroborated. It is possible to argue (as Walt does) that Vasquez should not have chosen MSRP, but if you accept the metatheory, one cannot then say "it doesn't apply to theories in different research programs." It does.

Accordingly, acknowledging that Vasquez's weak specification allows him to mistakenly group different scholarship in the same research program does not undermine the position that MSRP is applicable to appraise this work. Since Vasquez does not try to hold the research to a particular positive heuristic, that error is more nominal than substantive. Because he still requires the new research to satisfy the two novel fact criteria that both inter and intra program problemshifts must fulfill, the hard core error is not fatal to his efforts. Ironically, in this case, Vasquez's partial description of MSRP (exclusion of the positive heuristic and ad hoc$_3$ criterion) protects him from the consequences of his misdescription of realism and its subsets.

That being said, Vasquez still has to demonstrate that the problemshifts were ad hoc$_1$ and ad hoc$_2$, and here I would argue he has a much more serious problem. In addition to an underspecified definition of novelty, Vasquez does not include all the work that might be considered probative in making a determination of a progressive or degenerating trajectory. In particular, Vasquez only looks at the innovating piece of work, the scholarship that introduced each theoretical amendment described above. He does not include other work by the same or different scholars that might use the innovation to make novel predictions. I would hypothesize that the reason for this is a confusion between anomaly solution and the absence of novel fact.

Vasquez concentrates on establishing that subsequent theories in the trajectory solved what he considers anomalies for Waltz's theory (failures of balances to form or of states to balance), but he pays little or no attention to demonstrating the absence of novel fact. Anomaly solution and the absence of novel fact are not the same thing. To be sure, MSRP finds the presence of anomaly solution suspicious, but it is not determinative. The appraiser has to satisfy herself that scholars did not subsequently use that amendment to make novel predictions. The fact that an amendment solved an anomaly is not, by itself, sufficient to establish that the trajectory is degenerating.

This is a different critique from that raised by Walt in his chapter, that Vasquez used a limited sample size and so reached a biased conclusion that undercounted realism's recent accomplishments. To be sure, there is something to the claim that a critique of realism that leaves out work by scholars such as John Mearsheimer, Steven Van Evera, Dale Copeland, and Christopher Layne is going to be less than comprehensive.[14] But Vasquez can reasonably respond that he was answering a narrower, more technical question about a particular type of realist scholarship, rather than attempting a broad survey of the tradition as a whole. My concern is that addressing even this more limited procedural question required casting a wider net in the hope of catching more novel facts.

Where might Vasquez have looked for such novel predictions? One possibility is in the later works of the same scholars he critiques. For example, he correctly notes that the balance of threat theory in Stephen Walt's *Origins of Alliances* was designed, in part, to account for lacunae in Waltz's *Theory of International Politics*. Accordingly, if we were to only consider that iteration of balance of threat theory, we might conclude that the shift from balance of power was regressive. One could argue, however, that the clearest demonstration of *theoretical* novelty arising from Walt's balance of threat theory did not take place until 1996, when he extended the theory to explain the connection between revolutions and war. Since revolutions did not figure in the process that produced balance of threat theory, Walt's (1996) use of the theory to make predictions about whether revolutions lead to international conflict can be considered heuristically novel. Similarly, Walt (2000) employs balance of threat theory to hypothesize whether the acquisition of weapons of mass destruction by rogue states will encourage or impede the formation of defensive coalitions to contain, coerce, or disarm them.

Nor does the theoretical innovation have to be used by the originating scholar. Elman and Elman (1998) made a similarly premature critique of Joseph Grieco's (1995) essay on the European Monetary Union. Grieco uses neorealism to explain international institutional innovation. We suggested that, although explicitly invoking MSRP, Grieco's claim that his new "voice opportunity" and "binding" hypotheses are progressive in Lakatosian terms is problematic. In the article, Grieco engages in a purely anomaly-solving exercise: He shows how neorealism can account for an instance of institutionalized cooperation that appears inconsistent with the theory. He argues that his new theoretical emendation "sheds additional light on several key aspects of EMU" and that it can "resolve puzzles about the politics of institutional cooperation that may not be fully covered by alternative approaches." Our conclusion was premature, since it did not include subsequent work by John Ikenberry that applies the binding hypothesis to new domains.[15]

If Vasquez's application of MSRP fails to support the conclusion that realism is degenerating, the contributions by the five additional critics of balance of power theory in the volume do not strengthen his case. Jack Levy (Ch. 10 herein, 130) acknowledges that his "focus is more on the level of theory specification and research design than on metatheory, and [he] leave[s] aside the question of the progressive or degenerative nature of the realist research program as a whole or of its theory of balancing in particular." Bruce Bueno de Mesquita fails to engage Vasquez's argument on either epistemological or substantive grounds. Epistemologically, Bueno de Mesquita (Ch. 12 herein, 169–170) is intent on hoisting Waltz by his own petard and demonstrating his failure to satisfy the criteria laid out in Chapter 1 of *Theory of International Politics*. Substantively, Bueno de Mesquita mainly focuses on logical and empirical problems with Waltz's hypothesis about the stability of bipolarity, not balancing, and in advancing Bueno de Mesquita's preferred alternative. Bueno de Mesquita makes little or no attempt to support Vasquez's argument that the Waltz-Walt-Christensen & Snyder-Schweller discourse is degenerating when judged by Lakatosian criteria.

Richard Rosecrance concentrates on demonstrating the inadequacy of a strong version of manual balance of power theory, which predicts that equilibrium is produced by states that value a balanced system and are willing to bear the costs of bringing the system into balance in order to enjoy that benefit. The problem is that none of the scholars critiqued by Vasquez (with the possible exception of Schweller) make that argument.[16] In addition, Rosecrance's (Ch. 11 herein, 155–156) simplified discussion of ad hoc theory amendments appears to be all stick and no carrot: It incorporates the Lakatosian club to punish theorists for making linguistic extensions but excludes the possibility that such changes are valuable if they satisfy MSRP's novel fact criteria.

Paul Schroeder (Ch. 9 herein, 114) acknowledges being an outsider in the "debate over Lakatosian theory and international relations theory in general, and in particular over the proposition that realism, especially structural realism, represents a degenerate IR research program." He comes at the question of whether balance of power theory is valuable as, and using the tools of, an (admittedly, unusually able and distinguished) historian. He is also, not unreasonably, interested in concluding an ongoing disagreement with Waltz. This was sparked by Schroeder's 1995 essay in which he critiqued *Theory of International Politics*, and which Waltz in turn vigorously criticizes in Chapter 3.

Michael Barnett's critique of Walt's *Origins of Alliances* (Ch. 14 herein) suggests that the incorporation of ideology into his balance of threat theory removes it from the realist camp. This account follows the initial stages of a metatheoretic critique, since it makes a serious attempt to delineate a hard core and to demonstrate that Walt's theoretical iteration disobeys it. However, even if everything Barnett writes is true (and Walt would dispute that), all he has demonstrated is that Waltz and Walt's respective theories belong in different research programs. Lakatos's novel fact criteria still need to be applied, and this step is not carried out. Barnett overstates the extent to which the degree of conformity with the hard core provides grounds for assessment in MSRP. For Lakatos, the existence of a hard core is one of the minimal requirements for a research program to subsist, and obedience/disobedience to the core can trigger the applicability of different assessment criteria. But conformity is not a virtue in and of itself. Straying from the hard core is permissible if it results in a fruitful problemshift; that is, if it produces another research program that tells us something new about the world. The reasons for permitting disobedience are fairly straightforward: If authenticity was an overriding virtue, scientists would still be sitting on a flat Earth around which the Sun revolved.

In sum, the answer to the charge "Is contemporary realism or some sub-set thereof dealing with balance of power theory degenerating?" is "not yet proven." It may well be that a more complete application of MSRP will demonstrate that contemporary realism has the failings Vasquez identifies. His essay has provoked a reconsideration of the subfield's epistemological paradigmatic underpinnings, and makes such a review both much more likely and much more likely that it will reach reliable conclusions. But we are not there yet.

## SECTION III   THE FUTURE OF THEORY APPRAISAL

We leave this book much more hopeful than we were when we entered the debate, both about the possibility of the field of international relations engaging in serious theory appraisal as a regular part of the discipline's agenda, and the possibility of advancing in fruitful directions the debate on the balancing of power.

One of the immediate beneficial consequences of the *APSR* forum debate (herein, Part I) was that theory appraisal and in particular the work of Imre Lakatos received more widespread attention. Almost immediately after the publication of the debate, Colin Elman and Miriam Elman (independently of Vasquez, but provoked by their participation in the *APSR* forum) convened a conference on Progress in International Relations Theory (PIRT) to examine how IR theorists could better equip themselves to determine whether their work is getting any better. The resulting project adopts a somewhat different approach than the present volume, which takes realism and the balancing of power as its deep focal point. By contrast, the PIRT project (see Elman and Elman 2002b) complements this book's concentrated application by taking a broader and more diverse approach. Leading scholars attempt a Lakatosian appraisal of several different research programs: Robert O. Keohane and Lisa L. Martin on institutionalist theory; Jonathan M. DiCicco and Jack S. Levy on the power transition research program; Andrew Moravcsik on the liberal research program; James Lee Ray on the democratic peace research program; and Stephen G. Walker on operational code analysis. In addition, Robert Jervis discusses the gap separating realism and neoliberalism, and Randall Schweller, Jack Snyder, David Dessler, Roslyn Simowitz, John Vasquez, and Andrew Bennett debate the pros and cons of Lakatosian and other theory appraisal metrics.

The chapters in this book, and those in Elman and Elman 2002b, show that theory appraisal is no easy task. Yet while there may be problems that need to be overcome, the attempt to explicitly specify appraisal criteria and justify them is an important contribution and an advance over the past. As James Lee Ray observes in Elman and Elman 2002b, "The broader the base of agreement in the field regarding the issue of how we know what we feel we know, the larger and more accommodating will be the platform accessible to all of us for fruitful dialogue. . . ." Specification and stipulation of definition makes it clearer to all involved where and why there is disagreement and more importantly where the strengths and weaknesses of various theories, research programs, and paradigms may lie. The discussion in this book makes these matters much clearer about the balancing of power and the research related to it than before the debate began.

A second contribution of specifying criteria for appraisal is that it affects how we do our research and our theorizing. By having explicit criteria in mind we frame our research designs, and we construct and emend theories in a certain way. After the debate in this book, we would expect that authors who work on theories of balancing of power will be more self-conscious and sophisticated users of both metatheory and theory. Thus, the question of whether something is a novel fact, whether an emendation is an ad hoc explanation (and of what type) are useful questions to consider, not only in terms of appraising theory but in terms of constructing it and testing it in the first place. In this way, we see theory appraisal as helping to move work on the balancing of power in a direction that will improve discourse and research on it, so that even if more of a consensus does not emerge on all of the key areas at least the work will become more precise and rigorous.

One of the ways in which this might occur is to get more agreement, even if it is only tacit, about what kinds of evidence or arguments would need to be presented in order to get scholars to accept some of the claims of the other side. Here, we think some of the conceptual work and the call for various empirical tests (historical case studies and quantitative tests) will help resolve some key controversies. In this sense some of the suggestions made by Waltz (Ch. 3), Vasquez (Ch. 8), and Levy (Ch. 10) all seem to point in the same direction. Of course, ultimately, it is not just the participants themselves that will need to be convinced, but members of the subfield as a whole.

If precision and rigor can aid the quality of work within a specific research program, it can provide even greater benefits for more diffuse and wide-ranging debates, like that over paradigms. Paradigm debates are sometimes scorned as paradigm wars, but in many ways they provide useful benefits for a discipline. They prevent the fracturing of a discipline into schools of thought that have little to do with each other. A discipline debating the merits of competing paradigms is a community of scholars engaged in each others' work, still keeping an open mind, and learning from each other. We would think that such a community of scholars would also more quickly uncover their mistakes and illusions than one that devolved into a community of like-minded people.

For years there had been discussion and debate about paradigms, in particular the merits of the realist paradigm, but only a few scholars have approached this debate through an attempt at systematic appraisal (Keohane and Nye 1971; Keohane 1983; Burton et al. 1974; Vasquez 1979, 1983; Banks 1985; Smith 1987; Simowitz and Price 1990; among others). With the rise of the debate on the democratic peace and the end of the Cold War, the field returned to a discussion of the merits of the realist paradigm, this time by comparing it to more fully developed alternative paradigms (see Lebow and Risse-Kappen 1995; Moravcsik 1997; Maoz 1998). The debate on the balancing of power comes in the middle of this larger debate on paradigms and provides an illustration of how criteria from philosophy of science can be applied to international relations theory.

There are dangers in a discipline wracked by debate over fundamentals. Sometimes everything can be reduced to debate, and no serious research is being done or published because there is so little consensus on the ground rules that one cannot tell what is competent research and what is not. Taking theory appraisal and philosophy of science seriously is a way of avoiding that kind of fracturing. It is our hope that the work in this book has made a small contribution to bringing rigorous theory appraisal more into the mainstream of the field.

## NOTES

1. This section draws on Elman and Elman 2002a and 2002b.
2. Laudan 1977, 85.
3. Elman and Elman 2002a.
4. Vasquez, Ch. 2 herein, 28.
5. See also Diesing 1991, 61.
6. While Lakatos himself very occasionally used the term *paradigm* when referring to metatheoretical units in general, (see, for example, Lakatos 1970, 155, 177–180) he clearly believed that MSRP was distinct from Kuhn's approach See, for example, Lakatos 1971b, 120.
7. Vasquez 1998, 7–9, 30–31, 250. Vasquez is not the only IR scholar who combines these epistemologies. See, for example, Helga Haftendorn (1991, 12), who questions whether "our present research programs are adequate to construct new paradigms." There are, however, several IR scholars who register the differences between Kuhn and Lakatos, recognizing in particular that, contra Kuhn, Lakatos's MSRP aspires to provide rational and universal criteria for scientific appraisal (for example, Kratochwil 1984, 314; Krasner 1985, 137; Snyder 1985, 92; Keohane 1989, 37; Simowitz and Price 1990, 442–443; and Wohlforth, Ch. 15 herein).
8. Vasquez, 2002.

9. Vasquez 1998, 245n2. In the book chapter version of his essay, Vasquez also provides several definitions of novel fact, variously "something about the world and its regularities other than what was uncovered by the discrepant evidence"; "new propositions and predictions (or observations) that the original theory did not anticipate"; and facts that "tell us things we did not (theoretically) know before." Vasquez 1998, 244, 246, 247. Although all describe "increased content," these definitions do not make it clear what type of novel fact he is applying.
10. Vasquez 1998, 254.
11. Waltz, Ch. 3 herein, 52–53; Schweller, Ch. 6 herein, 74; Christensen and Snyder, Ch. 5 herein, 66; and Walt, Ch. 4 herein, 60–61.
12. Jack Levy suggests in his chapter that the two versions become indistinguishable where a state makes a bid for hegemony, since both manual and dyadic theories predict that other states will countervail.
13. Waltz, Ch. 3 herein, 52–53.
14. There is, of course, another sense in which Walt's complaint about a biased sample holds true: All the other scholars Vasquez critiques (Waltz, Snyder, Christensen, Schweller, Elman and Elman) received their doctorates from Columbia University.
15. Ikenberry (2001) uses Grieco's binding hypothesis to help answer the question, "What do states that have just won major wars do with their newly acquired power?"
16. It is ambiguous whether Schweller's (1998a, 84) lions are dyadic or manual balancers, since "they are willing to pay high costs to protect and defend the existing international order."

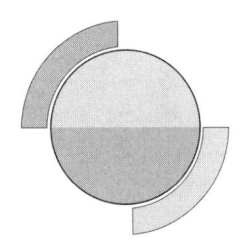

# REFERENCES

Alexander, Jeffrey. 1987. *Twenty Lectures: Sociological Theory Since World War II*. New York: Columbia University Press.
Altfeld, Michael. 1984. "The Decision to Ally: A Model and a Test." *Western Political Quarterly*, 37 (3) (December): 523–544.
Anderson, Olive. 1967. *A Liberal State at War: English Politics and Economics during the Crimean War*. New York: St. Martin's.
Anderson, M. S. 1966. *18th-Century Europe, 1713–1789*. New York: Oxford University Press.
Aron, Raymond. 1966. *Peace and War: A Theory of International Relations*. Translated by Richard Howard and Annette Baker Fox. Garden City, NY: Doubleday.
Aron, Raymond. 1973. *Peace and War*. Translated by Richard Howard and Annette Baker Fox. Garden City, NY: Doubleday/Anchor Press.
Arquilla, John. 1992. "Balancing, Bandwagoning, and Bystanding." Paper presented at annual meeting of the American Political Science Association, Chicago, Illinois.
Ashley, Richard K. 1986. "The Poverty of Neorealism." In *Neorealism and Its Critics*, ed. Robert O. Keohane. New York: Columbia University Press.
Ayoob, Mohammad. 1994. *Third World Security Problematique*. Boulder, CO: Lynne Reinner
Backhouse, Roger E. 1998 "Paradigm/Normal Science." Pp. 352–354 in *The Handbook of Economic Methodology*, ed. John B. Davis, D. Wade Hands, and Uskali Maki. Northhampton, MA: Edward Elgar.
Bagby, Laurie M. Johnson. 1994. "The Use and Abuse of Thucydides in International Relations." *International Organization* 48 (1) (winter).
Baldwin, David, ed. 1993. *Neorealism and Neoliberalism: The Contemporary Debate*. New York: Columbia University Press.
Banks, Michael. 1985. "The Inter-Paradigm Debate." In *A Handbook of Current Theory*, ed. Margot Light and A. J. R. Groom. London: Frances Pinter.
Barnett, Corelli. [c. 1972] 1984. *The Collapse of British Power*. Gloucester, UK: A. Sutton.
Barnett, Michael N. 1996. "Identity and Alliances in the Middle East." Pp. 400–447 in *The Culture of National Security: Norms and Identity in World Politics*, ed. Peter J. Katzenstein. New York: Columbia University Press.
Barnett, Michael. 1998. *Dialogues in Arab Politics: Negotiations in Regional Order*. New York: Columbia University Press.
Barnett, Michael, and Jack Levy. 1991. "The Domestic Sources of Alignments and Alliances: The Case of Egypt, 1962–1973." *International Organization* 45 (3) (summer): 369–396.

Bedford, David and Thom Workman. 2001. "The Tragic Reading of the Thucydidean Tragedy." *Review of International Studies* 27 (1) (January): 51–67.
Bell, P. M. H. 1986. *The Origins of the Second World War in Europe*. London: Longman.
Bennett, Andrew, and Alexander George. 1999. *Case Studies and Theory Development*. Cambridge, MA: MIT Press.
Bennett, D. Scott, and Allan Stam. 1998. "Comparative Theory Testing: Expected Utility versus All Comers." Paper presented at the Annual Meeting of the International Studies Association, Minneapolis, Minnesota.
Berger, Thomas. 2000. "Set for Stability? Prospects for Conflict and Cooperation in East Asia." *Review of International Studies* 26 (3) (July): 405–428.
Biddle, Stephen. 1998. "Recasting the Foundations of Offense-Defense Theory." Paper presented at the annual meeting of the American Political Science Association, Boston.
Biles, Peter. 2000. "Bitter Foes." *The World Today* 56 (7) (July): 11–13.
Blainey, Geoffrey. 1973. *The Causes of War*. New York: Free Press.
Blaug, Mark. 1976. "Kuhn versus Lakatos or Paradigms versus Research Programmes in the History of Economics." In *Method and Appraisal in Economics*, ed. Spiro J. Latsis. New York: Cambridge University Press.
Blaug, Mark. 1991. "Afterword." Pp. 499–512 in *Appraising Economic Theories: Studies in the Methodology of Research Programs*, ed. Neil de Marchi and Mark Blaug. Brookfield, VT.: Edward Elgar.
Blaug, Mark. 1992. *The Methodology of Economics: Or How Economists Explain*. 2nd ed. New York: Cambridge University Press.
Bobrow, Davis B. 1972. *International Relations: New Approaches*. New York: Free Press.
Bochenski, J. M. 1965. *The Methods of Contemporary Thought*. Translated by Peter Caws. Dordrecht, Holland: D. Reidel Publishing.
Boswell, Terry, and Mike Sweat. 1991. "Hegemony, Long Waves, and Major Wars: A Time Series Analysis of Systemic Dynamics, 1496–1967." *International Studies Quarterly* 35 (June): 123–149.
Boulding, Kenneth E. [c. 1962] 1963. *Conflict and Defense*. New York: Harper.
Brecher, Michael. 1999. "International Studies in the Twentieth Century and Beyond: Flawed Dichotomies, Synthesis, Cumulation." *International Studies Quarterly* 43 (2): 213–264.
Bremer, Stuart. 1992. "Dangerous Dyads: Conditions Affecting the Likelihood of Interstate War, 1816–1965." *Journal of Conflict Resolution*, 36 (2): 309–341.
Bremer, Stuart. 1993. "Democracy and Militarized Interstate Conflict, 1816–1965." *International Interactions*, 18 (3): 231–249.
Bridge, F. R. 1972. *Great Britain and Austria-Hungary 1906–1914: A Diplomatic History*. London: Weidenfeld and Nicolson.
Bridge, F. R. 1990. *The Habsburg Monarchy among the Great Powers, 1815–1918*. New York: Berg.
Brodie, Bernard. 1941. *Sea Power in the Machine Age*. London: H. Milford.
Brooks, Stephen. 1997. "Dueling Realisms." *International Organization* 51 (3) (summer): 445–477.
Brooks, Stephen G., and William C. Wohlforth. 2002. "American Primacy in Perspective." *Foreign Affairs* 81 (July/August): 20–33.
Brown, Michael, Sean Lynn-Jones, and Steven Miller, eds. 1995. *The Perils of Anarchy: Contemporary Realism and International Security*. Cambridge, MA: MIT Press.
Bueno de Mesquita, Bruce. 1975. "Measuring Systemic Polarity." *Journal of Conflict Resolution* 19 (2) (June): 187–216.
Bueno de Mesquita, Bruce. 1978. "Systemic Polarization and the Occurrence and Duration of War." *Journal of Conflict Resolution* 22 (2) (June): 241–267.
Bueno de Mesquita, Bruce. 1981a. "Risk, Power Distributions, and the Likelihood of War." *International Studies Quarterly* 25 (4) (December): 541–568.
Bueno de Mesquita, Bruce. 1981b. *The War Trap*. New Haven, CT: Yale University Press.
Bueno de Mesquita, Bruce. 1984. "A Critique of 'A Critique of *The War Trap*.'" *Journal of Conflict Resolution* 28 (2) (June): 341–360.

Bueno de Mesquita, Bruce. 1989. "The Contribution of Expected-Utility Theory to the Study of International Conflict." In *Handbook of War Studies*, ed. Manus Midlarsky. Boston, MA: Unwin Hyman.
Bueno de Mesquita, Bruce. 1999a. "Neorealism's Logic and Evidence: When Is a Theory Falsified?" Paper presented at the 50th annual meeting of the International Studies Association. Washington, D.C., February 16–20.
Bueno de Mesquita, Bruce. 1999b. *Principles of International Politics: People's Power, Preferences, and Perception.* Washington, D.C.: CQ Press.
Bueno de Mesquita, Bruce. 2001. "Neorealism's Logic and Evidence: When Is a Theory Falsified?" Stanford, CA: Hoover Institution, unpublished paper.
Bueno de Mesquita, Bruce, and David Lalman. 1988. "Empirical Support for Systemic and Dyadic Explanations of War." *World Politics* 41 (1) (October): 1–20.
Bueno de Mesquita, Bruce, and David Lalman. 1992. *War and Reason: Domestic and International Imperatives.* New Haven, CT: Yale University Press.
Bueno de Mesquita, Bruce, Stephen Krasner, and Robert Jervis. 1985. "Symposium: Methodological Foundations of the Study of International Conflict." *International Studies Quarterly* 29 (2) (June): 121–136.
Bull, Hedley. 1977. *The Anarchical Society: A Study of Order in World Politics.* New York: Columbia University Press.
Bullen, Roger. 1980. "France and Europe, 1815–48: The Problem of Defeat and Recovery." Pp. 122–145 in *Europe's Balance of Power, 1815–48*, ed. Alan Sked. London: Macmillan.
Burton, John W., A. J. R. Groom, Chris Mitchell, and A. V. S. de Reuck. 1974. "The Study of World Society: A London Perspective." Occasional Paper, No. 1, International Studies Association.
Butterfield, Herbert. 1953. *Christianity, Diplomacy and War.* London: Epworth Press.
Butterfield, Herbert. 1966. "The Balance of Power." Pp. 132–148 in *Diplomatic Investigations: Essays in the Theory of International Politics*, ed. Herbert Butterfield and Martin Wight. Cambridge, MA: Harvard University Press.
Caldwell, Bruce J. 1991. "The Methodology of Scientific Research Programmes in Economics: Criticisms and Conjectures." Pp. 95–107 in *Economics, Culture and Education: Essays in Honor of Mark Blaug*, ed. G. K. Shaw. Brookfield, VT: Edward Elgar.
Carr, Edward Hallett. 1939. *The Twenty Years' Crisis: 1919–1939.* London: Macmillan.
Carr, Edward Hallett. 1945. *Nationalism and After.* London: Macmillan.
Carr, Edward Hallett. [1946] 1964. *The Twenty Years' Crisis, 1919– 1939: An Introduction to the Study of International Relations.* New York: Harper and Row.
Carrier, Martin. 1988. "On Novel Facts: A Discussion of Criteria for Non-ad-hoc-ness in the Methodology of Scientific Research Programmes." *Zeitschrift für Allgemeine Wissenschaftstheorie* 19 (2): 205–231.
Chace, James. 1998. "The Balance of Power." *World Policy Journal* 15 (4): 105–106.
Christensen, Thomas J. 1996. *Useful Adversaries: Grand Strategy, Domestic Mobilization, and Sino-American Conflict, 1947–1958.* Princeton, NJ: Princeton University Press.
Christensen, Thomas J. 1997. "Perceptions and Alliances in Europe, 1865–1940." *International Organization* 51 (winter): 65–98.
Christensen, Thomas J., and Jack Snyder. 1990. "Chain Gangs and Passed Bucks: Predicting Alliance Patterns in Multipolarity." *International Organization* 44 (2) (spring): 137–168.
Christensen, Thomas J., and Jack Snyder. 1997. "Progressive Research on Degenerate Alliances." *American Political Science Review* 91 (December): 919–922.
Churchill, Winston S. 1948. *The Gathering Storm.* Boston, MA: Houghton Mifflin.
Claude, Inis L., Jr. 1962. *Power and International Relations.* New York: Random House.
Claude, Inis L., Jr. 1989. "The Balance of Power Revisited." *Review of International Studies* 15 (April): 77–85.
Cobden, Richard. 1878. *Political Writings.* London: W. Ridgway.
Conant, James B. 1947. *On Understanding Science.* New Haven, CT: Yale University Press.
Copeland, Dale. 2000. *The Origins of Major War.* Ithaca, NY: Cornell University Press.
Cross, Rod. 1982. "The Duhem-Quine Thesis, Lakatos and the Appraisal of Theories in Macroeconomics." *Economic Journal* 92: 320–340.

Damasio, Antonio. 1994. *Descartes's Error: Emotion, Reason, and the Human Brain*. New York: G. P. Putnam.
Danilovic, Vesna. 2001. "Conceptual and Selection Bias Issues in Deterrence." *Journal of Conflict Resolution* 45 (February): 97–125.
Dann, Uriel. 1989. *King Hussein and the Challenge of Arab Radicalism: Jordan, 1955–67*. New York: Oxford University Press.
David, Stephen. 1991. "Explaining Third World Alignment." *World Politics* 43 (2) (summer): 233–256.
Davis, James W., Jr., and Bernard I. Finel, Stacie E. Goddard, Stephen Van Evera, Charles L. Glaser, and Chaim Kaufmann. 1998/99. "Correspondence: Taking Offense at Offense-Defense Theory." *International Security* 23 (winter): 179–206.
Dawn, C. Ernest. 1996. "The Other Arab Responses." In *The Six-Day War: A Retrospective*, ed. Richard Parker. Gainesville, FL: University Press of Florida.
de Marchi, Neil. 1991. "Introduction: Rethinking Lakatos." In *Appraising Economic Theories: Studies in the Methodology of Research Programs*, ed. Neil de Marchi and Mark Blaug. Brookfield, VT: Edward Elgar.
Dehio, Ludwig. 1961. *The Precarious Balance*. New York: Vintage.
Dehio, Ludwig. 1962. *The Precarious Balance: Four Centuries of the European Struggle*. New York: Knopf.
Desch, Michael. 1996. "Why Realists Disagree about the Third World (and Why They Shouldn't)." *Security Studies* 5 (3) (spring): 358–384.
Desch, Michael. 1997. "When Culture Matters (and When It Doesn't)." Paper presented at the Program on International Politics, Economics, and Security, January 23.
Desch, Michael. 1998. "Culture Clash: Assessing the Importance of Ideas in Security Studies." *International Security* 23 (1) (summer): 141–170.
Dessler, David. 1999a. "Explanation and Scientific Progress." Paper prepared for the conference on "Progress in International Relations Theory: A Collaborative Assessment and Application of Imre Lakatos's Methodology of Scientific Research Programs," January 15–16, 1999, Scottsdale, AZ.
Dessler, David. 1999b. Scientific Inference as Reasoning to the Best Explanation. Paper prepared for the 50th annual meeting of the International Studies Association. Washington, D.C., February 16–20.
Dessler, David. n.d. *Positivism in World Politics*. Manuscript in progress.
Dessouki, Ali Hillal. 1989. "Nasser and the Struggle for Independence." In *1956: The Crisis and Its Consequences*, ed. Roger Owen and Wm. Roger Louis. New York: Oxford University Press.
Deudney, Daniel. 1993. "Dividing Realism: Structural Realism and Security Materialism on Nuclear Security and Proliferation." *Security Studies* 2 (314) (summer): 7–36.
Deutsch, Karl W., and J. David Singer. 1964. "Multipolar Power Systems and International Stability." *World Politics* 16 (3) (April): 390–406.
Deutsch, Karl, and J. David Singer. 1969. "Multipolar Power Systems and International Stability." Pp. 315–324 in *International Politics and Foreign Policy*, ed. James N. Rosenau, rev. ed. New York: Free Press.
Devlin, Keith. 1997. *Goodbye Descartes: The End of Logic and the Search for a New Cosmology*. New York: John Wiley.
DiCicco, Jonathan M., and Jack S. Levy. 1998. "Power Shifts and Problem Shifts: The Evolution of the Power Transition Research Program." Paper prepared for the conference on "Progress in International Relations Theory: A Collaborative Assessment and Application of Imre Lakatos's Methodology of Scientific Research Programs," January 15–16, 1999, Scottsdale, AZ.
DiCicco, Jonathan M., and Jack S. Levy. 2002. "The Power Transition Research Program: A Lakatosian Analysis." In *Progress in International Relations Theory: Appraising the Field*, ed. Colin Elman and Miriam Fendius Elman. Cambridge, MA: MIT Press.
Diesing, Paul. 1991. *How Does Social Science Work? Reflections on Practice*. Pittsburgh, PA: University of Pittsburgh Press.

Donnelly, Jack. 1995. "Realism and International Relations." In *Political Science in History: Research Programs and Political Traditions*, ed. James Farr, John S. Dryzek, and Stephen T. Leonard. New York: Cambridge University Press.
Donnelly, Jack. 2000. *Realism and International Relations*. Cambridge, MA: Cambridge University Press.
Donovan, Arthur, Larry Laudan, and Rachel Laudan. 1992. *Scrutinizing Science: Empirical Studies of Scientific Change*. 2nd ed. Baltimore, MD: The Johns Hopkins University Press.
Dorn, Walter L. 1940. *Competition for Empire, 1740–1763*. New York: Harper & Row.
Doyle, Michael W. 1986. "Liberalism and World Politics." *American Political Science Review* 80 (4) (December): 1151–1169.
Doyle, Michael W. 1997. *Ways of War and Peace*. New York: W. W. Norton.
Duchhardt, Heinz. 1979. *Studien zur Friedensvermittlung in der frühen Neuzeit*. Wiesbaden, Ger.: F. Steiner.
Duchhardt, Heinz, ed. 1991. *Zwischenstaatliche Friedenswahrung im Mittelalter und früher Neuzeit*. Cologne, Ger.: Böhlau.
Dunne, Tim, Michael Cox, and Ken Booth, eds. 1998. "Special Issue: The Eighty Years' Crisis 1919–1999." *Review of International Studies* 24 (5) (December).
Edelstein, David. 2000. *Choosing Your Enemy: Perceived Intentions and International Politics*. Ph.D. Dissertation, University of Chicago.
el-Gamasy, Mohammed. 1993. *The October War*. Cairo, Egypt: American University in Cairo Press.
Elman, Colin. 1996a. "Horses for Courses: Why Not Neorealist Theories of Foreign Policy?" *Security Studies* 6 (1) (autumn): 7–53.
Elman, Colin. 1996b. "Cause, Effect, and Consistency: A Response to Kenneth Waltz." *Security Studies* 6 (1) (autumn): 58–61.
Elman, Colin. 2001a. "Parsing Realism: How (Not) to Adjudicate Authenticity and Adjustment in IR Theory." Paper prepared for presentation at the Program on International Security Policy, University of Chicago, April 24.
Elman, Colin. 2001b. "History, Theory, and the Democratic Peace." *International History Review* 23 (December): 757–766.
Elman, Colin. 2002. "Recovering Realism: John Mearsheimer's *The Tragedy of Great Power Politics*." Paper prepared for delivery at the Annual Meeting of the American Political Science Association, Boston, August 29–September 1, 2002.
Elman, Colin, and Miriam Fendius Elman. 1995. "Correspondence: History vs. Neorealism: A Second Look." *International Security* 20 (1) (summer): 182–193.
Elman, Colin, and Miriam Fendius Elman. 1997. "Lakatos and Neorealism: A Reply to John A. Vasquez." *American Political Science Review* 91 (4): 923–926.
Elman, Colin, and Miriam Fendius Elman. 1998. "Progress in International Relations Theory: Information and Suggestions for Project Participants." Paper prepared for participants in "Progress in International Relations Theory: A Collaborative Assessment and Application of Imre Lakatos's Methodology of Scientific Research Programs," January 15–16, 1999, Scottsdale, AZ.
Elman, Colin, and Miriam Fendius Elman. 2002a. "How Not to Be Lakatos Intolerant: Appraising Progress in IR Research." *International Studies Quarterly* 46 (2) (June): 231–262.
Elman, Colin, and Miriam Fendius Elman, eds. 2002b. *Progress in International Relations Theory: Appraising the Field*. Cambridge, MA: MIT Press.
Farber, Henry S., and Joanne Gowa. 1995. "Polities and Peace." *International Security*, 20 (2): 123–146.
Farber, Henry S., and Joanne Gowa. 1997. "Common Interests or Common Polities? Reinterpreting the Democratic Peace." *The Journal of Politics* 59 (2) (May): 393–417.
Fearon, James D. 1992. "Threats to Use Force: The Role of Costly Signals in International Crises." Ph.D. dissertation. Berkeley, CA: University of California.
Fearon, James D. 1994. "Signaling versus the Balance of Power and Interests: An Empirical Test of a Crisis Bargaining Model." *Journal of Conflict Resolution* 38 (2) (June): 236–269.
Fearon, James D. 1995. "Rationalist Explanations for War." *International Organization* 49 (3) (summer): 379–414.

Fearon, James D. 1998. "Domestic Politics, Foreign Policy, and Theories of International Relations." *Annual Review of Political Science* 1:289–313.
Feaver, Peter D., Gunther Hellman, Randall L. Schweller, Jeffrey W. Taliaferro, and William C. Wohlforth. 2000. "Correspondence: Brother Can You Spare a Paradigm? (Or Was Anybody Ever a Realist?)" *International Security* 25 (summer): 165–184.
Feyerabend, Paul K. 1975. *Against Method: Outline of an Anarchistic Theory of Knowledge*. London: NLB.
Fierke, K. M. 1998. *Changing Games, Changing Strategies: Critical Investigations in Security*. Manchester, UK: Manchester University Press.
Finifter, Ada. 1997. Editor's Notes. *American Political Science Review* 91 (4): viii.
Finnemore, Martha, and Kathryn Sikkink. 1998. "International Norm Dynamics and Political Change." *International Organization* 52 (autumn): 887–918.
Fischer, Fritz. 1967. *Germany's Aims in the First World War*. New York: W. W. Norton.
Foucault, Michel. 1972. *The Archaeology of Knowledge*. New York: Pantheon.
Fogel, Robert. *Railroads and American Economic Growth: Essays in Econometric History*. Baltimore, MD: Johns Hopkins University Press.
Forde, Steven. 1995. "International Realism and the Science of Politics: Thucydides, Machiavelli, and Neorealism." *International Studies Quarterly* 39 (June 1995): 141–160.
Frank, Robert H. 1991. "Positional Externalities." In *Strategy and Choice*, ed. Richard J. Zeckhauser. Cambridge, MA: MIT Press.
Frankel, Benjamin, ed. 1996a. *Roots of Realism*. London: Frank Cass.
Frankel, Benjamin, ed. 1996b. *Realism: Restatements and Renewal*. London: Frank Cass.
Frankel, Benjamin. 1996c. "Restating the Realist Case: An Introduction." *Security Studies* 5 (spring): ix–xx.
French, David. 1986. *British Strategy and War Aims, 1914–1916*. London: Unwin Hyman.
Friedman, Thomas L. 1999. *The Lexus and the Olive Tree*. New York: Farrar, Straus, Giroux.
Gaddis, John Lewis. 1980. *The Long Peace: Inquiries into the History of the Cold War*. New York: Oxford University Press.
Gaddis, John Lewis. 1992/1993. "International Relations Theory and the End of the Cold War." *International Security* 17 (3) (winter): 5–58.
Gallman, Waldemar. 1964. *Iraq under General Nuri: My Recollections of Nuri al-Said, 1954–58*. Baltimore, MD: Johns Hopkins University Press.
Garnham, David. 1991. "Explaining Middle Eastern Alignments during the Gulf War." *Jerusalem Journal of International Relations* 13 (September): 63–83.
Garst, Daniel. 1989. "Thucydides and Neorealism." *International Studies Quarterly* 33 (1) (March): 3–27.
Gartzke, Erik. 1998. "Why Kant We All Just Get Along? Opportunity, Willingness and the Origins of the Democratic Peace." *American Journal of Political Science*, 42 (1): 1–27.
Gartzke, Erik, and Michael W. Simon. 1998. "A General Test of Alliance Theory." Mimeographed, Penn State University.
Geller, Daniel S., and J. David Singer. 1998. *Nations at War: A Scientific Study of International Conflict*. Cambridge, MA: Cambridge University Press.
Gelpi, Christopher, and Joseph Grieco. 1998. "Democracy, Crisis Bargaining, and Audience Costs: Analyzing the Survival of Political Elites." Paper presented at the Annual Meeting of the American Political Science Association, Boston, MA, August 31–September 3.
George, Alexander L., and Richard Smoke. 1974. *Deterrence in American Foreign Policy: Theory and Practice*. New York: Columbia University Press.
George, Jim. 1994. *Discourses of Global Politics: A Critical (Re)Introduction to International Relations*. Boulder, CO: Lynne Rienner.
Gerges, Fawaz. 1994. *The Superpowers and the Middle East: Regional and International Influences*. Boulder, CO: Westview Press.
Gilpin, Robert. 1981. *War and Change in World Politics*. New York: Cambridge University Press.
Gilpin, Robert. 1986. "The Richness of the Tradition of Political Realism." In *Neorealism and Its Critics*, ed. Robert O. Keohane. New York: Columbia University Press.
Gilpin, Robert. [1981] 1987. *The Political Economy of International Relations*. Princeton, NJ: Princeton University Press.

Gilpin, Robert. 1996. "No One Loves a Political Realist." *Security Studies* 5 (spring): 3–26.
Glaser, Charles L. 1994–95. "Realists as Optimists: Cooperation as Self-Help." *International Security* 19 (3) (winter): 50–90.
Glaser, Charles L. 1997. "The Security Dilemma Revisited." *World Politics* 50 (1) (October): 171–210.
Glaser, Charles L., and Chaim Kaufmann. 1988. "What Is the Offense-Defense Balance and Can We Measure It." *International Security* 22 (spring): 44–82.
Goldgeier, James, and Michael McFaul. 1992. "A Tale of Two Worlds: Core and Periphery in the Post–Cold War Era." *International Organization* 46 (spring): 467–492.
Gorodetsky, Gabriel. 1999. *Grand Delusion: Stalin and the German Invasion of Russia.* New Haven, CT: Yale University Press.
Gowa, Joanne. 1999. *Ballots and Bullets: The Elusive Democratic Peace.* Princeton, NJ: Princeton University Press.
Green, Donald P., and Ian Shapiro. 1994. *Pathologies of Rational Choice Theory: A Critique of Applications in Political Science.* New Haven, CT: Yale University Press.
Grieco, Joseph M. 1988. "Anarchy and the Limits of Cooperation: A Realist Critique of the Newest Liberal Institutionalism." *International Organization* 42 (3) (summer): 485–507.
Grieco, Joseph M. 1990. *Cooperation among Nations: Europe, America, and the Non-Tariff Barriers to Trade.* Ithaca, NY: Cornell University Press.
Grieco, Joseph M. 1993. "Anarchy and the Limits of Cooperation: A Realist Critique of the Newest Liberal Institutionalism." Pp. 116–140 in *Neorealism and Neoliberalism: The Contemporary Debate,* ed. David Baldwin. New York: Columbia University Press.
Grieco, Joseph M. 1995. "The Maastricht Treaty, Economic and Monetary Union and the Neorealist Research Programme." *Review of International Studies* 21 (January): 21–40.
Grunbaum, Adolph. 1976a. "Can a Theory Answer More Questions Than One of Its Rivals?" *British Journal for the Philosophy of Science* 27 (March): 1–23.
Grunbaum, Adolph. 1976b. "Ad Hoc Auxiliary Hypotheses and Falsificationism." *British Journal for the Philosophy of Science* 27 (December): 329–362.
Gulick, Edward Vose. 1955. *Europe's Classical Balance of Power.* New York: Norton.
Gulick, Edward Vose. 1967. *Europe's Classical Balance of Power: A Case History of the Theory and Practice of One of the Great Concepts of European Statecraft.* New York: W. W. Norton & Co.
Haas, Ernst B. 1953. "The Balance of Power: Prescription, Concept, or Propaganda?" *World Politics* 5 (April): 442–477.
Haftendorn, Helga. 1991 "The Security Puzzle: Theory-Building and Discipline-Building in International Security." *International Studies Quarterly* 35 (March): 3–17.
Hahn, H. W. 1984. *Geschichte des Deutschen Zollvereins.* Göttingen, Ger.: Vandenhoeck and Ruprecht.
Hands, D. Wade. 1991a. "The Problem of Excess Content: Economics, Novelty, and a Long Popperian Tale." In *Appraising Economic Theories: Studies in the Methodology of Research Programs,* ed. Neil de Marchi and Mark Blaug. Brookfield, VT: Edward Elgar.
Hands, D. Wade. 1991b. "Reply to Hamminga and Maki." In *Appraising Economic Theories: Studies in the Methodology of Research Programs,* ed. Neil de Marchi and Mark Blaug. Brookfield, VT: Edward Elgar.
Harris, Errol E. 1970. *Hypothesis and Perception.* London: Allen and Unwin.
Hartmann, Frederick H. 1978. *The Relations of Nations.* 5th ed. New York: Macmillan.
Heikal, Mohammad. 1987. *Cutting the Lion's Tail: Suez Through Egyptian Eyes.* New York: Arbor House.
Heikal, Mohammad. 1996. *Secret Channels.* London: Harper Collins.
Hensel, Paul. 2000. "Territory: Theory and Evidence on Geography and Conflict." Pp. 57–84 in *What Do We Know About War?* ed. John A. Vasquez. Lanham, MD: Rowman & Littlefield.
Herz, John. 1962. *International Politics in the Atomic Age.* Paperback ed. New York: Columbia University Press.
Hirsch, Fred. 1976. *The Social Limits to Growth.* Cambridge, MA: Harvard University Press.
Hoffmann, Stanley, ed. 1960. *Contemporary Theory in International Relations.* Englewood Cliffs, NJ: Prentice Hall.

Hoffmann, Stanley. 1968. "Balance of Power." *International Encyclopedia of the Social Sciences.* Vol. 1. New York: Macmillan, 506–510.
Hoffmann, Stanley, and David Fidler, eds. 1991. *Rousseau on International Relations.* New York: Oxford University Press.
Hollis, Martin, and Steve Smith. 1990. *Explaining and Understanding International Relations.* Oxford: Clarendon Press.
Holsti, K. J. 1985. *The Dividing Discipline: Hegemony and Diversity in International Theory.* Boston, MA: Allen & Unwin.
Hopf, Ted, and John Lewis Gaddis. 1993 "Correspondence: Getting the End of the Cold War Wrong." *International Security* 18 (2) (fall): 202–215.
Hotelling, Harold. 1929. "Stability in Competition." *Economic Journal* 39 (March): 41–57.
Hufbauer, Gary Clyde, Jeffrey J. Schott, and Kimberly Ann Elliot. 1990. *Economic Sanctions Reconsidered.* 2 vols. Washington, D.C.: Institute for International Economics.
Hui, Victoria Tin-bor. Forthcoming. *War and State Formation in Ancient China and Early Modern Europe.* New York: Cambridge University Press.
Huntington, Samuel P. 1993. "Why International Primacy Matters." *International Security* 17 (spring): 68–83.
Hussein, King. 1962. *Uneasy Lies the Lion.* New York: Heineman.
Huth, Paul K. 1988. *Extended Deterrence and the Prevention of War.* New Haven, CT: Yale University Press.
Huth, Paul K. 1996. *Standing Your Ground: Territorial Disputes and International Conflict.* Ann Arbor, MI: University of Michigan Press.
Huxley, Tim. 1998. "The Changing Balance of Power in East Asia: Implications for Regional and International Security." *Issues and Studies* 34 (11/12) (November/December): 90–120.
Ikenberry, G. John. 2001. *After Victory: Institutions, Strategic Restraint, and the Rebuilding of Order After Major Wars.* Princeton, NJ: Princeton University Press.
Ingram, Edward. 2001. "Hegemony, Global Reach, and World Power: Great Britain's Long Cycle." Pp. 223–251 in *Bridges and Boundaries: Historians, Political Scientists, and the Study of International Relations*, ed. Colin Elman and Miriam Fendius Elman. Cambridge, MA: MIT Press.
Israel, Jonathan. 1989. *Dutch Primacy in World Trade, 1585–1740.* Oxford, UK: Clarendon Press.
Jaggers, Keith, and Ted Robert Gurr. 1995. "Tracking Democracy's Third Wave with the Polity III Data." *Journal of Peace Research* 32 (November): 453–468.
Jervis, Robert L. 1970. *The Logic of Images in International Relations.* Princeton, NJ: Princeton University Press.
Jervis, Robert L. 1976. *Perception and Misperception in International Politics.* Princeton, NJ: Princeton University Press.
Jervis, Robert L. 1978. "Cooperation under the Security Dilemma." *World Politics* 30 (January): 167–214.
Jervis, Robert L. 1991/92. "The Future of World Politics: Will It Resemble the Past?" *International Security* 16 (winter): 39–73.
Jervis, Robert L. 1993. "International Primacy: Is the Game Worth the Candle?" *International Security* 17 (spring): 52–67.
Jervis, Robert L. 1997. *Systems Effects: Complexity in Political and Social Life.* Princeton, NJ: Princeton University Press.
Jervis, Robert L. 2001. "International History and International Politics: Why Are They Studied Differently?" Pp. 385–402 in *Bridges and Boundaries: Historians, Political Scientists, and the Study of International Relations*, ed. Colin Elman and Miriam Fendius Elman. Cambridge, MA: MIT Press.
Jervis, Robert L., and Jack Snyder, eds. 1991. *Dominoes and Bandwagons.* New York: Oxford University Press.
Jervis, Robert L., Richard Ned Lebow, and Janice Stein, eds. 1985. *Psychology and Deterrence.* Baltimore: Johns Hopkins University Press.

Joffe, Josef. 1999. "Germany: The Continuities from Frederick the Great to the Federal Republic." In *A Century's Journey: How the Great Powers Shape the World*, ed. Robert A. Pastor. New York: Basic Books.
Jones, Charles. 1998. *E. H. Carr and International Relations: A Duty to Lie*. Cambridge, MA: Cambridge University Press.
Jones, Daniel M., Stuart Bremer, and J. David Singer. 1996. "Militarized Interstate Disputes, 1816–1992: Rationale, Coding Rules, and Empirical Patterns." *Conflict Management and Peace Science* 15 (2) (fall): 163–213.
Kahler, Miles. 1997. "Inventing International Relations: International Relations Theory After 1945." Pp. 20–53 in *New Thinking in International Relations Theory*, ed. Michael W. Doyle and G. John Ikenberry. Boulder, CO: Westview.
Kahn, Herman. 1960. *On Thermonuclear War*. Princeton, NJ: Princeton University Press.
Kaiser, David. 1990. *Politics and War: European Conflict from Philip II to Hitler*. Cambridge, MA: Harvard University Press.
Kaplan, Morton. 1957. *System and Process in International Politics*. New York: John Wiley.
Kapstein, Ethan B., and Michael Mastanduno, eds. 1999. *Unipolar Politics: Realism and State Strategies After the Cold War*. New York: Columbia University Press.
Katzenstein, Peter J., ed. 1996. *The Culture of National Security: Norms and Identity in World Politics*. New York: Columbia University Press.
Katzenstein, Peter J., Robert O. Keohane, and Stephen D. Krasner, eds. 1998. International Organization at Fifty: Exploration and Contestation in the Study of World Politics. *International Organization* 52 (4) (autumn).
Kaufman, Robert G. 1992. "To Balance or to Bandwagon? Alignment Decisions in 1930s Europe." *Security Studies* 1 (spring): 417–447.
Kaysen, Carl. 1990. "Is War Obsolete?" *International Security* 14 (spring): 42–64.
Kecskemeti, Paul. 1958. *Strategic Surrender: The Politics of Victory and Defeat*. Stanford, CA: Stanford University Press.
Kegley, Charles W., Jr. 1993. "The Neoidealist Moment in International Studies? Realist Myths and the New International Realities." *International Studies Quarterly* 37 (June): 131–146.
Kegley, Charles W., Jr., and Gregory A. Raymond. 1994. *A Multipolar Peace? Great-Power Politics in the Twenty-First Century*. New York: St. Martin's.
Kegley, Charles W., Jr., ed. 1995. *Controversies in International Relations Theory: Realism and the Neoliberal Challenge*. New York: St. Martin's.
Kennan, George F. 1951. *American Diplomacy, 1900–1950*. Chicago, IL: University of Chicago Press.
Kennedy, Paul. 1984. "The First World War and the International Power System." *International Security* 9 (1) (summer): 7–40.
Kennedy, Paul. 1987. *The Rise and Fall of the Great Powers: Economic Change and Military Conflict from 1500 to 2000*. New York: Random House.
Keohane, Robert O. [1983] 1989. "Theory of World Politics. Structural Realism and Beyond." In *Political Science: The State of the Discipline*, ed. Ada W. Finifter. Washington, D.C.: American Political Science Association. Reprinted in Robert O. Keohane, *International Institutions and State Power*. Boulder, CO: Westview.
Keohane, Robert O. 1984. *After Hegemony: Cooperation and Discord in the World Political Economy*. Princeton, NJ: Princeton University Press.
Keohane, Robert O. 1986a. *Neorealism and Its Critics*. New York: Columbia University Press.
Keohane, Robert O. 1986b. "Realism, Neorealism, and the Study of World Politics." In *Neorealism and Its Critics*, ed. Robert O. Keohane. New York: Columbia University Press.
Keohane, Robert O. 1986c. "Theory of World Politics: Structural Realism and Beyond." In *Neorealism and Its Critics*, ed. Robert O. Keohane. New York: Columbia University Press.
Keohane, Robert O. 1988. "Alliances, Threats, and the Uses of Neo-Realism." *International Security* 13 (1) (summer): 169–176.
Keohane, Robert O. 1993. "Institutional Theory and the Realist Challenge after the Cold War." Pp. 269–300 in *Neorealism and Neoliberalism: The Contemporary Debate*, ed. David Baldwin. New York: Columbia University Press.

Keohane, Robert O., and Lisa Martin. 2002. "Institutional Theory as a Research Program." In *Progress in International Relations Theory: Appraising the Field*, ed. Colin Elman and Miriam Fendius Elman. Cambridge, MA: MIT Press.

Keohane, Robert O., and Joseph S. Nye, Jr. ed. 1971. *Transnational Relations and World Politics*. Cambridge, MA: Harvard University Press.

Keohane, Robert O., and Joseph S. Nye. 1977/1989. *Power and Interdependence: World Politics in Transition*. Boston, MA: Little, Brown.

Keohane, Robert O., and Joseph S. Nye. 1989. *Power and Interdependence*. 2nd ed. New York: Harper Collins.

Kerr, Malcolm. 1970. *The Arab Cold War*. New York: Oxford University Press.

Khalil, Muhammad. 1962. *The Arab States and the Arab League: A Documentary Record*. Vols. 1 and 2. Beirut, Lebanon: Khayat's.

Kim, Woosang, and James D. Morrow. 1992. "When Do Power Shifts Lead to War?" *American Journal of Political Science* 36 (November): 896–922.

King, Gary, Robert Keohane, and Sidney Verba. 1994. *Designing Social Inquiry: Scientific Inference in Qualitative Research*. Princeton, NJ: Princeton University Press.

Kissinger, Henry A. 1964. *A World Restored*. New York: Grosset and Dunlap.

Kissinger, Henry A. 1979. *White House Years*. Boston, MA: Little, Brown.

Kissinger, Henry A. 1994. *Diplomacy*. New York: Simon & Schuster.

Klein, Ira N. 1968. "British Imperialism in Conflict and Alliance: Anglo-French and Anglo-Russian Relations in Asia, 1885–1914." Ph.D. dissertation. Columbia University, New York.

Kraehe, Enno E. [1963] 1983. *Metternich's German Policy. Vol 1: The Contest with Napoleon, 1799–1814. Vol. 2: The Congress of Vienna, 1814–1815*. Princeton, NJ: Princeton University Press.

Krasner, Stephen D. 1978. *Defending the National Interests*. Princeton, NJ: Princeton University Press.

Krasner, Stephen D. 1985. "Toward Understanding in International Relations." *International Studies Quarterly* 29 (June): 137–144.

Kratochwil, Friedrich. 1984. "Errors Have Their Advantage." *International Organization* 38 (spring): 305–320.

Krüger, Peter. 1985. *Die Aussenpolitik der Republik von Weimar*. Darmstadt, Ger.: Wissenschaftlicher Buchverlag.

Kugler, Jacek, and Douglas Lemke, eds. 1996. *Parity and War*. Ann Arbor, MI: University of Michigan Press.

Kuhn, Thomas. 1962. *The Structure of Scientific Revolutions*. Chicago, IL: University of Chicago Press.

Kuhn, Thomas. 1970a. *The Structure of Scientific Revolutions*. Chicago, IL: University of Chicago Press.

Kuhn, Thomas S. 1970b. "Reflections on My Critics." Pp. 231–278 in *Criticism and the Growth of Knowledge*, ed. Imre Lakatos and Alan Musgrave. New York: Cambridge University Press.

Kuhn, Thomas S. 1971. "Notes on Lakatos." Pp. 137–146 in *Boston Studies in the Philosophy of Science, Volume VIII: PSA 1970*, ed. Roger C. Buck and Robert S. Cohen. Dordrecht, Holland: D. Reidel.

Kupchan, Charles. 1994. *The Vulnerability of Empire*. Ithaca, NY: Cornell University Press.

Kydd, Andrew. 1997a. "Game Theory and the Spiral Model." *World Politics* 49 (April): 371–400.

Kydd, Andrew. 1997b. "Why Security Seekers Do Not Fight Each Other." *Security Studies* 7 (autumn): 116–117.

Labs, Eric J. 1992. "Do Weak States Bandwagon?" *Security Studies* 1 (spring): 383–416.

Labs, Eric J. 1997. "Beyond Victory: Offensive Realism and the Expansion of War Aims." *Security Studies* 6 (summer): 1–49.

Lakatos, Imre. 1970. "Falsification and the Methodology of Scientific Research Programmes." Pp. 91–196 in *Criticism and the Growth of Knowledge*, ed. Imre Lakatos and Alan Musgrave. Cambridge, UK: Cambridge University Press.

Lakatos, Imre. 1971a. "Replies to Critics." In *In Memory of Rudolf Carnap*, ed. Roger C. Buck and Robert S. Cohen. *Boston Studies in the Philosophy of Science*. Vol. 8. Dordrecht, Holland: D. Reidel.

Lakatos, Imre. 1971b. "History of Science and Its Rational Reconstructions." In *In Memory of Rudolf Carnap*, ed. Roger C. Buck and Robert S. Cohen. *Boston Studies in the Philosophy of Science*. Vol. 8. Dordrecht, Holland: D. Reidel.

Lakatos, Imre. 1974. The Role of Crucial Experiments in Science. *Studies in History and Philosophy of Science* 4 (4): 309–325.

Lakatos, Imre. 1978. *The Methodology of Scientific Research Programmes*. Cambridge, UK: Cambridge University Press.

Lakatos, Imre. 1999. "History of Science and its Rational Reconstruction." In *The Methodology of Scientific Research Programmes, Philosophical Papers*. Vol. 1, ed. J. Worrall and G. Currie. New York: Cambridge University Press.

Lakatos, Imre, and Elie Zahar. 1975. "Why Did Copernicus's Research Program Supersede Ptolemy's?" In *The Copernican Achievement*, ed. Robert S. Westman. Berkeley, CA: University of California Press.

Langer, William L. 1950. *European Alliances and Alignments, 1871–1890*. New York: Alfred Knopf.

Langer, William. 1964. *European Alliances and Alignments, 1871–1890*. 2nd ed. New York: Vintage Press.

Lapid, Yosef. 1989. "The Third Debate: On the Prospects of International Theory in a Post-Positivist Era." *International Studies Quarterly* 33 (September): 235–254.

Larson, Deborah Welch. 1991. "Bandwagon Images in American Foreign Policy: Myth or Reality?" In *Dominoes and Bandwagons*, ed. Robert Jervis and Jack Snyder. New York: Oxford University Press.

Larvor, Brendan. 1998. *Lakatos: An Introduction*. London and New York: Routledge.

Latsis, Spiro J. 1976. "A Research Programme in Economics." In *Method and Appraisal in Economics*, ed. Spiro Latsis. Cambridge, UK: Cambridge University Press.

Laudan, Larry. 1977. *Progress and Its Problems: Towards a Theory of Scientific Growth*. Berkeley, CA: University of California Press.

Layne, Christopher. 1993a. "The Unipolar Illusion: Why New Great Powers Will Rise." *International Security* 17 (spring): 5–51.

Layne, Christopher. 1993b. "The Unipolar Illusion: Why New Great Powers Will Rise." Pp. 244–290 in *The Cold War and After*, ed. Sean M. Lynn-Jones and Steven Miller. Cambridge, MA: MIT Press.

Layne, Christopher. 1994 "Kant or Cant: The Myth of the Democratic Peace." *International Security* 19 (2) (fall): 5–49.

Layne, Christopher. 1998. "Rethinking American Grand Strategy: Hegemony or Balance of Power in the Twenty-First Century." *World Policy Journal* 15 (2) (summer): 8–28.

Lebow, Richard Ned. 1994. "The Long Peace, the End of the Cold War, and the Failure of Realism." *International Organization* 48 (2) (spring): 249–277.

Lebow, Richard Ned. 2001. "Thucydides the Constructivist." *American Political Science Review* 95 (3) (September): 547–560.

Lebow, Richard Ned, John Mueller, and William C. Wohlforth. 1995. "Correspondence: Realism and the End of the Cold War." *International Security* 20 (2) (fall): 185–187.

Lebow, Richard Ned, and Thomas Risse-Kappen, eds. 1995. *International Relations Theory and the End of the Cold War*. New York: Columbia University Press.

Leffler, Melvyn, P. 1992. *A Preponderance of Power: National Security, the Truman Administration, and the Cold War*. Stanford, CA: Stanford University Press.

Legro, Jeff, and Andrew Moravcsik. 1999. "Is Anybody Still a Realist?" *International Security* 24 (2): 5–55.

Lemke, Douglas, and William Reed. 2001. "War and Rivalry among Great Powers." *American Journal of Political Science* 45 (2) (April): 457–469.

Leplin, Jarrett. 1997. *A Novel Defense of Scientific Realism*. New York: Oxford University Press.

Levy, Jack S. 1983. *War in the Modern Great Power System, 1495–1975*. Lexington, KY: The University Press of Kentucky.
Levy, Jack S. 1984. "The Offensive/Defensive Balance of Military Technology: A Theoretical and Historical Analysis." *International Studies Quarterly* 28 (2) (June): 219–238.
Levy, Jack S. 1985. "Theories of General War." *World Politics* 37 (3) (April): 344–374.
Levy, Jack S. 1987. "Declining Power and the Preventive Motivation for War." *World Politics* 40 (1) (October): 82–107.
Levy, Jack S. 1989. "The Causes of War: A Review of Theories and Evidence." Pp. 209–333 in *Behavior, Society, and Nuclear War*. Vol. 1, ed. Philip E. Tetlock, Jo L. Husbands, Robert Jervis, Paul C. Stern, and Charles Tilly. New York: Oxford University Press.
Levy, Jack S. 1990/91. "Preferences, Constraints, and Choices in July 1914." *International Security* 15 (3) (winter): 151–186.
Levy, Jack S. 1994. "The Theoretical Foundations of Paul W. Schroeder's International System." *International History Review* 16 (4) (November): 715–744.
Levy, Jack S. 2002a. "War and Peace." Pp. 350–368 in *Handbook of International Relations*, ed. Walter Carlsnaes, Thomas Risse, and Beth A. Simmons. Thousand Oaks, CA: Sage Publications.
Levy, Jack S. 2002b. "Qualitative Methods in International Relations." Pp. 432–454 in *Millennial Reflections on International Studies*, ed. Michael Brecher and Frank P. Harvey. Ann Arbor, MI: University of Michigan Press.
Levy, Jack S., and Michael N. Barnett. 1992. "Alliance Formation, Domestic Political Economy, and Third World Security." *Jerusalem Journal of International Relations* 14 (4) (December): 19–40.
Liberman, Peter. 1993. The Spoils of Conquest. *International Security* 18 (2) (fall): 125–153.
Liddell-Hart, B. H. [c. 1970] 1982. *History of the Second World War*. New York: Putnam.
Lieber, Keir A. 2000. *The Offense-Defense Balance and the Prospects for Peace*. Ph.D. Dissertation, University of Chicago.
Liska, George. 1962. *Nations in Alliance*. Baltimore, MD: Johns Hopkins University Press.
Luard, Evan. 1992. *The Balance of Power: The System of International Relations, 1648–1815*. London: MacMillan.
Lukacs, John. 1999. *Five Days in London, May 1940*. New Haven, CT: Yale University Press.
Lundestad, Geir. 1986. "Empire by Invitation: The United States and Western Europe, 1945–1952." *Journal of Peace Research* 23 (August): 263–277.
Lustick, Ian S. 1997. "Lijphart, Lakatos, and Consociationalism." *World Politics* 50 (October): 88–117.
Lynn, John A. 1999. *The Wars of Louis XIV, 1667–1714*. London: Longman.
Lynn-Jones, Sean M. 1995. "Offense-Defense Theory and Its Critics." *Security Studies* 4 (summer): 660–691.
Maddy-Weitzman, Bruce. 1993. *The Crystallization of the Arab State System: 1945–1954*. Syracuse, NY: Syracuse University Press.
Maier, Charles S. 1987. *In Search of Stability: Explorations in Historical Political Economy*. New York: Cambridge University Press.
Mannheim, Karl. 1991. *Ideology and Utopia*. New York: Routledge.
Mansbach, Richard W., and John A. Vasquez. 1981. *In Search of Theory: A New Paradigm for Global Politics*. New York: Columbia University Press.
Maoz, Zeev. 1990. *Paradoxes of War: On the Art of National Self-Entrapment*. Boston, MA: Unwin Hymann.
Maoz, Zeev. 1996a. *Domestic Sources of Global Change*. Ann Arbor, MI: University of Michigan Press.
Maoz, Zeev. 1996b. The Strategic Behavior of Nations, 1816–1986. Paper presented at the annual meeting of the Peace Science Society (International), Houston, TX, October 25–27.
Maoz, Zeev. 1997. "The Renewed Controversy Over the Democratic Peace: Rearguard Action or Cracks in the Wall?" *International Security* 23 (1): 162–198.
Maoz, Zeev. 1998. "Realist and Cultural Critiques of the Democratic Peace: A Theoretical and Empirical Reassessment." *International Interactions* 24 (1): 3–89.
Maoz, Zeev. 1999. The Dyadic MID Dataset, 1.1. http://spirit.tau.ac.il/zeevmaoz/dyadmid.html.

# References

Maoz, Zeev. 2000. "The Street-Gangs of World Politics: The Origins, Management, and Consequences of International Alliances, 1816–1986." In *What Do We Know about War?* ed. John A. Vasquez. Lanham, MA: Rowman and Littlefield.

Maoz, Zeev. 2001. "Democratic Networks: Connecting National, Dyadic, and Systemic Levels-of-Analysis in the Study of Democracy and War." In *War in a Changing World*, ed. Zeev Maoz and Azar Gat. Ann Arbor, MI: University of Michigan Press.

Maoz, Zeev, and Bruce Russett. 1993. "Normative and Structural Causes of Democratic Peace, 1946–1986." *American Political Science Review* 87 (September): 620–638.

Martin, Lisa L. 1992. *Coercive Cooperation: Explaining Multilateral Economic Sanctions.* Princeton, NJ: Princeton University Press.

Martin, Lisa L., and Beth Simmons. 1998. "Theories and Empirical Studies of International Institutions." *International Organization* 52 (4) (autumn): 729–757.

Mastanduno, Michael. 1997. "Preserving the Unipolar Moment: Realist Theories and U.S. Grand Strategy after the Cold War." *International Security* 21 (spring): 49–88.

Masterman, Margaret. 1970. "The Nature of a Paradigm." In *Criticism and the Growth of Knowledge*, ed. Imre Lakatos and Alan Musgrave. Cambridge, UK: Cambridge University Press.

Mastny, Vojtech. 1996. *The Cold War and Soviet Insecurity: The Stalin Years.* New York: Oxford University Press.

Mattingly, Garrett. 1955. *Renaissance Diplomacy.* Baltimore, MD: Penguin.

Mautner, Thomas. 1996. *A Dictionary of Philosophy.* Cambridge, MA: Blackwell Publishers Inc.

Mayo, Deborah G. 1996. *Error and the Growth of Experimental Knowledge.* Chicago, IL: The University of Chicago Press.

McCloskey, Donald N. 1994. *Knowledge and Persuasion in Economics.* Cambridge, UK: Cambridge University Press.

Mearsheimer, John J. 1990. "Back to the Future: Instability in Europe after the Cold War." *International Security* 15 (4) (summer): 5–56.

Mearsheimer, John J. 1994/95. "The False Promise of International Institutions." *International Security* 19 (3) (winter): 5–59.

Mearsheimer, John J. 2001. *The Tragedy of Great Power Politics.* New York: W. W. Norton.

Meckstroth, Theodore. 1975. "'Most Different Systems' and 'Most Similar Systems': A Study in the Logic of Comparative Inquiry." *Comparative Political Studies* 8 (July): 133–177.

Milliken, Jennifer. 2001. *Conflict Possibilities: The Social Construction of the Korean War.* Manchester, UK: University of Manchester Press.

Milner, Helen V. 1988. *Resisting Protectionism: Global Industries and the Politics of International Trade.* Princeton, NJ: Princeton University Press.

Milward, Alan. 1992. *The European Rescue of the Nation State.* Berkeley, CA: University of California Press.

Mishan, Edward J. 1982. *What Political Economy Is All About.* Cambridge, UK: Cambridge University Press.

Modelski, George, and William R. Thompson. 1989. "Long Cycles and Global War." In *Handbook of War Studies*, ed. Manus Midlarksy. Boston, MA: Unwin Hyman.

Monger, George M. 1963. *The End of Isolation: British Foreign Policy, 1900–1907.* London: T. Nelson.

Moravcsik, Andrew. 1997. "Taking Preferences Seriously: A Liberal Theory of International Politics." *International Organization* 51 (4) (autumn): 513–553.

Morgan, T. Clifton, and Anne C. Miers. 1999. "When Threats Succeed: A Formal Model of the Threat and Use of Economic Sanctions." Paper presented at the 33rd annual meeting of the Peace Science Society, Ann Arbor, MI, October 8–10.

Morgan, T. Clifton, and Jack S. Levy. 1990. "Base Stealers versus Power Hitters: A Nation-State Level Analysis of the Frequency and Seriousness of War." Pp. 43–56 in *Prisoners of War?* ed. Charles S. Gochman and Alan Ned Sabrosky. Lexington, MA: Lexington Books.

Morgenthau, Hans J. 1946. *Scientific Man vs. Power Politics.* Chicago, IL: University of Chicago Press.

Morgenthau, Hans J. 1948. *Politics among Nations: The Struggle for Power and Peace.* New York: Knopf.

Morgenthau, Hans J. [1948] 1960. *Politics among Nations: the Struggle for Power and Peace*. 3rd rev. ed. New York: Knopf.
Morgenthau, Hans J. [1948] 1967. *Politics among Nations: The Struggle for Power and Peace*. 4th ed. New York: Knopf.
Morgenthau, Hans J. [1948] 1973. *Politics among Nations: the Struggle for Power and Peace*. 4th rev. ed. New York: Knopf.
Morgenthau, Hans J. [1948] 1978. *Politics among Nations*. 5th rev. ed. New York: Knopf.
Morgenthau, Hans J. [1948] 1985. *Politics among Nations: the Struggle for Power and Peace*. 6th rev. ed. New York: Knopf.
Morrow, James D. 1991. "Alliances and Asymmetry: An Alternative to the Capability Aggregation Model of Alliances." *American Journal of Political Science* 35 (4): 904–933.
Morrow, James D. 1993. "Arms versus Allies: Trade-offs in the Search for Security." *International Organization* 47 (spring): 207–233.
Morrow, James D. 1997. "A Rational Choice Approach to International Conflict." In *Decision-Making on War and Peace: The Cognitive-Rational Debate*, ed. Alex Mintz and Nehemia Geva. Boulder, CO: Lynne Rienner Publishers.
Morrow, James D. 2000. "Alliances: Why Write Them Down?" *Annual Review of Political Science* 3:63–83.
Mueller, John E. 1989. *Retreat from Doomsday: The Obsolescence of Major War*. New York: Basic Books.
Mufti, Malik. 1996. *Sovereign Creations: Pan-Arabism and Political Order in Syria and Iraq*. Ithaca, NY: Cornell University Press.
Musgrave, Alan. 1974. "Logical versus Historical Theories of Confirmation." *British Journal for the Philosophy of Science* 25 (March): 1–23.
Musgrave, Alan. 1976. "Method or Madness? Can the Methodology of Research Programmes Be Rescued from Epistemological Anarchism?" In *Essays in Memory of Imre Lakatos*, ed. R. S. Cohen, P. K. Feyerabend, and M. W. Wartofsky. *Boston Studies in the Philosophy of Science*. Vol. 39. Dordrecht, Holland: D. Reidel.
Mutawi, Samir. 1987. *Jordan in the 1967 War*. New York: Cambridge University Press.
Mutawi, Samir. 1996. "The Jordanian Response." In *The 1967 War: A Retrospective*, ed. Richard Parker. Gainesville, FL: University of Florida Press.
Nagel, Ernst. 1961. *The Structure of Science: Problems in the Logic of Scientific Explanation*. New York: Harcourt, Brace and World.
Neilson, Keith. 1996. *Britain and the Last Tsar, 1894–1914*. Oxford, UK: Oxford University Press.
Nicholson, Michael. 1989. *Formal Theories in International Relations*. Cambridge: Cambridge University Press.
Nicolson, Harold. 1939. *Diplomacy*. London: Oxford University Press.
Niebuhr, Reinhold. 1940. *Christianity and Power Politics*. New York: Scribner's.
Niou, Emerson, Peter C. Ordeshook, and Gregory F. Rose. 1989. *The Balance of Power: Stability in International Systems*. New York: Cambridge University Press.
Nunan, Richard. 1984. "Novel Facts, Bayesian Rationality, and the History of Continental Drift." *Studies in History and Philosophy of Science* 15 (4): 267–307.
Nye, Joseph S., Jr. 1988. "Neorealism and Neoliberalism." *World Politics* 40 (January): 235–251.
Nye, Joseph S., Jr. 1993. *Understanding International Conflicts*. New York: Harper Collins.
Olson, William C., and A. J. R. Groom. 1991. *International Relations Then and Now: Origins and Trends in Interpretation*. London: Harper Collins Academic.
Oren, Ido. 1990. "The War Proneness of Alliances." *Journal of Conflict Resolution* 34 (2): 208–233.
Organski, A. F. K. 1958. *World Politics*. New York: Knopf.
Organski, A. F. K. 1968. *World Politics*. 2nd ed. New York: Knopf.
Organski, A. F. K., and Jacek Kugler. 1980. *The War Ledger*. Chicago, IL: University of Chicago Press.
Organski, A. F. K., and Jacek Kugler. 1989. "The Power Transition: A Retrospective and Prospective Evaluation." In *Handbook of War Studies*, ed. Manus Midlarsky. Boston, MA: Unwin Hyman.

Parsons, Talcott. 1937. *The Structure of Social Action, Vol I: Marshall, Pareto, Durkheim.* New York: Free Press.
Paul, T. V. 1994. *Asymmetric Conflicts: War Initiation by Weaker Powers.* Cambridge, UK: Cambridge University Press.
Podeh, Eli. 1995. *The Quest for Hegemony in the Arab World.* New York: E. J. Brill.
Pollard, A. F. 1923 "Balance of Power." *Journal of the British Institute of International Affairs* (2) (March): 51–64.
Polyani, Michael. 1962. *Personal Knowledge: Toward a Post-Critical Philosophy.* Chicago, IL: The University of Chicago Press.
Popper, Karl. 1959. *The Logic of Scientific Discovery.* London: Hutchinson.
Popper, Karl. 1970. "Normal Science and Its Dangers." Pp. 51–58 in *Criticism and the Growth of Knowledge,* ed. Imre Lakatos and Alan Musgrave. New York: Cambridge University Press.
Popper, Karl R. 1989. *Conjectures and Refutations: The Growth of Scientific Knowledge.* 5th ed. London: Routledge.
Posen, Barry R. 1984. *The Sources of Military Doctrine: France, Britain and Germany Between the World Wars.* Ithaca: Cornell University Press.
Powell, Robert. 1999. *In the Shadow of Power: States and Strategy in International Politics.* Princeton, NJ: Princeton University Press.
Powell, Robert. 1990. *Nuclear Deterrence Theory: The Search for Credibility.* New York: Cambridge University Press.
Powell, Robert. 1996a. "Stability and the Distribution of Power." *World Politics* 48 (January): 239–267.
Powell, Robert. 1996b. "Uncertainty, Shifting Power, and Appeasement." *American Political Science Review* 90 (December): 749–764.
Price, Richard. 1997. *The Chemical Weapons Taboo.* Ithaca, NY: Cornell University Press.
Price, Richard. 1999. "Isms and Schisms: Culturalism versus Realism in Security Studies." *International Security* 24 (1) (summer): 169–72.
Priess, David. 1996. "Balance-of-Threat Theory and the Genesis of the Gulf Cooperation Council: An Interpretative Case Study." *Security Studies* 5 (summer): 143–171.
Przeworski, Adam, and Henry Teune. 1970. *The Logic of Comparative Social Inquiry.* New York: Wiley.
Quester, George. 1977. *Offense and Defense in the International System.* New York: Wiley.
Rabinovich, Itamar. 1972. *Syria under the Ba'ath, 1963–66.* New York: Halstead.
Rabinovich, Itamar. 1991. *The Road Not Taken.* New York: Oxford University Press.
Rasler, Karen A., and William R. Thompson. 1994. *The Great Powers and Global Struggle, 1490–1990.* Lexington, KY: The University Press of Kentucky.
Ray, James Lee. 1995. *Democracy and International Conflict: An Evaluation of the Democratic Peace Proposition.* Columbia, SC: University of South Carolina Press.
Read, Anthony, and David Fisher. 1988 *The Deadly Embrace: Hitler, Stalin, and the Nazi-Soviet Pact, 1939–1941.* New York: W. W. Norton.
Reiter, Daniel. 1996. *Crucible of Beliefs: Learning, Alliances, and World Wars.* Ithaca, NY: Cornell University Press.
Richards, Robert J. 1987. *Darwin and the Emergence of Evolutionary Theories of Mind and Behavior.* Chicago, IL: University of Chicago Press.
Risse-Kappen, Thomas. 1995. *Cooperation among Democracies: The European Influence on U.S. Foreign Policy.* Princeton, NJ: Princeton University Press.
Robinson, Ronald, and John Gallagher. 1953. "The Imperialism of Free Trade." *Economic History Review* 2nd series. 6:1–25.
Rose, Gideon. 1998. "Neoclassical Realism and Theories of Foreign Policy." *World Politics* 51 (October): 144–172.
Rosecrance, Richard. 1961. "Categories, Concepts, and Reasoning in the Study of International Relations." *Behavioral Science* 6 (3) (autumn): 222–231.
Rosecrance, Richard. 1963. *Action and Reaction in World Politics.* Boston, MA: Little Brown.
Rosecrance, Richard. 1995. "Overextension, Vulnerability, and Conflict." *International Security* 19 (spring): 145–163.

Rosecrance, Richard. 1999. *The Rise of the Virtual State: Wealth and Power in the Coming Century*. New York: Basic Books.
Rosecrance, Richard, and Arthur Stein, eds. 1993. *The Domestic Bases of Grand Strategy*. Ithaca, NY: Cornell University Press.
Rosecrance, Richard, and Chih-Cheng Lo. 1996. "Balancing, Stability, and War: The Mysterious Case of the Napoleonic International System." *International Studies Quarterly* 40 (December): 479–500.
Rosecrance, Richard, and Zara Steiner. 1993. "British Grand Strategy and the Origins of World War II." In *The Domestic Bases of Grand Strategy*, ed. Richard Rosecrance and Arthur Stein. Ithaca, NY: Cornell University Press.
Rosenberg, Alexander. 1986. "Lakatosian Consolations for Economics." *Economics and Philosophy* 2 (April): 127–139.
Ross, Dorothy. 1991. *The Origins of American Social Science*. New York: Cambridge University Press.
Rourke, John T. 2001. *International Politics on the World Stage*. 8th ed. McGraw-Hill/Dushkin.
Roy, A. Bikash. 1997. "Intervention across Bisecting Borders." *Journal of Peace Research* 34 (August): 303–314.
Ruggie, John G. 1983. "Continuity and Transformation in the World Polity: Toward a Neorealist Synthesis." *World Politics* 35 (January): 261–285.
Rule, James B. 1997. *Theory and Progress in Social Science*. Cambridge, UK: Cambridge University Press.
Rummel, R. J. 1983. "Libertarianism and International Violence." *Journal of Conflict Resolution* 27 (1) (March): 27–71.
Russett, Bruce M. 1993. *Grasping the Democratic Peace: Principles for a Post–Cold War World*. Princeton, NJ: Princeton University Press.
Russett, Bruce M. 1995. "Processes of Dyadic Choice for War and Peace." *World Politics* 47 (January): 268–282.
Russett, Bruce M., and John Oneal. 2000. *Triangulating Peace: Democracy, Interdependence, and International Organization*. New York: W. W. Norton.
Russett, Bruce M., John Oneal, and David R. Davis. 1998. "The Third Leg of the Kantian Tripod: International Organizations and Militarized Disputes, 1950–85." *International Organization* 52 (3): 441–467.
Sagan, Scott D., and Kenneth N. Waltz. 1995. *The Spread of Nuclear Weapons: A Debate*. New York: W. W. Norton.
Salibi, Kamal. 1993. *The Modern History of Jordan*. New York: I. B. Taurus.
Sartori, Giovanni. 1994. "Compare Why and How: Comparing, Miscomparing, and the Comparative Method." Pp. 14–34 in *Comparing Nations: Concepts, Strategies, Substance*, ed. Mattei Dogan and Ali Kazancigil. Cambridge, MA: Blackwell.
Satloff, Robert. 1994. *From Abdullah to Hussein*. New York: Oxford University Press.
Scheffler, Israel. 1967. *Science and Subjectivity*. Indianapolis: Bobbs-Merrill.
Schelling, Thomas C. 1978. *Micromotives and Macrobehavior*. New York: W. W. Norton.
Schroeder, Paul W. 1972a. "World War I as Galloping Gertie: A Reply to Joachim Remak." *Journal of Modern History* 44 (September): 319–345.
Schroeder, Paul W. 1972b. *Austria, Britain and the Crimean War: The Destruction of the European Concert*. Ithaca, NY: Cornell University Press.
Schroeder, Paul W. 1976. "Alliances, 1815–1945: Weapons of Power and Tools of Management." In *Historical Problems of National Security*, ed. Klaus Knorr. Lawrence, KS: University of Kansas Press.
Schroeder, Paul W. 1989. "The Nineteenth Century International System: Balance of Power or Political Equilibrium?" *Review of International Studies* 15 (April): 135–153.
Schroeder, Paul W. 1993. "The Transformation of Political Thinking." Pp. 47–70 in *Coping with Complexity in the International System*, ed. Jack Snyder and Robert Jervis. Boulder, CO: Westview.
Schroeder, Paul W. 1994a. "Historical Reality versus Neo-Realist Theory." *International Security* 19 (summer): 108–148.

Schroeder, Paul W. 1994b. *The Transformation of European Politics, 1763–1848*. Oxford: UK: Oxford University Press.
Schroeder, Paul W. 1995. "History vs. Neo-realism: A Second Look, The Author Replies." *International Security* 20 (summer): 193–195.
Schuman, Frederick. 1933. *International Politics*. New York: McGraw-Hill.
Schwarzenberger, Georg. 1941. *Power Politics*. New York: Prager.
Schweller, Randall L. 1992. "Domestic Structure and Preventive War: Are Democracies More Pacific?" *World Politics* 44 (January): 235–269.
Schweller, Randall L. 1993. "Tripolarity and the Second World War." *International Studies Quarterly* 37:73–103.
Schweller, Randall L. 1994. "Bandwagoning for Profit: Bringing the Revisionist State Back In." *International Security* 19 (summer): 72–107.
Schweller, Randall L. 1996. "Neorealism's Status-Quo Bias: What Security Dilemma?" *Security Studies* 5 (spring): 90–121.
Schweller, Randall L. 1997. "New Realist Research on Alliances: Refining, Not Refuting, Waltz's Balancing Proposition." *American Political Science Review* 91 (December): 927–930.
Schweller, Randall L. 1998a. *Deadly Imbalances: Tripolarity and Hitler's Strategy of World Conquest*. New York: Columbia University Press.
Schweller, Randall L. 1998b. "The Progressive Nature of Neoclassical Realism." Paper prepared for the conference on "Progress in International Relations Theory: A Collaborative Assessment and Application of Imre Lakatos's Methodology of Scientific Research Programs," January 15–16, 1999, Scottsdale, AZ.
Schweller, Randall L., and David Priess. 1997. "A Tale of Two Realisms: Expanding the Institutions Debate." *Mershon International Studies Review* 51 (3) (April): 1–32.
Schweller, Randall L., and William C. Wohlforth. 2000. "Power Test: Evaluating Realism in Response to the End of the Cold War." *Security Studies* 9 (3) (spring): 60–107.
Seale, Patrick. 1986. *The Struggle for Syria*. New Haven, CT: Yale University Press.
Seabury, Paul. 1965. *Balance of Power*. San Francisco: Chandler Publishing Co.
Sheehan, Michael. 1996. *Balance of Power: History and Theory*. New York: Routledge.
Shubik, Martin. 1971. "Games of Status." *Behavioral Science* 16 (March): 117–129.
Signorino, Curtis S. 1998. "A Strategic Probit Random Utility Model of International Conflict." Paper presented at the Annual Meetings of the American Political Science Association, Boston, MA.
Signorino, Curtis S., and Jeffery M. Ritter. 1999. "Tau-b or Not Tau-b: Measuring the Similarity of Foreign Policy Positions." *International Studies Quarterly* 43 (1): 115–144.
Simon, Michael W., and Erik Gartzke. 1996. "Do Democracies Flock Together, or Do Opposites Attract?" *Journal of Conflict Resolution* 40 (1): 617–653.
Simowitz, Roslyn. 1998. "Evaluating Conflict Research on the Diffusion of War." *Journal of Peace Research* 35 (March): 211–230.
Simowitz, Roslyn. 2002. "Measuring Intra-programmatic Progress." In *Progress in International Relations Theory: Appraising the Field*, ed. Colin Elman and Miriam Fendius Elman. Cambridge, MA: MIT Press.
Simowitz, Roslyn, and Barry Price. 1990. "The Expected Utility Theory of Conflict: Measuring Theoretical Progress." *American Political Science Review* 84 (June): 439–460.
Singer, J. David. 1961. "The Level-of-Analysis Problem in International Relations." *World Politics* 14 (1) (October): 77–92.
Singer, J. David. 1990. "Reconstructing the Correlates of War Data Set on Material Capabilities of States, 1816–1985." In *Measuring the Correlates of War*, ed. J. David Singer and Paul F. Diehl. Ann Arbor, MI: University of Michigan Press.
Singer, J. David, and Melvin Small. 1968. "Alliance Aggregation and the Onset of War." Pp. 247–286 in *Quantitative International Politics: Insight and Evidence*, ed. J. David Singer. New York: Free Press.
Singer, J. David, Stuart Bremer, and John Stuckey. 1972. "Capability Distribution, Uncertainty, and Major Power War, 1820–1965." In *Peace, War, and Numbers*, ed. Bruce Russett. Beverly Hills, CA: Sage.

Siverson, Randolph J., and Harvey Starr. 1994. "Regime Change and the Restructuring of Alliances." *American Journal of Political Science* 38 (February): 145–161.

Siverson, Randolph M., and Michael P. Sullivan. 1983. "The Distribution of Power and the Onset of War." *Journal of Conflict Resolution* 27 (September): 473–494.

Smith, Alastair. 1995. "Alliance Formation and War." *International Studies Quarterly* 39 (December): 405–426.

Smith, Alastair. 1998. "Strategic Estimation in International Relations." Paper presented at the Annual Meeting of the American Political Science Association, Boston, MA, August 31–September 3.

Smith, Michael Joseph. 1986. "Antecedents in Classical Political Thought: Thucydides, Machiavelli, and Hobbes." Pp. 4–15 in *Realist Thought from Weber to Kissinger*, ed. Michael Joseph Smith. Baton Rouge, LA: Louisiana State University Press.

Smith, Steve. 1987. "Paradigm Dominance in International Relations: The Development of International Relations as a Social Science." *Millennium* 16 (summer): 123–136.

Smith, Steve. 1995. "The Self-Images of a Discipline: A Genealogy of International Relations Theory." In *International Relations Theory Today*, ed. Ken Booth and Steve Smith. Cambridge, MA: Polity Press.

Smith, Steve. 1996. "Positivism and Beyond." In *International Theory: Positivism and Beyond*. Cambridge, UK: Cambridge University Press.

Snyder, Glenn. 1997. *Alliance Politics*. Ithaca, NY: Cornell University Press.

Snyder, Jack L. 1991. *Myths of Empire: Domestic Politics and International Ambition*. Ithaca, NY: Cornell University Press.

Snyder, Jack. 1984/85. "Richness, Rigor, and Relevance in the Study of Soviet Foreign Policy." *International Security* 9 (winter): 89–108.

Snyder, Jack, and Robert Jervis, eds. 1993. *Coping with Complexity in the International System*. Boulder, CO: Westview.

Spiezio, K. Edward. 1990. "British Hegemony and Major Power War, 1815–1935: An Empirical Test of Gilpin's Model of Hegemonic Governance." *International Studies Quarterly* 34 (June): 165–181.

Spiro, David E. 1994. "The Insignificance of the Liberal Peace." *International Security* 19 (2) (autumn 1994): 50–86.

Spirtas, Michael. 1996. "A House Divided: Tragedy and Evil in Realist Theory." *Security Studies* 5 (3) (spring): 385–423.

Spykman, Nicholas John. 1942. *America's Strategy in World Politics: The United States and the Balance of Power*. New York: Harcourt, Brace.

Stent, Gunther S. 1973. "Shakespeare and DNA." *New York Times*, January 28, sec. E.

Strauss, Barry S. 1991. "Of Balances, Bandwagons, and Ancient Greeks." In *Hegemonic Rivalry: From Thucydides to the Nuclear Age*, ed. Richard Ned Lebow and Barry S. Strauss. Boulder, CO: Westview.

Sumner, William Graham. [1911] 1968. "War." In *War: Studies from Psychology, Sociology, Anthropology*, ed. Leon Bramson and George W. Goethals. New York: Basic Books.

Suppe, Frederick. 1977a. "The Search for Philosophic Understanding of Scientific Theories." Pp. 3–307 in *The Structure of Scientific Theories*. 2nd ed. Ed. Frederick Suppe. Chicago, IL: University of Illinois Press.

Suppe, Frederick, 1977b. "Afterword." In *The Structure of Scientific Theories*. 2nd ed. Ed. Frederick Suppe. Chicago, IL: University of Illinois Press.

Suvorov, Viktor. 1990. *Icebreaker: Who Started the Second World War*. Trans. Thomas B. Beattie. London: Hamish Hamilton; New York: Viking Press.

Taylor, A. J. P. 1954. *The Struggle for Mastery in Europe, 1848–1918*. New York: Oxford University Press.

Tetlock, Philip E., and Aaron Belkin. 1996. "Counterfactual Thought Experiments in World Politics: Logical, Methodological, and Psychological Perspectives." Pp. 3–38 in *Counterfactual Thought Experiments in World Politics: Logical, Methodological and Psychological Perspectives*, ed. Philip E. Tetlock and Aaron Belkin. Princeton, NJ: Princeton University Press.

Thompson, William R. 1988. *On Global War*. Columbia, SC: University of South Carolina Press.

Thompson, William R. 2001. "Martian and Venusian Perspectives on International Relations: Britain as System Leader in the Nineteenth and Twentieth Centuries." Pp. 253–292 in *Bridges and Boundaries: Historians, Political Scientists, and the Study of International Relations*, ed. Colin Elman and Miriam Fendius Elman. Cambridge, MA: MIT Press.
Thompson, William R., and Gary Zuk. 1986. "World Power and the Strategic Trap of Territorial Commitments." *International Studies Quarterly* 30 (September): 249–267.
Thucydides. 1954. *The Peloponnesian War*. Translated by Rex Warner. New York: Penguin Books.
Thucydides. 1972. *History of the Peloponnesian War*. Rev. ed. Translated by Rex Warner. New York: Penguin Books.
Torbjørn, L. Knutsen. 1997. *History of International Relations Theory*. Manchester: Manchester University Press.
Torrey, Gordon. 1964. *Syrian Politics and the Military, 1945–58*. Columbus, OH: Ohio State University Press.
Toulmin, Stephen. 1961. *Foresight and Understanding: An Enquiry into the Aims of Science*. New York: Harper and Row.
Toulmin, Stephen. 1972. *Human Understanding*. Princeton, NJ: Princeton University Press.
Trachtenberg, Marc. 1999. *A Constructed Peace: The Making of the European Settlement, 1945–1963*. Princeton, NJ: Princeton University Press.
Van Evera, Stephen. 1984. "The Cult of the Offensive and the Origins of the First World War." *International Security* 9 (summer): 58–107.
Van Evera, Stephen. 1990/91. "Primed for Peace: Europe after the Cold War." *International Security* 15 (winter): 7–57.
Van Evera, Stephen. 1997. *Guide to Methods for Students of Political Science*. Ithaca, NY: Cornell University Press.
Van Evera, Stephen. 1998. "Offense, Defense and the Causes of War." *International Security* 22 (spring): 5–43.
Van Evera, Stephen. 1999. *Causes of War: Vol. I: The Structure of Power and the Roots of War*. Ithaca, NY: Cornell University Press.
Vasquez, John A. 1979. "Coloring It Morgenthau: New Evidence for an Old Thesis on Quantitative International Politics." *British Journal of International Studies* 5 (October): 210–228.
Vasquez, John A. 1983. *The Power of Power Politics: A Critique*. New Brunswick, NJ: Rutgers University Press.
Vasquez, John A. 1992. "World Politics Theory." In *Encyclopedia of Government and Politics*, ed. Mary Hawkesworth and Maurice Kogan. London: Routledge.
Vasquez, John A. 1993. *The War Puzzle*. Cambridge, UK: Cambridge University Press.
Vasquez, John A. 1995. "The Post-Positivist Debate: Reconstructing Scientific Enquiry and International Relations Theory after Enlightenment's Fall." In *International Relations Theory Today*, ed. Ken Booth and Steve Smith. Cambridge, MA: Polity Press.
Vasquez, John A. 1996a. "When Are Power Transitions Dangerous? An Appraisal and Reformulation of Power Transition Theory." In *Parity and War*, ed. Jacek Kugler and Douglas Lemke. Ann Arbor, MI: University of Michigan Press.
Vasquez, John A. 1996b. "Distinguishing Rivals That Go to War from Those That Do Not: A Quantitative Comparative Case Study of the Two Paths to War." *International Studies Quarterly* 40 (4) (December): 531–558.
Vasquez, John A. 1996c. "The Causes of the Second World War in Europe: A New Scientific Explanation." *International Political Science Review* 17 (April): 161–178.
Vasquez, John A. 1997. "The Realist Paradigm and Degenerative versus Progressive Research Programs: An Appraisal of Neotraditional Research on Waltz's Balancing Proposition." *American Political Science Review* 91 (December): 899–912.
Vasquez, John A. 1998. *The Power of Power Politics: From Neorealism to Neotraditionalism*. Cambridge, UK: Cambridge University Press.
Vasquez, John A. 2002. "Kuhn versus Lakatos? The Case for Multiple Frames in Appraising IR Theory." In *Progress in International Relations Theory: Appraising the Field*, ed. Colin Elman and Miriam Fendius Elman. Cambridge, MA: MIT Press.

Vasquez, John A., and Marie T. Henehan. 2001. "Territorial Disputes and the Probability of War, 1816–1992." *Journal of Peace Research* 38 (2): 123–138.
von Ranke, Leopold. 1973 [1833]. "The Great Powers." In *The Theory and Practice of History*, ed. Georg G. Iggers and Konrad von Moltke. Indianapolis, IN: Bobbs-Merrill.
Wagner, R. Harrison. 1986. "The Theory of Games and the Balance of Power." *World Politics* 38 (July): 546–576.
Wagner, Harrison. 1993. "What Was Bipolarity?" *International Organization* 47 (winter): 77–106.
Wallerstein, Immanuel Maurice. 1974. *The Modern World-System: Capitalist Agriculture and the Origins of the European World-Economy in the Sixteenth Century*. New York: Academic Press.
Walt, Stephen M. n.d. "Containing Rogues and Renegades: Coalition Strategies and Counterproliferation." Pp. 191–226 in *The Coming Crisis: Nuclear Proliferation, U.S. Interests, and World Order*, ed. Victor A. Utgoff. Cambridge: The MIT Press.
Walt, Stephen M. 1985. "Alliance Formation and the Balance of World Power." *International Security* 9 (spring): 3–43.
Walt, Stephen M. 1987. *The Origins of Alliances*. Ithaca, NY: Cornell University Press.
Walt, Stephen M. 1988. "Testing Theories of Alliance Formation: The Case of Southwest Asia." *International Organization* 42 (spring): 275–316.
Walt, Stephen M. 1991. "Alliance Formation in Southwest Asia: Balancing and Bandwagoning in Cold War Competition." Pp. 51–84 in *Dominoes and Bandwagons*, ed. Robert Jervis and Jack Snyder. New York: Oxford University Press.
Walt, Stephen M. 1992a. "Revolution and War." *World Politics* 44 (April): 321–368.
Walt, Stephen M. 1992b. "Alliances, Threats, and U.S. Grand Strategy: A Reply to Kaufman and Labs." *Security Studies* 1 (spring): 448–482.
Walt, Stephen M. 1996. *Revolution and War*. Ithaca, NY: Cornell University Press.
Walt, Stephen M. 1997. "The Progressive Power of Realism." *American Political Science Review* 91 (December): 931–935.
Waltz, Kenneth N. 1959. *Man, the State, and War: A Theoretical Analysis*. New York: Columbia University Press.
Waltz, Kenneth N. 1967. *Foreign Policy and Democratic Politics: The American and British Experience*. Boston, MA: Little Brown.
Waltz, Kenneth N. 1979. *Theory of International Politics*. Reading, MA: Addison-Wesley.
Waltz, Kenneth N. 1986. "Reflections on *Theory of International Politics*: Response to My Critics." In *Neorealism and Its Critics*, ed. Robert O. Keohane. New York: Columbia University Press.
Waltz, Kenneth N. 1989. "The Origins of War in Neorealist Theory." Pp. 39–52 in *The Origin and Prevention of Major Wars*, ed. Robert I. Rotberg and Theodore K. Rabb. New York: Cambridge University Press.
Waltz, Kenneth N. 1990. "Realist Thought and Neorealist Theory." *Journal of International Affairs* 44 (spring/summer): 21–37.
Waltz, Kenneth N. 1993. "The Emerging Structure of International Politics." *International Security* 17 (fall): 44–79.
Waltz, Kenneth N. 1996. "International Politics Is Not Foreign Policy." *Security Studies* 6 (autumn): 54–57.
Waltz, Kenneth N. 1997. "Evaluating Theories." *American Political Science Review* 91 (December): 913–917.
Waltz, Kenneth N. 1999. "Globalization and Governance." *PS* 32 (December): 693–700.
Waltz, Kenneth N. 2000. "Structural Realism after the Cold War." *International Security* 25 (summer): 5–41.
Ward, Michael D. 1981. *Research Gaps in Alliance Dynamics*. Beverly Hills, CA: Sage.
Watt, Donald Cameron. 1989. *How War Came*. New York: Pantheon.
Wayman, Frank W., and Paul F. Diehl, eds. 1994. *Reconstructing Realpolitik*. Ann Arbor, MI: University of Michigan Press.
Wayman, Frank W., and T. Clifton Morgan. 1990. "Measuring Polarity in the International

System." In *Measuring the Correlates of War*, ed. Paul F. Diehl. Ann Arbor, MI: University of Michigan Press.
Weinberg, Gerhard L. 1994. *A World at Arms*. New York: Cambridge University Press.
Weinberg, Steven. 1992. *Dreams of a Final Theory*. New York: Pantheon Books.
Wendt, Alexander. 1992. "Anarchy Is What States Make of It: The Social Construction of Power Politics." *International Organization* 46 (spring): 391–425.
Wendt, Alexander. 1999. *Social Theory of International Politics*. Cambridge, UK: Cambridge University Press.
Wentker, Hermann. 1993. *Zerstörung der Grossmacht Russland? Die britischen Kriegsziele im Krimkrieg*. Göttigen and Zürich: Vandenhoek, and Rupprecht.
Wernham, R. B. 1966. *Before the Armada: The Emergence of the English Nation, 1485–1588*. New York: Harcourt, Brace & World.
White, Ralph K. 1966. "Misperception and the Vietnam War." *Journal of Social Issues* 22 (July): 1–164.
Wight, Martin. 1946. *Power Politics*. "Looking Forward" Pamphlet No. 8. London: Royal Institute of International Affairs.
Wight, Martin. 1966. "The Balance of Power." Pp. 149–175 in *Diplomatic Investigations: Essays in the Theory of International Politics*, ed. Herbert Butterfield and Martin Wight. Cambridge, MA: Harvard University Press.
Wight, Martin. 1986. *Power Politics*. 2nd ed. Ed. Hedley Bull and Carsten Holbraad. Harmondsworth, UK: Penguin Books.
Williamson, Samuel R., Jr. 1969. *The Politics of Grand Strategy: Britain and France Prepare for War, 1904–1914*. London: Ashfield Press.
Wilson, Keith M. 1985. *The Policy of the Entente: Essays on the Determinants of British Foreign Policy, 1904–1914*. New York: Cambridge University Press.
Wilson, Keith M. 1987. *Empire and Continent*. London: New York: Mansell Pub.
Wilson, Mary. 1988. *King Abdullah, Britain, and the Making of Jordan*. New York: Cambridge University Press.
Wohlforth, William C. 1993. *The Elusive Balance: Power and Perceptions during the Cold War*. Ithaca, NY: Cornell University Press.
Wohlforth, William C. 1994/1995. "Realism and the End of the Cold War." *International Security* 19 (3) (winter): 91–129.
Wohlforth, William C. 1998. "Reality Check: Revising Theories of International Politics in Response to the End of the Cold War." *World Politics* 50 (July): 650–680.
Wolfers, Arnold. 1962. *Discord and Collaboration: Essays on International Politics*. Baltimore, MD: Johns Hopkins Press.
Worrall, John. 1978. "The Ways in Which the Methodology of Scientific Research Programmes Improves on Popper's Methodology." Pp. 45–70 in *Progress and Rationality in Science*, ed. Gerard Radnitzky and Gunnar Andersson. Boston, MA: D. Reidel.
Wright, Moorhead. 1975 "Introduction." Pp. ix–xxii in *Theory and Practice of the Balance of Power 1486–1914: Selected European Writings*, ed. Moorhead Wright. Totowa, NJ: Rowman and Littlefield.
Wright, Quincy. [1942] 1964. *A Study of War*. Abridged by Louise Leonard Wright. Chicago, IL: University of Chicago.
Wright, Quincy. 1965. *A Study of War*. 2nd ed. Chicago, IL: Chicago University Press.
Zahar, Elie. 1973. "Why Did Einstein's Programme Supersede Lorentz's? (I)" *British Journal for the Philosophy of Science* 24 (June): 95–123.
Zakaria, Fareed. 1992. "Realism and Domestic Politics." *International Security* 17 (fall): 177–198.
Zakaria, Fareed. 1998. *From Wealth to Power: The Unusual Origins of America's World Role*. Princeton, NJ: Princeton University Press.
Zakaria, Fareed. 2001 "America's New Balancing Act." *Newsweek*, August 6.
Zinnes, Dina A. 1967. "An Analytical Study of Balance of Power Theories." *Journal of Peace Research* 4 (3): 270–288.
Zubok, Vladislav, and Konstantin Pleshakov. 1996. *Inside the Kremlin's Cold War*. Cambridge, MA: Harvard University Press.

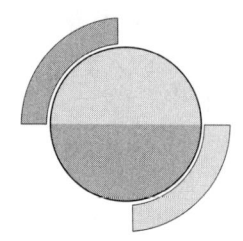

# INDEX

## A

Actors, essential, 167, 175–176, 184
Ad hoc adjustments. *See also* Problemshifts
  as standard practice, 60, 104–106
  in theory appraisal, 288–289, 299
  types of, 81–82
Aggressive intentions, variable of, 227–228, 245
Aggressor, balancing against, 91
Alliance
  formation, 205–210, 229
  initiation, 208–211, 215
  paradox, 203
  portfolios, 204
Anarchy
  Arabism vs., 228–229
  realist assumptions of, 31, 39–40, 83, 168
  regional absence of, 140–141
  in structural realism, 267
  threat vs., 245
Anticipatory compliance, 138
Anticolonialism, 229, 235–241
Appeasement, 69–70
Arab Collective Security Pact, 232–235, 236
Arabism, 100, 227–232, 249n5
Arab-Israeli conflict, 229–230, 241–245
Arab summit system, 241–243
Arab unification, 232–235, 249n5
Automatic balance of power, 10–11, 14, 297, 298

## B

Baghdad Pact, 235–241
Balance
  defined, 9
  holder of, 21n51, 90, 141, 144
Balance of interest theory, 16–17, 33–34, 46. *See also* Balancing
Balance of power, term, 13, 22n58
Balance of power theories, types of, 296–298
Balance of threat theory. *See also* Balancing; Bandwagoning; Threat
  Arab Collective Security Pact and, 235
  Baghdad Pact and, 240–241
  defended, 61–63
  as degenerative problemshift, 31–33, 45, 98–100
  as foreign policy application, 54
  historical critique of, 118–121
  Middle East and, 227–232
  outlined, 15–16, 64
Balancer. *See* Holder of the balance
Balancing. *See also* Balance of interest theory; Balance of threat theory; Bandwagoning
  defined, 8
  defining criteria for, 90–94, 134–136, 139–146, 148, 154–159
  as law, 30–31
  polarity and, 68

against threat, 48n8
unobserved, 137–139, 149
Bandwagoning. *See also* Balance of interest theory; Balance of threat theory; Balancing
  balance of interest theory and, 46, 52–53
  contra balancing, 31–35, 46
  defined, 48n8, 79
  domain of, 100
  foreign policy implications of, 129–130
  normative, 232, 240
  opportunistic, 76–79
  as positive feedback, 11
  PRIEs and, 206
Basic War Theorem, 191–192
Bipolarity, 67–68, 172–180, 182–183, 186
Black box, 267, 269–270, 274. *See also* Uncertainty
Blocking coalition, 175
Boundary concept, 123–124
Buck-passing. *See also* Chain-ganging
  defined, 73
  as degenerative problemshift, 35–37
  as discrepant evidence, 46
  as neutral feedback, 11, 15
  offense-defense balance and, 14
  polarity and, 67

## C

Capabilities, distribution of, 251–254. *See also* Power, distribution of
*Ceteris paribus* clauses, 9, 51
Chain-ganging. *See also* Buck-passing
  defined, 73
  as degenerative problemshift, 35–37
  domain of, 100–102
  offense-defense balance and, 14
  polarity and, 67
  as positive feedback, 260
Chinese multistate system, 142
Classical realism, 49, 57
Competition
  in defensive realism, 268
  in neoclassical realism, 272
  in offensive realism, 270–271
Compliance, anticipatory, 138
Competition
  balancing and, 154, 158
Concert of Europe, 119–120
Conflict, international. *See* War
Conflict involvement, 215
Constructivism, 100, 248
Critical test, 193–194

## D

Defensive realism, 61, 151n15, 267–270, 277. *See also* Structural realism
Defining criteria, 111, 169–171
Degenerative research programs, 26–27, 47, 260
Demanding test, 193–194
Democratic dyads, 210–211
Dependent variable, 139, 215, 219
Discrepant evidence, 99
Diseconomies of scale, 161
Distribution of capabilities, 22n58, 251–254. *See also* Power, distribution of
Domain, 97–98, 111, 139–146, 149
Domestic politics, 168. *See also* Arab Collective Security Pact; Baghdad Pact; 1967 War
Doves, 190–191
Dyad, 220
Dyadic alliance formation, 204–205
Dyadic balance of power, 10, 11, 14, 296–297
Dyadic expansion, 11
Dyadic level analysis, 214
Dyads, democratic, 210–211

## E

Economic sanctions, 138
Empire by invitation, 145
Empirical content
  contra balancing, 115–118
  defined away, 156
  testing of, 88–94, 170, 180–189, 193–194
  in theory appraisal, 60, 105
Endogeneity, 137–139
Enlightened self-interest, 123
Essential actors, 167, 175–176, 184
Eurocentric bias, 141–145
Explanatory power, 105
*Ex post facto*, 98
External balancing, 13, 91

## F

Falsification
  defined, 197
  impossibility of, 285–286
  in MSRP, 26
  of MSRP, 259–263
  of neorealism, 193–195

Falsification (cont.)
  Popperian, 2, 19n4
  rejection of, 50–51
  in theory appraisal, 105
  Waltz's criteria for, 170, 171
First image. See Levels of analysis
Free-riders, 164
Free trade, imperialism of, 144

**G**

Great power bias, 140
Greed. See Neoclassical realism
Grouping, 119–121, 127

**H**

Hawks, 190–191
Hegemonic bid, 89–90, 127
Hegemonic realism, 150n2, 152n37
Hegemonic stability theory, 142. See also Hegemonic realism
Hegemonic threat. See Hegemonic bid
Hegemony
  absence of, 133, 160–161, 251
  defined, 131
  undefined, 141
  U.S., 144–145
Holder of the balance, 21n51, 90, 141, 144

**I**

Identity, shared, 100
IIG. See International interaction game (IIG)
Imperialism of free trade, 144
Independence of states, 151n11
Independent variable, 216, 219
Interest, balance of, 16–17, 33–34, 46. See also Balancing
Internal balancing, 13, 91, 101
International conflict. See War
International interaction game (IIG), 185–194
Intrawar balancing, 134–135

**J**

Jackals, 16

**L**

Lakatos, Imre, 3, 20n20. See also Methodology of Scientific Research Programs (MSRP)

Leadership long cycle theory, 142–143. See also Hegemonic realism
Levels of analysis, 275–276, 278
Liberalism (in international relations), 206–207, 220
Limiting concept, 123–124
Lions, 16
Longevity, 180–181
Long peace, 182–183

**M**

Manual balance of power, 10, 11, 297, 300
Manual expansion, 11
Maritime powers, 143–144, 293
Metatheory. See Theory appraisal
Methodology of Scientific Research Programs (MSRP), 3, 59–60, 259–263, 281–289. See also Lakatos, Imre
MID. See Militarized Interstate Disputes (MID)
Militarized Interstate Disputes (MID), 211–213
"Most likely" case, 147, 149–150
MSRP. See Methodology of Scientific Research Programs (MSRP)
Multipolarity, 67–69, 172–180, 182–183
Multistate system, Chinese, 142
Mutual expansion, 11, 12

**N**

Neoclassical realism, 271–273
Neoliberalism, 47n1
Neorealism. See also Structural realism
  hard core of, 83, 107–108, 122
  summary of, 167–169
  term coined, 20n31
1967 War, 241–245
Non-events, 139, 149, 150
Normal science, 3, 35, 36
Norms, 228–232, 240–241, 247, 248
Novel fact criteria
  balance of threat theory and, 62–63, 99
  defined, 85–86
  definitions of, 304n14
  prediction and, 299–300
  validity of, 81, 288
Nuclear deterrence, 182

# Index

## O

Offense-defense balance
  alliance formation and, 67–68
  in defensive realism, 269
  as domain, 101–102
  feedback mechanisms, effect on, 15
  measurement of, 48n11, 273–274
  in offensive realism, 271
  polarity and, 67–68
Offensive realism, 61, 151n15, 270–271
Other-regarding behavior, 122–123
Overexpansion, 92

## P

*Pacta de contrahendo.* See Grouping
Pacts of restraint. See Grouping
Palestine, 241–245
Paradigmatism, 2–3, 281–284
Paradigms, 23, 25, 286–287
Paradigm wars, 258
Peace, 125, 131, 148, 182–183
Politically relevant international environment (PRIE), 205, 221n4
Politics, domestic, 168. See also Arab Collective Security Pact; Baghdad Pact; 1967 War
Positional competition, 75–76
Positivism, 50
Power
  bandwagoning and, 77
  in classical realism, 49
  distribution of, 90, 174–177, 187–188. See also Distribution of capabilities
  land-based, 142–143
  maritime, 143–144
  measuring of, 256–257
  in neorealist theory, 108, 168–169
  offense-defense balance vs., 269
  in offensive realism, 270–271
  role of, 102
  in structural realism, 267
Power parity hypothesis, 132
Power transition theory, 142
Predators' quarrel, 11, 12, 16–17
Predictive power of theories, 55, 105
Preponderance, 90
Preventive war, 136–137, 149
Prewar balancing, 134–135
PRIE. See Politically relevant international environment (PRIE)
Prisoners' dilemma, 180
Problemshifts. See also Ad hoc adjustments
  defined, 47
  as degenerative indicators, 81–82
  progressive vs. degenerative, 26
  in theory appraisal, 103–105, 286
  as theoryshifts, 47n5
Progressive research programs, 27, 47, 52
Protean, 46, 47
Proteanshift, 37
Public good, 157–158, 164
P value, 219–220

## R

Rational actor assumption, 173–174
Realism
  defined, 23
  elements of, 74–75
  history of, 5–7
  protean character of, 35, 40, 46
Realpolitik, elements of, 199n16
Regime survival, 230–231
Regional systems, 140–141
Research program. See also SRPs, elements of
  defined, 86
  elements of, 82
  nonexistence of, 259–263
  paradigms vs., 286–287
  selection of, for testing, 28–30
Revolutionary science, 3

## S

Sanctions, economic, 138
Scientific method, 219
Scope condition. See Domain
Second image. See Levels of analysis
Security
  bandwagoning and, 77
  competition vs., 75–76
  dilemma, 268–269, 270–271, 272
  in neorealist theory, 53, 168, 179, 267
Self-encirclement, 11, 12
Self-regarding behavior, 122–123
Semantic relabeling, 97, 98
Significance level, 219–220
Six Day War, 241–245
SRPs, elements of, 3, 58–59. See also Research program
States, independence of, 151n11
Strategic affinity, 204–208, 211, 215
Strategic selection, 138

Structural realism. *See also* Defensive realism; Neorealism; Offensive realism
  claims of, 115
  elements of, 267
  outlined, 56, 57
  prediction and, 53–54
Sucker bets, 41
Summit system, Arab, 241–243
System, defined, 21n36

## T

Tables, reading of, 219–220
Theory, 47n3, 50, 55, 57
Theory appraisal
  criteria for, 281–289
  defined, 44, 47
  development of, 2–4
  MSRP, use of in, 25–28, 259–263
  rigor, lack of in, 41
Theoryshifts. *See* Problemshifts
Threat. *See also* Balance of threat theory
  alliance formation and, 205–206
  anarchy vs., 245
  Arabism and, 225
  definition of, 121
  evaluation of, 15
  norms as, 231
Transcending, 119
Tripartite Alliance, 239

## U

Uncertainty. *See also* Black box
  in defensive realism, 269–270
  defined, 197
  in neoclassical realism, 272
  polarity and, 172–175, 177–180
  war and, 185, 192–194
Unification, Arab, 232–235, 249n5
Unipolarity, 54
Unitary rational actor assumption, 173–174, 267
United Nations, 182
Unobserved balancing, 137–139, 149

## V

Variables, types of, 215–216, 219–220

## W

War
  alliance formation and, 211–213
  Arab-Israeli, 241–245
  balance of power and, 90–91, 188–189
  balancing vs. nonbalancing, 157
  IIG and, 189–194
  preventive, 136–137, 149
  stability and, 140
  uncertainty and, 185–186
Wolves, 16
Worst-case planning, 269, 279n8

## Z

Zero-sum games, 180, 260